The
MODERN
WITCHCRAFT
Grimoire

The

MODERN WITCHCRAFT
Grimoire

YOUR COMPLETE GUIDE TO
CREATING YOUR OWN
Book of Shadows

Skye Alexander

Adams Media

New York London Toronto Sydney New Delhi

Adams Media
An Imprint of Simon & Schuster, Inc.
100 Technology Center Drive
Stoughton, MA 02072

For information about special discounts for bulk purchases, please contact Simon & Schuster Special Sales at 1-866-506-1949 or business@simonandschuster.com.

The Simon & Schuster Speakers Bureau can bring authors to your live event. For more information or to book an event contact the Simon & Schuster Speakers Bureau at 1-866-248-3049 or visit our website at www.simonspeakers.com.

Interior images © F+W Media, Inc.; iStockphoto.com/Nocturnus; iStockphoto.com/ilbusca; iStockphoto.com/ARTappler; iStockphoto.com/VeraPetruk.

Manufactured in China

10 9 8 7 6 5 4 3 2 1

Library of Congress Cataloging-in-Publication Data
Alexander, Skye, author.
The modern witchcraft grimoire: your complete guide to creating your
  own book of shadows / Skye Alexander.
Avon, Massachusetts: Adams Media, 2016.
Includes bibliographical references and index.
LCCN 2016007697 (print) | LCCN 2016017136 (ebook) | ISBN
  9781440596810 (pob) | ISBN 1440596816 (pob) |
  ISBN 9781440596827 (ebook) | ISBN 1440596824 (ebook)
LCSH: Witchcraft.
LCC BF1566.A54732016 (print) | LCC BF1566 (ebook) | DDC
  133.4/3--dc23

LC record available at https://lccn.loc.gov/2016007697ISBN 978-1-4405-9681-0
ISBN 978-1-4405-9682-7 (ebook)

To the witches of the next generation—
you are the torchbearers who illuminate our future

Acknowledgments

Many thanks are due to my astute and supportive editors Rebecca Tarr Thomas and Peter Archer, to Stephanie Hannus for her beautiful book design, and to the rest of the Adams Media staff—no author could work with a better team.

CONTENTS

Introduction

RECORDING YOUR MAGICKAL JOURNEY

Perhaps you're accustomed to keeping a journal in which the story of your life unfolds. There you confide your hopes and dreams as well as the events that make up the fabric of your existence. In *The Modern Witchcraft Grimoire*, you'll learn how to keep another book. Although it's similar in some ways to a journal, it is much more. It is your *grimoire* (pronounced grim WAR).

If you are Wiccan or follow another magickal path, your grimoire is an essential tool—an intimate account of your spiritual journey, the steps you take on the road to self-discovery, and what you learn along the way about the Craft of the Wise. As well, it's a resource for you, containing spells and other magickal lore that are aids in finding serenity and happiness.

Between its covers you reveal your soul's secrets, as well as your expressions in the outer world—particularly those of a magickal and spiritual nature. Here you pen information about your practice as a witch, the spells and rituals you perform, and your ongoing exploration of the mysteries that lie beyond the ordinary mundane world. Insights, visions, dreams, meditations, and musings all may grace the pages of your grimoire. Your experience is both personal and universal, for as a witch you know that everything in the cosmos is connected, wisdom is timeless, and truth is enduring.

Perhaps you feel inspired to discuss how you interpret the presence of the Divine Feminine in your life. How does she reveal herself to you and guide you on your spiritual path? Your grimoire is also the place to relate the magickal knowledge you've gained and the revelations you've discovered. As a practitioner of the Craft, you are continually unfolding and growing and transforming. You are continually deepening your relationship with yourself, the Goddess, nature, the universe, and everything around you. Each day opens new doors; each moment the spirit world slips extraordinary messages into your psychic mailbox. And you don't want to forget a single thing, so write it down!

The Modern Witchcraft Grimoire is a guide to designing and using this amazing resource. Part I explains the tradition of keeping a grimoire and why you'll want to create your own. I discuss various ways to fashion your book, how you might like to organize it, and what things you may consider including in it. Are you an artist? Perhaps you'll enjoy adding illustrations, photographs, and other inspiring imagery to enrich your book. Are you a poet? Compose original incantations to call up the magickal forces in the cosmos and write your poems in your grimoire. Do you have a dramatic bent? Choreograph personal rituals and record what you did, with whom, and what resulted. You can even fabricate your own grimoire from scratch. This is your chance to be creative and to express yourself, without fear of criticism or censorship.

In Part II I suggest ways to work with your grimoire. Celebrate and chart the sacred holidays. Catalog your spells. Discuss your interactions with deities, spirits, and other nonphysical entities. Let the spark within you shine, let the music in you sing. All the details of your quest here on earth and beyond could end up on the pages of your book.

I also share things here that I've found worth including in my own book: favorite spells and rituals, chants and affirmations, signs and symbols, insights and inspirations. I offer them as suggestions only, to help you get started in this wonderfully creative and richly rewarding endeavor. Take what you like and leave the rest. Your grimoire can contain anything you feel is significant to you as a witch and as a person. It is a record of your awakening and your evolution, what you've received and what you're giving back. It is uniquely yours—no two witches will create a grimoire in the same way.

Above all, I urge you to embrace your own truth. Delve deeply into your heart of hearts. Engage your imagination. Enjoy knowing that you are part of a long-standing, time-honored, and incredibly exciting tradition that connects you with witches past, present, and future. Invite the Goddess to join you in the process. Whatever you do will be amazing! Blessed be.

> *"You have more than enough to do, be, create and have everything you desire! In order to have EVERYTHING you desire, you must shift your beliefs and begin to see yourself in a new and strong way. It's about creating a powerful mindset shift . . . the first step is connecting with your Inner Goddess."*
>
> —LISA MARIE ROSATI

PART I

Designing Your Grimoire

Chapter 1

WHY CREATE A GRIMOIRE?

A grimoire is a witch's personal journal of her or his magickal experiences. Here, you keep track of your spells, rituals, and other things related to your development as a magick worker. It's like a cook's collection of recipes. Some people refer to it as a "book of shadows." Old grimoires served as collections of spells and rituals. A book of shadows today might also include its author's musings and insights related to a spell, as well as her dreams, feelings, poems, lore, and other asides.

Your grimoire is a record of your growth and of the changes you and others bring about in your life. Above all, it is a tool you can use in your search for and discovery of the path of the Goddess.

THE WAY OF THE GODDESS

The Egyptians called her Isis. The Sumerians knew her as Inanna, the Babylonians as Ishtar. Long before the advent of Christianity, Islam, and other patriarchal religions, our ancestors stood in awe of the Goddess's power and revered her in all her splendor. For as much as 30,000 years they drew nurture from her spirituality and strength. Now you have chosen to tread a special path in this world, a path rooted in antiquity that respects the Goddess as well as the God. You seek to know her, to learn of her great mysteries and feel her hand guiding you as you journey through life in the manifest world. Call to her and she will welcome you.

The Reawakening of the Goddess

In recent years we have seen a great re-emergence of interest in the Divine Feminine. Our modern world, where science and logic and materialistic thinking dominate, has become increasingly unbalanced. Many of us experience a thirst for deeper wisdom, a hunger in our souls, and realize that something essential has been missing from our lives. We seek a stronger connection with nature and the spiritual realm, and long to rediscover our true place in the universe. In our quest for a more fulfilling way of life, many of us have turned within and found the Goddess waiting there for us.

Wicca and Neopaganism, belief systems that honor the Goddess, resonate with us because they speak to issues about which we feel most deeply: respect for the environment, gender equality, and overcoming religious biases and narrow-minded thinking. They also encourage us to respect and develop our own, unique powers so we can take charge of our lives and be everything we choose to be.

Growing Wiccans

A growing number of both women and men now follow the Wiccan path. According to an American Religious Identification Survey in 2008 (the 2008 ARIS), 682,000 people in the United States identified themselves as Wiccan or Neopagans, although the real figure is probably much larger. Even the U.S. military now recognizes Wicca as a bona fide religion.

As you progress along your chosen path, you'll want to chronicle your spiritual journey—just as you might keep a travel log while on a trip. For Wiccans, your grimoire is the tool you use to do this. In writing your story, you preserve the intimate details of what you do and experience along the Wiccan Way, as well as your unique relationship with the Divine. You also make it possible for other seekers to share in your search for wisdom and to benefit from the knowledge you gain during your quest.

EARLY GRIMOIRES

Originally, a grimoire referred to a book of spells, incantations, invocations, and other practices used to call forth spirits. Grimoires existed in ancient Babylonia and early Middle Eastern civilizations. Later they made their way through Europe during the medieval and Renaissance periods. People have been writing grimoires since the invention of writing, and these works have been connected to three of the world's major religions—Judaism, Christianity, and Islam. They influenced the development of early science and the arts in Europe and parts of Asia. Grimoires thus are an important part of our cultural history.

The word "grimoire" is related to the word "grammar," which pertains to the rules and the relationships of language. Derived from the Middle English *gramere* and the Old French *gramaire*, the root of the word is an alteration of the Latin *grammatica*, which we can trace back to its source from the Greek feminine of *grammatikos*, meaning "of letters." It seems appropriate that this feminine derivative from the language of one of the earliest classical pantheistic civilizations has evolved to describe what many witches now consider a sacred text devoted to practices honoring the Mother Goddess.

Famous Ancient Grimoires

Since ancient times, magicians and mystics have compiled grimoires. These early texts and our knowledge of them are limited, though, mainly because the Church considered them heretical and destroyed those they found. However, some old grimoires managed to survive, and today they give us insight into the magickal thinking and workings of our ancestors.

One of the earliest and most influential grimoires, *The Clavicule of Solomon* or *The Key of Solomon*, was supposedly written by the great King Solomon and is believed to have appeared in the Middle East some 2,000 years ago. By the fifteenth century, copies of the book had found their way into the hands of European scholars and others who sought to learn the secrets of the wise king. The *Clavicule* included spells for summoning demons as well as the spirits of the dead, along with information about using magick tools and lots more. Another ancient spell book, the *Sepher Ha-Razim*—which is said to have passed down through many generations from Noah to King Solomon—contained techniques for divination, healing, and attracting good fortune.

Summoning Spirits Solomon-Style

Back in the old, old days, people put a lot of faith in spirits of all kinds. Some of those spirits, our ancestors believed, wanted to wreak havoc in our lives, whereas others could be called upon to block the malicious nature of the bad guys' curses. Therefore, early grimoires included invocations, rituals, and other practices for eliciting the aid of spiritual allies. Here's a brief excerpt from *The Key of Solomon* designed to conjure the powers of nonphysical beings. You can read the text in its entirety (translated into English) online at *http://hermetic.com* to get an idea of what early magicians believed.

"O ye Spirits, ye I conjure by the Power, Wisdom, and Virtue of the Spirit of God, by the uncreate Divine Knowledge, by the vast Mercy of God, by the Strength of God, by the Greatness of God, by the Unity of God; and by the holy Name of God EHEIEH, which is the root, trunk, source, and origin of all the other Divine Names, whence they all draw their life and their virtue, which Adam having invoked, he acquired the knowledge of all created things. . . ."

—THE GREATER KEY OF SOLOMON, BOOK I,
TRANSLATED BY S. LIDDELL MACGREGOR MATHERS

Astrological magick played an important role in some early grimoires including the Arabic *Picatrix*, attributed to mathematician Ahmad Al-Majriti and translated into Latin in the mid-thirteenth century. The *Liber Juratus*, supposedly penned by a legendary magus named Honorius of Thebes, also became popular during the medieval era. It contained techniques for gaining visions from God, commanding demons, and avoiding Purgatory, as well as scientific knowledge of the times. A fifteenth-century collection of Kabbalist magick, the *Book of the Sacred Magic of Abra-Melin the Mage*, offered information about love and prosperity magick, plus the secrets of invisibility and flying—pretty heady stuff for any age!

Grimoires in the Age of Enlightenment

Mysticism flourished in the eighteenth century, as spiritual reaction to the Age of Enlightenment's emphasis on logic and reason. Advanced printing techniques made books cheaper too, which enabled esoteric texts to reach a wider audience than ever before. One of these, a collection of magick symbols and spells for conjuring spirits called *The Sixth and Seventh Books of Moses*, gained prominence in Germany and then in the nineteenth century found its way to the United States. Around the same time, a grimoire known as *Petit Albert*, said to contain spells for invisibility, attracted attention in France as did another called *Le Grand Grimoire ou Dragon Rouge* (although it claimed an older pedigree), which provided instructions for raising demons. In Scandinavia and on the Iberian Peninsula, spell books purported to have been written by St. Cyprian that offered information for finding hidden treasure became popular. For centuries, metaphysicians in Europe and the New World who had kept their views and practices hidden now hungered for knowledge and sought to share it throughout the Western world.

Skeptics might say that this was a period of superstition and fanciful thinking, or that charlatans were trying to dupe gullible people with mystical hocus-pocus. However, the grimoires compiled then—and the much earlier material their authors drew upon—suggest that for centuries magickal workers have been in touch with occult forces. Intuitively we realize, as Shakespeare wrote, "there are more things in heaven and earth . . . than are dreamt of in your philosophy."

Leland's Grimoire

At the end of the nineteenth century, an American folklorist named Charles Godfrey Leland published one of the first grimoires in English. According to Leland, a mysterious Italian witch named Maddalena gave him a collection of magick lore titled *Vangel*, reputedly from a secret group of Goddess worshippers. The document, which Leland claimed Maddalena had written in her own hand, lies at the heart of his book *Aradia, Gospel of the Witches.*

To this day, however, there's a debate about the authenticity of the material. Did it actually come from a secret history of Italian witchcraft? Did Maddalena pass on an account of her own family's mystical practices to Leland, pretending their traditions were more arcane and ancient? Or did Leland make up the whole story, drawing information from various folkloric sources, and insist he'd discovered an early Italian coven's grimoire? Despite questions about the text's origins, Leland's book strongly influenced contemporary Neopaganism and Wicca, and still intrigues witches today.

Some historic grimoires now reside in museums and private collections, and some pricey (and perhaps dubious) books periodically show up for sale online and in auctions internationally. Although many modern witches might find the information contained in these early texts confusing or questionable, it's interesting to examine the rich tradition of grimoires handed down through the ages and to appreciate our ancestors' efforts to preserve esoteric knowledge for future generations, even when doing so might have led to persecution.

THE GRIMOIRE OF GERALD GARDNER AND DOREEN VALIENTE

The most influential book of shadows for contemporary witches is attributed to Gerald Gardner and Doreen Valiente, often considered the Father and Mother of modern witchcraft. Valiente, a prolific English author and poet, began demonstrating her interest in witchcraft and magick at age seven. In 1952—shortly after the 1735 Witchcraft Act was repealed, decriminalizing the practice of witchcraft in England—she met Gerald Gardner. An English witch and noted occultist who owned the Museum of Magic and Witchcraft on the Isle of Man, Gardner initiated Valiente into the Craft on Midsummer's Eve 1953. Their association spawned the modern-day religion we know today as Wicca.

More than a decade prior to meeting Valiente, Gardner discovered fragments of a text that he believed had been written by a group of earlier European witches. He included these findings in his book of shadows—although he didn't call it a "book of shadows" at the time—along with other rituals and practices he'd learned about during his many years of studying esoteric traditions from both the East and the West. His book's contents drew upon the work of Aleister Crowley (perhaps the most notorious magician of the modern era), Celtic folklore, the practices of the Hermetic Order of the Golden Dawn, Tantric yoga, Enochian wisdom, and other sources of mystical and occult knowledge. Valiente revised the material—chucking much of the Crowleyisms, in particular—and added information of her own as well as her poetry. The result was a compilation of inherited rituals from the past blended with original and modern elements. It became the core ethical guide and central spiritual text of the Gardnerian tradition of Wicca (there are several other Wiccan traditions as well).

Today, many witches use a similar method for creating their own grimoires—we draw upon traditional practices and add new ones. Some Wiccans choose to hand-copy material from a book of shadows created by the High Priestess or High Priest who initiated them into the Craft, and then put their personal insights and experiences into their magickal journals. Others prefer to create their own, original grimoires from scratch.

Thus, the Craft continues to evolve.

How Did the Term "Book of Shadows" Originate?

According to Doreen Valiente, Gardner stumbled upon a 1949 edition of a magazine called *The Occult Observer* in a Brighton, England, bookstore, which contained an article written by an Indian palmist named Mir Bashir. The article talked about a Sanskrit manuscript, ostensibly thousands of years old, that Bashir had come across in 1941. The document revealed an ancient Hindu technique for divining a person's future by measuring his or her shadow. Bashir titled his article "Book of Shadows" and Gardner latched onto it. Supposedly, the article appeared on the page opposite an ad for Gardner's book *High Magic's Aid*, a fantasy novel about witchcraft in Victorian-era England. Perhaps he saw this as a fortunate sign, but whatever the reason the term "book of shadows" stuck, and witches still use it today.

SHARE IT OR KEEP IT SECRET?

As mentioned already, some witches choose to keep their grimoires completely private, solely for their own use—after all, the spiritual journey is a very personal one and you may not feel you can be totally honest if you know someone else will read the intimate details of your experience. Other witches share their books with magickal partners or members of their covens. Still other witches decide to reveal some of their magick practices publicly—as I've done in *The Modern Guide to Witchcraft* and *The Modern Witchcraft Spell Book* and my other books—in hopes that by doing so we can assist other people on the path.

A History of Secrecy

In earlier times, occult knowledge was passed down orally to neophytes by more experienced practitioners. Most likely, small groups of witches and other magicians met in secret, and they may have possessed little knowledge of the whereabouts or practices of other groups. Few kept written records of their activities. They did this not only because in those days hardly anyone could read or write, but also because they needed to protect themselves. In many parts of the world, for many years, people suspected of practicing witchcraft were imprisoned, tortured, and killed. Even today, witches who reveal their beliefs publicly may suffer ridicule, prejudice, and worse.

Destroy the Evidence

Consider this excerpt from Gerald Gardner and Doreen Valiente's book of shadows:

If you would Keep a book let it be in your own hand of write. Let brothers and sisters copy what they will, but never let the book out of your hands, and never keep the writings of another, for if it be found in their hand of write, they well may be taken and enjoined. Each should guard his own writings and destroy it whenever danger threatens. Learn as much as you may by heart, and when danger is past, rewrite your book an it be safe. For this reason, if any die, destroy their book if they have not been able to, for an it be found, 'tis clear proof against them, And our oppressors well know, "Ye may not be a witch alone" So all their kin and friends be in danger of torture. So ever destroy anything not necessary. If your book be found on you. 'tis clear proof against you alone. You may be enjoined. Keep all thoughts of the Craft from your mind. Say you had bad dreams; a devil caused you to write it without your knowledge. Think to yourself, "I know nothing. I remember nothing. I have forgotten everything." (For more, see The Gardnerian Book of Shadows, *by Gerald Gardner, at* www.sacred-texts.com.*)*

When witches and practitioners of other magickal arts faced the threat of capture with such dire consequences, it's no wonder they insisted on keeping their grimoires secret. During the Burning Times in Europe, which lasted from the fourteenth until the eighteenth centuries, at least tens of thousands of people were executed as witches. The majority of these were women and girls.

Unfortunately, this fragmented approach has left us severely wanting in the area of verifiable information. It is very difficult to piece together the rites and rituals of an oral tradition when few written records exist and where fear and suspicion force people into hiding. Even today, some of us may worry about reprisals from our families, communities, or religious or political groups. Therefore, use your best judgment as to whether you wish to keep your book of shadows to yourself.

MODERN GRIMOIRES

The term "grimoire" is generic and may be used in place of the title of an actual book that its author chooses to keep secret. Today's grimoires are usually handwritten by individuals for their own personal use, although you can also create an effective and wonderful book of shadows digitally. A grimoire may include information and instructions related to a particular tradition, or it may contain strictly personal records and reminiscences intended only for the use of the author. Sometimes portions of a grimoire are passed down over time, copied by initiates from a master book.

Some Wiccans choose to keep more than a single book of shadows. One of these books contains the rituals upheld and enacted by a particular coven or circle to which the witch belongs. These rituals may have their roots in earlier times and, as such, preserve traditional practices and wisdom. The information in one coven's "core" grimoire will probably differ from that of other covens. Members of a select group are permitted to copy material from this book into their own grimoires for their own purposes. In a separate book a witch might record information of a more personal nature—the intimate thoughts and experiences of her or his sojourn along the road less traveled.

However, some covens share information or make certain practices and beliefs available to other "kindred spirits." The necessary secrecy that once existed when a witch's life depended on hiding her thoughts is loosening in modern-day witchcraft. Still, many people choose to preserve their private practices and ideas by limiting access to their grimoires.

What Should You Include in Your Book?

Every grimoire is essentially a book of shadows, but not every book of shadows conforms to the strict definition of a grimoire. As discussed earlier, what we call a book of shadows today includes elements of the grimoire (such as directions for spells and rituals), but it is not necessarily an exclusively instructive tome. Instead, it's an intimate record of your spiritual journey.

Purists insist that a grimoire should be entirely instructional, full of information, annotation, and practical application. They argue that a book of shadows more closely resembles a journal and that personal musings have no place in the grimoire. Fortunately for our purposes, no officially designated criteria for creating a book of shadows exist, nor is there a correct or incorrect way of building, blessing, and using your personal grimoire. As you read on, you'll see that I use the terms "grimoire" and "book of shadows" interchangeably. That's because I believe a witch's thoughts and feelings cannot be separated from the work she does—each stitch builds upon other stitches to create a whole cloth.

What goes into your book, how you create it, and how you use it will be as unique as you are. The goal is to document physically the spiritual journey of an individual who follows the path of the Goddess and the Craft of the Wise—whatever that means to you.

Online Grimoires

We're fortunate today to have an amazing resource that allows us to share knowledge while remaining anonymous: the Internet. A quick Google search will direct you to lots and lots of Wiccan websites and blogsites, as well as sites that provide historical information about witchcraft, Neopaganism, and various other magickal systems. You'll even find some that interpret early esoteric texts into modern languages and that let you glimpse the thinking and workings of the ancients.

Witchcraft's popularity has grown exponentially in recent years, in part because witches can now disseminate their wisdom widely and safely in the form of e-grimoires. Not only does this protect us from discrimination, it also enables us to gain information from a wider range of sources than ever before.

As you grow in your magickal practice, you may decide to start your own blog to share what you've learned during your spiritual journey in the Craft of the Wise. In doing so, you may meet many fellow travelers from around the world whose knowledge and experiences will enrich your own path. In turn, your wisdom will enhance theirs.

Writing the story of your spiritual awakening and subsequent journey can be an empowering method of self-discovery. You may become passionate about recording your spiritual and psychic progress. In the process, you'll strengthen the connections between divine power and personal power, and open yourself to greater intimacy with the Goddess.

You'll come to see that writing in your grimoire is a ritual in itself—you're creating a sacred tool that contains the chronicle of the magick unfolding within you. As you write, you'll chart your path—like an early seaman using the stars to map his course into previously unknown territory—and look back to see your growth, both as a person and as a witch. You'll forge new perspectives on old traditions and ancient rites, adapting them to your present-day needs and the needs of the world in which you live. You'll rediscover the seasons; you'll honor the passing of time; you'll celebrate life, death, and rebirth—each account recorded in your own hand.

"Magic is believing in yourself, if you can do that you can make anything happen."

—JOHANN WOLFGANG VON GOETHE

If you so choose, your grimoire can be more than a personal record. Inspired by those who have preceded you, it also can serve as a guide for novices just discovering the Wiccan path. It can remind us of where we came from and how far we still have to go. By writing your story, you take responsibility for the idea that the clearest pathway to the Goddess is through direct experience.

Chapter 2

CRAFTING YOUR GRIMOIRE

Early grimoires were handwritten, usually on parchment (a material made from animal skin) or paper. Depending on the author's ability to procure materials and work with them, the book's binding might have been made of richly tooled leather, carved wood, tapestry or velvet, or engraved metal. A wealthy witch or wizard might have decorated the cover of his or her book of shadows with gemstones, ornate silver hinges, gold leaf accents, or other precious adornments. A poor witch, understandably, would have chosen much more modest materials, perhaps inscribing spells on pieces of tree bark.

As you go about crafting your own grimoire, keep your purpose in mind. Whether elegant or plain, elaborate or simple, your book of shadows is a tool—a very special and personal tool—that you create in order to further your growth as a magick worker. Although you may draw upon the rich tradition that precedes you and let it guide the creation of your personal grimoire, remember there are no rules about what's right or wrong. Each grimoire is as unique as the witch to whom it belongs, and the most important thing is that it serves your objectives.

BEFORE YOU BEGIN

In the coming years, your grimoire will become a close confidant, an intimate account of your personal and spiritual evolution, a valuable reference guide, and, if you so desire, an inspiration for others. You'll keep this precious tool for the extent of your magickal journey on earth. Therefore, you'll want to take some time before you begin in order to determine the design and format that will serve you best.

Ask yourself some questions:

- Does your book need to be portable? If so, size matters. Will you carry your grimoire with you at all times, or only on special occasions?
- How often do you intend to write in your book of shadows? Daily? On new or full moons? After performing a spell? On the sabbats?
- What do you plan to include in your grimoire? Spells and rituals only? Personal musings, insights, and asides? Artwork? Experiences outside those of a magickal nature?
- What intentions do you hold for your grimoire? What role do you envision it playing in your magickal practice? In other areas of your life?
- Will you write in your book of shadows only in the privacy of your own home? In conjunction with a magickal partner or coven members?
- Do you intend to keep the contents of your grimoire completely private, or share them with certain people you trust?
- Will writing in your grimoire be part of a magick ritual, either with other people or solo?
- Where will your book reside? Displayed openly on your altar? In a secret hiding place in your home or office, or perhaps a safe-deposit box? In your backpack?
- Would you consider crafting the book yourself?

The Modern Witchcraft Grimoire

• What do you want to happen to your grimoire after you leave the physical world? Will you entrust it to someone else's use, or do you want it destroyed?

Considering these things can aid you in the process of crafting and maintaining your book of shadows. Although many witches have similar reasons for keeping grimoires, your actual practice and your individual objectives may differ from those of other people. My goal in writing *The Modern Witchcraft Grimoire* is to guide you through the process and to provide tips, information, and suggestions along the way.

YOUR GRIMOIRE'S COVER: A REFLECTION OF YOU

Can you judge a book of shadows by its cover? That's up to you. Your grimoire's binding is its outer skin. Each time you take it in hand, even before you begin to write in it, it sparks your magickal thinking and the vision you have of yourself as a witch. Running your fingers over its cover reminds you that you're on a spiritual journey, engaging in an age-old quest for wisdom, evolving as a human being and as a magician. What you hold in your hands is intensely personal, and yet also transcendent, for it draws upon the past and invites input from the spirit realm. Your grimoire is a representation of your deepest and most profound self. What do you want it to say about you?

Choosing Your Book's Cover Imagery

Wicca and witchcraft come in many "flavors": Gardnerian, Alexandrian, Dianic, Saxon, Celtic, and so on. Some witches don't align themselves with any specific group. If you do subscribe to a particular tradition or cultural heritage, you might like to reflect that on your grimoire's cover. For example, because I'm of Irish and Scottish descent, I have a book with a leather cover that features Celtic imagery and fastens with a pewter Celtic knot.

Many witches choose to include magick symbols on the covers of their grimoires: pentagrams, spirals, elemental or alchemical symbols, etc. If you're interested in astrology, you might opt for solar or lunar images, zodiac glyphs, your sun-sign "animal," or stars. If tarot's your thing, you could place a picture of a tarot card that speaks to you on the cover, perhaps The High Priestess or The Magician. Green witches might enjoy enriching their books' covers with botanical imagery. Pictures and symbols that represent the Goddess—or a favorite deity—may appeal to you. Or, you can honor your spirit animal guide by depicting it there. Some people like to use mythological creatures (such as dragons, phoenixes, griffins, or unicorns) on their grimoires; others add angels. The Kabbalah's Tree of Life, the Druids' World Tree, the Egyptian Eye of Horus . . . the list goes on.

Your book's cover may be simple or elaborate, depending on your preference. An online search will turn up lots of intriguing ideas and trigger your imagination. You may also find it helpful to visit a few New Age stores, shops that sell blank journals and scrapbooking materials, or art supply stores that stock sketchbooks. Whatever pleases you, reflects who you are as a person and a witch, and enhances your magickal experience is appropriate. Whatever feels right to you *is*.

Securing Your Grimoire

In order to keep their contents secret, some early grimoires—and some modern ones as well—were kept locked. Spellcasters didn't want the information contained within their books to fall into the wrong hands. Nor could they risk allowing people who might persecute them to gain access to potentially incriminating material. If you feel a need to protect your grimoire's contents from other people, by all means consider placing a lock on the cover.

If you aren't worried about anyone else getting his or her hands on your book of shadows, you can tie it shut with a strip of leather, a silken cord, a string of beads, or whatever strikes your fancy. Additionally, some witches like to slip their grimoires into drawstring pouches or wrap them in silk to protect them from dust and unwanted ambient energies.

INNER BEAUTY

Although the cover of your book of shadows sets the stage for what's inside, the contents matter most. Here's where you will record the story of your journey, chronicle your personal growth, and write down the secrets you hold dear. In a sense, the pages on which you note your thoughts and experiences are like picture frames that display a photo or painting. What "setting" do you feel will best frame your testimony?

Sensory Delights

Spend some time checking out readymade journals and examining scrapbooks/scrapbooking supplies. Some commercial books feature gorgeous, richly textured paper, perhaps embossed with images that resonate with you, or embedded with flowers or other adornments. Others come with lovely patterns and designs. You might also wish to examine books by artisans who have taken the time to fabricate handmade paper pages. (Later in this chapter, I'll give instructions for making your own from scratch.)

The sensory appeal of these journals can help start your creative juices flowing and inspire you to begin recording your steps on the magickal path. In fact, it's a good idea to get all your senses involved in your spellworking, for the more you can enrich the experience, the more power you bring to your spells. Choose a book that you love to look at and touch, one that invites you to grace its pages with your reminiscences. Writing in your grimoire should be a joyful experience.

As you record your spells, rituals, and other activities, consider adding a variety of images and objects that contribute to the beauty, tactile quality, and overall richness of your grimoire: milagros or other charms, feathers, small gemstones, scraps of lace, photographs of special places, pictures from magazines. If you did a candle spell, you might want to drip a bit of molten wax onto a page of your grimoire and engrave it with a symbol to remind you of the experience. If you used an essential oil in a spell, you may wish to dab a little of that fragrant oil on a page to remind you at a later time of your intention and the spell's results.

Keeping It Simple

If you prefer something simpler, that's okay. A loose-leaf binder might suit your purposes, allowing you to easily update your grimoire by adding pages or rearranging them. You can even type your grimoire on your computer or iPad. Although this method lacks the sensory appeal that many witches enjoy, the convenience could be an advantage—especially if you're on the go a lot.

Organizing Your Book of Shadows

How you choose to organize the material in your book of shadows will depend on how you decide to use it. The questions you asked yourself earlier may dictate the flow of your grimoire. No one way is better than any other. A table of contents at the beginning of your book will help you locate your spells easily. Ribbon markers can designate favorite or frequently used spells. If you choose to divide your book into categories, you may want to use tabs to indicate where different sections start. In Chapter 3, I'll discuss some ways you might like to organize your book.

One Book or Many?

If you've selected a design that lets you change or move around your entries, your grimoire can be as large as you like. If you've chosen a book with a fixed binding that doesn't allow you to add pages, however, you're going to fill it up eventually. Therefore, you'll need to continue writing in another book, creating a series. You may decide to use different books for different types of spells, instead of dividing a single grimoire into sections. Whether to keep one book or several is entirely up to you.

CRAFT IT YOURSELF

If you're the crafty type (no pun intended), you may enjoy making your book of shadows from scratch. By doing so, you follow in the footsteps of early spellworkers who fabricated their own grimoires. When you're finished, you'll have a book that is absolutely unique, imbued with your personal energy from the very start. This rewarding project, although time-consuming and (if you make your own paper) rather messy, lets you express your creativity and imagination. Your commitment can also bring you a deep sense of satisfaction.

Fashioning a book from recycled items is not as difficult as you might think and may appeal to ecologically minded witches. If creating the entire book seems too daunting, consider making just a few pages for

The Modern Witchcraft Grimoire

special incantations and spells to add to your book. Even if you buy your grimoire in a store, you can add herbs and flowers, or sketch in it to customize and personalize the pages.

Make Your Own Paper

The art of papermaking originated in China and ancient Egypt. If you resonate strongly with the goddess Kuan Yin or Isis, this may inspire you. Making your own paper from recycled items does not require any special equipment—you only need simple household products, many of which you may already possess.

The basis of paper is pulp. You can make pulp from almost any kind of paper, but avoid using anything with a glossy surface, such as pages out of magazines, because it is treated with chemicals.

MATERIALS NEEDED

Paper, such as tissue wrap, computer paper, writing or typing paper, paper bags (about ½ cup paper to 2 cups water; the more pulp you add, the thicker your finished paper will be)

Plastic bucket

Warm water

A piece of mesh (such as window screen) to fit in frames—the finer the mesh, the smoother the paper—or papermaking screen

2 wooden frames slightly larger than the size you intend your pages to be. You can use picture frames, but the corners must be tight and secured, or a deckle.

Staples

Electric blender (purchase one at a thrift store specifically for this purpose; don't use the one you make smoothies in)

Food coloring or dyes suitable for cotton fabrics (optional)

Large spoon or ladle

Plastic dishpan, large bowl, or other waterproof container big enough to easily accommodate the frames

Liquid laundry starch

Palette knife, butter knife, or athame

Absorbent cloths, such as dishtowels (one for each page of paper you
   intend to make)
Dried or fresh flowers, leaves, or bits of lace (optional)
Plastic wrap or waterproof cloth
Heavy book, cutting board, or brick

1. Tear the paper into postage stamp-sized pieces, stir, and soak the
pieces in a plastic bucket of water so that all the pieces are covered.
As you tear the paper into bits, focus positive energy into it and make
your intentions known by reciting the following: "Goddess, bless this
endeavor of art. By my hand, let the transformation begin, for the benefit
of all. So mote it be." Let the brew soak overnight.

2. Stretch the mesh over one of the frames and staple it so that it's very
taut. This covered frame will pick up the pulp and keep it flat. If the mesh
is loose, the paper will be saggy and difficult to remove from the frame.
Place the empty frame on top of the mesh frame to keep it taut and give
your paper a nice edge. Set the frames aside until step 7. (If you prefer, you
can purchase a papermaking screen and deckle at a craft/hobby store.)

3. After your paper has soaked overnight, pour off the excess water and
begin transferring the pulp into a blender, spoonful by spoonful.

4. Add water until the pitcher of the blender is no more than three-
quarters full. If you plan to color your paper, add food coloring or dye
now. Run the blender for about 15 seconds, and then check the pulp to
make sure it has broken down evenly. If necessary, stir the pulp, and then
run the blender for another 5 seconds or so. The mix should be about the
consistency of split-pea soup.

5. Gently pour the pulp into the plastic dishpan. At this point, you
can add a spoonful of liquid laundry starch to the pulp. This will make
the paper absorb ink better, so it will be less likely to bleed when you're
writing in your book.

6. Stir the pulp gently and wait for the movement of the water to
cease. At the moment when the water is still—but the pulp has not yet
settled—hold the frames securely in your hands with the empty frame
on top and the mesh frame with the mesh facing up directly underneath
it. Slide the frames under the water in a smooth motion, scooping up a

layer of pulp. It may take some practice to get the pulp evenly distributed over the mesh frame.

7. Keeping the frames steady and flat, lift them out of the water and allow the water to drain away. Remove the top frame. A layer of pulp should cover the mesh screen.

8. While the paper is still wet, but not dripping, gently remove the paper from the screen. This can take some practice—if the paper sticks to the mold, you may need to drain or sponge more water from it. Loosen the edges with a palette knife or butter knife—or if you wish, use your athame, consecrating each page instantaneously as you make it.

9. After you have removed the paper, lay it carefully on one-half of the absorbent cloth.

10. Consider pressing fresh herbs and flowers into the paper surface. Are you thinking about writing a protection spell on this sheet of paper? You might want to add basil leaves or a sprig of rosemary along the edges. Perhaps you have a love spell in mind. Adorn some of your pages with red rose petals.

11. Without bending your page, fold the other half of the cloth over the paper to absorb excess water. (You can even roll it with a rolling pin to squeeze out excess water.) Continue stacking individual pages in this fashion, making sure layers of cloth alternate with sheets of paper.

12. Put something waterproof (such as plastic wrap) at the top of the stack of paper, then place a heavy book, cutting board, or brick on the top. This will weigh the paper down and keep it flat while drying.

13. You can add positive energy to your paper by embossing magickal symbols in it. Emboss the paper by pressing an object, such as a pentagram, into the paper while the paper is still wet, and then remove the object. If you want a well-defined motif, leave the object there while the paper is weighted and don't remove it until the paper has dried completely.

Feel free to experiment. The more personal energy and thought you put into creating your book of shadows, the more you'll enjoy using it. Check out the website *http://paperslurry.com* for good instructions with pictures that show various methods for making paper.

Bind Your Book

Now it's time to bind your book of shadows. Even if you decide not to make your own paper, you can still create your cover, assemble the blank pages, and bind the book yourself. The following steps will explain some finishing options as you complete the construction of your book of shadows.

MATERIALS NEEDED

Binding board or heavy stock paper from a craft store; you can wrap the cover in cloth, securing the cloth with good PVA glue (see end of material list)

Scissors

Ruler

Scoring tool, such as a box cutter or X-Acto knife

Binder clips or similar clamps

Heavy book, cutting board, or brick

Pencil

If you'd rather not use glue to bind, use a cord or ribbon. You'll also need a drill or hole punch and a template for placing the holes.

If you plan to use glue to bind, use a heavy brush and PVA (polyvinyl acetate) glue, which is the most durable. If you want to avoid chemicals, use a natural type of paste or glue, such as fish glue.

1. Choose the material for your cover.

2. Cut two equal-sized pieces that are slightly larger than the pages of the book.

3. Measure about ¼" from the edge of each piece and score lightly so your book will open and close easily.

4. Set aside a strip of the cover material or an extra sheet of paper to use for covering the spine.

5. Assemble all your pages and the front and back covers in a stack. Clamp them together firmly with binder clips or clamps. Put small pieces of wood under the clamps so you don't have clamp marks on your cover. Make sure to stack the pages neatly, for they will be permanently assembled in the configuration you have them in now. Make adjustments at this point or you'll have crooked pages in your book.

The Modern Witchcraft Grimoire

6. Line up the pages so that the unclamped edge of the stack hangs slightly over the edge of the table you are working on. This edge will become the spine of the book.

7. Use a heavy book, cutting board, or brick to weigh down the pages and keep them in place.

Note: If you are not going to use glue to make the spine, skip to step 12 for instructions on binding with ribbon.

8. With a brush, spread glue very thickly all along the edges of the pages at the spine. Allow the glue to dry thoroughly.

9. The piece used for the spine should be the same length as the cover of your book and three times the thickness of the book. You can determine the thickness of your book by measuring the total height of the stacked pages. Multiply this number by three, and you will get the correct width of the spine. Draw two parallel lines with a pencil on the inside of the spine (the side you intend to glue onto the book so the pencil marks won't show), dividing the spine into three equal parts. These lines will serve as your scoring guide.

10. Score the cover material along the edge of a metal ruler with your scoring tool. Be careful not to cut through the spine—just score it deep enough so that you can fold it easily.

11. Glue the strip along the edge of the book so that it hides the previously glued area. Allow the spine cover to dry.

12. If you prefer to try a different technique, use cord or ribbon. This method does not require a spine. After you've clamped the pages, punch or drill at least three holes along one side of your book. If you are using a hole punch, first make a template so all the holes will be the same size and distance from the left edge of the pages. Do not attempt to punch holes through the template; use the template to mark in pencil where the holes should be on each page, and then punch them out individually. This will make the holes more accurate, and your finished book will be more attractive. If you're handy with power tools, you can drill very slowly through the clamped stack and achieve the same result in less time. Be sure your pages are securely clamped together so they don't slip while you're drilling.

13. Use a ribbon or cord that is five times the length of your book. Choose a color that pleases you or holds symbolic meaning. Push the ribbon through the first hole at the top of the book, leaving a tail of 2" or more.

14. With the tail in place, weave the ribbon through all the remaining holes. When you reach the end, wrap the ribbon around the bottom and go back again through the hole you just used. Continue weaving the ribbon back through the holes up to the top, envisioning the spiral dance of the Goddess as you go.

15. When you've finished threading the ribbon through the last hole, wrap it tightly around the top, as you did at the bottom, and tie it together with the tail end.

The Modern Witchcraft Grimoire

Chapter 3

ORGANIZING YOUR GRIMOIRE

Unless you feel like shuffling through hundreds of pages in your grimoire, you'll need some sort of organizing system so you can find the spell you want when you want it. Just as you organize your kitchen cabinets and your closets for convenience, you'll naturally determine a method that works best for you. Each witch is unique and so is her book of shadows—both the type of book she chooses and the way she puts it together.

How you configure your book depends on your personality, your lifestyle, your individual needs and preferences, the types of spells and rituals you perform, your spiritual path, your goals and objectives, and a whole lot more. Remember the questions you asked yourself at the beginning of Chapter 2? How you answered those questions will guide you as you go about organizing the material in your grimoire.

WHERE TO BEGIN

In the previous chapter, we talked about choosing the style and form for your book of shadows—even the possibility of making your own from scratch. However, the first book you create probably won't be your last. You might even decide to start a new book of shadows each year, on Samhain or another date that holds meaning for you, such as your birthday.

Assess Yourself and Your Objectives

As discussed earlier, old grimoires contained incantations, invocations, and rituals for calling forth spirits. Most witches today don't limit themselves to those practices alone. However, you might decide you only want to record magick spells and rituals in your book of shadows: no poems, no dream scenarios, no doodles in the margins. That's fine. Conversely, you may take an "anything goes" approach and choose to include whatever strikes your fancy. That's fine too. Your grimoire is a sacred tool you create to serve your purposes. Go with whatever facilitates your goal.

- If you're a green witch, your book might emphasize spells that incorporate botanicals and other natural ingredients. Because you have a special relationship with nature, you may find it useful to organize your grimoire according to the seasons.
- If you enjoy drama, you may opt to focus on rituals and ceremonial practices. Arranging your material around the eight sabbats might make sense for you.
- Are you a healer? If so, you could create categories for different healing methods: potions and elixirs, salves and balms, talismans and amulets, etc.
- Do you travel a lot? Perhaps you'll find it useful to keep a small travel journal in which you record some of your favorite spells, in addition to your primary grimoire. You could even keep a selection of spells on your iPad or laptop.

Allow for Updates

As you progress along your spiritual path, you'll continue refining your practice, your techniques, and your objectives. Coven members or other people you work with will influence you. Things you read about the Craft and various magickal traditions will influence you. The outcomes of your spells will influence you. And the world you live in—as well as the nonphysical worlds that interface with our material one—will influence you. Therefore, you can expect to continually update your grimoire as you journey along the course you've chosen.

Your first grimoire might be a three-ring binder or an electronic book. This allows you to experiment with various formats and make adjustments as you see fit—before you invest a lot of time and/or money in a gorgeous grimoire that inspires awe every time you look at it. You can always hand-copy your material into a beautiful bound book later.

METHODS FOR ORGANIZING YOUR GRIMOIRE

As I've said before, each witch's priorities, perspective, and practices are unique; therefore, each book of shadows will reflect its author's individuality. You probably won't configure your book the same way as someone else does, just as you probably don't arrange documents in your computer the same way another person does. The following suggestions for organizing your grimoire are just that: suggestions. If one of them suits your purposes, great. If not, feel free to devise your own system. Or you might start with one method, then later switch to another after you've got more spellcasting experience under your belt.

Keep a Daybook

The easiest way to begin a grimoire is to use a chronological approach, writing in your book on a daily basis, as a sort of journal or daybook of your experiences. This method works well if your book's binding doesn't allow you to add or rearrange the pages. It also enables you to chart your personal and spiritual growth day-by-day. Be sure to date your entries.

Take a Seasonal Approach

Maybe you'd like to align yourself more closely with nature's seasons and organize your book of shadows accordingly. You can designate a section for springtime spells, another for summer spells, another for spells to do in autumn, and another for winter magick. Consider pressing seasonal flowers and leaves between the pages to enhance your appreciation of nature's cycle of growth and decline during the year.

Follow the Moon

In Wicca, the moon represents the Great Goddess and the Divine Feminine. Therefore, many witches tap the moon's energy in spellcraft and time their magickal workings around the moon's phases. You might like to organize your book of shadows according to the movements of the moon through the heavens. We'll take a closer look at this in Chapter 9.

Spell to Protect Your Home

Because the moon rules the home, the moon's phase and sign are especially important in spells you do for your home. If possible, cast this spell while the moon is in Cancer, the moon's sign. Or, perform it 3 days before the new moon.

TOOLS AND INGREDIENTS

An image of your totem animal

Basil leaves (dried or fresh)

1. Do you have a totem animal? Totems serve as guardians and helpers—you can call upon them to aid you in times of need. Your totem is an animal, bird, reptile, or insect with which you feel a strong sense of kinship and which, to you, represents protective power. Select an image of your totem animal—a figurine, illustration, or photograph—and place it near your front door.

2. Say aloud, to your animal guardian:

"Protect this home,
High to low,
Fence to fence,
Door to door,
Light to dense,
Roof to floor."

3. Scatter the basil leaves around the outside of your home, making a big circle. Start in the east and move in a clockwise direction until you've completed the protective circle.

4. If you live in an apartment, you can either scatter the leaves around the entire building or place them in a bowl; set the bowl and your animal image just inside the door to your apartment.

Separate Everyday Spells from Special Occasion Spells

Some witches designate certain spells, rituals, and practices for sabbats and special occasions, such as birthdays or handfastings. Other spells may be performed anytime, or on an as-needed basis. These might include ritual baths, cleansing/clearing practices, and protection or healing spells. Perhaps you'd like to organize your book of shadows this way.

Arrange Your Book by Topic

Some people find it convenient to organize their spells into categories, according to the topic or purpose of the spells. For example, you might have a section for love spells, another for prosperity spells, and so on. Consider using different colored paper for the various types of spells: pink for love spells, green for money spells, etc. In Chapter 10, we'll discuss this method more extensively.

Sort Your Spells by Type

Maybe you'd prefer to sort your spells into categories according to how you create and use them. For instance, you might devote a section to magick potions, another to healing balms and salves, and another to ritual baths. This method can be useful when you're collecting the components you need for your spells or shopping for ingredients. It also lets you see what spells you can do on the spur of the moment, based on the materials you have on hand. In Chapter 14, we'll cover this method in more detail.

The Drink of Love

This magick potion should be shared with a romantic partner to improve the relationship. Perform the spell on a Friday night during the waxing moon, or when the moon is in Libra.

TOOLS AND INGREDIENTS

The Lovers card from a tarot deck

Spring water in a clear glass

A drop of melted honey or a pinch of sugar

A silver (or silver plate) spoon

1. Place the tarot card face-up on a windowsill where the moon will shine on it.
2. Set the glass of water on top of the card and leave it overnight. The image of the card will be imprinted into the water.
3. In the morning, add the honey or sugar to the glass of water.
4. Stir the potion with the silver spoon, using a clockwise motion, to sweeten the water and, symbolically, your relationship.
5. Return the tarot card to your deck.
6. Drink the water with your partner to strengthen the love between you.

Organize Spells by Their Components

Cookbooks often arrange recipes according to their main ingredients—for example, meat, fish, poultry, pasta, vegetables. You can organize your grimoire this way too by setting up sections for herbal spells, gemstone spells, candle spells, and so on. As with sorting your spells by type, this method can simplify things when you're shopping for ingredients or when you need to perform a spell on the spur of the moment using materials you already have on hand.

Gemstone Protection Amulet

This spell provides protection while traveling. Put it in your car's glove compartment to ensure protection on a daily basis, or carry it in your pocket, purse, or suitcase for safety during a long-distance trip.

TOOLS AND INGREDIENTS

1 piece of amber

1 piece of quartz crystal

1 piece of jade

1 piece of turquoise

1 piece of topaz

1 piece of agate

Amber essential oil

1 white pouch, preferably made of silk (or another natural fabric)

1 black ribbon

Saltwater

1. Wash the gemstones with mild soap and water, then set them in the sun for a few minutes to remove any unwanted energies.

2. Rub a little amber essential oil on each of the stones, then slip them into the pouch.

3. Tie the bag closed with the ribbon, making 9 knots.

4. Each time you tie a knot, repeat this affirmation: "This amulet keeps me safe and sound at all times and in all situations."

5. When you've finished, sprinkle the amulet with a little saltwater to charge it.

Have these suggestions started you thinking about how you might organize your own grimoire? In Part II, we'll explore these and other options in greater depth and look at details that can support your journey as a witch and spellworker.

Chapter 4

WHAT TO INCLUDE IN YOUR GRIMOIRE

What does it mean to practice magick? In Wicca, we see "magick" as working harmoniously with the natural forces all around us—in both the material world and beyond—to generate outcomes. A witch uses her attunement and influence to manipulate these forces, in order to elicit a series of controlled coincidences that will achieve a desired result. She seeks to move, bend, or otherwise change the natural flow of energy in the universe to bring about a condition that will benefit herself or someone else, and finally, all other beings as well.

Because your book of shadows will become your personal collection of spells and rituals—as well as an intimate account of your magickal journey—it's important to have a clear idea why you've chosen this path and what you hope to achieve by following the Wiccan Way. Take some time to think about why practicing magick is important to you. Begin to define what you believe. Then write your thoughts in your grimoire. Putting your ideas and desires down on paper helps to clarify them.

What do you consider the dominant aspects of your magickal practice? Are you primarily concerned with affecting your personal life (love, career, money)? Or do you seek to deepen your spiritual connection to the universe and the Divine? Is your magick based in obtaining practical results or enhancing your intuition? Most likely, you will combine all of these, but at various times different motivations will dominate.

Although magick is as limitless as the imagination, it should always be grounded and based in reality. Grounding and centering, as you may know, play a part in many spells and rituals. Effective spells need a structure, and you can best evaluate your structure by recording it. You can only truly observe the results of your work if you write down your spells from conception to outcome. No matter how good your memory is, you can't possibly remember everything—nor can you share your knowledge and experiences with others (if you choose to) unless you create a body of information to pass on.

AT THE BEGINNING

Before you actually start recording spells, incantations, invocations, rituals, etc. in your grimoire, consider writing down the rules, ethics, and principles you choose to follow. These will guide you as you journey on your spiritual path and as you progress in your magickal work. Many witches abide by what's known as the "law of three." This means that whatever intention and energy you send out returns to you like a boomerang, but threefold. As you can see, this serves as a strong deterrent against mischief, manipulation, or other kinds of deceptive practices.

The Wiccan Rede

"Bide the Wiccan law ye must
In perfect love, in perfect trust,
Eight words the Wiccan Rede fulfill:
An' ye harm none, do what ye will.

The Modern Witchcraft Grimoire

What ye send forth comes back to thee,
So ever mind the Rule of Three.
Follow this with mind and heart,
And merry ye meet, and merry ye part."

Although your principles may conform to those of a group with which you work or the stated rules of a particular tradition you follow, ultimately they grow out of your individual convictions. Your personal code of ethics may be as simple as "Harm none." In time and with experience, your early beliefs may change, just as your mundane beliefs have likely changed since childhood. Allow your ideas to evolve, as you follow your own truth and inner guidance.

> *"I think the highest purpose of ritual or magickal work is to seek our gods, to commune with the cosmic 'mirror' and the spirits of nature in order to learn more of the divinity within ourselves and reach evermore toward personal growth in its highest expression."*
>
> —MARIA KAY SIMMS, *A TIME FOR MAGICK*

Begin with a Blessing

You might like to bless what you write in your grimoire by starting each entry with a prayer, poem, or inspirational saying. Many witches call upon the Goddess or another divine being before engaging in magick work and request that entity's protection and guidance. Writing in your grimoire is a magick ritual; therefore, beginning with a blessing makes perfect sense. Use a different blessing for every entry or the same one each time you write. Here's an example:

A Celtic Blessing
"Calm me, Goddess
as you calmed the storm,
Still me, Goddess
keep me from harm.
Let all tumult within me cease.
Enfold me, Goddess, in your peace."

Date Your Entries

I recommend dating each entry you make in your grimoire. This enables you to see how much time elapsed between casting a spell and the manifestation of its outcome. It also helps you place your experiences within a context and lets you witness your personal evolution over time.

RECORD YOUR MAGICKAL WORKINGS

As soon as possible after completing a spell, ritual, or other magickal working, record it in your grimoire. Include any information you consider relevant, such as the following:

- Describe your purpose (intention) for doing what you did. If you performed a spell for another person, you may want to say so (use initials or a pseudonym if you prefer not to mention the person's real name).
- Where did you perform the spell or ritual?
- Did anyone else participate? (Use initials or a pseudonym if you prefer.)
- What tools/ingredients/components did you use?
- What did you actually do? Write down the steps you took, in the order you did them: cleansed the space, cast a circle, called upon deities, lit candles, or whatever you did.
- What did you experience? How did you feel during the process? Did you receive any insights, visions, sensations, etc.? Did anything unexpected occur?
- Describe the results of your spell. How long did it take to manifest? Was the outcome what you intended? What went right or wrong?
- Would you do this spell again? What, if anything, would you do differently next time?

Feel free to adapt this basic list to suit your own needs. Include anything you feel is significant or might be beneficial to your spellworking. You can go back later and add further insights, developments, or information.

Here's an example of what an entry in your book of shadows might look like:

Spell to Get a Raise

December 1, 2016—sun in Sagittarius, waxing moon in Capricorn

TOOLS AND INGREDIENTS

Ballpoint pen

Gold candle

Peppermint essential oil

Candleholder

$20 bill

Matches

1. Cleared the space with sage incense.
2. Cast a circle. (See Chapter 13 for details on how to cast and open circles.)
3. With the pen, inscribed "+ wealth" and three $ signs on the candle.
4. Dressed the candle with peppermint oil and put it in the candleholder.
5. Laid the $20 bill on my altar.
6. Set the candleholder on top of the $20 bill.
7. Lit the candle.
8. Said the following incantation aloud while staring at the flame:

"Element of fire,
Fulfill my desire,
The raise I seek,
I receive this week."

9. Let the candle burn for 20 minutes, then snuffed it out.
10. Opened the circle.
11. Repeated this again on 12/2/16 and 12/3/16, letting the candle burn down completely on the third day. Felt empowered, relaxed, and confident.
12. Success! On 12/8/16, received notice of a forthcoming raise after the first of the year. Thank you, Goddess!

WHAT ELSE GOES IN YOUR GRIMOIRE?

Let's use the kitchen analogy again. If you love to cook, you may keep all sorts of special equipment and cool gadgets in your pantry and cabinets. If you entertain regularly, you may consider it important to have beautiful dishes, sterling silverware, crystal glasses, linen tablecloths, and so on. If you live alone or rely heavily on takeout and frozen meals, your needs will be much simpler. The same holds true for your grimoire. The good news is, you get to choose what to include and what to omit—and you can change that at any time.

When you first begin keeping a grimoire, you may be tempted to put everything you come across within its pages. Over time, however, you'll probably become more selective. Perhaps you'll decide to weed out some material, just as you'd weed your garden to showcase what you consider important. William Morris, a nineteenth-century English textile designer, artist, and poet, said, "Have nothing in your houses that you do not know to be useful, or believe to be beautiful."

I think the same can be said for your book of shadows. Although it can be useful to look back at early entries to track your journey, don't be afraid to discard anything you no longer need.

Keep Track of Celestial Influences

As you record your magickal journey, you may find it helpful to keep track of the cosmic conditions that affect you. In addition to dating each entry in your book of shadows, I suggest you also include the moon's phase, and if you know astrology, note other celestial activity that might be relevant. For instance, Venus's placement could have an impact on love spells. If you're doing a spell for career success, the positions of the sun, Jupiter, and Saturn could factor in. You could even cast a chart for the day, print it out, and add it to your grimoire beside what you write for that day. Many online sites—including *www.astro.com*—offer free charts that you can calculate in a few minutes.

Track Your Health Cycles

Your health can also affect your magickal workings. Therefore, you may want to note any physical or emotional conditions you are experiencing at the time you perform a ritual or spell. Did you feel particularly energized? Tired because the baby kept you awake most of the night before? Did you have a cold or headache when you cast the spell? Women may also find it useful to track menstrual cycles, as these often influence your emotions and, consequently, the magick you do. You may discover that you feel more powerful or more intuitive at certain times of the month.

Note Situations in Your Everyday Life

It's hard to separate our magickal lives from our everyday lives—even for seasoned witches. If something in your mundane world is troubling you and sucking up a lot of your energy, you may not feel as focused or powerful in your spellworking—and you may not achieve the results you desire. Note this in your grimoire. On the other hand, if you're riding the crest of the wave and everything seems right at the moment, note that too. Maybe you've met a new person who shares your path or you started a yoga class or returned from a restful vacation. Occurrences such as these may influence your magick practice, directly or indirectly, so it's a good idea to keep track of them.

> *"Let my worship be within the heart that rejoices,*
> *for behold: all acts of love and pleasure are my rituals.*
> *And therefore, let there be beauty and strength,*
> *power and compassion, honor and humility,*
> *mirth and reverence within you."*
> —Doreen Valiente, "The Charge of the Goddess"

Pay Attention to Your Dreams

Many dream researchers and therapists believe your subconscious communicates with you through your dreams. Some metaphysicians suggest that your guides, angels, or other nonphysical entities may also send messages to you via dreams. Record any dreams that seem especially vivid, meaningful, or strange, or that recur again and again—they may provide valuable insights or even glimpses of the future. Also note dreams that have a direct correlation to things you're focusing on in your spiritual or magickal work. In Chapter 18, we'll talk more about dreams and how to work with them creatively.

Record Your Readings

Do you do tarot or rune readings? Consult the *I Ching* or use a pendulum to gain advice? If you work with one or more oracles, you'll probably want to keep a record of your readings. You may designate a separate journal in which to chronicle these, but your grimoire is a good place to write them down too. Date each reading and note the reason you did it or the question you asked. Draw the spread, indicating the positions of the cards, runes, etc. Add your own interpretation—what does the reading mean to you? Later on, you can revisit what you've written and describe how things turned out. You might record your reading like this:

Past, Present, Future Tarot Reading

October 12, 2016

"Please provide insight into my relationship with A"

Past	Present	Future
2 of swords	7 of wands	Temperance

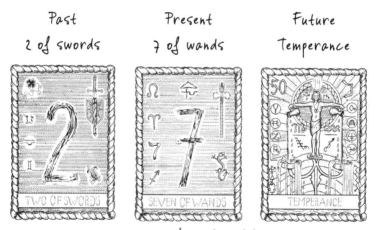

Interpretation: In the past I've felt helpless and confused about what to do. Now, I'm trying to hang in there and be strong; I'm determined to make this relationship work and I'm learning ways to handle problems better, without giving up or giving in. Temperance in the future position suggests things will be more peaceful, and I sense we'll establish a more balanced and harmonious arrangement.

The Modern Witchcraft Grimoire

Other Things to Include

Do you have a favorite poem or song that resonates with you at a deep level? Have you just read an inspiring passage in a book? You may wish to jot these down in your book of shadows—especially if they figure into your spiritual and/or magickal path in some way. Musings about things you noticed while walking in the park, comments on what's transpiring in the world around you, thought-provoking ideas raised by a friend—all these, and much more, may have a place in your book of shadows too.

Many witches like to include visuals in their grimoires. Early grimoires often contained drawings of occult symbols and other illustrations as well. Even if you don't consider yourself an artist, you can still sketch images in the margins—you don't have to show them to anyone else, so don't censor yourself. Pictures from print sources or downloaded from the Internet can aid your visualization process. Do you want to take a trip to an exotic land? Why not paste a photo of that place in your book to help you focus on your goal? If you check out online images of grimoires, you'll see that lots of books—both ancient and modern—feature artwork of all kinds. Remember the old saying, a picture's worth a thousand words? This is definitely true in spellcasting.

We've already mentioned affixing dried leaves, herbs, and flowers to your grimoire. Don't limit yourself to these alone, however. Feathers, bits of lovely lace, a scrap of patterned silk, a remnant of an antique Japanese fan, a lock of your lover's hair, tiny seashells, a piece of your favorite sheet music, photos of loved ones, ribbons tied into magick knots . . . the possibilities are endless. What triggers your imagination? The ability to imagine a result, after all, must precede the result you seek to manifest.

Purists might frown on such diversions from tradition, but hey, it's your book, right? Whatever holds meaning for you has the potential to enrich your personal growth and enhance your magickal workings. Your book of shadows is a safe place to explore those parts of yourself that you may never have felt free to unveil before, to face your inner shadow, to acknowledge what holds meaning for you, and to connect with the beautiful being you are in your heart of hearts.

Chapter 5

PREPARING TO USE YOUR GRIMOIRE

You've acquired a book that will become your grimoire—or fabricated your own—and given thought to how you'll organize it. Now it's time to prepare yourself and your book for the ongoing relationship that will develop between you.

Writing in your book of shadows is a magickal act, so you'll want to treat it as such. This means you'll likely do your journaling within a sacred space you've created for your spellwork and other ritual practices. Perhaps you've already established a sacred place in your home. You may also have set up an altar there, where you could display your grimoire. If you haven't done this yet, you can use the following instructions or design your own ritual to create a sacred space for all your magickal workings.

CREATING SACRED SPACE

The purpose of defining and consecrating a sacred space is to give yourself a dedicated realm in which to perform magick and ritual, where you can move beyond your ordinary world when you so choose. You are, in essence, raising a temple (though not necessarily a brick-and-mortar one) for meditation, worship, divination, spellcasting, or any other aspect of magickal practice you wish to do here—including writing in your grimoire. You can create a more or less permanent sacred space or a temporary one, depending on your intentions and circumstances.

The Power of the Circle

In *The Spiral Dance*, Starhawk describes the circle as "the creation of a sacred space . . . Power, the subtle force that shapes reality, is raised through chanting or dancing and may be directed through a symbol or visualization. With the raising of the cone of power comes ecstasy, which may then lead to a trance state in which visions are seen and insights gained."

Cleansing Your Sacred Space

Once you've determined the location of your sacred space, take a broom and sweep the area thoroughly to clear away dust, dirt, and clutter. This is the real reason witches use brooms, not to fly through the sky. After you finish physically sweeping the area, focus on cleansing the psychic space. In this way, you remove unwanted energies or influences—any "bad vibes" that might linger there. Begin in the east and work your way counterclockwise around the area, in a circular fashion. Sweep the air, from the floor up to as high as you can comfortably reach. When you have gone around your area three times, lay the broom on the floor and visualize all the negative energy breaking up and dissolving.

Some spellworkers also like to "smudge" the area with the smoke from burning sage. Light a sage wand/bundle (available at New Age shops and online) or a stick of sage incense. Walk in a circle, starting in the east and moving counterclockwise, letting the smoke waft through the area. Then walk in an X across the space to finish cleansing your space. Now stand in the center of your space and feel the fresh, light, clean energy around you.

Purifying Your Sacred Space

For this next level of cleansing you'll need two chalices or tall glasses. Fill one with spring (or bottled) water. The water should be kinetic, not static, during this process for it is the essence of running water that generates potency. In the other chalice, place four pinches of salt, one to represent each of the four directions.

1. Hold the chalice that contains the water in your left hand and the chalice with the salt crystals in your right.
2. Pour the water into the chalice of salt, combining the two elements of water and earth.
3. Pour the now salted water back into the chalice in your left hand, dissolving the salt crystals so that the two distinct elements mix thoroughly. Continue pouring the water back and forth from hand to hand, as you repeat this intention:

"With salt I purify
With water I cleanse
All things in accord
From beginning to end."

If you prefer, you can create your own original incantation or blessing.

Dedicating Your Sacred Space

The next step is to dedicate your sacred space. You can begin by anointing the area you've chosen with frankincense essential oil (or another oil you prefer). Just put a little dab in each corner, starting in the east and moving clockwise around the space, creating a cross within a circle. This symbol represents the balance of female and male energies, the circle of creation, the four directions, and the four elements.

You may also opt to place a stone or crystal that has meaning for you at each of the four compass directions. (If your sacred space is outdoors, you can bury the stones in the ground.) Or you might like to design symbols that signify peace, holiness, protection, power, etc. and position them in your space. Some people display images of beloved deities in their sacred spaces. If you wish, you can create an elaborate ritual for dedicating your space—the choice is up to you.

Protecting Your Sacred Space

After you've finished setting up your sacred space, you'll want to protect it from intrusive energies. Consider these suggestions:

- Place a stone associated with protection, such as onyx, hematite, or peridot, in the area.
- Lay dried basil leaves in your sacred space.
- Position or draw a pentagram or other protective symbol there.
- Sprinkle some sea salt in the corners.
- Set a clove of garlic in your space.

"As a magician, you use ritual in order to create within yourself a mental state that allows you to give clear and direct instructions to your unconscious mind . . . Ritual is a means to an end, not an end in itself."
—NANCY B. WATSON, PRACTICAL SOLITARY MAGIC

CONSECRATE YOUR GRIMOIRE

The next step is to dedicate your book of shadows to its sacred purpose. Now you affirm your intention to do good works in the world and to record what you do so that it may benefit all beings.

1. Light a yellow candle on your altar (or other place where you do your magick work). If you wish, call upon Sophia, goddess of wisdom, or another deity to guide you.
2. Light frankincense incense in an incense burner.
3. Hold your book slightly opened above the rising smoke. Turn the pages slowly and gently, allowing the fragrant smoke to drift through the pages.

The Modern Witchcraft Grimoire

4. Speak the following words, or improvise your own:

"Blessed be this instrument of art,
By my hand [or human hands] you were made,
By magick, be now changed.
No more an ordinary book in my eyes but a grimoire dedicated to the Craft of the Wise.
By all the power of three times three
As I will, so mote it be."

5. Hold the book on your right hand and place your left hand on top of the book as you open yourself to the changes and lessons yet to come.
6. Imagine all the witches you know of and admire, both contemporary and historical. Picture yourself in the middle of a growing circle. To your left envision those who are older than you, and the elders who have passed on. To your right see the younger ones and those who will come in the future.
7. Recognize your place in the spiral of time and acknowledge this task that you have chosen. See yourself within the context of humanity and companionship. When the image is clear in your mind, speak these words aloud, or improvise your own:

"Wisdom of the ages, be with me here now.
Sacred book of changes, this promise I vow:
To honor those who have gone before;
To preserve the secrets, legends, and lore;
To hold my place in the spiral of time;
Within this sacred grimoire of mine."

When you've finished, take some time to think about the blessing ceremony you just performed. Did you experience a shift in the energy around you? Did you receive any insights, sensations, visions, or guidance? Do you sense that your book of shadows is now ready to serve as a sacred tool for furthering your purpose as a witch? If you called upon a deity to aid you, thank that deity now. Take some time to record the very first entry in your personal book of shadows—the experience of consecrating your book.

WRITING IN YOUR GRIMOIRE

The authors of secular books often dedicate them to people they love or to those who have assisted them in the writing process. You may choose to dedicate your grimoire to a deity to whom you are devoted, one who has played a special role in your life, or one whom you want to guide you in the magickal work you do—including the process of writing in your book of shadows. Therefore, the very first page of your book might be your dedication page.

Protecting Your Secrets

Consider putting a protection symbol at the beginning of your book to help safeguard it. A pentagram is a frequently used symbol of protection, but you can choose any emblem that holds meaning for you. You might even like to design a special symbol for this purpose. In Chapter 12 you'll learn how to create magick symbols known as *sigils*.

In keeping with the tradition of secrecy, you may want to use your magick name or Craft name when writing in your grimoire. If you mention anyone else within its pages, you'll probably want to disguise that person's identity too, referring to him or her by a pseudonym or initials. The same holds true for the names of private locations, such as the homes of fellow witches. This is a good precaution to take if you're worried that your book might fall into the wrong hands.

Writing in Code

Some witches choose to exercise yet another method for ensuring that the information in their grimoires remains secret. They write in code. Then, if an inappropriate person discovers their books, that individual won't be able to read the contents. You can explore this option if you wish. Or you could consider writing only certain parts of your book in a secret script if you want some portions to remain accessible to others.

SECRET SCRIPTS

Since ancient times, magickal workers and others who sought to protect their knowledge—and themselves—have written in secret scripts. Some authors wrote in languages other than those used in the culture or country where they lived, such as Sanskrit or Coptic, which worked well enough in the days when few people could read or write and even fewer knew the languages spoken in foreign lands. Today, however, with the availability of online translation sites, you'll have to go to greater lengths if you really want to keep what you write secret.

The Theban Alphabet

Although we cannot say for certain what the Theban alphabet's origins are, it is a beautiful and widely used magickal alphabet, especially among Gardnerian Wiccans. The Golden Dawn also adopted it in the nineteenth century. Sometimes referred to as the Witch's Alphabet or the Runes of Honorius, this ceremonial text came into use during the medieval period. Heinrich Cornelius Agrippa mentioned the script in Book III of the *Three Books of Occult Philosophy* published in the 1530s, and attributed it to Honorius of Thebes. Agrippa credited Pietro d'Abano (or Peter of Abano), an Italian writer and magician who lived during the thirteenth century, with preserving the Theban alphabet.

A		B		C		D	
E		F		G		H	
I		J		K		L	
M		N		O		P	
Q		R		S		T	
U		V		W		X	
		Y		Z			

The Futhark Runes

Known as the Older Rune Row or the Elder Futhark, these runes were used by Germanic ceremonial magicians for divination and inspiration, and as inscriptions in talismans and amulets. The word "rune" means a secret or mystery. Although they have phonetic correlations, the Futhark runes never evolved into a spoken language. The name "futhark" derives from the first six characters that appear in this system. According to Nordic legend, the god Odin (or Woden) first spied the runes as he hung from the World Tree, Yggdrasil, for nine days and nights.

The runes can also serve as an oracle for divination; each individual rune contains a specific esoteric message. For 2,000 years, this oracle was used throughout Northern Europe and Scandinavia, until 1639 when the Christian church banned it. Viking and Saxon invaders brought the runes to the British Isles. In the United States, J.R.R. Tolkien's *The Lord of the Rings* introduced many readers to the runes, and Ralph Blum's bestseller *The Book of Runes* taught people how to use the oracle.

FUTHARK RUNES			
Number	**Shape**	**Phonetic Value**	**Name**
1	ᚠ	F	Fehu
2	ᚢ	U	Uruz
3	ᚦ	TH	Thurisaz
4	ᚨ	A	Ansuz
5	ᚱ	R	Raidho
6	ᚲ	K	Kaunaz
7	ᚷ	G	Gebo
8	ᚹ	W	Wunjo

FUTHARK RUNES			
Number	**Shape**	**Phonetic Value**	**Name**
9	ᚺ	H	Hagalaz
10	ᚾ	N	Nauthiz
11	ᛁ	I	Isa
12	ᛃ	J	Jera
13	ᛇ	EI	Eihaw
14	ᛈ	P	Perthro
15	ᛉ	Z	Algiz
16	ᛋ	S	Sowilo
17	↑	T	Teiwaz
18	ᛒ	B	Berkano
19	ᛗ	E	Ehwaz
20	ᛗ	M	Mannaz
21	ᛚ	L	Laguz
22	◇	NG	Ingwaz
23	ᛞ	D	Dagaz
24	ᛟ	O	Othala

The Ogham Runes

The early Celts used an alphabet known as Ogham, based on trees. Because the Celts and Druids considered trees sacred, the Ogham letters also serve as mystical symbols. Each of the twenty letters in this system corresponds to a particular tree. B (Beith), for instance, is linked with the birch; N (Nion) represents the ash tree. The letters are composed of a series of straight and angled lines, or notches, cut along a central line or stave. A word or phrase written in Ogham looks a bit like a tree limb with branches sprouting from it. Throughout Ireland and Britain you can see standing stones engraved with Ogham glyphs. Early Celtic manuscripts also feature Ogham script.

Another unique characteristic of Ogham is that it can be signed with the fingers. Using a part of the body—the torso, nose, or leg—as a center dividing line, you can extend your fingers on either side to form letters.

OGHAM ALPHABET			
Shape	**Letter**	**Name**	**Tree**
├	B	Beith	Birch
⊨	L	Luis	Rowan
⊫	F	Fearn	Alder
⊯	S	Sail	Willow
⊰	N	Nion	Ash
⊣	H	hÚath	Hawthorn
⊨	D	Dair	Oak

OGHAM ALPHABET			
Shape	**Letter**	**Name**	**Tree**
⊐|	T	Tinne	Holly
⊐|	C	Coll	Hazel
⊐|	Q	Quert	Apple
⊥	M	Muin	Vine
⊁	G	Gort	Ivy
⊁	NG	nGéatal	Reed
⊁	Z (st)	Straif	Blackthorn
⊁	R	Ruis	Elder
⊥	A	Ailm	Silver Fir
⊥	O	Onn	Gorse
⊥	U	Úr	Heather
⊥	E	Eadha	Poplar
⊥	I	Iodhadh	Yew

Other Options

The Greek mathematician and philosopher Pythagoras, who lived in the sixth century B.C.E., is usually credited with having developed the system of numerology that we use today. This study of numbers, known as *gematria*, attaches a number equivalent to each letter in a word. Each number has an esoteric meaning as well as a mundane one. Someone who understands the hidden correspondences between letters and numbers can read a word and comprehend a secret meaning behind the obvious one.

TABLE OF NUMBER–LETTER CORRESPONDENCES								
1	2	3	4	5	6	7	8	9
A	B	C	D	E	F	G	H	I
J	K	L	M	N	O	P	Q	R
S	T	U	V	W	X	Y	Z	

Various other magickal alphabets exist too, such as the Masonic/Rosicrucian system. In his comprehensive book, *The Magician's Companion*, Bill Whitcomb presents a collection of different secret scripts including an intriguing one based on configurations of daggers. You can even design your very own magick language that only you can interpret.

PREPARING YOURSELF TO WRITE

Before you begin writing in your grimoire, you'll want to prepare your body and your mind. Open yourself to the guidance of the Goddess or a particular deity with whom you've chosen to work. You want to move into a realm beyond the mundane, where you align with Spirit. Begin your preparation by making a conscious decision to enter the time and space we refer to as "between the worlds."

Turn off the TV. Shut down your computer. Silence your phone. Dim the lights. Light a candle or two or three. Do not let the outside world intrude. Invite benevolent forces to assist you. Relax and breathe slowly, deeply. Clear your mind.

One by one, begin to release your distractions, letting them flow further and further away from you.

1. Sit in a comfortable place with your spine straight, facing your altar if you have one. Picture a radiant ball of energy located in the center of your being, your solar plexus, about halfway between your heart and your navel. As you continue to breathe, allow the light to expand. As you inhale, understand that as you take the surrounding air into your body, you transform it into energy. As you exhale, you release your cares and concerns. Get in touch with this cycle of breathing, of energy released and replenished, replenished and released.

2. If you are sitting in a chair, bend down and touch the floor with the palms of your hands as you breathe in, imagining that you are gathering energy from the earth beneath you, beneath your home. Picture the earth. Now send your energy outward so that you can psychically touch things beyond your physical reach. Your reach extends beyond the floorboards, beyond the foundations of your home, deep into the sacred earth.

3. Call up this energy as you breathe in. Sit up straight again, and let the energy flow through you. As you exhale, send it spiraling into your center. Envision it transforming into a glowing light that you hold within the core of your being. When this image becomes very clear, visualize the glowing ball of energy moving slightly, first spiraling within itself, and then traveling up and down a bit. Realize that as you breathe, you are taking in energy from the air and transforming it into living breath. You are also taking in energy from the earth and transforming it into active power.

4. Stay focused and let the rising ball of energy reach your heart. Experience this as an embrace from the Goddess, the power of the earth moving through you according to your will. Envision the ball of energy separating and becoming two distinct spheres. As the spheres separate, they travel to your shoulders. Feel the warmth surrounding your shoulders as you would if you were walking in bright sunlight.

5. Let the spheres of pulsing, glowing light travel slowly down your arms; experience each movement as a distinct sensation. Your shoulders drop and become more relaxed. Any residual tension in

your arms completely dissipates. Your wrists grow limp. You are surrendering to the beauty of this power, even as you are directing it. The energy fills your hands and permeates all the way to your fingertips.

6. Turn your hands over so that your palms face-up. Slowly raise your arms. Imagine sending this energy outward to touch all beings. Extend your arms with your palms facing outward in an invoking gesture. Breathe deeply and feel how this transforming energy changes you.

7. Open your eyes and look around the room. Notice how your perception has changed. Lower your arms slowly and let your hands touch the floor once again. Continue focusing on the cycle of breath, releasing and replenishing energy. As you exhale, send the energy back into the earth from which it came. Breathe deeply.

8. You should feel relaxed, but not the least bit sleepy. Tranquil, but invigorated and alive, in touch with the earth and with the delicate energies to which the intuitive mind is open. Think about how a simple act such as grounding your energy and opening your psychic center can heighten your awareness. Now you are ready to begin writing.

"Magick happens when you step into who you truly are and embrace that which fulfills your soul."
—Dacha Avelin, *Embracing Your Inner Witch*

Set aside time to write in your grimoire on a regular basis. Incorporate writing into your magickal practice and into your regular routine. Find some time to write in the morning, remembering your dreams and delineating your hopes for the day. Write in the evening to reflect on the day's events. A line or two will suffice. Honor the moments in life that could be easily forgotten by jotting down a word or two about the sunrise or the approach of twilight.

Your grimoire can be anything and everything you want it to be. It is the place for you to explore and express your spirituality: a safe place free from other people's judgment, criticism, and skepticism. No one but you need be aware of the secrets kept within its pages. Creating your own grimoire lets you deepen awareness of your magickal life. By writing your story, you may also become an inspiration for others. Your book of shadows will enhance your knowledge of yourself, your aspirations, your dreams, and your personal growth. May it comfort you in times of darkness and bring you joy in times of light. May it keep your secrets as a trusted friend would, protect the stories of your lifetime, and hold your personal mythology securely.

Merry meet, and merry part, and merry meet again. Blessed be.

—❖— PART II —❖—

Using
Your
Grimoire

Chapter 6

EVERYDAY MAGICK

Magick isn't something you do, it's what you are. As a witch, you will make magickal workings an integral part of your everyday life. We usually think of the sabbats as times to perform spells and rituals. The sabbats, however, only make up eight days out of 365 each year—what about the rest? Why wait for the next sabbat to cast a spell, communicate with the spirit realm, or engage in a meaningful ritual?

Every day is a magickal day, if you choose to see it that way. Wondrous happenings and amazing revelations occur each day of the year. All we have to do is open our eyes and minds and hearts to these occurrences. Each day also affords unique opportunities for spellworking. By understanding the distinct qualities of the days of the week and the forces behind them, you can attune yourself to their special energies and thus enhance the power of your spells. Of course, you'll want to record your experiences in your grimoire.

"To work magic, I need a basic belief in my ability to do things and cause things to happen. That belief is generated and sustained by my daily actions."

—STARHAWK

MORNING RITUALS

You may enjoy writing in your book of shadows as soon as you awaken, thus making it part of your morning routine. This way, the images from your dreams will still be fresh and you can record them in detail. Later on, the busyness of the day will likely cloud your memory. Early morning is also a good time to set out your intentions for the day.

In addition to writing, you may want to design a simple ritual that will start the day on a pleasant note. Anything that you do every day with awareness becomes a ritual, such as taking a refreshing shower or savoring a morning cup of coffee. The challenge is to make the ritual sacred, and to receive the benefits of divine grace. You may only need a few moments to transform your morning experience from mundane to magickal, thus paving the way to a more inspired and productive day.

Use the following suggested ritual to start your day, or design one of your own. Personalize the ritual, if you wish, by inserting the names of other goddesses or deities with whom you feel a special affinity.

1. Begin by sitting or standing before your altar. Place a small quartz crystal, a cup or chalice of water, a candle, a little essential oil that you find pleasing, and some incense on the altar. Light the candle to symbolize the rising sun, and then take a moment to reflect silently on the energies you'd like to call to yourself during the unfolding day. Imagine your perfect day and try to form a clear image of it in your mind. You may want to accomplish something specific. Perhaps you'd like to change something in your regimen, such as eating a healthy breakfast instead of grabbing a doughnut.

2. Picture yourself in a state of attainment. See yourself achieving whatever your heart desires. Imagine doing all the things you mean to do and need to do in a state of joy and satisfaction. When the image of what you intend is clear, speak the following words aloud, or improvise your own: "Rosy-fingered Eos, goddess of the dawn who paints the morning sky with light, I ask for your blessing and rejoice as you set the sky alight. I anoint myself as your child, alive and anew with your radiant energy."

The Modern Witchcraft Grimoire

3. Place a small drop of essential oil on your fingertip. Touch your fingertip to your third eye (on your forehead, between your eyebrows). See yourself bathed in the light of the breaking dawn.

4. Light the incense and let its perfume waft over you. Inhale its aroma and speak the following words: "The fires of day have risen. Let my heart's desire rise up to the feet of the Goddess, that she may gather and direct my sacred intention with her wisdom and power. As the sun climbs through the sky, bless me, Lady of the Morning, who bestows abundance to us, her children. So mote it be."

5. Grasp the cup/chalice of water and hold it aloft to toast the day. Bring it down to chest level, near to your heart. Dip your fingers in the water, close your eyes, and place a little water on each eyelid. Say aloud, "Goddess Iris, who adorns the sky with rainbows of light, bring me clarity of vision that I may see the true nature of everything around me. May I be blessed in your eyes."

6. Hold the crystal in your hands, feeling it come alive with your energy. Imbue the stone with the intentions of what you most desire to manifest on this day. As you hold the crystal, speak the following words or improvise your own: "Blessed Mother Earth, I honor you and your unending generosity. May your sacred treasure enrich my existence. May I share the abundance of the Goddess on this day."

7. Extinguish the candle. Carry the crystal with you as a talisman to help you maintain your focus throughout the day.

Note in your grimoire any impressions, sensations, insights, or other experiences that arise during your morning ritual. Quite possibly you'll receive some sort of awareness or guidance now that can help you as the day unfolds.

EVENING RITUALS

Twilight is an utterly magickal time—a liminal zone that's not wholly day or night, but betwixt and between. The sun sinks low in the horizon, painting the sky with brilliant light. Behind the sunset darkness approaches in indigo and violet hues, and finally the black of hidden wisdom descends. At this time of transition, the clarity of light merges with the mysteries of darkness. Celebrate with an evening ritual such as the following, or create your own. Personalize it, if you wish, by inserting the names of other goddesses or deities with whom you feel a special affinity.

1. Begin by reflecting on the day that has just passed. Contemplate what you have experienced. Which things went as you had hoped and which things would you have changed if given the chance?
2. Place a cup or chalice of water, a candle, and a moonstone on your altar. Light some incense as you invoke the mysteries of the night with this charge: "Queen of the Night, radiant goddess Nut who shines forth in her many aspects through the moon and stars, bless this coming darkness. I ask for your blessing as one who honors you and seeks to learn your great mysteries."
3. Hold the incense aloft and say: "As the curling whispers of smoke rise to greet the night sky, so does my mind rise along the rivers of dreamtime to welcome you, beloved Goddess, into my dreams. I invoke you and I invite you to inspire my dreams that I may experience your divine grace."
4. Light the candle and meditate on its softly glowing flame, as you say: "I step between the worlds into a world both in and out of time. The candle lights my path as the moon lights the night sky. I gaze upon your great beauty in wonder, Goddess of the Ages, Lady of Mystery, thou who art brighter than all the stars."
5. Hold your cup or chalice and take a sip of water as you say: "May your abundance flow through me, may dreams and visions come to me. May the unseen be seen and the power of sight granted to me that I may perceive in the night that which is unknowable by day."
6. Pick up your moonstone and hold it to your third eye as you say: "Rare gem of the night, send forth your light to guide me through the darkness. I enter into your starry realm in love and trust, abandoning all fear with the knowledge that you are with me always, in my thoughts and in my dreams. I do not merely sleep, but awaken to your presence."

The Modern Witchcraft Grimoire

7. Think about what you would like to glean from your dreams. Inspiration? Prophecy? Self-knowledge? When you're ready, extinguish the candle.

Take a few minutes to write in your grimoire your ideas and intentions, as well as any insights or impressions you may have received during the ritual.

"It is only by working the rituals, that any significant degree of understanding can develop. If you wait until you are positive you understand all aspects of the ceremony before beginning to work, you will never begin to work."
—LON MILO DUQUETTE, *THE MAGICK OF ALEISTER CROWLEY*

POWER DAYS

According to astrology and mythology, each day of the week is ruled by one of the heavenly bodies in our solar system. Each day also has a rich Pagan history of its own. Different days have different qualities and characteristics, therefore some days are better suited than others to specific types of spellwork. By casting a spell on the day that corresponds to your intention—based on the deity who presides over the day—you can increase your potential for success. Most love spells, for instance, should be done on Friday because Venus, the planet of love and relationships, governs that day.

Day of the Week	Ruling Planet/Deity
Sunday	Sun
Monday	Moon
Tuesday (*Mardi* in French)	Mars (Tiw in Norse mythology)
Wednesday (*Mercredi* in French)	Mercury
Thursday	Jupiter (Thor in Norse mythology)
Friday (*Vendredi* in French)	Venus (Freya in Norse mythology)
Saturday	Saturn

When you prepare yourself to enact a ritual or cast a spell or a charm, you are agreeing to suspend reality for a time to get in touch with energies greater than your own limited scope of individual perception. By entering the space and time "between the worlds," you make an agreement with yourself and with the spirits. You agree to acknowledge their divine presence by inviting them into your sacred space. You agree to accept physical manifestations of the divine presence. And you agree to suspend your sense of disbelief in order to accept that magick and psychic experiences are indeed possible and desirable. You might not hear a clap of thunder to show that the goddesses and gods have acknowledged your work—but, then again, you just might.

Your Personal Best

When's the best time to cast a spell? On your birthday. On that special day each year, the sun shines brightly on you (even if it's raining outdoors) and spotlights your unique talents and abilities. The day's vibrant energy enhances whatever you undertake. As a result, whatever spells you do on your birthday have a better than usual chance of succeeding.

Sunday

As suggested by its name, the sun rules Sunday. The sun's golden rays brighten everything they touch. The sun's light enables us to clearly distinguish one thing from another, and it nurtures growth on our planet. Therefore, Sunday's energy supports spells that involve creativity, inspiration, self-expression, career success, and public image. This is also a good time for celebration and bringing people together— consider performing group rituals on Sundays. Because witches connect the sun with God energy, you may want to call upon the sun gods such as Ra (Egyptian), Apollo (Greek), or Aidan (Celtic) to lend strength and meaning to your efforts.

Monday

The moon rules Monday. Because we associate the moon with Goddess energy, magickal work planned for a Monday should involve aspects of the Goddess. The changing phases of the moon make Monday a good time to do spells and rituals designed to stimulate change. The moon governs the tides, so spells involving water are also appropriate for this day. Think of purification and cleansing work that you may need to do. Consider consecrating your chalice on a Monday. Astrologers associate the moon with home and family; therefore, it's best to cast spells involving these things on a Monday. Lunar energy enhances fertility spells too. Meditate on the aspects of the Greek moon goddess, Artemis, or on her Roman counterpart, Diana, and request her assistance.

Tuesday

Tuesday is ruled by the planet Mars and named for the Nordic god Tiw (or Tyr), the invincible warrior whose attributes include strength, attainment of desire, and manifestation of the will. Perform spells and rituals for strength, courage, daring, or success in any type of competition on Tuesday. If you're doing a spell to help you stand up to an adversary, overcome an obstacle, or reverse an attack on you, Tuesday would be a good day to perform it. It's also a good time to build your psychic defenses through protection rituals.

Wednesday

The planet Mercury rules Wednesday. In Roman mythology, Mercury is the messenger of the gods. Astrologers connect the planet with communication—both spoken and written—as well as with various types of mental activity and short trips. Rituals and spells for Wednesday involve communication, education, sending and receiving messages, and intellectual pursuits. This is also a good day to connect with spirits or do divination, perhaps by using a pendulum, runes, or the tarot.

Mercury's Retrograde Periods

Every four months, the planet Mercury goes retrograde for approximately three weeks when it appears to be moving backward through the sky. Mercury rules communication and thinking in general, so your mind might not be as clear as usual during retrograde periods. Your ability to communicate with others may be hampered as well. Usually, these aren't good times to do magick, as confusion, lack of clarity, and mistakes can occur.

Thursday

The planet Jupiter rules Thursday, and the day gets its name from the Norse god Thor. In mythology, Thor, the god of thunder, wields a mighty hammer; thus he's sometimes linked with strength, justice, and legal matters. If you are trying to influence the outcome of a legal proceeding or political matter, you may find that enacting a spell on a Thursday gives you an edge. Astrologers connect Jupiter—the largest planet in our solar system—with growth, abundance, and good fortune. Do spells for prosperity, career advancement, or any type of expansion on Thursdays. Because Jupiter also governs the zodiac sign Sagittarius, which astrologers associate with long-distance travel, Thursday is a good time to do travel spells.

Friday

Venus, the goddess of love and relationships, governs Friday. The Nordic goddess Freya, the patroness of powerful women, passion, and love, gave her name to this day. As you might expect, spells, rituals, and charms relating to matters of the heart are best performed on Friday. Venus also rules the arts and beauty, so if you want to stimulate your creativity or make yourself more attractive, do a spell on Friday. Friendships and social occasions can also benefit from Venus's influence—hold group rituals and celebrations on a Friday.

Saturday

As its name indicates, Saturday is ruled by the planet Saturn. Astrologers connect Saturn with limitations, endings, and the past, as well as structure, stability, and the business world. Do spells on Saturday to end an unwanted relationship, to bring a successful close to an endeavor, or to create strong boundaries. Protection spells and banishing rituals can benefit from Saturn's power. Do spells to strengthen a business venture, rein in spending, or encourage stability in any area of your life on this day. Saturday is also a good time for past-life work and rituals to honor those who have left the physical world.

The Modern Witchcraft Grimoire

BRING MAGICK INTO EVERYDAY TASKS

We spend most of our daily lives engaged in mundane activities and routine tasks. However, you can enrich ordinary undertakings with magickal energy—and why not? Kitchen and hearth witches embrace this concept; they consider everything in their homes sacred and imbue every household chore with magickal significance. For example, you can view sweeping the floor free of dust and dirt as simultaneously cleansing the space of negative energy.

Nowhere is this practice more evident than in cooking. When you prepare food, you put your personal energy, intention, and love into nourishing those who will eat what you cook. And the herbs you use to season your dishes contain magickal properties—you'll learn about these in Chapter 16. Consider incorporating the following practices into your daily routine:

- As you cook and clean, use affirmations to bless your home and loved ones.
- When you open the kitchen door say: "May only health, love, and joy come through this door into this home."
- While stirring a pot on the stove or a mixture in a bowl say: "Thanks be to all beings who contributed to this meal."
- While serving food say: "May the food I share nourish my loved ones in both body and soul."
- While sweeping or vacuuming say: "May all harmful, disruptive, or unbalanced energy be removed from this place."
- When you turn off the kitchen light at night say: "Bless this kitchen, and keep those of us who use it safe and healthy through the night."

Design your own household rituals and magick practices. You may also enjoy studying the ancient Chinese art known as feng shui, which associates each sector of your home with certain parts of your life. Feng shui teaches you how to magickally manipulate energies and bring about results in your world by making adjustments in your living space.

A Kitchen Witchery Spell

This spell uses "kitchen witchery" to sweeten a frustrating situation. You don't have to be a gourmet cook to carry it off—your intention is what counts.

Piece-of-Cake Spell

Things aren't going as smoothly as you'd hoped. Perhaps a project is taking longer or costing more than expected; a romance has hit a snag; you have to deal with a lot of uncooperative people at work or at home. It's time to use your witchy talents to rectify the unpleasant situation.

TOOLS AND INGREDIENTS

A cake mix (or ingredients for making your favorite cake recipe)

Food coloring

A large bowl

Spoon

Cake pan(s)

Candles

Matches or a lighter

1. Collect the ingredients needed for this spell and preheat the oven.

2. Cast a circle around the area where you will do your spell—in this case, your kitchen.

3. Follow the directions for making the cake, according to the package or your favorite recipe. You may want to choose a flavor that suits your intentions: chocolate or strawberry for love, cinnamon or mint for money, almond or vanilla for peace of mind, anise for protection. As you work, focus on your objective and imagine you are sending your intention into the batter.

4. If you like, add food coloring to tint the batter to match your intention: pink for love, green for money, and so on (see Chapter 12 for information about color symbology).

5. Stir the batter using a clockwise motion if your goal is to attract something or to stimulate growth of some kind. Stir counterclockwise if you want to limit, decrease, or end something.

The Modern Witchcraft Grimoire

6. Pour the batter into the pan(s) and bake.

7. When the cake has finished cooking, let it cool, and then ice it with frosting in a color that relates to your intention. You may want to decorate it with symbols, pictures, and/or words that describe your objective.

8. Add candles of an appropriate color. The number of candles should also correspond to your goal: 2 for love, 4 for stability, 5 for change, and so on.

9. Light the candles and concentrate on your wish. Blow out the candles.

10. Share the cake with other people who are involved in the challenging situation, so that everyone benefits. Each person who eats some of the cake takes the intention into him- or herself and becomes a co-creator in the spell's success.

"We come into this world with precious gifts that are meant to be shared, if each one of us takes the time to send healing and love to the world, we truly can change the lives of many and the world around us."

—JASMEINE MOONSONG

Treat Your Entire Home As Sacred

The Buddha once said, "Wherever you live is your temple if you treat it like one." Sacredness is more a matter of attitude and behavior than of trappings, and it doesn't require a building or props. Nonetheless, creating a sacred space is an important part of practicing magick, and witches often use tools and processes to establish safe havens in which to work.

We talked about creating sacred space in Chapter 5. You can designate a specific area as the sacred space where you'll perform your spells and rituals, write in your grimoire, meditate, and so on. However, if you prefer, you can see your entire home as sacred. Sacred space is a place of peace and calm, but it is not necessarily "between the worlds" as defined by a magick circle. Sacred space is what goes into the circle, or it can simply exist on its own.

When you're in your sacred space you can still interact with the ordinary world—you don't erect barriers. When you use sacred space, you make the existing environment holy, as opposed to creating a whole new surrounding. You remain open to the good energies in the area instead of sealing yourself away.

Sacred space is a wonderful alternative to a circle if you seek to create a harmonious atmosphere for a gathering of people, particularly if the attendees are of mixed spiritualities. You can create it without anyone else's knowledge by purifying and harmonizing the energy of the area. Envision the area cleansed of all "bad vibes" and project your intention for peace and joy into the space. Thus you remove distracting, harmful, or stale energy and in its place leave a positive, comfortable feeling.

Creating sacred space for other people who may not share your beliefs does not manipulate them in any way, nor does it disrespect their own religions. You are offering them a peaceful and balanced environment in which to study, discuss, eat, or mingle. Try creating sacred space before a dinner gathering during the week, when everyone is tired and stressed out, or before a family get-together where conflicts are likely to arise. Watch how everyone relaxes in the serene energy. That's everyday magick at its best.

The Modern Witchcraft Grimoire

Chapter 7

SPECIAL OCCASION SPELLS

For millennia, people on earth have observed the sun's apparent passage through the sky and the seasonal changes that resulted. Ancient structures, such as Stonehenge and Newgrange, Ireland, accurately marked the solstices, indicating that our ancestors carefully tracked the ever-changing relationship between the sun and our planet.

Across many lands and many centuries, myths explained earth's seasons as the Goddess's journey. During summer, she brings life to earth. During winter she descends into the underworld and loses everything—her power, her identity, her true love, or all of the above. Through recognition of her divine essence, her supremacy is restored, and life on earth once again flourishes. In some tellings, the Goddess's consort—the Sun King—undertakes an annual trip through the sky, arriving at significant places at certain times of the year to mark what we call the "sabbats."

Wiccans today divide the sun's annual cycle, known as the Wheel of the Year, into eight periods of approximately six weeks each. Each "spoke" corresponds to a particular holiday (or holy day). These special days or sabbats, based in early agrarian cultures, afford unique opportunities for performing magick spells and rituals.

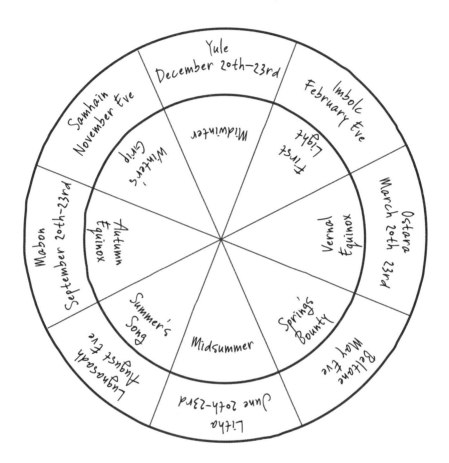

You may choose to organize the sections of your grimoire around these sabbats. Some witches like to start a new book of shadows each year on Samhain. Be sure to record in your book what you experience on these important days—not only the practices in which you engage, but your thoughts, insights, feelings, and dreams as well. Do you celebrate the sabbats with special festivities? If so, describe what you did on each one, with whom, what you ate, what you wore, the results of your spellcasting, and so on.

The Modern Witchcraft Grimoire

Song of Amergin

The "Song of Amergin" is one of the earliest examples of Celtic poetic mythology. Dating back to circa 1268 B.C.E., the song is an Irish liturgical hymn and could very well be used as a charge of the god. Consisting of metaphoric statements interspersed with queries, the "Song of Amergin" has been interpreted by Robert Graves to have direct correlations with the ancient Celtic calendar and alphabet. In Graves's translation, the "Song of Amergin" describes a journey through the Wheel of the Year told through the beautiful poetic imagery of a Druidic bard:

"I am a stag: of seven tines,
I am a flood: across a plain,
I am a wind: on a deep lake,
I am a tear: the Sun lets fall,
I am a hawk: above the cliff,
I am a thorn: beneath the nail,
I am a wonder: among flowers,
I am a wizard: who but I
Sets the cool head aflame with smoke?
I am a spear: that roars for blood,
I am a salmon: in a pool,
I am a lure: from paradise,
I am a hill: where poets walk,
I am a boar: ruthless and red,
I am a breaker: threatening doom,
I am a tide: that drags to death,
I am an infant: who but I
Peeps from the unhewn dolmen arch?
I am the womb: of every holt,
I am the blaze: on every hill,
I am the queen: of every hire,
I am the shield: for every head,
I am the tomb: of every hope."

The rich images contained in this verse suggest that the spirits of nature are irrevocably connected to the spirit of the gods and goddesses. Divine grace can be discovered anywhere—in hopes and fears, in achievements and disappointments, in shadow and light, in joy and pain, in life and death. All are valid expressions of Divine Consciousness.

SAMHAIN

The most holy of the sabbats, Samhain (pronounced SOW-een) is observed on the night of October 31, when the sun is in the zodiac sign Scorpio. Better known as Halloween or All Hallows' Eve, this is the holiday people usually associate with witches and magick. Most of the ways the general public marks this sabbat, however, stem from misconceptions—it's a solemn and sacred day for witches, not a time for fear or humor. Some religious groups that don't understand its true meaning feel threatened or offended by Halloween and have even tried to ban it.

The Holiday's Significance

Considered the witches' New Year, Samhain begins the Wheel of the Year. Thus, it is a time of death and rebirth. In many parts of the Northern Hemisphere the land lies barren now; the last of the crops have been plowed under to compost, and the earth rests in preparation for spring.

Witches view Samhain as a time to remember and honor loved ones who have passed over to the other side. That's why Halloween is associated with the dead. No, skeletons don't rise from graves nor do ghosts haunt the living on Samhain, as movies and popular culture tend to portray it—though you may connect with spirits and departed friends on this magickal night.

Samhain Magick

Witches believe the veil that separates the seen and unseen worlds is thinnest at Samhain. Consequently, you may find it easy to contact spirits in other realms of existence or to request guidance from ancestors and guardians. Samhain is also a good time to do divination, because insights and information can flow more easily on this sabbat than at any other time of the year.

In keeping with the concept of an ongoing cycle of destruction and renewal, witches often choose to shed old habits or attitudes at this time, replacing them with new ones. Consider doing a psychological housecleaning on Samhain. On a slip of paper, write whatever you want to leave behind when the old year dies—fear, self-limiting attitudes, bad habits, unwanted relationships, and so on. Then burn the paper in a ritual fire. Samhain is also a good time to perform banishing spells.

Rune Reading

October 31, 2016

"How can I improve my career path?"

Situation	Obstacle	Action	Outcome
ᚾ	ᛁ	ᛟ	ᛒ
Nauthiz	Isa	Othala	Berkano

Interpretation: Nauthiz clearly describes my feelings of being constrained and frustrated in my present job situation. Isa as the obstacle indicates I'm at a standstill and there's no opportunity for advancement where I am now. Othala in the action position suggests I need to leave my current job and seek something else. Berkano as the outcome heralds growth in the future.

WINTER SOLSTICE OR YULE

The Winter Solstice occurs when the sun reaches 0 degrees of the zodiac sign Capricorn, usually around December 21. This is the shortest day of the year in the Northern Hemisphere. Also known as Yule, the holiday marks the turning point in the sun's descent into darkness; from this point, the days grow steadily longer for a period of six months.

The Holiday's Significance

Pagan mythology describes the apparent passage of the sun through the heavens each year as the journey of the Sun King, who drives his bright chariot across the sky. Some tellings describe the Sun King as the Goddess's consort; in other stories he is her son. In pre-Christian Europe and Britain, the Winter Solstice celebrated the Sun King's birth. This beloved deity brought light into the world during the darkest time of all—a theme echoed in Christianity's story of the birth of Jesus in this season of the year. Thus, witches celebrate this sabbat as a time of renewal and hope.

Yule Magick

Decorating our homes at Christmas with ornamented pine trees and holiday greenery dates back to pre-Christian times. Because evergreen trees retain their needles even during the cold winter months, they symbolize the triumph of life over death. Do spells for strength, courage, endurance, and protection now. In a magickal sense, pine is used for its cleansing properties. The crisp, clean scent of pine needles can help eliminate negative energies from your home. You can clear bad vibes from your environment by burning pine-scented incense or candles.

Burning the Yule log is another ancient tradition with which Wiccans mark the Winter Solstice. On the eve of Yule, build a fire from the wood of nine sacred trees. The central element in the Yule fire is an oak log, for the oak tree represents strength and longevity. After the fire burns down, collect the ashes and wrap them in a piece of cloth. If you place the package under your pillow, you'll receive dreams that provide guidance and advice for the coming year. Write about the experience in your grimoire and perhaps paste some pine needles into these pages of your book of shadows.

Yule Greenery

The Druids considered the evergreen holly a sacred plant and valued its incredible hardiness. According to Celtic mythology, holly bushes afforded shelter for the earth elementals during the wintertime. The Druids also valued mistletoe, an herb of fertility and immortality. It has long been used in talismans as an aphrodisiac—perhaps that's the reason people still kiss beneath it today.

IMBOLC OR BRIGID'S DAY

This sabbat honors Brigid, the beloved Celtic goddess of healing, smithcraft, and poetry. A favorite of the Irish people, Brigid was adopted by the Church when Christianity moved into Ireland and was canonized as Saint Brigid. Her holiday is usually celebrated on February 1, though some witches mark it around February 5, when the sun reaches 15 degrees of Aquarius. In the Northern Hemisphere, daylight is increasing and the promise of spring is in the air.

The Holiday's Significance

Brigid is one of the fertility goddesses, and Imbolc means "in the belly." This holiday honors all forms of creativity, of the mind as well as the body. Illustrations of Brigid sometimes show her stirring a great cauldron, the witch's magick tool that symbolizes the womb and the receptive, fertile nature of the Divine Feminine. As goddess of inspiration, Brigid encourages everyone, regardless of gender, to stir the inner cauldron of creativity that exists within.

Although Brigid represents an aspect of the Divine Feminine, her day falls under the zodiac sign Aquarius, a masculine air sign in astrology. Her blazing hearth brings to mind both the metalsmith's forge and the homemaker's cook fire. Thus, she represents mind and body, a blend of yin and yang energies, and the union of polarities necessary for creation.

Imbolc Magick

On Imbolc, the Sun King's chariot ascends in the sky; the sun's rays grow stronger and days grow longer. Witches celebrate this spoke in the Wheel of the Year as a time of hope and renewal, a reaffirmation of life, and a time to plant "seeds" for the future. You may wish to build a fire in a magick cauldron to honor Brigid. On a piece of paper, write wishes you want to materialize during the year, then drop the paper into the cauldron. As the paper burns, the smoke rises toward the heavens carrying your requests to Brigid.

In keeping with the holiday's theme of fire, many people light candles to honor the Goddess. Candles are the most common tool in the witch's magick toolbox, used in all sorts of spells and rituals. Engrave words that represent your wishes—love, prosperity, health, etc.—into the candle's wax. Then light the candle and focus your attention on its flame, while you envision your wishes coming true.

The Name of the Goddess

Brigid goes by many names, including Lady of the Flame, Goddess of the Hearth, and Bright One. Her feast day is sometimes called Candlemas because of her association with fire. In magickal thinking, the fire element fuels inspiration and creativity.

SPRING EQUINOX OR OSTARA

Pagans and witches celebrate Ostara when the sun enters 0 degrees of Aries, around March 21. In the Northern Hemisphere, the Spring Equinox ushers in warmer weather, days that are longer than nights, and the advent of new life. Ostara gets its name from the German fertility goddess Eostre; the word "Easter" derives from the same root. Both holidays celebrate the triumph of life over death.

> *"This is the time of spring's return, the joyful time, the seed time, when life bursts forth from the earth and the chains of winter are broken. Light and dark are equal: It is a time of balance, when all the elements within us must be brought into a new harmony."*
> —STARHAWK, FROM AN OSTARA RITUAL IN *THE SPIRAL DANCE*

The Holiday's Significance

The Sun King's chariot continues climbing higher in the sky, reaching the point at which day and night are of equal length on Ostara. The Spring Equinox marks the first day of spring and the start of the busy planting season in agrarian cultures. Farmers till their fields and sow seeds. Trees begin to bud, spring flowers blossom, and baby animals are born. Ostara, therefore, is one of the fertility holidays and a time for planting seeds—literally or figuratively.

Ostara Magick

On Ostara, sow seeds that you want to bear fruit in the coming months. This is an ideal time to cast spells for new beginnings: launch new career ventures, move to a new home, or start a new relationship. If you're a gardener, you'll start preparing the soil and planting flowers, herbs, and/or vegetables now. Consider the magickal properties of botanicals and choose plants that represent your intentions (see Chapter 16 for more information). Even if you don't have space for a garden plot, you could plant seeds in a flowerpot to symbolize wishes you hope will grow to fruition in the coming months.

According to an old German story, a rabbit laid some sacred eggs and decorated them as a gift for the fertility goddess Eostre. The goddess liked the beautiful eggs so much that she asked the rabbit to share them with everyone throughout the world. Eggs represent the promise of new life, and painting them bright colors engages the creative aspect of the sabbat. And rabbits, of course, have long been linked with fertility. You might enjoy decorating eggs with magickal symbols, such as pentagrams and spirals.

BELTANE

Wiccans usually celebrate Beltane on May 1, although some prefer to mark it around May 5, when the sun reaches 15 degrees of Taurus. The sabbat is named for the god Baal or Bel. In Scottish Gaelic, the word *bealltainn* means "fires of Belos" and refers to the bonfires Pagans traditionally light on this sabbat. The joyful festival celebrates the earth's fertility, when flowers bloom and plants begin sprouting in the fields.

The Holiday's Significance

The second fertility holiday in the Wheel of the Year, Beltane coincides with a period of fruitfulness. To ancient and modern Pagans alike, this holiday honors the earth and all of nature. In early agrarian cultures, farmers built fires on Beltane and led livestock between the flames to increase their fertility.

Sexuality is also celebrated on this sabbat—the Great Rite has traditionally been part of the holiday's festivities. In pre-Christian days, Beltane celebrants engaged in sexual intercourse in the fields as a form of symbolic magick to encourage fertility and a bountiful harvest. Children conceived at this time were said to belong to the Goddess.

Beltane Magick

If possible, celebrate Beltane outdoors in order to appreciate nature's fullness. Because Beltane is a fertility holiday, many of its rituals contain sexual symbolism. The Maypole, around which young females dance, is an obvious phallic symbol. You can decorate the Maypole with flowers in recognition of the earth's beauty and fruitfulness. Consider pressing one or two of those flowers between the pages of your grimoire.

Sometimes a woman who seeks a partner will toss a circular garland over the top of the pole, signifying the sex act, as a way of asking the Goddess to send her a lover. Another fertility ritual utilizes the cauldron, a symbol of the womb. Women who wish to become pregnant build a small fire in the cauldron, and then jump over it. If you prefer, you can leap over the cauldron to spark creativity in the mind instead of the body.

Beltane's connection with the earth and fullness makes this sabbat an ideal time to perform prosperity magick. Incorporate peppermint, parsley, cedar, or money plant into your spells. This is also a good time to make offerings to Mother Earth and the nature spirits.

SUMMER SOLSTICE OR MIDSUMMER

In the Northern Hemisphere, the Summer Solstice is the longest day of the year. The Sun King has now reached the highest point in his journey through the heavens. Wiccans celebrate Midsummer around June 21, when the sun enters 0 degrees of the zodiac sign Cancer. This is a time of abundance, when the earth puts forth her bounty.

The Holiday's Significance

In early agrarian cultures, Midsummer marked a period of plenty when food was abundant and life was easy. Our ancestors celebrated this joyful holiday with feasting and revelry. At this point, however, the

The Modern Witchcraft Grimoire

sun has reached its pinnacle and begins its descent once again. Celtic Pagan mythology depicts this as the end of the Oak King's reign as he is overthrown by the Holly King, who presides over the waning part of the year. This myth sees the two "kings" as two separate aspects of the God. These rivals are the Goddess's lovers, and each has his season.

Folklore says that at Midsummer earth spirits abound—this belief inspired Shakespeare's delightful play *A Midsummer Night's Dream*. Apparently, life on every level rejoices in the fullness of the season. If you wish, you can commune with the elementals and faeries at this time.

Midsummer Magick

Just as we've done for centuries, witches today celebrate the Summer Solstice with feasting, music, dancing, and thanksgiving. Remember to share your bounty with the animals and birds too, and return something to Mother Earth as a sign of gratitude.

Midsummer is also a good time to collect herbs, flowers, and other plants to use in magick spells. Legend says that if you wish to become invisible, you must wear an amulet that includes seeds from forest ferns gathered on Midsummer's Eve. Perform spells for success, recognition, and abundance on the Summer Solstice.

LUGNASADH OR LAMMAS

Named for the Irish Celtic god Lugh (Lew in Wales), this holiday is usually celebrated on August 1, although some witches prefer to mark it around August 5, when the sun reaches 15 degrees of Leo. According to Celtic mythology, Lugh is an older and wiser personification of the god Baal or Bel (for whom Beltane is named). Lugnasadh (pronounced LOO-na-sah) is the first of the harvest festivals. The early Christians dubbed the holiday *Lammas*, meaning loaf-mass, because farmers cut their grain at this time of the year and made it into bread.

The Holiday's Significance

In agrarian cultures, this holiday marked the time to begin preparing for the barren winter months that lay ahead. Our ancestors cut, ground, and stored grain, canned fruits and vegetables, and brewed wine and beer in late summer. The old English song "John Barleycorn Must Die" describes the seasonal ritual of rendering grain into ale.

Early Pagans sold their wares at harvest fairs and held athletic competitions at this time of the year. You can see this age-old tradition carried on today at country fairs throughout rural parts of the United States.

> *"Threshing of the harvest was considered a sacred act and the threshing barn a sacred place. An old fertility custom is still practiced when a new bride is carried over the threshold."*
> —DEBBIE MICHAUD, *THE HEALING TRADITIONS & SPIRITUAL PRACTICES OF WICCA*

Lugnasadh Magick

Today, Wiccans enjoy sharing bread and beer with friends on Lugnasadh, just as we've done for millennia. You might like to bake fresh bread from scratch or even brew your own beer as part of the celebration. While you're kneading the bread, add a dried bean to the dough. When you serve the bread, tradition says that whoever gets the bean in his or her piece will be granted a wish.

If you like, you can fashion a doll from corn, wheat, or straw to represent the Sun King. To symbolize the time of year when his powers are waning, burn the effigy in a ritual fire as an offering to Mother Earth. The custom of decorating your home with dried corncobs, gourds, nuts, and other fruits of the harvest also has its roots in Lugnasadh.

AUTUMN EQUINOX OR MABON

The Autumn Equinox usually occurs on or about September 22, when the sun reaches 0 degrees of Libra. Once again, day and night are of equal length, signifying a time of balance, equality, and harmony. Mabon is also the second harvest festival, and witches consider it a time for giving thanks for the abundance Mother Earth has provided.

The Holiday's Significance

This sabbat marks the last spoke in the Wheel of the Year. From this day until the Winter Solstice, the Sun King's path arcs downward toward earth. As the days grow shorter in the Northern Hemisphere and the cold, barren winter approaches, reflect on the joys and sorrows, successes and failures of the year that is nearing its conclusion.

Mabon Magick

Mabon is a good time to do magick spells that involve decrease or endings. Do you want to let go of self-destructive beliefs or behaviors? Lose weight? End an unfulfilling relationship? Now is the time to break old habits and patterns that have limited you. Anything you wish to eliminate from your life can now be released safely, before the New Year begins with Samhain.

Because the Equinox signifies a time of equality and balance, try to balance yin and yang, active and passive on this day. Seek rest and activity, solitude and socializing in equal portions. You may also enjoy engaging in creative endeavors to mark the sabbat.

At each turn of the Wheel, note in your grimoire your feelings, insights, and the results of your magickal workings. Each year, you may enjoy rereading what you wrote the previous year. It's interesting to look back over time to reminisce about your sabbat celebrations and compare your experiences as you grow in the Craft.

Chapter 8

SOLAR SPELLS

Without the sun, life on our planet would not exist. As the center of our solar system, the sun plays a central role in our lives. Therefore, you'll want to describe in your grimoire your relationship to the sun and the seasons that result as the earth revolves around it.

Witches understand the close connection between magick and the heavenly bodies. The positions of the sun, moon, planets, and stars influence our personal cycles, plant growth, animal behavior, weather patterns, the secular and sacred rituals we enact, and the spells we perform. The Wheel of the Year bases the eight Wiccan holidays (known as sabbats) on the sun's movement through the twelve signs of the zodiac, as discussed previously in Chapter 7.

If you're like many people, you notice that your emotions and energies shift with the seasons. You may feel more physically vital, sociable, or adventurous during some months and more introspective, imaginative, or sensitive during others. Most likely, you're reacting to the natural energies of the zodiac signs and the movements of the heavenly bodies. By keeping track of your reactions in your grimoire, you'll discover the most auspicious times to do magick work and when to perform certain types of spells for best results.

ASTROLOGY AND MAGICK

When doing magick spells, it's a good idea to take celestial influences into account in order to choose the most auspicious times to perform spells and rituals. The sun and moon, and their ever-changing relationships to our planet, have fascinated human beings since the beginning of time. Our ancestors noticed that the sun's apparent movement brought about the seasons and that the moon's phases altered the tides and affected fertility in both humans and animals. Even today, we can easily see how solar and lunar forces operate in everyday life.

The ancients believed gods and goddesses inhabited the heavenly bodies. From their celestial abodes, the deities governed every facet of life on earth. Each deity—and each planet—possessed certain characteristics and powers. Modern astrologers don't usually think of the planets as the actual homes of gods and goddesses; however, we still connect each of the celestial spheres with specific properties, influences, and powers that affect human and earthly existence.

Planetary Powers

Aligning yourself with planetary powers that support the nature of your spells can improve the effectiveness of your magickal workings. The following table shows each planet's areas of influence. (Note: For convenience, astrologers often lump the sun and moon under the broad heading of "planets" although, of course, we know they're not.)

Planet	Areas of Influence
Sun	Sense of self/identity, public image, career, creativity, leadership, well-being, masculine power
Moon	Emotions, intuition, dreams, home/domestic life, family/children, feminine power
Mercury	Communication, mental skill/activity, learning, travel, commerce
Venus	Love, relationships, social interactions, art, creativity, beauty, women
Mars	Action, vitality/strength, competition, courage, men
Jupiter	Growth/expansion, good luck, knowledge, travel
Saturn	Limitations, responsibility, work/business, stability/permanence
Uranus	Change, independence, sudden or unexpected situations, unconventional ideas or behavior
Neptune	Intuition, dreams, imagination/creativity, the spirit realm
Pluto	Hidden power/forces, transformation, death and rebirth

When you're doing spells, you may want to refer to this table. Venus's energy, for instance, can enhance love spells. Jupiter's expansive power can be an asset when you're doing spells for career success or financial growth. You can use the planets' symbols on candles, in talismans and amulets, and lots of other ways. You may also wish to consult an astrologer or check an ephemeris (tables of daily planetary movements) to determine when the celestial energies are favorable for your magickal workings.

TRACKING SOLAR CYCLES IN YOUR GRIMOIRE

Consider organizing your grimoire around the solar cycles. Each month write down your spells, rituals, and experiences along your magickal journey. Astrologers begin the solar year with the Spring Equinox, when the sun enters the zodiac sign Aries on about March 21. In the witches' Wheel of the Year, this is the sabbat of Ostara. During each solar month, record how you feel, what you see happening around you in nature, what you experience (especially in terms of your magickal and spiritual development), significant dreams and insights, and, of course, the spells you do. You may also enjoy pressing seasonal flowers, leaves, and other botanicals between the pages of your grimoire to mark the beauty of the changing seasons. Some witches begin a new book of shadows every year, and you may choose to do this at the Spring Equinox instead of on Samhain. If you prefer, you could annually revisit the sections designated for each solar month and add updates.

The Modern Witchcraft Grimoire

Planets and Signs

Each planet rules one or more signs of the zodiac. You probably know your birth sign—that's the astrological sign in which the sun was positioned on the day you were born. What you may not know, though, is that the moon and all the planets in our solar system also spend periods of time in each of the twelve signs of the zodiac and they continually move through these signs/sectors of the heavens. These signs affect the energy of the planets. Therefore, it's good to check the positions of the planets when you're doing spells—especially the placements of the sun and moon. In Part II, I frequently advise doing spells when the sun or moon is in a particular astrological sign, in order to tip the scales in your favor. The following table shows the connections between the planets and the signs they govern.

Planet	Zodiac Sign(s)
Sun	Leo
Moon	Cancer
Mercury	Gemini, Virgo
Venus	Taurus, Libra
Mars	Aries
Jupiter	Sagittarius
Saturn	Capricorn
Uranus	Aquarius
Neptune	Pisces
Pluto	Scorpio

Now, refer back to the table presented earlier in this chapter that lists the planets and their areas of influence. When the sun or moon is positioned in a sign, it takes on characteristics of that sign and the planet that rules the sign, which can be important in spellwork. For example, it's usually best to do love spells when the sun or moon is in Taurus or Libra—signs ruled by the planet Venus. If you're doing a travel spell, consider casting it when the sun or moon is in Gemini or Sagittarius.

The moon remains in a sign for about two and a half days and completes a circuit of all twelve zodiac signs each month. Check an ephemeris or an online astrology site to determine which days will support your objectives.

Sun Signs

When someone asks "What's your sign?" he's really asking "Where was the sun positioned in the sky on the day you were born?" Astrology divides the sky into twelve sectors and links them with the signs of the zodiac. From earth, the sun appears to travel through all twelve sectors during the course of a year, spending approximately thirty days in each sign.

Aries

The sun enters Aries at the Spring Equinox, around March 21, and remains in the sign until about April 20, although this can vary a day or so from year to year. In many parts of the Northern Hemisphere, the earth now begins to awaken after a period of slumber. Plants start to sprout; baby animals are born; migrating birds return from their winter habitats. Thus, we consider Aries a time of beginnings and planting seeds, physically or symbolically.

Do you sense something stirring in you now? Do you feel inspired to begin something new, break new ground, or "birth" a part of yourself? Because the war god Mars (Ares in Greek tradition) rules this sign, you may seek out challenges, adventures, and physical activities this month. The fiery energy of the period can help fuel your ambitions and desires.

Taurus

The sun enters Taurus around April 21 and remains in this sign until about May 20, although this can vary a day or so from year to year. In many parts of the Northern Hemisphere, the days now grow warmer and the earth begins to bring forth the first of its bounty. Therefore, we consider Taurus a fruitful sign and connect it with abundance.

Are your creative juices stirring? Do you feel a desire to express yourself or use your talents in a productive way that others can appreciate? The earthy energy of Taurus can help bring your ideas to fruition. Do

The Modern Witchcraft Grimoire

you feel more sexual than usual? Because Venus, the goddess of love and beauty, rules this sign, you may focus on relationships or devote yourself to sensual pleasures now.

Gemini

The sun enters Gemini around May 21 and remains in this sign until about June 20, although this can vary a day or so from year to year. In many parts of the Northern Hemisphere, flowers blossom profusely now, spreading their pollen far and wide. In a similar way, Gemini's energy spreads ideas far and wide, "pollenating" our minds and cultures.

Do ideas blossom in your head now? Do you seek out people with whom to share your ideas and interests? Are you hungry for knowledge? Because Mercury, the god of communication, rules this sign you might choose to read, write, study, communicate with friends, or engage in other intellectual endeavors now.

Cancer

The sun enters Cancer around June 21, and remains in this sign until about July 21, although this can vary a day or so from year to year. This period of fullness in the Northern Hemisphere begins with the Summer Solstice, the longest day in the year, and the Wiccan sabbat Midsummer. As the earth blossoms with abundance, you may become aware of the abundance in your own life and express gratitude for it.

Do you feel a desire to celebrate your tribe, culture, and/or heritage? Do your loved ones seem dearer to you than usual? Do you experience strong nurturing feelings toward others or long to be nurtured by someone else? Because the moon rules Cancer, which astrologers link with home and family, you may enjoy spending time at home with your family now or reconnecting with your ancestors.

Leo

The sun enters Leo around July 22 and remains in this sign until about August 22, although this can vary a day or so from year to year. In many parts of the Northern Hemisphere, the sun shines brilliantly now and illuminates our world. Likewise, Leo's light shines brightly on each of us, illuminating our special gifts.

Are your creative juices flowing? Do you feel inspired to express your unique talents and seek recognition for your abilities? Now's the time to step out of the shadows, into the spotlight. Leo's fiery energy gives you the confidence and courage to show your stuff, and to make your mark in the world.

Virgo

The sun enters Virgo around August 23 and remains in this sign until about September 22, although this can vary a day or so from year to year. In the Northern Hemisphere, the days are growing shorter and cooler temperatures remind us that winter lurks just around the corner. Now we must work to prepare ourselves for bleaker times ahead.

Do you feel a need to tend to the details in your life, to put things in order? Do you seem busier than usual? If you've taken a break during the summer, you may sense pressure to get back to work. Virgo's practical energy helps you see things in perspective and organize your plans for the future.

Libra

The sun enters Libra around September 23 and remains in this sign until about October 21, although this can vary a day or so from year to year. This is one of the most beautiful times of the year in many parts of the Northern Hemisphere, and it begins with the Fall Equinox—the harvest celebration Wiccans call Mabon.

Do you feel a sense of "gathering" as winter approaches, a desire to collect and store the rich abundance of the period (literally or symbolically) in preparation for the future? Do you experience a heightened appreciation for the beauty around you? Venus, the planet of relationships, rules Libra. It makes you aware of your connection to other people and your need for them, inspiring you to gather your loved ones around you.

Scorpio

The sun enters Scorpio around October 21 and remains in this sign until about November 20, although this can vary a day or so from year to year. As the nights grow longer and colder in the Northern

Hemisphere, we tend to draw into ourselves and shift away from outer-world activities, becoming more introspective. Samhain, the most sacred of the witch's sabbats, occurs during this solar month and recognizes the continuing cycle of death and rebirth as the earth slips into a period of decline and rest.

Do you feel like pulling into yourself to explore your innermost depths? Are you shedding things you no longer need, so something new can emerge? Do you sense a connection with the spirit realm, hidden forces, and a desire to delve into regions beyond the material world? The transformative energy of Pluto, the planet that rules Scorpio, can guide you beyond the mundane into the extraordinary.

Sagittarius

The sun enters Sagittarius around November 21 and remains in this sign until about December 20, although this can vary a day or so from year to year. As winter closes in (in the Northern Hemisphere), we feel an urgency to do all that needs to be done in preparation for the harsh time ahead; therefore, this month is often a busy one.

Astrologers connect this sign with questing for knowledge and experiences that broaden us physically and/or spiritually. In some countries, it coincides with a period of travel, generosity, and social celebrations. Do you seek to expand your horizons through study, travel, or exploring the spiritual realms? Do you reach out to others, offering your time, energy, and material benefits in an expression of gratitude and giving back for the abundance you've enjoyed? Do you feel restless and curious about what lies just beyond your reach? The benevolent energy of Jupiter, the planet that rules Sagittarius, can help you find what you're looking for.

Capricorn

The sun enters Capricorn on the Winter Solstice around December 21—also the Wiccan sabbat Yule—and remains in this sign until about January 20, although this can vary a day or so from year to year. During the darkest time of the year (in the Northern Hemisphere), solar forces withdraw to shelter and renew themselves in preparation for the fruitful times ahead. Early cultures recognized this as a time of courage during a harsh period of cold and scarcity and celebrated humankind's strength when faced with difficulty.

Do you find yourself retreating, regrouping, and repairing in preparation for the future? Are you assessing your resources and using them productively? Are career or financial issues a priority now? It's time to get realistic about your goals and start formulating plans—it's no coincidence that we make New Year's resolutions during Capricorn. Let pragmatic Saturn, which rules this sign, guide you.

Aquarius

The sun enters Aquarius around January 21 and remains in this sign until about February 19, although this can vary a day or so from year to year. Even though this can be the coldest period of the year in many parts of the Northern Hemisphere, the days are growing longer and hope for better times glimmers on the horizon. Change hovers in the air, heralded by Uranus, the planet of change, which rules Aquarius.

Do you feel restless and ready for new adventures? Do you sense a change within yourself and/or see change beginning to happen around you? Are your senses and ideas awakening after a period of withdrawal, leading you to seek out the company of like-minded individuals? Let the energy of Aquarius guide you to express your true self.

Pisces

The sun enters Pisces around February 20 and remains in this sign until about March 20, although this can vary a day or so from year to year. The last sign of the zodiac, Pisces bridges the mundane and the spirit realms, showing us that we are not merely physical beings but sparks of the Divine. Even though the days are growing longer, this can still be a cold, dreary, isolating month in many parts of the Northern Hemisphere, during which we spend time looking within ourselves. Draw upon the wisdom of the hidden dimension now and the knowledge that abides in your own deepest regions.

Is your intuition sharper than usual? Are your dreams more vivid? Do you recognize the presence of the Divine acting through you? Do you feel inspired to express artistically what's being conveyed to you?

The visionary power of Neptune, which rules Pisces, can reveal what lies beyond the material world and connect you with spiritual forces that can guide you on your path.

Celestial Charts

You can look up the exact positions of the sun, moon, and planets on any given day in a book called an ephemeris. These tables of planetary motion list the heavenly bodies according to the signs and degrees in which they're located on every day of the year. Usually the data are arranged by month and grouped into a volume that covers a year, a decade, or even an entire century. You can find ephemerides online too.

SPELLS FOR EVERY SEASON

"To everything there is a season," says Ecclesiastes 3:1. That's certainly true in the art of spellcraft. Aligning yourself with cosmic energies that support the nature of your spells can improve their effectiveness. Keep a record in your grimoire of the spells you do during each solar month and note their outcomes. I like to date the spells I perform, so I can go back later and compare my experiences year after year. This also helps me to better understand how the energies operating at different times of the year influence my magickal workings.

Following you'll find information about the types of spells best suited to each month of the solar year. If, however, you can't wait until the "right" month to cast your spell, perform the spell when the moon passes through that sign (which it does for approximately two and a half days each month)—we'll discuss this more in Chapter 9.

Aries

The strong, activating energy present this month helps jump-start spells for new endeavors. If you're facing a challenge, hope to best an opponent, or need some extra vitality or courage—in an athletic event, for example—consider doing a spell at this time. Want to stimulate movement in a situation or remove an obstacle? Aries's fiery energy can provide zing and speed up the process. Spells cast at this time often manifest quickly, but their results don't always endure long-term. Candle spells can be especially effective now.

Taurus

The fruitful and down-to-earth nature of this sign supports spells to attract material goodies. Now's the time to do magick for wealth, comfort and security, and abundance of all kinds. Taurus's creative energy also encourages fertility, whether you're trying to start a family or birth a great work of art. Love spells can benefit from the cosmic forces at work now too. Tap the power of plants and gemstones this month to enhance your spells.

Gemini

This mentally oriented sign supports the use of affirmations, incantations, and chants in spellwork. During this month, you can also benefit from studying magickal traditions and/or sharing your knowledge with other like-minded people. Your ability to communicate may be sharper now, so try contacting spirit guides or use telepathy to send messages to other people. This is a good time to receive guidance from oracles as well.

Cancer

Now's the time to develop your intuition, for Cancer's energy increases your sensitivity to everything in the cosmos. Spells to protect your home and family, bless a new home, or increase fertility can benefit from Cancer's energy too. You might also consider doing past-life regressions this month or connect with loved ones who've left the physical plane. The Summer Solstice occurs when the sun enters Cancer, making this a good time to do magick to attract abundance and to celebrate your blessings.

Leo

Leo's energy supports spells to strengthen your self-esteem, advance your position in the world, improve your public image, or get the recognition you seek. The creative energy of this sign can also boost

The Modern Witchcraft Grimoire

your own creative ability—use this period to let the artist in you shine. Enrich all your spells and rituals with an extra dash of drama and imagination now.

Virgo

Virgo's practical energy supports spells to improve your work situation and/or relationships with coworkers, clients, and colleagues. This is also an ideal time to perform healing spells, especially using botanicals. Working with plant/tree magick can be rewarding now— invite the nature spirits known as devas to assist you. Connecting with your spirit animal guides may prove fruitful as well. Consider doing spells to heal the earth this month too.

Libra

This sign, ruled by Venus—the planet of love and relationships— strengthens loves spells and spells to improve relationships of all kinds. Spells to enhance your beauty, expand your social network, or encourage people to view you more favorably can benefit from Libra's power of attraction. If you're seeking more peace and harmony in your life, this is the time to perform magick for that purpose—consider doing spells for world peace now too.

Scorpio

Most types of magick can benefit from Scorpio's energy, for astrologers connect this sign with hidden knowledge and occult forces. Your intuition may grow stronger now and your dreams may provide important insights. Consider shamanic journeying, past-life regression, working with spirits and nonphysical entities, divination, and scrying this month. You may also wish to do spells for financial growth and personal power at this time.

Sagittarius

Use the expansive nature of Sagittarius for travel spells—whether you're traveling in the physical world or the realms beyond. Consider shamanic journeying or engaging in a vision quest now to gain wisdom. This is also a wonderful time to expand your knowledge of the Craft or to study other magickal traditions. Growth spells of all kinds can benefit from Sagittarius's energy—use it to get a raise or a promotion.

Capricorn

The pragmatic nature of this sign can aid spells for business and career endeavors, as well as magick to improve your financial savvy. If you wish to bolster your public image or need to ward off attacks from adversaries, tap Capricorn's energy. Do spells for protection, strength, security, and banishing, and to bring something to a successful close.

Happy Birthday!

Pay special attention to the month in which your birthday falls. Your magickal energies increase on your birthday, so this is usually the ideal day to work spells for your own well-being and empowerment.

Aquarius

If you want to make changes in your life, do magick while the sun is in Aquarius. This stimulating sign can help break up stagnant conditions, sometimes quite quickly. Aquarian energy can also aid spells to encourage new adventures, gain new knowledge, or attract new people. Under its influence, you can acquire amazing insights that advance not only your own way of thinking, but other people's too. Consider doing magick with a group of like-minded people now.

Pisces

Your intuition may improve while the sun is in Pisces, so consider engaging in practices such as divination, telepathy, and psychic healing at this time. You could find it easier to communicate with the spirit realm now too. The imaginative energy of Pisces can aid spells to enhance creativity as well as those that use creative visualization. Because Neptune, the planet that rules liquids, governs this sign, you might enjoy concocting magick potions this month—make sure to record your recipes in your grimoire.

The Modern Witchcraft Grimoire

Chapter 9

LUNAR SPELLS

One of the most important connections we have in the magickal universe in which we live—and one of the most obvious—is to earth's closest neighbor: the moon. Earthlings can't help being captivated and mystified by the moon. Poets, artists, musicians, lovers, astrologers, and, of course, witches all find the moon juicy subject matter for study and inspiration. For Wiccans, as you know, the moon symbolizes the Goddess and the archetypal feminine power in the universe.

Since ancient times, cultures around the world have connected the moon with the Divine Feminine. In early agrarian cultures, our forebears sowed crops and bred animals in accordance with the moon's cycles. Even today, despite the many sophisticated scientific developments in modern-day agribusiness, the *Farmers' Almanac* still publishes information about lunar cycles—it's not uncommon for farmers who employ advanced technical methods to also consider the moon when planting and harvesting.

If you're like many people, you experience the moon's ever-changing energy in your everyday life—your emotions, your sleep patterns, your mental alertness, your vitality, and your intuitive power. Wiccans know that the moon also plays a key role in spellwork. In your grimoire, keep track of how you relate to the moon and how it influences your mundane and magickal affairs.

The moon rules the night, affects the tides, and influences women's fertility cycles. In Wicca, the moon's phases represent the three stages of a woman's life and the Triple Goddess:

- The waxing crescent moon symbolizes the maiden aspect of the Goddess.
- The full moon signifies the mother aspect of the Goddess.
- The waning crescent moon represents the crone aspect of the Goddess.

"I have called on the Goddess and found her within myself."
—MARION ZIMMER BRADLEY, *THE MISTS OF AVALON*

Moon Goddesses

- Anunit (Babylonian)
- Arianrhod (Celtic)
- Artemis (Greek)
- Candi (Indian)
- Cerridwen (Celtic)
- Chang-o (Chinese)
- Dae-Soon (Korean)
- Diana (Roman)
- Hecate (Greek)
- Ishtar (Babylonian)
- Isis (Egyptian)
- Ix Chel (Mayan)
- Kuan Yin (Chinese)
- Luna (Roman)
- Mawu (African)
- Sarpandit (Sumerian)
- Selene (Greek)
- Sina (Polynesian)
- Yemaya (African/Caribbean/South American)

Some goddesses depict the maiden, some the mother, and some the crone. We often associate maiden goddesses with purity, independence, and joy. Mother goddesses usually represent fertility and fruitfulness, love and relationships, nurturance, and creativity of all kinds. Crone goddesses epitomize wisdom, courage, power, and sometimes death and destruction.

- Maiden goddesses: Artemis, Diana, Bast, Athena, Rhiannon
- Mother goddesses: Brigid, Isis, Demeter, Astarte, Inanna, Ishtar, Tara, Sekhmet, Yemaya, Oshun
- Crone goddesses: Hecate, Cerridwen, Kali, Sophia

Because the moon holds such significance for witches, you may choose to organize your book of shadows around your esbat rituals.

"'Tis the witching hour of night,
Orbed is the moon and bright,
And the stars they glisten, glisten,
Seeming with bright eyes to listen—
For what listen they?"

—John Keats

In a magickal practice known as "drawing down the moon," a witch goes into a trance and invites the Goddess (or divine feminine energy) to enter her body. While the witch is in the trance, the Goddess speaks through her. Margot Adler wrote in depth about this in her book *Drawing Down the Moon,* and it's usually considered a more advanced technique for working with lunar energy. However, novices can connect with the moon's power in simpler ways:

1. Go outside at night and observe the moon. Let its silvery light wash over you. How do you feel standing in the moonlight, under the dark bowl of the night sky? How is this different from how you feel in the daytime?
2. Follow the moon's passage through the heavens, from new to full and back to new again. Pay attention to how you feel during different phases of the moon. Many people feel more energized during the full moon and less vital during the last three days before the new moon.

3. The moon moves into a different sign of the zodiac approximately every two and a half days. You might notice that your moods and feelings change every time the moon passes through a different astrological sign. For instance, you may feel more impulsive when the moon is in Aries, more sensitive when it's in Cancer.

Keep notes in your grimoire about what you experience, so you can refer back to them later. What you learn from strengthening your connection with the moon will be useful to you when casting spells and doing rituals—and perhaps in other areas of your life too.

THE LUNAR YEAR

The ancient Druids used a lunar calendar with thirteen months, rather than a solar one as we do today. They associated each month of the year with a tree.

THE DRUID LUNAR CALENDAR	
Tree	**Month**
Birch	December 24–January 20
Rowan	January 21–February 17
Ash	February 18–March 17
Alder	March 18–April 14
Willow	April 15–May 12
Hawthorne	May 13–June 9
Oak	June 10–July 7
Holly	July 8–August 4
Hazel	August 5–September 1
Vine	September 2–September 29
Ivy	September 30–October 27
Reed	October 28–November 24
Elder	November 25–December 23

ESBATS

Witches often come together for esbats, usually on full and/or new moons, to enjoy community and fellowship. On the full moon, the radiance of the Goddess illuminates the night sky, and her brilliance dims the brightness of the stars. Her shining body hangs like a voluptuous pearl against the surrounding darkness. The full moon calls witches to gather and honor her divine power.

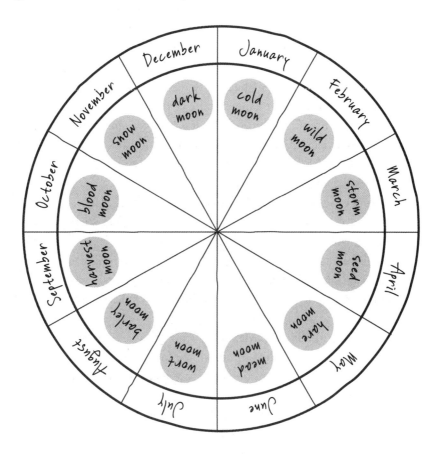

Each full moon has its own unique characteristics, often based on seasonal energies. Use the specific qualities of each full moon to guide you as you create your rituals. Esbat rituals draw upon nature's patterns, as well as mythology, cultural traditions, and astrology. Whether or not your magickal practice involves gathering with a coven or other people, you may wish to mark the full moons with rituals and/or spellwork. The following list briefly describes some of the attributes of each full moon. (Note that different cultures call the moons by different names.)

1. January—Known as the Cold, Frost, Ice, and Quiet Moon, it marks a time for renewal, discovery, resolve, and focusing on your purpose. Now is the time to set goals and to do spells for wealth and prosperity.
2. February—Called the Wild, Snow, Ice, and Starving Moon, it represents a period of healing and purification. Spells that prepare you for initiation, encourage healing or new growth, or foster physical or financial well-being are appropriate at this time.
3. March—The Storm, Wind, or Death Moon ushers in a time of change and awakening after a bleak, dormant period. Goals set under January's Cold Moon now begin to manifest. Do spells for personal growth and change now.
4. April—The Seed, Water, Growing, or Awakening Moon is a time of opening to new opportunities and experiences. Do spells for love, cleansing, growth, and strength at this time.
5. May—Known as the Hare, Bright, Grass, and Corn-planting Moon, it encourages joy, pleasure, sexuality, and fertility. This is a good time to do love spells, as well as spells for healing from emotional trauma and loss.
6. June—During the Honey, Mead, Planting, or Horse Moon, focus on strengthening relationships of all kinds: love, family, friendship, etc. This is also a good time to do spells to enhance communication and domestic harmony.
7. July—The Wort, Raspberry, or Rose Moon represents a time of maturation and fulfillment. Spells for career success, prosperity, and protection can benefit from the energy of this full moon.
8. August—Known as the Barley, Gathering, or Lightning Moon, this marks a time for gathering together all that holds meaning for you. Celebrate your blessings now and show gratitude, which will bring more blessings your way. Work with others of like mind during this time to share ideas, goals, and information.

9. September—The Harvest, Singing, or Spiderweb Moon is another period of reaping rewards for your efforts, and for seeing your dreams come to fruition. Give thanks for goals realized, projects completed, and wisdom gained. Focus on completion and bringing your life into balance.

10. October—During the Blood, Harvest, or Leaf-falling Moon, release old patterns and clear away emotional/psychic debris. Do spells to help you let go of whatever or whoever is standing in the way of your dreams' fulfillment. This is also a time to remember and honor loved ones who have moved on to another realm of existence.

11. November—The Snow, Dark, or Tree Moon is a time to look beyond the mundane world, into the magickal one. Scry to gaze into the future; do divination to gain guidance and wisdom that will aid you in the coming months. Open your mind to receive prophecies of things to come.

12. December—Under the Dark, Cold, or Long Night Moon, release your fears and banish those things in your life that are harmful or no longer useful. This is a time for silence, meditation, and introspection. Do spells to break old bonds, overcome obstacles, and end self-limiting habits/behaviors.

Decorate Your Altar for Esbats

A beautiful way to align yourself with the changing lunar cycles is to decorate your altar in accordance with each esbat. A bowl of pinecones or evergreen branches might grace your altar on the Cold Moon, along with bayberry candles to represent financial stability. In the spring and summer months, place a vase of seasonal flowers on your altar along with candles in a color that harmonizes with the moon's energy. Where you live on Planet Earth will influence what you choose to place on your altar each month. You may also like to display artwork, crystals and gemstones, figurines of deities—and of course, your grimoire—on your altar. Keep notes about what you did. You might also take a picture of your altar on each esbat and include it in your book of shadows.

Whether you belong to a group of magick workers or practice solitary witchcraft, during full-moon nights you will experience the sense of community and fellowship of like-minded individuals. You can be certain that on any full moon, witches around the world are casting circles and performing spells, celebrating and chanting, scrying and meditating. You are an integral part of this global community. By realizing your part in the whole, you will bring yourself into closer connection with your fellow beings and the Divine.

> "The moon does not fight. It attacks no one. It does not worry. It does not try to crush others. It keeps to its course, but by its very nature, it gently influences. What other body could pull an entire ocean from shore to shore? The moon is faithful to its nature and its power is never diminished."
> —DENG MING-DAO, *EVERYDAY TAO: LIVING WITH BALANCE AND HARMONY*

MOON PHASES IN MAGICK

The term *moon phase* refers to the part of the moon's face that you see illuminated in the night sky. The relative positions of the sun, moon, and earth shift as the moon orbits the earth, causing the changing phases. For the purposes of magick, witches are mainly interested in four lunar phases: new, waxing, full, and waning. Astronomically these phases are further defined as the new moon, waxing crescent, first quarter, waxing gibbous, full moon, waning gibbous, third quarter, and waning crescent.

You're more likely to reap the rewards you desire if you do magick during favorable phases of the moon. When casting spells or performing rituals, pay particular attention to the new moon, the full moon, and the waxing and waning phases. Each has its own unique energy that can add to the power of your spells:

- The new moon, as you might expect, encourages beginnings. Are you looking for a new job? A new romance? A new home? The best time to start anything is during the new moon. As the moon grows in light (and seemingly in size), your undertaking will grow too.
- The waxing moon—the two weeks after the new moon and leading up to the full moon—supports growth and expansion. Do you want to boost your income? Turn up the heat in a relationship? Get a promotion at work? Cast your spell while the moon's light is increasing to generate growth in your worldly affairs.

The Modern Witchcraft Grimoire

- The full moon marks a time of culmination. It allows you to start seeing the results of whatever you began on the new moon. Want to bring a project to a successful conclusion? Receive rewards, recognition, or payments that are due to you? Perform a spell while the moon is full for best results—its bright glow puts you in the spotlight. If your goal is to attract attention—from a lover, boss, or the public—the full moon illuminates you favorably. The full moon can also shine light on secrets and deception to help you get to the truth of a murky situation.
- The waning moon—the two weeks after the full moon and before the new moon—encourages decrease. Do you want to lose weight? End a bad relationship? Cut your expenses? Reduce your responsibilities at work or home? Cast your spell while the moon is diminishing in light (and size) to diminish the impact of something in your life.

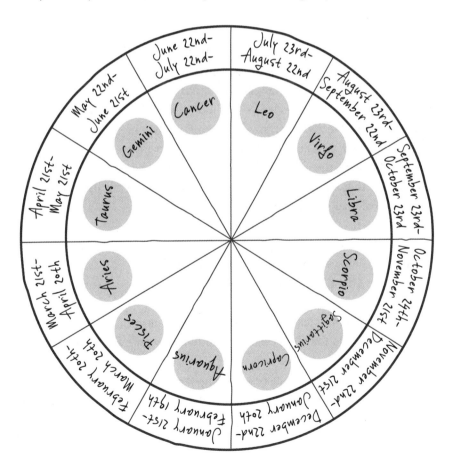

Record in your book of shadows what you experience while working with the energies of the different moon phases. To fine-tune your magick, consider both the moon's phase and its zodiac sign.

Blue Moons and Black Moons

When two full moons occur in the same month, the second is dubbed a blue moon. During the blue moon, you may find you get bigger or better results than on an ordinary full moon, or that you experience a lot more activity or vitality. When two new moons occur in the same month, the second one is called the black moon. This is considerably more powerful than a regular new moon, so any seeding spells you do under a black moon may manifest more quickly.

MOON SIGNS AND MAGICK

Witches have always placed great importance on the moon's role in magick, and astrology helps to explain why. Astrologers associate the moon with emotion, intuition, and creativity—the very things witches rely on when doing magick. As the moon circles the earth, it travels through all twelve zodiac signs in approximately a month, remaining in a sign for about two and a half days. Each sign favors certain types of magick. To make the most of a spell or ritual, perform it while the moon is in a sign that supports your intentions. The following list shows the best types of spells to do during each moon sign:

- Aries: Confronting obstacles and adversaries, courage, competition, starting new ventures, vitality, masculine virility
- Taurus: Abundance, fortitude, fertility, sex, plant or earth magick, spells for home or property
- Gemini: Communication, learning, mental pursuits, short trips
- Cancer: Spells for the home, protection, security, feminine fertility, children
- Leo: Leadership, career success, courage, recognition, creativity, vitality
- Virgo: Health and healing, job-oriented spells, discernment, mental clarity, pets

The Modern Witchcraft Grimoire

- Libra: Love, legal matters, peace, artistic endeavors, social situations, balance within and without
- Scorpio: Power, sexuality, psychic pursuits, overcoming obstacles and fears, banishing, transformation
- Sagittarius: Travel, spiritual growth, knowledge, expansion, creating opportunities, good luck
- Capricorn: Firm foundations, self-control, financial stability, career success, public image, manifesting goals, binding or banishing
- Aquarius: Change, new opportunities, adventure, liberation, friendship, group endeavors
- Pisces: Creativity, emotional healing, spiritual pursuits, developing psychic awareness

Let's say, for example, you want to find a better job. Virgo is most closely linked with work and work relationships. But if your main concern is to make more money, do magick while the waxing moon is in Taurus. If financial stability and status are more important, cast your spell while the moon is in Capricorn. If you're seeking fame or recognition, a Leo moon will support your intention. Study the unique properties of each sign to help you choose the right one for your purpose.

Moon Magick Communication Oil

Use this versatile oil to anoint candles, gemstones, ritual tools, and other spell components. It aids all forms of communication, with human beings and nonphysical entities. You can also use it as a massage oil or add it to a ritual bath.

TOOLS AND INGREDIENTS

3 ounces of olive or grape seed oil

A glass jar

3 drops of essential oil of sandalwood

A pinch of cinnamon

3 marigold (calendula) petals

A small quartz crystal

1. Pour the vegetable oil into the jar.

2. Add the essential oil, cinnamon, and marigold petals.

3. Add the quartz crystal.

4. Put a top on the jar and shake it 3 times to charge the mixture.

5. Massage your palms and the soles of your feet with the oil. Put a drop of oil on your throat chakra (the center of communication).

Record the results of your spell in your book of shadows. Also note your experiences, feelings, insights, and sensations while doing the spell, as well as anything that you believe to be relevant.

ECLIPSES

The ancients regarded eclipses with awe and even fear. Astrologers witness the powerful energies produced during eclipses and how these celestial events affect human affairs. Often you'll notice a series of related events occur in connection with a series of eclipses; each eclipse brings further development on what happened at the previous eclipse. You can tap the high-octane energy of solar and lunar eclipses in your magick work too; however, eclipses can sometimes spark unpredictable results, so proceed with caution.

Solar Eclipses

A solar eclipse occurs when the moon is new. At this time, both the sun and moon occupy the same sign and degree in the zodiac. The moon passes between the sun and earth, blocking our vision of the sun. In her book *Lunar Shadows*, Dietrech J. Pessin writes, "This time is filled with a mystery and unseen influences are yet to be developed in our lives . . . it is a time to observe, dream and plan—not to initiate action." Because the moon shadows the sun now, emotion and intuition—things we associate with the moon—tend to take precedence over the solar activities of logic, intellect, and outer world endeavors. Focus on inner growth, dreamwork, and psychic practices during a solar eclipse.

Lunar Eclipses

A lunar eclipse occurs when the moon is full, and the sun and moon are in opposite signs of the zodiac. The earth passes between the two heavenly bodies, blocking the sun's light to the moon. Because the moon is overshadowed, things we associate with the sun—such as logic and intellectual activities—become highlighted. A lunar eclipse brings matters to light that may have lain hidden for some time, but with more force than an ordinary full moon. Pessin calls this a time when "all the cards are on the table." During a lunar eclipse, do magick to bring projects to fruition or to conclude situations in your life.

Familiarizing yourself with the energies of the celestial bodies and their shifting relationships to our earth will benefit not only your spellwork but also your understanding of your place in the cosmos. You'll develop a richer connection with nature and her cycles. You'll witness the meaning of the old axiom "as above, so below" in action. And by studying this information, as recorded in your grimoire, you'll come to a deeper appreciation of the physical expression of the Goddess and the God, as symbolized by the moon and the sun that light up our world.

Chapter 10

SPELLS FOR SPECIFIC PURPOSES

Many cookbooks organize recipes according to types of food: meat, fish, vegetables, bread, pasta, and so on. In a similar way, many witches find it convenient to arrange their grimoires according to the types of spells they do: love, money, health, protection, etc. This method makes it easy to locate the spell you want when you want it. It also lets you see what spells you do most frequently and select some favorite "go-to" spells that you can turn to with confidence.

FIND IT FAST

If you decide to configure your book of shadows in this way, you may want to insert tabs or dividers to mark the various sections of your book. Some people like to "color code" their books, using colored paper to indicate different categories of spells: pink for love spells, green for money, and so on. This works especially well if you're using a book that allows you to shift the pages around, such as a three-ring binder.

If your grimoire has a fixed binding that won't let you add pages, you can demarcate the various "chapters" of your book with bookmarks. Do you have an artsy nature? You may enjoy handcrafting pretty bookmarks to designate the sections of your grimoire. The more personal you make your book and the more imagination you put into it, the better. Try these suggestions:

- Cut strips of posterboard or heavy construction paper, each about 2" wide by 7" long. Onto the strips glue pictures from magazines that represent the topics you've included in your grimoire: happy couples or hearts for love, dollar signs or diamonds for prosperity, airplanes or cruise ships for travel, and so on.
- Dry flowers, herbs, or other botanicals that have magickal connections to the categories you've chosen for your book: roses for love, mint for money spells, etc. (Refer to the charts in Chapter 16 for more information.) Then affix these botanicals to strips of posterboard or heavy construction paper.
- Select posterboard or heavy construction paper in various colors that correspond to the topics in your book. Cut the paper into strips, then draw symbols or other images on the strips to represent the subjects of the spells. You could decorate these strips with magick sigils, which are spells in themselves (see Chapter 12), to mark sections in your grimoire.
- Purchase ribbons in colors that symbolize the topics you've chosen to include in your book. Lay the ribbon markers between the pages to define the different sections. Or, if you opt to craft your own grimoire from scratch, fasten the ribbons in place when you bind your book (see Chapter 2 for instructions). Attach tiny charms, gemstone beads, or other symbolic adornments to the ribbons, if you like.

INVITE DIVINE ASSISTANCE

When you prepare yourself to enact a ritual or cast a spell or a charm, you agree to suspend reality for a time to get in touch with energies greater than your own limited scope of individual perception. By entering the space and time "between the worlds" you make a pact with yourself and with the myriad spirits who share the cosmos with us. You acknowledge their presence by inviting them into your sacred space. You accept them as manifestations of the Divine.

Whether you choose to interact only with the forces of the Divine Feminine and/or the Divine Masculine or to invite assistance from other deities, spirits, and nonphysical beings is up to you. Later in this book, we'll talk more about some of the entities who may assist you in your magickal work.

Devote Each Section of Your Grimoire to a Goddess

Ancient cultures revered certain qualities and characteristics in each goddess, and saw her as having dominion over specific areas of life on earth. Today, many witches and Neopagans continue to honor a pantheon of deities and call upon these deities to aid us in our magickal practice.

As you go about compiling your grimoire, think of the goddesses traditionally associated with the many and diverse parts of your life. Think about the types of spells you intend to perform. Most likely, you'll feel a special attraction to certain goddesses, perhaps based on your own heritage or personal affinities. You may want to dedicate each section of your grimoire to a different goddess and then invoke her power and assistance when you perform spells and rituals in the areas she governs.

Many deities play a number of roles and can be called upon to assist you in numerous areas of your magickal practice. The following list suggests some to consider, but you can find a wealth of additional information online and in other books.

- Love: Venus, Aphrodite, Freya, Hathor, Hera, Juno
- Protection: Tara, Artemis, Tiamat, Frigg, Beset
- Prosperity/Abundance: Venus, Lakshmi, Gaia, Demeter, Ceres, Epona, Renenet

- Healing: Brigid, Isis, Ceres, Freya, Kuan Yin
- Creativity: Brigid, Isis, Venus, Selena
- Wisdom: Sophia, Cerridwen, Hecate, Hestia, Morgan, Saraswati
- Success: Nike, Isis, Cybele, Amaterasu, Cerridwen
- Home: Brigid, Cerridwen, Coatlicue, Beset
- Children/Fertility: Yemaja, Axo Mama, Cybele, Oshun, Demeter, Frigg, Heket
- Happiness: Bast, Hathor, Lilith, Freya
- Strength/Power: Inanna, Artemis, Sekhmet, Tiamat, Pele, Kali, Persephone, Selket

Working with Goddess Energy

Begin by researching various goddesses. Learn all you can about the goddesses with whom you might like to work and to whom you plan to dedicate the different sections of your grimoire. Familiarize yourself with ancient rites of worship and decide how these relate to your modern-day experience. How might you adapt early ideas to your present-day practice?

Next, dedicate each section of your book of shadows to a particular goddess who will help you by lending her powers to your magickal workings. On the first page of each section, write a blessing to the deity who will preside over that portion of your book and the spells and rituals you perform. Let's say, for example, you've devoted the love section of your book of shadows to Venus. Write the following blessing or one of your own creation:

"Most beautiful Venus, whose light shines brightest in the night sky, and whose loving energy embraces all humankind, I dedicate the spells and rituals I perform for love and relationships to you. Fill me with the power and perfection of your love, so that I may channel your divine energy into the magick I do. I ask your guidance as I seek to bring more love to myself, other people, and the manifest world. May I and all beings know the blessedness of your divine love that transcends all worldly love, and may it sustain us, uplift us, and bring us joy."

The Modern Witchcraft Grimoire

If you like, add pictures of the deity as you interpret her and other symbols or objects that you attribute to her.

Before you perform a spell or ritual, invite the goddess with humility. Explain your reasons for calling upon her. What, exactly, do you hope to accomplish? Whether you are seeking love, knowledge, protection, or abundance, your invocation must include your statement of intent.

When the Goddess is effectively evoked, she does not merely announce "Here I am!" She will make her true self known to you through images, inspiration, insights, emotions—and often she will have a message to impart. When she speaks through you, you may find that words and visions flow as freely as a wild river, carrying you to places unimaginable heretofore. Remain open to this energy and try to retain the experience of receiving her communication. Record as many details in your grimoire as you can, in order to deepen your understanding of what has transpired.

LOVE SPELLS

Love makes the world go 'round, as the saying goes, and witches cast more spells for matters of the heart than for any other purpose. Therefore, you'll probably want to dedicate a section in your grimoire for love spells. Because emotion is one of the key ingredients in magick, it's logical that love spells would be among the most powerful of all. Usually the best times to perform love spells are during the waxing moon, when the sun or moon is in Libra, or on Fridays—unless you intend to block someone's attention or end an unwanted relationship. In that case, do your spell while the moon is waning, when the sun or moon is in Scorpio or Capricorn, or on Saturday.

Before you begin the spell, cleanse your space, and cast a circle (see Chapter 13 for details on how to cast and open circles). Call upon the goddess who presides over your love spells and ask her to assist you.

Here's a sample love spell you can use if you like:

Light My Fire

Use this spell to spark a new love affair or to fan the flames in an existing romance. You can cast it for yourself or someone else.

TOOLS AND INGREDIENTS

A ballpoint pen

A red candle

Essential oil of jasmine, rose, or patchouli

A ring large enough to slide over the candle

A candleholder

Matches or a lighter

1. With the ballpoint pen, carve the two individuals' names on the candle, so that the letters are alternated and interspersed. For example, you'd write Bill and Sue this way: B S I U L E L.

2. Rub some essential oil on the candle, then slide the ring onto it—the symbolism is obvious.

3. Place the candle in the holder and light it. As you stare into the flame, chant the word created by your joint names (don't worry if it doesn't make any sense or sounds discordant). Envision a union between you and your partner.

4. When you can no longer concentrate on this spell, snuff out the candle and open the circle.

5. Repeat each day until the candle has burned down to the ring.

6. Remove the ring and place it on your altar, or give it to the person for whom you did the spell, to "fire up" a romance.

7. Thank the goddess of love for her assistance.

Be sure to include the date(s) when you performed the spell and record the results. Each time you cast this spell, add more details and experiences in your grimoire, including any changes you may have made from the original.

PROSPERITY AND ABUNDANCE SPELLS

Spells for abundance are probably the second most popular among witches. Of course, prosperity and abundance mean different things to different people, but usually spellcasters perform these spells to attract money and/or material goods. Enact prosperity spells during the waxing moon, when the sun or moon is in Taurus, on a Thursday or Friday—unless your goal is to stabilize finances or cut your expenses. In that case, do your spell when the moon is waning, when the sun or moon is in Capricorn, or on a Saturday.

Before you begin the spell, cleanse your space, and cast a circle. Call upon the goddess who presides over your prosperity spells and ask her to assist you. Here's a sample spell you can use to draw money to you:

Buried Treasure Spell

This spell offers a new twist on the old legends about buried treasure. Instead of hunting for that pirate's hidden chest of gold doubloons or a leprechaun's pot of gold at the end of a rainbow, you symbolically stash treasure in order to "prime the pump" so greater riches can flow to you.

TOOLS AND INGREDIENTS

A small mirror

A tin box with a lid

9 coins (any denomination)

A magnet

A shovel

1. Place the mirror in the bottom of the tin box, with the reflective side up.

2. Lay the coins, one at a time, on top of the mirror while you envision each one multiplying exponentially.

3. Attach the magnet to the inside of the box (on the lid or on a side) and visualize it attracting a multitude of coins to you.

4. Put the lid on the box and open the circle.

5. Take your "treasure chest" and the shovel outside and dig a hole beneath a large tree. Bury the box in the ground near the tree's roots.

6. When you've finished, say this incantation aloud:

"By the luck of three times three
This spell now brings great wealth to me.
The magnet draws prosperity.
The mirror doubles all it sees.
My fortune grows as does this tree
And I shall ever blessed be."

7. Thank the goddess for her assistance.

Be sure to include the date(s) when you performed the spell and record the results. Each time you cast this spell, add more details and experiences in your grimoire, including any changes you made from the original.

Louise Hay's Prescription for Prosperity

In order to become prosperous, bestselling author and publisher Louise Hay in her book *You Can Heal Your Life* says you must:

- Feel deserving.
- Make room for the new.
- Be happy for other people's prosperity.
- Be grateful.

She also explains that "true prosperity begins with feeling good about yourself ... It is never an amount of money; it is a state of mind. Prosperity or lack of it is an outer expression of the ideas in your head."

PROTECTION SPELLS

Early grimoires contained lots and lots of spells for protection—some of them incredibly complex, and many of which invoked the assistance of spirits. Early spellcasters frequently called upon deities of all sorts to safeguard them, their homes, and their loved ones from both physical and psychic harm. People in many cultures have used evil eyes and hex signs since ancient times and still do today. As in earlier eras, the world presents many dangers today—as a quick glance at the nightly news will confirm—so you'll most likely want to devote a section in your grimoire to protection spells. Usually the best times to perform protection spells are during the waning moon, when the sun or moon is in Capricorn, and/or on a Saturday.

Before you begin the spell, cleanse your space, and cast a circle. Call upon the goddess whom you've chosen to preside over your protection spells and ask her to assist you. Here's a sample spell you can use to create a protection amulet for yourself or someone else:

Protection Amulet

Protection amulets are one of the oldest forms of magick. With this spell you create one to shield you (or someone else) from potential injury or illness.

TOOLS AND INGREDIENTS

A piece of amber (for protection from physical or nonphysical sources)

A piece of bloodstone (for protection from physical injury)

A piece of turquoise (for protection from illness)

Pine incense (for cleansing and purification)

An incense burner

Matches or a lighter

A photo of you (or another person if you're doing this spell for someone else)

A pen with black ink

Essential oil of rosemary

A white pouch, preferably silk

A black ribbon

Saltwater

1. Wash the stones with mild soap and water, then pat them dry.
2. Fit the incense into the burner and light it.
3. Across the photograph write the words "I am safe" as you envision yourself safe and sound, completely surrounded by a sphere of pure white light. If you're doing the spell for someone else, write "[person's name] is safe" and envision her or him protected by white light.

4. Dot each corner of the photo with essential oil. Inhale the scent of the oil and mentally connect it with a feeling of safety.

5. Slip the photo into the pouch (if necessary, fold it so it's small enough to fit).

6. Rub a little essential oil on each of the stones and add them to the pouch.

7. Tie the pouch closed with the black ribbon, making 8 knots. Each time you tie a knot repeat this incantation aloud:

"Anything that could cause harm
Is now repelled by this magick charm."

8. Sprinkle the amulet with saltwater, then hold it in the incense smoke for a few moments to charge it.

9. Open the circle and thank the Goddess for her help.

10. Wear or carry the amulet with you at all times to protect you from harm, or give it to the person you intend to protect.

As you record the spell in your grimoire, be sure to include the date(s) when you performed the spell and describe the results. Each time you cast this spell, add more details and experiences in your book, including any changes you made from the original.

SPELLS FOR HEALTH AND HEALING

In the days before modern medicine and technology, people relied heavily on magick to promote health and healing. Even today, we realize that a patient's attitude and beliefs influence his or her well-being and can have a huge impact on the person's recovery. Like the beneficial nature of prayer, which Dr. Larry Dossey wrote about in his book *Prayer Is Good Medicine*, magick's power can boost all sorts of healing. You may want to dedicate a section of your grimoire to healing spells and rituals. The best times to perform spells for health and healing depend on the nature of the ailment and your intention.

Before you begin the spell, cleanse your space, and cast a circle. Call upon the deity who presides over your health and healing work, and

The Modern Witchcraft Grimoire

request her assistance. If you're performing a spell for another person, ask his or her permission before you begin. Here's a sample spell you can use yourself or to aid someone else—even at a distance:

Heaven and Earth Healing Spell

This spell draws upon the powers of heaven and earth to help heal any condition. You can perform it anytime.

TOOLS AND INGREDIENTS

A magick wand

1. After casting a circle around yourself, stand in the center of the circle with your feet about shoulder-width apart. (If you're doing the spell for someone else and that person is physically present, cast the circle around both of you.)

2. Hold the wand over your head with both hands, with your arms outstretched and straight, pointing the tip of the wand at the sky.

3. Close your eyes and say aloud: "With this wand I draw down the healing force of the heavens." In your mind's eye see light flowing into the wand, filling it with cosmic energy and making it glow brightly.

4. Open your eyes and point the tip of the wand at the afflicted part of your body (or the other person's body). If the person for whom you are doing this spell is not physically present, aim the wand toward his/her location. Envision the light you collected from the heavens flowing into the injured or ailing body part, filling and embracing it with healing rays.

5. When you sense that all the light has been transferred from the wand to the body, point the wand at the ground.

6. Close your eyes and say aloud: "With this wand I draw up the healing force of Mother Earth." In your mind's eye see light flowing into the wand from the center of the earth, filling it and making it glow brightly.

7. Open your eyes and aim the tip of the wand at the afflicted part of your body (or the other person's body). Envision the light you collected from the earth flowing into the injured or ailing body part, infusing it with healing rays until all the light has been transferred from the wand to the body.

8. When you have finished, thank the Goddess as well as the forces of heaven and earth for assisting you, and then open the circle.

Be sure to include the date(s) when you performed the spell and record the results. Each time you cast this spell, add more details and experiences in your grimoire, including any changes you made from the original.

OTHER SPELLS TO INCLUDE

The other categories you choose to include in your book of shadows will depend on your preferences, your objectives, and the types of spells you do most frequently. If you travel a lot, you might add a section for travel spells. If your career is a primary focus, you may consider devoting a section to spells for success. You could dedicate portions of your grimoire to spells for personal power, spiritual growth, creativity, good luck, peace and harmony, children and pets, or just about anything else that fits your needs. You might want to establish a "Miscellaneous" category for all those great one-off spells you like as well as those that have many potential yet undefined applications.

Over time, as you become more proficient as a magician and collect more and more spells, you may even decide to create an entire book of shadows for each category. Or you could keep a big book that contains all your spells as well as a smaller one that holds some of your favorites.

Each time you perform a particular spell or ritual, note in your book of shadows when you cast the spell, what you actually did, what tools and ingredients you used, what you experienced, and the results you got. How long did it take to see results? What went right and what went wrong? Was anyone else involved in your spellworking? If so, what impact did that person's presence have? If you did a spell for someone else, how did she or he react? Also note anything you changed from your original working. If you did something differently, did this affect the outcome? How? Would you change something in the future? What and why?

CRAFTING YOUR OWN ORIGINAL SPELLS

In the beginning, as a novice witch, you'd probably be wise to stick with tried-and-true spells shared with you by spellworkers you respect. But after a while, when you are more comfortable with your knowledge and powers and have some experience under your magick belt, you'll probably want to try crafting your own spells. That's great! The more personal a spell, the better results it's likely to generate because you invest more emotion in it. Each of us has unique needs, preferences, talents, and strengths—use them to your advantage.

Readers frequently e-mail me and ask me to look at the spells they've designed themselves and to offer suggestions. In nearly every case, the writer has created a fabulous original work of art that shows he or she has invested a great deal of thought, time, and effort into the process. One of the most interesting of these was a woman who'd been nearly blind all her life. She explained that she found it difficult to relate to the visual spells I'd included in my previous books and wanted to adapt the spells to make the best of her other senses. This amazingly creative woman tackled the challenge with enthusiasm and insight. She designed some beautiful spells I could never have imagined that used her individual strengths in very special ways.

Planning Your Spells

Carefully plan your spells before you attempt to cast them. The old adage "Be careful what you ask for, you just might get it" is never more relevant than in spellwork. Consider the implications of every nuance— the color of the candles you choose to place on the altar, the manner in which you have prepared your tools, the conviction with which you consecrate, the spirits you invoke, every word that you speak, and, especially, the intention you hold in your mind and heart.

According to Wiccan theory, the energy you send out via a spell will return to you threefold. Therefore, it's in your best interest to plan carefully before casting your spell into the world, so that you avoid unexpected or undesirable results you didn't intend.

Your Grimoire As a Spellcrafting Companion

When you begin crafting your own original spells, your grimoire becomes an even greater ally than you may have realized earlier. It serves as your workbook while you build the framework of the spells you create. It lets you clearly define your intentions by writing them down—writing is the first step in bringing an idea to fruition in the manifest world. Your book of shadows also enables you to keep track of your steps as you progress on your journey. And it allows you to see whether you've gone astray or could have done something differently to produce a better result.

As you set out to craft a spell of your own design:

- Write down your intention and the ideas you have about what you hope to accomplish.
- Research the implications of the spell you plan to craft. What have other spellcasters experienced? What challenges do you foresee? What outcomes?
- Give your ideas time to settle. During the next few days or weeks, you may gain additional insight, perhaps from your dreams or meditations, into what you could do to enhance or refine your spell.
- Make a list of ingredients and tools you'll need. How will you acquire these? What do you need to do to prepare them for your spellwork?
- Will you include an affirmation or incantation? Practice writing it until it says exactly what you intend. (See the instructions in Chapter 11.)
- Do you plan to ask a deity to assist you? If so, which one? How will you invoke this deity? Write down the invocation you plan to use and study it to make sure it says what you want it to say.
- Determine the best time to cast your spell (see Chapters 6, 8, and 9 for more information).
- Decide where you'll perform your spell, and prepare the space.
- Will anyone else be involved in the process? If so, discuss the details with that person to make sure you're in agreement and clear about your intentions and outcomes, as well as what you plan to do.
- Organize the steps you'll take in casting your spell.
- Try to anticipate what might transpire and how your thoughts, words, and actions may manifest.
- Approach your work with serenity and patience, rather than feeling a need for immediate gratification.

The Modern Witchcraft Grimoire

Of course, after you've finished casting your spell, record everything in your book of shadows as soon as possible. Follow up with an explanation of the results and any other experiences related to your magick work. What occurred? How, when, where? In this way, you will gain greater confidence and a more personal understanding of the connections between each aspect of your process. You will be able to observe the results that manifest after you perform your spell. You'll become conscious of your role in what transpires.

In time, you'll notice patterns and synchronicities. You'll learn what works for you and what doesn't. You'll develop your techniques and expand your repertoire. You'll strengthen your magickal muscles and move into the next phase of proficiency. How amazing is that?

Chapter 11

VERBAL SPELLS

When you utter a spell aloud, you create a resonance that begins the process of manifestation. Sounds produce vibrations that echo through the cosmic web that connects everything in our universe. These vibrations stimulate effects in the visible world. Words also act as verbal symbols that convey your intentions. Even a word from a language with which you aren't familiar can serve as a magick symbol. In fact, many spellcasters choose to use words from ancient tongues, such as Sanskrit or Arabic, or from cultures other than their own because for them these words have no mundane associations.

It's safe to say that the earliest spells were most likely spoken ones, intoned by witches and wizards, shamans and sorcerers long before the advent of writing. Verbal spells figured prominently in early grimoires. They owed their popularity, in part, to the fact that the magick worker needed nothing other than a voice to cast the spell. Even if the magician couldn't read or write, he or she could memorize the words and say them at the appropriate time. Our ancestors called upon gods and goddesses, as well as angels, spirits, demons, and other nonphysical entities, via invocations, spoken charms, and incantations.

Witches today still use verbal spells to request the assistance of deities and other beings. Because affirmations, incantations, chants, charms, and blessings continue to play an important role in magickal workings, you may choose to devote a section of your grimoire to spoken and written spells.

Evoking and Invoking

When you *evoke* an entity—a spirit, an elemental, a ghost, or another nonphysical being—you summon it to appear before you and instruct it to do your bidding. When you *invoke* an entity, you invite it to actually enter your body. The entity becomes part of you, temporarily, and works or speaks through you. (Mediums also do this in séances when they channel spirits.) Witches sometimes invoke the Goddess or God in rites, and for the duration of the rite the deity abides within the witch until released. Before you evoke or invoke any being, it's a good idea to learn all you can about that entity so you know what you're getting into. An old saying warns: Don't raise any spirit you can't put down.

CHANTING

What comes to mind when you think of chanting? Medieval monks singing Gregorian chants in European cathedrals? Buddhists dressed in saffron robes sitting in lotus position, uttering the Sanskrit phrase *Om Mani Padme Hum*? Chants are typically phrases or words repeated aloud for a particular purpose. Saying a rosary is a form of chanting. So are the cheers sports fans shout to encourage players on the field.

Some people chant mantras while meditating. A mantra is a group of sacred sounds repeated for spiritual purposes. The mantra not only helps you to focus your mind; it lets you become aware of the spirit housed within your body. Witches sometimes chant in their rituals to raise energy and to unify all the participants in the ritual. Maybe you've heard this popular chant, for instance, or intoned it yourself: "The Goddess is alive, magick is afoot."

The repetitive sounds in a chant—as well as the actual words that compose it—act on your subconscious to generate results. Interestingly, chanting has the power to quiet or enliven. It can help you concentrate, shift your consciousness to an altered state, affect physical processes such as blood pressure and heart rate, connect you to the divine realm, and more.

"She changes everything she touches,
And everything she touches changes!"

Do you have a few favorite chants that help you get into the mood for magick? Some that you recite to calm your mind before meditating? Perhaps you chant to cleanse sacred space or to chase away unwanted energies before spellworking. In your book of shadows, jot down the chants you find valuable. You can use them alone or in conjunction with other magickal processes.

Consider setting some to music or accompanying your chants on a hand drum to boost their power. Although most chants are quite simple, you could add bits of sheet music to accompany the words in your grimoire, or sketch the notes yourself on the pages of your book—this adds both an instructive and an illustrative element. If you are raising magickal children, you may enjoy singing favorite chants to your kids just as you would sing nursery rhymes.

"We all come from the Goddess
And to her we shall return
Like a drop of rain
Flowing to the ocean."

AFFIRMATIONS

In the last few decades, affirmations have gained popularity in psychological and self-help circles, as well as among spellcasters. Affirmations are short positive statements that you formulate to produce a desired result. They express clearly and succinctly what you intend to attract, eliminate, manifest, or change in your life. Whether you write your affirmations or say them aloud, putting your intentions into words helps to focus your mind, clarify your objectives, and empower your spells.

Designing Effective Affirmations

As is true with anything else in life, some ways are better than others when it comes to designing affirmations. These tips will help you to word yours effectively:

• Keep it short.
• Use only positive imagery.
• State your intention in the present tense, as if the condition already exists.

Let's try a couple examples to help you get a feel for creating affirmations.

Right: I am completely healthy in body, mind, and spirit.

Wrong: I don't have any illnesses or injuries.

See the difference? The first sentence affirms what you seek: health. The second makes you think of conditions you don't want: illnesses and injuries.

Right: I now have a job that's perfect for me.

Wrong: I will get the perfect job.

In the first sentence you state that the job you seek is yours *right now.* The second indicates that you'll eventually get the job you want, but doesn't specify when—it could be some time way off in the future. Yes, it may take a while for all the pieces to fall into place, but the first step to achieving success is believing (and affirming) that you already have what you desire and that the situation is already determined in your favor.

Being specific is usually a good thing when creating affirmations. If your goal is to lose twenty-five pounds or you've got your heart set on acquiring a 1965 red Mustang convertible, for instance, list the pertinent details in your affirmation. But sometimes you don't know all the ins and outs of a situation, or you don't want to limit your options—as in the job example we just considered. In such cases, simply state that whatever you achieve is right for you in every way and let the universe work out the fine points.

Consider designing some general, all-purpose affirmations and use them regularly. List these in your book of shadows and, if you like, enrich them with illustrations.

Your list might look something like this:

- My life is rich with abundance of all kinds.
- I have everything I need and desire.
- I am happy, healthy, wealthy, and fulfilled in every way.

You can recite these favorite affirmations first thing in the morning and last thing at night, while driving to work, taking a shower, folding laundry—whenever you have time. In this way, you make magick part of your daily routine and attract good things into your life on a continual basis.

Using Affirmations

The versatility of affirmations makes them the darlings of many modern witches. Each time you read the words of an affirmation you've created, you are reminded of your objective. Seeing the written affirmation makes an imprint on the visual part of your brain; hearing it stated aloud impacts the auditory sense. Together, they provide a one-two punch in spellcasting.

Here are some ways you can use affirmations:

- Say your affirmation aloud several times a day—or at least first thing in the morning—to set your objective into motion.
- Post an affirmation in a place where you'll see it often: near your computer, on your bathroom mirror, on your refrigerator, on the dashboard of your car, and so on.
- Write an affirmation on a slip of paper and add it to a medicine pouch, talisman, or amulet.
- Write an affirmation on a slip of paper and burn it in a cauldron or ritual fire to release something you want to eliminate from your life, such as an unwanted habit or relationship.
- Carve a short affirmation on a candle, and then light the candle to ignite the affirmation.

Once you understand the basics of creating affirmations, you'll probably find lots of original ways to include them in your spells and rituals. Record them in your grimoire, and comment on the results you get from using affirmations. Over time, you may refine the affirmations you've noted in your book of shadows, based on your experiences.

Affirmations and Healing

Bestselling author and publisher Louise Hay, in her book *You Can Heal Your Life*, includes a lengthy section of affirmations intended to aid specific health issues. For example:

Problem	Affirmation
Allergies	"The world is safe and friendly. I am safe. I am at peace with life."
Lower back pain	"I love and approve of myself. Life supports and loves me."
Indigestion	"I digest and assimilate all new experiences peacefully and joyously."
Sore throat	"I speak up for myself with ease. I express my creativity."

By repeating an affirmation regularly, you reprogram your thinking process. Your updated perspective enables you to remedy the problem.

INCANTATIONS

One of the oldest known incantations—believed to be more than 3,000 years old—was discovered by archaeologists in the ancient Mesopotamian city of Kish. The author inscribed this ancient love spell in cuneiform on a clay tablet, calling upon Akkadian deities:

"By Ištar and Išhara
I conjure you:
As long as his neck
And your neck
Are not entwined,
You shall find no peace!"

Incantations can be as short as two lines or as long as your imagination and intention dictate (the Mesopotamian one excerpted here, for instance, contains a total of thirty-eight lines). Although early spellcasters used incantations to curse as well as to charm, witches today usually frown on the practice of performing magick to harm or manipulate someone against his or her will.

What's the difference between an affirmation and an incantation? Incantations are usually written as rhymes. The catchy phrasing makes them easy to remember. You don't have to be a poet laureate to create an effective incantation—just follow the same basic rules when writing an incantation as you would when writing an affirmation: keep it simple, use positive imagery, and state it in the present tense. Here's an example of a simple incantation for healing:

"I am healed
In body and mind
Of imbalances
Of any kind."

Although it's perfectly okay to merely write incantations, they become even more effective when spoken aloud. Because incantations feature both rhyme and meter, you may enjoy putting them to music and singing them.

THE FORCES OF THE FOUR DIRECTIONS

Many spells and rituals petition gods, goddesses, and other entities for assistance. You may choose to call upon a deity with whom you feel a particular kinship. Or, if you're performing a ritual on one of the sabbats, you might seek the aid of the deity connected with that day: for example, Brigid on Imbolc, Lugh on Lugnasadh.

Witches often summon the forces associated with the four directions and the four elements. You may envision these as angels, guardians, or other spirits. The archangel Raphael, for instance, is said to oversee the east, Michael the south, Gabriel the west, and Uriel the north.

Here's a simple practice you can use as part of a circle-casting ritual:

1. Stand in the center of the circle, facing east. Outstretch your arms at your sides, with your left palm open and facing down toward the earth and your right palm upturned toward the sky.
2. Say aloud: "Before me Raphael, angel of air, guardian of the east. Please guide, protect, bless, and empower me."
3. Next, say aloud: "Behind me Gabriel, angel of water, guardian of the west. Please guide, protect, bless, and empower me."
4. Next, say aloud: "To my right Michael, angel of fire, guardian of the south. Please guide, protect, bless, and empower me."
5. Next, say aloud: "To my left Uriel, angel of earth, guardian of the north. Please guide, protect, bless, and empower me."
6. Finally say: "About me shines the five-pointed star, and within me the six-rayed star. Blessed be."

While you call to these angelic beings, envision them standing around you and offering their support. Perhaps you'll see Raphael dressed in yellow, Gabriel in blue. Maybe Michael wields his famed sword. See the five-pointed star—the pentagram—overlaid on your body, its points aligned with your head, arms, and legs.

You can design your own ritual, but before you begin calling the quarters, gain as much knowledge as possible about their energies and correspondences. This will enrich your experience and enhance your magickal work.

East, Realm of Dawn

The east corresponds to daybreak. When contemplating the energies of this direction, find an eastern-facing spot and rise early enough that you can see and feel the tranquil transition of the awakening world. This will give you a very real experience of new beginnings, as night surrenders her darkness to the power of the rising sun. Birds emerge from sleep and herald the start of the day. The grass is wet with dew and the world seems fresh and undisturbed. Open yourself to the sensations of dawn and the promises she proffers, then write down your experiences in your book of shadows.

South, Realm of High Noon

Preferably on a bright and sunny day, find a place where you can sit quietly and be undisturbed. Face the south. Do not look directly into the sun overhead, but feel its heat and warmth on your face and shoulders. As you breathe, envision the glowing center of energy contained within you as an internal echo of the sun itself. Notice the heightened activity of the day, when everything seems to be at its very peak. The sun nurtures life on earth, but it can also dangerous, scorching the land and your own skin. Contemplate this duality and other insights or sensations that come to you, and then record your experiences in your book of shadows.

West, Realm of Sunset

In many mythologies, the western lands are seen as a magickal place. To the west lay the Summerlands, the Isle of Apples, Avalon, Tír na nÓg, and the Isle of Man. At the time of the setting sun, when the earth begins to grow quiet again after the day's activities, face the west. Notice the changes in the sky. The sun descends toward the horizon, the temperature cools, and nocturnal creatures emerge from their lairs. Twilight paints the sky with many colors and, on the seacoast, land and ocean appear to be one. As you relax, breathe deeply and observe day surrendering to night. In your grimoire, note your experiences in this place of twilight and mystery.

North, Realm of Midnight

At midnight, when the moon is bright and other humans sleep, begin your contemplation of the north. Gaze at the stars. Find Polaris, the North Star, which has guided sailors and navigators for centuries. Once you find the North Star, you can never truly be lost. The north pulls the compass point to itself, thus its magnetism and power are undeniable. Picture the earth in the sleep of winter, trees bare of their leaves, the earth frozen and solid, icicles dangling from branches and twigs. Feel yourself standing upon the earth, the Great Mother who gave life to us all and who will one day cradle our bones. Turn inward and open yourself to the wisdom and secrets of this direction. Write down your experiences in this time of silence and solitude.

CALLING THE FOUR QUARTERS

When you feel comfortable in your knowledge of the four directions and their energies, you're ready to evoke and/or invoke the deities who reign there. You may do this alone or with other like-minded people, as a ritual in itself or as part of a more extensive ritual or rite. Before performing a spell, you may choose to invite the assistance of the powers and elements of the four directions. Use the following to call the deities who guard the quarters, or better yet, write your own "script."

Call to the East

Start in the east, the realm of new beginnings, of the dawn and of springtime. The east corresponds to the element of air, and represents possibility and awareness. Look to the east when you seek to renew hope and faith. Face east to summon the power inherent there for strength in communication, mental clarity, and wisdom. Call the forces of this direction with this charge:

"I call upon the spirits of air who guard and protect the gateway to the eastern realm. I beckon and call you forth from the far corner of the universe wherein you dwell. Winds of change, strength of tornadoes, bear witness to this ritual and give us your aid. Gentle breeze that carries the seed to fertile soil, descend into this circle and grant us your blessing. Realm of the Dawning Star, bestow upon us your gifts of vision, insight, and song. We seek to know you, we seek to honor you. By the air that is our breath, we charge you, be here now! To the East and the spirits of air, we bid you hail and welcome!"

Call to the South

Proceed clockwise around the circle and face south, the direction of noontime and of summer. The south corresponds to the element of fire, and represents fullness and vitality. Turn to the south when you seek fulfillment of desire, when you need passion, inspiration, or courage. Face the south and call the powers of the direction with this charge:

"I call upon the spirits of fire who guard and protect the gateway to the southern realm. I beckon and call you forth from the far corner of the universe wherein you dwell. Candle flame and hearth fire, come into this circle and warm our hearts.

Strength of wildfire and volcano, descend into this circle and grant us your blessing.
Golden orb of the high noon sun, realm of heat and brilliance, bestow upon us your
gifts of passion and inspiration. We seek to know you, we seek to honor you. By the
fire in our hearts, we charge you, be here now! To the South and the spirits of fire,
we bid you hail and welcome!"

Call to the West

Continue around the circle to the western "corner" and face the direction of sunset and of autumn. The west corresponds to the element of water. Turn to the west when you seek to enhance your intuition, uncover mysteries, and balance your emotions. Face the west and call the powers of the direction with this charge:

"I call upon the spirits of water who guard and protect the gateway to the western
realm. I beckon and call you forth from the far corner of the universe wherein you
dwell. Ocean depths, cradle of life, come into this circle and reveal the truth of our
inner visions. Strength of storm, rushing rivers, and rolling tides, descend into this
circle and grant us your blessing. Gentle rain that nourishes and cleanses, realm of
the setting sun, bestow upon us your gifts of intuition and mystery. We seek to know
you, we seek to honor you. By the water in our blood, we charge you, be here now! To
the West and the spirits of water, we bid you hail and welcome!"

Call to the North

Finally, you come to the north, the powers of elemental earth, representing both the womb and the grave, the source of all life and that which awaits at the end of life. North corresponds to the season of winter and to midnight. Turn to the north when you wish to manifest outcomes and reveal truth. Face the north and call the powers of the direction with this charge:

"I call upon the spirits of earth who guard and protect the gateway to the northern
realm. I beckon and call you forth from the far corner of the universe wherein you
dwell. Gaia, Demeter, Earth Mother, come into this circle and manifest the power
of your divine law. Strength of earthquake and of mountain, foundation beneath
our feet, descend into this circle and grant us your blessing. North Star, navigator's
guide, that which calls all other directions unto itself, bestow upon us your gifts of

strength. We seek to know you, we seek to honor you. By the earth that is our body, we charge you, be here now! To the North and the spirits of earth, we bid you hail and welcome!"

Wiccan Words

Wiccans often greet one another with the words "Merry meet." Another phrase, "Blessed be," may be spoken as a welcome, at the end of a ritual, in parting, or any time you want to wish someone well. This simple blessing contains the vibrations of love, and it thus attracts positive energy, dispels harmful vibrations, and confers protection.

ENDING A SPELL OR RITUAL

Spells, like books, have a beginning, middle, and end. Properly concluding a spell or ritual is just as important as the other parts. These final actions seal your spell, activate it, and allow you to step back into your everyday world. Witches do this with actions as well as with words.

Binding a Spell

It's customary to close a spell with a definitive statement. Wiccans often use the phrase "So mote it be" to bind a spell. If you prefer, you can say "So be it now" or "So it is done" or "Amen." The number three represents creativity, form, and manifestation in the three-dimensional world. Therefore, you can end a spell by repeating a statement three times or performing a gesture three times. In her book *The Spiral Dance*, Starhawk offers this closing statement to bind a spell:

"By all the power
Of three times three,
This spell bound around
Shall be.
To cause no harm,
Nor return on me.
As I do will,
So mote it be."

To make sure your spell only generates positive results, say something in conclusion like, "This spell is done for the good of all, harming none." Put the finishing touches on your spell in this way, before you open the circle and allow your intentions to flow out into the manifest world.

Releasing Deities and Spirits

If you've summoned deities, spirits, angels, guardians, or other entities to assist you during your magickal workings, you must release them at the end of the spell or ritual. Do this with gratitude and respect. Just as you called forth these beings with chants, incantations, invocations, or other utterances, you'll say so long to them verbally. You can design a personalized ending ritual or use a "readymade" one from another source. Here's a simple way to release entities, so they can return to their usual realms of existence:

1. Face east, and say aloud: "Guardian of the east, spirit of air, we thank you for your presence here. Depart now and return to your home, harming none, and let there be peace between us. Hail, farewell, and blessed be."

2. Turn to face north, and say aloud: "Guardian of the north, spirit of earth, we thank you for your presence here. Depart now and return to your home, harming none, and let there be peace between us. Hail, farewell, and blessed be."

3. Face west, and say aloud: "Guardian of the west, spirit of water, we thank you for your presence here. Depart now and return to your home, harming none, and let there be peace between us. Hail, farewell, and blessed be."

4. Face south, and say aloud: "Guardian of the south, spirit of fire, we thank you for your presence here. Depart now and return to your home, harming none, and let there be peace between us. Hail, farewell, and blessed be."

If you've asked for assistance from specific beings, include their names in your parting statements. For instance, if you've called upon the four archangels, say something like: "We thank you, Raphael [Uriel, Gabriel, Michael], for your guidance and protection during this ritual/rite."

In this way, you bring your ritual to a close in a pleasant way that honors those who have lent their energies to your joint endeavor. Just as you might say goodnight to valued guests after a dinner gathering, you thank these beings for their participation and wish them a safe return to their homes.

Chapter 12

VISUAL SPELLS

Most of us are visually oriented people, and a vibrant image has the power to strongly impact us. Advertisers know this very well—just watch a commercial for some sort of drug, in which the pictures show happy, healthy people while the voiceover describes all the drug's unpleasant side effects. The viewer's mind reacts to the pictures rather than the words. Because images are so powerful, witches use them to enrich spells and rituals—when you're doing a spell, a picture truly is worth a thousand words.

You may like to add drawings, symbols, and other images to your book of shadows. A quick look at Pinterest will reveal lots of gorgeously illustrated grimoires and may give you some ideas for decorating your own. Many witches sketch in their grimoires. Others affix photos or visuals from magazines. I like to draw Celtic knots in mine because I'm of Irish descent. I also enjoy creating collages that combine pictures, words, fabric, dried flowers and leaves, and all sorts of other objects— the collages serve as spells in themselves.

How about designing what's known as a "vision board" in your book? Write an affirmation that describes your objective, and then decorate the page with pictures that show what you intend to bring about. Look at it in the morning and before going to bed at night to spark your mind's creative power.

CREATIVE VISUALIZATION

In the late 1970s, author Shakti Gawain brought the concept of creative visualization into widespread public awareness. But witches have long known that visualization is the first step in working magick and precedes manifestation. Imagination is at the heart of a spell. If you can't imagine something, you won't be able to attain it. Forming a picture in your mind of the result you intend to manifest begins the process—in so doing, you mentally plant the seeds that will grow into the outcome you desire.

Don't think about the problem or condition you wish to change—instead, focus on the end result you seek. For instance, if your goal is to heal a broken leg, don't think about the injury; instead, envision the leg strong and healthy. If you want to attract prosperity, envision yourself driving an expensive car, living in a luxurious mansion, flying in your own private jet—anything that signifies "wealth" to you. Give yourself permission to dream big! Enrich your mental images with lots of color and action—clear, vivid images generate faster and more satisfactory results than bland ones.

Use Visual Aids

When doing a healing spell for someone you know, paste a photo of the person in your grimoire next to the written spell. This helps you focus your mind and channel the positive energy of the spell to that person.

THE POWER OF COLOR

Most people aren't aware of it, but we are constantly affected by the colors in our environment. Psychological studies show that our responses to color can be measured physically—red stimulates respiration and heart rate, blue lowers body temperature and pulse.

The Modern Witchcraft Grimoire

Colors contain myriad symbolic associations too. Blue, for instance, reminds you of the sky; green suggests foliage, grass, and healthy crops; orange is the color of fire and the sun. The Druids considered blue a sacred color that denoted someone who'd achieved the rank of bard (a formally trained storyteller entrusted with the oral history of a group). Early Christians associated blue with peace and compassion, which is why artists often depicted the Virgin Mary wearing blue. The beautiful stained glass windows in European cathedrals drew upon color symbolism to convey information to congregations who were largely illiterate. Because these connections are deeply rooted in our psychology, you can use color to influence the mind in your magickal workings.

The intensity of a color signifies its intensity in spellworking. Bright golden-yellow, for example, brings to mind the sun and fire; therefore it can activate and invigorate a spell. Pastel yellow has a gentler vibration that's usually associated with the air element and ideas. Red denotes sexual passion in a relationship, whereas pink symbolizes a gentler type of love, affection, and friendship.

The Power of Black

Black, a color that witches frequently wear, has many negative connotations to the general public, including death and mourning. To witches, however, black represents mystery and power, for it contains all the colors of the rainbow. It's also reminiscent of the night, the time when witches often gather to work magick.

Color Symbolism

Once you understand the energetic correspondences of colors, you can incorporate them into your spells and rituals. Witches often keep a stash of candles in various colors for spells and rituals. If you fashion medicine pouches or crane bags, use cloth in colors that relate to your objectives. Working with the plant kingdom helps you understand how flower colors can add meaning to spells—even people who know nothing of magick intuitively connect red roses with passion, which is why lovers give them on Valentine's Day. Gemstones, too, come in a wide range of colors that can influence your spells. The clothing you wear during a ritual, how you decorate your altar, and the images you include in your grimoire may also depict your associations with colors. Choose colors carefully in order to bring their energies to the spells.

Consider writing your spells with pens, pencils, markers, or crayons in colors that correspond to your intentions. As mentioned earlier, you may want to include colorful pages in your grimoire to denote specific types of spells: pink for love, green for money, and so on.

Color	Correspondences
Red	passion, anger, heat, energy, daring
Orange	confidence, activity, warmth, enthusiasm
Yellow	happiness, creativity, optimism, ideas
Green	health, fertility, growth, wealth
Light blue	peace, clarity, hope
Royal blue	independence, insight, imagination
Indigo	intuition, serenity, mental power
Purple	wisdom, spirituality, connection with higher realms
Pink	love, friendship, sociability
White	purity, clarity, protection
Black	power, wisdom
Brown	stability, practicality, grounding in the physical world

In your book of shadows, describe your responses to colors. What emotions do different colors spark in you? What associations do you have with various colors? Do you find some colors more appealing than others?

Colors and the Elements

In magick work, each of the four elements corresponds to a specific color. So do the four directions, which we discussed in Chapter 11.

The Modern Witchcraft Grimoire

Element	Direction	Color Correspondence
Fire	South	Red
Earth	North	Green
Air	East	Yellow
Water	West	Blue

When you cast a circle, you may want to place a yellow object (such as a candle) in the east, a red one in the south, a blue one in the west, and a green one in the north. If you set up altars at each of the four directions, consider decorating each in the appropriate color.

Chakra Colors

Holistic healing links the body's main energy centers, known as the chakras, with the seven colors of the visible spectrum. Red is associated with the root chakra, at the base of the spine; orange with the sacral chakra; yellow with the solar plexus chakra; green with the heart chakra; blue with the throat chakra; indigo with the third eye; and purple with the crown chakra, at the top of the head. Knowledge of these chakra-color connections can help your healing spells.

THE MAGICK OF THE TAROT

The beautiful oracle known as the tarot provides a rich source of magick imagery that you can tap for spells as well as divination. Many tarot decks display colorful palettes, but the colors shown on the cards are not purely decorative—they embody specific symbolic, spiritual, psychological, and physiological properties as well.

You'll find many familiar—and some not so familiar—images on the cards in your deck. Tarot artists intentionally choose symbols from various spiritual, cultural, magickal, and psychological traditions to convey information directly to your subconscious. Like dream imagery, the pictures on the cards speak to us at a deeper level and trigger insights in a more immediate and succinct way than words can.

The cards in the Major Arcana, in particular, offer powerful imagery, although many decks include vivid symbolism on the Minor Arcana cards as well. Some of the symbols are universal in nature, found in many cultures and time periods. Others may reflect the individual designer's intentions or beliefs, rather than holding broader meanings for all users.

The Suits of the Tarot

Each of the four suits in a tarot deck is linked with an element: Wands with the element of fire, Cups with water, Pentacles with earth, and Swords with air. As we discussed earlier, each of the four elements corresponds to a color. Therefore, many tarot artists emphasize red on the cards in the suit of Wands, blue on the Cups cards, green on the Pentacles cards, and yellow on the Swords cards.

Each suit also represents a particular area of life, so in spellwork choose cards from the suit that best relates to your intention. You can use cards from the suit of wands, for instance, in spells for career success or creativity. Choose cards from the suit of cups for love spells, pentacles for money spells, and swords for spells involving communication, intellectual pursuits, and legal matters.

Spellworking with Tarot Cards

Tarot cards make wonderful visual tools for spellcasting. Among the seventy-eight cards in a standard deck, you'll find one or more cards to represent any objective you may have.

I recommend purchasing a deck specifically for spellwork and another for doing readings. Some of the spells you perform require you to leave the cards in place, rather than returning them to the deck afterward. For example, you may wish to slip a card into a talisman or amulet pouch. To do the following spell, you'll need to tape three cards together. Perhaps you'd like to paste some of your favorite cards in your grimoire. I have a miniature deck that's perfect for this purpose.

Tarot Triptych Love Spell

A triptych is an altarpiece or decoration composed of 3 panels joined together. Perform this spell during the waxing moon, when the sun or moon is in Libra, or on a Friday.

TOOLS AND INGREDIENTS

3 tarot cards

Tape

Essential oil of rose, jasmine, patchouli, ylang-ylang, or musk

1. Choose 3 cards from a tarot deck (one you don't use for readings). These cards should depict things you desire in a romantic relationship. For instance, you might select the 10 of Pentacles if financial security is important to you or the Ace of Cups if you want to attract a new partner.
2. Lay the cards face-down, side by side, and tape them together.
3. Dab some essential oil on each card, while you envision yourself enjoying the loving relationship you seek.
4. Stand the triptych up on your altar or in another place where you'll see it often. (If you know feng shui, put it the Relationship Gua of your home.)

If you have a mini deck or a third deck, you can affix three cards from it in your book of shadows when you record the spell. You might also want to dab a bit of essential oil on the page where you write your spell. You can adapt this spell for other intentions too; simply select three cards that symbolize your objective.

RUNE MAGICK

Like tarot cards, runes serve as symbols that you can incorporate into your magick spells. In Chapter 5, we discussed different types of runic alphabets and the significance of these images. If you wish to use runes as a secret code when you write in your grimoire, that's fine, but they also have many other applications in spellcraft. Like the tarot, runes speak directly to your subconscious, bypassing the analytical, left-brain part of your mind. That's one reason why they come in handy in magick work.

Runes in Spellcraft

One of the beauties of runes as visual elements in magick work is their simplicity. You don't have to be a Rembrandt or a Michelangelo to draw runes. Most runes (Norse, Ogham, etc.) can be formed with a few lines, yet their stripped-down imagery doesn't detract from their power. In fact, sometimes a very simple graphic can best convey your meaning. Consider the logos companies choose to represent them—a great logo depicts a company's mission via a strong, uncomplicated, and meaningful design that you can easily remember.

Witches today, like spellcasters centuries ago, use runes in many ways. Divination is one popular practice—see the rune reading example in Chapter 7. However, you can also draw runes on paper, stones, or pieces of wood and add them to talisman and amulet bags. Inscribe them on candles. Decorate your magick tools with runes. Embroider them on ritual clothing or altar cloths. (See the charts in Chapter 5.)

Using Rune Imagery in Your Grimoire

In your grimoire, sketch runes in the margins, alongside your spells and incantations—anywhere you like—to represent your intentions. Not only will these designs dress up a page, they also help you focus on your objectives and imprint your subconscious with their energy. Of course, you'll want to write down the spells you perform using runes, as well as your rune readings. But you can incorporate runes into your book of shadows in other ways too:

- Choose a rune to define the nature of each spell you do and draw that rune on the page where you record that spell. The glyph serves as a visual shortcut for the spell.
- Have you chosen to organize your grimoire according to the types of spells you perform? If so, you could separate the categories with divider pages and draw a rune on each of those pages to signify the subject. The Norse rune Gebo, which looks like an X, could illustrate love spells. Berkano or Fehu could introduce the section where you record spells for abundance.
- Write your intentions in Ogham runes as a decorative border around the pages in your grimoire. Centuries ago, people in Ireland and the

British Isles carved rows of Ogham script on standing stones in this way. Even if you don't comprehend the meanings of the glyphs, your subconscious will understand.

- Drip hot candle wax on a page in your book and imprint a significant rune in the wax.

SIGILS

A sigil is a uniquely personal symbol you draw in order to produce a specific result. The word comes from the Latin *sigillum*, meaning sign. In a sense, a sigil is a way of communicating with yourself via secret code, because no one else can interpret the symbol. Although there are various techniques for designing sigils, the easiest one involves fashioning an image from letters.

Creating Sigils

Start by writing a word or a short affirmation that states your intention. Delete any letters that are repeated. For example, the word SUCCESS contains three Ss and two Cs, but you only need to put one of each into your sigil. Entwine the remaining letters to form an image—this is where you get creative. You can use upper- and/or lower-case letters, block or script. Position them right-side up, upside down, forward, or backward. The end result depicts your objective in a graphic manner that your subconscious understands. You'll instantly recognize its meaning at a deep level, and that reinforces your intention.

The following sigil combines the letters S U C C E S S to create an image. Of course, you could configure the letters in a zillion different ways, according to your own preferences, and each design would be uniquely powerful. That's what makes sigils so special.

Sigils in Spellwork

The processes of creating the sigil and applying it are magick acts. Treat them that way. You may wish to design the sigil as a spell in itself.

Or you can fashion the sigil and then use it later as a component of another spell. In this way you both craft and cast, and both produce effects. You can incorporate sigils into spells in myriad ways. For instance:

- Draw a sigil on a piece of paper and slip it into a talisman or amulet pouch.
- Display a sigil on your altar to remind you of your intention.
- Hang one on the door to your home to provide protection.
- Carve one on a candle, and then burn the candle to activate your objective.
- Draw or embroider a sigil on a dream pillow.
- Add them to paintings, collages, or other artwork you create.
- Paint one on a glass so it can imprint water, wine, or another beverage with your intent.
- Have a jeweler fabricate your sigil as a pendant or pin and wear it as a talisman.
- Get a sigil tattooed on your body.

There's no limit to how many sigils you can draw or how many ways you can use them. Give your imagination free rein.

Creating Sigils on a Magick Square

A magick square is an ancient configuration of smaller, numbered squares arranged in rows and columns in such a way that the numbers in each column and row add up to the same sum. One of the simplest squares, which magick workers associate with the planet Saturn, consists of nine small squares within a larger one.

4	9	2
3	5	7
8	1	6

The Modern Witchcraft Grimoire

To design a sigil on a magick square:

1. Decide on a word that represents your intention. Let's say, for example, you want to increase your strength (physically, emotionally, mentally, or spiritually).
2. Refer back to the table of letter and number correspondences in Chapter 5. Write down the numbers that correspond to the letters in STRENGTH: 1 2 9 5 5 7 2 8.
3. Place a sheet of tracing paper over the magick square.
4. Locate the square with the number 1—the number that corresponds to the first letter of your word, the letter S. Draw a small circle on the tracing paper where you see square 1.
5. Next, draw a line on the tracing paper from that circle to the square with the number that relates to the second letter in your word, in this case the square for 2 because that's the number linked with the letter T.
6. The third letter in STRENGTH corresponds to the number 9, so find this square and draw a line to it.
7. If your word contains two letters side by side with the same number value, draw >< on the line where it crosses the box that contains the repeated number.
8. Continue in this manner until your line drawing "spells out" the word. Make a small circle at the end of the last line to denote the end of the word.

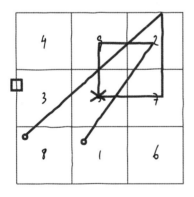 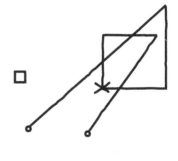

The finished design is your magick sigil. Affix the tracing paper with the image on it into your grimoire. Or, if you prefer, redraw the sigil directly into your book. (If you'd like to learn more about using magick squares, see my book *Magickal Astrology*. You can also see methods for designing sigils on YouTube.)

Add Sigils to Your Grimoire

Not only are sigils the perfect way to encode a spell or anything else you want to keep private, they can be beautiful additions to your grimoire. As with runes, sigils can define the various sections in your book of shadows. They can also stand alone as visual spells. Use them to illustrate the core meaning of an affirmation or incantation. You can even design a sigil that encompasses the entire affirmation. If you like, add other images to a sigil, such as astrological glyphs, runes, stars, spirals, flowers—anything that holds meaning for you.

Chapter 13

ACTIVE SPELLS

Most spells have an active component to them, even if it's just lighting a candle on your altar. The "Buried Treasure Spell" in Chapter 10 is a good example of an active spell. So is the "Spell to Protect Your Home" in Chapter 3. Even writing in your grimoire is an active spell.

Some rituals involve many complex, carefully choreographed steps. When you're doing complicated magickal workings, you may find it necessary to write down the steps in your book of shadows so you can remember them—especially if you don't perform them often. Although you can cast a spell simply by envisioning it in your mind's eye, witches often combine physical movements with words, visualization, and sound. The more you engage your senses in magick work, the more powerful your spells and rituals are likely to be.

CASTING A CIRCLE

Casting a circle is one of the most fundamental and widely used practices in magick work. This circle functions as a shield against any undesirable influences, as well as a container for the energy generated during spells and rituals. It also separates magickal space from mundane space. A circle isn't a flat ring, nor is it a dome over you. Your circle is a sphere surrounding you above and below the place where you do your magick work, as if you were standing in a bubble. You draw a circle, but envision a sphere growing out of the line you draw—it's a circle in three dimensions, a shell that allows the sacred space within the circle to exist between the worlds.

Yes, you can cast a circle by imagining yourself surrounded by a sphere of pure white light—and that circle will work just fine. But many witches enjoy a more active ritual. You'll find lots of suggestions and instructions for circle-casting online and in other books, including many of mine. You can also design your own method. Do whatever you feel inspired to do, whatever engages your senses and your imagination. You may want to try a number of different ways to cast a circle to see which one best suits you. In your grimoire, write what you did, what tools (if any) you used, who else (if anyone) took part, what you felt, and what results you experienced.

Basic Circle-Casting Steps

You can design an elaborate ritual for casting a circle, or you can follow these easy steps:

1. Stand in the center of the space you will define as your circle.
2. Facing east, point your magick wand or athame outward toward where you're going to draw the circle's wall. (If you don't have a wand or athame, you can point your finger. We'll talk more about magick wands, athames, and other tools in Chapter 15.)
3. Center your personal energy within your body. Then ground your energy by envisioning it flowing down through your feet and into the earth, where it connects with the energy of the earth.
4. Draw energy up from the earth, through your body, and out to your hand, into your wand or athame.

The Modern Witchcraft Grimoire

5. Allow this energy to flow out to the point where you intend to begin forming your circle.

6. Slowly turn in a clockwise direction until you are again facing the original starting point and the flow of energy joins up with where it started, forming a seamless ring.

7. Visualize the ring thickening and curving inward until it meets above your head and below your feet, forming a perfect sphere of energy.

8. Lower your wand or athame to shut off the energy flow.

You are now ready to enact your magick spell or ritual within the circle you've cast.

Circle-Casting with a Sword

Some witches use a ceremonial sword to cast a circle. Hold the sword with the point facing outward. Beginning in the east, walk clockwise three times around the space where you will work, delineating the outer edge of the circle with the point of the sword. Chant the following incantation (or one you compose yourself) as you walk:

"Thrice around the circle bound
Evil sink into the ground.
This charge I lay by the number three
As is my will, so mote it be."

Circle-Casting with Pentagrams

If you're using a wand or athame to cast your circle, you may want to stop at each of the four directions—east, south, west, and north—to draw a pentagram in the air before you. (You can use your hand if you don't have a wand or athame.) The pentagram represents protection, so this added step in your ritual reinforces the protective nature of the circle.

1. Hold your wand or athame in your hand, with your arm outstretched before and slightly above you, pointing outward.

2. With the tip of your tool, draw a pentagram in the air.

3. Visualize energy flowing from the cosmos into your tool, down your arm, through your body, and into the ground.
4. Repeat this action at each of the four directions.

Calling the Quarters While Casting a Circle

Some witches call the quarters while casting a circle. As you walk around the circle, stop at each of the four directions and call out to the guardians of those directions. You can craft an eloquent incantation or use this simple one:

> *"Guardian of the eastern sphere*
> *Now we seek your presence here.*
> *Come, East, come.*
> *Be with me (us) tonight."*

Repeat this directive at each of the four directions (substituting the name of the specific direction). You may choose to light a candle at each point. Select a color that corresponds to each direction, as discussed in Chapter 12.

The Four Elements Technique

This technique combines the four elements—earth, air, fire, and water—to cast a circle.

1. Fill a bowl with saltwater, which symbolizes the elements of earth and water.
2. Beginning in the east, walk in a clockwise direction, sprinkling the saltwater on the ground to define a circle as you say: "With earth and water I cast this magick circle."
3. Next, light a stick of incense, which represents fire and air (smoke).
4. Again, start in the east and walk clockwise around the circle, trailing the fragrant smoke behind you while you say: "With fire and air I cast this magick circle."

If you prefer, two people can perform this circle-casting ritual together. In this case, one person holds the bowl of saltwater and the other carries the stick of burning incense.

The Modern Witchcraft Grimoire

"In Witchcraft, we define a new space and a new time whenever we cast a circle to begin a ritual. The circle exists on the boundaries of ordinary space and time; it is 'between the worlds' of the seen and unseen . . . a space within which alternate realities meet, in which the past and future are open to us."

—STARHAWK, *THE SPIRAL DANCE*

Opening the Circle

At the end of your spell or ritual, you must open the circle in order to return to your ordinary realm of existence. Once you've removed the "psychic fence," your magick can flow out into the world and manifest. Additionally, you must release the entities you've called upon (if any). An easy way to do this is to retrace the steps you took while casting the circle, but in reverse order. Instead of walking clockwise, walk counterclockwise. Imagine the circle you erected dissolving behind you as you move.

Did you call upon the guardians of the four directions or invite other nonphysical entities to join you in your spell or ritual? If so, now's the time to thank them for their assistance and bid them adieu until next time. Pause at each direction and say aloud:

"I thank you for your presence here
And for the aid you gave to me.
Until we meet another time,
Hail, farewell, and blessed be."

If you lit candles at the four directions, snuff them out as you release the spirits of each direction.

Ending your spell or ritual is just as important as beginning it. After you finish your working, record all the details in your grimoire. Describe the actions you took during the ritual. Write down the incantations, invocations, or other chants you used. Later, when you see the results of your spell or ritual manifest, note what happened, how the results came about, how long it took for the outcome to materialize, and anything else you consider significant.

"A spell involves words and actions chosen to achieve a certain goal or desire, and is driven by the will of the person performing it. Words, symbols, and tools are combined to produce a ritual. Power is raised and directed out to the Universe to do its work."

—DEBBIE MICHAUD, *THE HEALING TRADITIONS & SPIRITUAL PRACTICES OF WICCA*

MAGICK MUDRAS

Mudra is the Sanskrit word for seal or gesture and refers to a special movement used in a spiritual ritual. Perhaps you've seen people employ a familiar mudra during meditation; they press their thumbs and index fingers together while extending the other fingers. Folding your hands in prayer is another example of a mudra. Although we often associate mudras with Eastern religions, witches in all parts of the world use them in spellwork and ritual practices.

In a broader sense, mudras are gestures or postures that depict your intentions. Purists might argue that the term refers only to sacred gestures, but we use "mudras" all the time to convey our intentions—when we wave to a friend, cross our fingers for good luck, or clap our hands to applaud someone. Think of a police officer directing traffic by waving his arms, or a dog trainer using hand signals to instruct her animal. Holding out your hand with your palm facing away from you clearly says: Stop. These and other gestures serve as active symbols. They also enable you to communicate with other people via sign language during a group ritual.

Witches know that where your attention goes, energy flows. When you point your finger, you steer attention (yours or someone else's) in a particular direction. That's what you do when you extend your hand to cast a circle. Mudras may involve only the hands or the entire body. Try some of these mudras to direct energy for magickal purposes:

- With your hand, draw a pentagram in the air for protection.
- Stretch your arms up above your head to draw down energy from the heavens.

- To invoke a deity, hold one arm outstretched above your head, then draw the energy into yourself by pulling your hand down to your heart center.
- Hold your arms up and outward from your body, curving them in the shape of a crescent moon to invoke the blessing of the moon goddesses.
- Clear sacred space by sweeping your arms and hands about the area to disperse unwanted energies.
- Ground energy by bending down and placing your palms flat on the ground (or floor).
- Touch your index finger to your third eye to stimulate intuition.
- Stand with your arms outstretched at your sides with your right palm turned up to draw down the energy of the heavens and your left palm turned down to draw up the energy of the earth. Then cross both palms over your solar plexus to bring both energies into your body.
- Push away unwanted energies by holding your arms outstretched before you, palms open and facing away from you. Then turn in a counterclockwise direction until you've made a complete circle.
- Lay your hand over a body part or chakra to send healing energy.
- Sign Norse or Ogham runes (see Chapter 5 for charts of rune symbols).

In your grimoire, sketch the mudras you enacted. Describe why and how you used them. How did you feel performing these magickal movements? Could you sense or see energy shifting in connection with your actions? Did you experience anything else? What, if anything, might you do differently to produce a different effect?

You can read about traditional mudras online and in many books. Consider incorporating them into your meditations, yoga, breathwork, healing, and/or other practices. If you like, you can design your own symbolic gestures that have significance for you.

MAGICKAL DANCE

Dancing may be one of the oldest forms of magick. The early Celts incorporated dancing in many of their rituals and festivals. Dancing around the Maypole on Beltane, for instance, symbolized and encouraged fertility. Ancient magicians danced to raise energy, chase away unwanted spirits, petition deities for assistance, align themselves with divine powers, facilitate healing, and more. Today, modern witches still dance for these and other reasons. In group work, dancing stimulates positive energy and unites the individuals participating in the ritual. Besides, dancing is fun!

"Dance is the hidden language of the soul, of the body."
—Martha Graham

Mystical Movements

In classical Indian dance, mudras carry special meanings—the dancer conveys a range of ideas, both mystical and mundane, through hand and body movements. Sufi dancing encourages peace and harmony, in the dancer and in the outer world. In Iran, the Sufi dance samā' includes movements that correspond to the planets, the cycle of the seasons, the elements, and humankind's search for union with the Divine. Expressive hand movements also play an important role in Middle Eastern belly dancing.

In Native American traditions, dancing offers a way to connect with Mother Earth and Father Sky. Dancing awakens intuition, inner wisdom, and healing powers as well. A dancer who wishes to invoke a spirit animal's assistance enacts movements similar to those of the flesh-and-blood animal. Shamans may also dance to gain visions or enter trance states.

The Spiral Dance

In a group dance known among Wiccans as the spiral dance, participants weave their energies together to celebrate community and creativity, honor loved ones who have transitioned into the afterlife, and symbolize the cycle of life, death, and rebirth. Starhawk, author of the bestselling book *The Spiral Dance: A Rebirth of the Ancient Religion of the Great Goddess* and a founding member of the Reclaiming Collective, designed the basic movements in the ritual, which was first performed publicly in San Francisco in 1979.

Performed on Samhain, the ritual dance marks the turn of the Wheel and the witches' New Year. Dancers hold hands and twine in both clockwise and counterclockwise directions. Drumming, music, and chanting often accompany the dancers' movements, raising power for ritual work. You can see the dance enacted on YouTube.

Want to participate in a spiral dance? You can. Wiccans and Neopagans in many parts of the world celebrate this uplifting ritual—if you search online you can probably find one being held someplace near you. Or, learn the steps and invite a group of like-minded friends to join you in reenacting this tradition. Record your experiences in your grimoire.

MAGICKAL LABYRINTHS

When you hear the word "labyrinth" what comes to mind? Perhaps you think of the mythical structure in Crete, designed by the architect Daedalus to contain a frightful beast known as the Minotaur, half human and half bull. However, that convoluted prison, rich with psychological symbolism, was really a maze, not a labyrinth. Mazes are puzzles with many blind alleys and dead ends. Labyrinths are magickal, unicursal systems used throughout the world for millennia as tools for spiritual development.

In the mid-1990s, the Reverend Dr. Lauren Artress popularized the thirteenth-century labyrinth on the floor in France's Chartres Cathedral by having it replicated in San Francisco's Grace Cathedral. Labyrinths date back many thousands of years and had mystical and magickal purposes long before the advent of Christianity. This ancient pattern features a single, winding path that leads into the center of the circle and symbolizes the journey to your own center or to the Source.

Walking a Labyrinth

Labyrinths can be found in many different designs in different parts of the world (see Sig Lonegren's *Labyrinths: Ancient Myths and Modern Uses*), but the one many Wiccans and Neopagans favor has seven concentric circuits. Each circuit corresponds to a color, a note on the musical scale, a chakra, and one of the heavenly bodies visible to the naked eye.

You can walk a labyrinth as a form of meditation—the process makes you feel relaxed and centered. A labyrinth can also be a sacred space where you do magickal workings. A potent sending and receiving device, a labyrinth focuses, amplifies, and transmits energies. From its center, you can project intentions with greater power. You can receive messages from deities, spirits, and other entities more easily too.

If you have an outdoor space large enough to allow for a labyrinth, you might like to build one of stone or plantings, or carve the pattern into the ground. Or you can draw one on a large piece of paper or fabric (you'll probably have to tape several pieces together). This portable option allows you to fold up your labyrinth and store it when it's not in use.

Labyrinth Ritual

This active group ritual helps you get in touch with astrological energies and understand how they operate in your own life. It's also a wonderful way to celebrate your connection with the cosmos and nature, as well as with other magickal practitioners.

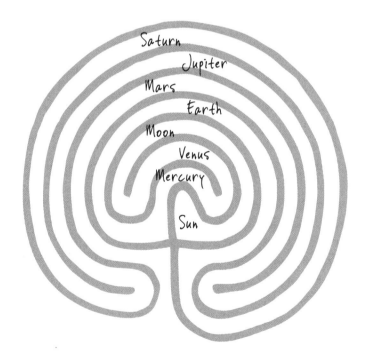

The Modern Witchcraft Grimoire

1. Choose eight people to represent the sun, moon, Mercury, Venus, Earth, Mars, Jupiter, and Saturn. It's more fun and dramatic if everyone dresses up in costumes or wears masks that represent the planets' energies. (See Chapter 6 for information about planetary powers.)
2. Each of these people stands at the entrance to the circuit that corresponds to his or her planet or luminary (see illustration).
3. Each participant in the ritual takes a turn walking through the labyrinth. As you come to the entrance of each circuit, the person representing the corresponding planet says a keyword that relates to the planet's nature. For instance, the person representing Venus might say "love" or "beauty."
4. Contemplate the meaning of the keyword(s) associated with each planet while you walk through that planet's circuit.
5. As you move inward toward the center of the labyrinth, reflect on how you respond to each planet's energy. How does it feel to you? How does it affect you personally?
6. Continue in this manner until you have passed through all the circuits and reached the center of the labyrinth.
7. Spend as much time in the center as you wish.
8. As you move back out of the labyrinth, walking through the circuits again but in reverse order, contemplate how you express each planet's energy in the outer world. How does it affect your relationships with other people? How can you handle each planet's challenges better?
9. After everyone has had a chance to walk through the labyrinth, share your experiences.

Be sure to write down in your grimoire what transpired during this ritual. What did you feel? What insights did you gain? Did you have any visions? What reactions did you have to the other participants in the ritual? Did you notice any nonphysical beings in the labyrinth with you? Did you sense a closer or clearer connection with the planets and their powers?

Some people say you can tap the energy of a labyrinth without actually walking it. Draw a labyrinth pattern in your grimoire and then slowly run your finger through the circuits, into the center and back out again. What do you experience?

Chapter 14

MAGICKAL CONCOCTIONS

Let's use our cookbook analogy again. Many cookbooks organize recipes according to the role they play in a meal, how they're prepared, or how they're consumed. You might see a section for appetizers, another for beverages. This method lets the cook quickly locate what's appropriate for her purposes. You can arrange your grimoire in a similar way for convenience.

Most witches do lots of different types of spells. We concoct potions and lotions, salves and balms, talismans and amulets, and so on. Organizing your book of shadows according to this method can be useful when you're collecting the components you need for spells or shopping for ingredients. It also lets you see what spells you can whip up on the spur of the moment, based on the materials you have on hand.

CHOOSING YOUR CATEGORIES

Begin by making a list of the types of spells you do regularly. If you're a healer, your work may focus largely on spells designed to remedy ailments and encourage well-being. If you're a green witch, you'll likely rely heavily on botanicals.

Next, consider what sorts of practices you enjoy most. For instance, I know a woman who agrees with Hippocrates's advice: "The way to health is to have an aromatic bath and a scented massage every day." She formulates all kinds of lovely soaps and bath products with essential oils and other natural substances; the medicinal and magickal properties of her ingredients promote good health. What natural talents do you possess? Maybe you're a great cook and can brew up some fabulous magickal meals. If you have sewing skills, you may lean toward fashioning dream pillows, ritual clothing, or crane bags. A jeweler friend of mine works with gemstones and metals to fashion wonderful magick jewelry.

Where you do your spellwork could influence your choices too. Do you have a designated room or area for magickal activities? Do you live with other people who might not understand or support your beliefs and Craft practices? How much space do you have for storing materials? These considerations may influence the types of spells you do.

Other factors such as your finances, mobility, age, health, availability of ingredients, and so on may dictate the types of spells you choose to perform. If you're new to the Craft, you may want to try a bit of everything in order to discover what you like best and where your strengths lie. After a while, you'll probably emphasize some types and pay less attention to others. Most of us have favorite spells that we do frequently, and you may give those "pride of place" in your grimoire. You might relegate other spells to a back burner—or even toss them out. Remember, your grimoire is your workbook as well as your magick journal. The things you choose to include should be ones you find useful, joyful, interesting, and effective.

POTIONS

Magick potions rank way up there on the list of legendary concoctions. Remember the potion labeled "Drink Me" that shrank Alice down to a height of only ten inches during her adventures in Wonderland? And the one

The Modern Witchcraft Grimoire

the Little Mermaid quaffed that transformed her fishy tail into legs? Harry Potter and his pals learned to formulate all sorts of potions at Hogwarts, including one to attract good fortune, aptly nicknamed "Liquid Luck."

Of course, love potions are among the most popular of all and people have sought them since ancient times. The first-century Roman philosopher Pliny the Elder recommended making an elixir from hippopotamus snout and hyena eyes. Reportedly, Cleopatra sipped pearls dissolved in vinegar to heighten her sex appeal.

> *"The juice of it on sleeping eye-lids laid*
> *Will make man or woman madly dote*
> *Upon the next live creature that it sees."*
> —WILLIAM SHAKESPEARE, *A MIDSUMMER NIGHT'S DREAM*

Love Potion #9

This brew calls for 9 components—hence its name. The magickal correspondences of the ingredients give the potion its power.

TOOLS AND INGREDIENTS

A chalice	A drop of vanilla extract
Red wine (or apple juice)	Grated chocolate
A drop of honey	¼ teaspoon ground red rose petals
A pinch of ground ginger	A silver spoon
A pinch of cayenne	

1. If you have a chalice, use it for this spell. If not, wash a pretty glass goblet and substitute it.
2. Cast a circle around your workspace.
3. Pour the wine (or apple juice) into the chalice.
4. Add the honey, ginger, cayenne, and vanilla to the wine.
5. Grate a little chocolate on top of the liquid.
6. Sprinkle the rose petals on the beverage.
7. With the silver spoon, stir the blend 3 times using a clockwise motion to combine the ingredients.
8. Drink the potion to increase the love in your life.
9. Open the circle.

Ingredients for Potions

Usually, we think of magick potions as liquids that a person ingests to produce a desired condition. Because someone consumes these drinks, it's imperative that you use only nontoxic ingredients in your concoctions. The brew needn't taste good, however—many don't. Potions for healing often contain medicinal herbs; other drinks rely mainly on symbolic correspondences, although some potions include substances with recognized physiological properties. Chocolate, for example, stimulates a release of endorphins in the brain, giving you a high similar to being in love, hence its place in love spells.

If you've decided to assign a section in your grimoire to potions, you may want to break it down into additional categories for the types of spells you do most often: love, prosperity, healing, protection, and so on. The following table lists some ingredients you may want to keep on hand for these potions.

COMMON INGREDIENTS FOR MAGICK POTIONS		
Purpose	**Herbs and Spices**	**Other Foods and Beverages**
Love	ginger, cayenne, marjoram, vanilla, cinnamon, rosemary, cardamom, saffron	red wine, apples, apricots, raspberries, strawberries, honey, maple syrup, sugar, chocolate, asparagus, chestnuts, oysters
Prosperity	mint, cinnamon, clove, parsley, dill	champagne, beer, caviar, alfalfa, barley, corn, sunflower seeds, cashews, pecans, hops, spinach, figs
Protection	basil, anise, fennel, parsley, rosemary, sage, cayenne	garlic, pine nuts, witch hazel, salt, mustard, mushrooms, onions, cranberries
Good luck	allspice, bay leaves, cloves, cinnamon, pepper, nutmeg	hazelnuts, cashews, olives, sunflower seeds, coffee, bamboo shoots, bell peppers, cabbage
Healing	chamomile, ginger, yarrow, peppermint, comfrey, calendula	vinegar, aloe, coconut, green tea, molasses, salmon, yogurt, almonds, dandelion greens, bok choy, watercress

LOTIONS, BALMS, AND SALVES

Many lotions, balms, and salves intended for healing purposes contain ingredients with known medicinal properties. Eucalyptus and spearmint, for example, help clear sinus congestion. Aloe soothes burned skin. And although many witches engage in healing practices, we also prepare magickal concoctions for other purposes. In such cases, a spell's power usually comes from the symbolic nature of its components. (In Chapter 16 you'll find charts to guide you.)

If you choose to formulate lotions, balms, or salves, be sure to use nontoxic ingredients that won't cause adverse reactions in the person for whom you've made them. Dilute essential oils in a "carrier oil" such as olive, grape seed, jojoba, or coconut. Ask the person for whom you are doing the spell if he or she is allergic to certain items, such as nuts or wheat. Always test a little bit of the substance on the skin before slathering on a whole lot.

Although many lotions are designed to rub on the body, some may be applied to other objects in spellwork. Witches use oils to dress candles and to anoint magick tools, gemstones, crystals, talismans, and amulets. You may even like to dab a drop of a favorite essential oil on a page in your grimoire.

Prosperity Oil

This versatile magick lotion has many applications—use it alone or in conjunction with other spells to attract money as well as other forms of abundance. Blend it during the waxing moon, preferably on Thursday.

TOOLS AND INGREDIENTS

A green glass bottle with a lid or stopper

4 ounces of olive, almond, or grape seed oil

A few drops of peppermint essential oil

Gold or silver glitter

A small piece of tiger's eye or aventurine

1. Wash the bottle and gemstone with mild soap and water, and then dry them.
2. Cast a circle around your workspace.
3. Pour the olive, almond, or grape seed oil into the bottle.
4. Add the peppermint essential oil and glitter.
5. Drop the tiger's eye or aventurine in the mixture, then put the lid or stopper on the bottle and shake 3 times to charge the potion.
6. Open the circle.

In your grimoire, write down the various ways you use this Prosperity Oil. Of course, you'll also want to note the outcomes you obtain from each use. Did you get better results from rubbing the oil on your body? On candles or gemstones? Did you try dabbing some on your wallet? If you used it in conjunction with other spells, which ones? What happened?

RITUAL BATHS

If you agree with Hippocrates, aromatic healing baths may be your thing. For millennia, people have "taken the waters" for therapeutic reasons—and still do. Spas around the world offer all sorts of delicious treatments that involve immersing yourself in a pool, spring, or tub of water that contains mystical healing properties.

Although witches may embrace the idea of "water cures"—soaking in mineral-rich natural springs or a bathtub to which essential oils have been added—we also bathe for esoteric purposes. A ritual bath not only washes away physical dirt and germs; it also allows you to remove the stress (and outside interferences) of the day, relax, and shift your mood in preparation for magickal work. It's a bit like cleansing your sacred space of bad vibes; in this case, your "temple" is your body. Love spells sometimes call for taking a ritual bath with a partner prior to spellcasting.

As part of your cleansing ritual, consider these additional steps:

• Light candles and/or play soft music.
• Place citrine crystals at each corner of your bathtub. (Golden-colored citrine possesses clearing properties.)

- Add bath salts and/or fragrant essential oils that correspond to your intention: rose for love, mint for prosperity, lavender for peace of mind.
- Sprinkle flower petals that represent your objective into your bathwater.
- Invite the undines or a favorite water deity—Oshun, Mami Wata, Aphrodite, Anuket, Thalassa, Eurybia, Poseidon, Ganga, Nymue—to join you.

Afterward, record your experiences in your grimoire. What did you include in your ritual bath? What did you sense, see, or feel? Did the ritual bath contribute to the magickal work that followed? In what way?

Purifying Ritual Bath Scrub

Try this fragrant purifying scrub before doing a ritual or spell. Use warm—not hot—water. Do not use this scrub on your face. If you have sensitive skin, blend the herbs and essential oils into the oil and omit the salt. Rub the oil gently into your skin prior to your bath, and then rinse it off.

TOOLS AND INGREDIENTS

2 teaspoons lavender flowers (fresh or dry)

2 teaspoons chamomile flowers (fresh or dry)

½ cup sea salt or Epsom salt

A lidded jar

A small glass bowl

½ cup vegetable oil (such as sweet almond, olive, grape seed, or jojoba oil)

3 drops lavender essential oil

3 drops frankincense essential oil

A damp washcloth

1. Purify all the ingredients first. You can do this by visualizing white light around them.

2. Grind the dried flowers finely while you state aloud that they will cleanse and purify your body, mind, and spirit.

3. Put the salt in the jar.

4. In the bowl, mix the oils.

5. Add the oil blend to the salt, then close the jar and shake to combine thoroughly.

6. Open the jar and sprinkle the herbs over the oil and salt blend. Close the jar and shake to blend a final time.

7. Place about a tablespoon of the mixture in the center of a clean, damp washcloth or in the palm of your hand. Gently rub the salts against your skin. Imagine them loosening any negative energy that may cling to you. Feel the purifying ingredients soaking into your body, cleansing your aura and calming your mind.

8. When you feel cleansed, immerse yourself in the bathwater and rinse away the salt scrub along with any negative energy.

9. Step out of the bath and dry yourself gently with a clean towel. If you wish, dress in ritual clothing before engaging in magickal work.

TALISMANS, AMULETS, AND FETISHES

Do you have a special token that you carry to keep you safe or to bring good fortune? If so, you're following a time-honored tradition. The early Egyptians placed good-luck charms in the tombs of royalty to ensure their souls would pass safely into the world beyond. Ancient Greek soldiers carried amulets into battle to protect them. An amulet or talisman may be a single object that has special meaning for its owner, or may be a combination of several items—gemstones, botanicals, magick images, etc.—contained in a charm bag or medicine pouch, designed for a specific purpose. The energies of the ingredients plus your belief in their magickal properties give the talisman or amulet its power.

"Witchcraft is more than just a practice, it is a way of life. A way of looking at the physical and spiritual as a collaborative source of manifestation."

—DACHA AVELIN, EMBRACING YOUR INNER WITCH

Amulets

Many people use the words *charm, amulet,* and *talisman* interchangeably. However, these three types of portable magick are not the same. Each has its own, distinct purpose and application.

The word "amulet" comes from Latin *amuletum,* which means "a charm"—so it's no wonder people still confuse one with the other. The Greeks called amulets *amylon,* or food. This definition implies that people used food offerings to ask gods and goddesses for protection. They may have even eaten or carried a small bit of that food as an amuletic token. For example, ancient Greeks carried leaves with Athena's name written on them to safeguard themselves from hexes. And, of course, we're all familiar with the idea of hanging garlic to scare away harmful entities.

Witches mainly use amulets for protection. An amulet wards off danger and guards the owner from all manner of harm: illness, assault, accident or injury, theft, natural disasters, evil intent, or black magick. Until something external creates a need for their energy, amulets remain passive. Consequently, an amulet's power might stay latent—but still present—for a very long time.

Amulets and the Moon

Usually it's best to create amulets during the waning moon. You could also consider making an amulet when the sun and/or moon is in Capricorn or on a Saturday.

You can fashion amulets from all sorts of materials: stone, metal, or bundled plant matter. A symbol drawn on a piece of paper will work too. Just make sure whatever you include represents your intention.

Gemstone amulets are perennial favorites—our ancestors prized them, just as people do today. Amulets were sometimes chosen for their shape or where they were found. A stone with a hole through it supposedly protected a person from malicious faeries (who got trapped in the hole). Carrying a crystal found adjacent to a sacred well known for its healthful qualities could encourage well-being. Witches also use plants for protective purposes. Some botanical amulets contain herbs valued for their healing or cleansing properties; others rely on their symbolic nature.

The ancient magi gave precise instructions on how to make amulets. The base components must be organized and measured precisely, and any carving is done in an exact order. Say, for example, you want to create a healing amulet for a sick person. You could use copper as the base material. First you'd apply an emblem for recovery to the copper base, because recovering from the ailment is your primary objective. Afterward, you might choose to add a symbol for ongoing protection to keep sickness from returning.

Protection Amulet

Do you feel a need for some extra protection? This amulet helps to shield you from potential injury or illness. Perform the spell during the waning moon, preferably on a Saturday.

TOOLS AND INGREDIENTS

A piece of turquoise

Black paint or nail polish

Rosemary essential oil

Pine incense

An incense burner

Matches or a lighter

Saltwater

1. Wash the piece of turquoise with mild soap and water, then pat it dry.

2. Cast a circle around the area where you will do your spell.

3. With the paint or nail polish, paint the protection rune Algiz (see Chapter 5) on the stone.

4. Rub a little rosemary essential oil on the other side of the stone.

5. Fit the incense into the burner and light it.

6. Sprinkle the stone with saltwater, then hold it in the incense smoke for a few moments to charge it.

7. Open the circle.

8. Carry the gemstone amulet with you at all times to protect against harm, or give it to the person you wish to protect.

TALISMANS

Talismans serve as active participants in magick work. Unlike amulets, which remain inactive until an outside force stimulates their energy, talismans instigate conditions. Today the word "talisman" refers to any token that has been created specifically to attract or activate a desired result: love, prosperity, success, and so on.

When to Make Talismans

In most cases, talismans should be made or acquired while the moon is waxing. Also consider the position of Venus when fashioning love talismans. Jupiter's placement will affect a talisman for success or abundance.

Unlike amulets, talismans can influence conditions from a distance. For example, a love talisman can attract a partner from all the way on the other side of the world. Although talismans are more potent than amulets—at least in terms of how far their energy extends—their power tends to get used up rapidly because they're constantly projecting it rather than sitting back waiting for a need to arise.

Like amulets, talismans must include materials appropriate to their functions. For example, when making a love talisman you could use rose quartz, rose petals, small heart-shaped tokens, or other components that symbolize love. An effective talisman could be as simple as a single gemstone or quite complex, including numerous carefully chosen ingredients. (See Chapter 16 for lists of correspondences.) As you fashion a talisman, recite affirmations or incantations over it, instructing it to carry out your intentions. Charge it by sprinkling it with saltwater or holding it in the smoke of burning incense.

Aladdin's Lamp

Many old stories tell us that spirits dwelled in talismans and could be commanded by the magician to do specific tasks. Aladdin's lamp, which held a powerful spirit known as a jinni, was a kind of talisman.

How to Use Talismans and Amulets

Most people wear or carry talismans and amulets on their persons, but you can use them in other ways too:

- Display one on your altar.
- Set one on your desk, near your computer.
- Hang one above the entrance to your home.
- If you know feng shui, place them in the sectors of your home that relate to your intentions.
- Slip one under your pillow at night.
- Put one in your car's glove compartment.
- Attach one to your pet's collar.
- Bury them in your yard or garden.
- Put one in the cash register in your place of business.

FETISHES

The word "fetish" probably comes from Latin *facticius* (meaning artificial), by way of Portuguese *feitiço* and French *fétiche*. A fetish can be any object, so long as the person who carries it has a strong emotional connection to the object or regards it as representing a higher authority (such as a spirit or deity).

The Modern Witchcraft Grimoire

A fetish represents only one objective—you wouldn't carry a single fetish for love, protection, *and* success. Many fetishes serve as "one shot" magick spells—you need a different one for each instance when help is sought. A witch might make up a bunch of fetishes at the same time, all of them designed for the same purpose. For example, she might fabricate a number of fetishes to stimulate artistic endeavors by wrapping bay leaves (to represent the sun god Apollo) in pieces of yellow cloth (the color of creativity) and empowering those bundles with an incantation. Then whenever she needs a little inspiration, she can use one of the bundles.

You activate the energy of single-use fetishes by carrying them, burning them, burying them, or floating them on moving water. Burning releases your wishes to the heavens and disperses the energy. Burying helps the energy grow. Floating in water transports the energy where it's desired or needed.

In your grimoire, record information about the amulets, talismans, and fetishes you create. When did you fashion them? Did you make them for yourself or someone else? What did you feel, sense, see, or experience during the process? Note the ingredients you included, the steps you took during your spellworking, incantations you recited, and anything else of significance. Be sure to write down your results, how long the outcomes took to manifest, and anything you might consider changing in the future.

Chapter 15

WORKING WITH MAGICK TOOLS

Practitioners in every field of endeavor rely on certain tools to help them do their jobs well. Gardeners work with shovels and hoes, carpenters need hammers and saws, cooks use pots and skillets. Magick workers utilize special tools too. The tools of the Craft speak to the subconscious mind in forms that help support spellwork. A tool's shape, the material from which it's fabricated, and other features provide clues to its symbolism and thus its role in magick.

Of course, you don't really need any equipment to craft and cast spells—the most important "tool" of all is your mind. The implements in a witch's toolbox, however, are good aids to magick work. They serve as centering devices that focus your attention. Wielding magick tools in a spell or ritual also adds drama and excitement, which can kick the magick up a notch.

If you choose to use magick tools in your work—and most witches do—you'll want to discuss them in your grimoire. How did you acquire these tools? Did you purchase them readymade or fabricate your own? Describe the process(es) you used to consecrate and charge them. How do you work with your tools? Record the spells and rituals in which you employ certain tools. How do you feel using them? How do they influence your work? You might even designate a special section in your book of shadows for each tool and the spells and rituals that use it.

"Magic . . . uses all of reality, the world itself, as its medium."
—BILL WHITCOMB, *THE MAGICIAN'S COMPANION*

THE ROLE OF SYMBOLISM

We've talked a lot already about symbols and their role in magick work. When you use a witch's tools, you draw upon their symbolism. If you already own a selection of magick tools, you're probably familiar with their associations. However, if you haven't yet acquired the tools of the Craft, take some time to learn their correspondences and their purposes in spellwork.

Masculine and Feminine Symbolism

Notice that the shapes of the tools of the Craft correspond to the human body. The five points of the pentagram signify the five "points" of the body: head, arms, and legs. The wand and the athame, which symbolize masculine power or yang energy, look distinctly phallic. So do the ritual sword and the rod (or stave). The chalice and cauldron, shaped like the womb, represent feminine or yin energy. So do bells and bowls. Witches often use the wand and athame to project energy, whereas the chalice and cauldron contain and nurture it.

Elemental Symbolism

Additionally, the four primary tools correspond to the four elements: fire, water, air, and earth. The wand represents the element of fire, the chalice signifies the water element, the athame symbolizes air, and the pentagram represents earth. You'll notice that these tools show up in the tarot as the four suits of the Minor Arcana. Usually called Wands (sometimes Rods or Staves), Swords (or Daggers, meaning athames), Cups (or Chalices), and Pentacles (or Pentagrams, sometimes referred to as Coins or Disks), the suits describe fundamental life energies and ways of interacting with the world. It's a good idea to keep these correspondences in mind when you're doing tarot readings as well as when you're performing a spell or ritual.

> "The four elements . . . are the basic building blocks of all material structures and organic wholes. Each element represents a basic kind of energy and consciousness that operates within each of us."
> —STEPHEN ARROYO, *ASTROLOGY, PSYCHOLOGY, AND THE FOUR ELEMENTS*

THE WAND

Contrary to popular opinion, witches don't tap people with magick wands to turn them into toads or make them invisible. Witches use wands to direct energy. You can either attract or send energy with your wand. Aim it at the heavens to draw down cosmic power and bring it into the material world. Point it toward a person, place, or thing to project energy toward your goal. You may wish to use your wand to cast a magick circle too.

Choosing or Creating Your Magick Wand

Magick workers traditionally fashioned wands from wood, cut from a living branch of a tree in a single stroke (after asking the tree's permission and making an offering in thanks). The Druids favored yew, hazel, willow, and rowan; however, you may prefer another wood instead for your wand. You don't have to choose wood, if you'd rather use something else—you can find some gorgeous wands made of crystal, metal, or glass rods adorned with gemstones. Perhaps you'd like to mount a quartz crystal at the end of your wand to enhance its power.

You can personalize your wand and enhance your relationship with it by decorating it with elemental symbolism:

- Attach objects to it made of brass, iron, bronze, or gold—metals that correspond to the fire element.
- Paint it fiery colors, such as red, orange, or gold.
- Decorate it with the glyphs for the astrological fire signs Aries, Leo, and Sagittarius, or the elemental symbol for fire (an upward-pointing triangle).
- Engrave it with words of power and/or runes (such as Teiwaz) that signify your intentions.
- Tie red, orange, or gold ribbons onto your wand.
- Affix fiery gemstones to it: ruby, golden topaz, carnelian, bloodstone, tiger's eye.

In your grimoire, describe your relationship with your wand. Did you fashion it yourself? Why did you purchase, fabricate, or otherwise acquire this particular wand? How did you personalize it? Did you imprint it with signs or symbols? What did you experience during the process? How do you plan to work with your wand?

How Long a Wand?

Tradition says a wand should be the length of its owner's forearm from the elbow to the tip of the middle finger. However, that may be unwieldy for some people. Choose a wand that is at least six inches long, but only as long and thick as you find comfortable to handle.

Consecrating and Charging Your Wand

Until you consecrate your wand and charge it with your intention, it's just a stick of wood or an inert rod of metal or glass. The ritual you design to imbue your wand with your own energy can be simple or complex, depending on your personality and your objectives. You may call on a beloved deity to assist you, or invite the fire elementals known as salamanders to join in. You may want to create an incantation or other charge to direct your wand.

Before you begin, cleanse your wand of all unwanted ambient energies. I recommend holding it in the smoke from burning incense or from a ritual fire to purify it. Cast a circle, then proceed with the ritual you've designed. You may want to anoint your wand with essential oil—cinnamon, sandalwood, cedar, and frankincense are good choices. Perhaps you'll want to command your wand to do your bidding with a chant or incantation. Create a poetic directive or say something as simple as "I now consecrate this wand to do the work of the Goddess and God, and charge it to assist me in my magickal work, in harmony with Divine Will, my own true will, and for the good of all concerned."

Match the Tool to the Element

Some witches design rituals that incorporate the element to which the individual tool corresponds. For example, you could charge your chalice by submerging it in a sacred pool of water. Similarly, you could bury a pentagram in the ground beneath a venerable tree or place your wand in the sunshine to let the sun's rays charge it.

After you've finished the ritual and opened the circle, write in your grimoire what you did to consecrate and charge your wand. What steps did you take to infuse it with your energy? Did a god or goddess participate? If you anointed your wand with an essential oil, you may want to dab a bit on the page where you describe your ritual. If you uttered a magickal charge, write it here too. Discuss how you felt during the process. What did you sense, see, intuit, or otherwise experience?

The Pentagram

The tool most often connected with witchcraft, the pentagram symbolizes the element of earth. In magickal work, it's associated with protection, and many Wiccans wear pentagrams as protection amulets. Usually, a pentagram is depicted as a five-pointed star with a circle around it; however you may also see it as a five-pointed star without the circle. (If you visit Texas, where I live, you'll spot pentagrams everywhere—though most people think of them as "Texas stars." The Texas Rangers wore pentagram-shaped badges, and I often wonder how many lives those magick emblems saved.)

Choosing or Creating Your Pentagram

Unless you have metalsmithing talents, you probably won't craft your own pentagram jewelry, but you can purchase some really beautiful pentagram pendants, earrings, and rings. Many witches wear pentagrams made of silver—a metal associated with the Goddess, the moon, and feminine energy—but that's up to you. Perhaps you'd like one decorated with earth-related gemstones, such as jade, moss agate, aventurine, onyx, or turquoise.

In addition to choosing a pentagram to wear, you might acquire another to place on your altar. Consider hanging one near the door of your home for protection, and keeping one in your car as a safety measure. If you're handy at sewing, you could embroider pentagrams on ritual clothing and/or an altar cloth. Some witches even have them tattooed on their bodies.

On one of the beginning pages of your grimoire (or on the cover) draw a pentagram to protect your secrets from prying eyes. Within the pages of your book of shadows, describe how you selected your pentagram. How will you use it? If you purchased a readymade pentagram, did you do anything to personalize it? What did you experience during the process?

Consecrating and Charging Your Pentagram

The ritual you design to consecrate and your pentagram can be simple or complex, depending on your preferences. Before you begin, however, purify your pentagram of all unwanted ambient resonances. The easiest way to do this is to hold it under running water while you envision it cleansed of all harmful, disruptive, or unbalanced energies. Then cast a circle and proceed with the ritual you've planned. If you decide to anoint your pentagram with essential oil, select one that corresponds to the earth element and/or protection such as rosemary, pine, or basil.

Direct your pentagram by saying something as simple as "I now consecrate this pentagram to do the work of the Goddess and God, and charge it to assist me in my magickal work, in harmony with Divine Will, my own true will, and for the good of all concerned." Or write a more elegant and personal incantation. If you wish, invite a favorite deity to join you in performing the ritual.

The Modern Witchcraft Grimoire

After you've finished the ritual and opened the circle, write in your grimoire what you did to consecrate and charge your pentagram. How did you infuse it with your energy? Did a god or goddess participate? If you anointed your pentagram with an essential oil, you may want to dab a bit on the page where you describe your ritual. If you uttered a magickal charge, write it here too. Describe how you felt during the process. What did you sense, see, intuit, or otherwise experience?

THE ATHAME

The origins of the word "athame" have been lost to history. Some people speculate that it may have come from *Arthana*, a term for a knife mentioned in the early grimoire *The Clavicule of Solomon*. This ritual dagger is usually a double-edged knife about four to six inches long, although some Wiccans prefer crescent-shaped athames that represent the moon. It needn't be sharp because you're unlikely to cut anything physical with your athame, except perhaps to inscribe symbols on candles. One of its main purposes is to symbolically remove negative energies. You can also use it to slice through obstacles and sever bonds, again symbolically. If you wish, you can cast a circle with an athame instead of a wand—and if someone needs to leave a circle during a ritual, you can "cut" a doorway with your athame to allow passage.

Choosing or Creating Your Athame

Unless you have smithing and carpentry skills you'll probably acquire a readymade athame. Tradition says you should procure your athame yourself, and it should never be used by anyone else. However, if you feel drawn to purchase a vintage dagger for your magick work, make sure it hasn't drawn blood in the past. Some magicians believe that an athame used to physically harm another will never again be functional in magick work, although in ancient times witches often "fed" special ritual knives with blood. Before you use any tool for magick work, you must cleanse it of all energies other than your own.

Like the wand, the phallic-shaped athame represents the masculine force. It corresponds to the element of air too, so you could decorate its handle with symbols such as those for the zodiac signs Gemini, Libra, and

Aquarius or the elemental symbol for air (an upward-pointing triangle with a horizontal line through the center). To personalize it, you may want to:

- Engrave your Craft name on the handle.
- Add runes, sigils, or other images and words that hold meaning for you.
- Decorate it with gemstones that relate to the air element: clear quartz, aquamarine, garnet, or zircon.
- Tie yellow ribbons—the color associated with the air element—to its handle.
- Fasten feathers to its handle.

In your grimoire, describe how you acquired your athame. How do you plan to work with it? How did you personalize it? How did you decorate it? What signs or symbols did you choose (if any) and why? What did you experience during the process?

Consecrating and Charging Your Athame

Before you begin working with your athame, purify it to disperse all unwanted energies. Wash it first with mild soap and warm water, then dry it. Next, hold it in the smoke of burning incense. You can design a complex ritual for consecrating and charging your athame or keep it simple. Call upon deities or spirits to assist you, if you like. Compose a special incantation or affirmation to direct it for your purposes. If you decide to anoint your athame with essential oil, select one that corresponds to the element of air, such as carnation, clove, or ginger.

After you've completed your ritual, write in your grimoire what you did to consecrate and charge your athame. Did a god or goddess participate in the ritual? If you anointed your athame with an essential oil, you may want to dab a bit on the page where you describe your ritual. If you uttered a magickal charge, write it down too. Describe how you felt during the process. What did you sense, see, intuit, or otherwise experience?

THE CHALICE

What's the most famous chalice of all? The Holy Grail, of course. Many people believe it now lies submerged in the sacred Chalice Well in Glastonbury, England. In rituals and rites, witches often drink a ceremonial beverage from a chalice. That's why many chalices feature long stems—so they can be passed easily from hand to hand. Sharing the cup with coven members signifies connectedness and unity of purpose. You may choose to drink magick potions you've concocted from your chalice too, as we discussed earlier.

Choosing or Creating Your Chalice

A symbol of the feminine force, the chalice's shape clearly suggests the womb. Therefore silver, because it's ruled by the moon, is a good material for your magick chalice. Some people prefer crystal, blue or indigo glass, or ceramic chalices, however—the choice is entirely yours. A quick online search will turn up pictures of many fabulous chalices, some dating back more than a thousand years. The chalice also symbolizes the water element, and water is linked with the emotions, intuition, imagination, and dreams. Therefore, you could think of your chalice as the cradle of the emotions, as well as a vessel that holds and nourishes your hopes and dreams.

To personalize your chalice, you may wish to mark it with symbols of the water element, such as those for the astrological signs Cancer, Scorpio, and Pisces, or the elemental glyph for water (a downward-pointing triangle). Or, decorate it with "watery" gems such as moonstones, pearls, or sapphires. Perhaps you'd like to paint your chalice to resemble a flower, such as the blue-and-orange crocus favored by members of The Golden Dawn (be sure to use lead-free paint).

Within the pages of your book of shadows, describe how you selected your chalice and how you plan to work with it. Did you do anything to personalize it? What did you experience during the process? Note anything you consider relevant.

Consecrating and Charging Your Chalice

Wash your chalice in warm water with mild soap (or vinegar and water) before using it for magick work. This removes both dust and unwanted ambient energies that could interfere with your intentions.

The ritual you design to consecrate and charge your chalice may be complex or simple—whatever works for you. A brief blessing may be all you need, but if you feel drawn to plunge your chalice into a sacred well for a lunar month, go for it. Alternately, you could sprinkle it with "holy" water from a spring, sea, or lake that is special to you. Maybe you'd like to invite a particular deity, such as Oshun, Mami Wata, or Poseidon, to join in your ceremony. Chant, sing, or recite a special incantation to dedicate your chalice to the Goddess and to your magickal work. If you decide to anoint your chalice with an essential oil, select one that corresponds to the element of water such as jasmine or ylang-ylang. Make sure the oil you use has no toxic properties.

After you've completed your ritual, write in your grimoire what you did to consecrate and charge your chalice. Did a god or goddess participate in the ritual? If you anointed your chalice with an essential oil, you may want to dab a bit on the page where you describe your ritual. If you uttered a magickal charge, write it here too. Describe how you felt during the process. What did you sense, see, intuit, or otherwise experience?

OTHER TOOLS FOR MAGICKAL WORK

Although the four tools we've already discussed serve as the primary implements of the Craft, you may decide that you'd like to add other items to your collection. If you're new to the Craft, I suggest you start slow and assess your needs, your intentions, and your practice before you go on a magickal shopping spree. Some tools, such as candles, are inexpensive and readily available. Others, such as crystal balls, are not only costly but bring powerful energies into your environment and you must be willing to assume responsibility for them.

Here's a short list of some favorite witchy tools you may want to work with:

- Cauldron—great for brewing magickal concoctions, cooking celebratory meals, and containing small ritual fires
- Sword—use it for circle-casting, to slice through obstacles (symbolically), or in banishing work
- Bell—marks the steps in a ritual or meditation, and may summon a deity or spirit

- Besom (broom)—sweeps unwanted energies from a sacred or ritual space
- Crystals—augment the power of spells, aid scrying and meditation, assist in healing, and much more
- Singing bowls—attune the chakras and attract harmonious cosmic energies for rituals, spellworking, and journeying
- Cords and ribbons—seal spells, bind unwanted entities, and hold energies for future use
- Scrying mirror or crystal ball—lets you gaze into areas beyond your normal range of vision
- Oracles (tarot cards, runes, pendulums, etc.)—predict the future, guide the present, and augment spells and rituals

As you deepen yourself in magickal practice you may find that objects you once considered ordinary now have mystical uses. Treat the tools you bring into your practice as the sacred implements they are. Respect and care for them as you would dear friends, and they will serve you for a lifetime.

No Worries Spell

Worrying never makes things better—in fact, it can exacerbate a troublesome situation. Instead, take out your magick tools and chase those fearful thoughts away. Perform this spell at midnight, during the waning moon.

TOOLS AND INGREDIENTS

A dark blue candle

A candleholder

Matches or a lighter

A hand drum or gong

An athame

A bell

1. Cast a circle around the area where you will do your spell.

2. Fit the candle in its holder, set it on your altar (or other surface where it can burn safely), and light it.

3. Begin playing the drum or gong to break up negative thoughts and vibrations. Feel the sound resonating through you, stirring up your power and confidence. Play for as long as you like.

4. When you feel ready, chant the following incantation aloud. If possible, shout it out—really assert yourself!

"Doubt and fear
Don't come near.
By the dawn
Be you gone.
By this sign [with your athame draw a pentagram in the air in front of you]
And light divine
Peace is mine.
I am strong
All day long.
My worries flee
Magickally.
I ring this bell [ring the bell]
To bind this spell,
And all is well."

5. As you chant, envision your fears receding into the darkness, losing their strength. When you're ready, extinguish the candle and open the circle.

The Modern Witchcraft Grimoire

Chapter 16

INGREDIENTS FOR SPELLS

Today, few people use eye of newt and toe of frog in spells. Witches are more likely to choose everyday ingredients we can find in any supermarket or New Age store—or better yet, in the natural environment. Utilizing objects from nature is a wonderful way to enhance your connection with Mother Earth and to increase the power of your spells by adding the energies of plants, stones, and so on.

Since ancient times, witches, shamans, sorcerers, and other magicians have looked to nature for spell materials. They used herbs and flowers to make healing potions, salves, poultices, and tonics. Gemstones and crystals provided protection, augmented personal powers, and attracted blessings. The natural world still provides a cornucopia of plants, minerals, and other treasures that you can incorporate into your own magickal workings.

SYMPATHETIC MAGICK

The basic philosophy of sympathetic magick is simple: like attracts like. This means that in spellwork, an item can serve as a representative or stand-in for another item that's similar to it in some way. It also means that the similarities are not coincidental and that they signify a connection—physical, spiritual, energetic, or otherwise—between the two items. Ginseng root, for example, resembles the human body, a similarity that some healers believe contributes to ginseng's medicinal properties. When you do spells, you can utilize associations between objects in order to make your spells more effective. In some instances, you may be aware of these connections; in other cases, the understanding happens at a subconscious level.

Because similarities exist between items, you can often substitute one ingredient for another in a spell. As we've already discussed, the color pink corresponds to the energy of love. So if you're doing a love spell, you could use a pink rose or a piece of rose quartz—both resonate with loving vibrations. The energy of the flower is quicker, the stone's more enduring.

CANDLES

Early sun-worshipping civilizations considered fire the embodiment of the Divine on earth. The ancient Greek story of Prometheus illustrates this link. Prometheus, one of the race of Titans, stole the sacred fire from Zeus on Mount Olympus and brought it to humankind. For this act, Prometheus suffered horribly—but his gift enabled human beings to enjoy a better existence on earth. Today, witches still associate the sun with the God and the moon with the Goddess, and burn candles to express the power of the fire element.

Candles are probably the most popular component in spells and rituals. The concept of illumination carries both a practical meaning—visible light that enables you to conduct your work—and an esoteric one—an inspiration or awakening that enlivens your spell's energy and expands your understanding. Candles provide a focal point for your attention, helping you to still your mind, and their soft, flickering light creates an ambiance that shifts you out of your ordinary existence.

Light in the Dark

The term "candle" comes from *candere*, a Latin word meaning "to shine." Candles represent hope, a light in the darkness, a beacon that shows the way to safety and comfort. Five thousand years ago, the Egyptians formed beeswax into candles similar to the ones we use today. Beeswax candles with reed wicks have been discovered in the tombs of Egyptian rulers, placed there, perhaps, to light their souls' journey into the realm beyond.

Spellworking with Candles

When you consecrate a candle to a magickal purpose, you infuse it with your intention and thereby transform it from something mundane into something magickal. Lighting the candle links you to the Divine. The burning wick consuming the wax symbolizes the deities infusing the material world with their power, so that a desired outcome may manifest.

Witches usually keep on hand a supply of candles in a range of colors. When you cast spells, it's important to remember these color connections (refer to the table in Chapter 12). If you're doing a love spell, for example, burn a red or pink candle that represents passion, affection, and the heart. Prosperity spells call for green, gold, or silver candles, the colors of money.

Candles can enhance just about any spell. Many magick workers set candles on their altars: white, red, or gold to symbolize male/yang/god; black, blue, or silver to represent female/yin/goddess energies. Some formal rituals involve carefully placing candles in specific spots and moving them according to prescribed patterns, perhaps over a period of days or weeks.

Candle Spell to Increase Your Influence

Begin this spell during the waxing moon, preferably on a Sunday. It increases the light you shine into the world and simultaneously turns the "spotlight" on you.

TOOLS AND INGREDIENTS

A candle (in a candleholder) to represent you

7 candles (in candleholders) each one a different color of the visible spectrum

Matches or a lighter

1. Set the candle that represents you on your altar.
2. Arrange the other candles close together in a circle around "you."
3. Light all the candles and let them burn for several minutes—until your attention starts to wander—then snuff them out.
4. The next day, move the 7 candles out a bit, expanding the circle on your altar and symbolically your circle of influence. Light all the candles and let them burn for several minutes, then snuff them out.
5. Repeat this for 7 days. On the last day, let all the candles burn down completely.

You can also cast a circle with candles in which to perform spells and rituals. Position candles around the space where you plan to do your magick, and then light them in a clockwise manner, beginning at the easternmost point. To open the circle after you've finished your working, snuff out the candles in reverse order.

Engraving Candles

Many spells call for engraving candles with symbols that represent your intentions. Select one or more symbols that resonate with you—runes, sigils, astrological glyphs, names, numbers, etc.—and that depict the purpose of your spell. Practice drawing these images in your book of shadows beforehand. In candle carving, you can't erase a mistake!

When you're ready, hold the candle in your hand and close your eyes. Visualize your thoughts permeating the wax and becoming one with the candle itself. Then, using a ballpoint pen, toothpick, nail, or pin, etch the word or symbol into the wax. (If you're really careful, you can use your

The Modern Witchcraft Grimoire

athame.) Don't become overly concerned with the artistic renderings of symbols, however. Your intention is the most important aspect of this work, not whether you can draw well. The magick is in performing the task and imbuing the candle with your intention.

When you've finished engraving your candle, you can dress it (see the following) or burn it as is. As the wax burns, your intention is released into the atmosphere where it can begin manifesting.

Dressing Candles

Dressing or anointing candles gives your spell a bit more "octane" by adding the scent (and natural energy) of essential oils. The act of anointing also carries the implication of sanctifying something, making it sacred.

Choose an oil that corresponds to your intention. You could use rose, ylang-ylang, or patchouli for love spells, peppermint oil for money spells, cinnamon or sandalwood for success spells. (For an example, see "Spell to Get a Raise" in Chapter 4.) Start applying the oil to the middle of the candle and then work it gradually in each direction to balance the polarity of the two ends—as above, so below. Think of your request or intention rising into the heavens as you rub oil upward toward the top of the candle. Envision the completed work coming down to reality and materializing on earth as you rub the oil toward the bottom of the candle. Inhale the fragrant aroma and let it trigger impressions in your mind of how your spell will manifest.

Apply a thin, even layer, letting the oil seep into the carvings. Want to dress up your candle even further? Sprinkle a little glitter on the surface—or mix glitter into the oil beforehand. The oil will make the sparkly glitter stick to the candle.

If you wish, you may say an incantation to bind the spell, such as the following. Better yet, improvise your own.

"Blessed be thou creature of wax.
You were made by the art of the hand
And now by magick you are changed.
Thou art no more a candle, but [state your intention].

Blessed by the sweetness of the Goddess,
Consecrated by my will and hand,
You are bound now to this charge,
For strengthening the greater good,
For manifesting intention on earth,
As an agent of the Tripart Goddess.
Charged with the power of three times three
As I will, so mote it be."

How you choose to burn your candle will be determined by the nature of the spell you are doing. Some candles should be burned completely and without interruption—in this case, mini candles and small votives in glass containers are best. Other spells call for burning a candle for a period every day, at a specific time. Pillar candles lend themselves to this. Tapers can set the mood for any spell or ritual, in the same way their lovely soft light enhances a dinner party.

Safety First!

Remember never to leave a burning candle unattended! If you want to burn a candle without interruption but need to leave your altar, consider placing the candle in the fireplace with the screen closed or in the center of your bathtub with the shower curtain removed. But do this only if you don't have rambunctious pets or kids who might be tempted to investigate, knock the candle over, or otherwise interfere.

After you finish your spell, write down what you did in your grimoire. What color candle did you use, and why? What symbols did you engrave on it? What oil(s) did you select to anoint it? Utter an incantation or petition a deity? You may want to drip some of the candle wax on the page where you recorded the spell, and perhaps dot the page with essential oil as a reminiscence. How about inscribing the soft wax with the symbol you carved into the candle? Of course, you'll want to note the results of your spell and any other relevant experiences.

Scrying with Candles

The term "scrying" refers to tapping into your second sight to see what you can't see with your physical eyes. This may mean peeking into the future or glimpsing something that's going on in another place beyond your ordinary range of vision. Often we think of scrying as something a witch does by gazing into a crystal ball. It's not the only way, though. You can look at clouds or into a body of water—or a candle's flame. Here's how:

1. In a dark room, light a candle (set it on your altar or in another place where it can burn safely).
2. Watch its flickering flame, allowing it to gradually quiet your thoughts and bring on a state of relaxation.
3. As you gaze at the flame, allow your vision to "soften"—that is, don't try to focus clearly or intently on the flame. You might even want to let your eyes drift slightly to the side of the flame, rather than staring directly at it.
4. As images begin to arise in the flame, permit them to develop as they will, without trying to direct them. Just observe, as if you were watching a movie.
5. Gaze into the smoke rising from the flame. Do you see images there as well? Allow them to unfold before you, without attempting to control them or even make sense of them.
6. Notice any emotions, sensations, or impressions you experience—prickling on the back of your neck, a fluttering in your heart, or the presence of an unexpected scent, for example.
7. Continue gazing at the candle's flame and smoke for as long as you like, or for as long as the images remain.
8. When you're ready, snuff out the candle and ease yourself back into ordinary reality.

Write in your grimoire what you experienced. What did you see in the flame and/or smoke? Did you recognize any of the images as relating to your everyday life or to the purpose for which you sought visions? What did they mean to you? Describe anything else you sensed or felt. Note details that may seem insignificant at the time—they may turn out to be meaningful. Revisit your grimoire at a later date and record anything that you feel ties into what was revealed to you while scrying. Practicing this technique regularly will strengthen your psychic muscles and enable you to gain insight readily.

Wax Poppets

You can shape candle wax into a human or animal form to create what's known as a "poppet." Typically, a witch creates a poppet to represent someone he or she wishes to send magickal energy to, usually at a distance. Whatever you do to the poppet symbolizes what you intend to do to whomever the poppet represents. For instance, if you fashion a poppet to signify a beloved pet and carefully wrap it in white cloth to protect it, the animal will receive the benefit of that protection.

Wax Heart Spell

This spell is sure to melt your beloved's heart. Perform it during the waxing moon, preferably when the sun or moon is in Libra, or on a Friday.

TOOLS AND INGREDIENTS

A ballpoint pen (or other engraving tool)

1 red candle

1 pink candle

An essential oil that corresponds to love and that you find pleasing

Matches or a lighter

Aluminum foil

1. With the pen carve your name on one candle and your beloved's on the other.
2. Dress both candles with the essential oil.
3. Light both candles, then tilt them so the melting wax drips onto the foil, blending to form a single mound of wax.
4. When you have enough wax to mold, allow it to cool slightly, but don't let it harden. Form a heart out of the wax.
5. Place the wax heart on your bedside table. If you prefer, you can insert a wick into the wax heart while the wax is still pliable and use it as a candle to fire up your romance.

BOTANICALS

It's reasonably safe to say that every plant has probably been used at one time or another in spellcraft. A Greek myth explains that the daughters of Hecate (one of the patronesses of witchcraft) taught witches how to use plants for both healing and magick. The Druids considered trees sacred. According to green witchcraft, all plants contain spirits—to work effectively with plants, you must communicate with them at a spiritual level, not just a physical one. Even the pages of the grimoire in which you are writing come from plant material.

To practice plant magick you'll need to reconnect with nature. You can't honor something you don't feel an intimate connection with, and you certainly can't call on the plant spirits to assist you unless you develop a rapport with plants. If you live in a concrete jungle, this may present some challenges. But even in the heart of the city, you can find parks, botanical gardens, greenhouses, or garden centers where you can commune with plants.

Earth Spirits at Findhorn

In the early 1960s, Eileen and Peter Caddy and their associate Dorothy Maclean began a spiritual community in a wild and windswept area of northern Scotland known as Findhorn. Even though the soil there was mostly sand and the climate inhospitable, Findhorn became famous for its amazing gardens, which produced tropical flowers and forty-two-pound cabbages. How could this happen? According to Dorothy, the spirits of the plants—she described them as "living forces of creative intelligence that work behind the scene"—guided Findhorn's founders in planting and maintaining the incredible gardens. In the book *Faces of Findhorn*, Professor R. Lindsay Robb of the Soil Association writes, "The vigor, health and bloom of the plants in this garden at mid-winter on land which is almost barren, powdery sand cannot be explained . . ." Well, not by ordinary thinking anyway.

Spellworking with Botanicals

Every plant is unique, with its own special energies and applications. Rowan, for instance, hung above a doorway protects your home from harm. Mugwort improves psychic awareness. Healing plays an important role in the work many witches do, and in this work they often draw upon the powers of botanicals. For thousands of years and into the present, people have relied on herbal medicine to heal everything from the common cold to a broken heart. Here are some other ways you might choose to work with the magickal properties of plants:

- Press pretty flowers and herbs in your book of shadows.
- Watch plant behavior for omens and signs.
- Mix leaves and petals into magick potions.
- Use plant matter in amulets and talismans.
- Add plant matter to incense and candles.
- Blend herbs for poultices and healing teas.
- Mix healing plant oils into lotions, salves, and ointments.
- Decorate your altar with flowers.
- Plant flowers in a magick garden to attract nature spirits.
- Make fragrant potpourris to perfume your closets and dresser drawers.
- Place live plants in various parts of your home or yard to encourage personal growth and well-being.

Lavender

The Modern Witchcraft Grimoire

Red Clover

Rosemary

Some plants may be burned in ritual fires, as offerings or for purification. Sage is one of the most popular plants to use for this purpose. Many botanicals also come in the form of incense (sticks, cones, coils) that you can burn in spells and rituals. You can make an herbal infusion by boiling water, removing the water from heat, and then letting the plant material steep in the water for several minutes. If you wish, set flowers in water and leave them in the sun to "steep." The essence of the flowers will be imparted to the water. Add a tiny amount of liquor such as brandy or vodka to the water to preserve it. Mist a room with flower water to purify it or sprinkle a little on an amulet or talisman to charge it.

As any good cook will tell you, the key to great food lies both in the ingredients and how the cook combines them. The same holds true for spells. If you think of a spell as a magickal recipe, you begin to understand why the components (that is, the ingredients) are so important. If you don't measure them correctly, add them to the mix at the right time, and give them enough time to "bake" properly, the magick goes awry.

Choosing Botanicals for Spells

So what constitutes a good spell component? Anything that's essential to the recipe—anything that builds the energy until it's just right. All the ingredients must mesh on a metaphysical level. Of course, the witch herself is the key component of any spell, adding a word, a touch, or a wish.

When selecting botanicals, choose organic plants if possible. You don't want the poisonous vibes of pesticides present in your spellwork! If you are purchasing your herbs and do not know under what conditions they were grown, wash them thoroughly to remove any residual chemicals that may have been used. If you're harvesting a plant that you've grown yourself or found in the wild, ask the plant's permission before picking it, and thank it for its help.

The Magickal Properties of Botanicals

- Acacia: For meditation; to ward off evil; to attract money and love
- Aloe: To soothe burns or skin ailments; for digestion and internal cleansing

- Angelica: For temperance; to guard against evil
- Anise: For protection; burn seeds as a meditation incense
- Balm: To soothe emotional pain, mitigate fears
- Bay: For purification, divination, psychic development, heightened awareness
- Basil: For protection, balance, purification, divination
- Burdock: For purification, protection, psychic awareness; to ward off negativity; aphrodisiac
- Catnip: For insight, love, happiness
- Cayenne: To stimulate courage, sexual desire, or enthusiasm
- Cedar: For wealth, abundance, success
- Chamomile: For relaxation, peace of mind; as a digestive aid; to bless a person, place, or thing
- Cinnamon: For financial and career success, love spells, mental clarity
- Cinquefoil: To stimulate memory, aid communication; for divination or psychic dreams
- Clove: For success, prosperity; to remove negativity; to numb pain
- Clover: For love spells, psychic awareness, luck
- Comfrey: For protection, cleansing, endurance
- Daisy: To attract good luck
- Elder: For protection, healing rituals
- Fennel: For protection
- Foxglove: To heighten sexuality (poisonous)
- Frankincense: To aid meditation, psychic visions, mental expansion, purification
- Garlic: For protection, healing; to lift depression
- Ginger: For love, balance, cleansing; to speed manifestation
- Hawthorne: For success, happiness, fertility, protection
- Jasmine: For love, passion, peace, harmony; to sweeten a situation or relationship
- Kava-kava: To heighten psychic awareness, to calm anxiety
- Laurel: For success and victory
- Lavender: For relaxation, spiritual and psychic development, purification
- Marigold: For happiness, psychic awareness, success in legal matters
- Marjoram: For acceptance of major life changes

- Mint: For prosperity; to speed up results
- Mugwort: For divination, psychic development and awareness; good for washing crystals
- Myrrh: For protection, healing, consecration
- Nettle: To mitigate thorny situations such as gossip and envy
- Parsley: For prosperity, protection, health
- Rosemary: For protection, love, health; to improve memory
- Rue: For protection; to strengthen willpower, to speed recovery from illness and surgery, to expel negativity
- Sandalwood: For consecration, spiritual communication, travel spells, success
- Skullcap: For relaxation before magickal practices
- Thyme: To focus energy and prepare oneself for magickal practice
- Vervain: For protection, divination, creativity, self-confidence; to remove negative energy
- Willow: For love, protection, conjuring of spirits, healing, dowsing
- Wormwood: For spirit communication; to enhance psychic ability (poisonous if burned)
- Yarrow: For divination, love, protection; to enhance psychic ability

"And above all, watch with glittering eyes the whole world around you because the greatest secrets are always hidden in the most unlikely places. Those who don't believe in magic will never find it."

—ROALD DAHL, *THE MINPINS*

GEMSTONES

Today, people wear precious and semiprecious gems mostly because they're so pretty. Witches, however, realize that crystals and gemstones can also be used for spellworking, divination, shamanic journeying, meditation, and dowsing. Stones also play important roles in healing, and each of the body's seven major chakras corresponds to one (or more) gems based on their colors and resonances.

Gemstones and jewelry have long been favored as talismans and amulets. The Chinese, for example, prize jade and wear it to bring health, strength, and good fortune. During the Crusades, ladies gave opals to soldiers to keep them safe in battle. Originally, people wore birthstones to enhance, balance, or moderate their own personal characteristics. Birthstones resonate with the qualities of the zodiac signs to which they correspond. By the way, you should look at your sign, not the month of your birth, to discover your true birthstone. If you're an Aquarian, for example, your birthstone is garnet, regardless of whether you were born in January or February.

> *"When you wear certain gems on your left side you can consciously control and modify stresses from your environment. . . . [W]hen you wear gems on your right side, your gems can aid your productivity."*
> —DOROTHEE L. MELLA, *STONE POWER*

Spellworking with Gemstones

Like plants, crystals and gemstones are living entities, although they resonate at a rate so slow that most people can't perceive it. However, their slow, concentrated energy enables them to keep working their magick for a long time. You can include gemstones and/or crystals in virtually any spell to increase, focus, stabilize, or fine-tune your spell's potency. Here are some suggestions:

- Wear them to enhance your personal energy field.
- Put them in amulets or talismans to augment your intentions.
- Set them near the windows and doors of your home to provide protection.
- Meditate with them.
- Infuse magick potions with them.
- Dowse with a gemstone or crystal pendulum.
- Display them on your altar to attract positive energy.
- Offer them to deities or nature spirits as gifts in return for assistance.
- Gaze into them to see the past or future.

Choosing Gemstones for Spells

As you might suspect, different stones possess different qualities and serve different functions in spellworking. A general rule of thumb is that clear stones are best for mental and spiritual issues, translucent or milky stones for emotional situations, and opaque stones for physical matters. You can use gems alone or in combination with other substances to produce the results you desire.

A stone's color or pattern can provide clues to its abilities. Pink gems, such as rose quartz and morganite, are perfect for love spells. Jade, aventurine, and other green stones can benefit money spells. Since ancient times, people have valued stones with eye-like markings as protection charms against the "evil eye" and all sorts of misfortune.

The following guidelines offer suggestions for using gems in spellwork. In time, you'll develop your own ideas about which stones you find best for which spells. Be sure to note these in your grimoire.

STONES AND THEIR MAGICKAL PROPERTIES	
Amber	For physical and psychic protection
Amethyst	For meditation, enhancing and remembering dreams, calming emotions, increasing psychic ability
Aquamarine	For clarity and mental awareness, encouraging spiritual insight, stimulating creativity
Aventurine	To attract wealth or abundance
Bloodstone	For healing, strength, and physical protection
Carnelian	To stimulate passion, sexual energy, courage, and initiative
Citrine	For clearing vibrations from other stones and crystals
Coral	To attract love or increase affectionate feelings; to enhance self-esteem; to calm emotions
Diamond	To deepen commitment and trust, especially in a love relationship; to absorb and retain energies and vibrations; for strength and victory

STONES AND THEIR MAGICKAL PROPERTIES

Emerald	To aid clairvoyance and divination; to promote healing, growth, mental and emotional balance
Hematite	For grounding; to help stabilize emotions
Jade	For prosperity; to enhance beauty and health
Jasper	Red jasper is good in love spells to stir up passions; brown jasper is excellent for healing purposes; poppy jasper breaks up blockages that prevent energy from circulating through the body
Lapis lazuli	For opening psychic channels, dealing with children; to stimulate the upper chakras
Moldavite	To energize psychic talent, to quicken spiritual evolution, to open the upper chakras; moldavite is regarded as an extraterrestrial stone because it resulted from a meteor collision with the earth nearly 15 million years ago
Moonstone	To enhance the vividness of dreams and dream recall; to calm emotions
Onyx	For banishing and absorbing negative energy, grounding and stabilizing; to help break deeply ingrained habits
Opal	For protection; to encourage psychic ability and visions; to attract love
Pearl	To strengthen self-esteem; for balance in love relationships; to increase femininity
Quartz (clear)	To retain information; to amplify the energy of other stones; to transmit ideas and energy; for psychic awareness
Rose quartz	To attract love and friendship; for emotional healing and balance; to amplify psychic energy
Ruby	To stimulate the emotions, passion, love; to open your heart to divine love
Sapphire	To increase spiritual knowledge and connection with the Divine; for wisdom, insight, and prophetic vision; star sapphires provide hope and clarity of purpose

STONES AND THEIR MAGICKAL PROPERTIES	
Smoky quartz	For endurance; to hold problems until you are ready to deal with them
Tiger's eye	For abundance, self-confidence, the freedom to follow your own path
Tourmaline	Green and black tourmaline are good for cleansing, healing, and absorbing negative vibrations; pink and watermelon tourmaline attract friendship, love, and fulfillment; use them to transmit messages and energy
Turquoise	For protection, healing, prosperity; to ease mental tension and emotional anxiety

You can combine several stones to address various aspects of a spell. Let's say your goal is to find a job that pays well and brings you into contact with interesting people—aventurine plus watermelon tourmaline should do the trick. In a love spell, you might seek both passion and affection, in which case you'd choose carnelian and rose quartz. After a while, you'll start to intuit which stones are right for your intentions. Stones play such an important role in magick work that you'll probably want to spend time familiarizing yourself with their many properties. Judy Hall's books provide extensive information about how to use stones for a wide range of purposes.

Caring for Your Stones

Gemstones hold on to thoughts, emotions, and information programmed into them for a long time, even for centuries. You've probably heard of the Hope Diamond, a 45-carat blue diamond that for more than a century supposedly bore a curse that brought death and misfortune to the people who owned it. Although you probably have nothing to fear from the stones you acquire, nonetheless it's a good idea to cleanse and purify them before you use them for magickal work.

Wash them in running water, with mild soap if you like, while you envision them cleansed by pure white light. You can also purify gemstones energetically by gently rubbing them with a piece of golden citrine.

Try one of these other methods for cleansing stones, if you prefer:

- Leave them in sunlight or moonlight for a specific period, say twenty-four hours or a week—it's your call. Do what you feel is necessary.
- Bury them in a small dish of soil or sand for a time.
- Hold the stone in the smoke of burning sage or purifying incense.
- Immerse the stone in water for a time. Holding it in a running stream or the ocean's waves will purify it faster, but leaving the stone in a small bowl of water will work too. Don't worry; you cannot remove the innate energy of a stone, so it's impossible to over-purify or wipe out its powers.

Each time you use a stone for a magickal purpose, it is important to cleanse it before working with it again. You'll also want to purify your stones if someone else handles them—you don't want that person's energy to interfere with your own.

Keep a record in your grimoire of the stones you use in spells. Can you perceive different resonances emanating from different stones? Do you feel an affinity for some more than others? If you combined gems with other ingredients in a spell, how did that work out? Do you sense that certain gems enhance one another's powers? Do you use some stones for healing, others for meditation, others for scrying, and so on? Note any impressions, insights, sensations, or other reactions you experience while working with gemstones and crystals—sometimes these can be pretty amazing. You might even choose to affix small gemstones to the pages of your grimoire, to remind you of spells you did with these gems or because they add a decorative element to your book of shadows—or both.

Chapter 17

SYMBOLS IN SPELLWORK

We've talked a lot about symbols and the importance of symbolic association in spellwork. Symbols are such powerful magickal tools because they speak to us at an unconscious level, evoking hidden truths, archetypes, emotions, and spiritual qualities that lie at the core of our psyches. As a result, we often experience profound feelings in connection with them. Observe the way patriotic people respond to their nation's flag, how Christians relate to the cross, or how the Nazis reacted to the swastika and you'll see the power of symbols at work.

We respond to symbols in collective ways as well as personal ones. Many symbols are universal, appearing in the art and artifacts of numerous cultures from different times and places. The spiral, which represents life energy, is one such symbol. In addition, each of us has a set of individual symbols that have special meanings for us alone. When you use a symbol in spellwork, you draw upon the energy of whatever it represents. Simultaneously, you project your intentions through it to generate a result in the manifest world.

"Witchcraft promotes the advantages of learning and applying new symbolism into one's psyche; this is the Witch's code."

—Gede Parma, Spirited: Taking Paganism Beyond the Circle

What symbols speak to you? Keep a record in your grimoire of the symbols with which you feel a special connection—especially the "secret" ones known as sigils that you create yourself. Note your personal symbols and what they mean to you. Draw symbols in your book of shadows and spend time reflecting on them, allowing their secrets to rise into your consciousness. Meditate on various symbols to intuit their deeper meanings. How do you feel when you hold a symbol in your mind's eye? What insights do you gain? Do you see representations of these symbols in the material world? In your own life?

Intricate or Simple?

Intricate shapes strengthen concentration and your ability to perceive detail, beauty, and complexity. Simple shapes free your mind to imagine what lies beyond the pattern.

SHAPES AS SYMBOLS

Remember the saying, "As above, so below"? This means that all things in the spirit realm have some kind of representation here on earth. Spiritual energies manifest themselves as shapes in the mundane world—and because witches understand this we can tap these energies for our own purposes.

Numbers, letters, and geometric shapes are common symbols you see around you every day, usually without giving them a second thought. The average person only recognizes the obvious meanings of these familiar images. To someone versed in occult knowledge, however, symbols reveal something much deeper.

"An idea, in the highest sense of that word, cannot be conveyed but by a symbol."

—Samuel Taylor Coleridge

The Shapes of Things

Geometric shapes contain symbolism that transcends time and place. The cross, for example, isn't unique to Christian belief; it existed in ancient Celtic, Egyptian, and Native American cultures too. This simple yet powerful image represents the union of the archetypal male energy or sky (the vertical line) with female energy or earth (the horizontal line). The intersecting lines also designate the four directions that divide the four quarters we've talked about in earlier chapters.

The star is a common symbol of hope, the circle a well-known symbol of wholeness. Spirals represent life energy in many cultures. Triangles signify trinities, whether Father-Son-Holy Spirit, maiden-mother-crone, past-present-future, or some other threefold concept. The following list gives the symbolic meanings of basic geometric shapes:

Shape	Meanings
Arrow	warrior energy, direction, movement, hitting the mark
Circle	union, wholeness, life's cycles, the full moon, containment
Circle with a slash	refusal or banishing
Cross	intersection of male and female/heaven and earth/spirit and matter, the four corners of creation
Spiral	life energy, the spiritual path that leads inward and outward
Square	foundations, stability, permanence, truth and rightness
Star	hope, wishes and dreams, protection
Triangle (point down)	feminine energy, the element of water
Triangle (point up)	masculine energy, the fire element

According to green witches, the shape of a natural item provides a blueprint for how it should be used magically. If you find a heart-shaped stone or leaf, for example, you can apply it to spells that involve matters of the heart. You see a heart, you think love—and that thought produces positive energy to support your intention.

Elemental Symbols

Alchemy uses triangles to depict the four elements we've talked about in earlier chapters. Triangles that point upward toward the sky and spirit symbolize the masculine force. A simple triangle stands for the element of fire; one with a horizontal line through it signifies the air element. Downward-pointing triangles aim toward the earth and the realm of matter. They represent the feminine force and the elements of water and earth. The emblem for earth has a horizontal line through the center of the triangle, the one for water doesn't.

Historically, symbols have offered one meaning for the masses and another, deeper meaning for initiates. The Star of David is a good example. To most people, the six-pointed star is an image associated with the Jewish faith. However, when you view it as the intersection of two triangles—one pointing up and one pointing down—it depicts the union of masculine and feminine, spirit and matter. The merger of these two energies creates life.

The ancient grimoire known as *The Clavicule of Solomon* or *Key of Solomon* (discussed in Chapter 1) says that the archangel Michael gave King Solomon a magick ring. Its power lay in the symbol engraved on the ring—the Seal of Solomon—which enabled the king to trap demons in jars so they could do no harm. This symbol geometrically depicts the union of all four elements.

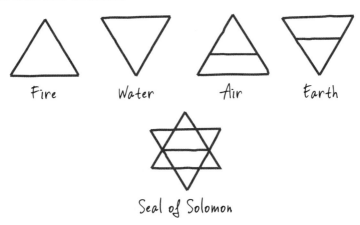

Fire   Water   Air   Earth

Seal of Solomon

The Modern Witchcraft Grimoire

Magick Numbers

We usually credit the Greek mathematician and philosopher, Pythagoras, who lived in the sixth century B.C.E., with having developed the system of numerology that's still used today. The study of numbers, known as *gematria*, is also based in esoteric Judaism and the Kabbalah. This practice attaches a number equivalent to each letter in a word (see Chapter 5 for details). Viewed in this way, every word contains a secret meaning based on the number values of its letters, as well as its outer meaning.

Additionally, each number possesses certain characteristics or resonances, as the following list explains:

Number	Meanings
0	wholeness, all and nothing
1	beginnings, individuality, initiative
2	polarity, partnership, duality, balance
3	creativity, self-expression, expansion
4	form, stability, permanence, order
5	change, instability, communication
6	give-and-take, cooperation, beauty, harmony
7	retreat, introspection, rest, spirituality
8	material mastery, manifestation, responsibility, sincerity, practical matters
9	transition, completion, fulfillment, abundance
11	humanitarianism, higher knowledge, insight
22	spiritual power, wisdom, mastery beyond the physical realm

You can tap the qualities inherent in numbers to enhance, activate, bind, or otherwise influence a spell. Witches often use the number three to complete a spell. This number signifies bringing an intention into the realm of form, literally making it three-dimensional.

SHAPES AND NUMBERS IN SPELLS AND RITUALS

Once you understand the symbolism inherent in shapes and numbers, you can utilize them in spells and rituals to emphasize specific energies or intentions. As you know, witches cast circles around a space where a spell or ritual will take place. The circle represents union, wholeness, life's cycles, the full moon, and containment. Tarot cards beautifully depict a smorgasbord of symbols, including numbers. We've talked about carving symbols on candles, using runes and astrological glyphs in talismans and amulets, and creating your own symbols known as sigils.

Let's say you want to do a candle spell to attract a romantic partner. Because two is the number of partnership, you'd light two candles to represent you and your prospective partner. If you're fashioning a prosperity talisman, you could place eight items in a medicine pouch or seal the pouch with a ribbon into which you've tied eight knots. That's because eight is the number of material mastery and manifestation. You can mix and match symbols to customize a spell, as in the one that follows. The important thing is to get your imagination involved. Remember, visualization precedes manifestation.

Candle Spell for Prosperity

This spell incorporates number, image, botanical, shape, and color symbolism to light the way to prosperity and brighten your financial prospects. Start the spell 8 days before the full moon.

TOOLS AND INGREDIENTS

8 green or gold candles	8 candleholders
Ballpoint pen (or another sharp instrument)	Matches or a lighter
Peppermint essential oil	

1. On each candle use the pen to inscribe a symbol or word that represents prosperity to you. You can use the same symbol on all 8 candles, or choose several different images.
2. Pour a little essential oil in your palm and rub it on the candles, coating everything except the wicks.

3. Put the candles in the candleholders and position them on your altar, making a square pattern to represent the 4 directions, the 4 quarters, and stability.

4. Light the candles and gaze at the flames.

5. Say aloud: "As these candles burn, prosperity flows to me from all directions, in harmony with Divine Will, my own true will, and with good to all."

6. Let the candles burn for a few minutes, then snuff them out.

7. Repeat this ritual each day for 8 days. Complete the spell on the day of the full moon.

After you've completed the spell, write in your grimoire what transpired. What images did you inscribe on the candles? How did you feel working the spell? Did your experiences change from day to day? What insights did you gain? What results did you get and how long did they take?

Experiment with using symbols in spellwork, trying out different combinations to see which ones you like best. Record the variations you use and describe your experiences in your book of shadows.

THE MAGICK OF DATES

We've talked about the significance of choosing certain days of the week for magickal work, but what about dates? Dates contain numbers and those numbers can be important in spellcasting. The first day of the month, for example, might be a good time to do a spell to launch a new venture.

> *"Those who deepen themselves in what is called in the Pythagorean sense 'the study of numbers' will learn through the symbolism of numbers to understand life and the world."*
> —RUDOLF STEINER, FOUNDER OF ANTHROPOSOPHY
> AND THE WALDORF SCHOOLS

Your Life Path Number

Your birth date forms a very important personal number and its energy influences you throughout your lifetime. Numerologists refer to this as your "life path" number because it indicates your direction or role in this lifetime. To find this powerful number, add the month, date, and year of your birth together. Keep reducing the sum by adding the digits until only a single digit remains. (Note: Usually the double or so-called "master" numbers 11 and 22 are left as is, rather than being reduced to the sum of their digits.) For example, if you were born on August 21, 1986 you would figure your life number this way:

Add 8 + 2 + 1 + 1 + 9 + 8 + 6 = 35

Reduce the sum to a single digit by adding $3 + 5 = 8$

The following brief interpretations describe the life roles that each number indicates:

Number	Interpretation
1	Leader, initiator, pioneer, a person who breaks new ground
2	Diplomat, mediator, agent, a go-between who assists others
3	Artist, musician, creator, someone who brings beauty into the world
4	Builder, artisan, technician, someone who makes practical, useful things
5	Teacher, writer, communicator, an idea person
6	Caretaker, homemaker, farmer, someone who nurtures and supports others
7	Truth seeker, religious leader, philosopher, mystic, wise wo/man
8	Businessperson, manager, industrialist, a person who uses money and resources in a productive way
9	Humanitarian, social worker, healer, a person who helps improve conditions for everyone
11	Inventor, visionary, avatar, someone who leads by positive example
22	A master builder who organizes people, nations, or institutions on a large scale

Calculate your life path number and note it in your grimoire. Does this describe you? Are you fulfilling the purpose to which you were born? How do you see the characteristics inherent in this number operating in your life? In your spiritual and magick work?

Life Cycles

Our lives are never static. Indeed, change is essential for personal growth. If you understand the influences guiding you, you can align yourself with them and utilize them to your advantage. Numerologists examine what they call "life cycles," which are based on your birthdate, to determine what you're likely to experience in any given year. By working with these cycles you can increase your success and satisfaction in life. You'll be more effective in your magickal work too, because you can harmonize it with the energies influencing you.

Let's look at the numerological cycle known as your "personal year." This changes each year and tells you what forces are operating in your life during a particular twelve-month period. To determine this, add the numbers of your birth month, date, and the year at your last birthday. If you were born on May 16 and you want to know what personal year cycle you will be experiencing from May 16, 2016, through May 15, 2017:

Add 5 + 1 + 6 + 2 + 0 + 1 + 6 = 21

Reduce the sum to a single digit by adding 2 + 1 = 3

Your personal year number for this period is 3. Therefore, you'll want to do things that correspond to a 3 vibration: have fun, enjoy more leisure time, express your creativity, expand your horizons physically and spiritually.

The following table briefly describes the essence of the nine yearly cycles and indicates where you are likely to focus your attention during those years.

Personal Year Cycle	Your Focus for the Year
1	New beginnings, action, independence, self-interest
2	Cooperation, partnerships, balance, developing plans
3	Expansion, travel, creativity, opportunity, personal growth
4	Stability, building, organization, financial matters, security
5	Communication, change, movement, sharing ideas
6	Give and take, balance, domesticity, love, comfort, beauty
7	Rest, retreat, withdrawal, introspection, healing
8	Manifestation, responsibility, power, managing resources
9	Fulfillment, completion, endings, transition, wisdom

In addition to personal year cycles, you also experience personal month cycles. You can tap the energy of these shorter periods in magickal work and in other areas of your life. To find your personal month, add the number of your personal year to the number equivalent of the current month (or any month in the future that you want to know more about). For example, if this year is a "7" for you, and you want to see what March has in store:

Add 7 + 3 (March's number) = 10

Reduce to a single digit by adding 1 + 0 = 1

March is 1 month for you, so during this time plan to do things that correspond to a 1 vibration. Use the table that describes the characteristics of personal years given earlier—the energies for the months are similar, though of shorter duration. This will help you to determine how to tap the power of your personal cycles in your spellwork and your life.

Record in your grimoire what you experience during these monthly and yearly cycles, both in your everyday life and in your magickal practice. Where did you focus your energies? What spells and rituals did you do? What areas of interest called to you? What knowledge and insights did you receive? Write down everything that you consider meaningful: your feelings, ideas, areas of concern, successes and setbacks, interactions with other people, dreams, and so on. In the future, you can compare what you experienced now with what transpires later.

ANIMALS AS SYMBOLS

Animals hold symbolic meaning for us too. A robin serves as a herald of springtime. A lion represents courage; a dog signifies loyalty. Celtic and Old European clans believed that certain animal deities oversaw entire groups of people. Irish clans called their members griffins, wolves, deer, etc., and individuals took their names from these animals. Animal guardians performed numerous functions for a clan, including protecting its warriors in battle.

Many family crests or coats of arms include animals, and those animal symbols convey distinct meanings. The crest of the Rothschild family—one of the most powerful families in the world—features a lion, a phoenix, and a unicorn. We see a version of this symbolism expressed today by our athletic teams. The Denver Broncos, the Boston Bruins, the Miami Dolphins, the St. Louis Cardinals, and the Chicago Bulls are some of the dozens of animal-named teams among the professional leagues.

Both Western and Chinese astrology link zodiac signs with animals. Zodiac means "circle of animals." You likely share some traits with the animal that represents your zodiac sign. If you're a Capricorn with the goat as your symbol, you persevere one step at a time and can climb to great heights. If you're a Leo, you may have regal bearing like the lion and proudly assume your role as a leader.

> *"Animals are sacred. They are living expressions of the divine principle—the Goddess and the God manifest in living form."*
> —Timothy Roderick, *The Once Unknown Familiar*

Spellworking with Animals

Perhaps you've heard the term "familiar." In spellwork, a familiar is an animal that works with a witch. Remember Harry Potter's owl? Black cats have long been associated with witchcraft. Ravens, snakes, and other creatures also have special places as wise beings in magick and folklore.

You may want to work with a familiar, but not every animal is intended for this type of relationship. Your beloved Fido or Fluffy may be a wonderful companion, but that doesn't necessarily make him or her your familiar. Often a witch experiences a strong psychic link with her familiar. Your familiar may serve as a guardian, guide, or healer. It can help you connect more deeply with the natural world and your intuition. The witch and her familiar are allies in the work—you don't own your familiar, it is a free being that deserves your utmost respect and gratitude.

Regardless of whether you work with a flesh-and-blood animal, you can incorporate animal symbolism in your magick. Think about various creatures and their distinctive qualities. Cheetahs are known for their speed and hunting skills. Foxes are clever, expert at dodging difficulties. Which animal's characteristics will best serve and guide you now?

Animal Deities

In India, people call upon the elephant-headed deity Ganesh to give them the strength to overcome difficulties. For many indigenous people of North America, the spirit of the bear provides protection.

Spirit Animal Protection Spell

According to shamanic traditions, spirit animal guardians provide protection and guidance in this world and beyond. Think of a creature who symbolizes protection for you. When you've chosen an animal helper, find a photograph, small figurine, or another symbol of that animal.

TOOLS AND INGREDIENTS

A black candle

A white candle

2 candleholders

Matches or a lighter

A photo, figurine, painting, or other image of the animal whose help you
are soliciting

The Modern Witchcraft Grimoire

1. Cast a circle around the area where you will do your spell.

2. Fit the candles in their holders and set them on your altar (or another surface, such as a tabletop). As you face the altar, the black candle should be at your left and the white one on your right.

3. Light the candles and place the image of the animal between them. Gaze at the animal image. Sense this animal's presence near you, as a spirit being who will accompany you wherever and whenever you need him or her.

4. Breathe slowly and deeply, bringing into yourself the qualities you seek from that animal: strength, courage, speed, cunning, and so on. Feel your fear ebbing away, replaced by the knowledge that your animal guardian is there to take care of you.

5. Ask this animal to share any suggestions that might help you. Listen carefully for an answer—it may come in the form of a vision, insight, sensation, sound, scent, or inner knowing.

6. Commune with your spirit animal guide for as long as you wish. When you feel ready, extinguish the candles, pick up the image of your animal guardian, and open the circle.

7. Carry the image with you for protection and reassurance.

In your grimoire, write down the results of your spell. What animal did you choose and why? How did the animal help you resolve your problem? Also describe your experiences—feelings, thoughts, impressions, insights, and so on.

Animal Divination

Dream researchers believe that when an animal shows up in a dream it bears a message for you. Sometimes you'll see an animal in nature, and if it's a creature you wouldn't ordinarily find in your locale, this could be a sign for you. If you see a ram, for example, think about what it represents to you. Power? Daring? Aggression? Competitiveness? Is it telling you to tackle a matter head on? To engage an adversary forcefully and directly? Are you being too aggressive or not aggressive enough?

Notice your reaction when something like this happens. Record your experiences in your grimoire. When and where did the animal appear to you? How does it relate to what's going on in your life? What message did it convey to you? How can you benefit from drawing upon its traits? Sketch or paste pictures of the animal in your book of shadows. You might even design a sigil that includes the animal's image. To learn more about animal divination and how to understand animals as symbols, see my book *The Secret Power of Spirit Animals.*

Chapter 18

DREAMS AND MAGICK

Some of the greatest moments of inspiration occur while we sleep. In the dark of night, thoughts begin to take form and significance. Shimmering dreams materialize into energy that seems to emanate from an unknowable source. When traveling the river of dreamtime, your mind is unbound, uncensored, and released from ordinary daytime expectations. Images, whether comforting or frightening, flow freely in an endless succession of vivid possibilities. Your grimoire is the perfect place to record your dreams, as dreams often contain guidance and insights. Keeping a log of your dreams also allows you to review them periodically to gain deeper understanding.

Dreams let us explore what lies beneath the surface, the unspoken world of archetypes and mystery that usually lies dormant, ready to rise and make its presence known in our lives—what psychoanalyst Carl Jung called the collective unconscious. The Goddess may visit you in dreams through symbols and signs. She travels from a place beyond, both in and out of time. Enter into her temple with the intention to know her and to open your unconscious mind to her presence, her words, and her teachings.

ONLY A DREAM?

Since the beginning of time, dreams have fascinated and perplexed us. Why do they happen? Where do they come from? What do they mean? Are dreams merely the result of chemical changes in the brain, as some studies suggest, or vehicles for divine communication?

Sources of Wisdom

Dreams figure prominently in the literature and mythology of all cultures. The 4,000-year-old *Epic of Gilgamesh* speaks of temples built to Mamu, who was the ancient goddess of dreams. Early Egyptians believed the gods bestowed dreams on humans, and dedicated many temples in Memphis to Serapis, the Egyptian god of dreams. The ancient Greeks erected temples to Asclepius, the god of healing. People with illnesses spent the night there and received guidance in their dreams from the god; the priests then wrote the cures on the temple walls.

The ancient texts of the Egyptians and Hindus as well as the Old Testament of the Bible discuss dreams, indicating that for millennia people around the world have looked to dreams for guidance, prophecy, wisdom, and inspiration. Muslims believe that a divine source gave the Qu'ran to Muhammad in a dream. Both Native American and Celtic shamanic teachings tell us that the dream realm is a parallel universe, a place we journey to when we sleep—and it is every bit as real as the world we inhabit when we're awake.

In his book *Dreamlife* David Fontana proposes "we sleep partly *in order to dream.* Sleep . . . may be the servant of the dream." You've probably heard of Edgar Cayce, often referred to as the "Sleeping Prophet." Although he had little formal education or medical training, he could go into a sleeplike trance and discover cures for thousands of sick people who sought his aid. He psychically "downloaded" wisdom that great minds before him had placed in the cosmic web (this web is sometimes referred to as the Akashic records).

What secrets and wisdom are your dreams trying to convey to you? Is a spirit or deity attempting to communicate with you via dreams? When you learn to decipher the meanings of your dreams, you can move with greater ease and grace through both the mundane and the magickal worlds.

Recording Your Dreams

Many people keep dream journals to help them remember and understand their dreams. However, you can record your dreams in your book of shadows if you like. Doing so can reveal connections between the realm of dreams and the realm of magick.

As part of your morning ritual, write down your dreams immediately upon waking. You will be better able to capture the fleeting images before they vanish into the ether or get lost in the busyness of the day. You may feel groggy and inarticulate from sleep. Your writing may seem as disjointed and unusual as the dream itself. No problem. This is precisely the point! You don't want your brain fully engaged—you want to capture the images and symbols that linger in the shadowy recesses beyond rational thinking. Don't worry about writing in complete sentences. You're not trying to explain, entertain, or analyze your thought process at this time; you're merely recording what you feel, sense, and recall.

Try a stream-of-consciousness approach to writing and let the images flow freely. Attempt to capture on paper what occurs so easily to your dreaming mind. Don't place value judgments on what you write or censor yourself, just be honest. Record the dominant images, obvious symbols, emotions, or other events that occurred in your dream. Also note little things that might not seem significant at the moment—they may turn out to be important later. As you write, ideas may bubble up to the surface of your consciousness, vying for your attention. Jot down whatever comes to you, even if you don't understand it right away.

As a part of your evening ritual, write a few lines about your day in your grimoire. Did your dream relate to something you encountered during the waking hours? What do you see as significant between what transpired during the day and what you dreamt? Make sure to date your entries and include any other details that may be relevant, such as astrological influences or health issues. When this ritual becomes entrenched in your daily practice, you'll probably notice that your subconscious eagerly presents more and more information to you and you become more facile at working with your dreams.

The Earliest Dream

The earliest known recorded dream, which belonged to King Thutmose IV, is carved upon a granite tablet that rests between the paws of the Sphinx.

DREAM SYMBOLS

No one knows exactly why people dream, yet researchers and psychotherapists generally agree that your dreams are trying to tell you something that can benefit you in your waking life. Usually dream messages are presented in symbolic rather than literal form. Some symbols appear in many people's dreams; others are unique to the dreamer.

Over time, general interpretations have been attached to the most common dream symbols. Personal symbols, though, hold special meaning that only you can comprehend. The following list includes a number of familiar symbols that turn up in most people's dreams at one time or another, along with their usually accepted meanings.

Image	Interpretation
House	you and your life; the basement represents your unconscious, the main floor shows your daily living situation, the attic or upper floors describe your mental or spiritual side
Car	your body and your passage through life; the driver represents who's controlling your life; the car's condition reveals health and physical matters
Water	emotions; the type of water (deep, murky, cold, turbulent, etc.) indicates the quality of your feelings
Sex	merging your masculine and feminine sides, or incorporating another person's qualities into yourself
Death	a transition or change; something is moving out of your life

The Modern Witchcraft Grimoire

Image	Interpretation
Birth	a new direction, perspective, or endeavor; creativity; opportunity
School	learning lessons; taking an exam represents being tested in an area of life
Monsters	things you fear or parts of yourself you haven't integrated

Dreams about Gems

It's said that when you dream about gemstones you've received a message from the Divine. To understand the message, consider the meanings associated with the particular gem (see Chapter 16).

Keep a list in your grimoire of the symbols you encounter in your dreams and describe what they mean to you. Do some appear frequently? Do they usually turn up in similar scenarios, or in a variety of ways? How do you feel when you encounter a particular symbol in a dream? After a while, you may identify certain symbols that are unique to you, or that hold different meanings for you than those commonly associated with them—pay special attention to these.

INTERPRETING YOUR DREAMS

If we agree that our dreams are trying to tell us something, it behooves us to learn to interpret them. Whether dream insights emerge from the subconscious or are sent to you by entities in the spirit realm, they may provide valuable information you can use in your everyday life and in your magick work. Each night as you enter the dream world, you have an opportunity to delve into areas that may not be available to you while you're awake.

Although dreams rarely play out in logical, easily comprehensible ways, with a little patience you can learn to understand their symbolic language. Think of dreams as your own personal movies, intended solely for you. Therefore, your own impressions are more important than standard textbook interpretations.

The following tips can help you get to the essence of your dreams:

- Try giving your dream a title that relates to what you remember as the most vivid or distinct image. The title could reflect the strongest event that occurred, the main action around which the events of the dream revolved.
- Write down what happened around you, to you, or because of you. These circumstances may be within or outside the realm of your control.
- Look for the crossroads, or the point in the dream at which things began to change, either for positive or negative results. Did your dream spiral up or down, either into delightful pleasure or a nightmare?
- Did some sort of resolution to the situation occur? How did this come about?
- How did you feel during the dream? Happy, sad, frightened, angry, confident, peaceful? How did you feel when you awoke?
- Who was in your dream? Are these characters people you know in your waking life? What associations do you have with them? If you don't know these people in waking life, do they represent something or someone?
- How did you interact with these characters? What transpired between you and them in the dream?
- Did any animals appear in your dream? If so, what associations do you hold with these animals?
- What images, actions, or scenes stood out most?
- Did anything in the dream seem totally fantastic and impossible in earthly terms? Or did the dream scenario play out in a relatively realistic manner?

Words have many meanings, both literal and symbolic, and dreams often play on words to get a point across. Once I dreamt I was in a long-distance race with many other people, and although I wasn't a trained runner I managed to keep up with the leaders in the race. Later, I won a contest and realized the dream had signaled that I was "in the running" for the award. Pay attention to words and phrases in your dreams, and note them in your grimoire—they may contain hidden meanings or puns that can provide insights.

The Modern Witchcraft Grimoire

Magick takes you into the secret recesses of the mind and makes you aware of your connections with other levels of reality. Dreams provide access to these realities. Keeping records of your dreams will lead you to a better understanding of your inner dynamics and what goes on beneath the surface of your ordinary mental processes. While in a dream state, you could even tap into the reservoir of knowledge contained in the Akashic records, the great cosmic "Internet" in the universe where many people believe the wisdom of all time is stored.

> *"Your vision will become clear only when you look into your heart. Who looks outside, dreams. Who looks inside, awakens."*
> —CARL JUNG

Recurring Dreams

Scenarios and images that show up repeatedly in your dreams are especially significant. If you experience recurring dreams, your subconscious may be trying hard to get something across to you. For instance, most of us periodically dream of being in a classroom taking a test for which we feel unprepared. Not surprisingly, we tend to have this dream at turning points in our lives, when we're facing new challenges or moving into a new phase of life.

Pay close attention to your own recurring dreams. Does the dream replay pretty much the same way every time or do you notice variations? Examine any changes in the dream's narrative, setting, or characters—these will tell you how the situation is progressing. Once you comprehend the dream's message and address the situation, you'll probably stop having the dream.

Problem-Solving Dreams

Because dreams take you into a perceptual realm that's different from your waking one, they can provide answers that elude you in your everyday life. Many famous people have used dreams to help them solve problems. Albert Einstein, Thomas Edison, Harry Truman, and Benjamin Franklin were known to "sleep on it" when confronted with a problem or important decision.

One well-known example is Elias Howe, who patented the lock-stitch sewing machine. For ten years Howe had been struggling to perfect his machine. Then one night he dreamt cannibals captured him and told him he would die a horrible death if he didn't solve the problem. As he sat in a large cooking pot, waiting to be boiled alive, he glanced up at their spears and noticed holes near the pointed ends. Howe had his answer. He put the hole near the tip of the needle and the sewing machine was born.

Some researchers, including Michael Newton, PhD, author of *Destiny of Souls*, suggest that spirits or disembodied entities may slip information to you in your dreams. Others believe your subconscious already knows the answer to the conundrum, but the answer hasn't percolated through to your rational mind yet. If you have a dilemma and want help resolving it, write your request on a piece of paper and put it under your pillow at bedtime. Tell yourself you'll receive an answer while you sleep. Ask the Goddess or a favorite deity to assist you. If necessary, repeat the process for a few nights until the solution comes to you.

Healing Dreams

Sometimes dreams suggest cures when we're ill or offer advice about how we can heal ourselves physically and emotionally. They can also illuminate health problems that could develop if we don't take corrective action. Additionally, dreams may tell us that a treatment we're undergoing is right or wrong for us.

If you want your dreams to give you advice about a health situation, use the process described for problem-solving dreams. Also, pay attention to signs and symbols in your dreams that could warn of potential problems. I once dreamed I was driving dangerously fast and wrecked my car. My dream advised that if I didn't stop pushing myself so hard I could damage my health.

Want to help someone else with a health issue? Before you go to bed, hold in your mind an image of the person you wish to help. Ask him or her if it's okay to offer assistance. If you get the go-ahead, envision that person completely healthy, happy, and at peace (don't focus on the ailment or injury). Affirm that while you sleep, you will send healing energy to that person for his or her highest good. You may wish to invite the Goddess, a guide, a guardian, or a deity to aid you. Be confident that the good vibes you project during the dream state will reach your target.

Precognitive Dreams

Sometimes dreams reveal the future. When your perception is loosened during sleep it can range far and wide, even beyond the limitations of time. A dream that lets you see in advance what's coming may help you to prepare yourself or avoid a problem altogether. Some precognitive dreams are laden with poignant images. Others are straightforward and nearly devoid of symbolism. You actually witness an event before it happens in the physical world. For example, three months before his brother died, Mark Twain dreamed of the death and funeral—exactly as it happened, right down to the smallest detail.

The more aware you become of your dreams, the more likely you are to have precognitive dreams and to recognize them when they occur. Often the feeling content of precognitive dreams differs from what you experience during other types of dreams—you may get a sense of heightened clarity, immediacy, or authenticity. Keeping track of your dreams in your grimoire will strengthen your resolve to transcend time and space in order to glimpse the future. Think how useful that could be!

Dreams and Divination

Because dreams erase the boundaries between past, present, and future, you can use this colorful technique to tap the wisdom of your dreams for divination.

- From a sheet of posterboard, cut a dozen or more 4" × 6" rectangles.
- From magazines cut images, words, and/or symbols that represent what you witnessed in one of your dreams.
- Paste the images on one of the posterboard rectangles to create a picture card that depicts the key elements, emotions, actions, etc. in your dream.
- Do the same thing for at least a dozen dreams, until you have at least twelve dream cards. (You don't have to stop at twelve—you can make as many as you like.)
- Use these personal dream cards as you would tarot cards to do readings.
- Record your readings in your book of shadows, along with your interpretations.

Lucid Dreams

In what's known as a lucid dream, you realize you are dreaming. You experience a sense of detachment and clarity as you observe yourself and the action going on in your dream. From this place of clarity, you can guide the dream—like a director controlling the action in a movie. You can transform a nightmare into a sweet dream or make an upsetting scenario turn out the way you want it to. Learning to control your dreams can help you gain better control over situations in your waking life too.

Here's a technique you can try. While you're dreaming, look at your hands. Then give yourself some sort of hand signal, such as pointing or counting on your fingers. This lets you know that you are, indeed, aware and guiding the action. Or, you can say to yourself, "It's only a dream" while you are in the midst of the dream. Once you feel in control, you can guide your dream to help solve problems, peek into the future, journey to other realms, make connections with beings in the spirit world, and more.

Record your dreams in your grimoire. Also note how your experiences in the dream state influenced your waking life. The more you practice lucid dreaming, the better you'll get at taking charge of your dreams and their outcomes.

Herbal Dream Pillow

Crafty witches sometimes sew dream pillows to help them sleep better and/or to inspire meaningful dreams. You can too.

TOOLS AND INGREDIENTS

2 rectangular pieces of blue or purple cotton cloth, about 4" × 6" (or
   whatever size you choose)
Needle and thread
Dried mugwort leaves
Dried lavender blossoms
Pinch of mint
Flaxseeds

The Modern Witchcraft Grimoire

1. Sew the 2 rectangular pieces of cloth together on 3 sides.
2. Turn the cloth inside out and fill with the dried herbs. The mugwort induces psychic dreams and lavender has a calming effect. The touch of mint aids mental clarity.
3. Fill the remainder of the pillow with the flaxseeds.
4. Sew up the fourth side.
5. Sleep with the pillow and allow it to influence your dreams.

Write any significant results in your book of shadows.

Mugwort (*Artemisia vulgaris*), nicknamed cronewort, is considered sacred to the moon goddess Artemis because of the silvery color of the underside of its leaves. Mugwort symbolizes the gifts of vitality and freedom from repression. You can also use it for centering, grounding, and renewing strength. When burned in small bundles, mugwort can enhance psychic visions.

Chapter 19

DEITIES, ANGELS, AND OTHER NONPHYSICAL ENTITIES

Although ordinarily we can't see them, many beings share our world with us. Perhaps you're aware of nonphysical entities around you—you may see or hear them, or simply sense their presence. Some of them reside on earth, others exist in what is often thought of as heaven. These distinctions, however, are a bit misleading, as the various levels of existence aren't really separate—they interact with and permeate one another.

How you choose to view nonphysical beings is up to you. Most witches believe in at least some of these entities, although our conceptions may differ. In the magickal view of the world, all forces—physical and nonphysical—are linked energetically. When you improve your relationships with gods and goddesses, angels, faeries, elementals, and others in the spirit realms, everything in the universe benefits.

THE GOD

Wiccans, as we've already discussed, believe that instead of one Divine Source (as patriarchal religions teach) there are two distinct powers: Goddess and God. We often think of the God as the Goddess's consort and recognize that both feminine and masculine forces are essential for existence. But the concept of dual forces operating in the universe isn't limited to Wiccans. Many cultures speak of both principles existing in and around us. The Chinese refer to these two energies as *yin* (feminine) and *yang* (masculine). Native Americans respect Mother Earth and Father Sky. These two polarities function in tandem to balance one another and create wholeness.

Throughout this book, we've talked about the Goddess. In Chapters 9 and 10, you'll find lists of goddesses, their areas of influence, and how they can assist you in your magick work. Now let's look at some of the aspects, powers, and attributes of the God.

Aspects of the God

Since the beginning of time, cultures around the world have honored a masculine force. The yang energy of the universe has been depicted in various guises and personalities, as individual deities with specific natures, characteristics, and responsibilities. The many faces of the God express qualities associated with the male archetype: strength, virility, daring, leadership skills, logic, protection, knowledge, and courage. The following list includes some of the god figures found in cultures around the world and the attributes connected with them.

GODS OF THE WORLD		
Name	**Culture**	**Attributes**
Adibuddha	Indian	ultimate male essence
Aengus	Irish	youth, love

GODS OF THE WORLD		
Name	**Culture**	**Attributes**
Apollo	Greek	beauty, poetry, music, healing
Bunjil	Australian	vital breath
Ea	Chaldean	magick, wisdom
Ganesh	Indian	strength, perseverance, overcoming obstacles
Green Man	Celtic	fertility, nature, abundance, sexuality
Horus	Egyptian	knowledge, eternal life, protection
Itzamna	Mayan	written communication
Lugh	Celtic	craftsmanship, healing, magick
Mars	Roman	aggression, war, vitality, courage
Mercury	Roman	intelligence, communication, trade, travel
Mithras	Persian	strength, virility, courage, wisdom
Odin	Scandinavian	knowledge, poetry, prophesy
Osiris	Egyptian	vegetation, civilization, learning
Pan	Greek	woodlands, nature, fertility
Shiva	Indian	destruction, transformation
Thoth	Egyptian	knowledge, science, the arts
Tyr	Teutonic	law, athletics
Vishnu	Indian	preservation, stability
Zeus	Greek	authority, justice, abundance, magnanimity

Archetypes transcend nationalities and religions, appearing in similar forms in many different cultures. For example, the Greek god Zeus corresponds to the Roman god Jupiter. You can see overlaps between the Egyptian god Thoth and the Greeks' Hermes. Mars and Mithras, both gods of war, were worshipped by soldiers in Rome and Persia, respectively.

Gaining the God's Assistance

On days when a witch wishes to identify with certain godlike qualities, she or he can ask for help from a deity who embodies those attributes. If you want to ace an exam, you can call on Mercury, Thoth, or Hermes to assist you. If you hope to overcome a formidable challenge or obstacle, ally yourself with the god Ganesh. Regardless of your goal or concern, you'll find a god who can provide the help you need.

In your grimoire, make a list of some gods with whom you feel a particular kinship. Also list some from whom you may seek assistance or think you might like to work with magickally. Then take time to learn all you can about them before you call on them for aid. Study the myths associated with them. Read about their powers and the areas in which they operate. If you are part of a coven or other group of magicians, discuss with them how they've worked with the Divine Masculine. The more you know about a particular god, the more effectively you can use his energy.

Note in your book of shadows which god(s) you called upon to assist your spellwork and why. Describe how you experienced his energy and how he made himself known to you. What transpired during the spell or ritual? What results came about?

Spell to Overcome an Obstacle

When a daunting challenge looms before you, call in some extra muscle to handle the task. Since ancient times, the people of India have drawn upon the strength of the elephant-headed god Ganesh to help them overcome seemingly insurmountable obstacles. You can too.

TOOLS AND INGREDIENTS

An image of an elephant or of Ganesh (for example, a magazine photo or small figurine)

An athame

1. Cast a circle around the area where you will do your spell.

2. Close your eyes and imagine you're in a dark, dense jungle. The vegetation is so thick you can see only a foot or two ahead of you. All sorts of dangers lurk unseen. Your situation seems impossible. You feel trapped and helpless.

3. Suddenly you hear the trumpeting call of an elephant—it's Ganesh coming to your rescue. He rushes toward you and lifts you with his trunk onto his back.

4. Explain to him the nature of your problem. Visualize yourself riding on Ganesh's shoulders as he marches into the jungle, trampling everything in his path.

5. With your athame begin slashing away at the vines and branches in your way (the dense vegetation symbolizes the obstacles facing you). Envision yourself hacking through the obstacles as space opens up before you. Feel Ganesh's strength, lifting you high above your problems.

6. Keep chopping away. You don't have to see all the way to the end, just tackle each obstacle as it presents itself.

7. When you feel ready, climb down from Ganesh's back and thank him for his assistance. You now realize you have the ability to handle whatever challenges arise.

8. Open the circle.

In your grimoire, describe how you felt performing this spell. Note your impressions, emotions, insights, visions, etc. Also write down how this spell and the deity's aid helped you overcome obstacle(s) in your life, and the results you experienced. You might want to paste the picture of Ganesh in your book or carry a small figurine in your pocket to remind you that you have a powerful ally on your side.

PETITIONING DEITIES

How can you get a god or goddess on your side? Many witches believe that divine assistance is always available to you and that the deities gladly offer their guidance, help, and energy to humans to use for positive purposes. Some view divine beings as higher aspects of human consciousness, which can be accessed and activated through magickal means.

If you want to connect with a particular entity, first ask that god or goddess to hear your request and come to your aid. One theory states that deities will not interfere with your own free will—you must ask them sincerely for help.

Honoring Deities

If you aren't accustomed to having a divine being as a partner in your spiritual pursuits, you may wonder how to go about petitioning your favorite god or goddess for assistance. Here are a few suggestions:

- Make an offering to the deity. Burning incense is a popular offering, although you may prefer a method that more specifically corresponds to the nature of the deity whose help you seek. Bacchus, for instance, is extremely fond of wine, so you could set a glass of good Cabernet on your altar and dedicate it to him.
- Place a picture or figurine of the chosen deity on your altar.
- Offer prayers, chants, poems, or songs to the deity.
- Light a candle in honor of the deity you wish to petition.
- Design and perform a ritual to the deity.
- Choose a gemstone for which the deity has an affinity, such as golden topaz for Amaterasu or moonstone for Diana, and place the gem on your altar.
- Plant herbs or flowers in honor of the god or goddess, or set a vase of flowers on your altar. Choose plants that correspond to the deity; asters, for example, are linked with the Greek goddess Astraea.

Which Deity Is the Right One?

Throughout history, people have linked gods and goddesses with certain qualities, skills, and powers, and their unique attributes can help you in your magickal work. If you're doing a spell for a particular purpose—and usually that's the case—your best bet is to request aid from a deity who has a special affinity with your objective.

- In love spells, seek aid from Venus, Aphrodite, Freya, or Aengus.
- For prosperity spells, call upon Lakshmi, Zeus, or the Green Man.
- Ask Brigid, Ceres, or Lugh for assistance with healing spells.

The Modern Witchcraft Grimoire

- If you seek protection, call on Artemis, Tara, or Horus.
- To gain wisdom or inspiration, ask Brigid, Cerridwen, Sophia, Mercury, Odin, or Thoth for help.
- Spells for courage or strength could benefit from the help of Mars, Sekhmet, or Ganesh.

Sometimes all you have to do to enlist a deity's aid is ask. However, you can show your sincerity by placing an image of the god or goddess on your altar, or in another place of honor. If the deity has a holiday associated with him/her, celebrate it. As suggested previously, you could also make an offering to a deity—incense, flowers, gemstones, etc.

Creating Altars to Deities

In addition to your primary altar, you may choose to create another altar and dedicate it to a favorite deity. This could be a more or less permanent altar, if your living circumstances permit, or a temporary one that you set up for a particular ritual and dismantle when you're finished.

- Place a statue, picture, or other image of the deity on the altar.
- If the deity you're petitioning presides over a certain sabbat or season of the year, put emblems of his or her special time on the altar.
- Drape the altar with a cloth in a color that reminds you of the deity: blue-green for water gods and goddesses, such as Neptune, Aphrodite, and Oshun; red, orange, or gold for fiery deities such as Apollo, Brigid, and Pele.
- If the deity has a connection with a certain direction, position the altar there. The archangel Michael, for instance, presides over the south, so an altar to him should occupy a south-facing spot.

You may want to include pictures of your favorite deities in your grimoire. Draw them yourself, or download them from the Internet. How about taking a photo of the altar you create to honor the deity and affixing it in your book of shadows? If you've composed a poem, song, or incantation to the deity, write that down too. What else did you do to petition a god or goddess? How did he or she respond?

The Charge of the Goddess

At some time, nearly every witch has likely experienced the desire to draw the energy of the Goddess or God into herself or himself. For the veteran priestess and priest, invoking the Goddess is often done as a part of ritual known as "drawing down the moon."

In this ritual, the priestess and priest work in tandem, with the priest invoking the great Goddess and the priestess receiving the energy of the Goddess into herself. The priestess then radiates this power outward through the circle. This sacred invocation is not exclusive to female/male working relationships. It is possible to attain divine consciousness on your own—communion with the deities is bestowed directly by the Goddess and not by any other person.

As we discussed in Chapter 1, the American-born folklorist Charles Godfrey Leland published accounts of interviews he said he'd conducted with an Italian strega (sorceress or witch) whose true identity remains unknown. Among the material Leland presented in his 1899 book *Aradia, Gospel of the Witches* was the earliest known version of the "Charge of the Goddess." The strega's particular tradition of Italian witchcraft focuses on the Roman goddess Diana, who gives birth to a daughter, Aradia.

This is perhaps an older tradition of Dianic witchcraft, which is now primarily associated with exclusively female covens. In the past, Dianic witchcraft was more closely connected with the worship of the moon goddess, personified by Diana and Aradia, than with a strictly feminine agenda. In this passage, Diana has instructed Aradia how to craft spells and ward off enemies, and now Aradia imparts her knowledge to others:

"When I shall have departed from this world,
Whenever ye have need of anything,
Once in the month, and when the moon is full,
Ye shall assemble in some desert place,
Or in a forest all together join
To adore the potent spirit of your queen,
My mother, great Diana. She who fain
Would learn all sorcery yet has not won
Its deepest secrets, then my mother will
Teach her, in truth all things as yet unknown.

And ye shall be free from all slavery,
And so shall ye be free in everything;
And as the sign that ye are truly free,
Ye shall be naked in your rites, both men
And women also: this shall last until
The last of your oppressors shall be dead;
And ye shall make the game of Benevento,
Extinguishing the lights, and after that
Shall hold your supper thus."

Following, Leland gave instructions for consecrating the meal, conjuring sacred cakes with wine, salt, and honey, and then forming them into crescent shapes before baking. Consider the age of this verse, and compare it to the more modern versions of the Charge of the Goddess found in other books—you'll see the evolution of the modern charge from its origins in the Aradia text. This evolution is an excellent example of how you can take wisdom that has been handed down over time and make it truly your own.

ANGELS

Virtually every faith speaks of angels in its legends, myths, and religious texts. According to most views, angels are considered cosmic messengers and spiritual guardians. They protect and guide human beings. They also serve as celestial helpers who carry requests between earth and the divine realm—the word "angel" derives from the Greek *angelos*, meaning messenger.

Guardian Angels

Spiritual and magickal traditions present many different conceptions of angels. In general, angels are considered the "good guys" in the universe. The simplest and most common image is that of the guardian angel, a personal celestial guide who may or may not have been human at one time. Your angel hears your prayers, watches over you, and helps you handle challenges in your life.

The Qu'ran tells us, "For every soul, there is a guardian watching it." Both the Old and New Testaments of the Bible regularly mention guardian angels. In the gospel of Matthew, for instance, St. Jerome explains, "Each one has from his birth an angel commissioned to guard it." The Talmud speaks of guardian angels being assigned both to individuals and to nations.

> *"Angels are anthropomorphic winged forms personifying divine will. Possibly evolved from Semitic and Egyptian winged deities, they appear in a number of religions as intermediaries between material and spiritual planes."*
> —Jack Tresidder, *The Complete Dictionary of Symbols*

Because guardian angels are believed to be the first-step intermediaries between humans and the divine realm, you can call upon your angel(s) whenever you need assistance, and feel confident that you'll receive guidance. Here are some ways your guardian angel(s) can help you in your magick work:

- In protection spells, ask your guardian angel(s) to keep you safe and sound in the face of challenges.
- If you're doing a travel spell, invite your angelic guide to accompany you on your journey.
- Want to send a message to the higher realms? Write your request on a slip of paper, and then burn it in your cauldron; as the smoke rises to the heavens it carries your request with it.

Angelic Hierarchies

Another theory proposes the existence of an angelic hierarchy, composed of many types of angels with varying roles and powers. The mystic Dionysius the Areopagite devised a three-tiered system for categorizing the heavenly entities. According to his system, each level contains three groups of angelic beings, each with their own powers and responsibilities.

- In the uppermost tier, the highest order known as seraphim wear red and cluster around the throne of God where they aid creation.
- Beneath them the cherubim, garbed in gold and blue, worship God and keep the Akashic records.
- Thrones, dressed in judges' robes, confer divine justice on those under them.

Below these three rarified orders, we find three more groups of angelic beings at the second level:

- Divine managers known as dominions wear crowns; they direct the other angels and govern the elements.
- Under them, virtues carrying white lilies or red roses work miracles throughout the cosmos.
- The powers, at the bottom of the second tier, fight evil in the universe.

Beings on the lowest tier maintain connections between the spirit world and the manifest one, and convey God's will to earth.

- Princes guide the nations and territories of the material world.
- Archangels aid the forces of nature and oversee the angels.
- At the bottom of the system, just above the level of human beings, angels protect people and convey messages to us from the higher levels.

This system says humans can only communicate with the entities on the lower two levels: angels and archangels. In earlier chapters, we've talked about calling upon the archangels Michael, Raphael, Gabriel, and Uriel through ritual. Guardian angels, it appears, are always with us, willing to lend a helping hand when we need it.

If you choose to work with angels and/or archangels, your encounters can be, well, heavenly! Describe your experiences in your grimoire. How did you contact and interact with the deities? Which deities appeared to you? Did you sense their immediate presence? What did you see, hear, feel, smell, intuit? How did their assistance enhance your magick work, your spiritual growth, and/or other areas of your life?

ELEMENTALS

Many beings that ordinarily remain unseen live side by side with us in the physical world. Folklore and faery tales frequently refer to these entities. Seafaring legends, for instance, often mention mermaids, and leprechauns appear with regularity in Irish lore. Most people discount these creatures as pure fantasy, but witches recognize them as elementals.

Sometimes called nature spirits, these nonphysical beings could be considered ambassadors for the four elements—fire, earth, water, and air—hence their name. Each resides within its element and possesses unique qualities characteristic of the element from which it harkens. If you befriend them, elementals will serve as devoted helpers and eagerly assist you in performing magick spells. But be aware: elementals can be tricksters, so approach them with care.

Salamanders

These fire spirits are naturally drawn to people who exhibit courage, creativity, passion, and initiative. When you do spells that involve action, inspiration, or vitality, salamanders can serve as liaisons, marshaling the forces of the fire element to assist you. Need an infusion of inspiration to complete your novel or a boost of stamina to win an important athletic event? Call upon these lively beings for help.

Paracelsus, the sixteenth-century philosopher, physician, and occultist, described them as looking like balls of fire or flaming tongues flashing across the landscape. Sometimes salamanders are depicted as lizard-like in shape. The ancients said salamanders hailed from the southern regions and brought nature's heat, without which warm-blooded creatures could not exist.

Gnomes

Gnomes are earth spirits. Sometimes called trolls, elves, dwarfs, or leprechauns, these practical, no-nonsense creatures may appear a bit gruff. However, they possess a wonderful appreciation for material things and can be valuable aides when you're doing prosperity spells. They have power over the plant and mineral kingdoms, so when you do magick with botanicals or gemstones, you're also working with the gnomes.

Legends say gnomes reside in caves or underground, where they guard hidden treasure. The ancient Greeks believed earth spirits known as hamadryads lived in trees, and if the tree was cut down the spirit died too. We find many varying depictions of gnomes in folklore, though often they're described as resembling small, sturdy humans, sometimes with coarse hair or fur—rather like Snow White's dwarfs—who come from the northern regions.

Undines (or Ondines)

Mermaids are the most famous of these water spirits. These beautiful but sometimes capricious beings are drawn to emotional situations and relate best to sensitive, intuitive, and artistic people. Invite these elementals to assist you when you're doing love spells.

Usually considered female, undines live in oceans, rivers, lakes, waterfalls, marshes, even fountains. Legends refer to them by many names, including naiads, water sprites, sea maidens, and selkies. Sometimes they're depicted as diminutive blue-green creatures who live under lily pads; other myths describe them as looking like incredibly lovely women with long hair and fishtails or scales, perhaps riding on the backs of dolphins. Undines care for the waterways of the world and all the marine life therein. (See my book *Mermaids: The Myths, Legends, & Lore* for information about undines throughout history.)

Sylphs

These air spirits gravitate to intelligent, literary, and analytical people. Their specialty is communication—call on them when you need help with negotiating contracts, handling legal issues, or managing other concerns that involve communication. Sylphs can also assist you in test-taking, public speaking, or writing.

As you might suspect, sylphs reside in the air. Legends depict them as delicate flying creatures who flit rapidly from place to place, riding the winds of the world. The tiny winged beings usually referred to as faeries are most likely sylphs. Some reports describe them as shimmering lights, rather like fireflies.

Thank Your Elemental Helpers

Make sure to treat elementals with consideration and respect—if they don't like you, they might play tricks on you. Always remember to thank the elementals that assist you in your spellworking and offer them small gifts to show your appreciation.

- Salamanders like candles and incense. Burn these to honor your fiery helpers.
- Gnomes adore jewelry and crystals. Bury a token in the ground as a way of saying "Thanks."
- Undines are fond of perfume. Pour a few drops of essential oil in a stream, lake, or other body of water.
- Sylphs enjoy flowers. Place fresh blossoms on your altar or lay them in a sacred spot outdoors as an offering.

Salamander Courage Spell

When you encounter setbacks, disappointments, or frustrating circumstances, ask the fire elementals to bolster your vitality, confidence, and resolve. Perform this spell on Tuesday or when the sun and/or moon is in Aries, Leo, or Sagittarius.

TOOLS AND INGREDIENTS
9 small red votive candles
Matches or a lighter
A magick wand

1. Arrange the candles in a circle around you, in a place where you can safely leave them to burn down completely.
2. Beginning in the east, light the candles one at a time as you move in a clockwise direction to cast the circle.
3. When all the candles are burning, stand in the center of the circle and face south.
4. Call out to the salamanders and tell them you have lit these 9 candles in their honor. Explain your situation and request their assistance, by chanting the following incantation aloud:

The Modern Witchcraft Grimoire

"Beings of fire
Shining so bright
Fuel my desire
Increase my might.
Help me be strong
All the day long
So in each deed
I'll surely succeed."

5. You may notice faint flickerings of light (other than the candles) in the room or sense the energy around you quickening. Perhaps you'll feel an excitement in the air. It might even seem a bit warmer. That means the salamanders are present and willing to work with you.

6. Take up your magick wand and point it toward the south. Your movements should be strong and purposeful, not wimpy. Envision yourself drawing powerful energy in though the tip of your wand. You might even see the wand glow or feel it tingle.

7. Now turn the wand and aim it at yourself. Sense the energy you've attracted from the south—the region where the salamanders reside— flowing from the wand into your body. Feel yourself growing more powerful, more confident, more alive.

8. Continue using your wand to pull energy and courage from the south in this manner for as long as you like. Remain in the center of the circle until all the candles have burned down completely.

9. Thank the salamanders for their assistance and open the circle, feeling renewed with vitality and confidence.

Elemental Exercises

To increase your awareness and ability to work with the elements, practice these exercises:

- Light a candle and focus your attention on the flame. See if you can make the flame move or flicker more brightly (without blowing or otherwise physically affecting it).

- Hold a crystal in your hand and close your eyes. Try to feel the crystal vibrating, pulsing, or otherwise resonating with energy.
- Sit beside a body of water. Cast your gaze slightly above the surface of the water and allow your focus to soften. Can you see energy swirling just above the water?
- Stand in a private spot outdoors, with your arms stretched out at your sides. Slowly bring your arms together and cross them in front of you, then open them again. Do this three times to raise the wind.

If you choose to work with spiritual beings, record your experiences in your grimoire. Who did you call to and why? What did you see, sense, hear, feel, smell, intuit? What impact did the entities have on your magick? What powers did they impart to you? Will you work with them in the future, and how?

Chapter 20

LOOKING TOWARD THE FUTURE

Once you've embarked on a magickal path, you will probably continue following it for the rest of your life. As is often said, magick isn't something you do, it's something you are. Having peeled away the veil of secrecy and glimpsed the mysteries within, you'll never see things as you did before. Now that you've become familiar with the hidden dimensions of the natural world, embraced the mystical forces that underpin our universe, and felt the power of the Goddess's touch, you can never go back to ordinary thinking.

No matter how long you study and practice the art of the Craft, you'll never know it all. You could be at it your entire adult life and still barely scratch the surface. It's like any other subject: The deeper you dig, the more you discover. Around each corner lies something new and awe-inspiring! Your grimoire is the place to describe your mystical discoveries, your experiences in the magickal realm, and anything else that you feel plays a part in your spiritual journey.

WORKING WITH OTHER WITCHES

If you've been a solitary witch until now, perhaps you're wondering what it might be like to work with other people who share your views. Maybe you've considered studying with a teacher who can help you advance more quickly and steer you away from some pitfalls along the way. Perhaps you know someone else who is following the Wiccan Way and you think the two of you could combine your talents to mutual advantage. Or you might want to join a coven, a group of like-minded folks with whom you can celebrate the sabbats and engage in magick and ritual practices.

It's nice to have "kinfolk" with whom you can share ideas and information. Also, you can learn from other people and they can learn from you, thereby expanding everyone's knowledge. In a world that still doesn't completely accept witches and magick, you may long for a community where you can feel safe, accepted, and valued. If you decide you want to share your magickal path with other people, do your homework in order to find the right folks for you to befriend. Each witch and each coven is unique, and it's important that your energies, beliefs, goals, etc. are compatible.

Some covens hold open circles and allow people outside their immediate membership to participate in some events or gatherings— for example, esbat rituals. That could be a good way to start exploring your options. Check out online resources, such as The Witches' Voice at *www.witchvox.com* to learn about possibilities in your area. My book *The Modern Guide to Witchcraft* offers more information about finding and joining a coven or other group of magick workers.

If you do start practicing with other people, you'll undoubtedly make many discoveries—about the Craft and about yourself. Doors will open into areas where you haven't ventured before. Record your findings in your grimoire. What did you experience when working magick with other people? How did you sense their energies and yours intermingling? Was the interaction uplifting, invigorating, peaceful,

The Modern Witchcraft Grimoire

edgy, uncomfortable? Did a ritual or spell seem to have more power when you performed it with others? Note any impressions, insights, emotions, visions, sensations, etc. that seem relevant.

If you continue working with the same people over a period, you'll probably want to keep a running account of how you evolve as a group. Describe ways in which you support and enhance one another's workings, how you grow as a result of the group's input, challenges that arise within the group and how you solve them, and so on. In keeping with the tradition of secrecy, you may wish to mention other people by their Craft names, initials only, or pseudonyms to protect their identities should your grimoire fall into the hands of someone you don't want to know your business.

SHARING SPELLS AND SECRETS

As mentioned earlier, witches have often copied material from their teachers' grimoires. A High Priestess or Priest might make available some portions of her or his book to a chosen few within a small circle, as Gerald Gardner did in his Bricket Wood coven. In this way, ancient spells and incantations have been passed down through the centuries into the present day. This practice allows us to preserve witchcraft's rich heritage and observe its evolution over time. Everyone's experiences contribute to the development of the whole. Each witch is a torchbearer whose flame, when joined with others', lights up the world.

You may decide you want to let a magickal partner and/or the other members of your circle read what you write in your grimoire. Likewise, others in your group may give you permission to study their books. If you cast spells together, it can be useful to discuss what you did and what transpired. What went right and what went wrong? How might you do things differently in the future?

Depending on your personal perspective and preferences, you may choose to share your knowledge on a larger scale, as I do by writing books. A quick online search will reveal an amazing amount of information about all aspects of witchcraft, spellcasting, magick, the witchy life, and the occult in general. Maybe you'd like to contribute to an existing blog or even start one of your own. Now that Wicca and Neopaganism are becoming more accepted in many societies, lots of witches feel a desire to spread the word. Perhaps you will too.

Whether you decide to keep the contents of your grimoire private or share your experiences with other people is entirely up to you. So is the choice whether to hand down your knowledge to those who come after you or to have your confidences destroyed when you pass into the Summerland. If it is your wish, no one but you need know the secrets you keep in your book of shadows.

MORE THAN A BOOK

By now you've come to look upon your grimoire as more than just another tool. Few equally powerful methods of attaining self-awareness can be used so easily every day. This repository of your most private thoughts, spells, chants, musings, and meditations probably seems more like a friend than a book.

As you continue to learn, grow, and change, so will what you write in your grimoire. Looking back over earlier entries will reveal the arc of your journey and inspire you to keep going. Keeping your book of shadows will remind you of who you are during challenges and times of doubt. You also honor the precious moments in life by recording them. And, you preserve treasured memories for years to come.

Be passionate about yourself, even as you change, even in the face of the unknown. By writing your story, you may also become an inspiration for others. May your book of shadows deepen your knowledge of yourself, your aspirations, your dreams, and your loves. May it enrich your connection with the Goddess. May it comfort you in times of darkness and bring you joy in times of light. May it keep your secrets as would a trusted friend, protect the stories of your lifetime, and hold your personal mythology securely. Merry meet, and merry part, and merry meet again. Blessed be.

The Modern Witchcraft Grimoire

INDEX

Cancer, 109, 114, 126
Candle Spell for Prosperity, 236–37
Candles
anointing, 215–16
burning, 216
caution with, 216
dressing, 215–16
engraving, 214–15
essential oils for, 215–16
for influence, 214
lighting darkness, 213
for prosperity, 236–37
safety tips, 216
scrying with, 216–17
spells with, 213–14
symbols for, 214–15
wax poppets, 218
Capricorn, 111–12, 116, 127
Career spells, 142
Cauldrons, 208
Celestial charts, 113
Celestial influences, 54
"Celtic Blessing," 51
Chakras
color and, 165
gemstones and, 224–27
healing and, 224
magick and, 209
Chalice
charging, 207–8
choosing, 207
consecrating, 207–8
creating, 207
purpose of, 206–7
Chanting, 148–49
Charms, 192–96
Circle-casting

calling quarters, 154–56, 176
four elements technique, 176–77
love spells and, 135–36
opening circle, 177–78
with pentagrams, 175–76
steps for, 174–75
summoning forces, 154–56, 176
with sword, 175
Color
chakra colors, 165
elements and, 164–65
power of, 162–65, 212
symbolism of, 163–64
Communication oil, 128
Cords/ribbons, 209
Courage Spell, 270–71
Creative visualization, 162
Crystal balls, 209
Crystals, 209

Daily magick, 81–84
Dancing, 179–81
Dates, 237–41
Dawn, realm of, 154–56
Daybooks, 43
Deities. *See also* Goddesses; Gods
altars for, 263
animals as, 242
connecting with, 261–62
divine assistance from, 133–35
evoking, 156–58
honoring, 262

The Modern Witchcraft Grimoire

ABOUT THE AUTHOR

Skye Alexander is the award-winning author of more than thirty fiction and nonfiction books, including *The Modern Guide to Witchcraft*, *The Modern Witchcraft Spell Book*, *The Everything® Wicca & Witchcraft Book*, *The Everything® Spells & Charms Book*, *Naughty Spells/Nice Spells*, *Good Spells for Bad Days*, and *The Everything® Tarot Book*. Her stories have been published in anthologies internationally, and her work has been translated into more than a dozen languages. The Discovery Channel featured her in the TV special *Secret Stonehenge* doing a ritual at Stonehenge. She divides her time between Texas and Massachusetts. Visit her at *www.skyealexander.com*.

—

The
MODERN
GUIDE TO
Witchcraft

The

MODERN
⊷ GUIDE TO ⊷
Witchcraft

Your Complete Guide to

WITCHES, COVENS,
& SPELLS

Skye Alexander

Adams Media
New York   London   Toronto   Sydney   New Delhi

Adams Media
An Imprint of Simon & Schuster, Inc.
100 Technology Center Drive
Stoughton, MA 02072

Copyright © 2014 by Simon & Schuster, Inc.

For information about special discounts for bulk purchases, please contact Simon & Schuster Special Sales at 1-866-506-1949 or business@simonand-schuster.com.

The Simon & Schuster Speakers Bureau can bring authors to your live event. For more information or to book an event contact the Simon & Schuster Speakers Bureau at 1-866-248-3049 or visit our website at www.simonspeakers.com.

Manufactured in China

10 9 8 7 6 5 4 3 2 1

Library of Congress Cataloging-in-Publication Data has been applied for.

ISBN 978-1-4405-8002-4
ISBN 978-1-4405-8003-1 (ebook)

To Ron, always

Acknowledgments

I wish to thank my editors Tom Hardej and Peter Archer, and all the other talented folks at Adams Media for making this book possible.

CONTENTS

SO YOU WANT TO BE A WITCH

You've picked up this book because you're interested in witches. You wonder about who they are and what they believe. You know being a witch has something to do with finding a deeper connection to nature and to the entire cosmos. With finding an inner power and beauty that can help you accomplish what you want in life. In the back of your mind flits the image of an ugly old woman dressed in black, riding a broomstick, but you know that's wrong—and you want to find out more.

What does it mean to be a witch?

Witches come in all sizes, ages, colors, and personalities. They're doctors, computer programmers, teachers, landscapers, bartenders, and flight attendants. The person who cuts your hair or repairs your car might be a witch. Witches can be male or female—no, a male witch is *not* a warlock, and he might get angry if you call him that, for good reason. *Warlock* comes from an Old English word meaning "oath breaker" or "liar."

The simple fact that you're reading this book suggests that you think you, too, have witch potential. Guess what? You do. And with a little training, you can uncover your magickal power and learn to use it to shape your destiny.

WHY IS WITCHCRAFT GAINING POPULARITY TODAY?

Witchcraft resonates with us because it speaks to some key issues of today: respect for the environment, gender equality, and overcoming religious biases and narrow-minded thinking. It also encourages those who follow this path to discover and develop their own, unique powers so they can take charge of their lives and be everything they choose to be.

In general, most witches seek to improve themselves and humankind as a whole, and to live in harmony with the universe. This means working for the greater good—often through the use of magick—and harming none. It also means taking responsibility for your thoughts, words, and deeds because everything you do affects everything else.

Once you learn to harness your natural talents as a witch, you'll discover that a whole new world of possibilities exists. You'll be able to use what's known as the Law of Attraction to improve your financial situation, your relationships, your health, and your overall well-being. You'll also have the power to help others. And, you'll gain a greater sense of your place in the universe.

Magick won't help you finish a project for school or work, or make you taller, or fix a flat tire. However, it can strengthen your concentration and mental receptivity, make you more attractive to other people, or draw someone to you who can repair that flat.

It's a good idea to take it slow in the beginning—just as you would if you were training for a marathon. That way you'll have fun and avoid setbacks.

WHAT YOU'LL LEARN FROM THIS BOOK

We're all born magickal beings. As children we know this, but as we grow up we forget our true nature. We listen to other people whose limited views cause us to doubt our innate powers, and we get caught up in the stresses of everyday life. This book shows you how to reconnect with the magick in you. As you read these pages, you'll learn to pay attention to your intuition and let it guide you. You'll gain a greater appreciation and awareness of the natural world—the cycles of the moon, the energies of the seasons, your links with the animals, birds, and other creatures who share this planet with you. You'll also discover how to incorporate nature's tools—herbs and flowers, crystals and gemstones, and more—into your magickal workings.

You'll come to realize that witchcraft and magick aren't "hocus pocus." They are your birthright. They already exist deep within you. You already have the power to tap into the energies of the natural world and the cosmos; you just need to recognize that power and learn to direct it. That's what this book is about: reconnecting with your magickal self.

True magick lies in developing your inner potential and spirituality. This book is intended to help you on that journey toward getting in touch with nature, with the Divine, and with your own innate abilities—because ultimately, that's the real source of witchcraft.

PART I

Welcome TO THE WONDERFUL WORLD of WITCHCRAFT

Chapter 1

WHAT IS WITCHCRAFT?

Snow White, Cinderella, The Wizard of Oz, Alice in Wonderland, Beauty and the Beast, Peter Pan, Star Wars. Most of us first discovered wizards and witches, spells and potions, and the never-ending struggle between good and evil through these stories. Fairy tales showed us a world filled with magick—one where inanimate objects like mirrors, stones, and gems can have special powers; animals can talk; plants can think; and with a sprinkling of dust, kids can fly.

Then we grew up and forgot about magick. Our lives became a little less rich and our imaginations started to shrivel as we got mired in the mundane details of our daily lives. But every now and then, we recapture some of that early magick through books and movies like *ET*, *Lord of the Rings*, and *Harry Potter*. We find ourselves fascinated once again by the supernatural world and eager to reawaken the magick within us.

COMMON MISCONCEPTIONS ABOUT WITCHES

Before we go any further, let's get rid of those ridiculous ideas some people still hold about witches. Misconceptions about witches come from ignorance and fear. For centuries, mainstream religions have encouraged negative images about witches—and during a period known as "The Burning Times" these false ideas led to the deaths of countless innocent people in Europe and the New World. In recent times, the media continue to present a distorted picture of witches and magick, further confusing the issue. For the record:

- Witches do not steal or eat babies—this idea comes from old folklore, and fairies were often blamed for doing the same thing.
- Witches are not Satanists who sell their souls to the devil in return for special powers. Lots of witches don't even believe in Satan—he's a Christian conception.
- Witches don't ride brooms—they get around in cars, trains, and airplanes just like everyone else. (You might see a bumper sticker that says, "I'm driving this car because my broom's in the shop" but that's just a joke.)
- Witches prefer pizza over eye of newt any day.
- Witches don't inherit magickal powers from mysterious ancestors, although if Grandma was a witch and trained you in the Craft from childhood, you'll have a head start on other wannabe witches.
- Not all witches possess remarkable psychic powers, nor do they have the gift of prophecy. Some psychics may be witches, and many witches develop their intuition through practice. But the truth is, everyone has psychic ability, including you.
- Witches don't consort with or battle demons, vampires, zombies, or other monsters—they have better things to do.
- Not all witches worship ancient gods and goddesses—some don't believe in any type of deity.
- Witches aren't immortal; they live ordinary lifespans just like other humans.
- Witches aren't ugly old hags, they can be young and incredibly beautiful, but most of them are just average people like you and me.
- Witches don't engage in rivalries and conflicts with other magickal practitioners. The witches in Salem, Massachusetts, for example, don't have a long-standing rivalry with New Orleans's voodoo priestesses. Trust me on this. I've been a witch for twenty-five years and lived in Salem for eight—and I get along with people from New Orleans just fine.

If you choose to become a witch, you'll have to throw out all the silly and sensational things you've seen, heard, and read about witchcraft. At least for the time being, you'll have to live with being constantly offended by the ignorance of people who don't (or won't) understand witchcraft. Just put on your magick, protective shield and get on with practicing the real deal.

Wizards, Sorcerers, and Magicians

The words wizard and sorcerer can be used for either a man or a woman. Wizard derives from a term meaning "wise," and sorcerer means "witch" or "diviner." The word magician is also appropriate for both sexes and for witches of all stripes. Depending on the cultural setting, the term magician came to describe people adept in astrology, sorcery, divination, spellcasting, or other magickal arts.

In this book, we'll use some terms repeatedly. Let's clarify a few of them in order to avoid confusion:

- A witch is someone who uses his or her power along with the natural laws of the universe to shape reality in accordance with his/her purposes.
- Witchcraft is the practice of manipulating energy through various means to produce a desired result.
- Magick is the transformation that occurs when a witch/magician bends or shapes energy using paranormal techniques. The "k" at the end of the word distinguishes it from magic tricks and stage illusion (or sleight of hand).

As we go along, you'll see that witches follow any number of paths and use lots of different methods in the practice of their craft. They also perform many types of magick for a variety of reasons. As you explore the art of the witch and learn to use your own magickal ability, you'll discover what suits you best and what direction you wish to take in your own journey.

WITCHCRAFT AND RELIGION

Like people from other walks of life, witches share some concepts and disagree on others—we'll discuss some of these as we go along. Their ideas may be influenced by their cultural traditions and backgrounds, personal life experiences, or individual temperaments. That's okay. You don't have to subscribe to any particular belief system or set of rules to be a witch.

In the past, many witches learned their craft as part of a family tradition in which they were carefully trained, just as other people might learn carpentry or masonry. Villages had "cunning folk" to whom people turned for all kinds of help, from encouraging crops to grow to fixing a broken heart. Healing made up a large part of the witch's work, and many witches were knowledgeable herbalists and midwives. In exchange for such services, the witch might receive a chicken, a measure of grain, or other necessities.

Religious concepts weren't linked with the practice of witchcraft itself, though individual witches often embraced the beliefs of their families or culture. That's still true today. If you belong to a certain religion or are on a specific spiritual path, you needn't give it up to become a witch. In fact, you may choose to incorporate the ideas of your faith into your magickal practice. If you don't hold to any belief system at all, that's fine too. Witches can follow any religion or none. However, the lack of rules, dogma, or religious affiliation does not mean witches lack ethics.

Wicca and Witchcraft

People sometimes confuse the terms *witch* and *Wicca*. Witchcraft is a methodology, a skill, a way of working with energy to produce a result. Wicca is a spiritual philosophy, with its own code of ethics, concepts, rituals, deities, etc. Yes, many witches in the West today consider themselves Wiccan, and Wiccans generally practice witchcraft, but witches are not necessarily Wiccan.

Other Worlds of Existence

Many witches accept that one or more realms beyond our earth exist and that nonphysical beings share the cosmos with us. Some honor certain gods or goddesses, and we'll take a look at these in Chapter 6. Other witches converse with angels, fairies, and nature spirits. Still others believe that everything on earth—animals, plants, stones—possesses a divine essence or soul. But witches do not need to believe in divine beings in order to perform their work, just as computer programmers, electricians, and dental hygienists don't have to be members of a particular faith to do their jobs.

Life after Death and Reincarnation

The cycle of birth–life–death is obvious to all of us, but for many witches the cycle does not stop there. Instead of life ending when the body dies, they believe an individual's soul, spirit, or personal energy travels to a realm beyond the physical one and will eventually be reborn in another body in another time and place. Many of them view earth as a "school" and believe we come here as human beings to learn. This cycle continues until the soul has worked through all the lessons it set out to learn. Having completed the cycle, the soul retires to a place of joy and regeneration.

Of course, this idea isn't unique to witches. Christians, Muslims, and people of many other faiths believe our souls continue on after our bodies die, and Hindus have believed in reincarnation for thousands of years.

Where Do Witches Go When They Die?

Christianity has its heaven. Buddhism has nirvana. Where do witches go when they die? Many Wiccans believe that their souls go to the Summerland, a resting place before reincarnation into new bodies, in an ongoing cycle of birth, life, death, and rebirth.

THE WITCH'S CONNECTION WITH NATURE

Despite their differences and individual ways of practicing their craft, modern witches share some common ground. One of these is a respect for nature. This involves honoring the earth, attuning themselves to her cycles and seasons, and tapping natural forces in magickal workings.

Like shamans, witches see the earth as a living, breathing entity, their home to honor and protect, not a place to conquer and control. Witches regard the earth, its creatures, and everything that exists on our planet as teachers and part of the divine plan. From the witch's perspective, the planet itself and every living thing in this world has a spirit, a unique energy pattern. As a result, witches tend to think globally, mindful of nature and the cosmos.

Living in Harmony with the Earth

Witches celebrate life, and without our beautiful planet life as we know it could not exist. Therefore, witches attempt to establish a dialogue with Mother Nature. Yes, some of them may actually talk to trees, birds, animals, and stones, but more than that they try to observe and listen in order to understand their place in the natural order of things. Witches realize that we are dependent on the earth and therefore it makes sense to engage in practices that enrich both ourselves and the earth. "It's sacred ground we walk upon with every step we take," some witches sing. They seek to live in harmony with all of nature and to balance energies that have gone askew in our technology-driven society.

We often refer to our planet as Mother Earth, and indeed she is mother to us all. In a sense, that makes everyone and everything on earth part of a huge, extended family. When you know that you are a part of a greater whole it becomes more difficult to act against that whole. To do so would be counterproductive and would harm your kin, your friends, and yourself. Witches try to move gently, to respect all life, and to honor the sacredness in all things and in each other. If we can do this, we can heal the earth and the earth will heal us.

Green witches, in particular, devote themselves to this path. (You'll find out more about this in Chapter 7.) Some witches may work to protect endangered lands and wildlife, feeling that the loss of these would be a crime against Gaia (one name for the earth's spirit; in Greek mythology, goddess of the earth). Others donate money or time to ecological causes, and they often send out positive energy through spells and rituals. Later on, you'll learn more about how to do your part to create greater health, peace, and well-being in your own part of the world and beyond.

The Modern Guide to Witchcraft

Signs and Omens in Nature

A rock, a flower, an herb, a tree, or an animal may hold special meaning for a witch, depending on when and where it appears and what's going on in her life at the time. For example, if a wild rose suddenly blossoms in her yard, she might take it as a positive omen of love growing in the home. A clever witch will take this one step further: She'll thank nature for its gift, dry some of those petals, and turn this little treasure into love-inspiring incense. In this manner, a witch may find herself re-inspired by a childlike wonder toward the planet and the small things that we often overlook in our busy lives.

Natural Magick

If you are serious about being a witch and doing magick, you'll need to get in touch with the natural world around you—it has much to teach you and many gifts to offer you. Today, most of us are more familiar with computers and smartphones, offices and shopping malls sealed against the weather, than we are with the sight of crops growing in the fields, the sound of streams rippling over rocks, or the scent of moist leaves on the forest floor.

Go for a walk outdoors. Reconnect with the feeling of the wind blowing through your hair. Listen to the birds that live in a tree in your yard. Watch the sunset. Take time to smell the flowers that bloom in the park during the summer. The natural world is just as natural as it ever was, except there's less of it than there was twenty-five years ago—and most of us don't make a point of enjoying it often enough.

As you begin to rediscover the natural rhythms around you, you'll also start to notice how they affect the flow of your inner life. When you become accustomed to doing this, you'll find that you feel more in sync with everything around you, and with yourself. You may not be able to align your life with the changing seasons the way our ancestors did—nor is it really necessary. However, expanding your awareness of the cycles of the earth and the cosmos will put you in touch with powerful energies beyond your own immediate skills and enable you to do magick more effectively. In later chapters, we'll talk more about tapping into the magick of the natural world around you. You'll learn to make potions, conduct rituals, and cast spells for a happier, healthier, more fulfilling life.

GOOD WITCH, BAD WITCH: WHICH IS WHICH?

Despite the ugly face that religions have tried to put on witches, historically most have been concerned with helping individuals and communities. As we've already said, fear and misunderstanding underlie the foolish ideas many people hold about witches. Once you get to know them, witches are pretty much like everyone else; they just see the world a little differently.

Are there "bad" witches who use their knowledge and power for personal gain and ill will? Yes, of course, just as there are "bad" Christians, "bad" Muslims, and so on. Witches are people. If you shake any figurative tree hard enough, a couple rotten apples are likely to fall off. That's just human nature. The good news is that these rotten apples are the exception, not the rule.

Witchcraft and Ethics

Just like everyone else, witches confront issues that require them to make ethical choices. For instance, should magick be used as a weapon, even if it's only to fight back? Should you use magick to get what you want, even if that means you put someone else at a disadvantage? And where do you draw the line between white and black magick?

Some witches may not concern themselves with the ethical results of a spell or ritual—what counts is that the spell works. With a spell, you're attempting to stack the odds in your favor—or in another person's favor, if the spell is for someone else. You're attempting to influence something in the future. We all do this constantly, of course, in various ways, but when a witch casts a spell she brings her full conscious and creative awareness to the process.

Wiccans and some other witches believe that magick has a boomerang effect: Whatever you do comes back to you. If you do a spell that hurts someone else, you'll hurt yourself in the process or attract someone to you who will cause you harm. For that reason, witches often follow a version of the Golden Rule when doing spells: Be kind to others and be kind to yourself.

Magicians recognize that even though the human mind and spirit have unlimited potential, we can't possibly foresee all the possible outcomes of a spell. Human beings are not omniscient, and sometimes even good intentions lead to terrible results. Just to be on the safe side, you might want to end a spell or ritual with a phrase such as "This is done for the greatest good of all and may it harm none." In essence, this turns over responsibility for the outcome to higher (and wiser) powers who have a better understanding of how to bring about the best possible outcome.

What If Someone Important to You Is Opposed to Witchcraft?

Arguing about it is the worst thing to do. You're not going to change anyone's opinions about spells or anything else. Your best bet is to follow your practice in private. If possible, step back from the situation and try to look at the other person as a teacher. What lesson can you learn from this opposition?

Your Personal Code

Every magickal tradition, from the Druids to Wicca to Santería, has its own code—principles that guide the practitioner, boundaries that she won't cross, a core set of beliefs that permeate everything she does. These core beliefs define an individual's magickal practice. In Wicca, for instance, the primary principle is to harm nothing and no one.

But people also develop their own personal codes. Have you defined yours? As previously noted, cultural differences play a part in sculpting a particular individual's beliefs. In the end, however, each of us must refine our own codes as we evolve from children to adults. What's right for one person might not be okay for another. At the heart of any belief system lies a code by which you live your life, and it may not have any connection to what other people consider good and bad.

Following your own truth will become ever more important as you develop your magickal ability and grow more adept at using your powers. Each witch relies on her inner voice (or conscience, if you will) in determining how she wields magick. There is no cut-and-dried answer to whether anyone is a good or a bad witch.

As a beginner to the wonderful world of witchcraft, you will learn something new every day and experience new sensations and feelings as you explore your newfound path. Some may surprise you, some will challenge you, and lots will fascinate and excite you. One thing you can be sure of now that you've started down this road: You'll never be quite the same again.

Chapter 2

MAGICK AND HOW IT CAN HELP YOU

Have you ever wondered why some days you seem to breeze through life, but on other days nothing goes right? Why it is that when things start sliding downhill, they seem to go from bad to worse? How can you keep the good times rolling and prevent the bad ones from getting a foothold? Is there a way to turn your luck around?

Absolutely! That's what magick spells are for—to give you power over your destiny. Rather than being a victim of circumstances beyond your control, with magick you control the circumstances. Once you start viewing the world from a magickal perspective, you'll be able to see beyond everyday frustrations, disappointments, and aggravations. You'll maneuver around the obstacles that pop up in your path. It's similar to what athletes call being "in the zone."

Considering all the curves life throws us, it only makes sense to use whatever tools are available to give yourself an advantage. Magick spells are just that: tools to help you avoid pitfalls and attract blessings. For thousands of years people have been doing magick. You can, too, and once you start doing spells, you'll never want to stop!

Perhaps you're skeptical. You may be wondering, what's this magick stuff all about anyway? More important, can it really help me? The answer is *yes*. If you didn't believe in magick (at least a little bit), you wouldn't be reading this book.

YOU'RE ALREADY A MAGICIAN

You may not realize it yet, but you're already a magician. You've already done lots of magick spells without even knowing it. Now you're going to learn how to perform magick purposefully, to turn your luck around. Once you discover the secret, you'll be able to chart your own destiny, avoiding the pitfalls and setbacks that seemed inevitable before.

The word "magician" derives from the Latin *magi* meaning wise men or women (singular *magus*). Remember the wise men in the Christmas story? They were also called *magi*, or magicians, and they followed a star they'd seen that foretold of Jesus' birth, which suggests they knew astrology, too.

Every culture, stretching back long before the advent of written history, has had its magicians: medicine men, cunning folk, kahunas, Druids, witches, and shamans. By choosing a magickal path, you are following in the footsteps of ancient seers and healers who knew how to shape the forces of the universe with their intentions.

Simply put, magick is the act of consciously creating circumstances using methods that defy scientific logic. The notorious British magician Aleister Crowley said, "Every intentional act is a Magickal Act." Whenever you form an objective in your mind, then fuel it with willpower, you're doing magick.

TEN GOOD THINGS MAGICK CAN DO FOR YOU

Before we get into *how*, let's consider *why* learning to do magick is worth your time and effort. Here are ten ways magick can help to make your life better. It can:

1. Improve your love life
2. Attract prosperity
3. Keep you and your loved ones safe from harm
4. Enhance your health
5. Protect your home and personal property
6. Open up new career opportunities

7. Give you more control over your life
8. Improve interactions with family, friends, and coworkers
9. Ward off problems and enemies
10. Strengthen your intuition and psychic skills

People who don't understand magick have made it seem weird or evil, and Hollywood sensationalizes it to the point of absurdity. Actually, there's nothing scary, strange, or silly about magick—it's a natural ability you were born with, a talent you can develop just like musical or mathematical talent. All it takes is desire, a little training, and practice.

THE POWER BEHIND MAGICK

Fortunately, you don't really need any special tools to practice witchcraft. Yes, witches frequently do use a variety of tools to enhance their magickal workings—you'll learn about these later. The tools, however, aren't the source of power, the witch is. The truth is, magick is all in the mind—mostly the tools just help you to stay focused.

Thinking Makes It So

In the movie *What Dreams May Come*, the character played by Robin Williams dies and then wakes up in the afterlife. The place looks, smells, tastes, and feels more or less like the so-called real world. But he quickly learns that in this place, whatever he thinks or desires manifests instantly. All of it is a construct of consciousness.

Magick works in the same way. What you think is what you get. The manifestation may not be immediate—although it can be. If your belief and your intent are strong enough, if you bring passion to your spell, and if you can focus your energy clearly toward a specific goal, then you have a good chance of achieving what you want.

Knowing exactly what you want to accomplish and stating your intention with absolute clarity is essential whenever you perform a spell. Otherwise, your spell could backfire.

The fact is, you're doing magick all the time, whether or not you realize it. As noted later, the Law of Attraction states that your thoughts, emotions, and actions affect the energetic patterns around you, and the most significant "tools" in magick are your thoughts and feelings. That's why it's important to use your magickal power with clear intent, so you can produce the results you truly desire.

Underlying all magick is a simple principle of physics: For every action there is an equal and opposite reaction. Remember that old computer axiom, garbage in, garbage out? Magick is like that, too: If you put bad thoughts and feelings in, you'll get bad stuff back and vice versa. So, be careful what you ask for!

What You Believe Is What You'll Get

Belief is the core of magick. Without it, all you have are words and gestures, light and dust, nothing but bluster—rather like the Wizard in *The Wonderful Wizard of Oz* that Dorothy and her companions exposed as just an ordinary man behind a curtain. But what, exactly, is meant by belief? Go back to Oz. The Lion sought courage because he believed he was cowardly. That belief ruled his life until the Wizard pointed out how courageous he actually was. The Lion experienced a radical shift in his beliefs about himself when he realized that he had possessed what he desired most all along. Believing he didn't have courage was what crippled him.

Most of us are just like the Cowardly Lion. We let fear, doubt, and erroneous beliefs limit our power and our ability to create what we desire most in life. Let's say you want abundance. To you, that means financial abundance, money in the bank, freedom from worrying whether the next check you write is going to bounce. However, to those around you, your life appears to be incredibly abundant—you have a loving family, wonderful friends, good health. Sometimes a shift in our deepest beliefs happens because someone whose opinion we respect points out that we really *do* have what we desire. Other times, we reach the same conclusion on our own. One thing you can count on: When your beliefs change, so will your life circumstances.

When you do magick, you must believe in yourself and your ability to produce the result you seek. Doubt pours water on your creative fire. If you doubt you can achieve your goal, you won't. That's true whether you're playing a sport or casting a spell.

The Power of Your Beliefs

A belief is an acceptance of something as true. Thousands of years ago, people believed the world was flat. In the 1600s, men and women were burned at the stake because people in power believed they were evil and consorted with the devil. (You'd be surprised to discover how many people still believe witches are the devil's disciples—more about this later.)

On a more personal level, all of us face the consequences of our personal beliefs in all areas of our lives, every day. Your experiences, the people around you, your personal and professional environments—every facet of your existence, in fact is a faithful reflection of a belief.

Some common ingrained, self-limiting beliefs that many people hold on to include:

- I'm not worthy (of love, wealth, a great job, whatever).
- My relationships stink.
- I'll never amount to anything.
- People are out to get me.
- Life is a struggle.
- You can't be rich *and* spiritual.
- I live in an unsafe world.

The foundations for many of these notions are laid in childhood, when we adopt the beliefs of our parents, teachers, and other authority figures. Childhood conditioning can be immensely powerful. Inside the man or woman who lacks a sense of self-worth lurks a small child who may believe he or she is a sinner, unworthy, or not good enough.

On a larger scale, our beliefs also come from the cultures and societies in which we live. A woman living in the West, for example, is unlikely to have the same core beliefs about being female as a woman in, say, a Muslim country.

A belief system usually evolves over time. It's something that we grow into, as our needs and goals develop and change. Even when we find a system of beliefs that works for us, we hone and fine-tune it, working our way deeper and deeper into its essential truth. Everything we experience, every thought we have, every desire, need, action, and reaction—everything we perceive with our senses goes into our personal databank and helps to create the belief systems that we hold now. Nothing is lost or forgotten in our lives.

You don't have to remain a victim of your conditioning, however. You can choose for yourself what you believe or don't believe, what you desire and don't desire. You can define your own parameters. Once you do that, you can start consciously creating your destiny according to your own vision—and keying into your magickal nature to make that happen.

THE LAW OF ATTRACTION

Have you heard of something called the Law of Attraction? Actually, it's an ancient concept, but in recent years Esther and Jerry Hicks have popularized and expanded it so that now millions of people around the world are familiar with the idea. At its core, the Law says that you attract whatever you put your mind on. In their best-selling book *Money, and the Law of Attraction* the Hickses wrote, "Each and every component that makes up your life experience is drawn to you by the powerful Law of Attraction's response to the thoughts you think and the story you tell about your life." In *The Secret*, Rhonda Byrne explained that "Your life right now is a reflection of your past thoughts."

What they're saying is, you create your own reality. Your thoughts and feelings generate energy, and they interact with the energy all around you in your environment. Over time, your ideas—especially the ones you feel passionate about—produce "thought forms," which serve as patterns that eventually become physical forms. You could look at it this way: Let's say you're a fashion designer and in your mind you envision a fabulous dress. That creative idea or "thought form" must exist before you can start to develop the physical object. You keep refining your design, doing drawings and maybe even stitching a sample, and eventually produce the dress you'd imagined.

Magick works in essentially the same way. First you create an image in your mind of what you desire and then imbue that image with energy

The Modern Guide to Witchcraft

and emotion. In time, what you conjured up mentally will emerge into the material world.

A big part of becoming a powerful witch and performing effective magick is training your mind. This means focusing your thoughts, raising your energy to the highest level you can, and using your will to bring your intentions into fruition. Later in this book, we'll talk more about how to do this—and the more you practice, the better results you'll achieve.

One Thing at a Time

Most of us have grown accustomed to doing several things at once. While eating dinner we also watch TV, send texts to our friends, and make notes of things we need to remember to take care of tomorrow. When you do magick, however, multitasking actually diminishes your returns. As Esther and Jerry Hicks explain in *Money, and the Law of Attraction*, "When you consider many subjects at the same time, you generally do not move forward strongly toward any of them, for your focus and your power is [sic] diffused."

Start paying attention to your thoughts. Are you focusing on what you lack? If so, you'll continue to experience lack. Do you spend time lamenting the problems in your life? If so, you'll keep making more problems for yourself. Whenever you catch yourself thinking something that's *not* what you want, do a mental 180 and start thinking about what you do want instead.

MAGICK ISN'T JUST BLACK AND WHITE

Magick is ethically neutral, just like electricity is neutral. Both magick and electricity can be used to help or to harm. Magick is simply the intentional use of energy. Casting a magick spell is simply a means to an end. A witch uses willpower to direct energy toward a particular goal. Her intention is what colors the magick white, black, or gray.

You've probably heard people describe themselves as white witches, meaning they uphold the "do no harm" rule. The truth, though, is that most magick isn't black or white, it's gray—including the magick most self-proclaimed white witches perform. That doesn't mean it's bad or harmful, however. In fact, the spells of most witches and magicians fall into the gray area.

White, Black, or Gray?

Not every witch will agree with the following definitions of white, black, and gray magick. However, these guidelines can help you sort out the differences:

- White magick's purpose is to further spiritual growth, by strengthening your connection with the divine realm and/or gaining wisdom from a higher source.
- Black magick intends to harm or manipulate another person, or to interfere with his/her free will.
- Every other kind of magick is a shade of gray.

This means that if you do a spell to get a better job or to attract a lover you're operating in the gray zone. Nothing wrong with that. It's easy, though, to stray from the path and inadvertently cast a questionable spell—especially when you're having a bad day or dealing with difficult people. Let's say a coworker is a real pain in the neck and you do a spell to get even with her for a dirty deed. Your revenge may seem justifiable, but it's still black magick.

Here's another little-known fact: Most black magick isn't performed by evil sorcerers or wicked wizards, it's done by ordinary people who don't even realize what they're up to. Have you ever cursed some jerk for stealing your parking space or cutting in front of you in a long supermarket line? That's black magick, too.

Why Doing Black Magick Isn't Such a Good Idea

Maybe you're wondering, why *not* use magick to put someone who's wronged you in his place? It's tempting, for sure. Except remember that in the world of magick, whatever you do returns to you like a boomerang. Indeed, many magicians say it comes back magnified threefold. That's a good reason for keeping your thoughts focused on positive stuff. It's also why usually the best way to get what you want—especially on days when everything seems to be going wrong—is to bless instead of curse.

INTENTION IS EVERYTHING

Admittedly, it can be hard sometimes to determine if you're treading on the dark side of Magick Street. For many people, love spells seem to raise the most questions. What if you want to do a spell to get your yoga instructor to fall for you? Is that okay? It all depends on your intention. If he already has a partner and your goal is to win him away from her, obviously that's *not* a good idea.

Good spells respect other people's free will and right to make their own choices in life. Even if your yoga teacher isn't romantically involved with anybody else, it's manipulative to cast a spell to coerce him into doing something he wouldn't want to do otherwise. How would you feel if someone did that to you? There's another reason, too, to think carefully before casting a spell to win a person's heart. A well-executed love spell creates a strong bond between you and someone else. Later on, if you change your mind, breaking the bond could be tough, to say the least.

Instead, try another angle to accomplish your goal. You could magickally enhance your own attractiveness. You could do magick to remove any obstacles existing between you and the other person. You could do a spell to attract a lover who's right for you, rather than targeting a particular individual. Or you could turn the final decision over to a higher power and let your favorite god/dess, angel, or spirit guide find the perfect partner for you. This kicks your ego out of the driver's seat and lets the universe guide you toward an outcome that's right for you. Maybe you and your yoga teacher would live happily ever after together. On the other hand, maybe you'd be better off with somebody else, perhaps someone you haven't met yet.

Chapter 3

A CONCISE HISTORY OF WITCHCRAFT IN THE WEST

Witches have a rich cultural heritage that they continue celebrating today. Although witchcraft's origins are hidden in antiquity, most likely, people around the world have practiced magick and witchcraft in some form since the beginning of time. Anthropologists speculate that Stonehenge may have been a sacred site where magick rituals were performed thousands of years ago. The famous paintings on the Trois Frères cave walls in Montesquieu-Avantès, France, which date back 15,000 years, may have been put there by Paleolithic peoples as a form of sympathetic magick—by painting these images, cave dwellers sought the aid of spirit animals to help them succeed at hunting.

Today contemporary witches are reviving interest in the Craft. As you join their leagues, you'll become part of the new wave of magicians who are putting a modern spin on an ancient worldview. How exciting is that?

THE OLD RELIGION

Magick and witchcraft go hand in hand. Although not all magick falls under the broad heading of witchcraft, all witches practice magick in one form or another. At the dawn of the human race, when people first came to understand cause and effect, they began trying to explain the mysteries of earth and the heavens. If a wind blew down a tree and hurt someone, the wind might be thought of as "angry" or considered to be a spirit that needed appeasement. In this manner, people began to anthropomorphize aspects of nature. They imagined that gods and goddesses, spirits and demons, and all sorts of fantastic creatures lived in the unseen realms, where they governed everything that happened on earth. Magickal thinking was born.

Magickal Beginnings

As civilizations developed, each brought a new flavor and tone to magickal ideas. One of these ideas was that the universe is a huge web made up of all kinds of invisible interlocking strands. Everything is connected to everything else. If humans could learn to influence one of these connections, they could affect the whole web.

At first, these attempts to influence the world were very simple: one action to produce one result. The action usually corresponded symbolically to the desired result. For example, let's say someone wanted to bind an angry spirit and limit its power. He might tie a knot in a piece of rope and imagine that he'd caught the spirit in that knot. If the action worked, or seemed to work, it was used again. Eventually a tradition developed.

Wise Men and Women

Over time, attempts at guiding "fate" became more elaborate. Our ancestors delegated the tasks of influencing the universe to a few wise individuals, and elevated them to positions of authority in their community. They called these wise men and women shamans, priests and priestesses, magi, or witches. Their job included performing spells and rituals to coerce the ancestors, powerful spirits, or deities into doing their bidding. Although these witches all performed essentially the same basic functions—healing the sick, encouraging crops to grow, predicting the future—how they went about it depended on the culture and era in which they lived.

In early Celtic communities, for example, the Druids served as seers, healers, advisors, astrologers, and spiritual leaders. Their power was second only to the clan's chieftain. An ancient Norse text called the *Poetic Edda*, written in the tenth century, uses the term *völva* to describe a wise woman who did prophecies, cast spells, and performed healing for the community.

Modern witches no longer hand over magickal authority to a select few. Today, everyone is welcome to explore these paths and practices, not just an elite group. Using your personal power is encouraged. Each one of us has a special talent or skill, and ultimately that gift can benefit everyone. Every individual brings something unique to the Craft, which has caused the field of magick to evolve and expand greatly.

WITCHCRAFT IN EUROPE

It's been said that history is written by the victors. History is imperfect and is often clouded by societal, personal, or political agendas; therefore, the study of magickal history is no easy task. To trace the course of events from ancient times to the modern day, let's begin by examining the early practice of witchcraft in Europe.

Not everyone agrees about the evolution of witchcraft in Europe. Some historians believe it developed out of the old fertility cults that worshipped a mother goddess. Others think that the idea of witchcraft was all superstition—when people could not explain an unpleasant event, they blamed it on someone whom they labeled a witch. Still other researchers say witchcraft stemmed from a wide variety of practices and customs including Paganism, Hebrew mysticism, Celtic tradition, and ancient Greek folklore.

As people traveled from one country to another, they influenced the beliefs and practices of the native culture. When the Vikings and the Romans invaded the British Isles, for example, their legends, gods, and goddesses mixed with those of the indigenous people. Traders and travelers, too, brought stories and ideas to the lands they visited. All this cross-pollination had an impact on the way witchcraft evolved.

Additionally, because most people in earlier centuries couldn't read or write, magickal traditions were handed down through generations by oral teaching. The few literate individuals probably recorded information according to their own views. Therefore, it's difficult to figure out what's true and what's fantasy regarding long-ago witchcraft.

Fairy-Tale Witches

Witches show up frequently in our favorite fairy tales, where they're sometimes referred to as fairy godmothers. Certain of these witches can't resist putting enchantments on humans, turning them into hideous beasts ("Beauty and the Beast") or frogs ("The Frog Prince"), or condemning them to unpleasant plights ("Sleeping Beauty"). Others, however, such as the one in "Cinderella," wave their magick wands and make wishes come true. Some of these fairy-tale witches derive from old goddesses in ancient myths, such as the witch in "Hansel and Gretel" who originated in the Baltic fertility goddess Baba Yaga. In old French romance stories, witches and women who practiced magick were called "fairies."

CRIMINALIZING WITCHCRAFT

During the eighth and ninth centuries, the powers-that-be started laying down laws against witchcraft and linking age-old practices with evil doing. As the Christian Church gained power, it attacked the "old religion," which was based in nature and folk traditions. For example, the common people had a custom of leaving offerings for spirits—until 743, when the Synod of Rome declared it a crime. In 829, the Synod of Paris passed a decree against reciting incantations (simple verbal spells for good luck) and idolatry (worshipping the old gods and goddesses). By 900, Christian scholars were promoting the idea that the devil was leading women astray. These events helped prepare the scene for the fury of the Inquisition.

Between the 1100s and 1300s, the Church continued to hammer away at witches. Christian zealots presented a picture of witches as evil creatures who cavorted with the devil, ate children, and held wild orgies to seduce innocents. Witchcraft became a crime against God and the Church. In 1317, Pope John XXII authorized a religious court, known as the Inquisition, to go after anyone who was believed to have made a pact with the devil.

Thousands of trials proceeded. Punishments included burning, hanging, and excommunication. The interrogation process involved torturing people to get them to confess the "truth"—that is, to force them to admit to whatever the inquisitor wished—and to point a finger at other witches.

"In 1484, the Papal Bull of Innocent VIII unleashed the power of the Inquisition against the Old Religion. With the publication of the *Malleus Maleficarum*, 'The Hammer of the Witches,' by Dominicans Kramer and Sprenger in 1486, the groundwork was laid for a reign of terror that was to hold all of Europe in its grip until well into the seventeenth century." —Starhawk, *The Spiral Dance*

Accusing someone of witchcraft also became a bureaucratic convenience. Not only those who actually practiced the Craft were tortured, imprisoned, and killed—anyone whom the authorities disliked or feared was accused of being a witch. Conviction rates soared as many "undesirables" fell prey to the inquisitors.

The atmosphere in England was less radical than on the continent. Because Henry VIII had separated from the Catholic Church, practicing witchcraft in Britain was regarded as a civil violation, and courts handed down fewer death sentences. In part, this may have been due to the influence of John Dee, a well-known wizard who served as an advisor to Queen Elizabeth I.

THE BURNING TIMES

The witch-hunt craze picked up speed in the sixteenth century, during the Reformation period. The public, confused by the religious changes going on, was only too willing to blame anyone whose ideas seemed "different." If someone had a grudge against a neighbor, he could denounce her as a witch. It was the perfect environment for mass persecution.

The legal sanctions against witches became even harsher than before, and the tortures inflicted grew crueler. To force people to confess to witchcraft, inquisitors strapped them to the "rack" and pulled them apart limb by limb, crushed their hands and feet with thumbscrews and "boots," and placed hot coals on their bare skin. If found guilty, the alleged "witches" were burned at the stake.

During the so-called "Burning Times" in Europe, which lasted from the fourteenth until the eighteenth centuries, tens of thousands and possibly millions of people (depending on which source you choose to believe) were executed as witches—most of them women and girls. So thorough were the exterminations that after Germany's witch trials of 1585 two villages in the Bishopric of Trier were left with only one woman surviving in each.

Cats and Rats

During the Burning Times, cats were thought to be witches' familiars and zealots destroyed them by the thousands. It's theorized by some that the Black Plague, which devastated Europe's human population in the fourteenth century, resulted in part because the rat population increased and spread disease once their natural predators were eliminated.

As occurs in all tragedies, some individuals profited from the witch hunts. Payments were given to informants and witch hunters who produced victims. In some instances, male doctors benefited financially when their competitors—female midwives and herbalists—were condemned as witches. Powerful authorities confiscated the property of the victims.

It's hard to know for certain why the witch hysteria finally subsided. Perhaps people grew weary of the violence. In England, the hunts declined after the early 1700s, when the witch statute was finally repealed. The last recorded execution occurred in Germany in 1775.

WITCHCRAFT IN THE NEW WORLD

In the New World, witchcraft evolved as a patchwork quilt of beliefs and practices. Many different concepts, cultures, and customs existed side by side, sometimes overlapping and influencing one another. Each new group of immigrants brought with them their individual views and traditions. Over time, they produced a rich body of magickal thought.

The Modern Guide to Witchcraft

Medicine men and women of the native tribes in North, Central, and South America had engaged in various forms of witchcraft and shamanism for centuries. They tapped the plant kingdom for healing purposes and to see the future. They communed with spirits, ancestors, and other nonphysical beings, seeking supernatural aid in crop growing and hunting. Like witches in other lands, these indigenous people honored Mother Earth and all her creatures. And, like magicians everywhere, they worked with the forces of nature to produce results.

When European settlers migrated to the New World, they brought their customs with them. Not all of these early immigrants were Christians. Some followed the Old Religion and sought freedom to practice their beliefs in a new land. Evidence suggests that some of these people joined Indian tribes whose ideas were compatible with their own.

The slave trade introduced the traditions of African witches to the Americas. Followers of voudon (voodoo), Santería, macumba, and other faiths carried their beliefs and rituals with them to the Caribbean and the southern states of the United States, where they continue to flourish today.

Witchcraft in Salem

When William Griggs, the village doctor in colonial Salem Village (now Salem), Massachusetts, couldn't heal the ailing daughter and niece of Reverend Samuel Parris, he claimed the girls had been bewitched. Thus began the infamous Salem witch hunt, which remains one of America's great tragedies. Soon girls in Salem and surrounding communities were "crying out" the names of "witches" who had supposedly caused their illnesses.

Between June and October 1692, nineteen men and women were hung and another man was crushed to death for the crime of witchcraft. Authorities threw more than 150 other victims into prison, where several died, on charges of being in league with the devil.

Religious and political factors combined to create the witch craze in Salem. A recent smallpox epidemic and attacks by Indian tribes had left the community deeply fearful. Competition between rivals Rev. James Bayley of neighboring Salem Town (now Danvers) and Rev. Parris exacerbated the tension as both ministers capitalized on their Puritan parishioners' fear of Satan to boost their own popularity.

The hysteria also enabled local authorities to rid the community of undesirables and dissidents. Economic interests, too, played a role in the condemnation of Salem's "witches"—those convicted had their assets confiscated and their property was added to the town's coffers. A number of the executed and accused women owned property and were not governed by either husbands or male relatives, which didn't sit well with the male-dominated society of the time. Putting these independent women in their place may have been part of the motive behind the Salem witch trials.

Today, Salem commemorates the victims of the Salem Witch Trials with engraved stones nestled in a small, tree-shaded park off Derby Street, near the city's waterfront and tourist district. Visitors can walk through the memorial and remember Salem's darkest hour.

Hallucinating Witches

One theory suggests that the people supposedly afflicted by witchcraft in Salem were actually "high" on a fungus called ergot that grows on rye bread. The hallucinogen LSD was first derived from ergot. Therefore, the strange behavior exhibited by the "victims" was probably due to eating this psychedelic substance, not demonic possession.

WITCHCRAFT'S REBIRTH

Despite centuries of persecution, witchcraft never died. It just went underground. Witches continued to hand down teachings from mother to daughter, father to son, in secret. Through oral tradition, rituals, codes, and symbols, magickal information passed from generation to generation, at every level of society.

Some parts of the world, of course, never experienced the witch hysteria that infested Europe and Salem, Massachusetts. But even in those places where persecution once raged, witchcraft and magick reawakened during the nineteenth and twentieth centuries.

Magick in the Victorian Era

Interest in magick, mysticism, spiritualism, and the occult in general blossomed toward the end of the nineteenth century, perhaps as a reaction to the Age of Reason's emphasis on logic and science. The magicians of this era had a strong impact on the evolution of contemporary witchcraft and magick.

One noted figure of the time was Charles Godfrey Leland, a Pennsylvania scholar and writer who traveled widely studying the folklore of numerous cultures. His most famous book, *Aradia, or the Gospel of the Witches* became an important text that influenced the development of Neopaganism and modern-day witchcraft. Another was Madame Helena Blavatsky, a Russian-born medium and occultist who moved to New York and founded the Theosophical Society with Henry Steel Olcott. Theosophy, which means "divine wisdom," combines ideas from the Greek mystery schools, the Gnostics, Hindus, and others.

The Hermetic Order of the Golden Dawn, begun by Englishmen William Westcott, S.L. MacGregor Mathers, and William Woodman, was the most important magickal order to arise in the West during the Victorian period. All three men were Freemasons and members of the Rosicrucian Society, which influenced their beliefs and practices. The order's complex teachings drew upon the ideas and traditions of numerous ancient cultures and melded them into an intricate system of ceremonial magick (more about this in Chapter 7).

The Poetry of Ritual

The Golden Dawn's magick rituals were written by the noted British poet and mystic, William Butler Yeats, who was one of the order's most prominent members, in collaboration with founding father S.L. MacGregor Mathers.

The most notorious member of the Golden Dawn was Aleister Crowley, a controversial and charismatic figure who many say was the greatest magician of the twentieth century. After breaking with the Golden Dawn, he formed his own secret society, called Argenteum Astrum, or Silver Star, and later became the head of the Ordo Templi Orientis (Order of the Templars of the Orient or OTO). Much of his magick centered upon the use of sexual energy, which outraged the stuffy, uptight Victorians. The author of numerous books on magick and the occult, Crowley also created one of the most popular tarot decks with Lady Frieda Harris, known as the Thoth Deck.

Neopaganism

Pagan was originally a derogatory term used by the Church to refer to people, often rural folk, who had not converted to Christianity. Generally speaking, today's Neopagans can be described as individuals who uphold an earth-honoring philosophy and attempt to live in harmony with all life on the planet as well as with the cosmos. Pagans tend to be polytheistic, meaning they acknowledge many deities rather than a single god or goddess, although some Pagans may not honor any particular higher being.

The Pagan and Wiccan communities overlap a great deal and share many beliefs, interests, and practices. Not all Pagans are witches or Wiccans, although Wiccans and witches are usually considered Pagans. Because of the similarities between them, they often combine their resources for political, humanitarian, environmental, and educational objectives.

WITCHCRAFT TODAY

In the past few decades, the ranks of witches have swelled rapidly. Although it's impossible to accurately determine how many people practice witchcraft, a study done in 2001 by City University of New York found 134,000 self-described Wiccans in the United States. Certainly, that number has increased since then.

The American Academy of Religions now includes panels on Wicca and witchcraft. The U.S. Defense Department recognizes Wicca as an official religion and allows Wiccan soldiers to state their belief on their dog tags. As of 2006, an estimated 1,800 Wiccans were serving in the U.S. military.

Undoubtedly, the Internet has helped to spread information about the Craft. By enabling witches around the world to connect with one another in a safe and anonymous manner, the Internet has extended witchcraft's influence to all corners of the globe. Today you'll find thousands of websites and blog sites devoted to the subjects of Paganism, Wicca, witchcraft, and magick, along with lots of intelligent, thought-provoking ideas and scholarship.

Witchcraft isn't a static belief system or rigid body of rules and rituals; it's a living entity that's continually evolving and expanding. As education dissolves fear and misconceptions, magickal thinking and practices will gain greater acceptance among the general populace and influence the spiritual growth of all people, regardless of their specific faiths.

Chapter 4

THE MAGICKAL UNIVERSE IN WHICH WE LIVE

We live in a magickal universe. Children often understand this quite clearly, even if adults don't. To a child, the world is alive with possibilities. Most people miss this wondrous fact because they've been trained to look only at the physical world and to focus on the mundane aspects of daily life. Magick, however, teaches that the world most of us see is only the tip of the iceberg. As you develop your magickal abilities, you'll rediscover the awesome power that abides in the universe—and in you.

Maybe, in the deepest recesses of your mind, you have shadowy memories of an ancient time when you lived in constant contact with the earth, the cosmos, and your own instinctual nature. As you strengthen your relationship with nature and the universe, you may reawaken these memories. Perhaps you'll realize that you're a witch in your heart of hearts—and always have been.

There are many ways to tap your magickal power and many ways to harness the creative energy of the universe. This book introduces a number of philosophies, paths, and practices. Some will appeal to you, and some won't. Take what you like and leave the rest. Regardless of which course you choose to follow, when you become a witch and do magick, you enter into an agreement with the universe that if you do your part, the rest will unfold.

THE COSMIC WEB

From the perspective of science, everything is energy. Magicians see the world as surrounded by an energetic matrix that connects everything to everything else. This matrix, or "cosmic web," envelops our earth like a big bubble. It also permeates all things that exist here and extends throughout the solar system and beyond. The web pulses with subtle vibrations that magicians, psychics, and other sensitive individuals can feel. Regardless of whether you are consciously aware of these vibrations, you are affected by them—and your own personal energy vibrations continually affect the matrix.

Energy, Energy Everywhere

Everything in the world emits an energy vibration of some kind. Different things have different energy patterns, resonances, or "signatures." These resonances reach out to touch one another in a series of crisscrossing lines all around the world, rather like a big spider web. They also connect the physical and nonphysical worlds. These energetic connections are what enable witches and wizards to work magick—even over a long distance. You simply send a thought or emotion along one of these energy lines to wherever or whomever you wish to reach—it works faster than sending a text.

Consider this: How many times have you gotten a phone call from someone you were just thinking about? It's not an accident. Your thoughts and the other person's connected in the cosmic web before you spoke to one another in the physical realm. When you do magick, you purposefully tap into this infinite web. You tug a little on one of the lines. As you become skilled at using magick, you'll learn to navigate the cosmic web just as easily as you surf the Internet. The first step is to sensitize yourself to these vibrations and become aware of the energetic field around you.

Sensing Energy Currents

Try these simple exercises to start becoming aware of your own energy and the energy around you. If you like, you can do these exercises with a friend.

1. Close your eyes and hold your palms up in front of you, facing each other, about a foot or so apart. Slowly move your palms closer together but don't actually let them touch. Can you sense the energy flowing between your palms? You may feel warmth or coolness, various degrees of tingling, or something else. You might even sense a color or feel an emotion. Does the feeling grow stronger as your hands get closer together?

2. Choose an object, preferably a natural one such as a stone or plant. Run your hands around the object without touching it physically, trying to feel the energy it possesses. What do you sense? Can you feel warmth, coolness, or any other sensation coming from the object? Do you get any impressions or thoughts? Don't discount them, even if they seem weird.

3. Ask a friend to do this exercise with you. Sit with your eyes closed, while your friend stands behind you. Slowly, your friend moves her hand toward your head, without ever actually touching you. When you sense the energy from her hand, say so. Then switch places and try the exercise again.

Write down what you experienced in what will become your "grimoire" or "book of shadows," a journal of your magick spells and experiences. These notes will help you as you continue working with different energies, and as you grow more aware of how your own energies fluctuate with your mood, your health, and your circumstances.

THE COSMIC INFORMATION REPOSITORY

Like the Worldwide Web, the cosmic web teems with information. All ideas, words, actions, and emotions—going all the way back to the beginning of time—are stored in this energetic matrix. Anyone who knows the password can access this vast storehouse of knowledge.

Maybe you've heard of a psychic named Edgar Cayce, sometimes called the "Sleeping Prophet." Although he had little formal education or medical training, Cayce could go into a trance and discover cures for the thousands of sick people who sought his aid. How did he do it? He psychically "downloaded" wisdom that great minds before him had "blogged" into the cosmic web.

Not only psychics can access information in this way—lots of people do. They just don't realize it. Inventors, artists, musicians, and other creative people often claim to get insights without really knowing where they came from. Mozart didn't plan, structure, or analyze his compositions—he just listened to the music playing in his head and then wrote it down. Van Gogh said, "I dream of painting, and then I paint my dream." Scientific people, too, report having epiphanies that lead to new discoveries in technology, medicine, and other areas. All these people are connecting to the cosmic web and drawing knowledge from it.

Meditate to Quiet Your Mind

You, too, can tap into this awesome repository of information. Being able to key into the wisdom of the ages is a terrific asset to a witch. Wouldn't it be awesome to have the great wizard Merlin guiding you as you cast a spell?

First, you'll need to learn to quiet your mind. Most of us have minds that race like a hamster in a treadmill. In the world of magick, that's counterproductive. You can't "hear" the masters' advice if you're thinking about a zillion other things. One of the best ways to still the inner chatter is to meditate. If you've never meditated, you may think you have to sit in lotus position and chant "Oooommm" for hours. Not true. You can take a walk outside, listen to soothing music (without lyrics), watch the sunset, weed your garden, take a relaxing bath, or fold laundry. The point is to put all your attention on whatever you're doing, without letting distractions interfere. (My book *The Best Meditations on the Planet* includes 100 different meditations—something for everyone.)

Meditation enables you to clear the clutter from your mind and focus your thinking. It also opens the channels of communication between you and the cosmos. Because the mind is the force behind magick, it stands to reason that the more mastery you gain over your thoughts, the more effective your spells will be.

Trust Your Intuition

Whether you call it ESP, a hunch, a gut reaction, an inner knowing, or psychic power, everyone has intuition. It may raise hairs on the back of your neck, cause a twinge in your solar plexus, or make you feel lightheaded. It may speak to you in moments of crisis or utter calm, in the middle of a city traffic jam or while you're taking a shower. Regardless of how your intuition communicates with you, it's important to remember that your so-called sixth sense is just as normal and important as the other five senses.

Think how much you'd miss out on if you lacked the sense of sight, hearing, taste, smell, or touch. The world would be a much duller place. Now try to imagine how much more you could get out of life if you had another sense on top of those five. The good news is that you do!

Because intuition doesn't "make sense" (that is, it doesn't rely on our five physical senses), people tend to discount its validity. Yet many noted scientists have acknowledged that intuition played a significant part in their discoveries. In his later years, Nobel laureate Jonas Salk, who found a vaccine for polio, wrote a book about intuition titled *Anatomy of Reality*. In it he proposed that creativity resulted from the union of intuition and reasoning. Bill Gates said, "Often you have to rely on intuition." Albert Einstein believed "the only real valuable thing is intuition."

What we call intuition is the connection between your conscious mind and the cosmic web. Intuition is a witch's best friend. Sometimes intuition is the most important factor in spell-working. You can memorize the properties of different herbs, gemstones, or colors. You can follow all the prescribed steps in a ritual. But if you don't trust your intuition to guide you, you'll never develop your full potential. To connect with your intuition:

- Listen to the "voice within."
- Pay attention to hunches.
- Pay attention to your dreams and what they're trying to tell you.
- Notice "coincidences."
- Write down impressions and insights that you receive, even if they don't make sense in the moment—they may turn out to mean something more in the future.

As you start paying attention to your intuition, it will grow stronger and begin funneling more useful information your way. Being able to draw on your intuition will enrich your life and enhance your magickal ability in countless ways.

THE MOON AND YOU

One of the most important connections we have in the magickal universe in which we live—and one of the most obvious—is earth's closest neighbor: the moon. We can easily see the impact the moon has on our planet and its inhabitants. For example, the moon's twenty-eight-day cycle influences the oceans' tides; higher tides usually occur during the full moon. It also affects the weather, crop growth, animal and human fertility—as the *Farmers' Almanac* has professed for two centuries—as well as the way we feel and behave. More babies come into this world during the full moon than at other times of the month. Ask police officers or hospital workers about the full moon and they'll tell you they see more crises, more crimes, and more activity in general when the moon is full. No, the full moon won't turn you into a werewolf, but it might bring out your wild side.

Astrologers associate the moon with emotion, intuition, and creativity—the very things that witches rely on when they do magick. So, if you want your spells to be more powerful and effective, pay attention to the moon's cycles and learn to draw upon lunar energy.

Connecting with the Moon

Since ancient times, the moon has fascinated earthlings. Poets, artists, musicians, lovers, astrologers, and magicians all find the moon juicy subject matter for study and inspiration.

> *"Evidence of Moon worship is found in such widely varied cultures as those of the Anasazi Indians of New Mexico, the Greeks, Romans, Chinese, pre-Columbian Peruvians, Burmese, Phoenicians, and Egyptians. In the Craft, when we refer to the great god by the Hebrew names El or Elohim, we borrow terms that entered Hebrew from Arabic, where the god name 'Ilah' derives from a word that means 'moon.'"*
> —MORWYN, *SECRETS OF A WITCH'S COVEN*

Because the moon plays such an important role in magick—and in our lives—you might want to consider getting on closer terms with our planet's satellite. In a practice known as "drawing down the moon," a priestess goes into a trance and invites the goddess (or Divine Feminine energy) to enter her body. While the priestess is in the trance, the goddess speaks through her. Margot Adler wrote in depth about this in her book *Drawing Down the Moon*, but beginners can connect with lunar energy in simpler ways:

- Go outside at night and observe the moon. Let its silvery light wash over you. How do you feel standing in the moonlight, under the dark bowl of the night sky? How is this different from how you feel in the daytime?
- Follow the moon's passage through the heavens, from new to full and back to new again. Pay attention to how you feel during different phases of the moon. Many people feel more energized during the full moon and less vital during the last three days before the new moon.
- The moon moves into a different sign of the zodiac approximately every two and a half days. You might notice that your moods and feelings change every time the moon passes through a different astrological sign—you may feel more impulsive when the moon is in Aries, more sensitive when it's in Cancer, for instance.

Keep notes of what you experience, so you can refer back to them later. What you learn from strengthening your connection with the moon will be useful to you when you start casting spells and doing rituals.

The Moon and Magick

You're more likely to reap the rewards you desire if you do magick during favorable phases of the moon. When casting spells, pay particular attention to the new moon, full moon, the waxing and waning phases. Each has its own unique energy that can add to the power of your spells:

- The new moon, as you might expect, encourages beginnings. Are you looking for a new job? A new romance? A new home? The best time to start anything is during the new moon. As the moon grows in light (and seemingly in size), your undertaking will grow too.

- The waxing moon—the two weeks after the new moon and leading up to the full moon—supports growth and expansion. Do you want to boost your income? Turn up the heat in a relationship? Get a promotion at work? Cast your spell while the moon's light is increasing to generate growth in your worldly affairs.
- The full moon marks a time of culmination. It allows you to start seeing the results of whatever you began on the new moon. Want to bring a project to a successful conclusion? Receive rewards, recognition, or payments that are due to you? Do a spell while the moon is full for best results. The full moon's bright glow can also put you in the spotlight or shed light on murky issues. If your goal is to attract attention—from a lover, boss, or the public—the full moon helps illuminate you favorably. The full moon can also shine light on secrets and deception to let you get to the truth of a shady situation.
- The waning moon—the two weeks after the full moon and before the new moon—encourages decrease. Do you want to lose weight? End a bad relationship? Cut your expenses? Cast your spell while the moon is diminishing in light (and size) to diminish the impact of something in your life.

When two new moons occur in the same month, the second one is called the black moon. It is considerably more powerful than a regular new moon, so any seeding spells you do under a black moon might manifest more quickly. When two full moons occur in the same month, the second is dubbed a blue moon. During the blue moon, you may find you get bigger or better results than on an ordinary full moon, or that you experience a lot more activity or vitality.

THE FOUR DIRECTIONS

You're familiar with the four compass directions: north, south, east, and west. In magick, the four directions are more than mere geographical designations. They have special meanings and associations. Hindu mandalas, Native American medicine wheels, and Celtic stone circles all depict the four directions. Later on, when you learn to cast a circle before performing spells and rituals, you'll work with the four directions in greater depth. For now, let's just look at the directions in a way you've probably never considered them before.

Angelic Connections

Perhaps you've heard of four archangels known as Michael, Raphael, Gabriel, and Uriel. According to some schools of magickal thought, these archangels (an order of divine beings above angels) guard the four directions:

- Raphael guards the east.
- Michael watches over the south.
- Gabriel presides over the west.
- Uriel governs the north.

You can call upon these guardians and ask them to lend their assistance to your rituals and rites. Connecting with them and drawing upon their powers can greatly enhance the effectiveness of your magickal work.

Elemental Connections

When magicians speak of the elements, they're not referring to the periodic table you learned about in school. They mean the four elements: air, fire, water, and earth. These elements are the energetic building blocks that make up our world. We'll go into more detail and depth about the elements later on, but for now let's just note their relationships with the four directions:

- Air relates to the east.
- Fire is associated with the south.
- Water corresponds to the west.
- Earth is linked with the north.

Each has its own connections with the zodiac signs, the suits of the tarot, spirits and angels, the tools a magician uses, and lots of other things. The more you get into magick, the more you'll find yourself working with the elements.

Color Correspondences

Each of the four directions resonates with a certain color. Magickal art, including tarot cards, often depicts these color connections. You might also choose to incorporate them into spells. (Note, however, that Native American medicine wheels do not use these same color correspondences.)

* Yellow relates to the east.
* Red is associated with the south.
* Blue corresponds to the west.
* Green is linked with the north.

Learning to sense the four directions will give you a better understanding of your place in the cosmos. Working with these energies will strengthen your connection to both the earth and to the magickal universe around you.

Three More Directions

In addition to the four compass points, you'll want to consider three other directions when you do magick. The first of these, *Above*, refers to the heavenly realm and all the beings that live there: God, Goddess, angels, spirit guides, ancestors, and so on. The second, *Below*, corresponds to Mother Earth, the foundation of physical existence. *Within* means your own inner self. It's important to align yourself with all seven of these directions and to balance their energies when you're doing magick. They are all sources of power, and they all influence outcomes.

SENSING THE DIRECTIONS

You're going to work with the four directions and their correspondences a lot as your magickal practice expands. Before you actually start using these energies in spells and rituals, practice sensing what the energies feel like. If possible, try doing these exercises outside as well as inside your home. Many witches prefer to do magick while surrounded by nature whenever they can.

1. Stand facing east and close your eyes. Take a few deep breaths to quiet your thoughts. Keep an open mind as you try to sense the energy at this compass point. This is the energy of dawn, birth, and beginnings. It might take a few minutes, so give yourself time to receive the universe's vibrations. You might feel a slight tingling, warmth or coolness, a subtle emotional shift, or something else.
2. Turn to face south and, again, try to sense the energy flowing toward you. This is the energy of fullness and maturity. Does it seem any different from what you felt when you faced the east?
3. Turn to face west and, again, try to sense the energy flowing toward you. This is the energy of winding down and letting go. How does it seem to you?
4. Turn to face north and, again, try to sense the energy flowing toward you. This is the energy of turning inward, silence, and endings. What do you feel?

If at first you don't succeed in sensing these energies, remember the advice: Try, try again. With practice, you'll learn to pick up on the different resonances and attune yourself to them. Be sure to write down what you experience in your grimoire.

As you continue strengthening your magickal muscles, you'll come to a keen awareness of how intertwined you are with everything else in the cosmos. You'll realize that you can create your own reality by aligning yourself with the dynamic, magickal forces that exist all around you. And you'll notice that possibilities you never imagined before now open up for you.

Chapter 5

THE ELEMENTS OF THE WITCH'S PATH

Wiccans, green witches, shamans, and many other magicians believe that all things in nature—animals, plants, rocks, streams, hills—possess a type of consciousness. The term *animism* refers to this belief. The consciousness within even seemingly inanimate objects enables witches to use them in spellworking. The term *pantheism* is sometimes used to describe Neopagan paths. Often the term is misunderstood as meaning the worship of nature, but it actually means to recognize the Divine in all places, or to identify the Divine with the universe. The root word *pan* means "everywhere," and earth-honoring people believe that their deities are accessible in all places, at all times.

This doesn't mean that witches worship trees, rivers, and stones, any more than astrologers worship the sun, moon, and planets. It means they believe that the entire world, material and nonmaterial, possesses sacred energy, and that each of us holds a spark of divine energy within us.

In the previous chapter, we talked briefly about the four elements. Now let's examine the elements more fully, because earth, air, fire, and water are the four primary substances of creation—not only in nature and the material world, but magickally as well.

EARTH: THE SOLID ELEMENT

Planet Earth is the home of humans and other creatures, as well as a school for learning all kinds of spiritual lessons. When witches speak of the earth element, however, they don't mean simply the physical ground on which we stand. "Earth" in a magickal sense is also an energetic property.

In early agrarian cultures, farmers gave offerings of bread or mead to the soil to ensure a good crop. Soil also served as a component in many old spells. People buried symbolic items in the ground to banish something or to encourage growth. For example, to remove sickness, one healing spell instructs a sick person to spit in the soil and then cover that spot and walk away without looking back. To speed recovery from illness, patients were encouraged to grow health-promoting plants in the soil from their footprints. If you wanted to make sure your lover didn't cheat on you, you'd gather a little soil from beneath your foot and place it in a white cloth bag.

From the Womb of Gaia

Native American stories tell us that the soul waits for rebirth in the earth's womb (under the soil). You'll find dozens of myths, including those of ancient Sumer and Guatemala, that say humankind was shaped from soil. According to the ancient Greeks, the heavens were born into existence from the womb of Gaia, the mother who oversees all the earth's abundance.

Characteristics of the Earth Element

In the material sense, earth serves as our foundation. Thus it corresponds to the characteristics of stability, permanence, groundedness, security, and endurance. Earth energy moves slowly and steadily, so it's good to draw on when a situation or spell requires patience and/or gradual development. Magicians link the earth element with financial matters, material abundance, and fertility. People who have a lot of earth energy in their makeup tend to be practical, reliable, determined, tenacious, sensual, hard-working, cautious, no-nonsense individuals.

The Modern Guide to Witchcraft

Earth Correspondences

Lots and lots of things correspond to the earth element, such as the direction north as you learned in the previous chapter. We'll discuss more as we go along, but here are some that you'll most likely use in your spellworking:

- Zodiac Signs: Taurus, Virgo, Capricorn
- Tarot Suit: Pentacles/Coins/Discs
- Magickal Tools: Pentagram, Salt, Stones
- Colors: Brown, Green, Gray
- Stones: Opaque Stones (such as hematite, onyx, and agate)

AIR: THE ELUSIVE ELEMENT

Air is the most elusive of the elements because it is invisible, intangible, and changeable. The ancients believed that the wind is influenced by the direction from which it originates. This idea translated into magickal methods quite nicely. For example, if a wind blows from the south it can generate passion, warmth, or enthusiasm in spellcraft. If a wind moves from the west it stimulates intuition and imagination.

The Wind Beneath Your Spells

We see a fair amount of directional wind work in spellcraft. For example, always scatter components in a wind moving away from you to carry a message or to take away a problem. Perform magick for new projects with the "wind at your back," for good fortune. When trying to quell anger, opening a window to "air out" the negative energy has great symbolic value.

Think, too, of how the wind scatters pollen to fertilize plants. In a similar way, the air element describes how words are spread far and wide, fertilizing our minds and cross-pollinating our societies with new ideas. Air can be gentle or fierce, damp or dry, hot or cold, and each of these "moods" has slightly different magickal connotations. For example, a damp wind combines the power of water and air to raise energy that is dreamy and nourishing.

Characteristics of the Air Element

The air element relates to flexibility, instability, intellect, and detachment. Air energy moves quickly, so it's good to draw on when a situation or spell involves change, movement, or you want things to happen fast. You can also use air energy to contact spirits or other nonphysical beings. Magicians link the air element with mental activity, communication, the world of ideas, and social interaction—use it for spells that involve these things. People who have a lot of air energy in their makeup tend to be friendly, curious, fickle, adaptable, idealistic, talkative, and interested in all sorts of ideas.

Air Correspondences

As you continue your magickal studies, you'll find many things correspond to the air element, such as the direction east as you learned in the previous chapter. We'll discuss more as we go along, but here are some that you'll most likely use in your spellworking:

- Zodiac Signs: Gemini, Libra, Aquarius
- Tarot Suit: Swords/Daggers
- Magickal Tools: Athame, Incense
- Colors: Yellow, Pale Blue, White
- Stones: Transparent Stones (such as aquamarine, diamond, and clear quartz)

FIRE: THE ELEMENT OF CLARITY

For millennia, our ancestors gathered around fires to cook, tell stories, and celebrate life. Because of its warmth, fire represents our passions, enthusiasm, and kinship. Fire also allowed early people to see in the darkness, therefore, magicians connect it with clarity, vision, and enlightenment. When humans discovered fire and learned how to use it, their lives were transformed; thus the fire element is associated with transformation. Think of the mythical phoenix rising from the flames—a symbol of fiery transformation.

Characteristics of the Fire Element

The fire element conveys inspiration, enthusiasm, vitality, and daring. Fire energy moves rapidly; it's volatile and unpredictable—think of how a wildfire can rage out of control or how lightning bursts in the sky. You can draw on the element of fire when you want to kick your spell's power up a notch or you want to see rapid results. Of course, if you seek to transform something in your life—a relationship, career path, or health condition—you can tap into fire's dynamic power. Magicians link the fire element with creativity, action, and the will to make things happen. You can also employ fire energy to banish fear, see the future, or in purification spells and rituals. People who have a lot of fire energy in their makeup tend to be self-confident, passionate, impulsive, outgoing, vigorous, and courageous individuals.

Your Power Element

Each witch has one element to which she most strongly responds, called a power element. By working with and tapping into that element, a witch can energize herself and her magickal processes. Determine your power element by going to places where you can experience each element intimately. For example, sit beside a stream, lake, or ocean to connect with the water element; stand high on a windswept hill to feel the air element. Pay attention to your reactions. Once you determine which element energizes you, find ways to expose yourself to it regularly, to refill your inner well.

Fire Correspondences

You'll discover many more things that correspond to the fire element as you progress in your magickal studies. We'll discuss more as we go along, but here are some that you'll use often in your spellworking:

- Zodiac Signs: Aries, Leo, Sagittarius
- Tarot Suit: Wands/Rods/Staves
- Magickal Tools: Wand, Candles
- Colors: Red, Orange

- Stones: Stones that contain sparks of light or rutiles, such as fire opals, star sapphires, and red phantom quartz

WATER: THE ELEMENT OF MOVEMENT

Water comprises more than 70 percent of our earth's surface and about 60 percent of our bodies. Of course, water is essential for life. Consequently, we associate the water element with nourishment. Water moves constantly—the oceans' shifting tides, the rolling rivers and rippling streams, the rains that fall to earth—and so we sense change and movement in this element. Because we wash in water, we think of this element as cleansing, clearing, and healing. Even today, people go to hot springs and spas to "take the waters." Since ancient times, people have gathered at sacred wells and reported seeing holy visions in streams and other bodies of water. Thus, water relates to spirituality and mysticism.

Ancient Water Healing Practices

According to an old European custom, dew gathered at dawn banishes illness, making it a good base for curative potions. Bathing in the water from a sacred well, dipping your hands into the ocean's water three times and then pouring it behind you so the sickness is likewise "behind" you, or releasing a token that represents your sickness into the waves are old spells that you can still use today.

Characteristics of the Water Element

The water element embodies the characteristics of nourishment, healing, purification (physically and spiritually), intuition, emotion, and creativity. Tap this element to "water" spells for growth and abundance, or to nurture your creativity. Water energy is changeable and unpredictable—it can manifest as a gentle rain or a typhoon. Thus, it's a good energy to draw upon when you're doing spells for change or to stimulate movement—the trick is to control the energy so you get just the right amount. Because the moon affects the tides, it has connections with the water element. Purification spells and rituals also draw upon the water element. Magicians often take ritual baths before doing spells and wash magick tools with water to purify them. People who have a lot of water energy in their makeup tend to be emotional, sensitive, intuitive, imaginative, and compassionate individuals.

Water Correspondences

We've already talked a bit about the use of lunar energy and intuition in spellwork, and you'll learn more as you go along. We'll discuss the water element in later chapters, but for now make note of these correspondences that you'll most likely use in your spellworking:

- Zodiac Signs: Cancer, Scorpio, Pisces
- Tarot Suit: Cups/Chalices
- Magickal Tools: Chalice, Cauldron
- Colors: Blue, Aqua, Indigo, Purple
- Stones: Translucent stones and gems such as pearls, opals, moonstones, and rose quartz

SPIRIT: THE FIFTH ELEMENT?

Spirit (also known as ether) isn't an element *per se*, but you'll often see it included in a list of magickal elements as the fifth point of the pentagram. It's even harder to define than air. Spirit links the four quarters of creation and thus is the source of magick. Spirit resides within and without, around, above, and below all things. Although we can experience earth, air, fire, and water directly with our physical senses, spirit is elusive. You can only engage it with your spiritual senses.

In spells and rituals, spirit usually comes into play if a witch chooses to call upon a divine figure to bless and energize her magick. Or, it may become part of the equation if you invite devic entities (nature fairies) to work in harmony with you.

NATURE SPIRITS: THE WITCH'S ALLIES

No matter how much access a witch has to nature, she's likely to work closely with the earth. You can live on the forty-seventh floor of a high-rise apartment building in the middle of a metropolis and still have a meaningful relationship with the earth.

Among the witch's allies in the magickal world are the nature spirits. Sometimes called devas, elementals, or fairies, these spirits can be valuable partners and aides in your practice. Although most people don't see them, you can think of these spirits as the intelligence or awareness attached to a particular place, a plant or tree, a natural object such as a rock or stream, or a specific type of weather. They are not deities.

Do all witches work with nature spirits? No. Most do recognize that nature has an intelligence, or a sense of spirit, that varies according to the location. How each witch relates to these spirits or forces depends on how she perceives them.

How you visualize these spirits is completely up to you. You may see them as tiny people or orbs of light. You may not see them at all but experience emotions or sensations when you are near the tree, flower, standing stone, or phenomenon with which the spirit is associated. Whether your visualization matches the visualizations of other witches is unimportant. What *is* important is that if you choose to work with them, you must honor the spirits as allies and work with them to heal and harmonize the earth and its inhabitants.

You can encounter nature spirits in many places and through a variety of methods. The simplest method is to reach out and connect with the spirit of a single plant, then ask the plant spirit for information on the plant's uses and properties. In his book *Plant Spirit Medicine*, Eliot Cowan stresses that the energy possessed by each individual plant is entirely personal. The information and/or gift the spirit of that plant offers to you is exactly what you need at that moment. This gift is not necessarily an energy traditionally associated with the plant. For example, the energy you receive from a rose bush will not necessarily be love, even though we usually connect roses with love and romance. The spirit of the rose bush may perceive that you require something different and offer it to you. The key to working with nature spirits like this is to remain open to what they bring to you, without expectations or preconceived ideas.

The Modern Guide to Witchcraft

ELEMENTALS

Since ancient times, myths and legends have spoken about supernatural beings who fly through the air, burrow beneath the earth, or swim in the ocean's depths. But these magickal creatures don't simply reside in these regions; they serve as guardians and ambassadors of their respective realms. Some people might describe them as energetic forces, rather than specific entities, and they go by different names in different mystical traditions. Witches often choose to work with four elementals known as gnomes, sylphs, salamanders, and undines. These elementals correspond to the four elements: Gnomes are earth elementals, sylphs are air spirits, salamanders abide in the fire element, and undines are found in water.

The Earth Spirits at Findhorn

In the early 1960s, Eileen and Peter Caddy and their associate Dorothy Maclean founded a spiritual community in a wild and windswept area of northern Scotland known as Findhorn. Even though the soil there was mostly sand and the climate inhospitable, Findhorn became famous for its amazing gardens, which produced tropical flowers and forty-two-pound cabbages. How could this happen? According to Dorothy, the elementals who govern plant growth—she described them as "living forces of creative intelligence that work behind the scene"—guided Findhorn's founders in planting and maintaining the incredible gardens. In his book *Faces of Findhorn*, Professor R. Lindsay Robb of the Soil Association writes, "The vigor, health and bloom of the plants in this garden in midwinter, on land which is almost barren, powdery sand, cannot be explained . . ." Well, not by ordinary thinking anyway!

Gnomes: Earth Elementals

Those little green guys you see in the garden might be gnomes, though not all gnomes are green or little. Some of them look like leprechauns or trolls. Known as sprites or dryads in some cultures, these nature spirits aid the growth of flowers, trees, and other plants—if you look closely, you might spot them sitting in a tree or resting beneath a blackberry bush. When autumn comes, they change the leaves from green to red, orange, and gold. Earth elementals also play an important role in helping the earth heal from the effects of pollution, deforestation, mining, and other forms of destruction.

Practical, no-nonsense beings, they can seem a little gruff at times. However, they have a wonderful appreciation for material things and wealth—remember the leprechaun's pot of gold? Ask the earth elementals to lend a hand with prosperity spells.

Sylphs: Air Elementals

Most people think of fairies as small, flying creatures like Tinker Bell, but these are probably air elementals. Sylphs aren't just cute and delicate winged beings, as contemporary films and children's books portray them—they handle lots of things related to the air and sky. They have the power to manipulate the winds, influence air quality, and help earthlings breathe. They also assist birds and flying insects.

In magickal work, sylphs can help you with verbal spells such as incantations. If you want to ace a test, learn a new subject or skill, or communicate clearly with someone, ask a sylph for assistance. Air spirits also like to get involved with legal matters and contracts.

Salamanders: Fire Elementals

No, we're not talking about a type of lizard. Salamanders, in the magickal sense, are the fire elementals. You may see these shining beings in a candle flame or the sun's rays, and they abide in all types of fire. They stimulate inspiration—when you have an Aha! moment and suddenly "see the light" you may have connected with a fire elemental.

Salamanders like to work with people who have a spiritual bent and with those who exhibit initiative or daring. Invite them to join you when you do spells that involve passion, vitality, courage, or action.

Undines: Water Elementals

These spirits splash about in the waters of the world. The Greeks' water nymphs and mermaids fall into this category, too. Usually depicted as beautiful young females, undines perform a variety of tasks, from nourishing life on earth to regulating the tides to inspiring artists and poets. They also protect fish and aquatic creatures, and—if they choose—guide humans on sea voyages. In recent times, these elementals have been working hard to offset the effects of water pollution and the destruction of marine habitat.

Capricious creatures, they gravitate toward sensitive, artistic people and you can call upon them if you need help with a creative project. Want to get in touch with your psychic ability? Ask an undine for assistance. These elementals will also come to your aid when you're doing love spells.

Always remember to thank the elementals that assist you in your spellworking. These beings enjoy receiving small gifts that express your appreciation:

- Gnomes adore jewelry and crystals. Bury a token in the ground as a way of saying "Thanks."
- Sylphs enjoy flowers. Place fresh blossoms on your altar or lay them in a sacred spot outdoors as an offering.
- Salamanders like candles and incense. Burn these to honor your fiery helpers.
- Undines are fond of perfume. Pour some in a stream, lake, or other body of water.

If you behave disrespectfully toward the elementals, they may retaliate by playing nasty tricks on you. Be generous, however, and your elemental friends will continue to serve you faithfully.

Chapter 6

GODS AND GODDESSES

How do you envision the Divine? How do you integrate sacred energy into your own life? Do you believe in many gods and goddesses, one deity with many faces, or a single Supreme Being?

Throughout history, virtually every culture has entertained visions of a divine realm populated by one or more beings with supernatural powers. Early people who lived close to nature often revered female creator/fertility figures. A great Mother Goddess shows up in many different civilizations as Mary, Demeter, Ceres, Isis, and various other deities. The ancient Greeks, Romans, and Norse worshipped numerous gods and goddesses. The Hindu pantheon includes many diverse spiritual beings, too.

Witches, Wiccans, and Neopagans—just like followers of other belief systems—often disagree about the nature of the Divine. Some follow a specific faith and worship one or more gods or goddesses; some aren't religious at all. Wiccans honor a Goddess and a God as her consort; Neopagans often recognize a number of deities. Many witches consider all spiritual paths equally valid and that all lead to the same place. Who or what you believe in—if anything—is totally up to you.

FACETS OF THE DIVINE

Early people connected spirits with the wind, nature, the stars, and the forces behind phenomena they couldn't explain in other ways. These divine beings were said to watch over creation and guide human destiny. As the earth's population grew and cultures interacted with one another—through war, trade, and migration—our conceptions of the heavenly realm evolved.

Some spirits fell out of favor as our ancestors learned more about the actual workings of the physical world and the universe. In some instances, minor tribal gods and goddesses merged with or gave way to deities with greater powers. Some deities went by different names and faces in different countries—Venus in Rome, Aphrodite in Greece, Amaterasu in Japan—although their attributes were essentially the same.

A popular metaphor describes divine energy as a gemstone, and every facet on that gemstone as a different manifestation of the core energy. These manifestations present themselves differently, but they are all, in the end, from the same divine source.

Some witches naturally relate to the gods and goddesses that are part of their personal heritage. Scandinavians might gravitate to Freya, Greeks to Sophia, Irish to Brigid. Santeríans combine Catholicism with African Paganism, and honor deities from both traditions.

One Deity or Many?

- Monotheism means a belief in a single supreme being.
- A dualist believes in two deities; in a Wiccan context, this would be God and Goddess.
- Polytheism is the belief in many separate gods.
- Henotheists believe in one god without denying the existence of others.

DUAL FORCES IN THE UNIVERSE

Wiccans believe that instead of one divine source or entity, there are two distinct deities—Goddess and God—and they in turn manifest as the gender-related god-forms. But the concept of dual forces operating in the universe isn't limited to Wiccans. Many cultures speak of a feminine and a masculine principle that exist in and around us. The Chinese refer to these two energies as yin (feminine) and yang (masculine). Native Americans respect Mother Earth and Father Sky.

These two polarities function in tandem to balance one another and create wholeness.

The Divine Feminine

When we talk about feminine and masculine, we don't mean woman and man. Think energies instead. Receptivity, emotion, passivity, and intuition are all expressions of feminine energy. You can see it operating in water, earth, the moon, darkness, night, silence, cool colors, and lots of other things. When you do magick, you use these ingredients in order to bring a specific energy into your spells and rituals. (In later chapters you'll learn ways to combine certain ingredients to produce the outcome you seek.) The Goddess is merely a depiction of the feminine force—the face we put on the energy to personify it.

The Earth Mother

Perhaps the most omnipresent symbol of the Divine Feminine is Mother Earth herself. Concern for the environment and "green" practices show respect for the Goddess, who appears in all of nature. It's no accident that movements honoring the earth and the Goddess evolved simultaneously. Indeed, many witches believe that unless Goddess energy reawakens within each of us and in the world as a whole, the planet may be destroyed.

The Divine Masculine

The feminine is not complete without the masculine; together, these energetic polarities form a whole. Go online and look at the yin-yang symbol. The white part represents the masculine force, the black side the feminine. Notice how, when joined, they form a circle, the symbol of wholeness. Masculine energy expresses itself outwardly as action and assertiveness. You can see this principle operating in fire, wind, the sun, light, daytime, noise, warm colors, and many other things—and you'll use these in specific ways when you do magick. Gods such as Thor, god of thunder and lightning, and the war god Mars symbolize the qualities of the masculine force.

Tripartite Deities

Sometimes the God and Goddess are shown as tripartite beings. This means that they are represented by three different images that signify the three stages of human life. The Goddess is frequently depicted in three aspects—maiden, mother, and crone—that signify the three phases of womanhood. Likewise, witches often see the God as having three faces, which represent the stages of a human's life: youth, maturity, and old age.

Depending on the type of magick you're doing, you might choose to call upon a certain aspect of the God or Goddess. For instance, if you need extra vitality to win a big ballgame, invite the youthful side of the Divine Masculine to assist you. If you're trying to get pregnant, ask the mother aspect of the Divine Feminine to lend you her fertility.

SEEING THE DIVINE IN NATURE

Honoring the earth and being aware of the natural world are part of many modern alternative spiritualities. A person who honors the earth and considers the natural world her primary teacher is sometimes labeled a nature-worshipper or called a Pagan (see Chapter 3). In modern use, however, the terms are not generally pejorative. In New Age spiritual practice, the word "Pagan" is being reclaimed by people who resonate to the heartbeat of the earth itself. Green witches, for instance, see the Divine in all of nature. If you ask a green witch, "Is there a God or Goddess?" she'll probably reply, "Of course." If you inquire further, "Who is he or she?" the green witch might say, "God is everywhere in nature."

GODDESSES FROM AROUND THE WORLD

Whatever she's called, however her story is told, the characteristics of the Divine Feminine—fertility, creativity, compassion, wisdom, beauty, love, healing—can be seen in the goddesses of all cultures. Here are some of the world's many goddesses and the attributes usually associated with them.

Name	Culture	Attributes
Amaterasu	Japanese	beauty, leadership, brightness
Aphrodite	Greek	love, beauty, sensuality
Artemis	Greek	courage, independence, protection
Axo Mama	Peruvian	fertility
Bast	Egyptian	playfulness, joy
Brigid	Celtic	creativity, smithcraft, inspiration, healing
Ceres	Roman	nourishment, health
Ceridwin	Celtic	inspiration, wisdom
Cybele	Asia Minor	fertility
Diana	Roman	hunting, purity, independence
Freya	Norse	love, healing, sensuality
Hathor	Egyptian	love
Hecate	Greek	magick, death, wisdom
Inanna	Sumerian	journeys, facing fears, courage, grief
Isis	Egyptian	art, nourishment, wholeness, awakening
Kali	Indian	transformation, death, destruction, change
Kuan Yin	Asian	compassion, humanitarianism, mercy
Lakshmi	Indian	wealth, abundance
Pele	Hawaiian	fiery spirit, destruction and rebirth, vitality
Sekhmet	Egyptian	grace, dignity, strength
Siva	Slavic	fertility
Sophia	Greek	wisdom, power
Tara	Indian	nourishment, protection, compassion
Tiamat	Babylonian	power, magick, protection
Yemaja	Nigerian	secrets, dreams, childbirth, purification

On days when a witch wishes to connect with certain qualities in herself or wants to strengthen abilities she feels are weak, she can ask for help from a goddess who embodies the qualities she seeks. Say you have an important business meeting coming up and you want to make a good impression. The Egyptian sun goddess Sekhmet, depicted as a lioness, symbolizes the attributes you need. Ask her to help you accomplish your aims.

Goddess-Named Products

Goddesses have loaned their names to various products in popular culture. The sportswear company Nike, for instance, took its name from the Greek goddess of victory. But some associations seem a bit curious, such as Gillette's razor for women, called Venus—does this imply that shaving off all your body hair makes you more loving? Or how about Kali Mints, named after the Indian goddess of death—they don't sound very appetizing do they?

GODS FROM AROUND THE WORLD

Since the beginning of time, cultures around the world have honored a masculine force. The many faces of the God express qualities associated with the male archetype: strength, virility, daring, leadership skills, logic, protection, knowledge, and courage. Here are some of the gods found in various cultures around the world and the attributes connected with them.

Name	Culture	Attributes
Aengus	Irish	youth, love
Apollo	Greek	beauty, poetry, music, healing
Damballah	Haitian	wisdom, reassurance
Ea	Chaldean	magick, wisdom
Ganesh	Indian	strength, perseverance, overcoming obstacles
Green Man	Celtic	fertility, nature, abundance, sexuality
Horus	Egyptian	knowledge, eternal life, protection
Lugh	Celtic	craftsmanship, healing, magick
Mars	Roman	aggression, war, vitality, courage

Name	Culture	Attributes
Mercury	Roman	intelligence, communication, trade, travel
Mithras	Persian	strength, virility, courage, wisdom
Odin	Scandinavian	knowledge, poetry, prophesy
Osiris	Egyptian	civilization, learning
Pan	Greek	nature, fertility
Shiva	Indian	destruction, transformation
Thoth	Egyptian	knowledge, science, the arts
Tyr	Teutonic	law, athletics
Vishnu	Indian	preservation, stability
Zeus	Greek	authority, justice, abundance, magnanimity

Want to take a trip? Invite Mercury to help you plan your itinerary. Need some extra power on the gridiron? Consider adding Mars or Mithras to your team. You can develop a personal relationship with the gods and goddesses, no matter what their origin, and learn more about yourself through working with them.

GETTING HELP FROM GODS AND GODDESSES

Once you've familiarized yourself with a number of gods and goddesses, you may opt to petition one or more for help with a specific task. If you are facing a big challenge or obstacle, you could call on the Hindu god Ganesh to assist you. Perhaps you admire a certain deity's attributes and want to add them to your own character. If you'd like to be more compassionate, say, you could align yourself with Kuan Yin, the Asian goddess of mercy. Many witches believe that gods and goddesses are willing to help us if we ask and show them due respect.

Guides, Guardians, and Other Spirit Helpers

Most witches believe we share this universe with all sorts of nonphysical beings—not just gods and goddesses—including lots of good guys who are willing to help us. They guide, protect, and aid us in our daily lives. When things go wrong, we can call on them for assistance.

Some people envision these divine helpers as angels. Others prefer to think of them as sages, guardians, or parts of their own higher consciousness. Native Americans often look to revered ancestors and spirit animals for guidance. We've already talked about teaming up with fairies, nature spirits, and elementals. These supernatural beings can be tremendous assets in magickal work—indeed, they could be essential to a spell's success.

Tips for Working with Deities

When working with spirit helpers, certain rules of etiquette apply, as is the case in any personal or business relationship:

- Ask for assistance—guides, guardians, and deities recognize your free will and might not intervene unless you invite them to do so.
- Show respect—treat spirit helpers as honored teachers and allies, not servants.
- Don't try to micromanage deities—if you seek aid from spirit beings, turn over the reins and allow them to carry out your request as they see fit.
- Don't seek help to do harm—although some evil entities lurk out there, you don't want to join forces with them, and the good spirits won't get behind a bad cause.
- Express gratitude—remember to thank the beings who assist you, and perhaps give them an offering.

Ways to Attract Divine Assistance

How can you go about connecting with deities? They might come to you in a dream, meditation, or vision. Countless people throughout history have experienced visitations from divine beings. Myths and legends from many cultures speak of gods and goddesses interacting with humans in this way. Such appearances aren't just a thing of the past—they can happen to anyone, any time.

The Modern Guide to Witchcraft

But if that doesn't happen to you, don't despair. You have other ways to catch a favorite deity's eye. Consider these suggestions:

- Learn as much as you can about the god/dess you wish to attract. Read myths, spiritual literature, and folklore. Many websites and blog sites provide in-depth information about deities, from the best known to the most obscure.
- Set up an altar and dedicate it to the deity of your choice. In Chapter 9, we'll talk more about creating altars and shrines.
- Collect artwork depicting the deities you want to petition. Again, you'll find lots of images online, but New Age stores and some religious shops also sell spiritual artwork. Display these images in a prominent place where you'll see them often, such as on your altar.
- Find out what things certain deities like. Many of them have preferences for particular plants, foods, stones, etc. Place these on your altar or in a special place outdoors as offerings to the god, goddess, or other spirit.

Keep an open mind and an open heart when you're working with deities. Trust your intuition—when you're dealing with forces beyond the mundane world, you need to rely on a type of knowing beyond your everyday awareness, one that will let you tune in to higher frequencies. Finally, believe that the spirits will speak to you, in one way or another. Doubt slams the door between you and magickal beings. When you're dealing with other realities and supernatural forces, remember this: You'll see it when you believe it.

Chapter 7

DIFFERENT TYPES OF WITCHCRAFT AND MAGICK

Now that you have a better understanding of the magickal universe in which you live and perhaps have met some of your spirit helpers, it's time to start thinking about how you might like to proceed along your journey as a witch. Just as musicians approach their craft in very personal ways, so do witches. Some musicians are classically trained and perform complicated pieces in concert halls or with orchestras. Others can't even read music and prefer to jam in a more casual manner. Witches, too, may choose to tread a simple path or an incredibly complex one. Kitchen and hedge witches, for example, generally practice uncomplicated, natural magick. They usually don't belong to a coven—though they may join forces with other witches for special purposes. Solitary practitioners, they depend on self-study, insight, creativity, and intuition as their guideposts. Their practice usually includes plant and herbal magick, often for the purpose of healing.

Other witches perform magick with more ritualistic overtones, drawing inspiration from various mystical and spiritual movements, such as the Qabalah (a body of Jewish mysticism and magick). They look at every aspect of a spell or a ritual as part of a huge picture. Each piece must be in the right place for everything to turn out as it should. For instance, the astrological phase of the moon during which the spell is performed should be suited to the task. The witch might wear special clothing and move in carefully choreographed patterns. Every part of the working should be designed to build energy toward a desired outcome.

Which path you choose depends on your personality, preferences, and talents. Do you enjoy group activities and working with other people toward a common goal? Perhaps you'd like to join a Wiccan coven. Or are you a loner and a homebody? You may be a natural hedge witch. Do you feel a strong connection with the earth and love the outdoors? If so, green witchcraft might be your thing. If you have a flair for the dramatic, ceremonial magick might appeal to you. Where you live could be a factor too. In the Southwestern states, shamanism influenced by Native American traditions is popular; in Salem, Massachusetts, you'll find plenty of Wiccans. Let's look at a few of these different practices now—you may find one that intrigues you enough to investigate it further.

Origins of the Freemasons

During the Middle Ages, some Medieval tradesmen became members of secret, mystical guilds. Because they possessed special knowledge of magick and symbolism as well as skills in carpentry, masonry, or glasswork these artisans were hired to work on Europe's great cathedrals. The famous rose windows they created had unique healing properties, due to a type of magick that we still don't fully understand today. These early guilds spawned the Freemasons.

GREEN WITCHES

Green witches are the original "tree huggers." The green witch walks the path of the naturalist, the herbalist, the wise woman, and the healer. Earth is her primer, the natural world her classroom. The natural world offers many gifts, but comparatively few people in today's technology-driven society embrace them. With the resurgence of nature-based practices and environmental awareness, however, green witches are once again emerging as guardians of nature and of humanity's relationship with our planet.

The green witch uses nature's gifts to improve the well-being of the physical body, the spirit and soul, and the environment. In earlier times,

The Modern Guide to Witchcraft

many people practiced green witchcraft, whether or not they called it that. Midwives, herbalists, shamans, and other healers knew the powers of plants—both medicinal and magickal—and tapped botanicals for all sorts of purposes. They also felt a strong connection to the earth, the seasons, and the cycles of life. In fact, their very lives depended on existing in harmony with nature.

The Modern Green Witch's Work

Today's green witches follow in the footsteps of their ancestors. They honor the earth and all its inhabitants—rocks, plants, and animals. They utilize ingredients from nature to concoct remedies and in spellcasting, particularly herbs and crystals. (You'll learn more about this in Chapters 11 and 12.) They work to protect the environment and try to live in harmony with all of creation. They may interact with the devas, elementals, or spirits who guard nature. Using their intuition, they create a channel of communication between the natural world and the human one.

A green witch usually works alone with nature as her partner. Historically, green witches lived apart from the community. Those who needed the services of such a witch traveled to see her, perhaps high into the hills or at the edge of the forest. She used the properties of the plants and trees around her to heal others. These days, you're more likely to find a green witch living in the middle of a city or in the suburbs, and her garden is likely to be small—maybe just some containers on a porch or a kitchen window "greenhouse."

She might work in an office or in sales or in the service industry. Perhaps she's in the medical field. Or she's a teacher or a full-time parent. Today's green witch understands that she can't restore nature's balance by isolating herself in the wild, she must bring her knowledge and gifts into the rest of the world. Cities, superhighways, and deforested areas—places where humankind has damaged nature—need the green witch's healing powers.

Living the Green Path

A green witch isn't defined by where she lives or what she does to bring home a paycheck. Nor is she limited to working with flowers, trees, and herbs. What makes a green witch is her relationship to the world around her, her ethics, and her affinity with nature. She doesn't merely practice green witchcraft, making potions and lotions, healing salves and teas—she *lives* the green path.

The path of the green witch combines aspects of both witchcraft and shamanism, but is wholly neither. It is an intensely personal path that integrates ability, likes and dislikes, the climate of a particular geographic location, and interaction with the energy of the environment. Healing, harmony, and balance are all key to the green witch's practice and outlook on life. These concepts embody three distinct focuses:

1. The earth (your local environment, as well as the planet)
2. Humanity (in general, as well as your local community, friends, and acquaintances)
3. You

Whether you choose to grow your own garden, install solar panels on your home, pick up trash by the side of the road, or get involved in a movement to protect wildlife is totally up to you. Although rooted in the ancient past, green witchcraft isn't a tradition so much as a personal adaptation of an ideal. No body of formal knowledge is passed on through careful training, no established group mind to which you are connected by sacred ceremonies performed by elders.

The green witch's power comes from participating in the miracle that is life, from attuning yourself to the energies of the environment around you. Instead of striving to amass power, you tap into the flows of energy that already exist in and around the earth. The challenge is how to walk a green path today, in a time of environmental stress, mass industrialization, and urbanization.

HEDGE WITCHES AND KITCHEN WITCHES

The terms *hedge witch* and *kitchen witch* can refer to someone who follows a home-based, freeform spiritual path that can't be clearly defined or identified as an existing Neopagan path. In some circles they connote a person who engages in a shamanic practice involving spirit journeys or trancing (more about this later), often with the aid and support of herbal knowledge. A kitchen or hedge witch can also be someone who pursues a solitary nature-based spiritual path. In earlier times, wise women, cunning men, and other such practitioners were sometimes called green witches or hedge witches; they worked to heal individuals, communities, and any malaise in the natural world.

Home as a Sanctuary

Similar to green witchcraft, hedge witchcraft is nature based. Hedge witches are often solitary practitioners, meaning they work alone rather than with a coven or group of other people. They may be self-dedicated, but they are rarely publicly initiated into the field—they're more likely to have learned the Craft at Grandma's side or eased into it as an extension of growing herbs in a backyard garden.

Hearth and home occupy a central place in their spiritual and magickal work—often kitchen witches work out of their own homes, making those homes places of healing energy and knowledge. Their homes provide shelter and nourishment, for both the body and the spirit. The hedge witch's home is her temple and her sanctuary, which she tends in order to keep energy flowing smoothly and freely. She seeks to support, nurture, and nourish her family (and extended community), both spiritually and physically. That neighbor who always makes you feel comfortable and peaceful in her home, who serves you soothing herbal teas and healthy, homemade meals might be practicing kitchen witchery, even if she doesn't call it that.

Home-Based Spirituality

We find the concept of the home as a spiritual center in many cultures and throughout many eras. The home, and in particular the hearth, has often served as a point of connection for god/desses and humankind. In China, the Kitchen God is viewed as an important domestic deity, and families hang paper images of the god near their stoves. In the West, kitchen witches use two symbols as joint keystones: the cauldron and the flame. (We'll talk more about these symbols in later chapters.)

Traditionally, the cauldron represents abundance and hospitality. In magick, it also symbolizes rebirth, mystery, creation, fertility, transformation, and feminine power. The flame is a symbol of life, activity, the Divine, purification, inspiration, and masculine power, making it an excellent partner for the cauldron.

A Clean Sweep

The kitchen witch bases her magickal practice in her everyday household activities—cooking, cleaning, baking, and so forth, all form the basis for her magick. For example, sweeping the floor free of dust and dirt may simultaneously cleanse the space of negative energy. That's the real reason witches use brooms, by the way—not to fly across the sky.

Although we usually think of hedges as surrounding property, for witches the hedge is more than a physical barrier. It symbolizes spiritual protection from the stresses of the outside world. It can also be seen as a barrier between the world of humans and the spirit realm.

WICCA

The words *Wicca* and *witch* come from the Anglo-Saxon term *wicce* meaning "to bend or shape." Wicca's tenets reach back to the "Old Religion" of pre-Christian Europe, especially that of the early Celts. Its roots also dig deeply into prehistoric times and the ancient fertility goddesses worshipped by Paleolithic peoples.

Writer Gerald Gardner is commonly given credit for coining the term *Wiccan* and jump-starting the modern movement in the 1950s. During the 1960s and '70s as feminism emerged Wicca gained popularity because it offers greater balance and equality than patriarchal religions. It is one of the few faiths that honors a primary feminine deity; however, you needn't be female or a feminist to pursue a Wiccan path. Today, Wicca is among the fastest-growing religious systems in the United States; it is even recognized by the U.S. military.

As mentioned earlier, people sometimes mistakenly think Wicca and witchcraft are interchangeable terms. Wiccans generally practice witchcraft, but witches may not necessarily share Wiccan beliefs and therefore would not consider themselves Wiccan. Simply put, Wicca is a religion, like Christianity or Judaism. It has defined practices, beliefs, and ethical codes. Within this religion, however, you'll find plenty of room for personal expression.

How Many Wiccans Are There?

According to ReligionFacts (*www.religionfacts.com*) between 1 and 3 million men and women worldwide consider themselves adherents of Wicca. Other estimates put that number closer to 800,000. Indiana University of Pennsylvania places Wicca among the eight largest faith groups in the United States.

Although Wiccans observe certain customs, rituals, and practices, the religion is flexible with no dogma, no sacred texts, and no laws save one: Do no harm. Wiccans follow what's known as the threefold law. The law basically states that whatever you do, whatever energies you "put out," will return to you threefold (three times over) in this lifetime or in the next. Therefore, Wiccans attempt to abide by what's known as the Wiccan Rede.

The Wiccan Rede

Bide the Wiccan law ye must,

In perfect love and perfect trust,

Eight words the Wiccan Rede fulfill:

An' ye harm none, do what ye will.

What ye send forth comes back to thee,

So ever mind the Rule of Three.

Follow this with mind and heart,

And merry ye meet, and merry ye part.

Various branches of Wicca, each with somewhat different views, already exist. Dianic Wicca, for example, has a strong feminist component. Gardnerian Wicca is more formal and hierarchal than some other branches, and its practitioners perform rituals "skyclad" (nude). Visit *www.wicca.com* for more information about these and other types of Wicca. Like all belief systems, Wicca continues to evolve, and young enthusiasts coming to it today will surely expand its ideas, practices, and forms of expression in the future.

SHAMANISM

One of the earliest depictions of a shaman was found in France, in the cave of Les Trois Frères. Estimated to be at least 15,000 years old, the painting shows a man disguised as a bison and armed with a bow. Originally, the term *shaman* referred to a Siberian medicine man, but it can apply to anyone who engages in shamanistic practices, regardless of the era and society in which the person lives. In simple terms, a shaman is someone who understands both the spirit world and the natural world, and who uses that knowledge to provide healing, guidance, and protection to his people.

The Lessons of Don Juan

In the 1970s, the best-selling books of Carlos Castaneda introduced readers to the concepts of shamanism. Castaneda wrote about his five-year apprenticeship with a teacher whom he called Don Juan, and described his experiences in what he termed "nonordinary states of reality." He also discussed shape-shifting, a shamanic practice that involved projecting his own consciousness into animals and plants.

Among the indigenous people of North, Central, and South America, shamans have long served as medicine men, midwives, visionaries, wisdom keepers, and healers. These shamans worked with the forces of nature, the deities and ancestors in the spirit realms, and totem animals to ensure the well-being of their tribes.

Walking Between the Worlds

From the shamanic perspective, the physical world is only one facet of reality. Many other realms exist, and it's possible to travel to these other realities at will. Shamans have learned to erase the barriers that ordinarily separate the physical and nonphysical realms in order to "walk between the worlds."

The Modern Guide to Witchcraft

As seers and diviners, Native American shamans use drumming, dancing, herbs and botanical substances, fasting, and other practices to induce altered states of consciousness. While in these trance states, the shamans journey beyond the limitations of matter and space to gain knowledge, communicate with entities in the spirit world, effect healing, and observe the future. Dreams, too, provide access into other levels of reality. Although we tend to associate shamanism with Native Americans, you'll find shamans in many other cultures too. Celtic magicians might not use the term shamanism, but they engage in shamanic practices. They explore what's known as the Otherworld, a nonphysical place of wisdom, creativity, and imagination, as well as the fairie realm.

Often a shaman uses a technique called "astral projection" to visit other worlds beyond our earthly one. This allows the person's spirit to journey freely while the physical body remains in a trancelike state. The spirit is also able to temporarily leave the body during sleep and explore the nonphysical realms. In these other levels of reality, the shaman might meet spirits that once occupied human bodies as well as gods, goddesses, and other beings that have never incarnated.

Spirit Animals

When journeying in this way, shamans sometimes seek the assistance of spirit animals or other guides to provide protection and direction. In ancient times, people in many parts of the world believed spirit animals lived in an invisible realm that intersects with our own physical one. These spirit beings helped our ancestors in countless ways, from providing protection to offering healing wisdom to predicting the future. Early humans considered these animal guides and guardians as types of deities—somewhat like angels—and paid homage to them.

Native American tribes traditionally established special affinities with certain animals, which became the tribe's totems or sacred animals. They assisted the shamans' personal spirit guides in magickal work. Tribes carved totem poles with the images of various spirit and animal guides as a way of showing gratitude and to request continued aid in the future.

SORCERERS

Like shamans, sorcerers understand that our planet is not the only realm of existence, nor are we earthlings the only forms of intelligent life in the cosmos. Sorcerers believe the universe contains an infinite number of worlds just waiting to be explored. Furthermore, they're adept at traveling to these other worlds and interacting with the beings who reside there—and they don't need a passport to get in.

In her book *The Sorcerer's Crossing*, Taisha Abelar describes sorcerers as people whose goal is "breaking the perceptual dispositions and biases that imprison us within the boundaries of the normal everyday world and prevent us from entering other perceivable worlds." What she means is, we limit ourselves with narrow, conditioned thinking and miss out on a lot.

Through training and practice, sorcerers develop the ability to expand their sight beyond ordinary vision and see things the rest of us can't. They can perceive the life in rocks and trees, as well as see the spirits who live all around us. With practice, the sorcerer attunes herself with her nonphysical, energetic body—known as the "double"—controlling and expanding it in order to accomplish feats far beyond what most of us consider normal. For example, a sorcerer might project her double someplace other than where her physical body happens to be at any given time, so that she can be in two places at once. While she's sitting at her desk, performing her everyday job, she may simultaneously be chanting in a temple in India or visiting Machu Picchu in Peru.

DRUID MAGICK

The word *Druid* derives from the Indo-European root *drui*, meaning "oak," as well as "solid and true." Originally, Druids served as the bards, teachers, healers, judges, scribes, seers, astrologers, and spiritual leaders of the ancient Celts. They conducted rites and rituals, gazed into the future, healed the sick, kept the history of their people, and addressed legal matters within their communities. These wise men and women were highly revered and wielded authority second only to the king's.

Much of what we know today about the early Druids has been handed down through oral tradition, folklore, legends, songs, and poetry. As the Romans and Christianity moved into Ireland and Britain, the conquerors destroyed the Druids and their tradition. Thus, most of Druidic history remains shrouded in mystery.

Druids and Magick

Maya Magee Sutton, PhD, and Nicholas R. Mann, authors of *Druid Magic*, explain that in contemporary Irish dictionaries, the word *draiocht* means "magick" as well as "spells." Its root, *draoi*, translates as "magician," "sorcerer," or "Druid." This suggests a strong connection between the Druids and the practice of magick.

Modern-day Druids follow beliefs and practices associated with their early ancestors. With little actual information available about the old ways, however, neo-Druids interpret the spiritual tradition by blending ancient with contemporary wisdom. A reverence for nature, knowledge of astrology and divination, healing, and shamanic journeying continue to be part of today's Druidic practice.

The Druids consider trees to be sacred. Oaks, in particular, have long been linked with Druid spirituality. Sacred rituals were—and still are—performed in oak groves. Druids believe trees embody wisdom that can be passed along to human beings. Each tree possesses certain characteristics and unique properties that Druids use in their magickal work. Rowan trees, for instance, offer protection. Oaks give strength and endurance. Willows are associated with intuition and divination—they're a favorite wood for making magick wands.

CEREMONIAL MAGICK

Also called high or ritual magick, ceremonial magick evolved out of the teachings of early mystery schools in various parts of the world. Its practitioners are more likely to describe themselves as magicians than as witches. The Hermetic Order of the Golden Dawn, an organization that formed in the latter part of the nineteenth century as a secret society (see Chapter 3), has greatly influenced this type of magick and its practice today. The group's philosophy is founded on the Hebrew Qabalah and the doctrines of Hermes Trismegistus, and draws upon the belief systems of the Freemasons, Rosicrucians, Gnostics, and others.

More formalized and intellectualized than Wicca and other Pagan spiritual paths, ceremonial magick involves study of the Qabalah, astrology, alchemy, tarot, and many other subjects. It emphasizes the use of ritual and ceremony, along with mental training, to facilitate spiritual enlightenment, healing, extrasensory powers, and understanding of the cosmic order. Carl Weschcke, president of the publishing company Llewellyn Worldwide, has called this field of magick "spiritual technology." Indeed, if you have a fondness for highly developed systems, this path might be for you.

Why engage in complicated and sometimes lengthy rituals? Rituals focus the mind and transport you from the everyday world into a magickal one—that's a key reason for enacting them. Rituals rely on symbolic associations that the magician's senses and subconscious mind intuitively understand. Gestures, diagrams, postures, words, images, sounds, scents, and colors all play symbolic roles in magick rituals and ceremonies.

Ritual magick often involves elaborate and carefully orchestrated practices that are designed for various purposes. Purification rituals, for instance, cleanse the mind, body, and energy field. Protection rituals define sacred space and prevent unwanted influences from interfering. The rituals themselves are magickal acts.

The Magickal Qabalah

The Qabalah (sometimes spelled Kabbala, Cabala, and other ways) is a body of collected teachings that underlie Hebrew mysticism. It includes four sections that cover doctrines, magickal practices, orally conveyed wisdom, and techniques for working with words, letters, and numbers. It also describes the Tree of Life, which plays an important part in ritual magick and shows the stages of development and pathways to spiritual enlightenment.

The Modern Guide to Witchcraft

SEX MAGICK

Mystical rites, rituals, and ceremonies involving sex have been practiced in numerous cultures, East and West, for longer than anyone can document. The early Celts engaged in sexual activity, particularly during the spring planting season and on Beltane, as a form of sympathetic magick to encourage the land's fertility. Temple priestesses in ancient Greece combined sex and mysticism. Tantric yoga channels sexual energy toward spiritual goals and also promotes health and longevity. In Wicca's Great Rite, a couple invites the God and Goddess to enter their bodies during sex, and the act is considered sacred.

The Origins of Sex Magick

Western sex magick is rooted in the teachings of Sufis, adherents of a mystical branch of Islam, who supposedly shared their knowledge with the Knights Templar during the Crusades in the Middle East. The Templars brought these practices back to Europe, where they were incorporated into other mystical and occult philosophies. Magick's notorious bad boy, Aleister Crowley, did much to promote and influence the course sex magick has taken in the West. Crowley learned sex magick while traveling in India and Africa, and he emphasized its practice through the organization he headed, the Ordo Templi Orientis (OTO).

Sex magick can be great fun, but that's not its purpose. In simple terms, it's a way to supercharge your magickal work and generate results faster. According to sex magick's tenets, this creative force, which is responsible for all human and animal life, can be directed to create abundance, success, healing, spiritual growth, and so on—like other types of magick. It taps the powerful creative energy inherent in sexual activity for specific purposes other than human reproduction. Some witches engage in sex magick, others don't. It can be added to any other form of witchcraft, magick, or spiritual practice, and can be done by anyone. (For more information, see my book *Sex Magic for Beginners*.)

VOUDON OR VOODOO

When people hear the word *voodoo*, they often envision dolls stuck with pins, zombies, and hideous rituals carried out secretly in darkness. But voudon (or voodoo) is simply a belief system. First brought to Haiti by African slaves sometime during the sixteenth century, it emerged in Louisiana 200 years later.

Voudon involves the interaction of humans with spirits. Numerous deities and spirits play parts in voudon's elaborate rituals and spells. In a traditional voudon ceremony, worshippers work themselves into a frenzy through music, chanting, and dancing, sometimes accompanied by various forms of drugs and alcohol. During an altered state of consciousness, they become possessed by one of the spirits and collapse to the ground, writhing and speaking unintelligibly. Once possessed, a worshipper is believed to be able to bring about a cure, good fortune, or some other desire. In some instances, animal sacrifices might be offered to the spirits to win their favor.

The dark side of voudon, however, has captured the public's imagination. Some practitioners, it's said, turn the dead into zombies—reanimated corpses who are slaves without wills of their own. The extremes of voudon's black magick can include all the stuff of horror movies, including control over others, ritual murders, and cannibalism.

SANTERÍA

Often referred to as a Cuban mystery religion, the word *santería* literally means "the worship of saints." A blend of Catholicism and Nigerian Paganism that evolved centuries ago, when Yoruba slaves were taken from Nigeria to Cuba, santería consists of a pantheon of *orishas* who are a combination of Catholic saints and Yoruba gods and goddesses. If you were raised Catholic you might find this colorful tradition intriguing, a way to incorporate witchcraft into the religious training and experience you already have.

When a man joins the religion and becomes a *santero* (or *santera*, if she's female), he agrees to "worship the saints, to observe their feasts, obey their commands, and conduct their rituals," writes Migene

Gonzalez-Wippler, author of *The Santería Experience.* "In exchange for this absolute submission, he gains supernatural powers, protection against evil, and the ability to foresee the future and even to shape the future according to his will."

Casting spells and practicing witchcraft are part of a *santero*'s work. A *santero* often keeps icons or statues of the *orishas* and other saints on his altar, along with flowers, a bowl of water, and a bottle of Florida water (a type of cheap cologne used in many of the spells). The darker side of santería, known as mayomberia, is a type of black magick.

Of course, many other types of witchcraft and magickal practices exist around the world. The Polynesian spiritual path known as Huna teaches you to unite three aspects of yourself and channel your primal energy to bring about the results you desire. Practitioners of the ancient Chinese art of feng shui (pronounced *fung shway*) use a form of magick when they make changes in your home and workplace in order to attract money, love, health, etc. Wherever you go, you'll find people performing magick and doing witchcraft—even if they don't always call it that.

Chapter 8

SACRED SPACE

The Buddha once said, "Wherever you live is your temple if you treat it like one." Sacredness is more a matter of attitude and behavior than of trappings, and it doesn't require a building or props. Nonetheless, creating a sacred space is an important part of practicing magick, and witches often use tools and processes to establish safe havens in which to work.

WHAT IS SACRED SPACE?

Sacred space is an area you've cleansed of distractions and energy that you don't want to interfere with your magickal work. Within this purified zone you may choose to meditate, make offerings, and conduct spells or rituals. If you are lucky enough to have a temple or dedicated worship space in your home, then that is your permanent sacred space.

You've probably heard of magick circles. What makes sacred space different from a circle? A circle is a consciously constructed area that partially overlaps both our material world and the divine world. The resulting region is said to be "between the worlds," not wholly in one or the other. Sacred space is a place of peace and calm, but it is not necessarily "between the worlds." Sacred space is what goes into the circle, or it can simply exist on its own.

When you're in your sacred space you can still interact with the world beyond it—it doesn't set up a barrier the way a circle does. When you use sacred space, you make the existing environment holy, as opposed to creating a whole new surrounding. You remain open to the good energies in the area instead of sealing yourself away from them.

Sacred space is a wonderful alternative to a circle if you seek to create a harmonious atmosphere for a family gathering, particularly if the attendees are of mixed spiritualities or if the space you are using is unfamiliar to you. You can create it without anyone else's knowledge by purifying and harmonizing the energy of the area. You remove distracting, harmful, or stale energy and leave a positive, comfortable feeling instead.

Creating sacred space for other people who may not share your beliefs does not manipulate them in any way, nor does it disrespect their own religion. You are offering them a peaceful and balanced environment in which to study, discuss, eat, or mingle. Try creating sacred space before a dinner gathering during the week, when everyone is tired and stressed out. Watch how everyone relaxes in the serene energy.

CREATING SACRED SPACE

Creating sacred space includes four basic steps. The process takes place both inside you and outside, both in your mind and in a physical space.

- *Create*: This means eliminating thoughts, feelings, and energies that would distract you, so that your psyche is calm and all those everyday annoyances have been left behind.
- *Cleanse*: Clean up the area you will be using so that you have a tidy, pleasant place in which to work.
- *Purify*: This is the magickal counterpart to cleansing. Purification removes negative energy.
- *Consecrate*: This step involves blessing the space in some fashion.

From here you can go on to cast a circle if you so desire, or if your ritual requires it. (You'll learn how later in this chapter.) Otherwise, you're ready to begin doing whatever you choose to do within the sacred space you've created with these four steps.

Creating Internal Sacred Space

Before you perform any magick spells or rituals, you need to calm your spirit and your mind. Begin by putting aside your daily concerns and taking a few minutes to relax your body. Your goal is to shift your thinking and feeling from ordinary consciousness to a more serene and elevated consciousness. Giving yourself just five minutes to meditate will help you get in the right frame of mind to create sacred space.

Cleansing

Cleansing the physical space where you will work removes the distraction caused by dirt and clutter. Physical clutter and dust create chaotic energy, as any feng shui expert will attest. Cleansing also signifies your intention to honor this space and make it special. Sweep the floor with a regular broom and dustpan, clear off your altar or workspace, and tidy the general area. Put away loose papers, piles of books, clothes, toys, and other clutter from the area. Once you've removed the physical clutter, clean and polish the surfaces.

Cleanse yourself, too. Some witches like to take a relaxing bath or shower before a ritual. Although this step technically focuses on physical cleansing, it also helps you to mentally and emotionally prepare yourself to do magick.

Purifying Ritual Bath

Try this fragrant purifying scrub before doing a ritual or other magick work. Use warm—not hot—water. Do not use this scrub on your face. If you have sensitive skin, blend the herbs and essential oils into the almond or jojoba oil and omit the salt. Rub the oil gently into your skin prior to your bath or shower, and then rinse off.

CLEANSING BATH SCRUB

½ cup sea salt

1 teaspoon lemon zest (fresh)

1 cup fine Epsom salts

½ cup sweet almond or jojoba oil

3 drops lavender oil

3 drops frankincense oil

2 teaspoons lavender flowers (fresh or dry)

A lidded jar large enough to hold at least two cups of scrub

A small glass bowl

A damp washcloth

1. Purify the ingredients first. You can do this by visualizing white light around them. Grind the dried flowers finely while you state aloud that they will cleanse and purify your body, mind, and spirit.

2. In the covered jar, shake the two salts together. In the bowl, mix the oils. Open the jar and add the oil blend to the salt. Close the jar and shake to combine thoroughly. Open the jar and sprinkle the herbs over the oil and salt blend. Close the jar and shake to blend one final time.

3. To use the salt scrub once you are in the bath or shower, place about a tablespoon in the center of a clean, damp washcloth or in the palm of your hand. Gently rub the salts against your skin. Imagine them loosening any negative energy that may cling to you. Feel the purifying salt, lavender, frankincense, and lemon soaking into your body, cleansing your aura and calming your mind.

4. When you feel cleansed, rinse the salt scrub and the negative energy away with water.

5. Step out of the bath and dry yourself gently with a clean towel.

Purification

In this step, you purify yourself and the area where you'll be working. Cleansing deals with physical dirt; purification gets rid of the negative energy that clutters up an area. You can do this by sweeping in a counterclockwise motion with a besom (a witch's broom). If you enjoy aromatherapy, spritz some lavender scent into the air or burn your favorite calming incense. Some witches prefer to burn a smudge stick and waft the smoke around the area. Others sprinkle small amounts of salt in the space. Or, you can simply visualize a ball of white light materializing in the center, then growing outward and driving away negativity.

Purifying with a Stone

You can also purify your sacred space with a crystal or gemstone. Citrine, a yellowish-colored quartz crystal, is a good choice, although clear quartz will work as well. Before you use your chosen stone to purify a space, wash it in warm water and pat it dry. (Remember to cleanse your stone(s) often to get rid of any negative energy that may cling to them.) Then program or "charge" it with the purpose of purification. You can do this by speaking your intention to the stone. Rather than visualizing the negative energy being absorbed into the stone, imagine the stone pushing away unwanted vibrations.

1. Beginning at the perimeter of your area, slowly walk counterclockwise in circles that grow decreasingly smaller, spiraling in toward the center. As you do this, hold the crystal out and visualize it repelling the unwanted energy away from your space. If you notice a place that feels as if it has collected lots of negative energy, pause there and move the crystal around and up and down slowly, until you feel that the energy has been dispersed.

2. Finish in the center of the space. As an added precaution, you can leave the crystal lying on the floor to allow it to continue chasing away unwanted energy.

Consecration

Once both you and your ritual space have been physically cleansed and spiritually purified, you're ready to consecrate the space. To consecrate means to sanctify, and this is the definitive step that makes the space sacred.

One way to do this is to bring into your space the energies of the four elements we discussed in Chapter 5. Choose an object that represents each element; for example, a candle could symbolize the fire element, a stone could signify earth, a bowl of water could stand for the element of water, and a smoking stick of incense could bring in the air element.

Here's another method: Stand in the center of the area and feel yourself drawing up energy from the earth beneath your feet into the center of your body. Next, connect with the energy of the sky and sense it flowing down into the center of your body. Allow these two energies to mingle within you—feel them swirling around and blending in your core—then envision yourself radiating this dual energy outward until it fills the space. Stop the flow of energy from both sky and earth when you sense that your sacred space is filled.

After Your Ritual

Sacred space does not need to be dismantled, as a circle does, when you've finished your magickal working. You can leave it and come back whenever you choose, knowing that your sanctuary awaits you. To signal that your work here is finished, simply say something like, "This [ritual/spell/meditation] is ended. I go in peace." How long does sacred space last? It depends on where you created it. If your sacred space is in a room of your home, its sanctity will linger longer than if you set up a temporary space in a public mall. The more often you use this space, the more you reinforce its sanctity.

PREPARATION FOR CASTING A CIRCLE

Since ancient times, circles have symbolized both power and protection. When you cast a circle, you're working on several levels simultaneously. At a physical level you're defining the boundaries for your work, and on a spiritual level you're filling the space with your personal power. Modern witches still perform spells and rituals within a circle. Group work, especially gatherings and public rituals, frequently takes place in a circular sacred space. The circle represents unity, accord, and wholeness. It provides a protective psychic "fence" that keeps unwanted energies out and desired energies in, until you're ready to release them. A circle also shows that each person present is important to the success of the magickal working.

Creating the Proper Ambiance

The time spent creating sacred space is important psychologically for the participants. This allows everyone to adjust to spirit-thinking rather than mundane thinking. That attitude is important to the success of even the simplest magickal process. Everyone involved must be focused on your agreed-upon intention, in order to harness the energy needed for your spell or ritual. Once you're inside the circle, no one should leave unless absolutely necessary. The following guidelines will help you create the right ambiance for your sacred space:

1. Ensure that you (or the group) won't be interrupted. Turn off cell phones, TVs, etc.
2. Choose the right space for your task, taking into account weather, personal time, physical constraints, and what's going to take place in the sacred space.
3. Make sure the area is safe and tidy; get rid of anything that might distract you from the task at hand.
4. Set up your purified tools so they're readily accessible.
5. If you light candles, make sure you do it in a safe place to avoid the danger of fire. Keep them away from flammable materials (such as curtains).

Don't use potentially harmful chemicals in your sacred space. Whatever you put into sacred space—physical, emotional, and mental—gets amplified. Outdoors, use natural insect repellents, and salt or mulch to inhibit weed growth. Indoors, use only "green" cleaning materials.

Your Magickal Workspace

Your circle should be large enough to accommodate the number of people who will be working inside of it, as well as any objects that you'll bring into the circle. It's also your workspace, so if you'll be dancing, drumming, or otherwise moving about inside the circle, allow plenty of room for your activities.

Do You Need to Cleanse, Purify, and Consecrate Your Space Before Casting a Circle?

Some witches believe that you must always cleanse, purify, and consecrate the space where you will construct your circle. Others believe that cleansing and purifying are necessary, but that the act of creating the circle consecrates the space. Still others believe that you don't need to prepare the space in any way before you raise your circle. Do what feels right to you.

A circle isn't a flat ring, nor is it a dome over you. Your circle is actually a sphere surrounding you above and below your workspace, as if you were standing in a bubble. You draw a circle, but envision a sphere growing out of the line you draw—it's a circle in three dimensions, a shell that allows the sacred space within the circle to exist between the worlds.

CASTING A MAGICK CIRCLE

Casting a circle begins as an act of faith; you *believe* the circle is there. Although many methods exist for circle casting, some of them quite elaborate, you can begin by following these simple steps:

1. Stand in the center of the space you will define as your circle.
2. Facing east, extend your "projective" hand outward, pointing to where you're going to draw the circle's wall. (Your projective hand is the hand with which you send out energy.)
3. Center your personal energy within your body. Then ground your energy by envisioning it flowing down through your feet and into the earth, where it connects with the energy of the earth.
4. With your projective hand still extended, draw energy up from the earth, through your body and out to your hand.
5. Allow this energy to flow out to the point where you intend to begin forming your circle. Slowly turn in a clockwise direction until you are again facing the original starting point and the flow of energy joins up with where it started, forming a seamless ring.
6. Visualize the ring thickening and curving inward until it meets above your head and below your feet, forming a perfect sphere of energy.
7. Drop your hand to shut off the energy flow.

You are now ready to begin your magick spell or ritual.

Some witches prefer to use a tool to draw the circle, usually either an athame (ritual dagger) or a magick wand. We'll talk more about these and other tools later. Some witches like to actually walk the perimeter of the circle. If you want to do this, start in the east (make sure you know where the four compass directions are before you begin) and walk clockwise (or deosil), so that when the circle is completed you'll be inside of it. On a physical level, you create your circle by walking around its outer border, but for the circle to exist both in the physical realm and in the mental and spiritual realms, you must also visualize it with clear intent, channeling your energy and that of the earth into your visualization.

The Four Elements Technique

This technique combines the four elements—earth, air, fire, and water—to cast a circle. First, fill a bowl with salt water, which symbolizes the elements of earth and water. Beginning in the east, walk in a clockwise direction, sprinkling the salt water on the ground to define a circle as you say, "With earth and water I cast this magick circle." Next, light a stick of incense, which represents fire and air (smoke). Again, start in the east and walk clockwise around the circle, trailing the fragrant smoke behind you while you say, "With fire and air I cast this magick circle."

If you prefer, two people can perform this circle-casting ritual together. In this case, one person holds the bowl of salt water, and the other carries the stick of burning incense.

What If You Have to Leave a Circle?

Sometimes you just have to leave the circle, to retrieve something you forgot, go to the bathroom, or deal with some emergency. In this case, you'll need to open a door in the circle's "wall" to keep from breaking it—like popping a balloon—and letting all the power you've raised escape. You can cut a door with an athame, but the simplest method is to use your hands:

1. Hold your hands out in front of you, palms together. Slowly insert them into the energy of your circle wall.
2. Carefully pull your hands apart and visualize the wall of energy parting like a pair of curtains.
3. Step through and close the "curtains" behind you. Do what you need to do quickly and calmly, then return to the circle and open the curtains again, from the outside.

4. After stepping through the energy curtains and back into the circle, close the curtains.

DISMANTLING A BASIC CIRCLE

Dismantling the circle is just as important as raising it. Unlike sacred space, which slowly loses its energy over time, a circle must be taken down with as much care as you used to cast it. Perform the steps with reverence, closing the ritual with the same degree of respect as you entered into it. Basically, you dismantle a circle by repeating the motions you used to cast it, but in reverse:

1. Stand in the center of your circle and extend your "receptive" hand (the opposite of your projective hand) toward the wall of the circle. Center your personal energy, then ground it into the earth below.
2. Facing east, begin drawing the energy of the circle into your hand and let it flow through your body, then down into the earth. Turning counterclockwise, continue removing the energy in this manner until you face your original starting point again and the energy of the circle is all gone.
3. Drop your hand, shutting off the energy flow. Your hand may feel tingly or odd after collecting the energy—shake it a few times to get rid of any traces of the circle energy that may still be clinging to it. Disconnect your personal energy from the earth, bringing it back into your body.

You may wish to experiment with various circle-casting methods to see which ones you like best. Your circle may or may not be visible—it depends on you and your objective. Some magicians actually draw on the floor or ground with chalk. Some sprinkle flour or cornmeal to define the circle. Some witches light candles around the perimeter, or position stones in a circle. You might even choose to use a material that relates to the purpose of your spell; for example, if you're doing a love spell you could scatter rose petals in a circle. However, your intention and the love, passion, and joy that you project into the process are more important than the material you use.

Chapter 9

ALTARS AND SHRINES

If you plan to do magick frequently—and why wouldn't you?—you may decide to erect an altar in your home. An altar can be a TV table draped with a beautiful cloth, an ornate antique cabinet, or anything in between. Your altar is your basic "workbench" for doing magick. It establishes a sanctuary in your home and provides a focal point for casting spells, performing rites and rituals, and meditating. You go there to temporarily leave the ordinary, everyday world behind and enter sacred space.

SETTING UP YOUR ALTAR

Many witches include at least one central altar in a sacred space. Some believe it's important to place their altars in the east, others prefer the north, but wherever you choose to put yours is fine—go with what feels right. For practical purposes, setting the altar in the middle of your circle makes sense, especially if a number of people will join you there for rituals. Everyone can gather around it easily, and a central candle placed on the altar can symbolize Spirit as the guiding force for the ritual.

You can set up a permanent altar if your living circumstances permit. If you don't have enough space or share your home with other people who may not respect your altar, you can create a temporary one and dismantle it when you're finished doing your magick. If you're lucky enough to have a nice area outside to work in, you might position an altar there. Perhaps you could dedicate a special, large stone to that purpose.

What Goes on Your Altar?

Witches usually set up something depicting the four elements somewhere on their altars. These can be physical representations such as salt for earth, water for water, a candle for fire, and incense for air. Some magicians display their wands, pentagrams, athames, and chalices openly on their altars. If you decide to lay out your tools on your altar, be sure to include all four. (We'll discuss these tools in depth in the next chapter.) You might also like to place candles in handsome candleholders, some crystals, statues of favorite deities, flowers, and other meaningful objects there. Many people store their magickal gear in their altars. A cabinet with drawers is the perfect place to stash additional candles, incense, herbs, oracles, ritual clothing, and various other ingredients that you will use in your spells.

Your altar should bring you a sense of peace, joy, harmony, and personal power. Choose only things that hold positive associations for you to display on your altar.

Attuning Your Altar to Your Purpose

The items and symbols you bring to your altar largely depend on the purpose of your magick. Therefore, they may change regularly, depending on the type of spell or ritual you're doing. For example, for a ritual to honor your ancestors, you might want to include their photographs or personal effects. If you're doing a spell for love, you might set a vase of roses there.

Some witches enjoy decorating their altars according to the seasons or holidays. Spring flowers and some painted eggs add a pretty touch at Ostara. A cornucopia of fruits and vegetables could bring the flavor of the harvest festival Lughnasadh to your sacred space. At Yule, use evergreen sprigs and pinecones to set the scene. (We'll talk more about these holidays and how to celebrate them in Chapter 21.)

It's a good idea to cleanse and purify all the things you plan to use for magickal workings or to place on your altar beforehand. An easy way to do this is to light a stick of incense, such as cedar or sandalwood, and then pass the objects through the smoke.

Mobile Magick

You can even make a mobile altar to take along with you when you travel. You can transform a small box into a portable altar. Decorate it with images that imply "magick" to you, or pack a pretty scarf to drape over it. Fill the box with a few of the basics—tea light candles, incense cones, small crystals, etc. Or, consider putting an "altar" on your smartphone or iPad. Photograph your home altar or choose images that speak to you, and look at them whenever you want, wherever you go. Add some peaceful music to set the mood and you're good to go.

ADDING ALTARS IN YOUR CIRCLE

To connect with the four elements and the four corners of creation, some witches erect four small altars within their sacred spaces. If you decide to do this, position one altar at each of the four main compass points of your working space; these are known as the "quarters." You can either create permanent or temporary altars for a specific purpose. Consider placing items that represent the element on its respective altar—this can help to strengthen your connection with that element and enrich your experience during your magickal working. Here are some suggestions:

Direction	Element	Suggested Objects
East	Air	yellow candle, feathers, incense, wind chimes
South	Fire	red candle, red-colored stones (bloodstone, carnelian, ruby), figurine of a dragon
West	Water	blue candle, shells, bowl of water
North	Earth	green candle, stones or crystals, potted plants, marble or ceramic statue

An easy way to assign each altar to an element is to cover it with a cloth of the element's color: air/yellow, fire/red, water/blue, north/green. You might also consider putting a picture of the archangel who presides over each direction on the appropriate altar: east/Raphael, south/Michael, west/Gabriel, north/Uriel. Later in this chapter, you'll learn to call upon these deities to assist you in your magickal workings.

Elemental Shrines

A shrine is a place to honor something or someone, and to leave offerings. It serves as a physical point of contact where you can connect to a god or goddess, your guardian angel, a spirit animal, or an ancestor. Your altar can be used for these things as well, but a shrine is not a workspace for doing magick, like an altar. Shrines are easier to set up and maintain because they aren't as complex. A shrine can consist of a postcard, a specially charged crystal, a plant, or a small statue. If you don't want your family or roommate to know what you're doing, keep it simple. You know why those particular things are together; anyone else looking at them will think that it's just a decorative arrangement. Using a shrine as a focus for specific activities can also help unclutter your main altar area.

Famous Shrines

Since ancient times, all cultures have created shrines to honor deities and to mark sacred space. Stonehenge, a giant, megalithic circle in Wiltshire, England, remains a mystery today, but anthropologists think it might have been a sacred site for rituals or perhaps a shrine to deities. The Sekhmet Sanctuary at Luxor, Egypt, is a stunning shrine to the lion-headed goddess. Other amazing shrines include the Hanging Gardens of Haifa in Israel, Machu Picchu in Peru, and the Grand Mosque in Mecca. (See Judy Hall's book, *Crystals and Sacred Sites* to learn more.)

An element shrine is a place where you can connect with one element or all four. For example, if you build a water shrine, you can include a goblet of water, a small fountain, shells, river stones, or even just pictures of a waterfall or a calm lake. A fire shrine may be a collection of candles in reds and golds set on a crimson cloth, perhaps with a small brass figurine of a lion. The important thing is to think about what each element means to you and to gather a few items that represent your feelings and intentions regarding it.

Shrines for Harmony in the Home

Experiment with creating four separate shrines in four different places in your home. You can try building the earth shrine in the northern part of your house, the air shrine in the east, the fire shrine in the south, and the water shrine in the west. Make sure to have one shrine for each element so that your home remains balanced.

Does your home have a room where people tend to lose their tempers or energy runs too high? It may have an excess of fire energy that arises from its décor or as a result of how the energy flows through it. Try setting up an earth shrine or a water shrine in that room to ease tension and bring harmony. Choose a peaceful picture, a pretty blue or green stone, a shell, or a plant.

If an area of your home or workplace seems sluggish or heavy, consider building a fire shrine there. A photo of a sunny beach, a red stone, a vase of red or orange flowers—whatever feels right to you. You can do this in your office or workplace, too. Nobody has to know!

Memorial Shrines

Around the world, people create shrines to honor people who have died in battles or other catastrophes. These memorials, such as Footprints Fountain at Ground Zero in New York, serve as focal points for love, respect, prayers, gratitude, and hope. Not only do memorials such as these remind us of the victims and circumstances, they also hold the intentions of the people who visit, and invoke peaceful energies to help neutralize the traumas that took place there. Some people put up shrines at roadsides where fatal auto accidents occurred. When you visit the grave of a beloved friend or relative, and perhaps lay flowers or mementos there, you are showing reverence at a shrine created to honor that person.

CALLING THE FOUR QUARTERS/DIRECTIONS

Now let's put together some of the things you've learned in the previous chapters to do a more advanced form of circle casting. Many magickal traditions "call the quarters" as part of casting a circle. Not everyone uses the same words or gestures, however. Wiccans probably won't perform this practice in exactly the same way as ceremonial magicians do.

Before you cast your circle, erect four altars, one at each of the compass points. Decorate them as described earlier, with objects and symbols that represent the elemental energies of each direction. Of course, you'll want to cleanse, purify, and consecrate them first. Make sure you have everything in place before you actually cast the circle. Then once you and everyone else who will participate are inside it, you can light a candle at each altar and call in the quarters.

An Invoking Ritual

Some people invoke angels when calling the quarters. As we first discussed in Chapter 4, usually Raphael is associated with the east, Michael with the south, Gabriel with the west, and Uriel with the north. The deities are invoked in this order and released in the opposite order. Or, you might choose to invite gods, goddesses, animal totems, or other spirits to whom you feel a special connection or who have links to the purpose of your spell/ritual.

The following description is eclectic and generic, but nonetheless functional. As you call out to the four directions, visualize beams of pure white light stretching into the sky and connecting you at each of those directions to the powers of the universe. In time, you may wish to customize the ritual, adapting it to the season or your intention—you can even design your own entirely:

1. Begin at the east. Light a yellow candle here and face outward, with your back to the center of the circle. Call out to the forces of the east, saying, "Beings of Air, Guardians of the East, Breath of Transformation—Come! Be welcome in this sacred space. I/we ask that you stand firm to guard and protect, refresh and inspire me/us. Support the magick created here by conveying my/our wishes on every wind as it blows across the earth."

2. Move clockwise to the south and light a red candle. Invoke the deities of the south by saying, "Beings of Fire, Guardians of the South, Spark of Creation that banishes the darkness—Come! Be welcome

in this sacred space. I/we ask that you stand firm to guard and protect, activate and motivate me/us. Support the magick created here by conveying my/our wishes to the sun, the stars, and every beam of light that embraces the earth."

3. Continue to the west, light a blue candle, and call out, "Beings of Water, Guardians of the West, Rain of Imagination—Come! Be welcome in this sacred space. I/we ask that you stand firm to guard and protect, heal and nurture me/us. Support the magick created here by conveying my/our wishes to the dewdrops, rain, and the waves as they wash across the world."

4. Walk to the north, light a green candle, and say, "Beings of Earth, Guardians of the North, Soil of Foundation—Come! Be welcome in this sacred space. I/we ask that you stand firm to guard and protect, support and provide for me/us. Support the magick created here by conveying my/our wishes to every grain of sand, every bit of loam that is our world."

5. Move into the center of the circle and intone, "Ancient One, the power that binds all the elements into oneness and source of my/our magick—Come! Be welcome in this sacred space. I/we ask that you stand firm to guard and protect, guide and enhance all the energy created here. May it be for the good of all. So mote it be."

Once you've established your circle and feel the presence of the beings you've invited to join you in your sacred space, continue with your magick spell or ritual.

Closing the Circle and Releasing Magickal Energies

Releasing the sacred space is as important as erecting it. At the end of your workings, release the sphere you've created, thank the powers who've assisted you, ask them to keep guiding the energy you've raised. Bid them farewell until the next time:

1. Begin in the north quarter and move counterclockwise (as if you're unwinding something). See the beams of light that connected you to the rest of the universe slowly evaporating back into the Void.

Just because they leave your sacred space doesn't mean they're gone (energy can't be destroyed—it only changes form). They simply return to their source at the four corners of creation and attend to their tasks.

2. At the north point, say, "Guardians, Guides, and Ancestors of the North and Earth, I/we thank you for your presence and protection. Keep me/us rooted in your rich soil so my/our spirit(s) grow steadily, until I/we return to your protection again. Hail and farewell!" Then extinguish the candle.

3. Move to the west and say, "Guardians, Guides, and Ancestors of the West and Water, I/we thank you for your presence and protection. Keep me/us flowing ever toward wholeness in body, mind, and spirit, until I/we return to your protection again. Hail and farewell!" Then extinguish the candle.

4. Continue on to the south and say, "Guardians, Guides, and Ancestors of the South and Fire, I/we thank you for your presence and protection. Keep your fires ever burning within my/our soul(s) to light any darkness and drive it away, until I/we return to your protection again. Hail and farewell!" Then extinguish the candle.

5. Go to the east and say, "Guardians, Guides, and Ancestors of the East and Air, I/we thank you for your presence and protection. Keep your winds blowing fresh with ideas and hope, until I/we return to your protection again. Hail and farewell!" Then extinguish the candle.

6. In the circle's center say, "Great Spirit, thank you for blessing this space. I/we know that a part of you is always with me/us, as a still small voice that guides, protects, and nurtures me/us. Help me/us to listen to that voice, to trust it, and trust in my/our magick."

7. Before leaving the circle, some witches like to join hands and offer a closing chant, such as, "Merry meet, merry part, and merry meet again."

Calling the Quarters: An Alternative

Your invocation can be as simple or eloquent as you wish. Use your imagination. Here's a simpler and quicker technique if you're short on time. Stand in the center of the circle, facing east, while you say aloud:

Before me Raphael, guardian of the east.
Behind me Gabriel, guardian of the west.
To my right Michael, guardian of the south.
To my left Uriel, guardian of the north.
Be here now.

At the end of the spell or ritual, remember to release the energies you've called in and thank them for assisting you.

Working with the quarters and the spirits is a lot like being in an evolving relationship with someone you respect and admire. If you treat these entities accordingly, you will rarely be disappointed.

Chapter 10

THE WITCH'S TOOL KIT

If you were building a house you'd use a saw, hammer, carpenter's square, drill, and many other tools. Witches use special tools in their work, too. You've heard of magick wands, of course, but you might not be familiar with some of the other items in the witch's tool kit. And some objects you think you recognize may have magickal purposes that you wouldn't have guessed.

THE SYMBOLISM OF MAGICK TOOLS

In many cases a tool's symbolism is an important part of its magickal value and determines its function in casting spells. Its shape and/or the material from which it's made could be factors as well. The pentagram, the tool most often associated with witchcraft, is a good example. The five points of the star symbolize the five "points" of the human body: the head, arms, and legs. The circle surrounding the star represents wholeness, union, and boundaries, which is why magicians cast circles around themselves when doing spells. Thus, the pentagram's symbolism suggests one of its most popular uses: protection.

Da Vinci's Pentagram

Remember the pen-and-ink drawing artist Leonardo da Vinci did in 1490, called *Vitruvian Man*? Although the Renaissance master intended it as a diagram showing the ideal human proportions, it you look at it from a witch's perspective you'll notice it also depicts a pentagram.

Masculine and feminine symbolism appear in many magick tools. Don't think "man" or "woman" here; we're talking about energy forces. The wand, athame (ritual dagger), and sword are obviously phallic in shape. The shape of the chalice, cauldron, and bell represent the womb. Masculine tools activate, direct, and project energy; feminine tools hold, nurture, and give form to energy. Both forces are necessary in life and in magick.

The four primary magick tools—the wand, chalice, athame, and pentagram—also symbolize the four elements we've talked about in earlier chapters—fire, water, air, and earth, respectively. Each functions in accordance with its element's nature and brings its elemental force into play during a spell or ritual. For example, if your objective is to stabilize your finances, you might use the pentagram (symbol of earth) in your spellworking. If you want to fan the flames in a romantic relationship, the wand (symbol of fire) could have a role in your spell.

Are Magick Tools Really Necessary?

Witches and other magicians will tell you that tools are good helpmates to magick, but they are not necessary to the success of any spell or ritual. A tool is only something to help you focus your mind. Without your will and directed energy, the potential in any tool will remain dormant. A witch might talk about quartz crystals possessing energy-enhancing power, but until a crystal is charged and activated, that ability "sleeps" within. You awaken it. A focused will is all that any effective witch needs for magick. Everything else just makes the job easier.

THE MAGICK WAND

The best known of all magic tools is the wand, which gained even greater recognition through the Harry Potter stories. Although the scene in which Harry receives his wand is amusing, it's not accurate—the magician selects the wand, not the other way around. Until you fill your wand with power, it's just an ordinary rod.

The idea of using a magick wand to turn your boss into a toad or to make your rival vanish may be tempting, but that's not how it works. A wand's main purpose is to direct energy. If you want to send energy to a person, place, or thing, just aim your magick wand in that direction and *presto*—there it goes! You can also attract energy with a wand—point it at the sky to draw down power from the heavens, or at the ground to draw up the energy of Mother Earth. Magicians often cast protective circles around a designated space by using a wand to direct energy.

According to tradition, a wand should be at least 6" long, but only as big as is comfortable for you to handle. Early wands were wooden, cut from the branch of a tree the magician considered sacred (favorites included yew, rowan, and willow). Today, however, you can find wands made of metal, glass, and other materials as well—modern witches and wizards often prefer something with a little bling. Some magicians like to adorn their wands with gemstones and crystals, symbols, ribbons, beadwork, feathers, or painted images. Others opt for simplicity. If you decide to work with a magick wand, the decorations you choose should be ones that you find meaningful and that help you to focus your mind.

The wand corresponds to the element of fire. In the tarot, it appears as the suit of wands (sometimes called rods or staves). Therefore, you might select adornments that resonate with a fiery nature such as carnelians, red ribbons, or touches of gold or iron.

THE PENTAGRAM

As mentioned previously, a pentagram is a five-pointed star with a circle around it. The correct way to display it is with one point upright, two points down, and two out to the sides to represent the human body. Magicians use the pentagram for protection. You can wear one for personal safety. Hang one on your front door to guard your home, or place one in your glove compartment to protect your car. You can even put one on your pet's collar to shield her from harm. Some witches like to decorate their pentagrams with gemstones and crystals, or to combine it with other symbols, whereas others choose to keep it simple.

In rituals, a magician might draw pentagrams in the air as part of the circle-casting process. With a wand or athame he traces the symbol at each of the four directions to provide protection. Sometimes participants in a ritual mark pentagrams on their foreheads with essential oils (amber, basil, and pine are good choices) as additional safeguards. You can inscribe pentagrams on candles, paint them on stones, embroider them on mojo pouches and clothing—just about anyplace. You might even want to get a pentagram tattoo.

The pentagram corresponds to the element of earth. In the tarot, it appears as the suit of pentacles (sometimes called coins or discs). Thus, you may wish to decorate your pentagram with earthy gems: onyx, aventurine, turquoise, jade, or tiger's eye. (We'll talk more about gemstones and magick in Chapter 12.)

Texas Pentagrams

If you travel to Texas, you'll spot pentagrams everywhere—on houses, clothing, and jewelry, laid out in paving stones in a town square or above a courthouse's entrance—although most people don't realize the symbol's true meaning. Back in the late 1800s, the Texas Rangers (the lawmen, not the baseball team) began wearing Texas Star badges featuring a five-pointed star inside a circle. And who knows? Those pentagrams may have saved some lives.

THE ATHAME

This ritual dagger is never used for practical purposes (such as chopping vegetables) and certainly not to harm someone. Rather, a witch symbolically slices away negative energy or cuts through psychic obstacles with this magick tool. You can also cast a protective circle with it instead of a wand.

An athame is usually a double-sided knife about 4–6" long (although some witches and Wiccans prefer athames shaped like a crescent moon). It doesn't have to be sharp, however, because you probably won't cut anything physical with it. You can decorate your dagger with gemstones and crystals or other adornments if you like. Some people engrave or paint magick symbols on their athames. The choice is yours. Remember, however, that your athame is a weapon of the "spiritual warrior" and tradition says you shouldn't work with a knife that has drawn blood.

The athame corresponds to the element of air. In the tarot, it appears as the suit of swords (sometimes called daggers). Therefore, you might like to decorate your athame with air symbolism: aquamarine or fluorite, feathers, yellow ribbons, or the glyphs for Gemini, Libra, and/or Aquarius.

THE CHALICE

The most famous chalice of all is the legendary Holy Grail. As you might suspect, a chalice is used for drinking beverages—but not your everyday kind, such as a Coke with lunch. Your chalice should only hold ritual brews and magick potions. In some rituals a ceremonial drink is passed among participants, which is why chalices often have long stems that are easy to grasp.

A chalice may be made of any material: metal, crystal, glass, ceramic, even wood. Some people like to decorate their chalices with gemstones and crystals, or other adornments. You might choose to add symbols, words, and images that hold meaning for you. Ritual or high magicians traditionally paint their chalices to look like a crocus with eight petals, in blue and orange.

Site of the Grail

The Chalice Well in Glastonbury, England, is a sacred site for Celts and followers of Goddess religions. Many people believe it is the final resting place of the Holy Grail. For 2,000 years, this well has been in constant use and has never been known to run dry. A symbol of the life force, the well is revered as a gift from Mother Earth to her children.

The chalice corresponds to the element of water. In the tarot, it appears as the suit of cups (sometimes called chalices or bowls). Consider inscribing your chalice with the astrological symbols for the water signs Pisces, Cancer, or Scorpio, or adorning it with "watery" gems: pearls, aquamarines, sapphires, or coral.

CANDLES

Candles are essential ingredients in many spells. They symbolize the fire element and spirit, the energizing force that activates spells and rituals. In addition, they provide a focal point for your attention, helping you to still your mind. Their soft, flickering light creates an ambiance that shifts you out of your ordinary existence.

Witches usually keep on hand a supply of candles in a range of colors. Colors hold symbolic meanings and affect us psychologically and emotionally, so not surprisingly witches use them in lots of spells. If you're doing a love spell, for example, burn a red or pink candle that represents passion, affection, and the heart. Prosperity spells call for green, gold, or silver candles, the colors of money. Some formal rituals involve carefully placing candles in specific spots and moving them according to prescribed patterns.

Birthday Magick

Most people are familiar with a very simple and popular candle spell: making a wish and blowing out candles on a birthday cake. Because your birthday is a high-energy day, this is a good time to do magick spells as well as to eat cake and ice cream.

INCENSE AND ESSENTIAL OILS

For thousands of years, aromatic oils, gums, and resins have been used for both medicinal and cosmetic purposes, as well as in sacred rituals. Scents affect the limbic system, the portion of the brain associated with memory, emotions, and sexuality, which is why certain smells reawaken memories or stimulate the libido. Take a whiff of a certain perfume, of sea air, or of fresh-baked apple pie and, instantly, memories unfold. Because aromas immediately trigger moods, impressions, and associations, they can be assets in spells and rituals.

Essential Oils

Essential oils are extracted from plants rather than concocted from synthetic substances, as is the case with most modern perfumes. From the perspective of magick, essential oils are preferable to other scents because they contain the life energy of herbs and flowers.

Magicians use essential oils in many ways. Dressing candles is one popular practice. To dress a candle, choose an oil that relates to your intention. Pour a little oil in your palm and rub it over the waxy surface to add the properties of the scent to the candle. When the candle burns, the essence is released into the atmosphere to help manifest your intent. If you choose to make your own candles, you can incorporate essential oils into the mix.

Some essential oils can irritate skin or cause allergic reactions. A few oils are toxic. Research the oils you want to use before applying them to your skin or adding them to a ritual bath. Don't ingest the toxic ones!

Essential oils can also heighten the power of an amulet or talisman. Rub a little oil onto the charm or put a drop on a piece of paper and place it inside the charm. Magicians sometimes anoint their tools with essential oils to charge them. Of course, wearing fragrant oils is probably the most common way to enjoy them. You can even draw symbols on your body with essential oils to provide protection or to attract desired energies—and of course, for seduction.

Essential Oils and Their Magical Properties	
Acacia	Meditation, purification
Almond	Vitality, energy booster
Amber	Protection
Basil	Protection, harmony
Bay	Love spells, prophetic dreams
Bayberry	Money spells
Cedar	Prosperity, courage, protection
Cinnamon	Career success, wealth, vitality
Clove	Healing, prosperity, increased sexual desire
Eucalyptus	Healing, purification
Frankincense	Prosperity, protection, psychic awareness
Honeysuckle	Mental clarity, communication
Jasmine	Love spells, passion, to sweeten any situation
Lavender	Relaxation, peace of mind, healing, purification
Mint	Money spells
Musk	Love spells, vitality, to stimulate drive or desire
Patchouli	Love spells, protection, career success

Pine	Purification, protection, strength
Rose	Love spells, to lift spirits
Rue	Protection
Sage	Cleansing, wisdom
Sandalwood	Connection to the higher realms, knowledge, safe travel
Vervain	Money spells, fertility
Ylang-ylang	Aphrodisiac, love spells, to heighten passion or feminine power

Incense

In Latin, *incense* means "to burn." For centuries, churches and temples have used incense to clear the air and to send prayers to the deities. In Buddhist belief, burning an offering of incense invokes the Buddha into a statue of the holy being. The best incense is made from pure gums and resins, without synthetic binders.

Witches use incense to purify sacred space. Sage is the most popular herb for this purpose, but you can burn pine, frankincense, or eucalyptus if you prefer. As we discussed earlier, a witch may cast a protective circle by lighting a stick of incense and walking around the area in a clockwise direction, allowing the smoke to mark the space. You can also charge charms with incense by holding the amulet or talisman in the smoke for a few moments.

OTHER MAGICK TOOLS

Over time you may add to your magickal collection. Some of the spells in the following chapters use various tools for special purposes. Brooms sweep unwanted energies from a ritual space. Bells, gongs, drums, and rattles raise positive energy and disperse bad vibes. Magicians also use them to signal the steps in rituals. Swords, like athames, banish harmful forces and slice through obstacles. Staffs (or staves), like wands, direct energy.

The Cauldron

"Double, double, toil and trouble; / Fire burn, and cauldron bubble." Probably the best-known image of the witch's cauldron comes from

Shakespeare's play *Macbeth*, in which three crones stir into a cauldron all sorts of ghastly ingredients to brew up a magick potion. Contemporary witches still brew potions in cauldrons, but they don't use fillet of a fenny snake, lizard's leg, or howlet's wing to create a hell-broth, as the Bard's witches did.

A cauldron is a handy tool, especially if you don't have a fireplace, balefire pit, or barbecue grill, because you can build a small ritual fire in a cauldron. (Don't use regular barbecue charcoal if you're building a fire inside—the carbon monoxide can be deadly!) You can also concoct magick brews or cook ceremonial meals in it. Some people put flowers, water, crystals, or other objects in a cauldron during rituals. Because the cauldron represents the womb, it can nurture your intentions—write a wish on a slip of paper and drop it in the cauldron to slowly develop. A traditional cauldron is made of iron, but yours might be fashioned from ceramic, copper, stainless steel, stone, or another fireproof material.

Oracles

Oracles let you gaze into the future or to see things that lie beyond your ordinary range of vision. Pendulums and crystal balls provide glimpses into the unknown. Beautifully illustrated tarot cards are the most popular tools for reading the future—artists have created literally tens of thousands of different decks over the years. But divination isn't the tarot's only purpose. Some of the spells in Part II of this book use these cards in talismans, visualizations, and lots of other ways, as you'll soon see. (If you want to learn more about the tarot, see my book *The Everything® Tarot Book*.) Runes, too, can guide your path into the future; they also play roles in many spells. As you gain skill in working with these oracles, you may discover new applications for them in your magickal work.

CLEANING AND CHARGING YOUR MAGICK TOOLS

Before you use a tool for magickal purposes, it's a good idea to clean and purify it. This removes unwanted energies, as well as dust and dirt. In most cases the easiest way to do this is to wash the item with mild soap and water. Some people like to cleanse their tools in a running stream or sacred pool, but when that's not available ordinary tap water will suffice. If you prefer, you can "smudge" your tools by holding them in the smoke from burning sage for a few moments.

Four Elements Charging Technique

The next step is called "charging." A magick ritual in itself, charging consecrates your tools for your purposes and transforms that stick of wood or wineglass into a magickal object. One popular method for doing this involves the four elements: earth, air, fire, and water. Mix a little sea salt in water (or use ocean water, if available) and sprinkle it on the tool as you say to it: "With earth and water I charge you to do my will." Then, light incense and hold the tool in the smoke for a few moments while you say: "With fire and air I charge you to do my will." (Make sure to dry and rub down metal tools after sprinkling them with salt water so they don't tarnish or corrode.)

Charging with Essential Oils

Another technique calls for anointing your tools with essential oils. Rub a little essential oil—a single oil or a blend of several—on the tool while you say: "With this oil I charge you to do my will." The following table suggests appropriate oils for charging each tool.

Magick Tool	Charge with These Essential Oils
Wand	cinnamon, sandalwood, clove, musk, patchouli, cedar
Pentagram	mint, pine, amber, basil, fennel, anise
Athame	carnation, lavender, ginger, honeysuckle
Chalice	rose, ylang-ylang, jasmine, lily of the valley

These suggestions are just that: suggestions. You may decide to design a more elaborate or personal ritual for charging your magick tools. If you want to let your chalice bask in moonlight for twenty-eight nights or bury your pentagram beneath an oak tree for a week, by all means do it. Go with whatever feels right to you. The purpose, after all, is to make these tools yours, so the more personal the ritual the better.

The Modern Guide to Witchcraft

CARING FOR YOUR MAGICK TOOLS

How do you protect your expensive jewelry? Your heirloom silverware? Your favorite designer clothes? Devote the same care to storing your magick tools. If you have an altar, you may wish to display your tools on it. Many witches, however, prefer to store their tools safely out of sight, partly to prevent other people from handling them and partly to avoid uncomfortable questions. It's traditional to wrap your magick tools in silk, which protects them from dust and dirt as well as ambient vibrations. Alternately, you may choose to put them in velvet pouches, wooden boxes, or other containers and stash them in a drawer, trunk, closet, or cabinet. Like any precious possession, you want to safeguard them from damage and keep them from falling into the wrong hands.

Precautions and Protocols

When caring for and working with your magick tools, here are a few precautions and protocols to remember:

- Don't let anyone else use your tools or handle them, except perhaps a magickal partner with whom you work regularly.
- If someone else does touch a tool, smudge or wash it to remove that person's energy.
- If you do tarot readings for other people, use a different deck than the one you use to read for yourself. Keep a third deck for spells. The same goes for rune sets.
- Clean and smudge all tools before you begin using them to perform magick. After that, you needn't cleanse them unless someone else handles them. (Of course, if you drink or eat from a chalice or cauldron you'll want to wash it before storing it.)
- Use your tools for working magick only, not for mundane purposes.

Treat your magick tools with care and respect, and they'll serve you for a lifetime.

Acquiring Magick Tools

When you buy a car, you want to know something about its history. The same holds true for magick tools. If you purchase new items, you can check out the seller's reputation, get info about the craftspeople who actually made the objects, and read users' reports online. However, if you buy vintage items, well, tracking down their pedigrees can get a bit tricky. Antique chalices and swords may be exquisitely beautiful, reflecting a level of craftsmanship we no longer see today. But remember, magick tools used by someone else may hold that person's energy for a long time. This is especially true if the objects contain gemstones. Cleansing, purifying, and consecrating practices can remove old energies you wish to delete, but it's always a good idea to check out your tools' histories if possible before you start using them.

Once I found a handsome old knife in an antique shop, and thought it would make a fabulous athame—until the salesperson told me that it had previously been used as a bris knife. *Not* the energy I wanted tainting my ritual dagger!

You can also fabricate your own magick tools if you have skills in woodworking or metalsmithing. In earlier times, people fashioned wands from sticks of wood, and you can too. Choose a branch that has fallen from the tree, perhaps in a storm or as part of the natural aging process. Or, request permission from the tree to cut a twig and, after cutting, make an offering to the tree as a thank you. Unless you're a skilled glassblower, you're unlikely to create your own chalice from scratch. You can, however, buy special paints in crafts stores to decorate the glass with meaningful images. Even if you purchase new items from a metaphysical store, you may still want to add your own personal touches to make your tools uniquely yours.

Displaying Your Tools

As we've already said, some witches like to display their primary tools on their altars, along with candles to provide illumination, statues or deity representations, other items required for a particular spell or ritual, and maybe food and drink. If you like to have your book of shadows on hand when you do a ritual, you need room for it on the altar as well, which can make things a bit crowded. Just know that you're free to move things around as you require, which may mean setting up a secondary altar or, as we discussed in the previous chapter, four shrines within your sacred space. Do whatever you find comfortable and convenient. If you choose to leave your primary tools out on your altar, be sure to display all four for balance.

YOUR GRIMOIRE OR BOOK OF SHADOWS

A grimoire is a witch's journal of spells and rituals. Here's where you keep a record of the magick you perform, the ingredients and tools you use in spells, and your results. It's a bit like a cook's personal collection of favorite recipes.

From Days of Old

Originally, a grimoire referred to a book of spells and incantations used for calling forth spirits. Grimoires date back to the ancient Middle East, and later made their way through Europe during the Medieval and Renaissance periods.

Early grimoires were handwritten on parchment or paper, and perhaps bound in richly tooled leather or wood. Today, many witches still enjoy the process of recording spells and rituals by hand in beautifully bound journals. However, a grimoire or "book of shadows" keyboarded into your computer serves the same purpose. Most modern grimoires are written by individuals for their own use and generally they contain strictly personal records intended only for the author's purposes. However, sometimes a grimoire (or sections of it) may be passed down or copied from a master book. In such cases, the title of the original book is usually kept secret.

One of the most influential grimoires, *The Gardnerian Book of Shadows*, is attributed to Gerald Gardner and Doreen Valiente. This highly regarded book is a compilation of rituals that the authors blended and incorporated with original and modern elements between 1949 and 1961. *The Book of the Sacred Magic of Abramelin the Mage*, a fifteenth-century French manuscript translated by S.L. MacGregor Mathers in

1900, which includes spells for raising the dead and becoming invisible, had a major impact on contemporary ceremonial magick. Another amazing and rare grimoire, *The Magus*, composed by Francis Barrett in 1801, also covers astrology, alchemy, and Qabalistic knowledge, and remains an important source of information for magicians. You can see these texts online at *www.sacred-texts.com*, but be advised, they're not light reading.

Your Magickal Journey

Both a grimoire and a book of shadows hold spells, but a grimoire is intended to instruct, whereas a book of shadows is more of a personal record of a spiritual journey. Your book of shadows will not only include spells and incantations, but your observations, insights, and experiences as well. It might also contain dreams, poems, invocations, revelations, inspiration, and lore. If you like, you can draw in it, press flowers between its pages, add photographs—whatever tells of your journey.

Some people argue that a book of shadows more closely resembles a diary or a journal. Purists insist that a grimoire should be entirely instructional, full of information and practical application—no personal musings or little doodles in the borders. Fortunately, no "official" criterion exists for creating a book of shadows, so feel free to write in it whatever suits your purposes. Take the knowledge that is the gift of your elders and ancestors and combine it with your own practices and beliefs to create a new, useful work that is rooted in your tradition but remains unique and original. It's your journey, your story, and each book will be as individual as its author.

Traditionally, a witch keeps her book of shadows private—just as you'd keep your diary secret. You may, if you choose, share what you've written with people you trust, such as your teacher, a magickal partner, or an apprentice. The second part of this book is an open grimoire with spells for love, abundance, career success, health, and more. In the beginning, I recommend doing the spells as they're written. Later, when you have more magickal knowledge under your belt, you may enjoy adding your own touches or concocting original spells from scratch.

Chapter 11

PLANT MAGICK

It's reasonably safe to say that every plant has been used at one time or another for magickal purposes, especially in spellcraft. A Greek myth explains that the daughters of Hecate (one of the patronesses of witchcraft) taught witches how to use plants for both healing and magick, and throughout history witches have practiced herbalism. According to green witchcraft, all plants contain spirits. To work effectively with plants, witches communicate with them at a spiritual level, not just a physical one.

To practice plant magick you must first reconnect with nature. You can't honor something you don't feel an intimate connection with, and you certainly can't call on the energies of plant spirits without spending time with plants. If you live in the concrete jungle, this may present some challenges. But even in the heart of the city, you can find parks, botanical gardens, greenhouses, or garden centers where you can commune with plants.

Every plant is unique, with its own special energies and applications. Rowan, for instance, hung above a doorway protects your home from harm. Mugwort improves psychic awareness. Here are some ways you might choose to work with the magickal properties of plants:

- Watch plant behavior for omens and signs.
- Gather loosened leaves and petals for magick potions.
- Use plant matter in amulets and talismans.
- Add plant matter to incense and candles.

- Blend herbs for poultices and healing teas.
- Make fragrant potpourris to place in your closets and dresser drawers.
- Press pretty flowers in your book of shadows.
- Place live plants in various parts of your home or yard to encourage personal growth and well-being.

As any good cook will tell you, the key to great food lies in the ingredients and how the cook combines them. The same holds true for spells. If you think of a spell as a magick recipe, you begin to understand why the components (that is, the ingredients) are so important. If you don't measure the components correctly, add them to the mix at the right time, and give them enough time to "bake" properly, the magick goes awry.

So what constitutes a good spell component? Anything that's essential to the recipe—anything that builds the energy until it's just right. All the ingredients must mesh on a metaphysical level. Of course, the witch herself is the key component of any spell, adding a word, a touch, or a wish.

> *"But there are some things I know for certain: always throw spilt salt over your left shoulder, keep rosemary by your garden gate, plant lavender for luck, and fall in love whenever you can."*
> —SALLY OWENS, *PRACTICAL MAGIC*

In this chapter you'll learn about the magickal powers of many types of plants and how to use them in spellcraft. The lists that follow are by no means comprehensive, but provide enough information so that you can eventually design your own spells. You don't need to run out and buy everything on these lists; select a few staples that seem suited to the kinds of spells you want to cast—you can always add more later, just as a cook adds to her spice collection. As you become more proficient with spells, you'll compile your own lists of what works and what doesn't.

TREE MAGICK

Since ancient times, mythology and legends have talked about magickal trees. Early Greek myths said that certain trees could predict the future.

The Druids considered trees sacred, and liked to perform their rituals outdoors in groves of oak trees. The Celts believed that the sacred World Tree connected the upper, middle, and lower worlds. The Buddha gained enlightenment while sitting beneath a Bodhi tree.

Trees are the pillars of our world. They anchor our ground and seem to hold up the sky. They form the backbone of the green witch's practice. Although witches and herbalists tend to focus on herbs, they also work with wood, often when they want to create stability or permanence. Traditionally, magicians crafted their wands and staffs from wood. Sticks and twigs form the basis of many protective amulets; rounds cut from the cross-section of branches can be carved with magick symbols and carried as talismans. Witches also combine sacred woods in ritual fires, particularly at Yule. (You'll learn more about these practices later.)

The following list describes the magickal uses of trees, plus some associated lore. These trees grow in various areas of North America and elsewhere in the world. Depending on your purposes, you can use the bark, leaves, and/or inner wood:

- Apple: Apple trees grow in many parts of the Northern Hemisphere. Their widespread availability and fruitfulness link them with abundance, love, longevity, creativity, and fertility. Folklore associates the apple with the afterlife, fairies, and the otherworld. In Greek mythology, Paris awarded Aphrodite a golden apple because she was the most beautiful of the goddesses. If you cut an apple in half, you'll notice its seeds form a pentagram inside—a sure sign of its magick power.
- Ash: Some European cultures consider ash to be the World Tree. Magickally, ash is associated with water, strength, intellect, willpower, protection, justice, balance and harmony, skill, travel, and wisdom. Plant ash trees in your yard to protect your home and family.
- Birch: The traditional witch's broom is made of birch twigs. Magickally, birch has cleansing, protective, and purifying properties. Lore connects it with children, and cradles were often made of birch wood.
- Cedar: A precious wood that many cultures recognize as magickal and powerful, cedar has been known throughout the ages for its protective

qualities as well as its ability to repel insects and pests. Aromatic cedar was often given as an offering. Magickally, cedar is associated with healing, spirituality, purification, protection, prosperity, and harmony. Build a cedar fence around your home to attract abundance.

- Elder: Elder is also known as witchwood. Supposedly, bad luck will befall anyone who does not ask the tree's permission three times before harvesting any part of it—that's good advice when you're cutting any tree, not just elder. Folklore associates the elder with the crone aspect of the Goddess and with witches, thus elder wood is rarely used to make furniture or as firewood for fear of incurring their wrath. Herbalists prize elder for its many medicinal properties and use it as a laxative and diuretic, to treat irritated skin, sprains and bruises, and to loosen chest and sinus congestion. Magickally, elder wood is associated with protection (especially against being struck by lightning), prosperity, and healing.

- Hawthorn: Also known as May tree, mayflower, thorn, whitethorn, and haw, the hawthorn shrub often served as a boundary between properties. *Haw* is an old word for hedge. If a hawthorn grows together with an oak and ash tree, folklore says that the fairies dance among the trees. Like oak, the hawthorn's hard wood produces great heat when burned. Magickal associations include fertility, harmony, happiness, the otherworld, and protection.

- Hazel: European folklore links the hazel tree with wisdom. Thor, Brigid, Apollo, and other deities and mythological figures were associated with the hazel. Witches use both the nuts and branches in spells for luck, fertility, protection, and wish granting.

- Honeysuckle: Also known as woodbine or hedge-tree, the honeysuckle is associated with liminal or transitional (in-between) states. The scent of honeysuckle flowers is strongest in the evening, the time between day and night. Magickal associations include psychic awareness, harmony, healing, prosperity, and happiness.

- Maple: Used for furniture and other woodcrafts, maple also gives us sweet maple sugar and syrup. Magickally, maple relates to love, prosperity, life and health, and general abundance.

- Oak: A favorite of the Druids, oak's hardness and durability make it ideal for building homes, ships, and furniture. These qualities also link it magickally with strength, courage, longevity, protection, and good fortune. Traditionally, the Yule log is oak. Acorns, the fruit of the oak tree, are symbols of fertility. When found growing in oak trees, mistletoe was considered to be particularly potent by the Druids and important in their magickal work. Of course, today we think of mistletoe as something to kiss beneath—a nice application of its energies.
- Pine: Often pine is added to soaps and cleaning products. In magick, pine's cleansing properties make it useful for purification, clearing the mind, healing, prosperity, and protection from evil. Amber, one of the most beloved "gems" for magickal jewelry, is fossilized pine sap.
- Poplar: Also known as aspen, poplar's magickal associations include prosperity, communication, exorcism, and purification.
- Rowan: Rowan is also known as quicken, witchwood, and mountain ash (although technically not a true ash, it is so called due to the similarity of the leaves). A favorite of many witches, rowan's magickal associations include protection from evil, improving psychic powers, divination, healing, creativity, success, and transformation.
- Willow: The white willow, also known as the weeping willow, has long flexible branches and often grows near water. Folklore connects the willow with the Goddess and feminine cycles. Magickal associations include love, tranquility, intuition, harmony, protection, growth and renewal, and healing. Willow has traditionally been a favorite wood for magick wands and dowsers' rods.
- Witch hazel: Also known as snapping hazelnut because its seedpods spontaneously crack open, witch hazel has long been used in poultices for bruises and swelling, and for its astringent properties. Magickal associations include protection, healing, and peace.
- Yew: Yew is poisonous, which may be one reason it is associated with death. A European tree with hard, unyielding wood, it figures prominently in the lore of witchcraft and nature magick. Witches also connect it with spirits and the otherworld.

Some people have difficulty with the idea of cutting live wood away from a tree or bush because they don't know how to do it properly. When you use fresh wood, you capture a lot of life energy, which may be exactly what you're looking for in your ritual or spellwork. Deadfall is wood the tree has discarded as no longer useful, which may not be the kind of vibrant, living energy you're looking for. It depends on your personal view and the type of spell you're doing.

If you plan to cut fresh wood, you must first ask the tree or bush for permission. If you sense that the tree is okay with this, proceed with care and respect. Leave an offering for the tree as a "thank you."

Tree Attunement Exercise

Pick a tree. Stand next to it. Hold one hand about an inch or two away from the bark. Extend your awareness and feel the energy of the tree. Next, touch the bark. Explore how the tree feels to your hands. Bend close and smell the tree. Close your eyes and listen to the sounds the tree makes in response to the environment. Look closely at the tree and see the different textures, colors, and markings. If it has fruit you know to be safe, taste it.

Repeat these exercises with different kinds of trees. Compare and contrast your experiences. What are the similarities between the trees? What are the differences? After you've finished, make notes in your book of shadows.

FLOWER POWER

Flowers are the pretty parts of plants that hold essential reproductive information—in other words, they're the plants' sex organs. As such, the flower of a plant carries a tidy bundle of energy. In natural magick, the flower is often the part used. Flowers can be dried whole and woven into wreaths, pressed into a magickal collage, or made into potpourri or sachets. To fine-tune a spell, or cover all the bases if your objective is multifold, combine two or more flowers that offer the properties you seek. Here are some ways you might like to use flowers in spells:

- Fill mojo bags with dried petals.
- Add fragrant flower petals to candles.
- Wear floral essential oils that suit your purposes.
- Brew healing flowers, such as chamomile, in teas.
- Blend healing plant oils into lotions, salves, and ointments.
- Decorate your altar with flowers that relate to your intention.
- Plant flowers in a magick garden to attract nature spirits.

Do dried flowers carry a different energy than fresh flowers do? Yes and no; the intrinsic energy remains, but its expression is different. For certain rituals or charms you may want the vibrancy of fresh flowers, whereas amulets and talismans work better with dried flowers, whose energies tend to be slower acting and longer lasting.

In some cases, you might choose a particular flower for its physical properties especially if you're doing healing. Chamomile, for instance, has calming qualities that soothe mind and body. More often, however, you're looking for the symbolic value of the botanicals you use in spells. Roses, as you know, symbolize love. The following list includes flowers witches commonly use in magick, but it certainly isn't exhaustive. If you have a green thumb, you can grow your own plants for magick work. But you can find most of what you'll need at a nursery or large supermarket:

- Carnation: Also known as gillyflower, the carnation has a wonderful healing energy and makes an excellent gift for the sick. Use carnations magickally for protection, strength, energy, luck, and healing.
- Daffodil: Also known as narcissus and asphodel, the daffodil figures into charms for love, luck, and fertility.
- Daisy: We've all plucked the petals from a daisy and chanted, "He loves me, he loves me not." Not surprisingly, the daisy is commonly associated with love and flirtation, and is used in love spells.
- Gardenia: This fragrant flower brings tranquility, harmony, love, and healing. Add gardenia petals to a healing sachet or a talisman for love.
- Geranium: Grown indoors or out, geraniums carry strong protective energy, especially those with red flowers. Use rose-colored geraniums in spells for fertility, love, and healing.

- Hyacinth: Both grape and wild hyacinths have a lovely scent and a vibrant energy. Hyacinths are named for the youth of Greek legend, whose accidental death the god Apollo commemorated by creating the flower. Hyacinths are magickally associated with love, happiness, and protection.
- Iris: The iris's three petals are said to symbolize faith, wisdom, and valor. Witches use this lovely spring flower for purification and blessing, and to increase wisdom. You can grind the root, called orrisroot, and add it as a scent fixative in potpourri. Irises also play a role in love spells, especially when you want peace and harmony in a relationship.
- Jasmine: Also known as jessamine, jasmine possesses a heady but delicate scent that is usually stronger at night. Because of this, it is often associated with the moon and feminine energy. Magickally, jasmine relates to love, spirituality, harmony, and prosperity. Use it in spells for seduction and sensuality.
- Lavender: In aromatherapy, lavender calms body, mind, and spirit, and encourages relaxation and sleep. Magickally, lavender is associated with peace, tranquility, love, purification, and healing. Use it to restore harmony after a disagreement with a loved one.
- Lilac: The fragrant flowers of this shrub are usually white or a shade of purple. Magically, lilacs are used for protection and banishing negative energy.
- Lily: In general, lilies are associated with protection and removing hexes. Some cultures connect lilies (especially white ones) with death and the afterlife.
- Lily of the valley: This tiny cascade of white or cream-colored bell-shaped flowers has a delicate scent. Magickally, it enhances concentration and mental ability. You can also use it in spells to encourage happiness.
- Pansy: Also known as heartsease, love-lies-bleeding, love-in-idleness, and Johnny-jump-up, the pansy is a hardy, cheerful-looking plant with multicolored flowers, akin to the violet. Magickally, it is used for love spells, divination, communication, and happiness.
- Poppy: Although the red poppy is a gentle narcotic, the white poppy is toxic and the source of opium. Magically, the poppy is associated with fertility, prosperity, love, sleep, and invisibility.

- Rose: Throughout history, the rose has been one of our most beloved flowers. Folklore and literature have made the rose synonymous with love, and witches often use it in love spells. Magickally, roses also play roles in healing, divination, peace, harmony, psychic ability, and spiritual growth. Note the rose's color to understand its uses. (We'll talk more about color symbolism later.)
- Snapdragon: Witches link snapdragons with protection, particularly from illusion or deception. Plant white snapdragons along the perimeter of your home to protect it.
- Sunflower: The sunflower is, of course, associated with the sun. Use it magickally to bring happiness, success, and health. Because the plant has an abundance of seeds, it also relates to fertility. Bring sunflowers to a celebration or a summer solstice ritual to shine light on the event. Germinate the seeds and then plant them to attract abundance.
- Tulip: The tulip's chalice or cuplike shape represents a vessel to hold prosperity and abundance. Use tulips in spells for money, love, and happiness.
- Violet: Use this delicate flower in spells for love, peace, hope, harmony, good luck, fertility, and abundance. In charms and sachets, violets help to maintain tranquility and encourage peace between people. Combine violet with lavender in an herbal pillow to help a child sleep and prevent nightmares.

Caution: May Be Poisonous

Some beautiful flowers with strong magickal powers are poisonous—even deadly. Wolfsbane—a.k.a. aconitum, monkshood, and "the queen of poisons"—is a plant you probably want to steer clear of, or at least handle with extreme care (like wearing rubber gloves when you touch it). This pretty plant has deep blue flowers and witches value its magickal protective powers, but eating it or getting the juice from its root into a cut on your hand could stop your heart—literally. Lovely foxglove, or digitalis, is also toxic. Though long known for its healing properties, it can also cause a wide range of problems, even death. Essential oils are delightful, aromatic ingredients in spells, but some can irritate sensitive skin. Of course, you don't want to put anything you aren't sure of in food or beverages. Even plants that seem benign may cause allergic reactions in some people.

MAGICK HERBS

Generally, a plant referred to as an herb possesses some sort of medicinal or culinary value. Witches, however, use the term "herb" as a catch-all for the bits of trees, flowers, spices, and all sorts of plants, and use them for healing, food preparation, and of course, doing magick. The following list of herbs isn't all-inclusive, but describes many herbs that you might want to use in your spellworking. Quite likely, these herbs already sit in your kitchen's spice cabinet.

- Allspice: A common staple in the kitchen spice rack, allspice incorporates flavors such as clove, cinnamon, and pepper. Allspice berries make wonderful additions to prosperity blends and spells for increasing energy, love, healing, and luck.
- Angelica: Also known as archangel or angel's herb, this fragrant plant has been used for centuries to improve digestion. Witches use it magickally for protection and purification.
- Basil: Commonly found in spice racks and in kitchen gardens all over Europe and the Americas, basil is used magickally for prosperity, success, peace, protection, happiness, purification, tranquility, and love.
- Bay: Also known as bay laurel, it crowned the victor of games in ancient Greece and Rome. Witches use it to enhance success, wisdom, and divination. Write a wish on a bay leaf and burn it, or sleep with it under your pillow for prophetic dreams.
- Calendula: A type of marigold, calendula is used medicinally to treat skin irritations, such as eczema, bruises, scars, and scrapes. Use it in magick spells to bring happiness, prosperity, love, psychic powers, and harmony.
- Caraway: The seed of the caraway plant protects against negativity. It's also a good antitheft herb—add it to protection amulets or charms in your home.
- Chamomile: Therapeutically, chamomile aids digestion and soothes stomach problems, calms stress, and eases headaches. Magickally, it brings prosperity, peace, healing, harmony, and happiness.
- Cinnamon: This multipurpose herb possesses a great amount of energy, and a pinch can be added to rev up a spell's power. Use it in spells and charms for money, success, vitality, love, and purification.

The Modern Guide to Witchcraft

- Clove: The small dried bud of the clove plant is associated with protection, purification, mental ability, and healing. Add three cloves to an amulet or talisman to keep the charm's action pure and focused for a longer period of time. A sachet of rosemary, angelica, sage, three cloves, and a pinch of salt tied shut with red ribbon is a good all-purpose amulet to hang above a door or in your car for protection.
- Comfrey: Also known as knitbone, comfrey is renowned as a magickal healing herb, as well as for protection during travel and prosperity.
- Dill: Use either dill seed or weed to attract good fortune, tranquility, prosperity, passion, or protection.
- Ginger: When added to spells, ginger boosts their power. Use ginger to jump-start a romance, stimulate finances, and increase the potential for success in just about anything. Medicinally, it helps calm the stomach, fight colds, and suppress nausea.
- Marjoram: Also known as wintersweet, marjoram is similar to oregano, but sweeter and milder. The ancient Greeks crowned newly married couples with marjoram. Use it magickally to bring happiness, protection, love, and joy, particularly in family environments.
- Mint: Mint comes in many varieties and it's easy to grow in a garden or on the kitchen windowsill. It helps ease headaches, stimulates the appetite, and aids digestion. Use it magically for prosperity, love, joy, fertility, purification, and success.
- Mugwort: Also known as artemisia and sailor's tobacco, mugwort helps to open your mind before you try divination. Witches associate it with prophetic dreams, relaxation and tranquility, protection, banishing, and consecration.
- Nutmeg: Medicinally, nutmeg quells nausea and soothes digestive problems (although it can be toxic in large doses). Magickally, it boosts psychic abilities, happiness, love, and money.
- Parsley: The ancient Greeks made victors' crowns from parsley to celebrate success. Witches use the herb magickally for power, strength, passion, purification, and prosperity.
- Rosemary: You can use rosemary as a skin tonic applied externally and as a hair rinse to add shine to dark hair and soothe itchy scalp. Magickally, it provides protection, improves memory, and brings wisdom.

- Sage: Sage is perhaps the most popular herb for purification. Witches also use it in spells for protection, wisdom, health, and longevity.
- Verbena: Also known as vervain, enchanter's herb, and herb of grace, verbena helps calm headaches, eases stress, and makes a relaxing bedtime tea. Magickally it is associated with divination, protection, inspiration, abundance, love, peace, tranquility, healing, prosperity, skill in artistic performance, and reversing negative activity. Make a blessing/protection oil by infusing the fresh plant in light olive oil or grape seed oil. Add the dried herb to a charm bag to encourage success.
- Yarrow: Also known as milfoil, millefeuille, yarroway, or bloodwort, yarrow is a common garden herb whose leaves have traditionally been made into poultices to staunch blood. Witches use it for courage, love, and healing.

Don't overlook other greens for spellworking. Moss, for instance, is tenacious and grows even where you wouldn't think anything could survive. Use it in spells for patience, perseverance, and toughness. Ferns have connections with invisibility. Witchy folklore says that you should collect ferns before midnight on the eve of the summer solstice if you don't want to be seen. No, you won't actually vanish, but you can go about your business in secret. Grass, because it's so adaptable, can help you be more flexible and let things take their course. In Part II, you'll learn to tap the magick in plants to make amulets, talismans, and all sorts of charms.

Chapter 12

CRYSTALS AND GEMSTONES

Long before people began prizing gems for their monetary value, they used them as magick charms. In early societies, only rulers, members of royal families, priests, and religious leaders wore gems. The ancient Egyptians used stones for healing, protection, and other purposes, both physical and spiritual. According to Nancy Schiffer, author of *The Power of Jewelry*, our ancestors believed gemstones were "capable of human feelings and passions so that they could express jealousy and shock."

Many researchers believe crystals may have been sources of power and magick on the lost continents of Atlantis and Lemuria, and that crystals were used in building the pyramids and Stonehenge.

TAPPING THE MAGICK OF STONES

Today, we wear precious and semiprecious gems mostly because they're so pretty. Witches, however, realize that crystals and gemstones can also be used for spellworking, divination, shamanic journeying, meditation, and dowsing. Stones also play important roles in healing, and although witches connect some stones with longevity, none of them holds the elixir of life like the fabled Philosopher's Stone.

Birthstones resonate with the qualities of the zodiac signs to which they correspond. Originally people wore birthstones to enhance, balance, or moderate their own personal characteristics. By the way, you should look at your birth sign, not the month of your birth, to discover your true birthstone. If you're an Aquarian, for example, your birthstone is garnet, regardless of whether you were born in January or February.

You can include crystals or gemstones in virtually any spell to increase, focus, stabilize, or fine-tune your spell's potency. Here are some suggestions:

- Wear them to enhance your own personal energy field.
- Put them in amulets or talismans.
- Set them near the windows and doors of your home to provide protection.
- Meditate with them.
- Infuse magick potions with them.
- Dowse with a gemstone or crystal pendulum.
- Display them on your altar to attract positive energy.
- Offer them to deities or nature spirits in return for assistance.
- Gaze into them to see the past or future.

Like plants, crystals and gemstones are living entities, although they resonate at a slow rate that most people can't perceive. However, their slow, concentrated energy enables them to keep working their magick for a long period of time.

MAGICKAL POWERS OF DIFFERENT STONES

As you might suspect, different stones possess different qualities and serve different functions in spellworking. A general rule of thumb is that clear stones are best for mental and spiritual issues, translucent or milky stones for emotional situations, and opaque stones for physical matters. You can use gems alone or in combination with other substances to produce the results you desire.

A stone's color or pattern, too, can provide clues to its abilities. Pink gems, such as rose quartz and morganite, are perfect for love spells. Jade, aventurine, and other green stones can benefit money spells. Since ancient times, people have valued stones with eyelike markings as protection charms against the "evil eye" and all sorts of misfortune.

The following guidelines for stones and their magickal properties are simply a place to begin. In time, you'll develop your own ideas about which stones to use for which spells:

- Agate: A grounding stone, agate helps stabilize situations. Add it to a money mojo if you're having trouble holding on to money. Use it when you need extra strength or determination. Agates come in lots of colors, and the color influences the stone's powers. Green moss agate, for instance, has healing and calming qualities. Like all green stones, it works well in prosperity spells and also attunes you to nature spirits.
- Amber: Although it's not really a stone—it's fossilized pine sap—amber is highly prized by witches. Lore tells us that amber came from the tears of a setting sun, and as such it's still considered a solar/fire stone. A powerful protection gem, you can wear it or place it in an amulet to protect your home, car, business, etc.
- Amethyst: A purple quartz, this spiritual gem helps you to deepen meditation, remember dreams, and improve psychic ability. Want to attract divine assistance? Offer a favorite deity a pretty amethyst in return for her help.
- Aquamarine: A gift of the sea goddess, this lovely blue stone stimulates imagination and creativity. It can also increase intuitive awareness, mental clarity, and connection with your higher self. Use it when you want to work with the spirit world.
- Aventurine: This green stone with gold flecks in it is ideal for attracting wealth or abundance.
- Bloodstone: A green opaque stone with flecks of red, witches associate it with health (especially of the blood) and physical protection. You can also use it in spells for good luck, success, and courage.
- Calcite: Calcite comes in lots of colors, giving it a variety of potential magickal applications. Witches consider it a stone of purification and healing—use it to detoxify a situation. It also encourages spiritual growth, calms the mind, and aids intellectual processes.
- Carnelian: This milky red-orange stone is linked with success. It can also stimulate passion, sexual energy, courage, and initiative.

- Chrysocolla: In relationships and domestic situations, chrysocolla helps remove disruptive energies and restore stability. It can also help you deal with changes and heal emotional pain.
- Citrine: A yellow variety of quartz, citrine is a great stone for banishing nightmares and improving psychic abilities. Because it's also known for its cleansing properties, you can use it to clean your other stones and magick tools, or to clear the air after an argument or disturbance.
- Diamond: A popular stone for engagement rings, a diamond deepens commitment and trust, especially in a love relationship. It also enhances strength and bravery, and attracts victory.
- Emerald: Emeralds promote clairvoyance and can be used for divination. Witches also connect them with emotional healing, growth, love, and resourcefulness.
- Fluorite: Available in various colors, fluorite helps remove stress and negative energy. When things seem confused or disorganized, use fluorite to restore order. It also improves concentration, intuition, and mental clarity.
- Garnet: During the Middle Ages people wore garnets to drive away demons. Witches still consider garnet a stone of protection. It also increases love and passion, courage, and hope.
- Hematite: A dark silvery-colored stone, hematite is often used to ground unbalanced energy and to stabilize a spell. The stone also deflects negativity and is thus associated with defense, healing, and justice.
- Jade: A popular stone for prosperity magick, jade can also be used in spells to enhance beauty, increase fertility, and inspire love. Witches connect it with health and longevity, too.
- Jasper: Jasper comes in various colors and patterns, and each has its own distinctive properties. Use red jasper in love spells to stir up passion. Brown jasper aids physical healing; poppy jasper breaks up blockages that prevent energy from circulating harmoniously.
- Lapis lazuli: The most coveted lapis is a deep bluish hue, with almost no white flecks in it. Use it to increase your psychic ability and attract magickal insights. It's also a good stone to hold while meditating to

deepen your focus. Some of the best lapis comes from Chile, where it's often carved into animal figures. Shamans there use it in their spiritual practices.

- Malachite: This green stone is popular for prosperity magick. Long considered a stone of protection, it wards off evil and lets you sense forthcoming dangers or problems. It strengthens your connection to nature, and green witches use it for earth healing.

- Moldavite: This greenish stone came to us as a result of a meteor collision with the earth nearly 15 million years ago. A high-energy stone, it improves your ability to communicate with spirits, deities, and extraterrestrials. Use it to gain insight into your purpose in this lifetime.

- Moonstone: Ruled by the moon, this milky stone comes in various pastel colors and has long been used to aid dream recall. It also calms emotions, increases intuition, and benefits all sorts of female health conditions.

- Obsidian: Sacred to Hecate, the patroness of witches, obsidian is a favorite stone for scrying mirrors. Most likely, that's what the wicked queen in *Snow White* gazed into when she asked, "Who's the fairest of them all?" Obsidian also boosts strength—physically and emotionally—and can help break down blockages. Use snowflake obsidian—a black stone with whitish spots—for protection.

- Onyx: Use this black stone to banish negative energy and ground magick spells. It encourages self-confidence and determination. Onyx also helps you break deeply ingrained habits, whether physical or emotional. Wear onyx when facing adversaries in figurative or literal battles.

- Opal: This milky whitish stone encourages psychic ability and visions. Witches also use it in spells for love and seduction. In shamanic magick, it keeps potential enemies from seeing you. Opals can aid female health conditions too.

- Pearl: Ruled by the moon, pearls were considered sacred to the goddesses Isis and Freya. Use pearls in spells for love, happiness, and emotional balance. They can also aid intuition, fertility, and creativity.

- Peridot: Believed to repel evil and malevolent magick in earlier times, peridot is still used as a stone of protection. It can also help to neutralize toxins, physically and emotionally.
- Ruby: Rubies stimulate the emotions, passion, love, and sexuality. They also open your heart to divine love. Wear rubies for courage or to aid blood disorders. Folklore says they protect against vampires.
- Sapphire: Linked with Neptune, the sea god, this stone increases spiritual knowledge and connection with the Divine. Witches use it in spells for wisdom, insight, and prophetic vision; it also deepens meditation and can help you understand omens and signs. Star sapphires bring hope and clarity of purpose.
- Tiger's eye: A glossy, satiny, brown stone with bands of gold, tiger's eye is used for strength, courage, good fortune, and prosperity. Early Roman soldiers carried these into battle to keep them safe. The stone boosts self-confidence and gives you the freedom to follow your own path.
- Tourmaline: This stone comes in a variety of colors, including green, black, pinkish, and watermelon (a combination of red and green). The colors influence the stone's properties. Tourmaline clears negative energies and brings balance. Put one near your computer to dissolve electromagnetic fields. Green tourmaline aligns you with nature spirits; pink harmonizes the emotions; watermelon attracts love and friendship.
- Turquoise: A powerful stone of protection, turquoise is especially good for keeping you safe while traveling. Witches also use it for prosperity. Its healing properties help ease mental tension and emotional anxiety. Native Americans consider turquoise a sacred stone.

If you wish, you can combine several stones to address various aspects of a spell. Let's say your goal is to find a job that pays well and brings you into contact with interesting people—aventurine plus watermelon tourmaline should do the trick. In a love spell, you might seek both passion and affection, in which case you'd choose rose quartz and carnelian. After a while, you'll start to intuit which stones are right for your intentions. Stones play such an important role in magick that you'll probably want to spend time familiarizing yourself with their many properties. Judy Hall's books provide extensive information about how to use stones for a wide range of purposes.

QUARTZ CRYSTALS

Quartz crystals are the most versatile of all stones. Actually, many of the stones we've already talked about are mainly quartz with other minerals mixed in, such as the iron in aquamarine that turns it blue. If you only want to work with one stone, a beautiful clear quartz crystal can do it all. Crystal balls, in particular, are one of the most famous magick tools. You've seen crystal balls on TV and in movies, maybe even in real life, and you know witches use them to predict the future, a practice known as scrying. It is possible to view stuff you couldn't see otherwise by gazing into a crystal ball. But crystals can do oh so much more.

Quartz crystals are a combination of silica and water formed under certain conditions of pressure, temperature, and energy. These crystals possess amazing abilities to retain information, amplify energy, and transmit vibrations. That's why they're often used in watches, computers, laser tools, television and radio equipment, and many other familiar objects. Their properties also make crystals ideal for healing, storing knowledge, sending energy and thought patterns, and increasing the power of any substance they come in contact with. People who work with crystals believe they are actually unique life forms that possess innate intelligence and many diverse powers.

Quartz crystals come in various colors and shapes, both of which affect the crystal's characteristics and abilities. Let's take a look at some of the most common ones witches use.

Clear Quartz

Clear quartz crystals will probably become one of your go-to magick tools—and one of your favorites. An easily obtained stone, it looks like ice. Many have small inclusions that add to the crystal's properties. For example, those little silvery "plates" you see in some crystals are like tiny tablets where you mentally "write" your wishes. Those fine lines that look like sparkly threads, called rutiles, give the crystal a speedy quality that helps spells work faster.

You can wear crystals, put them in amulets and talismans, affix them to other magick tools, meditate with them, focus them in certain areas to promote healing, keep one in your glove compartment for protection, and on and on. Basically, they work in three ways:

1. They boost the powers of other substances. Let's say you're making a money talisman. You might put some dried mint leaves and an aventurine in a silk pouch, and then add a small clear quartz crystal to kick the power up a notch.
2. They hold on to thoughts, information, vibrations, energies, etc., for a long time. Many witches use clear quartz as protection amulets. You can "program" your crystal by either thinking or whispering your intention into it—tell it to keep you safe at all times and in all situations. Then wear it or carry it with you for safety.
3. They focus and direct energy. Want to send healing vibes to someone? First program a crystal with healing thoughts, then aim its pointed end toward that person. You can also draw power from the heavens by aiming the point at the sky and envisioning a beam of energy flowing down and into your crystal.

Caution: *Never* drill holes into your crystals—you'll kill them. If you decide to wear a quartz crystal as jewelry, make sure the stone is surrounded by wire, a band, or some other type of fastener, not pierced.

Rose Quartz

A favorite of many witches, rose quartz looks like a frozen strawberry daiquiri. It ranges in color from palest pink to deep rose, and a single crystal may contain a variety of shades, striations, and cloudy wisps. Both its color and its milky quality connect it with the emotions, and indeed, rose quartz is one of the best stones to use when doing magick for emotional issues. For witches, this crystal is synonymous with love. Use it in spells to attract romance, affection, and friendship.

But rose quartz can do more than bring romantic love. Its gentle, soothing energy also encourages emotional healing and balance. A stone of peace, it can help family members or coworkers get along together harmoniously. After a disagreement, rose quartz can smooth troubled waters and restore calm. It also can help you learn to love yourself better by increasing your self-esteem and self-acceptance. People who have suffered loss and grief can benefit from wearing rose quartz too.

Smoky Quartz

Smoky quartz ranges in color from palest gray to brownish gold to almost black. Its earthly tone connects it to security, permanence, and patience; it also increases strength and determination. Witches often use this crystal for grounding and stability. If you're dealing with a chaotic situation or upsetting changes, if everything around you seems to be spinning out of control, smoky quartz can help bring matters into balance. Its energy is slower than that of clear quartz, so it can help you reach long-term goals. Because it's associated with materialization, you can use it to bring ideas down to earth and make dreams come true.

If you're facing obstacles or blockages of some kind, smoky quartz can help you to slowly overcome them. It bolsters courage and strength, without bravado. If you need endurance to accomplish a task, smoky quartz is your friend. If you have a problem that you just can't deal with right now, you can give it to a smoky quartz crystal to hold for you until you feel ready to work through it.

Abundance Crystals

Some quartz crystals contain bits of greenish material, which magicians relate to prosperity and growth. These green inclusions may appear as specks of color scattered throughout the crystal or as slabs of green within the otherwise clear crystal. In some cases, it looks as if a smaller green crystal is actually growing inside the larger whitish one. Because we often associate green with money, healthy live plants, and growth, you can use these crystals to improve your finances or attract abundance of any kind.

CARING FOR YOUR STONES

By nature, crystals and gemstones hold on to thoughts, emotions, and information programmed into them for a long time, even for centuries. You've probably heard of the Hope Diamond, a forty-five carat blue diamond that for more than a century supposedly bore a curse that brought death and misfortune to the people who owned it. Although you probably have nothing to fear from the stones you acquire, nonetheless it's a good idea to cleanse and purify them before you use them for magickal work.

Wash them in running water, with mild soap if you like, while you envision the crystals cleansed by pure white light. This removes any unwanted vibrations as well as dust. You can also purify crystals energetically by gently rubbing them with a piece of citrine. It's a good idea to clean your crystals before using them in a magick spell or ritual. You also should wash them if they've been exposed to any strong emotions or unsettling events.

If you prefer, try one of these methods for cleaning a crystal:

- Leave it in sunlight or moonlight for a specific period of time, say twenty-four hours or a week—it's your call. Do what you feel is necessary.
- Bury it in a small dish of dirt for a time.
- Hold the stone in the smoke of burning sage or purifying incense.
- Immerse the stone in water for a time. Holding it in a running stream or the ocean's waves will purify it faster, but leaving the stone in a small bowl of water will work too. Don't worry; you cannot remove the innate energy of a stone, so it's impossible to over-purify.

Each time you use a stone for a magickal purpose, it is important to purify it. You'll also want to purify your stones if someone else handles them, so that person's energy doesn't interfere with your own in spellworking.

Some people like to display their crystals and stones on their altars or elsewhere in their homes—especially the really big, beautiful, and powerful ones. Others prefer to wrap them in silk or velvet and store them in a safe place. It's really up to you. Clear quartz crystals, in particular, love to sit in the sun, but amethysts can fade if exposed to bright sunlight. You may choose to designate certain stones for certain purposes. Witches often place stones in various places around their homes and workplaces—rose quartz or carnelian on your bedside table to attract love, aventurine or abundance crystal in your store's cash register to increase sales, and so on.

The relationship you establish with your stones and crystals will be unique. Treat your crystals and gemstones as valued partners. In time, they'll become your good friends. *Never* abuse your stones! Show them respect and they'll gladly work with you for a lifetime.

PART II

An

⊰ OPEN ⊱

GRIMOIRE

Chapter 13

CHARMS, AMULETS, AND TALISMANS

Myths, legends, and literature from cultures around the world mention talismans and amulets, tokens and totems. Our ancestors designed them to attract love, ward off evil, and bring health, wealth, and happiness. Museums display collections of artifacts believed to have served as power objects for Stone Age people. The early Egyptians placed charms in the tombs of royalty to ensure safe passage into the world beyond. Ancient Greek soldiers carried amulets into battle to protect them. Aztec priests used gemstones to invoke deities and for prophesying.

Is It Okay to Design Your Own Spells?

A lot of people who are new to magick often ask if it's okay to create their own spells. The answer is a resounding *yes*. After all, someone, somewhere had to come up with the first spell, and hundreds of thousands of spells have been created since then! It's probably a good idea in the beginning to use tried-and-true spells, such as the ones offered in the following chapters, until you get the hang of it. Once you feel confident in your knowledge and ability, use your imagination to come up with original spells that suit your purposes.

Good luck charms are as popular today as they were in ancient times. Even people who don't believe in magick often give special significance to certain objects, regardless of whether those objects have any monetary value. Is it just superstition, or do these items really work? Find out for yourself. In this chapter, you'll learn how to create charms, amulets, and talismans for love, money, career success, healing—whatever you choose.

THE LAW OF SIMILARS

To understand how spells work, you need to understand the Law of Similars. According to this law, colors, shapes, and various characteristics of a plant, stone, or other object give clues to an item's magickal function. For example, red stones might be used in magickal cures for blood problems; a heart-shaped leaf might be part of a love spell. Advertising certainly understands how symbolic images affect the subconscious in specific ways. It's no accident that Coca-Cola formed its bottles like a woman's figure, or that TV commercials show phallic-shaped champagne bottles spewing foam.

One of the ways witches apply the Law of Similars is with "poppets" or dolls made to represent people. You can fabricate a poppet from cloth, straw, wood, wax—whatever you prefer. You can even buy readymade poppets online. The magick happens when you do something to the doll that symbolizes your intention and the result you want to achieve.

I suspect you're probably thinking of voodoo dolls now. Voodoo priests supposedly inflict pain on a doll and that pain is magickally transmitted to the person whom the doll represents. Creepy, but that's not how you probably want to use this type of magick.

Instead, let's say you want to send healing energy to a friend who's broken her leg. First, you make a poppet to stand in for your friend. You might want to decorate the doll to look like your friend, dressing it in clothes your friend might wear or adding hair the color of your friend's—even pasting on bits of her real hair if she'll let you trim it. Then you bandage the doll's leg and send loving, healing energy to your friend in the form of a chant, thought, or visualization. Imagine your friend's leg is completely well. That's it. No pins, no blood, no harm. In later chapters, you'll find spells that rely on the Law of Similars to do their thing—even one using a doll.

CHARMS

Early charms were spoken spells. In a time when few people could read or write, witches used verbal spells. The word charm comes from a Latin term, *carmen*, that means "incantation" or "song." A charm is like a poem, and many charms rhyme or have a distinct rhythm, making it easier for the witch to commit them to memory—no need to carry a huge grimoire around, no scrolls to get damaged in the rain en route to the market!

Uttering chants, affirmations, and incantations serves two purposes: to focus your mind during spells and rituals, and to send your objectives out into the universe. If you like, you can incorporate other actions and symbolism into a verbal charm. For example, a witch might wait until the first night of a full moon to speak her charm, then recite it three times each night thereafter. The full moon represents fullness, completion, and coming into manifestation. The number three represents the body-mind-spirit connection. Witches often use the number three because it brings magickal thoughts into three-dimensional reality.

Here's an example of a simple verbal charm:

Leaf of ash,
I do thee pluck
To bring to me
A day of luck.

Abracadabra

One of the oldest and best-known written charms is the Gnostic spell that uses the word Abracadabra (no, we're not pulling a rabbit out of a hat). In the original Chaldean texts, Abracadabra translates as "to perish like the word," and it was customarily used to banish sickness. The process was relatively simple. Abracadabra was written in the form of a descending triangle on parchment, which was then laid on the afflicted body part. Then the parchment was stuck in the cleft of a tree and left there so that as time and the elements destroyed it, the magick would begin its work.

Okay, it's not a literary masterpiece, and your charms don't have to be either. The important thing is that a charm expresses your wish or goal, and that it's easy to remember. Repeat it often to give it more energy and to make the magick work faster. If you wish, you can add a physical action to the spoken charm. As you speak the word "pluck," take a leaf from a tree whose properties match your intention (see Chapter 11), and then carry it with you all day to attract good luck.

Affirmations

Affirmations are positive statements that you create to produce a result. Witches use them in all sorts of spells, both spoken and written. The important things to remember when designing an affirmation are:

- Keep it short.
- Be clear and precise.
- Only include images and situations that you desire.
- Always use the present tense, as if the condition you seek already exists.

Here are some examples of the right and wrong ways to create affirmations:

Right: I am healthy in body, mind, and spirit.
Wrong: I don't have any illnesses or injuries.
Right: I now have a job that's perfect for me.
Wrong: I want to get a better job.

See the difference? If you aren't exactly sure of all the details, it's okay to leave some things up to the universe to work out. The previous example, "I now have a job that's perfect for me," covers the bases without being specific.

Incantations

Incantations differ from affirmations in that they are usually written as rhymes. The catchy phrasing makes it easy to remember. You don't have to be a Wordsworth or Dickinson to create an effective incantation.

Just follow the same rules for designing an incantation as you did for an affirmation.

Here's an example of a simple love incantation:

As the day fades into night
I draw a love that's good and right.
As the night turns into day
We are blessed in every way.

The uses for affirmations and incantations are limited only by your imagination. Write one on a slip of paper and insert it into a talisman or amulet. Put it under your pillow at night. Repeat it regularly throughout the day, such as while you're in the shower or driving to work, and especially just before you go to sleep. Write it on a sheet of colored paper, decorate it with images that resonate with you, and post it in a place where you'll see it often. Be creative!

Using Colors in Magick Spells

Colors contain lots of symbolic associations. Blue, for instance, reminds you of the sky; green suggests foliage, grass, and healthy crops; orange is the color of fire and the sun. So deeply rooted are these connections that witches can use color to influence the mind and produce magickal results. When you're doing spells, remember these color correspondences and let them increase the power of your magick.

COLOR SYMBOLISM	
Color	**Correspondences**
Red	passion, anger, heat, energy, daring
Orange	confidence, activity, warmth, enthusiasm
Yellow	happiness, creativity, optimism, ideas, communication
Green	health, fertility, growth, wealth
Light blue	peace, clarity, hope
Royal blue	independence, insight, imagination, truth
Indigo	intuition, serenity, mental power, dreamwork

COLOR SYMBOLISM	
Color	**Correspondences**
Purple	wisdom, spirituality, connection with higher realms
Pink	love, friendship, sociability
White	purity, clarity, protection
Black	power, wisdom
Brown	stability, practicality, grounding in the physical world

Black, a color witches frequently wear, has many negative connotations to the general public, including death and mourning. To witches, however, black is a color of power, for it contains all the other colors. It's also reminiscent of mystery and the night, the time when witches often gather to work magick. In spellworking, black is associated with the planet Saturn and used for banishing, endings, and inner strength.

AMULETS

People often confuse charms, amulets, and talismans. Sometimes they use the word "talisman" to refer to both amulets and talismans, or the word "charm" to describe all three. Since ancient times, magicians have created these spells and, as a witch, you probably will, too, so you need to know the difference. A charm can either attract something to you or repel something. An amulet's main purpose is protection, or to prevent something from happening. It wards off unwanted magick and/or harmful situations, such as an auto accident or robbery. An amulet serves as a magick "shield" that blocks danger—it doesn't go on the offensive.

What Can You Use as an Amulet?

The early Greeks called amulets *amylon* meaning "food." This suggests that people used food offerings to ask gods and goddesses for protection—the petitioners might have even eaten or carried a small bit of that food as a token. Many items found in the natural world have been made into amulets, including plants, carved stones, and metal objects. Amulets were also commonly chosen for their shapes or where they were found. For example, our European ancestors often carried "holey stones" (any stone with a hole going through it) to guard against malicious fairies (who would get trapped in the hole). A crystal found near a sacred well known for its healthful qualities might be carried as an amulet to protect the bearer's well-being.

Amulets can be worn, placed with valuable items, affixed on pet collars, hung in windows, planted in gardens, or put anywhere you want them to provide protection. A horseshoe hung above a doorway is a familiar example of a protective amulet.

Amulets from Around the World

Brass ring (Lapland): Worn on the right arm to keep ghosts away

God figurines (Assyria): Buried near the home to protect all within

Lapis lazuli eyes (Egypt): Placed in tombs to safeguard the soul's journey

Metal rattles (Ancient Rome): Tied to children's clothing for overall protection

Miniature carved canoes (Iroquois): Protection from drowning

Monkey teeth (Borneo): For strength and skill

Peach stone (China): Protection against evil

Spruce needles (Shoshone): To keep sickness at bay

Amulets and talismans can consist of a single gem or object. Amethysts, for instance, have long been worn as amulets against drunkenness, because they increase self-control. Going to a big party this weekend? You might want to put on those amethyst earrings, just as a precaution. Or, an amulet may contain several items—just make sure that each item relates to your intention and holds special meaning for you. How about the amethyst earrings *and* some amber perfume (for protection against unwanted advances or accidents), but leave off the garlic necklace unless you think vampires might crash the party.

Creating an Amulet

After you've gathered all the ingredients for your magick amulet, go through the steps outlined in Chapters 8 and 9 for cleansing, purifying, and casting a circle. The ancient magi believed that when making amulets, you must work with the components in a precise order—the primary or most important ingredient should come first. Let's say, for example, you want to create a protection amulet for a relative who's going on a trip and you've decided to use a brass disc as your base. Start with that disc, then attach stones, beads, feathers, or other items to it in their order of importance. If you plan to carve magick symbols on the disc, begin with one for safety while traveling. Then inscribe another for ongoing protection while your relative is away, and finish with a symbol for a safe return. Just as early witches did, you'll probably want to recite affirmations or incantations over the amulet while you're fabricating it. When you've finished, open the circle as described previously and give the amulet to your relative.

Witches often make amulets (and talismans too) by filling cloth pouches with magick ingredients. If you're working with loose herbs and/or tiny objects, this is a good way to go. Choose a pouch of a color that relates to your intention: pink or red for love, gold or silver for money, etc. Insert the most important ingredient, say a small quartz crystal or other stone. Then add the rest of the items—flower petals, herbs, symbols written on paper—in the order of their significance. Tie the pouch with three knots to seal in your magickal components. Once you've sealed an amulet or talisman, don't open it.

How long will your amulet last? Because amulets remain passive until something external happens that creates a need for their energy, they can stay inert for a long time. However, once the magick energy has been activated and spent, the amulet has served its purpose. After showing gratitude, you can retire it: Burn it in a ritual fire, bury it, or otherwise dispose of it in a respectful manner.

A Talking Amulet

Disney jumped on the witchy bandwagon with a magick necklace, a big purple gemstone amulet fit for a princess, to wit, the princess Sofia. You can purchase a talking version of the playful amulet for your favorite little girl, complete with twelve action cards she can insert into the "amulet" to get insights from the stone.

TALISMANS

A talisman is designed to attract something its owner desires. Gemstones and jewelry have long been favored as talismans. The Chinese, for example, prize jade and wear it to bring health, strength, and good fortune. For centuries, women of many cultures have worn lockets that contain snippets of their lovers' hair as talismans.

You can also combine several items that relate to your objective (see Chapters 11 and 12 for suggestions). Slip the selected items into a cloth or leather pouch and wear it as a talisman. Or you could place meaningful items in a wooden box and set it on your altar to attract the object of your desires. If you know feng shui (a type of Chinese magick that focuses on harmonizing you and your environment) put the talisman in the part of your home that relates to your intention. A talisman can be made for yourself or for someone else. It's usually best to fashion a talisman while the moon is waxing (between new and full) because the waxing moon encourages increase and development.

Many old stories say that spirits lived in talismans and whoever possessed the talisman could command the spirit to do specific tasks. Remember Aladdin's lamp that held a powerful genie? The genie had to grant Aladdin three wishes. That's a mythological example of a talisman. For our purposes here, think of talismans as magick tokens created for a particular purpose.

What Goes Into a Talisman?

You create a talisman essentially the same way as you make an amulet, using one or more ingredients that relate to your objective. When choosing your ingredients, pay attention to both the purpose of the spell and your own associations with the objects themselves. If you (or the person you're making the talisman for) plan to carry it around, small, lightweight ingredients are essential. If you plan to wear an amulet or talisman, you'll need to design it with comfort, convenience, and beauty in mind.

Tokens as Talismans

You're enjoying a peaceful walk at a place that has special meaning for you, when you spot a pretty pebble lying on the ground. You pick it up, study its markings for a moment, rub its smooth surface, and then slip it into your pocket. From time to time, throughout the day, you touch the stone fondly. Back home, you place the stone on the mantel or coffee table, where it continues to bring pleasant thoughts. Perhaps you carry it with you on future sojourns.

This token now holds the positive energy you've given it. It has all the makings of a lucky talisman. In fact, many simple talismans are nothing more than ordinary objects that have been infused with meaning by their owners—the good feelings and thoughts associated with such objects are what give them their power. Objects found in this manner, and especially those that come from sacred sites, are ideal to use as talismans.

Because they actively send out energy to attract something you desire, talismans "burn out" faster than amulets do. If you don't get what you want in a reasonable amount of time, you might need to "feed" your talisman to reinforce its strength. You can do this by dabbing a little essential oil on it. Essential oils are extracted from plants and contain the life energy of herbs and flowers. Choose an oil from a plant that relates to the purpose of your talisman (see Chapter 11 for ideas).

TIMING SPELLS

If you're launching an ad campaign, applying for a job, or running for a political office, timing can be crucial to your success. The same holds true for magick. By performing a spell or ritual on an auspicious date, you increase the likelihood of accomplishing your goal quickly and effectively. In timing spells, the moon's cycle is usually the most important factor.

When casting spells, pay particular attention to these four significant lunar periods: the new moon, full moon, waxing, and waning phases. As we discussed in Chapter 4, each has its own unique energy that can help or hinder the power of your spells.

Superstition attaches all sorts of strange and scary things to the full moon especially. Despite all that nonsense about werewolves, the full moon is a high-energy period and it can be a great time to connect with the Goddess, nature spirits, and the earth. If you're interested in astrology, you'll also want to pay attention to the moon's passage through different zodiac signs—it changes signs about every two and a half days. Find a good book about astrological signs and choose a sign that relates to your intention—Libra for love, Sagittarius for travel—in order to boost the energy of your spell.

THE DAYS OF THE WEEK

Before powerful telescopes allowed astronomers to see beyond the range of the human eye, only seven heavenly bodies could be observed from earth: the sun, moon, Mercury, Venus, Mars, Jupiter, and Saturn. Early people believed that gods and goddesses inhabited these bodies, and named them for those deities.

Each god or goddess was said to possess particular characteristics and oversee certain aspects of life on earth. Venus, for instance, guided love and relationships. Mercury ruled communication and commerce. According to ancient tradition, each deity's power reigned supreme on one of the seven days of the week. By scheduling activities on a day when the deity who ruled your particular interest was in charge you could increase your chances of success.

When doing magick spells, the same holds true in modern times. Love spells, for example, can benefit from the energy of Venus if you perform them on Friday. The following table shows which days and deities govern which areas of life.

MAGICK DAYS		
Day of the Week	**Ruling Planet/Deity**	**Areas of Influence**
Monday	Moon	fertility, creativity, home and family matters, intuition
Tuesday	Mars	contests/competition, courage, strength/vitality, men
Wednesday	Mercury	communication, commerce, intellectual concerns

MAGICK DAYS		
Day of the Week	**Ruling Planet/Deity**	**Areas of Influence**
Thursday	Jupiter	growth/expansion, prosperity, long-distance travel
Friday	Venus	love, partnerships, the arts, women
Saturday	Saturn	limitations, authority, endurance, stability, protection
Sunday	Sun	public image, confidence, career pursuits, health/well-being

The Modern Guide to Witchcraft

Chapter 14

PROSPERITY SPELLS

Living gets more expensive every day. Each time you fill your car's tank with gasoline or buy groceries at the supermarket, it costs more. Most people's salaries aren't keeping pace with the rising cost of living and economic forecasts sound pretty grim. What's a person to do? When the going gets rough, witches start conjuring up some cash. Whether you're just trying to pay your bills or want a little extra to buy something special, magick can help.

WHAT DOES PROSPERITY MEAN TO YOU?

Do you define prosperity as a dollar amount, a cool million, for instance? Or do you think of it as a state of being, such as living comfortably? Does *abundance* mean having more of everything or having enough of everything? These distinctions may seem trivial, but before you begin doing prosperity spells, you need to be absolutely clear in your own mind about what these concepts mean to you.

If you're like most people, your beliefs about money and prosperity were instilled in you long ago, perhaps by your parents, a religious institution, or the society in which you lived. If these old attitudes are preventing you from having the abundance you desire, you'll have to get rid of them and replace them with new ideas.

If you were to conduct an informal survey among your friends, you might be surprised to discover how differently people view prosperity. Their responses would probably cover a wide spectrum: to have more money; to be in a better job; to enjoy a happy marriage or romantic relationship; to write a best-selling novel or screenplay; to own a house; to be self-employed; to be able to travel.

How about you? Finish the following sentences to see what your true feelings are. Don't try too hard or think about it too long.

1. I am happiest when . . .
2. My wildest dream is to . . .
3. Given the choice, I would most like to spend my time . . .
4. I thoroughly enjoy . . .
5. I would love to . . .
6. I now spend my free time . . .
7. I feel a sense of accomplishment when . . .
8. My greatest passion is . . .
9. One of my favorite hobbies is . . .

This list describes what makes you happy—and happiness is what "abundance" is all about. You can have all the money in the world, but if it doesn't make you happy, what good is it?

Write Your Wish List

Take a few minutes to define what prosperity and abundance mean to you today, right now, in this moment. Make a list of ten things that would make you feel prosperous if you had them. Now find an object that represents each entry on your list. Select these objects with care—you're going to use them to work magick.

Let's say that your wildest dream is getting your pilot's license. Perhaps you haven't yet accomplished this goal because you didn't have enough money for lessons or an airplane. Any number of objects might represent your dream: a model airplane, a photograph of the type of plane you would like to fly, or a child's plastic toy plane. The point is to choose something that immediately connects you to the feeling of flying.

When you've collected all ten items, put them in a place where you'll see them often: your desk, a windowsill, or your altar. Each time you look at them, you'll be reminded of your dreams of abundance and your intention to attract prosperity into your life.

Creating a Prosperity Consciousness

Do you think you're worthy of prosperity? Do you believe you are inherently valuable? Do you trust the universe to provide for you and always give you whatever you need? Or do you constantly worry about paying bills and fear poverty? Do you believe that money is the root of evil? Do you think you can't be both rich and spiritual?

Prosperity consciousness means you wholeheartedly believe you deserve to have whatever you desire. You know that your good fortune doesn't take away from anyone else's—the universe's warehouse of goodies is infinite. You welcome wealth of all kinds into your life. You use money to enrich your life and the lives of others. If you don't have a prosperity consciousness, you'll need to develop it before you can successfully do spells for prosperity.

Each time you notice yourself saying or thinking something that undermines your prosperity consciousness, such as "I can't afford that," cross it out in your mind's eye by drawing a line through it. Then rephrase the statement in a positive way.

We talked about affirmations in Chapter 13. Affirmations are good tools for reprogramming your ideas. Write down one or more affirmations related to prosperity and repeat them often. Say your affirmation(s) aloud at least a dozen times a day, until your subconscious gets the message. Here are a few suggestions:

- My life is rich with abundance of all kinds.
- I have everything I need and desire.
- All my bills are paid, and I have plenty of money to spare and share.
- I am happy, healthy, wealthy, and fulfilled in every way.

Try not to concern yourself with how you're going to get the money. Just trust that opportunities will begin to present themselves to you if you continue to say the affirmation and believe in yourself.

Timing Prosperity and Abundance Spells

For each of the spells in this chapter, I've noted the best time to perform the spell. In most cases, you'll be more successful if you do spells for prosperity and abundance while the moon is waxing. The seeds you plant with your spell will grow along with the moon. As the moon's light increases, so will your wealth.

Taurus is the zodiac sign of money, material goods, and physical resources. Therefore, an ideal time to do prosperity spells is when the moon and/or the sun is in Taurus. If your spell involves other people's money, insurance, taxes, inheritance, or litigation, you might be better off casting a spell when the moon and/or sun is in Scorpio.

The best days of the week for doing prosperity magic are Thursday and Friday, the days ruled by Jupiter and Venus respectively. These planets encourage growth, abundance, and good luck.

SO MANY BILLS, SO FEW FUNDS

Stop dreading those bills—that's the key to this spell's success. Instead, try looking at your bills in another light. Your creditors have provided goods or services up front, because they're confident you'll be able to pay. Now it's time for you to believe in yourself.

INGREDIENTS/TOOLS:
- A piece of green paper or paper designed to resemble money
- A pen that writes gold or silver ink
- A black ribbon
- A stick of peppermint incense
- An incense burner

BEST TIME TO PERFORM THE SPELL:
- Whenever you pay your bills

Gather together all bills that are due, plus your checkbook and a pen. Collect the listed ingredients. Cast a circle around the area where you will perform the spell. Cut the green paper into a rectangle the size and shape of paper currency and write $1,000,000 on it. Use the pen with gold or silver ink to write the following affirmation on the green paper: "I always have more than enough money to pay all my bills. My prosperity increases every day in every way."

After you've finished writing checks to cover your bills, stack the receipts and place the piece of green paper on top of them. Tie up everything with the black ribbon. Fit the stick of incense into its burner and light it. Hold the envelopes containing your checks in the smoke for a few moments. Put aside any fears and imagine you have everything you need, when you need it. Open the circle. Repeat this spell every time you pay your bills.

SPELL FOR UNEXPECTED EXPENSES

When you least expect it, often at the most inopportune time, the dishwasher breaks or your car's air conditioner dies. Here's a spell to generate extra cash to cover those emergency expenses.

INGREDIENTS/TOOLS:
- A ballpoint pen
- Three candles, one green, one gold, and one silver
- Three candleholders
- Enough coins (any denomination) to form a circle around all three candles
- Matches or a lighter

BEST TIME TO PERFORM THE SPELL:
- Preferably during the waxing moon, but in an emergency you can do this spell as necessary

Collect the ingredients needed for this spell. Cast a circle around the area where you will do your spell. Using the ballpoint pen, carve the word "money" on the green candle. Inscribe the gold candle with the word "abundance" and write "now" on the silver candle. Set the candles on your altar or another place where they can burn safely. Position them so they form a triangle, with the green and gold candles at the base and the silver one at the apex of the triangle.

Next, with the coins make a circle around the candles. Be sure all the coins are face up and that each coin touches those on either side of it. Light the candles and call upon your favorite spiritual helper—a guardian angel, totem animal, or other deity—and ask for assistance in acquiring the money you need.

Allow the candles to burn down completely, but don't leave the burning candles unattended. If you must leave the circle before the candles finish burning, extinguish them and light them again later to continue the spell. When the candles have burned completely, open the circle and thank the deity for helping you.

MAGICK MONEY OIL

This versatile magick potion has many possible applications. Rub it on candles to increase their power. Dab it on talismans. Anoint gemstones, crystals, or magick tools with it. Rub a little on your body. However you use it, this money oil helps you attract all forms of abundance.

INGREDIENTS/TOOLS:
- A green glass bottle with a lid or stopper
- A small piece of tiger's eye or aventurine
- 4 ounces of olive, almond, or grape seed oil
- A few drops of peppermint essential oil
- Gold or silver glitter

BEST TIME TO PERFORM THE SPELL:
- During the waxing moon, preferably on Thursday

Wash the bottle and gemstone with mild soap and water, then dry them. Gather all the listed ingredients. Begin by casting a circle around the area where you will do your spell. Pour the olive, almond, or grape seed oil into the bottle. Add the peppermint essential oil and glitter. Drop the tiger's eye or aventurine in the mixture, then put the lid or stopper on the bottle and shake three times to charge the potion.

Open the circle and apply your Magick Money Oil in whatever manner you choose. This magick oil can be incorporated into many of the spells in this chapter.

Oil Your Candles for More "Octane"

You can increase the power of the candles by rubbing Magick Money Oil on them before you burn them. Or, pour a little oil of cedar, sandalwood, mint, clove, or cinnamon—scents associated with money—in your palms, then rub the oil on the candles. Some witches say you should start at the middle of the candle, and if you wish to increase or attract something, rub the oil toward the top of the candle—just don't get oil on the wick. If you want to decrease or repel something, such as cutting expenses, start at the center and rub oil down toward the candle's base.

GOTTA HAVE IT SPELL

Whether you've got your eye on a pair of designer shoes, a new computer, or a sports car, this spell helps you obtain whatever your heart desires. You can magickally manifest big things as easily as little ones. The only limits are in your own mind.

INGREDIENTS/TOOLS:
- A clear quartz crystal or an abundance crystal (one that contains a greenish mineral called chlorite)
- A picture or other likeness of the object you've "gotta have"
- Essential oil of cedar (or the money oil from the previous spell)

BEST TIME TO PERFORM THE SPELL:
- During the waxing moon, preferably on Thursday

Collect the ingredients needed for this spell. Wash the crystal in mild soap and water. Cast a circle around the area where you will do your spell.

Hold the crystal in your left hand while you gaze at the picture of the item you've "gotta have" and imagine yourself already owning it. Really get your feelings and senses involved in the visualization—wearing the shoes, driving the car. The more vivid you can make the experience the better.

When your mind starts to drift, dab four dots of essential oil on the picture, one at each corner. Let the scent strengthen your intention to acquire the object you desire. When you feel confident that you'll receive your heart's desire, open the circle. Place the picture on your altar, desk, or another place where you'll see it often. Set the crystal on top of the picture to increase the power of your spell. Look at the picture regularly, reaffirming your intention, until the object materializes.

SIMPLE CAULDRON SPELL

The cauldron symbolizes abundance. In spells, it holds your intention along with whatever ingredients you use in your spells for a period of time, to let the spell brew. This is the easiest possible money spell you can do with your cauldron, but don't let that fool you into thinking it isn't powerful!

Put one penny in your cauldron every day. As you do, say aloud, "I invest in my financial well-being. Every day brings greater abundance to me." When the cauldron is full, take the pennies to your bank or donate them to a charity of your choice.

GOODBYE DEBT SPELL

The cauldron represents creativity and fertility; cedar is associated with wealth. Combine the two with the action of fire, and you've got a potent spell.

INGREDIENTS/TOOLS:
- A large iron cauldron (or a cooking pot if you don't have a cauldron)
- Cedar wood chips, sticks, or shakes
- The five of pentacles from a tarot deck you don't use for readings
- A shovel or trowel

The Modern Guide to Witchcraft

• During the waning moon

Place the cauldron in a spot where it's safe to build a fire. Cast a circle around the area where you'll do your spell. Put the cedar inside the cauldron. Set fire to the wood, and when you have a small blaze going, drop the tarot card into the flames. The five of pentacles signifies debt and poverty; as the card burns, envision your debts disappearing as well. Let the fire burn down completely, then collect the ashes. Open the circle. On the next new moon, bury the ashes someplace far away from your home.

BURIED TREASURE SPELL

Instead of hunting for a pirate's hidden chest of gold doubloons, in this spell you symbolically stash treasure in order to "prime the pump" so greater riches can flow to you.

INGREDIENTS/TOOLS:
• A small mirror
• A tin box with a lid
• Nine coins (any denomination)
• A magnet
• A shovel

BEST TIME TO PERFORM THE SPELL:
• During the waxing moon, preferably on a Thursday

Gather all the listed ingredients. Begin by casting a circle around the area where you will do your spell. Place the mirror in the bottom of the tin box, with the reflective side up. Lay the coins, one at a time, on top of the mirror while you envision each one multiplying. Attach the magnet to the inside of the box (on the lid or a side) and visualize it attracting an unlimited number of coins to you. Put the lid on the box and open the circle.

Take your "treasure chest" and the shovel outside and dig a hole beneath a large tree. Bury the box in the ground near the tree's roots. When you've finished, say this incantation aloud:

"By the luck of three times three
This spell now brings great wealth to me.
The magnet draws prosperity.
The mirror doubles all it sees.
My fortune grows as does this tree
And I shall ever blessed be."

YOUR GOOD LUCK COIN

Find a coin minted in the year of your birth (or in a year that has special significance for you). It can be any denomination—even a coin from another country if that country has positive associations for you. Say the following incantation aloud to give the coin its magickal power:

"By these words, my will, and coin,
Magick and good fortune join."

Carry the coin with you or place it where you need the most luck—your home, business, or elsewhere.

CRYSTAL ABUNDANCE SPELL

Some quartz crystals contain bits of greenish mineral matter in them. These are known as "money crystals" or "abundance crystals." If possible, use one of these in this spell. Otherwise, a clear quartz crystal will work fine.

INGREDIENTS/TOOLS:
- 1 quartz crystal
- An image that represents abundance to you

- On a Thursday when the moon is waxing

Select a magazine picture or download an online image that symbolizes prosperity to you. It might be an object or condition you desire, such as a new home, a sports car, or a European vacation. Lay the picture face up on a windowsill where the moon's light will shine on it.

Wash the crystal in warm water with mild soap to cleanse it of any unwanted energies. Dry the crystal, then hold it to your third eye (between your eyebrows) while thinking about your intention. Doing this sends the image into the crystal. Then set the crystal on the picture. Make sure the crystal's point faces toward the inside of your home, to draw what you want to you. Leave the crystal in place overnight. In the morning, remove the crystal and picture and give thanks for the bounty you are about to receive.

MONEY TALISMAN

If you like, you can decorate the pouch for this talisman with beads, tiny charms, embroidery, or symbols that represent wealth to you.

INGREDIENTS/TOOLS:
- 1 strip of paper
- A pen that writes green, gold, or silver ink
- Peppermint essential oil (or the Magick Money Oil from earlier in this chapter)
- 1 green pouch (preferably made of silk or velvet)
- 1 coin (any denomination)
- Cedar chips
- 3 whole cloves
- 1 pinch of cinnamon
- 1 gold or silver ribbon 9" long
- Incense burner
- Pine or sandalwood incense
- Matches or a lighter

- During the waxing moon

On the strip of paper, write this affirmation: "I now have plenty of money for everything I need and desire. Riches come to me from all directions." Dot the corners of the paper with essential oil, then fold it three times and slip it into the pouch. Add the coin, cedar, and herbs to the pouch.

Tie the pouch with the ribbon, making three knots. Each time you tie a knot, repeat your affirmation. When you've finished, say, "This is now accomplished in harmony with Divine Will, my own true will, and with good to all." Fit the incense into the burner and light it, then hold the talisman in the incense smoke to charge it. Carry the pouch in your pocket or purse. If you prefer, take it to your workplace to help you earn more money.

TAROT SPELL TO INCREASE YOUR INCOME

The vivid colors and images on tarot cards make them a wonderful addition to any spell. Even if you don't understand all the symbols on the cards, your subconscious will register them. The candles' colors are meaningful, too. Green is the color of paper money in some countries, and also reminds us of healthy, growing plants. White represents clarity and protection.

INGREDIENTS/TOOLS:
- 1 green candle and 1 white candle
- 2 candleholders
- An object that represents your desire
- 1 deck of tarot cards
- Matches or a lighter

BEST TIME TO PERFORM THE SPELL:
- During the waxing moon

Cast a circle around the area where you will perform this spell. Put your candles at opposite ends of your altar. Between them, place an object that signifies your desire to increase your income. This could be one of the items that you chose at the beginning of this chapter to symbolize the intentions on your wish list. It could also be a coin, a dollar bill, a piece of jewelry, or something else that suggests wealth.

From your deck of tarot cards, select the ace of pentacles (sometimes called coins or discs), which represents new financial undertakings and opportunities. Place it in front of the white candle. In front of the green candle, put the ten of pentacles. Sometimes called the "Wall Street" card, the ten symbolizes a financial windfall. In the middle, between the two candles, place the nine of cups—the "Wish" card—and the Star card, which symbolizes hope.

Light the candles and say:

"The money I spend
and the money I lend
comes back to me
in multiples of three."

See money flowing to you from all directions. The more vivid you can make your visualization, the faster your wish will manifest. End the spell by extinguishing the candles and giving thanks. Open the circle. Allow everything to remain on your altar overnight.

KEEPING TRACK OF YOUR SPELLS

Whenever you do a spell, record all the details in your book of shadows. That way, you can perform the spell again at a later date, adjust it, or adapt it to other circumstances. Following is a list of the basic information you should include about any spell or ritual you perform:

1. Name and type of spell. Write this at the top of the page.
2. Date and time you did the spell. If it's an original spell, you may also wish to add the date and time you composed it.

3. Who else was present, if anyone.
4. Moon phase. Add the moon sign if you know it, as well as other pertinent astrological information.
5. Weather. This is more important than you might think, as weather can affect your feelings as well as the place where you choose to perform your spell.
6. Location. Did you do the spell in the living room, backyard, etc.?
7. Your health. Your energy level and overall health can impact your spells. If you are female, also note where you are in your menstrual cycle.
8. Purpose of the spell. This may be obvious from the name of the spell, but a heading such as "Simple Cauldron Spell" might require a little more information about why you did the spell.
9. A complete list of the tools and ingredients used. This is vital for future reference and if you choose to repeat the spell.
10. Deities invoked, if any.
11. The entire text of the spell or ritual. You can write this down before the ritual, and just work from your text, if necessary.
12. How long it took to complete the spell.
13. The immediate reaction you felt to the ritual.
14. Short-term results. What did you notice over the first few days or weeks following the ritual?
15. Long-term results. What sort of changes have you observed over the following months or years?

You may choose to add other information you consider relevant, interesting, etc. Add drawings, poems, or other jottings if you like. Of course, you can always come back later and put in notations about things you thought of afterwards, dreams, discussions you may have had with fellow witches, and so on. It's your book to work with however seems best for you.

Chapter 15

LOVE SPELLS

Witchcraft and spellcasting are inseparable. Witchcraft, as you already know, is the practice of using your will, mind, emotions, and perhaps special tools to bring your intentions into being—magick is what happens during that process. Magick spells don't have to be complicated to be successful. If anything, the simpler the better—unless lots of details and drama enable you to create the magickal ambiance you desire. Some spells need nothing more than the witch's presence to activate them.

In myth, song, and poetry, love and magick are often linked. When we speak of falling in love we use such terms as enchanted, charmed, bewitched, under a lover's spell—and it often feels that way. But as Shakespeare wrote in his delightful play about magick and love, *A Midsummer Night's Dream*, "The course of true love never did run smooth." Therefore it's probably no surprise that the most frequently cast spells are—you guessed it—love spells.

Love spells, however, can be tricky and more than a few witches have performed questionable spells for romantic reasons. It's easy to let your heart rule your head. Before you do the spells in this chapter, give some thought to what you really want in a relationship and what your motives are for casting a spell. Do you really want to use magick to snag a guy who's not that into you? If your girlfriend is cheating on you, do you really want her back?

DEFINING WHAT YOU WANT

What's your reason for doing a love spell? Are you trying to attract a new romantic partner? Looking for your soulmate? Hoping to rekindle the spark in an existing relationship? The more specific you can be, the greater your chances of success.

Keep in mind that a love spell's primary purpose isn't to use magick to manipulate someone into falling in love with you. Its purpose is to balance your own energy so you attract the partner who is right for you. A relationship results from the interaction of two people, two individual forces—yin and yang—that merge to form a sum greater than the parts.

You'd think this should be easy, but for many people it's not. Your ideas may be influenced by the expectations of your family, your friends, or the culture in which you live. Your perceptions about your ideal mate might be conditioned by television and movies, books and magazines, and all sorts of societal stereotypes. The reasons a man in Zimbabwe marries could be quite different from those that unite a couple in Sweden. Even you and your best friend may not agree on what constitutes a good relationship.

Your Love List

Before you do any love spells, make a list of the qualities you seek in a partner. The act of compiling this list will prompt you to really think about your needs, desires, hopes, and priorities, and to put energy and intent behind the process of creating what you want. In a sense, your list becomes a spell. Like an affirmation, you state your intentions—what you intend to find in a partner—and focus your mind toward achieving your goal.

Your list can be as long and as detailed as you choose. As you write your list, be sure to state your desires in a positive way and in the present tense. Here are some examples:

- I now have a partner who respects and values me.
- I can trust and rely on my partner at all times and in all situations.
- My partner and I support and encourage each other's goals.
- My partner and I share a spiritual path.

- My partner and I have many common interests and enjoy one another's company.
- I now have a mate who is willing and able to enter into a committed, loving, primary partnership with me.

Be specific. Consider every angle. Cover all your bases. You might want to let a trusted friend read your list and provide feedback, so you don't overlook anything. You don't want to write a long and detailed love list that described all the qualities you seek in a mate, and then realize too late that you left out something important. I once drew up a list of things I wanted in a partner, and one qualification was "likes to travel." I should have stated "likes to travel *with me*" because the man I attracted loved to travel—and did, a lot—he just preferred to travel alone.

Timing Love Spells

Astrologers connect Venus with love and relationships, and Venus rules the zodiac signs Taurus and Libra. Libra is the sign of romantic partnerships and marriage, so you'll get an energy boost if you perform a love spell when the moon and/or the sun is in Libra. Taurus is connected with the physical side of love, so if you want to improve your sex life, consider doing your spell when the sun and/or moon is in Taurus.

If you're trying to attract a new partner, do a spell on the new moon. If you want to increase the joy or passion in an existing relationship, or to nudge a budding affair into full bloom, do your spell when the moon is waxing. To end an unfulfilling relationship, do magic while the moon is waning.

SPELL TO GET NOTICED

Does it sometimes seem like you're invisible? If you aren't getting the attention you seek, perhaps you need to boost your personal power. This spell helps you raise energy and project it into your environment, so that the person you've got your eye on will notice you.

INGREDIENTS/TOOLS:
- A clear quartz crystal
- A drum or gong

BEST TIME TO PERFORM THE SPELL:
- During the full moon

Collect the ingredients needed for this spell. Wash the quartz crystal with mild soap and water, then pat it dry. Cast a circle around the area where you will do your spell. Stand (or sit) in the center of the circle with the drum or gong. Place the crystal nearby.

Begin playing the drum or gong. Feel the vibration breaking down the invisible wall around you that has prevented that certain person from seeing you clearly. Now imagine you are drawing energy up from the earth, into your body. Envision it as a brilliant silver light moving up your legs and spine, until your entire body is filled with a silver glow.

Continue playing the drum or gong as you now imagine drawing energy down from the heavens. Visualize this as golden light flowing into the top of your head, down your spine, until your whole body is alive with a golden glow. Pick up the crystal and hold it to your heart. Strike the drum or gong one time as you imagine the mixture of silver and gold light radiating outward from your heart. As it flows through the crystal the light is magnified tenfold and spreads out, filling the room. Strike the drum or gong again as you send the light further, into the environment outside. You can project this powerful light as far and wide as you choose.

When you feel confident and secure in your newfound radiance, open the circle. Pick up the crystal and carry it with you at all times. It will retain the energy of the spell and continue resonating with it, enhancing your personal power wherever you go.

Clean Up Your Love Life

In the ancient Chinese magick system known as feng shui, everything in your home has symbolic value. If your love life is stuck, stressful, or nonexistent, take a look at your bedroom. Is it full of clutter? Does it feel unwelcoming? Get rid of old stuff that you don't need or use anymore—old stuff represents emotional baggage and things from your past that may be holding you back. Faded, worn-out objects represent a love life that's lost its sparkle. Broken items indicate broken dreams or a physical breakup. Organize what you choose to keep so your bedroom is neat and orderly.

SPELL TO ATTRACT A NEW LOVER

This is your chance to put to work that love list you so carefully compiled earlier. Use your magick to attract the perfect partner.

INGREDIENTS/TOOLS:
- Ylang-ylang, rose, or jasmine essential oil
- 1 rose-colored candle
- List of qualities you seek in a partner
- Matches or a lighter

BEST TIME TO PERFORM THE SPELL:
- The first Friday after the new moon

Cast a circle. Pour a little oil in your palm, and then rub it over the entire candle (except the wick). Set your list on your altar or other surface, and set the candle (in a candlestick or other fireproof container) on top of the list. Light the candle.

As the scent of the heated oil wafts into the air, vividly imagine your lover. Feel this person's presence right there in the room with you. How does this person look, act, speak, and dress? See as much detail as possible. What type of work does he or she do? What are his or her passions? Continue the visualization for as long as you like, making your mental images as rich as possible.

When you've spent as much time as you feel is necessary, snuff out the candle's flame and open the circle. Repeat this spell two more times before the full moon. On the night of the full moon, release your wish by allowing the candle to finish burning down completely. Express thanks for the love you are about to receive.

TURN UP THE HEAT

Has the spark gone out of your relationship? This spell uses spices to add spice to your love life, along with fire to heat up things between you and your partner.

INGREDIENTS/TOOLS:
- A fireplace, balefire pit, barbecue grill, hibachi, or other place where you can light a fire safely
- Matches or a lighter
- A piece of paper (hot pink or purple preferably)
- A pen that writes red ink
- Cayenne pepper
- Mustard seeds (or dry mustard)
- Ginger (freshly grated or powdered)

BEST TIME TO PERFORM THE SPELL:
- During the waxing moon, preferably on Tuesday

Collect the ingredients needed for this spell. Cast a circle around the area where you will do your spell. Build a small fire in a safe place.

On the paper, write what you find enticing about your partner and what you desire from him or her. Be as descriptive and explicit as you like—no one but you will read what you've written. When you've finished, draw the runes *Gebo*, which looks like an ✕, and *Teiwaz*, which looks like an arrow pointing up, around the edges of the paper. These two symbols represent love and passion respectively.

Place the spices on the piece of paper and fold it to make a packet that contains them. Visualize you and your lover in a passionate embrace. As you hold this image in your mind, toss the packet of spices into the fire. As it burns, your intention is released into the universe.

When you feel ready, open the circle.

MAGICK BALM TO HEAL A BROKEN HEART

She rejects your love. He finds someone else. We've all suffered with broken hearts. This spell eases the pain of losing the one you love and helps your heart begin to heal.

INGREDIENTS/TOOLS:
- A small piece of rose quartz
- A glass jar or bottle, preferably green, with a lid or stopper
- 3 ounces of olive, almond, or grape seed oil
- 6 drops of rose, jasmine, or ylang-ylang essential oil
- ¼ teaspoon dried chamomile leaves

BEST TIME TO PERFORM THE SPELL:
- Begin on the new moon and continue for as long as necessary

Collect the ingredients needed for this magick balm. Wash the rose quartz and the jar with mild soap and water. Cast a circle around the area where you will do your spell. Pour the olive, almond, or grape seed oil into the jar. Add the essential oil and inhale the fragrance, allowing it to relax your mind. Crush the chamomile leaves very fine and sprinkle them in the oil. Add the rose quartz. Cap the jar and shake it three times to blend and charge the ingredients. Open the circle.

Before going to bed, pour a little of the magick balm into your palm and dip your index finger in it. Then rub the oil on your skin at your heart. Feel it gently soothing the pain. Take several slow, deep breaths, inhaling the pleasant scent, letting it calm your thoughts and emotions. Repeat each night and each morning until your sadness diminishes.

Note: You can also try taking a flower essence called "Bleeding Heart," available online: *www.flowersociety.org* and in some large health food stores.

LOVE TALISMAN

This good luck talisman can help you attract a new lover or improve your relationship with your current partner. If you choose rich fabric, and perhaps add some beads, embroidery, or other decorative touches you can fashion a talisman that's pretty enough to wear.

INGREDIENTS/TOOLS:
- 1 strip of pink paper
- 1 pen with red ink
- 1 pink or red pouch, preferably made of silk or velvet
- 2 dried rose petals (a deep pink color is best)
- A pinch of cocoa
- 2 apple seeds
- 1 piece of rose quartz
- 1 small pearl
- 1 purple ribbon at least 6" long
- Red wine or apple juice
- 1 ritual chalice or cup

BEST TIME TO PERFORM THE SPELL:
- On the first Friday after the new moon

Cast a circle. On the strip of paper, write an affirmation such as, "I now have a lover who's right for me in every way and we are very happy together" if you want to attract new love. If you want to improve an existing relationship, write something like, "[Partner's name] and I are very happy together and everything is good between us." Fold the paper three times and slip it into the pouch. Add the rose petals, cocoa, apple seeds, and gemstones.

Tie the pouch with the ribbon, making six knots to tie in the ingredients and your magickal energy. Six is the number of give and take, and it signifies compatible energy between two people. Each time you tie a knot, repeat your affirmation. When you've finished say, "This is now accomplished in harmony with Divine Will, my own true will, and for the good of all."

Pour the wine or apple juice into your ritual chalice or cup and swirl it around three times, in a clockwise direction, to energize it. Dip your finger in the wine or juice, and then dot the talisman with the liquid to charge it. Drink the rest. Open the circle. Carry the pouch in your pocket or purse, or wear it. If you know feng shui, you can place the talisman in the relationship sector of your home.

SPELL TO REV UP YOUR SEX LIFE

Do you or your significant other work such crazy hours that you never have time for each other? Do you lack privacy in your home because of the kids, roommates, etc.? Are your schedules so frantic that you both constantly seem to be moving in opposite directions? If so, this spell might be just what you need.

INGREDIENTS/TOOLS:
- Sea salt
- Ylang-ylang oil
- Jasmine oil
- Aromatherapy diffuser/burner
- 4 red candles
- Matches or a lighter
- Your favorite music

BEST TIME TO PERFORM THE SPELL:
- During the full moon or on a Tuesday

A full moon on a Tuesday is best for this spell, although a full moon on any day of the week is good too. But don't worry if nature doesn't suit your schedule and you find you're in the mood some night when there isn't a full moon—you can still get good results. First, draw a bath and sprinkle sea salt into the water. Sea salt is an excellent psychic and spiritual cleanser. Soak as long as it takes to relax fully—not just your muscles, but down to the very center of your being. You and your partner can bathe together or separately, whichever you prefer.

When you're completely relaxed, dry off and put on loose and comfortable clothing (a sensuous silk robe is best). Cast a circle. If you have set up an altar, put several drops of both oils into an aromatherapy diffuser. Light the candle beneath it. (If you don't have an aromatherapy diffuser/burner, you can rub a little of each oil directly on the candles.) As soon as the fragrance begins to fill the air, place a candle in each of the four directions, beginning in the east and moving clockwise.

As you light each candle, say: "Goddesses of the [east, south, west, north], bestow your blessings, your power, your love, on [partner's name] and me, to make us one. So mote it be."

When you're finished, open the circle and put the candles, still lit, into the bedroom or wherever you and your significant other will be. Play your favorite music. Let the candles burn out safely on their own.

GEMSTONE FIDELITY SPELL

Are you just beginning a relationship and want to make sure your partner doesn't stray? Or, do you suspect he or she is interested in someone else? Either way, this spell can deepen the feelings and commitment between you.

INGREDIENTS/TOOLS:
- An oval- or circular-shaped piece of rose quartz
- An obelisk-shaped piece of carnelian
- 1 piece of dark blue ribbon long enough to tie around the two stones
- 1 piece of white silk large enough to cover the stones
- A metal box (preferably copper, brass, or lead) with a lid, large enough to contain the two gemstones
- A shovel

BEST TIME TO PERFORM THE SPELL:
- When the moon is in Capricorn or on a Saturday

The gemstones have two symbolic meanings in this spell. Not only do they represent you and your partner, but rose quartz is a stone of love and affection, and carnelian brings passion. The ribbon's color—dark blue—indicates strength, sincerity, and permanence; the white cloth offers protection.

In the morning, wash the gemstones with warm, soapy water, and then stand them side by side on your altar so that they are touching. Imagine one symbolizes you, the other your beloved (it doesn't matter which gem you choose to represent which person, although rose quartz has a feminine/yin resonance and carnelian a masculine/yang one). Tie the stones together with the ribbon, making two knots, while you visualize you and your partner connected by a strong bond of love and devotion. Cover the gems with the white cloth and leave them until evening.

Once the moon has risen, wrap up the gemstones in the white silk cloth, and then place the package in the box. Take the box outside and bury it in the ground, preferably beneath an oak or apple tree.

AMULET TO BLOCK UNWANTED ATTENTION

Some people just won't take "no" for an answer. If someone seems determined to push his or her way into your life and won't leave you alone, this amulet helps you repel unwanted attention and establish clear boundaries.

INGREDIENTS/TOOLS:
- A piece of amber
- A piece of onyx
- Pine incense
- An incense burner
- Matches or a lighter
- A piece of paper
- A pen with black ink
- A black pouch, preferably silk or leather
- Dried basil leaves
- Anise or fennel seeds
- An ash leaf

- A white ribbon 8" long
- Salt water

- During the waning moon, preferably on a Saturday

Collect the ingredients needed for this spell. Wash the amber and the onyx with mild soap and water. Cast a circle around the area where you will do your spell. Fit the incense in its burner and light it.

Envision yourself safe and sound, completely surrounded by a sphere of pure white light that no one can penetrate without your permission. On the paper, write the word "Protection." Draw a circle around the word and fold the paper so it's small enough to fit into the pouch.

Add the botanicals and stones to the pouch. Tie it closed with the white ribbon, making eight knots. Each time you tie a knot repeat this incantation aloud: "From energies I don't invite / This charm protects me day and night."

Sprinkle the amulet with salt water, then hold it in the incense smoke for a few moments to charge it. Open the circle. Wear or carry the amulet with you at all times, until the annoying person stops bothering you.

ADAPTING SPELLS

At times, you might want to adapt a spell to suit your specific needs, but where do you begin the process? Although adapting a spell is far easier than creating one, it still requires some forethought. When examining a spell, look for continuity and comprehensiveness. Ask yourself these questions:

1. Does the spell really target your goal with its words, actions, and components?
2. Does it do so on a multisensual level, engaging your senses of hearing, sight, touch, taste, and smell?
3. Does every part of the spell inspire you?

If the answer to any of these questions is no, you should try to find a substitute. For example, many old love spells call for blood as an ingredient. However, there are many health reasons why this may not be such a good idea today—plus, it might gross you out. Instead, you could substitute a red fruit juice or red wine—your intention is the most important component in the success of your spell. If you don't like some of the words in a particular incantation, there's nothing wrong with editing that poem or chant so it speaks to you. Lots of people have allergies to certain substances or just don't like the way an essential oil or incense smells—so go ahead and use something you do enjoy.

In many instances, it's great to do a love spell with your romantic partner (assuming he or she is willing and in agreement with you). You can even incorporate sex magick into your spellworking to increase the octane, so to speak—but make sure you know what you're doing before you start (my book *Sex Magic for Beginners* explains what you'll need to know to get started).

Chapter 16

SPELLS FOR SUCCESS

What does success mean to you? Some people consider themselves successful if they reach the highest ranks of their profession; others see money as a marker of success. In our celebrity-oriented society, fame is often the benchmark of success. In a broader sense, however, success means feeling a sense of purpose and joy in what you do. According to author Christopher Morley, "There is only one success—to be able to spend your life in your own way." Whether you want to ace an exam, land a great new job, or make your mark in the world, magick can help you succeed.

SETTING GOALS AND INTENTIONS

Just as travelers plot a route, companies design business plans to guide them where they intend to go. Without a road map of some sort, you can easily get sidetracked or your plans may be derailed. Some business people recommend establishing a five-year plan, whereas others opt for longer or shorter terms and update their plans periodically. Many experts suggest that entrepreneurs at least create a mission statement that describes the business's vision. You can apply this in other ways, too. Is your goal to finish college? Move to another part of the country where you'll have more opportunity? Start a home-based business?

Given what you already know about magick, you can probably see the value of setting a goal—an end result you wish to achieve. That's what you do every time you cast a spell. Once you've created an image of your goal, you can use your willpower to bring your dream into being. Your plans don't have to be etched in stone, but it's important to at least have a clear view of what you would like to accomplish. Remember, the more vivid you can make your images of your goals, the more likely they are to materialize in the way you desire.

Self-Esteem and Success

Your work life is connected with your beliefs about self-worth, prosperity, and success. If you feel unworthy, this will be reflected in your income and in your work situation. If, on the other hand, you believe you're valuable and deserving—of a raise, a promotion, or better working conditions—your self-image will be reflected in your outer-world image.

In the following brainstorming activity, you're going to take inventory of your work situation—the work you do, your bosses and other people who have power over you, your coworkers or colleagues, or your personal circumstances if you're self-employed:

1. Describe the work that you do; give specific details.
2. Is your work satisfying? Why or why not?
3. Do you get along with your boss?
4. Do you get along with your coworkers?
5. Are you passionate about your work?
6. What would you change about your work if you could?
7. Do you have moral or ethical objections to the work you do?
8. Do you feel you're paid fairly for what you do?
9. What are your professional goals for the next year? The next five years?
10. Do you have regrets about the career path you've chosen?
11. Have you gotten regular promotions and raises? If not, why?
12. Is your work life filled with struggles? If so, explain.
13. Are you earning enough doing what you do?
14. If you could choose to do anything you wanted, what would it be? Why?
15. If your passion lies elsewhere, can you imagine earning your living at it?

If your answers to the previous questions are mostly positive, then you're probably exactly where you want to be in life right now. If the answers are predominantly negative, it's time to start doing magick to change what you don't like.

"Obstacles are those frightful things you see when you take your eyes off your goal."

—Henry Ford

Write It Down

Don't just keep your goals in your head. Instead, write them down in a journal or loose-leaf binder. Writing your goals is the first step toward bringing them into the material world. The very act of putting words on paper takes them out of the realm of imagination. The tactile nature of writing, instead of keeping a folder in your computer, makes your ideas more tangible.

State your objectives in the form of affirmations. Your affirmations might be all-encompassing and general, such as "I now have a job that's perfect for me," or they may be very precise, such as "I graduate at the top of my class and [company name] hires me and pays me [$X/year]." Make a list that includes at least three and not more than ten goals. As soon as you've accomplished one objective, replace it with another.

Read through your affirmations twice daily, when you first wake up and just before going to sleep at night. Repetition imprints your goals on your subconscious and directs it to carry out your wishes.

TIMING SUCCESS SPELLS

Like other spells, the ones you do for success will be more powerful if you do them at the right time. In magick, as in other areas of life, timing counts. In most cases, you'll get better results if you do spells for work success while the moon is waxing. However, if your goal is to eliminate an obstacle or condition that's blocking your success, or you want to scale down your work-related responsibilities, do a spell during the waning moon.

Capricorn is the zodiac sign of business, goals, and public image. Therefore, an ideal time to do spells for career success is while the moon and/or the sun is in Capricorn. Virgo is connected with work, work relationships, and work-related health matters, so if your intention involves these things, do a spell when the sun and/or moon is in Virgo. If you seek status, recognition, or a promotion, do a spell while the sun and/or moon is in Leo, the sign of leadership and fame.

The best days of the week for doing success spells are Thursday, Saturday, and Sunday, which are the days ruled by Jupiter, Saturn, and the sun, respectively. These heavenly bodies govern growth, business, travel, public image, status, ambition, self-image, determination, and leadership ability. The best day(s) for doing each of the spells in this chapter is indicated for each spell.

SPELL TO CLARIFY YOUR GOAL

This spell helps you get clear about your goal. Often we think we want one thing and later on find that what we really wanted was something else entirely. So before you get to the "later on" point, do this simple spell for clarification.

INGREDIENTS/TOOLS:
- 1 dark blue candle
- 1 fireproof candleholder
- A few drops of essential oil of citrus
- Pen and paper

BEST TIME TO PERFORM THE SPELL:
- As you feel the need

Dress your candle with the oil, put it in the candleholder, and light it. As you smell the scent of citrus, write down your goal in the form of an affirmation. Keep it simple. Prop the paper on which you've written your goal up against the candleholder or lay it in front of the candle. Gaze into the candle's flame and sit quietly for a few moments, keeping

The Modern Guide to Witchcraft

your goal in mind. Imagine that you have already achieved this goal. How does it feel? Are you comfortable with it? How does it affect your family and friends? What is your life like now that you have gotten what you wanted?

The more vivid and detailed your visualization, the better. Hold the image in your mind until your mind starts to wander, then stop. Now read your goal again. Is it what you really want? If not, rewrite it. You may find that you merely need to fine-tune what you've written. If you rewrite your goal, let it sit for a day or two before you look at it again. Then ask yourself if it feels right. Chances are that it will. Once you're certain you've got it right, burn the piece of paper to release your intentions into the cosmic web.

SPELL TO GET THE RESPECT YOU DESERVE

Does your boss overlook your hard work and neglect to give you credit for what you do? Do clients and customers seem unappreciative when you go the extra mile for them? If you're feeling dissed lately, this spell can help you get the respect you deserve.

INGREDIENTS/TOOLS NEEDED:
- A ballpoint pen
- An orange candle
- A candleholder
- Cinnamon essential oil
- Dried bay leaves
- Matches or a lighter
- A piece of paper
- Colored pens, pencils, or markers
- Tape

BEST TIME TO PERFORM THE SPELL:
- During the full moon, on Sunday, or when the sun or moon is in Leo

Gather the ingredients needed for this spell. Cast a circle around the area where you will do your spell. With the ballpoint pen, inscribe a circle with a dot in its center on the candle; this is the astrological symbol for the sun. Dress the candle by rubbing the essential oil on it (not on the wick) and set it in its holder. Inhale the scent of cinnamon, letting it stimulate feelings of confidence and power. Lay the bay leaves in a circle around the base of the candle. Light the candle.

With the colored markers and paper, write the word "Respect." Add other images that represent status, honor, power, and recognition to you. (If you like Aretha Franklin, you could play her song "Respect" during the process.) While you work, imagine yourself being lauded by the people with whom you work. See them bowing down to you, offering you gifts, singing your praises, or whatever scenario pleases you. When you're happy with your design, put a dot of cinnamon oil on each corner of the piece of paper. Extinguish the candle and collect the bay leaves. Open the circle.

Take the paper and the bay leaves to your workplace. Tape the bay leaves, which represent victory and success, on your desk, computer, door, wall, or other spot in your work area; if you prefer, put them in a desk drawer or other safe place out of sight. Look at your respect drawing often—especially if someone treats you badly. Take a few deep breaths, inhaling self-confidence. Remember Eleanor Roosevelt's words: "No one can make you feel inferior without your consent."

SPELL TO ATTRACT SUPPORT

We all need encouragement and support in the work we do. This spell helps you attract someone who believes in you, sees your talent, and wants to nurture it.

INGREDIENTS/TOOLS:
- 1 ceramic pot
- Potting soil
- 9 seeds for a plant that blossoms with red or purple flowers
- Water

- On a Thursday during a waxing moon

Fill your ceramic pot with potting soil and place the nine seeds at various spots in the soil. As you plant the seeds, say aloud:

"I plant these seeds
And draw to me
The one who sees
What I can be.
So mote it be."

Once the seeds begin to sprout, the person who recognizes your genius should appear in your life. Until that happens, lavish your plant with tender loving care. Take every opportunity to make contacts—you never know who might become your "angel."

SPELL FOR A SUCCESSFUL START

Whether you're entering college, seeking a new job, or taking on a new project, this spell can help you make a successful start. Nothing can be as scary as the prospect of beginning something new. Most people wonder if they're smart enough, experienced enough, or talented enough to make a go of it. But if you listen to your fears, you'll never know how successful you might have been if you'd ignored them.

INGREDIENTS/TOOLS:
- A picture that represents what you are about to begin
- 1 quartz crystal

BEST TIME TO PERFORM THE SPELL:
- Nine days before the full moon

Cut out a picture from a magazine or download an online image that represents what you are about to start. Nine days before the full moon, lay the picture face up on your altar. Set the crystal on top of it. On the night of the full moon, burn the picture while you imagine yourself succeeding at your new effort, thereby releasing your intention into the cosmic web. Carry the crystal in your pocket or purse, or place it where you'll see it often to reinforce your self-confidence.

BITCHY COWORKER SPELL

There's one in every office—the coworker who makes everyone else's life miserable. The word "teamwork" isn't in his vocabulary. Her negativity drags down the rest of the staff's morale. Can a little magick sweeten this sour situation? Absolutely!

INGREDIENTS/TOOLS:
- A piece of tumbled rose quartz
- A piece of watermelon tourmaline
- A spray bottle
- Spring water
- Granulated sugar
- Jasmine essential oil
- Lavender essential oil

BEST TIME TO PERFORM THE SPELL:
- During the waning moon, preferably on Friday

Gather the ingredients needed for this spell. Wash the gemstones with mild soap and water. Cast a circle around the area where you will do your spell. Fill the bottle with spring water, then add the sugar and essential oils. Shake the bottle three times to charge the mixture.

Envision the annoying coworker surrounded by a sphere of pink light. Even though this person may be as prickly as a cactus, try to understand that negative people are filled with fear. This spell works by boosting your coworker's self-esteem, so projecting positive energy will actually defuse this person's bitchiness. Open the circle.

Take the magick potion and the gemstones to work with you. When your irritating coworker isn't around, mist his/her workspace with the water-and-oil mixture. Repeat as necessary. Hide the piece of tourmaline somewhere in the bitchy person's work area. (Tourmaline neutralizes and disperses negative energy.) Keep the rose quartz for yourself. Whenever you start feeling annoyed, rub the stone until you calm down. Before long you should notice a change in your coworker's attitude and behavior, and in your own reactions to him/her.

SPELL TO GET A RAISE

Everything seems to be going up except salaries. This spell uses growth symbolism to help you get a raise, even when the economy's bad and companies are cutting back.

INGREDIENTS/TOOLS:
- A clear glass bottle (no designs) with a lid or stopper
- Spring water
- A $20 bill (or larger denomination)
- Tape

BEST TIME TO PERFORM THE SPELL:
- During the waxing moon, preferably on Thursday or Friday

Collect the ingredients needed for this spell. Cast a circle around the area where you will do your spell. Fill the bottle with spring water. Tape the $20 bill on the side of the bottle. This infuses the water with the image of money. Cap the bottle and shake it three times to charge it.

Drink some of the magick water. As you do this, imagine you are being "watered" with wealth. See your boss calling you into his/her office and offering you a raise, or visualize yourself receiving a paycheck with a larger amount printed on it—choose an image that clearly expresses your intention. Open the circle. Continue drinking your "money water" daily—make more when you finish the first batch—and watch your income increase.

SPELL TO GET A BETTER JOB

You want to tell your boss to take this job and shove it, but times are tough and good jobs are hard to find. Instead, put your magick skills to work and get busy creating the perfect job.

INGREDIENTS/TOOLS:
- Pictures from magazines, the Internet, or other sources
- A piece of paper or cardboard large enough for you to stand on (if necessary, tape two or more sheets together)
- An orange marker
- Glue, paste, or tape

BEST TIME TO PERFORM THE SPELL:
- During the waxing moon, preferably on Sunday or Thursday

Spend some time thinking about the job you'd really like. What images come to mind? Is travel a factor? If so, a plane might be a good symbol. Perhaps a big walnut desk represents authority to you, or a TV screen suggests fame. Coins and paper currency signify money. Cut out magazine pictures that depict various aspects of your dream job or download images from the Internet.

Gather up all your images along with the other ingredients needed for this spell. Cast a circle around the area where you will do your spell. On the paper or cardboard, use the marker to draw a symbol that astrologers call the Part of Fortune. This lucky design looks like an ✕ with a circle around it. Make your drawing large enough so that you can paste all your pictures inside it. Begin attaching the pictures you've collected to the Part of Fortune. As you work, imagine yourself happy and successful in your new position.

When you've finished, lay the paper/cardboard on the floor. Remove your shoes and stand in the middle of it. Close your eyes and imagine yourself becoming one with your new job. Make the visualization as real as possible. Stand there until your mind starts to wander, then step off the paper/cardboard and open the circle. Repeat as necessary, until you land your ideal job.

The Modern Guide to Witchcraft

SPELL TO BIND A BACKSTABBER

She spreads damaging gossip about you at work. He steals your ideas and claims they're his. It's time to bring out the big guns—magick-wise, that is. This spell ties the backstabber's hands and prevents him/her from doing further harm.

INGREDIENTS/TOOLS:
- A small figurine (poppet) made of clay, wax, cloth, wood, or another material
- A black marker
- Black cord long enough to wrap around the figurine several times
- A shovel
- A large stone

BEST TIME TO PERFORM THE SPELL:
- During the waning moon, preferably on Saturday

Collect the ingredients needed for this spell. If possible, make the figurine (known magickally as a poppet) yourself, but if you aren't handy you can purchase an ordinary doll (the plainer the better, unless you can find one that resembles the backstabber). Cast a circle around the area where you will cast your spell.

With the marker write the troublemaker's full name on the poppet. Say aloud: "Figure of [whatever material the poppet is made of], I name you [the backstabber's name] and command you to cease your attacks on me now. I bind your ill will and render you powerless against me." Wrap the black cord around the figurine several times and tie it, making eight knots. Each time you tie a knot, repeat the last sentence of the affirmation: "I bind your ill will and render you powerless against me." When you've finished, open the circle.

Take the poppet and shovel to a place near your workplace and dig a hole in the ground. If that's not feasible, go to a remote area away from trees or water (and not on your own property). Place the poppet in the hole and cover it with dirt, then put the stone on top of it for good measure.

CREATING SPELLS FROM SCRATCH

After a while, you'll probably want to design some original spells. That's great. Following these steps will help you to create spells that can be just as effective as the ones you learn from this book and from other sources:

1. Boil down the purpose of the spell to a word or short phrase.
2. Find the ingredients suited to your goal.
3. Consider the best time to cast the spell.
4. Decide if you want to include an affirmation or incantation. If so, write one according to the instructions in Chapter 13.
5. Cleanse and purify all the objects you'll use in your spell.
6. Consider the order in which you'll do what you do.
7. Write your spell in your book of shadows, along with your experiences.

What kinds of results can you expect from your spellwork? Well, that depends on you. Like a computer, spells do what you tell them to do. That's why it's important to carefully consider what you really want and to state your objective accordingly. If you perform a spell to find a perfect companion and end up with a wonderful dog, your magick certainly has worked!

Chapter 17

PROTECTION SPELLS

The modern world is a dangerous place. Turn on the TV or read a newspaper and you'll see an ongoing parade of scary scenarios: hurricanes and earthquakes, car wrecks and plane crashes, robberies, kidnappings, and murders. Disease lurks just around the corner, threatening health and well-being. Accidents happen when you least expect them. How can you protect yourself against the evils of the world?

Since ancient times, people in all cultures have used magick to safeguard themselves, their loved ones, and their property. In fact, the earliest charms were probably created for protection—from wild animals, bad weather, and malicious spirits. The early Greeks, for example, carried leaves on which they'd written the goddess Athena's name in order to ward off hexes. The Egyptians believed the Eye of Osiris would protect them on earth and in the life beyond.

Before you start doing the spells in this chapter, consider what we've discussed already about the power of the mind. You can drive yourself crazy worrying about all the bad things that *could* happen, most of which never will. As Plato expressed it, "Courage is knowing what not to fear."

Magicians say you should never put your mind on anything you don't want to occur, lest you draw that thing to you. That's what the Law of Attraction teaches, too: You attract whatever you focus your attention on. So as part of your protection magick, you might consider turning off those violent shows on TV (including the news).

BREAKING THE FEAR BARRIER

The next time fear stares you in the face, don't turn around and run. Stare back. Confront it by asking yourself: What is the absolute worst that can happen? What is this fear really saying to me?

Here are a few tips for beating your fears:

- Identify your fear: If you don't identify your fears, they will unnecessarily spill into other areas of your life. Instead recognize the bottom line, or true root, of your fears. Maybe at some time in the long-ago past, that fear served a purpose, but you've outgrown it now. Once you do this, you can come to a better understanding of your fears and start to move past them.
- Release your fear: When confronted with a fear, try finding an object to represent your fear, then take a hammer to it, and smash it. Physical exercise sometimes serves the same purpose. When you find yourself in the grip of fear, head for the outdoors, if you can, and walk fast. Better yet, run. Run until your legs ache and you're panting for breath.
- Work through it: Sometimes in life, certain situations are so painful or difficult that nothing seems to work to break the hold a particular fear has on you. In that case, you simply have to keep working with it and live through it day by day, until you can finally get beyond it.

Taking slow, deep breaths can also help to calm anxiety. While doing this, you might try simultaneously pressing a spot on the center of your torso, about halfway between your heart and your belly button. Acupressurists call this the "Center of Power." With your index and middle fingers, apply steady pressure (but not so hard that it's uncomfortable) to this spot for a minute or two whenever you feel a need to ease fear and insecurity.

PENTAGRAM PROTECTION

As we discussed in Chapter 10, a witch's pentagram is a symbol of protection. Many witches wear pentagrams as jewelry to keep them safe and sound, and you may want to do the same. You could also put one in your car's glove compartment or hang one from the rearview mirror. Put one on the door of your home to keep would-be intruders and annoyances away. Place one in your desk at work. Decorate your clothes with pentagrams—you can even buy pentagram panties online. Paint pentagrams on your toenails. Some witches get pentagram tattoos for permanent protection. Or, if your need for safety is only temporary, try drawing or painting one on your chest near your heart.

WHITE LIGHT SAFETY SPELL

You're alone at night in a bad part of town. You're hiking in the mountains and the trail is more treacherous than you'd expected. It's time for some on-the-spot magick! This quick and easy spell can be done anywhere, in any situation, to provide instant protection.

INGREDIENTS/TOOLS:
• None

BEST TIME TO PERFORM THE SPELL:
• Any time

Begin breathing slowly and deeply. If possible, close your eyes. Imagine you are in the center of a sphere of pure white light that completely encloses you like a cocoon. Visualize the light spinning clockwise around you. See the light expanding, providing a thick wall of protection that extends outward from your body in all directions. If you're in a car, plane, or other vehicle, see the white light surrounding the vehicle as well.

Say or think this affirmation: "I am surrounded by divine white light. I am safe and sound, protected at all times and in all situations." Repeat the affirmation three times. Feel yourself growing calmer and more confident as you place your welfare in the hands of a higher force.

PROTECTION AMULET

A dicey situation has you worried and you feel a need for some extra protection. Protection amulets are one of the oldest forms of magick. This one helps to shield you from potential injury or illness.

INGREDIENTS/TOOLS:
- A piece of amber
- A piece of bloodstone (for protection from physical injury)
- A piece of turquoise (for protection from illness)
- Pine incense
- An incense burner
- Matches or a lighter
- A photo of you (or another person if you're doing this spell for someone else)
- A pen or marker with black ink
- Essential oil of rosemary
- A white pouch, preferably silk
- A black ribbon 8" long
- Salt water

BEST TIME TO PERFORM THE SPELL:
- During the waning moon, preferably on a Saturday

Collect the ingredients needed for this spell. Wash the stones with mild soap and water, then pat them dry. Cast a circle around the area where you will do your spell. Fit the incense into the burner and light it.

Across the photograph write the words "I am safe" as you envision yourself completely surrounded by a sphere of pure white light. Dot each corner of the photo with essential oil. Inhale the scent of the oil and mentally connect it with a feeling of safety. Slip the photo into the pouch; if necessary, fold it so it's small enough to fit.

Rub a little essential oil on each of the stones and add them to the pouch. Tie the pouch closed with the black ribbon, making eight knots. Each time you tie a knot repeat this incantation aloud:

"Anything that could cause me [other person's name] harm
Is now repelled by this magick charm."

Sprinkle the amulet with salt water, then hold it in the incense smoke for a few moments to charge it. Open the circle. Wear or carry the amulet with you at all times to protect you from harm, or give it to the person you wish to protect.

EVIL EYE AMULET

Do you feel you're under attack? Since ancient times, people in cultures around the world have used eye amulets to scare off evil of all kinds. Whether the evil force threatening you is human, animal, or supernatural, this all-seeing protection charm guards your home and its inhabitants.

INGREDIENTS/TOOLS:
- A disc of wood, ceramic, or stone about 1" in diameter
- Blue, black, and white paint
- A small paintbrush
- A white ribbon at least 1" wide and 4–6" long
- Tacky glue or something to attach the disc to the ribbon
- A small loop or hook for hanging
- Other adornments (optional)

BEST TIME TO PERFORM THE SPELL:
- On Saturday

Collect the listed ingredients. Cast a circle around the area where you will do your spell. Paint an eye with a blue iris, a black pupil, and white highlight on the disc—make it realistic or stylized, it's up to you. If you like, decorate the ribbon with symbols or designs that represent protection to you, such as pentagrams or circles. When the paint dries, attach the disc to the ribbon. Affix the loop or hook to the back of the disc. Open the circle.

Hang the amulet inside your home, near the front door. Each time you enter or leave your home, touch the eye amulet for good luck and to reinforce your sense of safety.

CIRCLE OF SECURITY

Here's another way to keep your home and everyone in it safe from harm of any kind—acts of nature as well as human menaces.

INGREDIENTS/TOOLS:
- Small clear quartz crystals
- A black cloth
- A garden trowel or shovel

BEST TIME TO PERFORM THE SPELL:
- Begin on Saturday during the waning moon

Collect the listed ingredients. If you live in a house and have a yard, you'll need enough crystals to completely circle your house. If you live in an apartment, you'll need one crystal for each window and each door to the outside. Wash the crystals with mild soap and water, then pat them dry. If you have a large area to cover and a lot of crystals, you might need to continue this spell over a period of days.

Draw or find a picture of a pentagram and lay it on your altar, or another surface. Place the crystals on it and visualize them absorbing the protection represented by the pentagram. Lay the black cloth over the crystals, covering them completely. Allow the crystals to sit overnight.

In the morning, remove the cloth. Pick up the crystals, put them in a bowl or other container, and take them outside. Beginning in the east, bury the crystals in your yard one at a time, making a protective circle that surrounds your home. Position them as close together or as far apart as feels right to you. If you live in an apartment, start at the east and place a crystal on each windowsill (inside) of your living space. Then set a crystal in a safe spot near or above each exterior door. As you work repeat this affirmation aloud:

"Crystals wise, crystals strong
Protect my home all day long.
Crystals clear, crystals bright
Keep it safe throughout the night."

You may also want to hang a pentagram on each door that leads into your home.

SPELL TO RELEASE NEGATIVITY

You already know that negative ideas and feelings attract negative situations. If you're concerned that your attitude may be drawing unwanted forces to you, this spell can help you let go of those bad vibes you've been putting out. After an unpleasant situation has occurred, perform this spell to shift the energy and prevent future problems.

INGREDIENTS/TOOLS:
- 1 piece of white paper
- 1 pen with blue ink
- White carnations in a clear glass container
- Matches or a lighter

BEST TIME TO PERFORM THE SPELL:
- During the waning moon

Write the following intention on the paper:

I now release [name the situation]
And create new, positive energy to carry me forward.
I trust this is for my highest good
And affirm my commitment to this new path.

Place the paper beneath the vase of flowers. Leave it there until the flowers wilt. When you throw out the flowers, burn the paper to complete the releasing process.

GUARDIAN ANGEL CHARM

Are you facing a challenge that seems bigger than you can handle? According to many spiritual traditions, everyone has a personal guardian angel who provides guidance and protection when you need it. This magick charm reminds you that your angelic helper is always near at hand.

INGREDIENTS/TOOLS:
- A small silver or gold hanging charm in the shape of an angel
- A white cord or ribbon 18" long
- Essential oil of amber

BEST TIME TO PERFORM THE SPELL:
- On Saturday

Collect the listed ingredients. Cast a circle around the area where you will do your spell. Slide the charm on the cord or ribbon and tie a knot to make a pendant necklace. As you tie the knot, visualize yourself safe, happy, and healthy. Say the following incantation aloud:

"Guardian angel, be with me.
Keep me healthy, safe, and free.
Guide my steps so I can see
What I must do. Blessed be."

Put a dot of amber essential oil on the angel charm. Inhale the scent and let it calm your nerves. You may sense your guardian angel nearby. Imagine yourself placing your concerns in the angel's hands, knowing that everything will be taken care of. Slip the necklace over your head and wear it for protection. Open the circle.

BASIL BATH

Locks on your doors and windows may deter human threats, but what about psychic ones? If you fear that someone is sending you "bad vibes" try this herbal protection spell.

INGREDIENTS/TOOLS:

- A large pot
- Two quarts of water
- A large bunch of fresh basil

BEST TIME TO PERFORM THE SPELL:

- On Saturday, preferably when the sun and/or moon is in Capricorn

Heat the water in the pot. Add the basil and let it simmer for several minutes. Allow the brew to cool. Strain the basil out and set it aside to dry—save it to use in other spells.

Run a nice, hot bath. As the tub fills, slowly pour in the basil-infused water. If you like, you can add Epsom salts or sea salts—salt has protective and purifying properties, too. While you're doing this, say the following affirmation aloud:

> *"I am now protected at all times,*
> *In all situations,*
> *Always and all ways."*

Soak in the bathwater for as long as you like. During this time, imagine yourself at peace, surrounded by pure white light, and sheltered from all harm.

PET PROTECTION SPELL

It's a dangerous world out there for animals, too. As anyone who's ever had an animal companion knows, the threat of cars, other creatures, and entrapment loom large and can endanger our beloved pets. This spell helps protect Fluffy or Fido from harm.

INGREDIENTS/TOOLS:

- A collar for your pet
- Sage incense, or loose sage
- A marker that will write on fabric or leather
- Amber essential oil

• Any time

Purchase a new collar, made of leather or fabric, for your pet. Cast a circle around the space where you'll be working. Light the sage and hold the collar in the smoke to cleanse it of unwanted energies. On the inside of the collar, write: "[Pet's name] is safe and sound at all times." Draw a pentagram at the end of the statement. The pentagram, as you know, is a symbol of protection. On the outside of the collar, write your name and phone number; or, get a pet tag made that includes this information and attach it to the collar.

Put four drops of essential oil on the collar, one at each end, on both sides of the collar. Open the circle. Place the collar in the sun for one day to charge it. Then fasten the collar on your pet to keep him safe.

(To be extra safe, ask your vet about having a tiny computer chip permanently implanted in your pet's skin that will identify him to city pounds, veterinarian's offices, and other agencies with scanners that can read such chips. See *www.homeagain.com* for information.)

WORDS OF POWER

Many spells, including those in this chapter, use affirmations or incantations. That's because words have power, as witches and magicians of all stripes know. Spiritual and occult literature frequently mentions the power of the human voice. For millennia people have been reciting magick words as a way of asking supernatural forces for assistance. This is usually done by calling out the deities' names. Speaking someone's name is said to be an act of power, giving the namer influence over the named.

Magicians recognize the power inherent in some words and, therefore, incorporate those words into spells and rituals. For example, if a witch wants to banish a spirit, he might order it to leave by saying, "Be gone." Many witches end spells with the words "So mote it be." This phrase (like "so be it") seals a spell.

You may choose to speak an incantation as part of a ritual or spell. Incantations, like prayers or blessings, can also be recited at mealtime or before going to sleep. If you prefer, write your incantation on paper and display it in a spot where you'll see it often. You might enjoy adorning your words with colorful pictures and framing your artwork—or even stitch an old-fashioned sampler like our great-grandmothers did. The more energy you put into your creation, the more effective it will be. Creating incantations is fun—use your imagination. In the process, you may even discover a talent for poetry that you never realized you had.

Chapter 18

SPELLS FOR HEALTH AND HEALING

Before we had modern surgery, pharmaceuticals, and state-of-the-art medical equipment, people turned to medicine men and wise women when they suffered health problems. These healers practiced magick to remedy diseases. Their knowledge of the spirit world and the healing energies in plants made them respected members of their communities. Today, healing remains a primary focus for many witches. Sometimes miraculous cures that baffle conventional doctors can be achieved through the same magickal practices that are used to attract wealth or love.

Holistic healing teaches that the mind and body are linked, and that our thoughts and emotions can produce illness or good health. This is most obvious in the case of stress, which we know can cause all sorts of problems, from headaches to digestive complaints to heart conditions.

The idea certainly fits in with what you know about magick and your ability to produce outcomes with your mind.

In magick, healing involves two steps:

1. Cleansing and/or purifying of the negative presence
2. Replacing the negative presence with something positive

In other words, you first need to clear away whatever is causing the problem, whether that's a virus, an emotional issue, or something else.

After you've accomplished this, you have to put into place something that will prevent the problem from coming back. That might mean a change in attitude, diet, or lifestyle. You may also want to do a protection spell to safeguard yourself or another person in the future.

Body Talk

Pay attention to the words you use to describe health conditions—they reveal the link between body, mind, and spirit. Is a situation at work giving you a "pain in the neck"? Are you having trouble "digesting" an idea? Eye problems may indicate you don't want to see something. Arthritis suggests you are emotionally or mentally inflexible. "Body talk" provides clues to an ailment's cause.

TAKING INVENTORY OF YOUR HEALTH

Just as doctors ask questions before they treat a patient, you'll have more success with healing spells if you understand your "patient" before you try to heal him or her. That's true even if the patient is you. By taking inventory of your health, you'll have a clearer idea about which spells will work best for you. Ask yourself these questions:

- Most of the time, is your energy high or low?
- In general, how would you describe your health?
- Have you noticed any particular patterns to your health?
- Describe your beliefs about illness and health.
- Are there certain times of the year when your health is better or worse?
- Do you worry a lot about your health?
- When was your last visit to a doctor? Why did you go?
- Do you have regular checkups?
- Do you have chronic health problems? If so, what are they?
- Do you get several colds a year?
- How much sleep do you need each night?
- When do you feel happiest and healthiest?
- Do you experience major fluctuations in your moods?

- Do you consider yourself a basically optimistic person?
- Have you ever sought "alternative" treatments for an illness or disease?
- Does anyone in your family have a chronic illness? If so, what?

Pay special attention to your answers for questions concerning your beliefs about health and illness. It may be that the three colds or the flu you get every year are directly related to your belief that getting three colds a year or coming down with the flu during the winter is normal. Read your answers several times. If you find that you hold negative or limiting beliefs concerning health, then changing these beliefs will do more for you than any spell.

THE HUMAN ENERGY FIELD

"Your body is designed to heal itself," writes Donna Eden in *Energy Medicine.*

In fact, we have all the tools we need to heal ourselves. It begins with an awareness of the subtle energies that give our bodies life. In China, this energy is called *chi* or *qi*. In India, the energy is known as *prana*. The Sufis call it *baraka*. It runs through pathways in our bodies called meridians and is focused in seven major centers, or *chakras*, which extend from the base of the spine to the crown of the head.

Chakra literally means disk or vortex. Imagine a swirling circle of energy of various colors and you'll have a pretty good idea of what it looks like. When your energy is balanced, you're healthy. When your energy centers are unbalanced or blocked, you get sick. Each energy center has a particular function and relates to certain organs and physical systems in your body.

Before it shows up as a physical problem, illness exists in the body's energy field. When a medical intuitive, psychic healer, or shaman looks at an energy field, he or she can read your psychological as well as your physical health history. However, you don't have to be psychic to pick up information about your own health or someone else's. Sometimes your first impression, going "from the gut," is enough. The more you develop your intuitive ability, the better you'll get at receiving this sort of information—and knowing what to do with it.

The following list of the chakras and the parts of the body associated with them is based on medical intuitive Caroline Myss's system:

ENERGY CENTERS (CHAKRAS) AND HEALTH		
Chakra	Location	Organs and Body Systems
1	Base of spine	Immune system, rectum, feet, legs, bones
2	Below navel	Sexual organs, large intestines, appendix, hips, bladder
3	Solar plexus	Abdomen and stomach, upper intestines, liver, kidneys, gallbladder, pancreas, middle vertebrae, adrenal glands
4	Chest center	Heart, lungs, shoulders, arms, circulatory system, diaphragm, ribs, breasts, thymus gland
5	Throat	Throat, neck, thyroid, parathyroid, trachea, esophagus, mouth, teeth, gums, hypothalamus
6	Middle of forehead	Eyes, ears, nose, brain, nervous system, pineal and pituitary glands
7	Crown	Skeletal system, skin, and muscular system

HEALTH SPELL CAVEATS AND CAUTIONS

You know someone who's suffering, and you know a little magick could help that person. Shouldn't you do a healing spell for her? Well, *maybe*. Physical pain is a red flag that something needs attention—not just the obvious symptom, but the underlying root of the problem. Perhaps the discomfort your friend feels is actually helping her get in touch with the deeper issues involved. If so, it may be a necessary and beneficial part of her healing process.

Respecting another person's free will is also important when you're doing magick. You can't change anyone else unless he wants to change.

As well, you may not fully understand the issues involved in another person's disease. Perhaps an injury is forcing an overachiever to slow down, work less, and spend more time with his family. Unless someone asks for your help, proceed with caution and reserve.

Finally, it's important to acknowledge that magick spells, no matter how powerful and well intentioned, aren't a substitute for professional medical care. Although you've perhaps heard of shamans who can cure broken bones by tying charmed sticks to the damaged limb, in most cases it's wise to have the bone set by a qualified doctor. You may have personally witnessed miraculous healings for conditions that orthodox medicine couldn't cure. But if you break a tooth, you'll probably be grateful for the skills of a competent dentist. Combine humility, patience, and common sense with magickal belief, for both your own good and everyone else's.

TIMING HEALTH SPELLS

Healing spells will be more powerful if you do them at the right time. It's usually best to do spells to increase vitality or repair damage to bone or tissue while the moon is waxing. But if your goal is to eliminate or reduce something, do a spell during the waning moon. Spells to lose weight, for example, should be done while the moon wanes.

The full moon is a high-energy day, and many people experience peak vitality at this time. However, the full moon can also increase stress and bring emotional or psychological issues out into the open. The three days prior to and including the new moon tend to be low-energy days. It may take longer to recover from an illness or injury during this period—don't push yourself too hard.

Virgo is the zodiac sign of health, so you may wish to do healing spells while the moon and/or the sun is in Virgo. The sun is connected with vitality, and Mars with physical strength. Therefore, you could do a healing spell when the sun and/or moon is in Leo or Aries, depending on your intention.

Spells to limit the spread of disease or to reduce problems associated with a condition should be done on Saturday. Spells to bolster strength and vitality are best done on Tuesday, Thursday, or Sunday.

Don't undergo surgery or other medical procedures unless you absolutely have to while Mercury is retrograde (meaning the planet looks as if it's moving backwards in the sky), as mental errors are more common at this time. If you have tests done while Mercury is retrograde and the results are unfavorable or inconclusive, consider having the tests redone. Mercury goes retrograde every four months for three weeks at a time; you can check online astrology sites such as *www.astro.com* to see when.

INGREDIENTS FOR SCENT-SATIONAL SPELLS

In recent years, aromatherapy—healing with scent—has entered the mainstream. But witches and healers have known about this practice for thousands of years. The ancient Chinese and Indians used these oils for both healing and spiritual purposes. Scented oils played an important role in the Egyptians' mummification process. And remember the frankincense and myrrh that the wise men gave Jesus at his birth?

This following list gives some common magickal correspondences for essential oils. If you're applying aromatics to your skin, be careful—some of these strong scents may cause irritation, and some people may be allergic to certain oils. Dilute them in a "carrier" oil such as olive, grape seed, or jojoba. Don't ingest them either. Although some are edible, others are toxic.

Aromatic	Correspondence
Almond	vitality, energy booster
Amber	protection
Apple	happiness, especially in love
Basil	protection, harmony
Bay	strength, prophetic dreams
Bayberry	money spells
Cedar	prosperity, courage, protection

The Modern Guide to Witchcraft

Aromatic	Correspondence
Cinnamon	career success, wealth, vitality
Clove	healing, prosperity, to increase sexual desire
Eucalyptus	healing, purification
Frankincense	prosperity, protection, psychic awareness
Gardenia	harmony, love
Ginger	cleansing, balance, awareness
Honeysuckle	mental clarity, communication
Jasmine	love spells, passion, to sweeten any situation
Lavender	relaxation, peace of mind, purification
Lilac	psychic awareness
Mint	money spells
Musk	love spells, vitality, to stimulate drive or desire
Narcissus	self-image
Patchouli	love spells, protection, career success
Pine	purification, protection, strength
Rose	love spells, to lift spirits
Rosemary	memory retention, banishing
Sage	cleansing, wisdom
Sandalwood	connection to the higher realms, knowledge, safe travel
Thyme	work with fairy folk
Vanilla	increases magickal power
Vervain	money spells, fertility
Violet	attraction
Ylang-ylang	aphrodisiac, love spells, passion, feminine power

Aromagick is one of the loveliest types of spellcasting. As you work with scents, consider both their mystical and physical effects. Combine two or more to "customize" your spells.

Aromagick Oils

An essential oil is prepared directly from the plant, which means that it carries the original energy of the plant. Synthetic scents and perfumes don't. Essential oils tend to be more expensive than perfume oils, but because they're stronger you only need a drop or two.

Here's an easy recipe you can use to make a versatile oil blend to boost energy, health, and happiness. If you'll only use it magickally, say to dot on talismans or to add to a ritual bath, you needn't dilute the essential oils. However, if you plan to apply the blend directly to your skin, be sure to mix the essential oils into a carrier oil.

AWAKE AND ALIVE OIL
- 1 part rosemary oil
- 1 part mint oil
- 1 part orange oil
- ½ part lemon oil
- ½ part thyme oil
- 20 parts carrier oil (depending on how you'll use it)

Wash a plain glass jar and let it dry. Then one by one, pour the oils into the container. Swirl them together. Empower the oil blend by holding it in your hands and visualizing your personal energy flowing from your hands into the oil. Cover the jar and label it: Write down the date, the ingredients, and the proportions. Store the oil in a cool, dark place.

Magick Healing Baths

For thousands of years, people have soaked in water for therapeutic reasons. Many spas such as those at Saratoga Springs, New York, Ojo Caliente in New Mexico, and Hot Springs, Arkansas, still attract visitors who seek healing through water cures (or hydrotherapy). The ancient Greek physician and Father of Medicine, Hippocrates, believed that "the way to health is to have an aromatic bath and scented massage every day."

You can put a couple spoonfuls of fragrant dried herbs inside an old sock or stocking, tie a knot in it, and toss it under the running water as you fill the tub. The result in an infusion brewed directly in your bath. Or, you can add essential oils to your bathwater. You'll probably only need a few drops if you're using the oils "neat," more if you've blended them in a carrier oil. In the beginning, add only a small amount because your skin may be sensitive to the oils. Mixing essential oils into Epsom salts and adding those to your bathwater is another good way to get their therapeutic benefits—use about ¼ cup of the scented salts in a bath, and store them in a glass container. You may also enjoy positioning scented candles at the corners of your bathtub and bathing by candlelight.

SIMPLE CHAKRA BALANCING SPELL

To do this spell you only need your imagination and willpower. Witches and healers link each of the chakras we talked about earlier with a color—it's sort of like having a rainbow running through your body.

- First (root) chakra: Red
- Second (sacral) chakra: Orange
- Third (solar plexus) chakra: Yellow
- Fourth (heart) chakra: Green
- Fifth (throat) chakra: Blue
- Sixth (brow or third eye) chakra: Indigo
- Seventh (crown) chakra: Purple

Sit in a quiet, comfortable place and breathe slowly, deeply. Focus your attention on the first chakra, and send beautiful, clear red light there. Do this for a minute or two, until you feel warmth at this energy center. Then shift your attention to the second chakra and focus orange light there. Repeat, moving up through your body, sending the appropriate-colored light to each chakra. By the time you reach the top of your head, you'll feel more relaxed and balanced in body, mind, and spirit. Try to do this every day to maintain personal harmony and well-being.

CASTING A HEALTH SPELL FOR ANOTHER PERSON

Once you've got the okay to go ahead and cast a spell for someone else, use sympathetic magick to provide healing.

INGREDIENTS/TOOLS:
- Something that represents the other person
- Sprig of sage

- Eucalyptus oil
- 1 gold candle
- 1 purple candle
- 2 fireproof candleholders
- Oil burner
- Matches or a lighter

- As needed

Find an object that represents the person for whom you're casting the spell. It could be a photograph of the person or an item that belongs to her, such as a piece of clothing or jewelry. Smudge your work area and the object that will stand for the other person with the smoke of sage. Cast a circle. Set the item in the middle of your work area or on your altar, and position a candle on either side of it. Place the oil burner behind it.

Pour several drops of eucalyptus oil into your burner. Light it, and then light the candles. After a moment of reflection during which you bring to mind the person's face and being, say:

"As the oil and candles burn,
Illness gone and health return,
For my [state relationship and the person's name]
Who is yearning and deserving."

Extinguish the oil burner. Open the circle and let the other two candles burn down naturally.

ENERGY ELIXIR

If you're like most people, you hit a slump late in the afternoon. When you need a quick pick-me-up that's all natural and caffeine and sugar free, drink this magick Energy Elixir to boost your vitality and clear your mind.

INGREDIENTS/TOOLS:

- A clear glass jar with a lid
- A small piece of rutilated quartz crystal
- Spring water
- A few drops of essential oil of peppermint or spearmint
- A few drops of essential oil of lemon
- A few drops of essential oil of sweet orange
- The Strength card from a tarot deck

BEST TIME TO PERFORM THE SPELL:

- Any time

Collect the ingredients needed for this spell. Wash the jar and the quartz crystal with mild soap and water, and let them dry. Cast a circle around the area where you will do your spell. Fill the jar with spring water. Add the essential oils, then the crystal. Cap the jar and shake it three times to charge it.

Lay the Strength card face up on your altar, table, or another surface. Set the jar on the card and leave it for at least ten minutes, so the water can absorb the energy of the image.

Remove the crystal, with your fingers, spoon, or tongs. Open the circle. Sip this supercharged elixir whenever you need an energy boost.

SPELL TO QUELL THE COMMON COLD

It's cold and flu season, and you're definitely feeling below par. A little herbal magick plus some TLC can relieve those miserable symptoms fast and make you feel better all over.

INGREDIENTS/TOOLS:

- Spring water
- Hyssop leaves and/or flowers
- An aqua beeswax candle with a cotton wick
- A candleholder
- Matches or a lighter

• As needed

Brew a strong tea from the hyssop leaves and/or flowers. Strain the herb residue from the water. Fill a bathtub with comfortably hot water and add the tea to it. Fit the candle in its holder and light it. Get into the tub and soak for as long as you like, inhaling the soothing scent of hyssop.

Focus your mind on loving thoughts and feelings. Envision yourself surrounded by love. As you inhale, imagine you are bringing love into your body. See and sense love circulating through your entire body, from head to foot. Spend several minutes doing this. Let the loving energy gently nourish you, strengthening your system so it can throw off the cold.

Remain in the tub for as long as you like. After you get out of the bathwater, extinguish the candle. Repeat this pleasant ritual whenever you like.

GREEN LIGHT SPELL TO SPEED RECOVERY

An illness or injury has sidelined you temporarily. This simple spell uses the color green, symbolizing health, to aid your recovery. Repeat it often and you'll be back in the game soon.

INGREDIENTS/TOOLS:
• A green light bulb or green filter that will color the light from an ordinary lamp
• A green ribbon long enough to tie around the afflicted body part

BEST TIME TO PERFORM THE SPELL:
• During the waxing moon to promote new tissue growth or to increase vitality; during the waning moon to eliminate an unwanted condition or to decrease unpleasant symptoms

Tie the ribbon comfortably around the part of your body that is injured or ailing. Make sure it doesn't interfere with an open wound or other skin damage. As you tie it, say aloud: "I am radiantly healthy and whole, in body, mind, and spirit." Shine the green light on the afflicted area for a few minutes, while you visualize yourself completely healed. *Don't* think about the injury or illness; imagine the end result you desire instead.

Repeat this "green light" treatment several times a day. Leave the ribbon in place until the condition is healed, then remove it and burn it.

HEAVEN AND EARTH HEALING SPELL

This spell draws upon the powers of heaven and earth to help heal any condition. You can do it for yourself or for someone else (remember to ask that person's permission first). Even if the other person is not physically present, you can still send him/her healing energy in this manner.

INGREDIENTS/TOOLS:
- A magick wand

BEST TIME TO PERFORM THE SPELL:
- Any time

Cast a circle around yourself. If you are doing the spell for another person who is physically present, cast the circle around both of you. Stand in the center of the circle with your feet about shoulder-width apart. Close your eyes. Hold the wand over your head with both hands, with your arms outstretched and straight. Point the tip of the wand at the sky and say aloud: "With this wand I draw down the healing force of the heavens." In your mind's eye see light flowing into the wand, making it glow brightly.

Open your eyes and point the tip of the wand at the afflicted part of your body (or the other person's). If the person for whom you are doing this spell is not physically present, aim the wand toward his/her location. Envision the light you collected from the heavens flowing into the injured or ailing body part, zapping it with healing rays.

When you sense that all the light has been transferred from the wand to the body, point the wand at the ground. Close your eyes and say aloud:

"With this wand I draw up the healing force of Mother Earth." In your mind's eye see light flowing into the wand from the center of the earth, making it glow brightly.

Open your eyes and aim the tip of the wand at the afflicted part of your body (or the other person's). Envision the light you collected from the earth flowing into the injured or ailing body part, zapping it with healing rays until all the light has been transferred from the wand to the body. When you've finished, thank the forces of heaven and earth for assisting you and open the circle.

SPELL TO EASE DIGESTIVE COMPLAINTS

This spell combines both physical and magickal healing to soothe problems with digestion.

INGREDIENTS/TOOLS:
- 1 glass cup
- A blend of chamomile tea and peppermint tea
- 1 piece of paper
- 1 pen with green ink
- Tape

BEST TIME TO PERFORM THE SPELL:
- Any time

On the paper, write the words *balance, harmony, peace, love,* and *acceptance.* Tape the paper to a clear glass cup, so that the words face in. Then brew some tea, combining chamomile and peppermint, and pour it into the glass cup. Let the tea sit for a few minutes to allow the words to imprint their message into the liquid.

Sip the tea slowly, feeling its soothing warmth in your stomach. Envision healing green light entering your stomach and abdomen, calming the upsets in your digestive tract. Feel yourself relaxing. Repeat this spell one or more times daily, until your problem improves.

STRESS-BUSTER RITUAL

You may not be able to avoid stress, but you can keep it from getting you down. This relaxing ritual helps you release stress and stay calm in the presence of everyday annoyances.

INGREDIENTS/TOOLS:
- Soothing music (new age or classical is best, either instrumental or chanting, without a catchy rhythm or lyrics)
- A tumbled chunk of amethyst
- A tumbled chunk of rose quartz
- A blue candle
- A candleholder
- A ballpoint pen
- Essential oil of lavender, vanilla, sweet orange, or ylang-ylang
- Matches or a lighter

BEST TIME TO PERFORM THE SPELL:
- Any time

Collect the ingredients needed for this spell. Wash the stones with mild soap and water, and then pat them dry. Start the music you've chosen. Cast a circle around the area where you will do your spell. With the ballpoint pen write the word "Peace" on the candle. Dress the candle by rubbing it with essential oil (not on the wick). Fit the candle in its holder and light it.

Hold one gemstone in each hand. Sit in a comfortable place and close your eyes. Begin breathing slowly and deeply. Inhale the soothing scent and allow it to calm your mind. Rub the smooth stones with your fingers. Feel the stones neutralize stress, irritability, and anxiety. Focus on your breathing. If your mind starts to wander, gently bring it back and say or think the word "peace."

Spend at least ten minutes this way, longer if you wish. When you feel ready, open your eyes and extinguish the candle. Open the circle. Let the music continue playing or shut it off. Carry the stones with you and rub them whenever stress starts to mount.

MAGICK HERB GARDEN

Early healers grew their own herbs to cure all manner of illness. You, too, can grow a magick herb garden and have fresh, healing herbs available when you need them for teas, poultices, lotions, and balms—and of course, for spells. If you don't have space for an outdoor garden, plant herbs in flowerpots or window boxes. Plant whatever you think you'll need for your magickal and healing work. Start with a few and add to your garden as your skills and needs expand.

Here are some suggestions:

- Lavender (for relaxation)
- Peppermint (for nausea and stomach ailments)
- Echinacea (for colds and flu)
- Dandelion (for skin disorders)
- Comfrey (for congestion and stomach complaints)
- Garlic (to clean wounds and prevent infection)
- Basil (for insect stings and bites)
- Aloe (for burns, constipation, and diverticulitis)
- Blackberry (for diarrhea, colds, and sore throats)
- Raspberry (for female complaints)
- Chamomile (for digestive disorders, nervous conditions, and insomnia)
- Calendula (for rashes, eczema, and skin irritations)
- Parsley (to cleanse the kidneys and liver)
- Rosemary (for headaches and insomnia)
- Sage (to staunch bleeding; for sore muscles)
- St. John's Wort (for bronchitis, low spirits, and lung congestion)
- Verbena (for coughs, breathing difficulties, and fevers)

BEST TIME TO PLANT:
- During the waxing moon, preferably when the sun or moon is in Taurus

Do some research to determine which plants to use for which health problems. Familiarize yourself with the magickal properties of the herbs you choose, too. (You'll find some information in Chapter 11.)

Consider every step of your gardening process—planting, watering, tending, and harvesting—as a magickal act. Invite the nature spirits to assist you. Talk to your plants and thank them for helping you, especially when you harvest them.

AN ATTITUDE OF GRATITUDE

Gratitude is the final step in doing a spell. Always end every spell by showing gratitude to whomever you consider the source or creative power in the universe. Even before you see results, say thank you. Gratitude has two purposes in magickal work. It indicates that you fully believe your intention will materialize, and it acknowledges the help you receive from forces outside yourself.

An expression of gratitude may be as simple as saying "Thank you" at the close of a spell. Some people like to make an offering of some kind. Others demonstrate gratitude for the help they've received by giving help to someone else. How you choose to show gratitude is less important than the intention behind it. Sincerity is what really matters.

Chapter 19

SPELLS FOR PERSONAL POWER

Personal power has a lot to do with having "presence." We all know people who just seem to shine, and everyone looks at them when they enter a room. Movie stars, powerful politicians, and celebrities have it. However, you don't need to be someone in the public eye to possess presence. In fact, your job or social position rarely has anything to do with it. Presence comes from within—from being present in the moment and in harmony with yourself. Some little kids have it. Some elderly people have it. You'll meet people from all walks of life who don't even realize they have it. In some instances, a person may be born with presence, but usually it's something you cultivate and nurture over time, with the development of self-knowledge.

Remember the old adage, know thyself? To know yourself and to use what you learn requires an act of will. As you know already, your will is the crux of every visualization, manifestation, and spell you cast. You don't simply say the words or use the right herbs. You don't just go through the motions. You plunge into yourself, you delve deep to discover your true motives, needs, and desires. You bring that self-knowledge into your daily awareness. Then you commit to your path and trust the process. The spells in this chapter will help you to expand self-awareness and increase your personal power.

YOUR SELF-IMAGE

Ironically, your self-image probably isn't something you created yourself. It's a patchwork affair made up of bits and pieces you've collected from lots of other people: family members, teachers, religious leaders, friends, your culture, and the media. Like donning clothing that's *in* style, rather than in *your* style, the self-image you wear might be uncomfortable or inappropriate. Maybe you even fashioned your self-image without questioning whether or not the "garment" was right for you.

Tailoring your self-image according to someone else's ideas usually results in unhappiness or frustration. If you see yourself in this picture, perhaps it's time to take a closer look at the person you think you are, the person you'd like to be, and where the ideas you hold about yourself originated.

From what you know about magick, your thoughts about yourself and what you deserve will produce conditions that fit with your ideas. Your life is your mirror. What you see is a reflection of what you believe about yourself. If you aren't happy with your situation, you can change it by changing your perceptions of yourself.

Remember, nobody else gets to decide whether you're worthy. Only you do. Nor can anyone else limit your personal power without your consent—and that's pretty sweet.

Your Self List

Make a list of your ideas about yourself. Consider your physical qualities, mental abilities, talents, job, relationships, lifestyle, and so on. What are your strengths and weaknesses? What things do you feel comfortable with, and which would you like to change?

Look at all areas of yourself. Make "plus" and "minus" categories if you like. Are you good at managing time? Do you have pretty eyes? Are you a skilled cook? Are you compassionate, a good listener, a loyal friend? Are you overweight? Are you always late for appointments? Do you buy things you don't need to make yourself feel better? Are you impatient, judgmental, or lazy? It can help to also examine where the negative ideas you hold about yourself originated.

Feeling Powerful

Think back to a time in your life when you felt powerful. Bring to mind the feelings that you experienced then, and reconnect with them. Hold these impressions in your mind and heart for a while, and remind yourself that inside you are still that powerful person.

This is the feeling you want to tap into when you do spells. The better you feel about yourself, the more positive energy you can bring to your magick. The more confident you are that your spells will succeed, the more likely it is that they will.

Go with the Flow

Although you may think this saying implies passivity, what it really recommends is that you put yourself into the stream of cosmic energy that flows through everything in the universe. What "go with the flow" really means is "stop resisting, and relax." Swimming is a good analogy. If you relax, the water will buoy you up, but if you flail about, you could drown.

Instead of struggling to figure out everything with your rational mind, allow your intuition to kick in. Trust that the universe, your higher self, Divine Will, Source, or whatever term you prefer has everything under control—all you have to do is stop interfering with the plan. When you hook into something larger than yourself, you discover that the big picture is way more amazing than you imagined.

The flow of a river is altered constantly by the curvature of the land that contains it, as well as by weather patterns and other factors. In the same way, the "flow" in your life changes as your goals and needs change. When you allow for that, you're better equipped to seize opportunities, to face challenges, and to fulfill your potential. In short, you are empowered.

INCANTATION FOR INSPIRATION

You're in a rut. You really need to come up with some great new ideas, but you just don't feel inspired. Chanting can spark your enthusiasm. Think how a crowd's cheers raise energy and fire up a ball team. Incantations operate on the same principle.

INGREDIENTS/TOOLS:
- A piece of paper
- A pen that writes red ink
- A drum, gong, or large bell

BEST TIME TO PERFORM THE SPELL:
- On a Tuesday during the waxing moon

Collect the ingredients needed for this spell. Cast a circle around the area where you will do your spell. On the paper, write an incantation that describes what you desire. It should praise you and your abilities with positive statements and imagery. Don't worry about its literary quality—no one but you will hear it. The point is to make it upbeat and catchy.

When you're satisfied with your rhyme, read it aloud. Then strike the drum, gong, or bell. Repeat the incantation again, and again, sounding the drum/gong/bell each time. If you prefer, you can strike the drum/gong/bell after each line or after each word of the incantation. Feel the sounds stimulating your energy. Feel the blockages within you crumbling. Feel your confidence growing. Continue for as long as you like. When you feel inspired, stop and open the circle.

Inspired Dreams

Some of the greatest moments of inspiration occur while we are sleeping. For example, the 2010 movie *Inception* starring Leonardo DiCaprio is based on director Christopher Nolan's own dreams. The Beatles's hugely successful song "Yesterday" came to Paul McCartney in a dream. So did the story for Stephen King's novel *Dreamcatcher.*

TALISMAN TO MAKE A GOOD IMPRESSION

You've got to make a good impression, but you feel anxious and uncertain. Whether you're going for a job interview, giving a presentation, or meeting with someone you admire, this lucky charm helps you shine. Remember, the key to success is believing in yourself.

INGREDIENTS / TOOLS:

- Sandalwood incense
- An incense burner
- Matches or a lighter
- Red nail polish or red paint
- A small brush
- A small stone
- A piece of paper
- A pen
- An orange cloth pouch, preferably silk
- Cedar chips
- Cinnamon
- Dried parsley
- A yellow ribbon 6" long
- Salt water

BEST TIME TO PERFORM THE SPELL:

- On Sunday, preferably when the sun or moon is in Leo

Collect the ingredients needed for this spell. Cast a circle around the area where you will do your spell. Fit the incense in its burner and light it. Use the nail polish or paint to draw the rune *Inguz*, which looks like two Xs stacked one on top of the other, on the stone. This rune represents new beginnings, fertility, and power.

While the nail polish or paint is drying, write on the paper what you intend to accomplish. Whom do you wish to impress? What results do you desire from this meeting? As you write your list of objectives, see yourself already achieving them. When you've finished, fold the paper so it's small enough to fit into the pouch and say aloud: "This is now accomplished in harmony with Divine Will, my own true will, and for the good of all."

Put the stone, paper, cedar, cinnamon, and parsley into the pouch. Tie the pouch closed with the ribbon, making three knots. Hold the image of your success in your mind as you tie the knots. Sprinkle the talisman with salt water, then hold it in the incense smoke for a few moments to charge the charm.

Open the circle. To bring good luck, carry this talisman in your pocket or purse when you go to your meeting. Just knowing it's there will increase your self-confidence and help you make a good impression.

POWER BELT

In karate, the belt you wear signifies your level of skill and accomplishment. The belt you create in this spell is not only a badge of your ability, it actually enhances your personal power.

INGREDIENTS/TOOLS:
- Music that energizes you and that signifies power to you
- A purple cord long enough to circle your waist three times (drapery cord is perfect, but you can use any material you like)

BEST TIME TO PERFORM THE SPELL:
- During the waxing moon, preferably on Sunday

Collect the items needed for this spell. Cast a circle around the area where you will do your spell. Begin playing the music you've selected. Close your eyes and allow the music to stimulate you, making you feel stronger and more energetic. Let your breathing become deeper.

Grasp the purple cord in your hands as you see yourself drawing up silvery light from the earth. Feel the light flow up your legs, into your torso, arms, and head. Next, visualize yourself drawing golden light down from the heavens, into the crown of your head. Feel this light flow into your torso, arms, and legs until your whole body resonates with it. Imagine these two forces blending harmoniously in and around you, increasing your vitality, confidence, and personal power.

Holding on to this sensation, open your eyes and begin tying knots in the cord. See yourself capturing some of the energy you've raised into each knot you tie. Tie as many knots as you like—just make sure the cord will still fit around your waist. When you're finished tying the knots, wrap the belt around your waist and secure it. Open the circle.

Wear this "power belt" to help you address whatever challenges you face. If at any time you need a quick rush of vitality or courage, untie one of the knots and release the energy it holds.

SALAMANDER COURAGE SPELL

Setbacks, disappointments, losses, or frustrating circumstances can make you feel like giving up. In this spell you draw upon the fire power of the universe and get assistance from the fire elementals we talked about in Chapter 5 to bolster your vitality and confidence.

INGREDIENTS/TOOLS:
- 9 small red votive candles
- Matches or a lighter
- A magick wand

BEST TIME TO PERFORM THE SPELL:
- During the waxing moon, preferably on Tuesday or when the sun and/or moon is in Aries, Leo, or Sagittarius

Arrange the candles in a circle around you, in a place where you can safely leave them to burn down completely. Beginning in the east, light the candles one at a time as you move in a clockwise direction around the circle (making sure that you'll be inside the circle when you're finished). When all the candles are burning, stand in the center of the circle and face south.

Call out to the salamanders, the elementals who inhabit the element of fire. Tell them you have lit these nine candles in their honor. Explain your situation and request their assistance, by chanting the following incantation aloud:

"Beings of fire
Shining so bright
Fuel my desire
Increase my might.

Help me be strong
All the day long
So I'll succeed
In every deed."

You may notice faint flickerings of light—other than the candles—in the room. Or, you might sense the energy around you quickening. It may even seem a bit warmer. That means the salamanders are present and willing to work with you.

Take up your magick wand and point it toward the south—the region where the salamanders reside. Imagine you are drawing powerful energy in through the tip of your wand. You might see the wand glow or feel it tingle. Now turn the wand and aim it at yourself. Your movements should be strong and purposeful, not wimpy. Sense the energy you've attracted from the south flowing from the wand into your body. Feel yourself growing more powerful, more confident, more alive.

Continue using your wand to pull energy and courage from the south in this manner for as long as you like. Remain in the center of the circle of candles until they have all burned down completely. Thank the salamanders for their assistance and release them. Open the circle and leave with renewed vitality and confidence.

SPIRIT ANIMAL SPELL

According to shamanic traditions, spirit animals provide power, protection, and guidance in this world and beyond. These animals can lend you their special powers to accomplish a particular task. For example, a cheetah can give you speed when you're up against a deadline. An elephant can bring you strength to overcome obstacles. Foxes are clever and can show you how to dodge difficulties. Think about various animals and their distinctive qualities. Which animal's characteristics do you need now? (See my book *The Secret Power of Spirit Animals* for more information.)

When you've chosen an animal helper, find a photograph, small figurine, or another symbol of that animal.

- A black candle
- A white candle
- Two candleholders
- Matches or a lighter
- A photo, figurine, painting, or other image of the animal whose help you are soliciting

BEST TIME TO PERFORM THE SPELL:
- Any time

Collect all the listed ingredients. Cast a circle around the area where you will do your spell. Fit the candles in their holders and set them on your altar (or another surface, such as a tabletop). As you face the altar, the black candle should be at your left and the white one on your right. Light the candles and place the image of the animal between them.

Gaze at the animal image. Sense this animal's presence near you, not necessarily as a physical creature but as a spirit being who will accompany you wherever and whenever you need it. Breathe slowly and deeply, bringing into yourself the qualities you seek from that animal: strength, courage, speed, cunning, and so on. Feel your fear ebbing away. Ask this animal to share any suggestions that might help you. An answer may come in the form of a vision, insight, sensation, sound, scent, or inner knowing.

When you feel ready, extinguish the candles and pick up the image of your animal guardian. Open the circle. Carry the image with you to give you the power you seek.

RITUAL TO RECLAIM YOUR ENERGY

Do you feel worn out at the end of the day, especially if you have to deal with a lot of people? When you're around a difficult person, do you notice your energy diminishing? According to ancient Toltec teachings, you leave a bit of your own vitality behind with every individual you meet during the day. This ritual lets you reclaim the energy you've given away so you don't get depleted.

INGREDIENTS/TOOLS:
• None

BEST TIME TO PERFORM THE SPELL:
• At the end of each day, before going to sleep

Choose a time when you won't be disturbed; turn off the TV, silence the phone, and so on. Sit in a comfortable chair and close your eyes. Start breathing slowly and deeply. Begin recalling all the people you encountered and all the incidents that occurred during the day, one at a time.

Turn your head to the left and remember something in which you participated in some way. Inhale as you recall the thoughts and feelings you had, as well as the actions that took place. Then turn your head to the right and exhale, releasing the experience with your breath. Continue doing this until you've recapped every event of the day, from beginning to end, the little things as well as the big ones. Feel yourself relaxing and gaining strength with each memory you cast out.

Repeat this procedure every night. Daily practice keeps you from draining your natural energy resources.

SPELL TO STRENGTHEN YOUR SELF-WORTH

This spell energizes the third chakra, located at your solar plexus. Energy healers connect this chakra with confidence and self-esteem.

INGREDIENTS/TOOLS:
• 1 ballpoint pen
• 4 yellow candles
• Almond oil
• 4 candleholders
• Matches or a lighter

BEST TIME TO PERFORM THE SPELL:
• On a Thursday, Friday, or Sunday night, or during the full moon

The Modern Guide to Witchcraft

With the ballpoint pen, carve a circle on each candle and make a dot in the center of the circle. This is the astrological symbol for the sun. Yellow, the sun's color, is also the color associated with the solar plexus chakra. Rub almond oil on the candles to dress them, and then position them in their holders. Dab a little almond oil on your solar plexus, too, to energize it.

Place the four candles at the four cardinal directions and stand at the center of the space you've defined. Starting at the east, move clockwise as you light the candles, making sure you'll be inside the circle when you're finished. After you've lit all four candles, spend a few minutes drawing the fire energy from the candles into yourself. Inhale the scent of almond oil and imagine a golden-yellow ball of light glowing in your solar plexus. Let this light expand until it fills your whole body with warmth and confidence.

Pinch your right nostril shut, inhale through the left, and hold to the count of ten. Release, and exhale through the right nostril. Repeat this five times, then switch sides. As you do this alternate nostril breathing, sense your power growing.

Spend as much time as you like in the circle of candlelight. When you're ready, extinguish the candles in reverse order from the direction you lit them and leave the circle.

SPELL TO EXPAND SELF-AWARENESS

Self-awareness is linked with personal power. Most of us underestimate ourselves and are more familiar with our weaknesses than our strengths. We may not even be fully aware of our many abilities. The more you practice witchcraft, the more you develop an appreciation for yourself and your power. If possible, do this spell outside, under the full moon.

INGREDIENTS/TOOLS:
- 1 amber-colored candle
- A candleholder
- Frankincense essential oil
- Myrrh essential oil

- An object that represents personal power to you
- 1 quartz crystal

- Preferably on a Thursday night during a full moon

Thursday is Jupiter's day, and Jupiter encourages expansion. If you can't do this spell on a Thursday, do it during a full moon on any day except Saturday (Saturn's day).

The object that represents your personal power should be something solid and three-dimensional: a stone or figurine, for instance, versus a photograph. Select the object with care. The amber-colored candle symbolizes the sun's golden light. The crystal you're using will amplify your desire.

Pick a spot where you won't be disturbed. Dress the candle with both essential oils, fit it in the candleholder, and set it on your altar, at your right. The object that represents your personal power and the crystal should be positioned directly in front of you. Light the candle, and then open your arms to "embrace" the moon. Vividly imagine its light filling you as you say:

> *"This light is presence,*
> *This light is power.*
> *It fills me*
> *Until I am presence,*
> *And I am power."*

Gaze at the crystal and your power object as the moon's light shines on them. Inhale the aroma of the oils for as long as you like, then snuff out the candle's flame. Carry your power object with you and touch it whenever you need a power boost.

THE POWER OF DREAMS

One way to expand your power is to learn how to gain info from your dreams. Your dreams are your friends, even if it doesn't always seem that way. Getting in touch with your dreams can help you understand what's going on during your waking hours. Dreams can help you work through problems. They may also present possibilities you might not have considered otherwise.

Dreams have fascinated us throughout history. The ancient Babylonians believed that spirits sent dreams to humans. In Egypt, people thought that dreams were gifts from the gods. The earliest known recorded dream, which belongs to King Thotmes IV, is carved on a granite tablet that rests between the paws of the Sphinx.

Often dreams give us a glimpse of the future, which can be immensely helpful to witches and others. What if you could see what's going to happen before it does? A practice called "lucid dreaming" allows you to control your dreams and direct them in the way you choose. Developing this technique while you sleep can help you direct your waking life, too.

Keeping a Record of Your Dreams

Dedicate a section of your book of shadows to dreamwork, and place your book and a pen or pencil near your bed. To get the most out of your dreams, write them down immediately upon waking—it's easier then to capture the fleeting images, before they vanish into the busyness of your day. You needn't write in complete sentences. Just make enough notes so you can come back later and revisit the dream and analyze it.

Don't make any value judgments about what you write. Just record your feelings and the images that stand out. Who appears in your dreams? Where do the dreams take place? Do you notice patterns or similarities in your dreams? Sometimes you'll realize that what takes place in your dream is a reworking of what happened during the day. The dream might even slip you a tip about how to handle something that occurred. Other times, a dream may serve as a warning to prepare you, or give you a glimpse into what lies ahead so you can take advantage of an opportunity when it comes. Always date your dreams, and include any information about what's going on in your waking life at the time that may be relevant.

The more you work with your dreams, the more they will reveal to you and the more guidance they'll provide—giving you the inside track. And, as you develop a better rapport with your subconscious, you'll discover your spellworking improves.

Chapter 20

MISCELLANEOUS SPELLS

For every desire, every worry, and every situation, there's a spell. You can use magick for the big deals in life and for all those little things as well. Whether you want to find the perfect life partner or the perfect pair of shoes to wear to an upcoming event, magick can help. And if a "readymade" spell doesn't already exist, you can always design your own or customize one to suit your needs.

The spells in this chapter address a variety of circumstances, both large and small, that show up in our daily lives. Some are so versatile they can be used in a number of different ways. A few of these spells may seem trifling, but hey, why wait until something major happens to flex your magickal muscles? Lots of witches use magick to get a parking space at a crowded shopping mall—nothing wrong with that. Every spell you do strengthens your power as a witch, so don't hesitate to use your talents whenever you have the occasion to do so.

PIECE-OF-CAKE SPELL

Things aren't going as smoothly as you'd hoped. A project is taking longer or costing more than expected; a romance has hit a snag; you have to deal with a lot of uncooperative people at work or at home. This spell uses "kitchen witchery" to sweeten a frustrating situation.

You don't have to be a gourmet cook to carry off this spell—your intention is what counts. When you've finished baking your magick cake, you may want to share it with the other people who are involved in the challenging situation, so that everyone benefits. Choose a flavor that suits your intentions: chocolate or strawberry for love; cinnamon or mint for money; almond or vanilla for peace of mind.

Ingredients/Tools:
- A cake mix (or ingredients for making your favorite cake recipe)
- Food coloring
- A large bowl
- A large spoon
- Cake pan(s)
- Candles
- Matches or a lighter

Best time to perform the spell:
- Depends on your intentions

Collect the ingredients needed for this spell. Cast a circle around the area where you will do your spell, in this case your kitchen. Preheat the oven.

Follow the directions for making the cake, according to the package or your favorite recipe. As you work, focus on your objective and imagine you are sending your intention into the batter. If you like, add food coloring to tint the batter to match your intention: pink for love, green for money, and so on. Stir the batter using a clockwise motion if your goal is to attract something or to stimulate an increase. Stir counterclockwise if you want to limit, decrease, or remove something. Pour the batter into the pan(s) and bake.

When the cake has finished cooking, let it cool. Ice it with frosting in a color that relates to your intention. You may want to decorate it with symbols, pictures, and words that also describe your objective. Add candles of an appropriate color. The number of candles should also correspond to your goal: two for love, four for stability, five for change, and so on.

Light the candles and concentrate on your wish. Blow out the candles. Share the cake with other people, if you like, or eat it yourself. Each person who eats some takes the intention into him/herself and becomes a cocreator in the spell's success.

The Modern Guide to Witchcraft

LUCKY CHARM BRACELET

When you were a kid you may have worn a charm bracelet with tiny symbols that represented your interests or achievements. The symbols on the magick charm bracelet you make in this spell, however, represent your desires and intentions. Keeping these symbols in your immediate energy field makes this bracelet work, well, like a charm.

INGREDIENTS/TOOLS:
- A silver or gold link bracelet
- Small charms that can be attached to the bracelet

BEST TIME TO PERFORM THE SPELL:
- Any time

Choose a bracelet that appeals to you and that can hold as many charms as you have wishes. You might want to wear a metal that relates to your goal. Silver embodies feminine qualities and corresponds to the moon. Its energy is receptive, intuitive, emotional, creative, and works through the power of attraction. Gold signifies masculine qualities and relates to the sun. Its energy is assertive, direct, logical, and works through the power of action.

Select charms that hold meaning for you and that depict your objectives. If your goal is to attract a lover, a heart is an apt symbol. A car or airplane might represent travel. Wear as many charms as you like. Add or remove them over time as your intentions change. Remember to wash your charms before wearing them, to get rid of any lingering energies left behind by other people who may have touched them.

SPELL TO END SHOPPING LINE WOES

Does it seem that you always get in the slowest checkout line at the store, especially when you're in a hurry? Let Sheila the Shopping Goddess put you in the fast lane.

INGREDIENTS/TOOLS:
• None

BEST TIME TO PERFORM THE SPELL:
• Any time

To make this spell succeed, you have to use your intuition—not logic. As you approach the checkout area of the store, close your eyes, clear your mind, and take a deep breath. Think or quietly say this incantation:

"Goddess Sheila so divine
Guide me to the fastest line."

Open your eyes and allow yourself to be drawn to a particular line. Don't analyze it or second-guess yourself. The shortest line may not be the fastest, and the shoppers with the fewest number of items in their carts might be the very people who'll dawdle. Trust your instincts.

BLESSING A NEW HOME

Whenever you move into a new home, it's a good idea to clear away the energies left behind by the former occupants, so they don't interfere with your comfort. This spell also blesses your home and brings happiness to you and anyone else who will share the home with you.

INGREDIENTS/TOOLS:
• Sage
• Broom
• 1 bottle of wine or apple cider
• 1 loaf of freshly baked bread

BEST TIME TO PERFORM THE SPELL:
• Before you move into your new home

The Modern Guide to Witchcraft

Begin by smudging your home with sage to cleanse it. Then, use the broom to sweep out the former occupants' vibrations. After you've done this, pour the wine (or cider) and slice the bread. The bread and wine ensure that you will always have enough to eat and drink in your new home. Share this magick meal with all who will live in the home with you and/or any friends who will enjoy visiting you there.

SMOOTH TRAVEL SPELL

No matter why you're traveling, where you're going, or what mode of transportation you'll take, this spell smooths the way. If possible, cast the spell in a place where you can see the moon. If you're traveling with someone else, add a piece of rose quartz for him or her.

INGREDIENTS/TOOLS:
- 1 ballpoint pen
- 1 white candle
- A candleholder
- Rosemary essential oil
- Matches or a lighter
- 1 piece of tumbled rose quartz

BEST TIME TO PERFORM THE SPELL:
- At night, within twenty-four hours prior to your departure

With the ballpoint pen, draw the astrological symbol for Jupiter (the planet that rules travel) in the candle's wax—it looks a bit like the number 4. Dress the candle with the rosemary oil, fit it in the candleholder, and light it. If you wish, you can burn a little dried rosemary in a fire-proof dish. Set the rose quartz in front of the candle.

Repeat this incantation while you gaze into the candle's flame and inhale the scent of the rosemary:

"By the light of Lady Moon,
I reach my destination soon.

The trip shall safe and happy be,
For all concerned, as well as me."

When you're finished, extinguish the candle and pick up the rose quartz. Rub a little rosemary oil on it and carry the stone with you while you're traveling.

NO WORRIES INCANTATION

Worrying never makes a problem better. This spell uses the power of sound plus your intention to chase fearful thoughts away and raise positive energy.

INGREDIENTS/TOOLS:
- A dark blue candle
- A candleholder
- Matches or a lighter
- A hand drum or gong
- An athame or wand
- A bell

BEST TIME TO PERFORM THE SPELL:
- At midnight, during the waning moon

Collect the ingredients needed for this spell. Cast a circle around the area where you will do your spell. Fit the candle in its holder, set it on your altar (or other surface where it can burn safely), and light it. Begin playing the drum or gong to break up negative thoughts and vibrations. Feel the sound resonating through your body, stirring up your power and confidence. When you feel ready, chant the following incantation aloud. If possible, shout it out—really express yourself!

"Doubt and fear
Don't come near.
By the dawn

The Modern Guide to Witchcraft

Be you gone.

By this sign [with your athame or wand draw a pentagram in the air in front of you]

And light divine

Peace is mine.

I am strong

All day long.

My worries flee

Magickally.

I ring this bell [ring the bell]

To bind this spell,

And all is well."

As you chant, see your fears disappearing into the darkness, losing their strength. When you're ready, extinguish the candle and open the circle.

BUBBLE MAGICK

This is fun to do with children, but even if you're a mature adult, you can still enjoy this playful magick spell. Let it bring out the child in you.

INGREDIENTS/TOOLS:
- 1 bottle of bubbles
- A power object (a special stone, charm, animal figurine, or other token)

BEST TIME TO PERFORM THE SPELL:
- Any time, weather permitting, but during the full moon is best

On a breezy evening when the moon is full, take the power object and bottle of bubbles to a hill, field, or park—someplace wide open. Place the power object on the ground between your feet, then make a wish and blow the bubbles. Project your wishes inside the bubbles. Let your power object direct the bubbles as the breeze carries them high into the air, where the gods and goddesses will hear the wishes and grant them.

As the bubbles, with your wishes inside, rise into the moonlit sky, say the following incantation:

"My wishes travel
The whole night through
So that magick's power
Can make them come true."

Watch the bubbles float off into the sky, and trust they will make your wishes come true.

A STEP IN THE RIGHT DIRECTION

This spell might sound a little silly, but a lighthearted approach is sometimes best when dealing with everyday troubles. Don't be put off by the playful quality of the spell—it can be quite powerful.

INGREDIENTS/TOOLS:
• Nail polish
• Polish remover
• Cotton balls and/or swabs

BEST TIME TO PERFORM THE SPELL:
• Depends on your intentions

Collect the ingredients needed for this spell. Select one or more bottles of nail polish, in colors that correspond to your intentions: pink or red for love, green or gold for money, and so on. Cast a circle around the area where you will do your spell.

Assign an objective to each toe. You can give all ten toes the same intention or pick ten different goals—or any other combination. Begin painting your toenails in colors that are appropriate to your objectives. As you paint each nail, concentrate on your intention and see it already manifesting. If you like, also decorate your nails with symbols that represent your intentions: dollar signs for money, hearts for love, and so on.

The Modern Guide to Witchcraft

Have fun and be creative. If you make a mistake or change your mind, simply remove the polish and start over.

Allow the polish to dry, and then open the circle. For the next week or so, or for as long as the polish lasts, know that each step you take will bring you closer to your goals.

SAFETY SHIELD FOR YOUR CAR

The average person drives about 12,000 miles each year. That exposes you to plenty of potential delays, accidents, and other problems. This spell protects you from harm whether you're driving your car in your own neighborhood or cross-country.

INGREDIENTS/TOOLS:
- 1 white paper square
- Colored markers
- Amber essential oil
- Tape, glue, or other adhesive

BEST TIME TO PERFORM THE SPELL:
- During the waning moon, preferably when the moon is in Gemini or Sagittarius

Cast a circle around the area where you'll be working. Cut a 4" square of paper. Within this square draw a circle. Write the word *safe* or an affirmation of your choice in the center of the circle. If you wish, add other symbols that represent safety (such as a pentagram) and travel to you. The pattern you've created is your safety shield.

Dot the four corners of the paper with amber essential oil. Open the circle. Attach the shield to the dashboard or window of your car. Each time you get into your car, look at the shield and touch it to activate its protective energies. Visualize yourself and your car surrounded by pure white light, and know that you are protected wherever you go.

MORNING RITUAL

We all engage in daily rituals. Anything that you do each day with awareness is a ritual, from your morning shower to reading in bed before you fall asleep. These rituals provide a sense of stability and continuity in our lives. Now that you are walking a witch's path, you'll naturally want to include magick in your routine.

Part of your morning routine should be writing in your book of shadows as soon as you awaken. While your mind is still fresh, jot down your dreams, first thoughts of the day, your intentions, and so on. In addition to your writing, you may want to come up with a simple ritual that will color the rest of your day. Maybe it's saying an affirmation or offering a blessing. You may only need a few moments of time to transform your morning into a more inspired experience. Here's a suggestion you might want to try:

1. Set a small crystal, a cup or chalice of water, a stick or cone of incense, and an essential oil that you find pleasing on your altar. Take a moment to think about the types of energies that you would like to call upon to influence the unfolding day. Imagine your perfect day and try to form a very clear image of it in your mind. You may have a specific accomplishment in mind. See yourself achieving whatever your heart desires. Imagine yourself doing everything you do throughout the day in a state of joy and satisfaction.
2. Put a small drop of oil on your fingertip and touch your fingertip to your third eye. See yourself bathed in the lovely morning light.
3. Light the incense and let its scent waft over you. Say an affirmation or blessing and focus your intentions for the day.
4. Hold the cup of water up to "toast" the day. Then bring it down to chest level, close to your heart. Dip your fingers in the water, close your eyes, and place a drop of water on each eyelid. Ask that your perception expand so you can see with clarity in all situations.
5. Hold the crystal and project into it your intentions for the day. Ask it to help you stay focused on your purpose throughout the day and to give you strength and determination when you need them.

The Modern Guide to Witchcraft

You may choose to carry the crystal with you throughout the day.

EVENING RITUALS

Twilight is a magickal time. Behind the setting sun's brilliant colors, the mystery of night approaches. You are moving "between the worlds." You'll want to mark the end of the day's activities and your entrance into the world of dreams with a well-crafted ritual. Here's a simple four-element ritual you may wish to use:

1. Begin by reflecting on the day that has just passed. Contemplate the energies you experienced, the things that went as you had hoped, and those you would like to have changed if you had the chance.
2. Place a cup of water and a crystal on your altar. Light a candle. Ask that you receive insight and guidance while you sleep.
3. Light a stick of incense and ask that your prayers rise up with the smoke and be heard by whatever deity you choose.
4. Take a sip of water and affirm that you'll enjoy a peaceful, restful night and awake refreshed in the morning.
5. Hold the crystal to your third eye. Trust that it will protect you throughout the night and anchor your spirit as it travels in the world of dreams. Place the crystal on your bedside table or under your pillow while you sleep.

Waking and Sleeping

You might want to choose different scents, stones, and candle colors for your morning and evening rituals. For example, a clarifying, energizing scent such as citrus, eucalyptus, or carnation could help awaken you to the day's possibilities, whereas lavender or chamomile can relax you at the end of the day. Light a yellow or orange candle in the morning, a blue or indigo one in the evening. A carnelian could jump-start your vitality as you begin the day; a piece of rose quartz or amethyst soothes you so you can sleep better.

Of course, these morning and evening rituals are merely springboards to get you started. In time, you'll develop your own daily rituals that hold special meaning for you and that enrich your days and nights in countless ways. In the next chapter, we'll discuss the eight special days of the magickal year and the rituals many witches and Pagans use to celebrate them.

Chapter 21

THE SEASONS OF THE WITCH

For centuries, earth-honoring cultures have watched the sun as it traveled through the sky (at least so it seems from our vantage point here on earth). Rather than thinking of the year as linear, witches view it as a circle. You'll often hear Wiccans, in particular, refer to it as the Wheel of the Year, and they divide that wheel into eight periods of approximately six weeks each. Each "spoke" in the wheel corresponds to a particular degree in the zodiac and marks a holiday (or holy day) known as a "sabbat." These high-energy days bring special opportunities for performing magick spells and rituals.

The wheel has its roots in the old agricultural festivals that marked the beginnings, peaks, and endings of the seasons. Four of the eight holidays relate to the four great Celtic/Irish fire festivals. Called the "cross-quarter" days, because they mark the midpoint of the seasons, these festivals were known to Pagans as Samhain, Imbolc, Beltane, and Lughnassadh. The four solar festivals—Yule (winter solstice), Ostara (spring equinox), Midsummer or Litha (summer solstice), and Mabon (fall equinox)—celebrate the dates when the sun enters 0 degrees of the cardinal signs of the zodiac: Capricorn, Aries, Cancer, and Libra respectively.

Even before recorded time, our ancestors celebrated these holidays. The ancient stone circles of Great Britain, such as Stonehenge, and the passage tombs of Ireland, such as Newgrange, clearly show that the early people noted the changes in the sun's position throughout the year. The Romans marked the winter solstice with the festivities of Saturnalia; the Greeks observed the Eleusinian mysteries during the fall equinox.

It's no coincidence that many of our modern-day holidays fall close to the dates when the early Greeks, Romans, Celts, and Germanic peoples of northern Europe celebrated these special days. In fact, we still enjoy some of the same customs and festivities as our distant ancestors, as you'll soon see. The Great Wheel is turning, and a magickal journey awaits you.

SAMHAIN

The most holy of the sabbats, Samhain (pronounced SOW-een) is usually observed on the night of October 31, when the sun is in the zodiac sign Scorpio. Better known as Halloween or All Hallow's Eve, this is the holiday people usually associate with witches and magick. Most of the ways the general public marks this sabbat, however, stem from misconceptions—it's a solemn and sacred day for witches, not a time for fear or humor.

The Holiday's Significance

Considered to be the witches' New Year, Samhain begins the Wheel of the Year. Thus, it is a time of death and rebirth. The word *samhain* comes from Irish, meaning "summer's end." In many parts of the Northern Hemisphere the land is barren at this time. The last of the crops have been plowed under for compost, and the earth rests in preparation for spring.

New Year, New Resolutions

Witches often choose to shed old habits or attitudes at this time, replacing them with new ones—similar to how nonwitches make resolutions on January 1. Consider writing on a slip of paper whatever you want to leave behind when the old year dies—fear, self-limiting attitudes, bad habits, and so on. Then burn the paper in a ritual fire to symbolically destroy what you no longer need.

For witches, Samhain is a time to remember and honor loved ones who have passed over to the other side. That's why people associate Halloween with the dead. No, skeletons don't rise from graves, nor do ghosts haunt the living on Samhain, as movies and popular culture tend to portray it. You probably won't be annoyed by uneasy or vengeful spirits, and it's highly unlikely that Grandpa's bones will rattle about in your living room.

Witches may attempt to contact spirits in other realms of existence, however, or request guidance from ancestors or guardians. The origin of the jack-o'-lantern is rooted in the belief that wandering spirits and ghosts turn up on Samhain. The lantern's glow was meant as a beacon so that the spirits of the dearly departed could find their way; the terrible faces carved on the pumpkins were meant to frighten away evil spirits.

Southwestern witches sometimes combine features from the Mexican Day of the Dead with Celtic Pagan customs on Samhain. People decorate their altars to mark the sabbat, often displaying photos of deceased loved ones. During the week before Samhain, they go house to house, visiting the altars of friends and relatives, saying prayers and paying respects. You, too, might wish to honor the memories of your deceased loved ones by placing photos, mementos, and offerings on your altar during Samhain.

Because the veil that separates the seen and unseen worlds is thinnest at Samhain, it's easier to communicate with beings on the other side at this time. You might also want to pull out your tarot cards or crystal ball during Samhain, to see what lies ahead in your future.

Psychic Babies

In earlier times, babies born on Samhain were thought to possess psychic power and could predict the future. No surprise, really, if you consider that these kids are Scorpios, and people born under this zodiac sign are notoriously perceptive and intuitive.

Ways to Celebrate Samhain

What would Halloween be without colorful costumes? This practice stems from the early custom of making wishes on Samhain, similar to making New Year's resolutions. Wearing a costume is a powerful magick spell, a visual affirmation of your goals. No witch would portray herself as a hobo or ghost! Instead, try dressing up as the person you'd like to be in the coming year in order to tap the magickal energies of this sabbat.

Samhain Spell to Free Yourself

Do you feel burdened or trapped by old beliefs, habits, or relationships? Now's the time to release yourself from figurative chains that may be holding you back. This spell breaks old bonds and sets you free to enjoy a happier life.

INGREDIENTS/TOOLS:
- A ball of red yarn (cotton or wool, no synthetics)
- An athame (or kitchen knife)
- A cauldron (or pot)
- Matches or a lighter

Cut the yarn into 9" pieces. Knot the ends together, forming a circle. Give each one a label, something in your life that you feel is holding you back. Perhaps it is a past hurt or a regret that you have been dwelling on. Cut as many pieces as you need. Slip them around your wrist and tell each of them specifically:

"[What you want to release], I have carried you long and far.
Your burden has been my teacher, and I accept your lessons.
Now I summon the strength to release you,
For your presence serves me no longer."

With your athame, begin cutting through the circlets. This might take a while, as an athame isn't normally sharp—your persistence is part of the spell. As you cut away your symbolic bonds, imagine yourself separating from your actual bonds. When you finish, burn the yarn in your cauldron, saying, "You are now consumed by the flames of transformation. You no longer bind me. Away you go, so that something new and blessed in me shall grow."

When the flames die and the cauldron cools, take it outside. (If your cauldron is too heavy to carry, scoop the ashes into something smaller.)

The Modern Guide to Witchcraft

Stand with the wind at your back and release the ashes into the air. As they blow away, prepare yourself to make a new start.

WINTER SOLSTICE OR YULE

The winter solstice occurs when the sun reaches 0 degrees of the zodiac sign Capricorn, usually around December 21. This is the shortest day of the year in the Northern Hemisphere. The word *solstice* comes from the Latin *sol stetit*, which literally means "sun stands still." Also known as Yule, the holiday marks the turning point in the sun's descent into darkness; from this point, the days grow steadily longer for a period of six months. Thus, witches celebrate this sabbat as a time of renewal and hope.

The Holiday's Significance

Pagan mythology describes the apparent passage of the sun through the heavens each year as the journey of the Sun King, who drives his bright chariot across the sky. In pre-Christian Europe and Britain, the winter solstice celebrated the Sun King's birth. This beloved deity brought light into the world during the darkest time of all.

It's easy to see parallels between the Old Religion's myth and the Christmas story. You can also see the theme expressed in the custom of lighting candles during Hanukkah and Kwanzaa, both of which fall near the winter solstice. In these religious practices, light symbolizes blessings, joy, and promise. However, the Yuletide celebration goes back even further, to the ancient Roman observance of Saturnalia, the festival of the Roman deity Mithras, which was held from December 17 until December 25. The cult of *Sol Invictus*, or "invincible sun," with which Mithras is often associated, may have predated the Romans by several hundred years.

Ways to Celebrate Yule

Before the Victorian era, Christians didn't decorate their homes at Christmas with ornamented pine trees and holiday greenery. That's a Pagan custom. Because evergreen trees retain their needles even during the cold winter months, they symbolize the triumph of life over death. Holly was sacred to the Druids. According to Celtic mythology, holly bushes afforded shelter for the earth spirits during the wintertime. The Druids valued mistletoe as an herb of fertility and immortality. It has long been used in talismans as an aphrodisiac—perhaps that's the reason we kiss beneath it today.

The Magickal Origins of the Christmas Tree

Magick trees show up in lots of contemporary stories and films; some of the best known include the Evil Talking Trees in *The Wonderful Wizard of Oz*, Treebeard in *Lord of the Rings*, the Tree of Life in *Avatar*, and Mother Willow in *Pocahontas*. But the concept of enchanted trees dates back to ancient times. In early Germanic and Norse cultures, people believed the King of the Forest made his home in a fir tree. Others thought benevolent nature spirits lived in firs. People danced around magick fir trees and decorated them with painted eggs, charms, and flowers. Quite possibly, Christmas trees have their origin in this old tradition.

Burning the Yule log is another ancient tradition by which Pagans mark the winter solstice. On the eve of Yule, witches build a fire from the wood of nine sacred trees. The central element in the Yule fire is usually an oak log, for the oak tree represents strength and longevity (although you can use any wood). The fire symbolizes the sun's return. After the fire burns down, anyone who wishes may collect ashes and wrap them in a piece of cloth. If you place the package under your pillow, you'll receive dreams that provide guidance and advice for the coming year. Tradition says you should save a portion of the Yule log and use it to kindle the fire the following year.

Harvesting your Yule log is a ritual in itself. If you live in the country in a wooded area, you may find just the right log lying dead on the ground. If you take a cutting from a live tree, do so with humility and clear intention. Ask for the tree's permission before you start cutting and leave a symbolic offering (such as a special crystal or an herbal charm) in its place. Select your Yule log long before the winter solstice because it will need some time to dry in order for it to burn properly.

Before you light your Yule log, cast a circle large enough to encompass your home and call in the guardians of the four directions (as discussed in Chapter 9). If you don't have a working fireplace or wood stove, you can place four candles in fireproof candleholders at the four directions and light them instead. Adapt the basic method to fit the season, as follows:

"Guardians of the east, we greet the dawn of the shortest day. We beckon you to join us in our celebration of the returning light and new beginnings. May the spirits of air bless us with the winds of winter. Hail and welcome!

"Guardians of the south, we honor the return of your radiant light. The lengthening of days is upon us. May the spirits of fire bless our home and hearth. Hail and welcome!

"Guardians of the west, the sun retreats to you and brings us to the longest night. You spirits of water, who take many forms, bless us with your purity and grace. Hail and welcome!

"Guardians of the north, yours is the place of all endings. In the depths of darkness, we dance upon the sleeping earth and ask for your blessing tonight. Hail and welcome!"

Light candles on your table and altar. Enjoy a special Yule feast either alone or with companions as you watch the fire and candles burn. Share gifts with your companions, such as the good luck charm that follows. When you've finished, release the directions, open the circle, and extinguish the candles and fire.

Yule Good Luck Charm

Would you like to help your friends and loved ones by increasing their good luck throughout the coming year? This Yuletide custom lets you make a unique magickal gift for everyone on your list.

INGREDIENTS/TOOLS:
- A Yule log
- Matches or a lighter
- A cloth drawstring pouch for each person on your gift list
- Dried pink rose petals (for love)
- Dried lavender buds (for peace of mind)
- Dried basil (for protection)
- Dried mint leaves (for prosperity)
- Dried echinacea (for health)
- A sheet of paper
- Scissors
- A pen

BEST TIME TO PERFORM THE SPELL:
- Yule (usually December 21)

On the night of the winter solstice, build a Yule fire in a safe place and burn an oak log in it. The next morning when the ashes have cooled, scoop some into each pouch. Add the dried botanicals. Cut the sheet of paper into slips, one for each person on your list. Write a personalized wish on each slip of paper. Fold the papers three times and add them to the pouches. Tie the pouches closed and give them to your loved ones.

IMBOLC, BRIGID'S DAY, OR CANDLEMAS

This sabbat honors Brigid, the beloved Celtic goddess of healing, smithcraft, and poetry. A favorite of the Irish people, Brigid was adopted by the Church and canonized as Saint Brigid when Christianity moved into Ireland. Her holiday begins on the evening of January 31 and concludes on February 2, although some witches celebrate it around February 5, when the sun reaches 15 degrees of Aquarius. This marks the midpoint between the winter solstice and the spring equinox.

In the Northern Hemisphere, daylight is increasing and the promise of spring is in the air. We begin to notice the first stirrings of new life. Therefore, Imbolc is considered a time of hope and renewal.

The Holiday's Significance

Brigid's association with the fires of the hearth and the forge represent both the strengthening of the sun's light and creativity. Brigid is one of the fertility goddesses, and Imbolc means "in the belly." In agrarian cultures, this is the time when baby animals grow in their mothers' wombs. This holiday honors all forms of creativity, of the mind as well as the body. Illustrations of Brigid sometimes show her stirring a great cauldron, the witch's magick tool that symbolizes the womb and the receptive, fertile nature of the Divine Feminine. As the goddess of inspiration, Brigid encourages everyone, regardless of gender, to stir the inner cauldron of creativity that exists within.

Ways to Celebrate Imbolc

Witches celebrate this spoke in the Wheel of the Year as a reaffirmation of life and a time to plant "seeds" for the future. In keeping with the holiday's theme of fire, you can light candles to honor Brigid. Fill your cauldron with soil or kitty litter. The cauldron symbolizes the womb of the Goddess. Take nine tapered candles and "plant" them into the "earth" in a spiral pattern, beginning in the center and continuing in a clockwise direction. With each candle, contemplate a different aspect of Imbolc:

1. Light the candle in the middle first, picturing light penetrating winter's darkness.
2. As you light the second candle, welcome the approaching spring.
3. Think of the possibilities contained in new life and new beginnings as you light the third candle.
4. With the fourth candle, imagine your own "rebirth" and your relationship to the Divine Mother.
5. As you light the fifth candle, consider the lessons your spiritual path has taught you. Give thanks for challenges met and knowledge gained.
6. The sixth candle represents the unknown, the lessons that lie before you and all the things you have yet to learn.

7. Light the seventh candle and meditate on things you wish to change. They can be mental, physical, emotional, or spiritual. Think of how you can use your magick to make positive changes in your life.

8. The eighth candle represents the things you wish to heal. These might be physical ailments, the suffering of the planet, rifts in relationships, and so on. Make room for the healing to begin within you. Release old wounds and past hurts. Take responsibility for your health. Focus on the best possible outcomes for situations that are beyond your control or influence.

9. As you light the ninth and final candle, welcome inspiration into your life. Sing or play music. Write a poem in Brigid's honor. Paint a picture. Even if you don't think you are particularly artistic, use the energy of the season and enjoy the creative process. Fashion a special charm or a new blend of incense. Whatever your chosen method of expression, ask the Goddess to inspire you and lend her beauty to your work.

SPRING EQUINOX OR OSTARA

Pagans and witches celebrate Ostara when the sun enters 0 degrees of Aries, around March 21. In the Northern Hemisphere, the spring equinox ushers in warmer weather, days that are longer than nights, and life reawakening. Birdsong fills the air and new buds sprout on bare tree limbs; baby animals are born and the greening of the earth begins.

Christianity adopted this joyful period of the year for the celebration of Easter (which usually falls near the spring equinox). Ostara gets its name from the German fertility goddess Ostare; the word *Easter* derives from the same root. Both holidays celebrate the triumph of life over death.

The Holiday's Significance

The spring equinox marks the first day of spring and the start of the busy planting season in agrarian cultures. Farmers till their fields and sow seeds. Ostara, therefore, is one of the fertility holidays and a time for planting seeds—literally or figuratively. Because day and night are the same length on the equinoxes, these holidays also signify balance.

Ways to Celebrate Ostara

On Ostara, sow seeds that you want to bear fruit in the coming months. This is an ideal time to launch new career ventures, move to a new home, or begin a new relationship. If you're a gardener, you'll start preparing the soil and planting flowers, herbs, and/or vegetables now. Consider the magickal properties of botanicals and choose plants that represent your intentions (see Chapter 11). If you don't have room for a garden, you could plant seeds in a flowerpot to symbolize wishes you hope will grow to fruition in the coming months.

Origins of the Easter Bunny

In an old German story, a rabbit laid some sacred eggs and decorated them as a gift for the fertility goddess Ostara. Ostara liked the beautiful eggs so much that she asked the rabbit to share the eggs with everyone throughout the world.

Some popular Easter customs have their roots in Ostara's symbolism. Eggs represent the promise of new life, and painting them bright colors engages the creative aspect of the sabbat. Some cultures connect the egg's golden yolk with the sun. You might enjoy decorating eggs with magickal symbols, such as pentagrams and spirals. Rabbits, of course, have long been linked with fertility.

Decorating Eggs for Ostara

Ukrainian folk art gives us some of the best examples of ritual egg decoration. Two main types of decoration are called *krashanka* and *pysanka*. *Krashanka* (plural *krashanky*) comes from the word *kraska*, meaning "color" and refers to an egg dyed a single brilliant hue. Believed to possess magickal powers, these eggs were usually eaten. People placed the shells under haystacks or stashed them in the thatched roofs of their homes as protective charms against high winds. *Krashanky* were also used for healing physical ailments. A sick person might wear a whole *krashanka* on a string around his neck, or place the egg on the infected part of the body as a cure.

Pysanky (plural of *pysanka*), which comes from the word *pysaty* meaning "to write," involves decorating the egg with a variety of symbols and a wide array of colors. Believed to provide protection against fire and lightning, these eggs were displayed in the home, carried as talismans, and exchanged as gifts. An old folk legend claimed that *pysanky* ruled the very fate of the world. Only *pysanky* could stem the flood of evil that threatened the earth, and if people ever gave up the custom a vicious monster would consume the world.

You can create your own magick *krashanky* by hard-boiling some eggs. Make natural vegetable dyes from red cabbage (for red dye), beets (purple), yellow onion skins (yellow), carrots (orange), and spinach (green). Combine chopped dye material with a quart of water and boil. Strain the liquid into a jar and add 2 tablespoons of white vinegar to set the dye.

Soak the eggs in the color of your choice, making sure that the liquid covers the eggs completely. The longer the eggs soak, the deeper the color will be; however, they will not be nearly as dark as the dye liquid itself. For the most intense color, allow the eggs to soak overnight in the refrigerator. Be careful when handling freshly dyed eggs, as some of the dye will rub off.

After you eat the eggs, burn the shells in a ritual fire or cast them into flowing water—it's bad luck to just toss them in the trash.

To make a *pysanka*, pierce both ends of the egg and carefully blow out the contents. With a wax crayon, draw magick symbols and images on the shell. Then immerse the egg in the dye—the wax will prevent the dye from adhering to the marked portions of the egg. The wax designs will be lighter and will stand out against the darker background. When you are satisfied with your work, allow the shell to dry completely. You can then remove the wax by warming the eggshell in an oven for a few minutes, then wiping the wax off with a paper towel.

BELTANE

Witches usually celebrate Beltane on May 1, although some prefer to mark it around May 5, when the sun reaches 15 degrees of Taurus. Flowers bloom and plants begin sprouting in the fields. Bees carry pollen from blossom to aromatic blossom. The sabbat is named for the god Baal or Bel, sometimes called "the bright one." In Scottish Gaelic, the word *bealtainn* means "fires of Belos" and refers to the bonfires Pagans light on this sabbat. This ancient holiday has been adopted as May Day, and some of Beltane's old rituals (*sans* the overt sexuality) are still enacted today.

The Holiday's Significance

The second fertility holiday in the Wheel of the Year, Beltane coincides with a period of fruitfulness. To ancient and modern Pagans alike, this holiday honors the earth and all of nature. In early agrarian cultures, farmers built fires on Beltane and led livestock between the flames to increase their fertility. The tradition of the Beltane fires survived in Wales until the 1840s; in Ireland, the practice continued into the mid-twentieth century; and in Scotland to this very day, the Beltane Fire Society holds an annual bonfire.

Sexuality is also celebrated on this sabbat—the Great Rite (the sacred union of God and Goddess) has traditionally been part of the holiday's festivities. In pre-Christian days, Beltane celebrants engaged in sexual intercourse in the fields as a form of symbolic magick to encourage fertility and a bountiful harvest. Children who were conceived at this time were said to belong to the Goddess.

Ways to Celebrate Beltane

It's best to celebrate Beltane outside in order to appreciate nature's fullness. Because Beltane is a fertility holiday, many of its rituals contain sexual symbolism. The Maypole, around which young females dance, is an obvious phallic symbol. Witches often decorate the Maypole with flowers in recognition of the earth's beauty and fruitfulness. Sometimes a woman who seeks a partner will toss a circular garland over the top of the pole, signifying the sex act, as a way of asking the Goddess to send her a lover. You may also choose to write wishes on colorful ribbons and tie them on a tree.

Another fertility ritual utilizes the cauldron, symbol of the womb. Women who wish to become pregnant build a small fire in the cauldron, then jump over it. If you prefer, you can leap over the cauldron to spark creativity in the mind instead of the body.

Beltane's connection with the earth and fullness makes this sabbat an ideal time to perform prosperity magick. Incorporate peppermint, parsley, lavender, alfalfa, cedar, or money plant into your spells. This is also a good time to make offerings of food and wine to Mother Earth and the nature spirits.

SUMMER SOLSTICE OR MIDSUMMER

In the Northern Hemisphere, the summer solstice is the longest day of the year. The Sun King has now reached the highest point in his journey through the heavens. Witches generally celebrate Midsummer around June 21, when the sun enters 0 degrees of the zodiac sign Cancer. This is a time of abundance, when the earth puts forth her bounty.

The Holiday's Significance

In early agrarian cultures, Midsummer marked a period of plenty when food was abundant and life was easy. Our ancestors celebrated this joyful holiday with feasting and revelry. At this point, however, the sun has reached its pinnacle and begins its descent once again.

Folklore says that at Midsummer earth spirits abound—this belief inspired Shakespeare's delightful play *A Midsummer Night's Dream*. If you wish, you can commune with the elementals and fairies at this time. Our ancestors regarded Midsummer's Eve as a time of intense magick, especially for casting love spells. Any herbs gathered at midnight on Midsummer's Eve were believed to have unparalleled potency.

Ways to Celebrate Midsummer

Just as they've done for centuries, witches today celebrate the summer solstice with feasting, music, dancing, and thanksgiving. Remember to share your bounty with the animals, too, and to return something to Mother Earth as a sign of gratitude.

Midsummer is also a good time to collect herbs, flowers, and other plants to use in magick spells. Some say that if you wish to become invisible, you must wear an amulet that includes seeds from forest ferns gathered on Midsummer's Eve. Spells for success, recognition, and fulfillment are best done on the summer solstice, too.

Candle Spell to Mark Midsummer
Candles represent the sun and the fire element, so burning them at the sun's peak is a common way to mark the holiday.

INGREDIENTS/TOOLS:
- 3 candles: 1 red, 1 orange, and 1 yellow
- Cinnamon or sandalwood essential oil
- 3 candleholders
- The Sun card from a tarot deck
- Matches or a lighter

On Midsummer's Eve, dress the candles with the essential oil and fit them in their holders. Arrange the candles in a triangle pattern with the point facing you, on your altar or another place where they can burn safely. Lay the Sun card face up in the center of the triangle. Light the candles. The Sun card represents fulfillment, abundance, recognition and respect, creative energy, and all the good things in life.

As you stand in front of your altar, feel the message of this card being directed toward you and visualize yourself absorbing all that it symbolizes. Sense the candle flames illuminating you and increasing your power on every level. Imagine yourself radiating with the sun's bright light. Stand this way for as long as you like, allowing the fiery force to fill you. When you feel ready, snuff out the candles and pick up the tarot card. Slip it in your pocket. Wherever you go, whatever you do the next day, you'll shine like the sun and enjoy the fullness of Midsummer.

LUGHNASSADH OR LAMMAS
Named for the Irish Celtic god Lugh (Lew in Wales), this holiday is celebrated either on August 1 or around August 5, when the sun reaches 15 degrees of Leo. This cross-quarter day falls halfway between the summer solstice and the fall equinox. According to Celtic mythology, Lugh

is an older and wiser personification of the god Baal or Bel (for whom Beltane is named). Lughnassadh (pronounced LOO-na-saad) is the first of the harvest festivals. The early Christians dubbed the holiday Lammas, meaning "loaf-mass," because the grain was cut at this time of the year and made into bread.

The Holiday's Significance

Corn, wheat, and other grains are typically harvested around Lughnassadh. In agrarian cultures, this was the time to begin preparing for the barren winter months that lay ahead. Our ancestors cut, ground, and stored grain, canned fruit and vegetables, and brewed wine and beer in late summer. The old English song "John Barleycorn Must Die" describes the seasonal ritual of rendering grain into ale.

Early Pagans sold their wares at harvest fairs and held athletic competitions at this time of the year. You can see this age-old tradition carried on today at country fairs throughout rural parts of the United States.

Ways to Celebrate Lughnassadh

Today, witches enjoy sharing bread and beer with friends on Lughnassadh, just as they've done for centuries. You might like to bake fresh bread from scratch or even brew your own beer as part of the celebration. While you're kneading the bread, add a dried bean to the dough. When you serve the bread, whoever gets the bean in his piece will be granted a wish.

If you like, you can fashion a doll from corn, wheat, or straw to represent the Sun King. To symbolize the time of year when his powers are waning, burn the effigy in a ritual fire as an offering to Mother Earth. The custom of decorating your home with dried corncobs, gourds, nuts, and other fruits of the harvest is also connected to Lughnassadh.

AUTUMN EQUINOX OR MABON

The autumn equinox usually occurs on or about September 22, when the sun reaches 0 degrees of Libra. Once again, day and night are of equal length, signifying a time of balance, equality, and harmony. Mabon is also a harvest festival, and witches consider it a time for giving thanks for the abundance Mother Earth has provided.

The Holiday's Significance

This sabbat marks the last spoke in the Wheel of the Year. From this day until the winter solstice, the Sun King's path arcs downward toward earth. As the days grow shorter and the cold, barren winter approaches, witches reflect on the joys and sorrows, successes and failures of the year that is nearing its conclusion. Like all harvest festivals, this is also a time to give thanks for the year's bounty and to recognize the fruits of your labors.

Mabon is a good time to do magick spells that involve decrease or endings. Do you want to let go of self-destructive beliefs or behaviors? Lose weight? End an unfulfilling relationship? Now is the time to break old habits and patterns that have been limiting you. Anything you wish to eliminate from your life can now be released safely, before the New Year begins with Samhain.

Ways to Celebrate Mabon

Because the equinox is a time of balance, try to balance yin and yang, active and passive on this day. Seek rest and activity, solitude and socializing in equal portions. Mabon marks the sun's entrance into the zodiac sign Libra, which astrologers connect with peace, diplomacy, harmony, and balance. Are you at odds with someone? If so, this is a good time to make peace. Is something causing you stress? Use the energy of this special day to find ways—magickal and/or practical—to ease that stress and restore balance in your life.

As our planet continues revolving in a great wheel around the sun, the seasons of the witch keep you attuned to the earth and the sky—even if you live in a high-rise in the middle of a city. They also link you to the past, the traditions of your ancestors, and the ongoing circle of birth, death, and rebirth.

Chapter 22

WHERE DO YOU GO FROM HERE?

As you can see from what we've touched upon in this book, the world of magick is vast and complex. Countless books have been written about magick, and more are published every day. Movies and television shows, no matter how silly, reflect a growing interest in magick. Now that witchcraft and wizardry have come out of the closet and people around the world are sharing their wisdom openly, the field will continue to grow ever richer. Everyone's experiences contribute to the development of the whole. Each witch is a torchbearer whose flame, when joined with others', lights up the world.

If you've managed to finish reading this book, you're surely ready for more. Maybe you're trying to decide which magickal path suits you best—the simplicity and earthiness of kitchen and hedge witchery, the drama of ceremonial magick, or something else? Maybe you're wondering if you should become part of a larger group or continue studying and practicing alone. The ever-expanding circle of witches worldwide provides opportunities to share your ideas with a supportive community and to align your abilities with other witches and magicians. You can even join an online coven. This chapter will help you decide what's best for you, at least for now.

SOLITARY WITCHCRAFT: IS IT RIGHT FOR YOU?

Some witches choose to work alone rather than with a group. Perhaps no coven is available in her community, or she may prefer to follow solitary practice because it suits her particular purposes, temperament, or lifestyle. Some people may work alone for a period, and then join a coven for a period, or vice versa. Witches who don't belong to a coven may still gather with "kindred spirits" to celebrate the sabbats or other events, in a sort of extended Circle.

For seasoned witches, a solitary path may be simply a matter of choice. For the beginner, however, working alone can be, well, lonely. It can also be more difficult to stumble along by yourself, instead of being guided by more experienced colleagues. Unfortunately, most of us didn't have the opportunity to learn from experts as children. On the other hand, a solitary pursuit enables you to develop your own style of magickal expression, rather than taking on the ideology or outward form of an established group.

As a solitary witch—especially if you're just starting out—some guidelines can help you proceed safely and successfully:

- Read lots of books by different authors, to gain a variety of insights and perspectives.
- Meditate regularly to improve your mental focus and your connection with your higher self.
- Set a schedule for yourself that makes magickal study and practice part of your everyday life, just like working out at the gym.
- Apply what you learn—study alone won't make you a witch.
- Start with simple rituals and spells, then work up to more complicated ones.
- Don't get discouraged if something doesn't turn out the way you'd planned; try to determine what went wrong and why, and learn from your mistakes.
- Practice, practice, practice. Magick is like every other skill—the more you do it, the better you get.
- Keep a grimoire of your experiences.

The Modern Guide to Witchcraft

After you've spent time studying and practicing on your own, you'll have a better idea of what type of magick appeals to you and which path you want to follow. At some point, you may decide to find a teacher or a group of like-minded individuals to work with. Working with a teacher can help you advance more quickly and may steer you away from some pitfalls along the way. Good teachers tend to be selective about the students they take on. If you can show that you've done your homework through solitary study, you'll have a better chance of convincing a teacher to help you reach the next level. Remember the old saying, "When the student is ready, the teacher will appear."

Witchcraft tends to appeal to people who dislike hierarchy and rigid dogma. In the past, witches often lived apart from the community they served, and even if people valued their wisdom and healing powers, the witches never quite fit in. Many modern witches were raised in patriarchal religions that didn't encourage free thinking; they have chosen Wicca (or another Pagan path) because it allows them to follow their own truth.

WHAT'S THE SCOOP ON COVENS?

The word *coven* originated from the Latin term *coventus*, meaning "assembly" or "agreement." (Covenant comes from the same root.) The term first appeared in Scotland around the 1500s to denote a witches' meeting or a local group of practicing witches. However, the word was rarely used until the modern witchcraft movement became more public and popularized.

In her book *The Spiral Dance*, Starhawk describes a coven as "a Witch's support group, consciousness-raising group, psychic study center, clergy-training program, College of Mysteries, surrogate clan, and religious congregation all rolled into one." That about sums it up. In short, a coven is a spiritual family in which each member is committed to the principles of the Craft and to one another.

It's nice to have "kinfolk" with whom you can share information about magick and your spiritual beliefs. Covens provide an opportunity for learning on all levels. It's also fun to celebrate meaningful holidays and events with people who feel as you do. In a world that still doesn't completely accept witches and magick, a coven brings you into a community where you can feel safe, accepted, and valued. Furthermore, the power a group can raise when working together far exceeds what one witch could muster alone.

The Magick Number Thirteen

A traditional coven has thirteen members, although some groups may choose to include more or fewer. Keeping the group small enables intimacy to grow among members and reduces the likelihood of developing into a pack of disciples led by a guru. Why thirteen? A year contains thirteen lunar months. Witchcraft is closely aligned with the moon and its feminine energy.

As you can well imagine, a group of independent-minded witches will likely have lots of differing opinions, ideas, and objectives. At times things can get pretty complicated. Some covens split up over trivial matters; others work through problems and find solutions. If you decide to become part of a coven, you'll want to ask yourself if you are willing to devote the effort necessary to make the coven work. Being part of something greater than yourself requires cooperation, respect, and tolerance.

Benefits of Working with a Coven

You can learn a lot—about magick and life—through working with a coven, especially a well-established one. In particular, you will have the opportunity to:

- Learn what modern magick really is, versus popular ideas and misrepresentations
- Discover the history of a specific magickal tradition
- Receive instruction on how to meditate and focus your mind effectively (in a group setting)
- Learn how to raise and direct energy through group spells and rituals
- Develop a closer relationship with deities that the coven considers important to its purposes
- Receive guidance on how to select your magick tools and use them effectively

Unless the group is eclectic, these points will be explained to you before you get involved. Usually, you'll have a chance to get to know the witches in a group and to work with them for a while before you (and they) decide if you should become a member.

Coven Culture

The best covens are made up of individuals who take their responsibility to the group seriously. You want a group whose practices honor both the individual and the group.

Consider the coven's traditions. Some covens follow specific "lineages" and ideologies, such as Celtic or Egyptian, Dianic or Alexandrian. If a coven holds to a particular tradition that doesn't interest you or makes you feel uncomfortable, you're in the wrong place. Ask yourself the following questions:

- What kind of attendance and study requirements are expected of you?
- Do these mesh with your schedule and responsibilities?
- Does the group have a specific initiation ritual? What is it like? Is there anything in that ritual that doesn't fit your vision?
- Does the group require secrecy? If so, what's the reason behind it and how hush-hush is everything?

Ask to attend an open Circle, celebration, or other function before you consider membership. This will allow you to observe how the coven operates and how the people involved interact.

Only you can determine whether joining a coven is right for you, and if it is, which coven best suits your objectives. Take your time. Bear in mind that every group will have its strengths, weaknesses, and idiosyncrasies—that's part of being human. Find a group with whom you feel a common bond and focus on the big picture; the nitpicky stuff you can work on over time.

FINDING A COVEN THAT'S RIGHT FOR YOU

After you've carefully considered the pros and cons of joining a coven, and decide to take the next step, how do you go about finding a group to join? It's not as if covens are listed in the Yellow Pages! You can, however, discover a wealth of resources and information online. The first place to look is *www.witchvox.com*. Since 1997, "The Witches' Voice" has provided a forum for Neopagans around the world, including news, information, services, festivals, and a list of covens.

You may find a coven in your own hometown, or at least in your state. Get in touch with a group's contact person—she should be able to give you more information about groups and gatherings. If none exists in your area, you could connect with one of the many online covens and Pagan groups.

Also check bulletin boards at bookstores, health food cooperatives, yoga centers, and New Age shops. A nearby Unity or Unitarian Universalist Church could steer you in the right direction—it may even provide space for Circles and other spiritual events.

Leaders and Members

If you're lucky, you'll find several groups to choose from. Pay particular attention to two key points: the aptitude of the leaders and the cohesiveness of the membership. These two factors can make or break a coven.

The best leaders don't seem to need titles. They are skilled facilitators, communicators, and diplomats. They remain sensitive to the individuals and to the greater whole. They teach, inspire, and motivate the members of the coven. When deciding between covens, ask yourself whether the leaders have these qualities and whether they have earned the respect of the coven for their wisdom, responsibility, openness, and consistency.

The best members are those who work together for the greater good, placing their individual preferences and desires second to the group's. They are dedicated to the group's goals and the magickal tradition to which they belong. They support and encourage one another, and refrain from gossiping, criticizing, or bickering among themselves.

The witches you want to work with will welcome you into the collective and respect you, without judging or trying to control you. They'll willingly share information with you and seek your input.

Cautions and Caveats

You'll want to keep in mind these things when considering a coven. If you see any of these warning signs, don't get near 'em with a ten-foot pole!

1. Any group that says you *must* do something in a particular way, even if it goes against your personal taboos or moral guidelines, is not for you.
2. Seeing members grovel before the coven's leader should raise a red flag. A leader needs help and assistance, but should not order members around like servants.
3. Be wary of any coven that charges dues for membership, unless there is a valid reason for fees, such as renting a place to gather (and proper accounting is in place). Most witches believe that learning should be free. It's okay to ask for help with the gas, or munchies for a meeting, but there's a huge difference between this and making a fast buck off someone's spiritual thirst.
4. A group whose members brag about their numbers, consider themselves all-powerful, or claim a 100-percent success rate in their magick isn't worth your time.

Many spiritual groups have been guilty of these problems—not just witches. Spiritual hubris is one of the most seductive and destructive forms of arrogance. Of course, witches aren't ego free, nor are they enlightened beings. They are humans, trying their best to become better people every day in every way.

Joining a Coven

If you have found your ideal coven and would like to join, the next step is to have an old-fashioned chat with the group's leader. Tell him or her of your interest and what attracted you to this particular coven. Ask if the coven is open to new members and how to go about getting more involved. Find out when they hold initiations. The initiation process will vary from group to group, but in any case you'll probably have some studying ahead of you and some things to learn before an actual initiation occurs.

Start thinking ahead. What role do you see for yourself in this group? Do you seek a specific function that utilizes your skills and talents? If, for example, you're a musician you might enjoy playing at rituals. Or, if you're a good writer, perhaps you could create some specialized spells, incantations, or rituals for the group.

This attitude will show your sincerity—and that you're thinking in terms of the group and not just about yourself. Also, it will help you define your place in the coven if and when you choose to take the next step (initiation).

Initiation Into a Coven

The initiation is a very important moment of bonding. At this stage, coven members extend their Circle, in all its quirky intimacy, to another person. Every person in the group should be present for this activity.

Each coven will enact its own, unique initiation ritual, even though there may be similarities from group to group. The ritual reflects the philosophy, traditions, objectives, and orientation of the group.

Welcoming Ceremony

One nice welcoming ritual involves braiding or knotting yarn to symbolize that the new member's path is tied in with the rest of the coven. The initiate brings a length of yarn, which is tied into the bundle created by the current members. In some cases, the coven's priest or priestess will keep the bundle or wear it as a belt as a sign of office.

At the time of initiation, new members can choose the magickal names they wish to use in sacred space. They then go to each person present, introduce themselves by that name, and greet them as brothers or sisters in the Craft (perhaps with a kiss on the cheek or a hug). Some covens have degrees of initiation and you may progress to higher levels in time.

If, down the road, you find you've made the wrong choice, there's nothing to prevent you from leaving a coven. Although covens would like people to stay for a while for the sake of continuity, witches recognize that each individual's path changes over time. Try to part on good terms. As witches say: "Merry meet, merry part, and merry meet again!"

FORMING YOUR OWN COVEN

Sometimes you can't find an existing coven that meets your needs. Or you may have belonged to a coven, but over time things have changed and it's time to try something else. If you don't wish to be solitary, you might consider forming your own group.

Remember, this isn't a social club, it's a spiritually mindful group and establishing it should be done with sincerity. Sometimes people form covens for the wrong reasons (for instance, to show off to friends or weird out their parents). Do some preliminary soul-searching—you really need to know yourself and be honest about your intentions.

Getting Down to Details

If you've determined this is the right move for you, decide how many people you want to be involved. Thirteen is the traditional number of witches in a coven, but you don't have to follow that custom. Set a reasonable limit on membership. Quantity is less important than quality—in fact, a large quantity may diminish quality.

Next, ask yourself what kind of coven you want. Do you intend to focus on a specific magickal tradition? Do you want your group to be religious or secular? Do you want a rotating leadership or one defined leader? How will you choose the leader(s)? In other words, consider all the factors that will define and flesh out your group. These guidelines will make it easier for others to decide whether your coven is right for them.

Here are some other things to consider:

- How will authority and responsibility be handled?
- Will your coven work magick for magick's sake, or will you bring religious aspects into your group?
- Where and when will you meet?
- Will you have requirements about how many meetings a year a person must attend to remain a member?
- Will you have study requirements?
- Will members participate in activities together outside the coven setting?

- Do you plan to keep a book of shadows for your group (and if so, how and where will it be maintained)?
- Will you need to have specific tools or clothing for your coven meetings?
- What festivals will you observe?
- What other types of gatherings do you want to hold (for instance, to respond to a member's personal needs)?
- What types of members' personal problems should the coven avoid getting involved in?
- How will someone attain the role of priest or priestess in your group?
- Who will make the decisions? Will you run your coven democratically, or will the leader's word be the final authority in matters?

After you've ironed out these details, politely approach individuals you think might be interested. Talk over what you envision and listen carefully to the way each person responds. It's okay for them to ask questions. If they don't, you should be worried. Nonetheless, somewhere at the bottom line, their vision of the group has to mesh with yours, or there are going to be problems.

Moving Forward with Your Group

Once you've found a core group, the next stage is the "shake 'n' bake" period. Consider setting a time period (for example, a year and a day) before anyone is considered a full, formal member of the coven (and before she's initiated into the group). This trial period gives everyone a chance to see if the relationships between the members work. It also allows time to learn the skills necessary for working magick together. Rome wasn't built in a day, and neither is a good coven.

During this growing stage, try out a variety of rituals, spells, and meditations together, keeping notes in your book of shadows about each event. Find out what sensual cues work best for everyone. Note what goes really wrong, and what goes really right. Review these notes regularly.

At the end of the trial period, everyone should sit down together and powwow. Discuss your accomplishments. Talk about what has and has not worked. Ask each person if he or she would like to continue in a more formalized manner. If the answer is yes, great! If not, separate as friends and spiritual helpmates. Just because you're not working magick together doesn't mean your friendship will end.

Those who decide to move forward now have an even greater task ahead, that of keeping things going. Establish a line of authority and really start organizing. And, of course, it's time to start formally meeting as a coven.

LIVING A MAGICKAL LIFE

As Donald Michael Kraig writes in his book *Modern Magick*, "Magick is not something you do, magick is something you are." Once you shift your way of thinking from mundane to magickal, you'll never see the world as you did before. Now, when you walk into a building, you'll sense its vibrations. Gemstones won't be just pretty baubles; instead, you'll see them as life forms that can aid you in your spellwork. Dreams will no longer be nightly happenstances, but messages from your inner self.

Magickal awareness brings you into intimate connection with all life on earth and with the cosmos beyond. You become conscious of how your thoughts produce results. You notice how your emotions and actions influence others and how they create the circumstances you experience. You sense the presence of nonphysical beings in your environment and allow yourself to be guided by your spiritual guardians. You recognize coincidences as meaningful events and learn from them.

Magick Isn't a Spectator Sport

At some point in your magickal process, you'll have to decide why you've chosen this path. Many people, especially teens and young adults, initially get interested in witchcraft and magick because they feel weak and seek to gain power over others. If you stick with it, however, you'll soon discover that witchcraft is really about gaining power over yourself and your ego.

When people ask me to do magick spells for them, I usually encourage them to get involved themselves. I'm happy to share spells with them, as I've done in this and other books. But often spells you do for yourself can be more effective, if only because the outcome is more important to you than to another person. You can pour your emotions into the spell. You feel a strong connection to any other people who may be involved in the spell. You know the outcome you desire.

Everyone possesses magickal ability. But magick isn't for couch potatoes. It's for people who genuinely want to take charge of their lives and their realities. Magick involves study, discipline, and practice. You'll have to build your mental muscles. It requires you to shift your old habit patterns and beliefs, which is easier said than done. It demands that you "clean up your act" and examine your motives. Most importantly, magick forces you to delve deep within yourself to discover who you truly are.

Setting Up Shop

You don't need to purchase a warehouse full of supplies in the beginning. Start with a few basics: candles, incense, ribbons, and kitchen herbs. As you progress, add some quartz crystals and gemstones. Later on, you may wish to invest in a wand, chalice, athame, and pentagram. Tarot cards, a crystal ball, and pendulum might follow at some point. Build your collection as your need or interest dictates.

Sometimes magick items find you. A friend gives you a tarot deck. You spot a crystal lying on the side of the road. In time, you might decide to grow your own magickal herbs. Some witches like to fashion their own candles or even distill their own scents. Others fabricate special ritual clothing or jewelry. Apply your talents however the muse guides you.

A Lifelong Pursuit

No matter how long you study and practice witchcraft, you'll never know it all. You could be at it your entire adult life and still barely scratch the surface. It's like any other subject: The deeper you dig, the more you discover.

Some people begin studying one type of magick and then move on to learn about another. In the course of your studies, you'll undoubtedly find yourself drawn to certain schools of thought and not others. Your heritage, temperament, interests, locale, companions, and many other factors will influence your decisions about which path to follow.

As you explore different types of magick, you'll discover that despite their outer forms of expression, they contain many common denominators. Gaining knowledge about one school of thought can increase your skill in another. Although some purists might disagree, many people think it's fine to combine features from different magickal traditions and schools of thought.

Magick transforms you. It becomes an integral part of your life and your worldview. You might study intensely at one period and then ease off temporarily. You may do lots of rituals for a time, then not perform any for a while. But once you assume the magician's mantle, you'll wear it forever.

Magick exists everywhere, all the time. You are part of the magick. Blessed be.

INDEX

ABOUT THE AUTHOR

Skye Alexander is the award-winning author of more than thirty fiction and nonfiction books, including *The Everything® Wicca & Witchcraft Book, 2nd Edition*; *The Everything® Spells & Charms Book, 2nd Edition*; *Naughty Spells/Nice Spells*; *Good Spells for Bad Days*; *The Secret Power of Spirit Animals*; and *The Everything® Tarot Book, 2nd Edition*. Her stories have been published in anthologies internationally, and her work has been translated into more than a dozen languages. The Discovery Channel featured her in the TV special *Secret Stonehenge*. She divides her time between Texas and Massachusetts.

The

MODERN
WITCHCRAFT

SPELL
BOOK

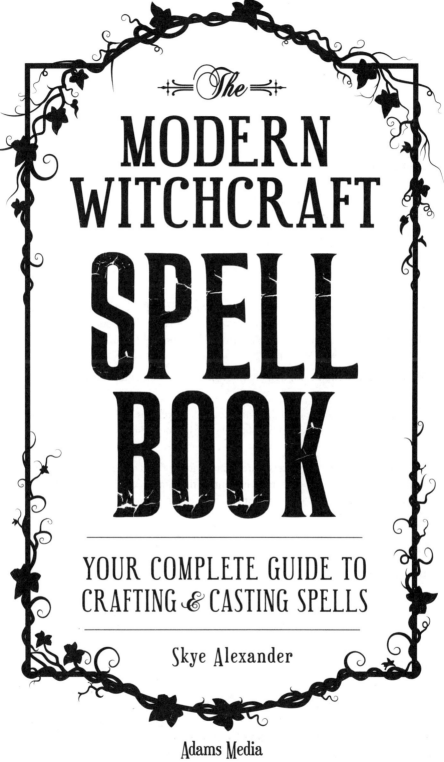

The
MODERN
WITCHCRAFT
SPELL
BOOK

YOUR COMPLETE GUIDE TO
CRAFTING & CASTING SPELLS

Skye Alexander

Adams Media
New York   London   Toronto   Sydney   New Delhi

Adams Media
An Imprint of Simon & Schuster, Inc.
100 Technology Center Drive
Stoughton, MA 02072

For information about special discounts for bulk purchases, please contact Simon & Schuster Special Sales at 1-866-506-1949 or business@simonandschuster.com.

The Simon & Schuster Speakers Bureau can bring authors to your live event. For more information or to book an event contact the Simon & Schuster Speakers Bureau at 1-866-248-3049 or visit our website at www.simonspeakers.com.

Manufactured in China

10 9 8 7 6 5 4 3 2 1

Library of Congress Cataloging-in-Publication Data has been applied for.

ISBN 978-1-4405-8923-2
ISBN 978-1-4405-8924-9 (ebook)

In memory of my mother, Joan Britton

Acknowledgments

Once again, I am indebted to my editors Tom Hardej and Peter Archer and all the amazingly talented folks at Adams Media for making this book possible.

CONTENTS

Introduction

SO YOU WANT TO BE A SPELLCASTER

Many of us were introduced to magick spells at an early age, through fairy tales, books, and movies. We saw Cinderella's fairy godmother transform a pumpkin into a jeweled coach drawn by a team of prancing horses. We witnessed a princess kiss a frog and turn him into a handsome prince. We watched Hermione Granger move trees with her magick wand. And we wanted to be able to wield that awe-inspiring power, too.

The good news is, you *do* have that power. Everyone has magickal ability—it's your birthright. And you know what else? You've probably already done lots of spells, but you just didn't realize it at the time. Blowing out candles on a birthday cake, for instance, is a popular good luck spell. Hanging an evergreen wreath on your front door is an ancient protection spell. Cursing a driver who steals your parking space, well, that's also a spell.

Simply put, a magick spell uses thoughts, words, and actions to cause certain changes to occur—and to generate outcomes through means that logic and conventional science can't explain. Have you ever made a wish that came true? That's magick at work. Would you like to be able to do that more often? You can. By training your mind and developing some natural skills that you already possess—and by aligning yourself with nature and the universe—you can create the reality you desire.

WHAT CONSTITUTES A SPELL?

Hollywood tends to focus on the sensational aspects of magick, witchcraft, and spellcasting, which can make the whole idea seem scary or weird or even ridiculous to many people. In reality, most witches and wizards don't put hexes on people; they don't turn frogs into princes or fly through the air on broomsticks; they don't brew eye of newt and tongue of dog in cauldrons for enchanted potions (although cauldrons still serve as handy tools in spellwork). Instead, modern-day magickal workers cast spells to help them get better jobs, attract love and friendship, safeguard their homes and families, and improve their health. You can even do a spell to find a parking space in a crowded shopping mall on the day after Thanksgiving.

According to Aleister Crowley, often recognized as the most powerful magician of the twentieth century, "Every intentional act is a magickal act." The purpose of a spell is to manifest something that you need or desire. That need or desire (or both) comprises your intent. When you cast a spell, your intent is vital to your success. Your *intention*, coupled with your *attention*, are the most important components in any spell— they're what make your wishes come true. That's why you'll often hear it said that magick is all in the mind. Beyond that, a spell might involve carefully orchestrated steps and procedures, exotic ingredients, cool clothes, and specialized equipment—all designed to increase the potency of the spell. It may also draw upon the forces of nature and/or supernatural powers.

The Modern Witchcraft Spell Book

WHAT YOU'LL LEARN FROM THIS BOOK

Few of us get the opportunity to attend Hogwarts for a magickal education. However, if you follow the guidelines in this book, you'll soon learn to cast spells for all sorts of purposes. You'll develop techniques for honing your mental and psychic powers. You'll find out how to tap the natural energies in plants and gemstones, and use them to augment your spells. You'll discover how to call upon spirits, deities, and other invisible beings to enhance your spellworking ability. Finally, you'll learn the best times to perform spells and rituals in order to produce the results you seek, safely and effectively.

Maybe you're not sure about all this stuff yet, but you're curious. Maybe you've dabbled with magick a bit and want to become more familiar with it. Maybe you're ready to take charge of your own destiny and start consciously creating the circumstances you desire in your life. If so, this book is for you.

⇥ PART I ⇤

Spellworking
BASICS

Chapter 1

THE ART OF SPELLWORK

Magick is the art of creating change in accordance with your will. It's also what happens when you manipulate energy to produce a result, using methods that conventional science can't explain. Witches, wizards, shamans, and others who work with the magickal forces of the universe sometimes add the letter "K" to the word *magic* to distinguish it from stage illusion, card tricks, and the like.

Many people think that magick, witchcraft, and the process of casting spells are weird—maybe even a little spooky or evil. Unfortunately, for centuries suspicion, skepticism, confusion, and fear have muddied the magickal waters and interfered with the widespread use of spells to attract health, wealth, happiness, and all the other good things in life. The truth is, nothing is more natural than doing a spell. A long tradition of spellworking exists in most cultures, including Western culture. People from all walks of life have engaged in magick and spellworking for millennia, for myriad purposes. Today, curiosity about the art of spellcasting is growing rapidly—and as we gain more knowledge and become more familiar with magickal practices, the scary factor diminishes.

You've probably already cast spells without knowing it. For instance, wearing a ring set with your birthstone is an ancient good luck spell. Maybe you've wished upon a star or made a wish before blowing out candles on a birthday cake. In essence, wishing for something really, really hard is a kind of spell. If you want something badly enough, and you think about it constantly, you send out energy to attract that new reality you seek and help it come into being.

Daydreams aren't spells, however. The difference boils down to what spellcasters call intent. Intent means determining your objective and then performing an action with awareness, consciously channeling energy and emotion into the action in order to produce a result. Throughout this book, we'll talk about intent, focusing energy, creating images, and fueling your spells with emotion and willpower, for these are the keys to doing successful magick.

Avoid Obsession

Obsessing over a desire or need can actually prevent you from getting what you want. If you keep desperately hoping that your wish will come true, you exhibit doubt. And doubt squelches a spell's success like water poured on a fire.

WHAT, EXACTLY, IS A SPELL?

Simply put, a spell is something you do with clarity, intent, and awareness to generate a result. A spell consists of a set of thoughts and symbolic actions performed in the physical world to initiate change on a higher level. Once a change takes place at that higher level, it filters down and materializes here on earth. When you do a spell, you alter a situation by introducing new energy or rearranging the energy that's already present.

A spell is *not* a religious act—although as you begin casting spells you may notice similarities in the actions you perform and the practices used by some religions. Spellcasting is a method; it's a secular activity with no dogma attached to it. Many religions use spells—or a form of energy transference or energy management—as part of worship, although they probably wouldn't describe it that way. For example, in Chapter 5, when we discuss affirmations and incantations, you might see a relation between these verbal spells and prayers.

When doing a spell, you are the agent of change. You draw upon your own resources to gather and direct energy. You make it happen, and you take responsibility for your actions and their results. You may request assistance from a higher power to accomplish your objective, if you wish. Or you may bring in the energies of various substances, such as plants and gemstones, to augment your own powers. Ultimately, though, you're the writer, director, and producer.

WHY USE SPELLS?

People perform spells for a variety of reasons. Crafting and casting a spell allows you to take control of a situation—you no longer have to sit and wait for life to sort itself out. Spellwork is an active method of dealing with life, instead of passively accepting what comes your way. Engaging in spellwork can boost your confidence—there's nothing quite like seeing one of your spells materialize. Your self-esteem ratchets up a few notches, and you realize that you possess power you never knew you had before. However, if you just do spells to impress your friends or make yourself seem more important, you're missing out on magick's greater value.

Spellcraft also exercises your creativity. You might not be able to play the saxophone or paint a masterpiece or win a flamenco dance competition, but you can craft a web of energy from a variety of objects and words, linked together by intent and desire, and cast that web out into the cosmos to draw your goal to you. Anyone can do spells, and everyone possesses magickal ability. Spellcraft combines the use of imagination, language, and action in a variety of ways, and the way you put it all together will be unique to you.

Spells aren't only about getting what you want, though—they can also be about giving back. You can raise positive energy and send it out into the world, as a way to say "thank you" for all the good things in your own life. You can do spells for other people, too, to aid them in their life journeys. Affirming your blessings and offering assistance to others can help you to draw more blessings to you. You can even do spells to heal the planet, encourage world peace, and other far-reaching objectives.

THE BENEFITS OF SPELLCASTING

Everything in our universe is composed of energy. As you craft and cast spells, you'll come to understand the flow of energy and its presence in and around you. Spellwork teaches you how energy moves, how you can handle it, and how you can direct it into various areas of your life. Once you understand how energy behaves, you can tap into it via different methods—that's what magick is all about.

Spellcraft is a deeply transformative process that touches the magician as well as her environment. Spells and magick are intended to make our lives happier and easier. However, if you think you can use spells to avoid work, forget it—you can't just twitch your nose and make your vacuum cleaner spiff up your home. Spellwork involves effort and dedication, particularly when you first begin, as you acquire new information and explore new techniques. Like everything else, it requires learning the principles and then practicing until you get it right—you must put energy into the equation if you want your outcomes to manifest.

That's not to say spellwork is onerous—anything but! It's a joyful and enlivening experience, one that may actually leave you feeling more vital and content after finishing a spell than you did before you began. Just the act of connecting with parts of yourself to which you ordinarily don't pay much attention can be exhilarating. You discover new strengths and abilities. Plus, knowing that you are linked with the other entities that share your world can give you a sense of belonging to a greater whole, a magickal universe with infinite possibilities.

Spellwork also helps you gain clarity and purpose. First of all, you must determine a precise goal. Often we think we know what we want, but we rarely take the time to seriously think about how deeply we desire something, and why—or how our lives will change if we get our heart's desire. You have to be completely honest with yourself in order to cast a successful spell, otherwise your hidden agendas may interfere or even materialize. If you do not have a defined goal, you'll end up throwing energy at a vague objective, wasting most of it. If you're confused or ambivalent about your intent, you'll get mixed results. Your spell won't succeed, or will succeed only partially.

By doing spells, you come to know yourself better. You learn to sift through the superficial and get to what really matters—and that benefits every part of your life.

HOW DO SPELLS WORK?

Everything in the world possesses an energy signature of some kind. Organic objects contain more energy than inorganic objects. A piece of wool or silk fabric, for instance, will hold more energy than a piece of polyester. The closer an organic object is to its natural state, the higher its energy. For example, a tree rooted in the wild has more energy than a stack of lumber created from that tree, and a varnished table built from that lumber retains even less of the tree's original energy.

All the energy possessed by these objects reaches out to connect with other energies. A web of energy links the physical and nonphysical worlds. That means you and I and everything else have a connection that enables us to communicate with one another, and, through the power of magick, to work together to consciously create our reality. When we seek to influence a situation by doing spells, we tweak the energy in one location, and that tweak sends ripples all over the web. A common metaphor is that of a spider's web. No matter where a spider sits on her web, when an insect strikes it the tiny shocks travel through all the strands of the web to alert her that she has a visitor for tea. Like the spider's web, strands of energy connect everyone and everything, enabling us to send out our intentions and receive input from our surroundings.

WHAT'S THE DIFFERENCE BETWEEN SPELLCRAFTING AND SPELLCASTING?

Spellcrafting and spellcasting are integrally connected, but they also have certain distinctions. To give a simple explanation, spellcrafting is the practice of fabricating the spell. You think about what you want to accomplish, gather ingredients to include in the spell, write down your objective, figure out the steps you'll take, and so on. Then you put it all together. It's a bit like preparing a recipe—and in fact, culinary recipes can be spells, as you'll learn in Part II of this book.

When you release the energy you've raised during the spellcrafting stage, you "cast" the spell. You send the energy and your intention out into the universe, so that your intention can manifest. Here's another analogy: Crafting the spell is like designing and assembling an automobile, whereas casting the spell is like driving the car. When you cast the spell, you put it to work.

WHERE CAN YOU USE SPELLS?

People use spells in every area of life, for all sorts of reasons. You can use magick spells for just about anything. However, spells for prosperity, love, health, and protection tend to be the most popular. In Part II of this book, you'll find dozens of spells that address these issues, and more.

One reason many of us don't enjoy the riches, well-being, and happiness we could is that we don't feel we deserve them. That lack of self-worth results in lack elsewhere in life. It can also sabotage your magickal workings. Perhaps you've heard of something called the Law of Attraction. This says that you attract what you think about. If you're constantly worrying about how you're going to pay your bills, if you see something you want but say to yourself "I can't afford that," your thoughts are about insufficiency. You think of yourself as being poor. Consequently, you attract poverty and lack. Before you can receive the blessings you desire, you must shift your thinking to prosperity consciousness. You must consider yourself worthy of obtaining your dreams and believe you can attain them.

"If you feel you are poor, you cannot attract prosperity."
Esther and Jerry Hicks, Money, and the Law of Attraction

Let's set something straight right now: Spellworking isn't selfish or greedy. When you do a spell to attract money or success or love, you aren't robbing anyone else of those goodies. The universe has plenty for everyone. Fulfilling your basic needs enables you to explore the higher potential of your life—your creativity, your spiritual calling, and so forth. When you no longer have to worry about having food, shelter, and the basic needs in order to survive on planet Earth, you can devote yourself to "loftier" goals that may benefit others as well as you.

As you become more proficient at doing spells, and you begin to see your spells materialize, you'll likely gain more self-confidence. If you're not sure of your abilities yet, it might help to start small. If you can't imagine manifesting $1 million, try a smaller sum, perhaps $100. Don't let yourself get stuck at a level below what's possible, though, because truly anything is within your grasp. The universe can just as easily give you something big as something little—but you have to be open to accepting it.

WHAT'S THE DIFFERENCE BETWEEN A SPELL AND A RITUAL?

Sometimes the words *spell* and *ritual* are used interchangeably, but they are two very different things. Yes, there's some overlap, and that can make things confusing. Think of it this way:

- When you do a spell, you use your mind, emotions, will, and natural powers to bring about an internal or external result.
- When you do a ritual, you perform a series of actions designed for a particular purpose.

In the secular world, we engage in rituals all the time, from dressing for work in the morning to readying ourselves for bed at night. Some secular rituals have traditional aspects, such as donning your favorite sports team's colors at homecoming, painting your face, and packing your cooler with plenty of beer. Spiritual rituals are often performed to honor a higher power or to celebrate your connection with that power, but they may have other purposes as well. A spell can be a part of a ritual, and a lengthy, detailed spell may include ritual actions, as well as interaction with deities.

BASIC STEPS TO SUCCESSFUL SPELLWORK

Although every spell is different, most involve a series of steps, as outlined here, or some version of them. Following these steps not only increases your likelihood of success, it also decreases your chance of mix-ups. An athlete wouldn't run a marathon without stretching first, nor would a surgeon perform a procedure without sterilizing his hands. The same holds true for spellwork. Setting the stage, cleansing your tools, and above all, preparing your mind are important to the success of your spells. Each step of a spell serves a purpose, and they all lead to your desired outcome.

1. Silence all distractions. Turn off the TV, phone, etc. Tell other people who won't be participating in the spell not to bother you—put a Do Not Disturb sign on your door. Put pets in a place where they won't demand your attention or upset your activity. You need to keep your attention focused on your task in order to produce good results. Additionally, when you do a spell, you move from mundane space into magickal space—being jerked back from that magickal place by some outside interference can be jarring, like being shaken out of a peaceful sleep.

2. Establish your intention. Unless you have a clearly defined reason for doing a spell, don't bother. It's simply a waste of time and energy, and your efforts may go awry. Write down your intention—this helps clarify your objective and starts the process of moving it out of your mind, into physical form. If you'll be working with other people, discuss your intention together beforehand so everyone understands what you're doing and why. It's essential that you're all in agreement and that you all focus on the same intention; otherwise, you might get mixed results.

The Modern Witchcraft Spell Book

3. Compose your spell. Think about your desired outcome and what energies you wish to harness in order to help you achieve this outcome. Write down what you'll do in your spell and the steps with which you'll proceed. If you plan to use an affirmation or incantation, make sure you either memorize it or write it down. (You'll learn more about this in Chapter 5.) If you'll be working with other people, go over the steps and details beforehand, so everyone is in accord and feels comfortable with his or her role.

4. Collect all the ingredients necessary for your spell. Cleanse each item, either by washing it with mild soap and water or by "smudging" it in the smoke of burning sage or incense. Bring all the objects you'll use into the space where you'll perform your spell. Ritual tools should have been consecrated beforehand (you'll learn more about these tools in Chapter 6). If you'll work with other spellcasters, decide whose tools will be used in the spell and who will wield them.

5. Establish your spellworking space. First, cleanse the area where you'll perform your spell. You can do this by smudging it with smoke from burning sage or incense or by sweeping it with a broom or both. Sometimes imagining the area filled with pure white light may be enough. Invite everyone who will participate to enter the space, and then cast a circle around it. (We'll discuss this in depth in Chapter 3.) A magick circle provides an energetic barrier that keeps unwanted energies out and holds desired energies in.

6. Shift your consciousness. Light a candle or incense, meditate, or do whatever helps you shift your thinking from mundane to magickal. From this point on, try not to let any ordinary thoughts intrude into your elevated mental state. If you're working with other people, don't talk unless you're chanting an affirmation or performing another verbal part of your spell.

7. Raise energy. Some people do this by chanting, humming, drumming, breathing deeply, or dancing—do what feels right to you. Envision yourself drawing energy up from the earth and into your body; also draw energy from the heavens down into your body, and let them blend within you. You'll sense your awareness change—you might feel more energized, calm, aware, centered, sensitive, tingly, or something else. If you're working with other people, allow your individual

energies to merge for the term of the spell. (We'll discuss this more in later chapters.)

8. If you choose, invite other entities to participate in your spell. Angelic presences, spirit guides and guardians, totem animals, ancestors, elementals, and other nonphysical beings can provide protection and assistance during spellwork. (We'll talk more about working with spirit beings in Chapter 7.)

9. Perform your spell, according to the plan you designed earlier.

10. After completing your spell, release the entities who've assisted you (if any) and thank them.

11. Open the circle. (You'll learn how in Chapter 3.) Send the energy you've raised during your spellwork toward your goal, and trust that it will materialize at the proper time, in the proper way.

12. Dismantle your magickal space. Extinguish the candles, collect your tools and any other items you brought into the circle, etc. Store your tools in a safe place until you choose to work with them again.

13. The final step is manifestation—this is when you achieve your goal.

In your book of shadows (your personal journal of spells), write down what you did and what ingredients/tools you used when you performed the spell, as well as what you felt, sensed, thought, witnessed, and so on. If you're working with other spellcasters, you may wish to discuss what transpired, how you felt about the spell and its enactment, and what (if anything) you might do differently in the future.

Chapter 2

TAPPING MAGICKAL POWER

What does it mean to practice magick? When we speak of magick, we mean the transformation that occurs when a witch, wizard, shaman, or other magick worker uses his or her power to shape energy, in order to accomplish an objective in the physical or nonphysical world (or both). When a witch does a magick spell, she doesn't send sparks flying from her fingertips, nor does she levitate objects and hurl them through space—that's pure Hollywood. Instead, she attunes her own innate abilities with the forces of nature to elicit a series of controlled coincidences that will achieve her desired result. She moves, bends, or otherwise alters the flow of energy in the universe to bring about a condition that will benefit her or someone else.

Each person who decides to take up the practice of magick has reasons for doing so. Before you begin performing spells, spend some time thinking about why spellcasting is important to you and what you hope to achieve by engaging in this practice. Write your thoughts in your book of shadows—putting something in writing helps you to clarify your thoughts. Begin to define what you believe. Do you seek out magick as a way to escape from the mundane aspects of life? Are you mainly concerned about making changes in your personal life (love, career, money)? Or do you want to deepen your spiritual connection to the universe? Do you intend to obtain practical results or to enhance your intuition? Most likely, your goals will include a combination of all these things, and maybe more.

The Law of Three

Ethical spellworkers abide by what's known as the "law of three." This means that whatever intention and energy someone sends out returns, like a boomerang, to the sender threefold. This is a strong deterrent against mischief, manipulation, or other deceptive practices.

CONSCIOUSLY CREATING CHANGE

It's been said that the only constant is change. We observe change all around us, all the time. The rising sun changes night to day; the setting sun changes day to night. Wind changes the face of the mountain. Rain changes the depth of the river, which wears away the rocks to carve the valley. Fire changes substance to ash. Planet Earth is constantly shifting, spinning, revolving, and renewing itself.

The purpose of doing magick is to create change intentionally. When you cast a spell, you bring about a change in some facet of your life and the world around you. When you cast a circle (as you'll learn to do in Chapter 3), you change a room or a grove of trees into a sacred temple. When you build an altar, you change a table or other surface into the stage upon which you interact with other forces and entities. When you consecrate a magick tool, you change an ordinary stick or wineglass into an instrument of Divine Will.

You possess the power to change just about anything in your life. As quantum physics has demonstrated, when you focus your attention on something, your energy influences the behavior of the molecules that you are watching (even though you can't actually see them). Focusing on something causes molecules to collect in the area where you direct your attention. What this means is, you quite literally change whatever you observe. That's magick! The goal—and the challenge—is to use magick with conscious awareness and intent. Spells are one way to do this.

WHERE DOES MAGICKAL POWER ORIGINATE?

We live in a magickal universe. Everything you see—and don't see—is imbued with magickal potential. We've been taught to believe that the things around us are material, tangible, and immutable substances, but none of that is true. A tree, a rock, the chair you're sitting on are all composed of energy. As I've said before, our world is surrounded by an energetic matrix that connects everything to everything else. This matrix, or cosmic web, not only envelops earth, it permeates all things that exist here, and it extends throughout the solar system and beyond. The web pulses with subtle vibrations, which witches and other sensitive individuals can feel. Regardless of whether you are consciously aware of these vibrations, you are affected by them—and your own energetic vibrations continually affect the matrix.

Let's talk some more about the Law of Attraction, because it's a fundamental part of magickal practice and spellwork. According to Esther and Jerry Hicks, whose bestselling books have done a great deal to popularize this ancient concept, "Each and every component that makes up your life experience is drawn to you by the powerful Law of Attraction's response to the thoughts you think and the story you tell about your life." This means that your ideas contain magnetic power, and that you're already bringing to yourself the outcomes you'll experience—even if you don't realize it.

What you get is what you see. The ideas and beliefs you hold in your mind are the source of what happens to you. They are the seeds from which your reality grows. Your thoughts, words, and deeds are at the root of your health, wealth, and happiness—or your illness, poverty, and misery. That's not meant to cast blame but to help you understand the amazing power you have at your fingertips.

In magickal work, learning to harness and direct your thoughts is essential to creating successful outcomes. Look around at your life circumstances. If you don't like something, know that you possess the power to change it, by first changing your thoughts.

Energy Signatures

Everything in the world emits energy of some kind, and everything has a unique energy "signature." Sometimes a signature is described as corresponding to a particular level of vibration. Higher vibrational levels usually are considered more spiritual and closer to the deities; lower vibrations indicate something more material.

YOUR PERSONAL ENERGY CENTERS

Just as your physical body has internal organs that enable it to perform various tasks necessary for survival, you also have nonphysical "organs" or energy centers that play an important part in your well-being. Asian health and healing practices, such as acupuncture, ayurvedic medicine, Reiki, and yoga, deal with the movement of energy through your body—especially as it relates to these dynamic energy centers known as the "chakras." The word *chakra* means "wheel" because to sensitive people who can perceive them these orb-like energy centers resemble spinning wheels or spirals. However, most individuals can't perceive them, nor can they be quantified using conventional medicine's tools.

Although many chakras exist throughout the body, we're primarily concerned with seven major chakras that roughly align vertically from the base of your spine to the top of your head. Each serves a particular function as a locus of energy that nourishes your body, mind, and spirit. When your chakras are in balance, your intuitive and psychic abilities are at their strongest, and you can draw upon their energy to work magick effectively. You'll find a number of spells in Part II of this book that involve working with the energy of the chakras.

The Modern Witchcraft Spell Book

Kundalini: The Mystical Serpent

According to mystical Eastern wisdom, the divine essence of all the chakras is *kundalini*. Kundalini is depicted as a serpent coiled around herself three and a half times. The serpent sleeps at the base of the spine and awakens (through yoga, breath work, or other practices) with a rattle or a hiss. She slowly uncoils herself and begins her ascent, traveling up through each chakra center, opening and activating it as she goes. Each major chakra is associated with a color and a significant symbol (which are all variations on the lotus flower). Use these symbols as guides to understanding and integrating these vital energies, so that you may experience the benefits. You'll find lots of pictures of the chakras online and in books, to help you connect with them further.

The Root Chakra

The root chakra is located at the base of the spine and is linked with the color red. This energy center deals with all issues pertaining to survival—it is your connection to the earth. Many fight-or-flight responses and animal instincts are stored here. The root chakra is also concerned with security, your sense of self, and your confidence. When you activate the root chakra you embrace your primal nature, as an integrated and necessary part of your higher self.

This chakra also affects your interactions with the material world. If your root chakra is balanced, you are likely to feel secure with your place in the world and your ability to cope with any hardships that may come your way. Blockages in the root chakra, however, may lead to feelings of inadequacy, insecurity, and a lack of self-confidence, which can interfere with everything you embark on, including spellwork. You can strengthen your root chakra by meditating and envisioning a glowing red ball of energy at the base of your spine, continually growing brighter and stronger.

The Sacral Chakra

Located just below the navel, the sacral chakra is associated with sex, desire, pleasure, and fulfillment. Its color is orange. Your carnal instincts reside here, in this realm of procreation and sensuality. When you open and balance your sacral chakra, you accept yourself as a sexual being who seeks pleasure. Obviously, this chakra affects spells you do for love. In addition to its correlation with sexuality, the sacral chakra impacts other kinds of desire as well. Your passionate hopes, dreams, and aspirations dwell here, too.

If your sacral chakra is balanced, you are likely to feel comfortable with your sexuality. You may also be adept at understanding and expressing your own needs on many levels, and you can find ways to make sure your needs are met. A deficiency or blockage in the sacral chakra may lead to excessive inhibition, as well as feelings of discomfort regarding sexuality and perhaps pleasure in general. Consequently, you might limit your ability as a creative being and as a spellworker, for doing magick spells is a creative endeavor. When your sacral chakra is balanced, you easily connect with your own needs and desires and your ability to attract what you seek. Visualize a spinning vortex of bright orange light just below your navel to activate your sacral chakra.

The Solar Plexus Chakra

The solar plexus chakra, located about halfway between your navel and your heart, is the center of your personal power. Its color is yellow. Its energy enables you to actualize your personal gifts and talents. Your willpower resides here, and when this chakra is functioning optimally, you take charge of your life and exercise your power—in the mundane world as well as the magickal one. When you open your solar plexus chakra, you take responsibility for your choices and feel confident acting upon them.

If your solar plexus chakra is balanced, you feel comfortable expressing your unique abilities. You use this chakra's energy to produce positive results for yourself and others, without fear or reluctance. In spellwork, your personal talents come to fruition, bringing you a greater sense of self-worth and helping you attain your goals. To strengthen this chakra, envision a brilliant yellow light, like sunshine, glowing there and radiating out into the world.

The Heart Chakra

The heart chakra, as its name implies, is located in the middle of the chest near your heart. Its color is green. This chakra deals with issues that pertain to the emotions, especially your ability to love and be loved, and obviously it plays an important role in love spells. It serves as the link between your physical body and your spiritual identity. The heart chakra is involved not only with romantic love but also love of self and love of community: family, friends, and humanity in general. It also connects you to nature and the spirits with whom you interact, whether or not you are aware of them.

When your heart chakra is open and balanced, you experience love without walls and can accept your own vulnerability without fear. Blockages in the heart chakra can lead to feelings of unworthiness, mistrust, and loneliness. People who have had their hearts broken often distance themselves from the heart chakra, saying things such as "I will never allow anyone to get that close to me again" or "No one will ever get the chance to hurt me like that again." To open this chakra, meditate and imagine spiraling green light all around your heart, sending forth love and receiving love as well.

The Throat Chakra

At the base of your throat, near the hollow where your collarbones meet, you'll find the throat chakra. Its color is light blue. All matters of communication relate to this energy center, as well as how you interact with other beings in the world around you and in the higher planes of consciousness. The manner by which you express your thoughts and speak your own truth is also affected by the throat chakra. Because many spells involve affirmations, incantations, or other verbalizations, this chakra affects the success of your spells.

If your throat chakra is blocked or imbalanced, you may take a dogmatic approach to discussing ideas or beliefs. Perhaps you talk excessively without listening or get caught up in arguing. Or you might be afraid to speak about your ideas or to share your talents with others for fear of criticism. To balance this chakra, imagine a beautiful, light-blue glow swirling at the base of your throat.

The Third Eye Chakra

The third eye or "ajna" chakra is located at your forehead where your eyebrows come together at the top of your nose. Its color is indigo. This is the site of psychic awareness, where matters pertaining to your intuition or "sixth sense" reside. It allows you to experience your spiritual nature through clairvoyance (seeing the unseen), memories of past lives, empathy (feeling what others feel), telepathy (accessing the thoughts of another), and astral travel (entering into nonphysical realms where the physical body cannot go).

When your third eye chakra is open and balanced, you experience your connection with other realms and may find you can communicate easily (intuitively) with beings who reside there. In magickal work, you can receive spiritual guidance and wisdom from higher sources—you may even be able to divine the future. A blockage or imbalance in this chakra may lead you to reject your own psychic gifts out of fear or skepticism. To activate your ajna chakra, picture the indigo light of the sky at night emanating from your third eye.

The Crown Chakra

Located at or just above the top of your head, this chakra is associated with the color purple, though some people see it as white. All spiritual matters pertaining to your soul's existence dwell here. The crown chakra serves as a portal through which you receive spiritual guidance and wisdom. A balanced crown chakra allows you to communicate with god/desses and divine beings on other levels of existence and to receive aid from them in magickal work.

When you activate and balance your crown chakra, your ego falls away; you live in a state of acceptance and assimilation with the Divine, a place beyond desire. You experience a sense of oneness with all beings. Because you know your spirit is indestructible, you fear nothing, not even physical death. An imbalance in the crown chakra can cause you to feel lost, alone, cut off from your Source and the higher forces that exist around you. Or you might suffer from delusions of grandeur. To bring this chakra into balance, visualize a brilliant, regal purple light emanating from the top of your head, flowing over you and through you, connecting you to All That Is.

CREATIVE VISUALIZATION

In the late 1970s, author Shakti Gawain brought the concept of creative visualization into widespread public awareness. But witches and other magickal practitioners had long known that visualization fuels magick and precedes manifestation. When you're doing a spell, a picture truly is worth a thousand words.

Creative visualization involves forming a mental picture of the result you intend to manifest. Don't think about the problem or condition you wish to change—instead, focus on the end result you seek. For instance, if your goal is to heal a broken leg, don't think about the injury; instead, envision the leg strong and healthy.

Images possess more power than words. Advertisers know this very well—just watch a commercial for some sort of drug, in which the pictures show happy, healthy people while the voice-over describes all the drug's unpleasant side effects. The viewer's mind reacts to the pictures rather than the words. Because images have such a strong impact, witches incorporate lots of visual and sensory components into magick spells, as well as words.

Imagination is at the heart of a spell. If you can't conceive of a situation or state of being, you won't be able to attain it. When you imagine the possibilities of what you may be able to create, you plant the first seeds. Remember how, as a child, you had fun letting your imagination run free? It's time to do that again. Give yourself permission to dream big. Enrich your mental images with lots of color and action—clear, vivid images generate faster and more satisfactory results than bland ones.

Try this exercise with a friend to explore your ability to form mental images:

1. Silence all distractions (phone, TV, etc.).
2. Sit in a comfortable place and close your eyes.
3. Ask your friend to say aloud a series of words, one by one, such as "apple," "horse," "campfire," "sailboat," or "ski chalet."
4. Notice the pictures that pop into your mind. Do you see a shiny red apple? A sleek, chestnut-colored horse with white stockings? A blazing fire shooting sparks into the night sky?

5. Choose one of those images, and let it spin out into something more. Do you envision a racehorse galloping toward the finish line? Girl Scouts seated around a campfire roasting marshmallows?
6. Now switch places, so your friend can exercise his imagination while you give him verbal "cues."
7. Record your images and impressions in your book of shadows.

Creative visualization will improve your psychic abilities as well. Once you learn to clear your psyche of all that useless clutter and chatter that take up space in your mind, you'll find your innate creativity can express itself. Furthermore, you can begin to form mental images that are in line with your purposes and that will attract the outcomes you desire.

What Is a Book of Shadows?

A book of shadows is a witch's personal journal of his or her magickal experiences. Here you keep track of your spells, rituals, and other things related to your development as a magician. It's like a cook's collection of recipes. Often you'll hear the words *grimoire* and *book of shadows* used interchangeably, although some differences existed in earlier times. Grimoires served as guidebooks that described spells and rituals. A book of shadows might also include its author's musings or insights related to a spell, as well as her dreams, feelings, and other asides.

LEARNING TO SENSE ENERGY

Magick spells draw upon the energies within you and around you. If you're going to become a successful spellworker, you'll benefit from learning to tap into the vast storehouse of energy that's available to you. Although energy currents flow in and around us all the time, invisibly wafting through our environment, most people don't pay attention to them. However, you can develop an awareness of them, and doing so will enhance your spellwork. Try these exercises to hone your ability to sense energy:

- Enter a building you've never been in before. Notice your reactions. Do you feel comfortable, welcomed, at ease? Or do you experience apprehension or hesitation? Do you want to continue further into the building, or withdraw? (This relates to an ancient Chinese magickal system known as *feng shui*.)
- Go to several different places, perhaps high on a hilltop and then near a body of water and finally deep in the woods. Spend some time sensing the "vibes" there. How do you feel in these different spots? Consider not just the obvious things, such as wind or sun or dampness, but also your personal reactions. Do you feel more enlivened in one place or another? Do you feel calm or agitated in a particular spot? Even if your impressions seem weird, don't discount them.
- Now go to several different places in a town or city. What do you experience there? How do you react to the faster pace? Does the energy seem more chaotic than it did in the natural places you visited? Do you find the energy invigorating or stressful? Exciting or draining?
- Go outside at night and look up at the sky. What do you see and sense? Many people are afraid of the dark—are you? And if so, why? In the world of magick, nighttime relates to mystery, the subconscious, and the realm beyond our everyday activities. In some magickal traditions, nighttime is the Goddess's time, when the feminine force is most active. Pay attention to your own experiences and remember to note them in your book of shadows.
- Go outside at dawn and again at dusk. These interim times, between day and night, are known as liminal zones. All around you, things are changing. Because change is essential to spellwork, you can align yourself with these transitions to perform powerful magick. Pay attention to the energetic shifts you sense as day and night switch places.

In Chapter 8, we'll look more closely at the energies inherent in the moon's phases, the earth's cycle around the sun, and other passages that can enhance or hamper your spellwork. You'll also learn how to time your spells to take advantage of the powers of nature and the cosmos that are available to you at various times throughout the year.

Chapter 3

A PLACE FOR SPELLWORKING

We've all had the experience of entering a place of reverence and sanctuary, whether it's a church or temple, a meditation room at a yoga center, or a grove of trees in a peaceful, natural setting. As soon as you step inside this special space, you sense a shift in the energy. You may feel serene, safe, suddenly removed from the busyness outside, or at one with something larger than yourself.

When you do spells or rituals, you want to go to a spot where you feel this sort of heightened awareness, connection, and peace. You need to leave the mundane world behind temporarily and slip into the world of magick. Creating sacred space is just as important as preparing yourself for spellwork. Maybe you're fortunate enough to have a place to call your sanctuary—a room in your home or a lovely, private spot in your yard. However, any place where you practice magick is your temple, and any place you treat with reverence is sacred space.

Your personal temple needn't be elaborate or large, like the ancient and awe-inspiring religious structures in India that occupy many acres. You can create a special area for magickal and spiritual practice in a corner of a room, on your back porch, or on the roof of your apartment building. In fact, if you live with people who might not understand or accept your beliefs, you may decide it's best to use a low-key, unobtrusive place to do your magickal work. You can place a vase of flowers, a candle, a colorful scarf, and a pretty stone on a shelf or dresser to designate your special place—you know the significance behind these everyday items, but no one else will.

BETWEEN THE WORLDS

When you prepare yourself to cast a spell or enact a ritual, you suspend your everyday concept of reality for a period of time. You expand your perception of the universe and your place in it, and get in touch with energies beyond your own. By entering the space and time "between the worlds," as it's often called, you can connect with the spirits who reside there. You acknowledge their presence by inviting them into your sacred space (we'll talk about this more in Chapter 7). You agree to accept physical manifestations of their divine presence. And you agree to suspend your sense of disbelief, in order to accept that magick and psychic experiences are indeed possible and even desirable.

At first, this may be difficult, as the rational mind often requires some type of tangible "proof" that a spiritual experience has occurred. This is where trust in yourself and the entities you work with comes in. Often your interactions will be subtle, but you'll learn in time to recognize gentle signs. You probably won't hear a clap of thunder to assure you that the goddesses and gods have acknowledged your work. Then again, you just might.

The Modern Witchcraft Spell Book

The Distinction Between Sacred Space and a Magick Circle

What makes sacred space different from a magick circle? A circle is a consciously constructed space that partially overlaps both our material world and the divine world. The resulting area is said to be "between the worlds," not wholly in one or the other. Sacred space is a place of peace and calm, but it is not necessarily between the worlds. Sacred space goes into the circle, or it can simply exist on its own.

CREATING SACRED SPACE

The purpose of defining and consecrating a sacred space is to give yourself a dedicated realm in which to perform magick and ritual, where you can move beyond your ordinary world when you so choose. You are, in essence, raising a temple (though not necessarily a brick-and-mortar one) for meditation, worship, divination, spellcasting, or any other aspect of magickal practice you wish to do here. You can create a more or less permanent sacred space or a temporary one, depending on your intentions and circumstances.

Cleansing Your Sacred Space

Once you've determined the location of your sacred space, take a broom and sweep the area thoroughly to clear away dust, dirt, and clutter. This is what witches really use brooms for, not to fly through the sky. After you finish physically sweeping the area, focus on cleansing the psychic space. In this way, you remove unwanted energies or influences, any "bad vibes" that might linger there.

Begin in the east and work your way counterclockwise around the room, in a circular fashion. Sweep the air, from the floor up to as high as you can comfortably reach. When you have gone around your area three times, lay the broom on the floor inside the circle and visualize all the negative energy breaking up and dissolving.

Some spellworkers also like to "smudge" the area with the smoke from burning sage. Light a sage wand/bundle (available at New Age shops and online) or a stick of sage incense. Walk in a circle, starting in the east, letting the smoke waft through the area. Now stand in the center of your space and feel the fresh, light, clean energy around you.

Dedicating Your Sacred Space

The next step is to dedicate your sacred space. You can begin by anointing the room or outdoor area you've chosen with frankincense essential oil (or another oil you prefer). Just put a little dab in each corner, starting in the east and moving clockwise around the space, creating a cross within a circle. This symbol represents the balance of female and male energies, the circle of creation, the four directions, and the four elements (about which we'll talk more later).

You may also opt to place a stone or crystal that has meaning for you at each of the four compass directions. If your sacred space is outdoors, you can bury the stones in the ground. Or you might like to design symbols that signify peace, holiness, protection, power, etc. and position them in your space. Some people display images of beloved deities in their sacred spaces. If you wish, you can create an elaborate ritual for dedicating your space—it is up to you.

Protecting Your Sacred Space

After you've finished setting up your sacred space, you'll want to protect it from intrusive energies. If you've designated your home or another building as sacred space, consider the following:

- Empower a mirror to deflect negative energy and hang it on your front door, facing outward (this is also a popular feng shui "cure"). Any disruptive energy that comes toward you will bounce back, away from your space.
- Bury protective stones such as onyx, hematite, or peridot under your doorstep, porch, or steps. (You can obtain these stones at your local New Age store.)
- Put a bunch of fresh basil in a pot with two quarts of water and simmer for ten minutes. Then strain out the basil (save it for other spells) and wash your doorstep with the basil-infused water.

- Hang a protective symbol on your door or near the entrance of your home: a pentagram, a Pennsylvania Dutch hex sign, or another image you associate with protection.
- Using saltwater, draw pentagrams or other protection symbols on the doors and windows of your home.
- Hang braids or wreaths of garlic, onions, and/or hot peppers in your home (don't eat them).
- Set a clove of garlic on each of your windowsills to absorb any negative energy before it can enter your home. Toss the old cloves and replace them with fresh ones on each new moon.
- Hang an iron horseshoe above your front door, with the open end turned up.

If you can't or choose not to consider your entire home (or another building) as sacred space, you can adapt the previous list according to your area. For example, if you have designated a portion of a room:

- Place a stone associated with protection there.
- Lay dried basil leaves in your sacred space.
- Position or draw a pentagram or other protective symbol there.
- Sprinkle some sea salt or spritz saltwater in the area.
- Set a clove of garlic in your space.

As you go about any daily routines that take place in your sacred space—especially if you've dedicated your entire home—be mindful of the energies around you. To attract positive energy, dust, mop, wash, and wipe countertops using a clockwise motion. To dispel unwanted energies, use a counterclockwise motion.

SETTING UP YOUR ALTAR

In my previous book *The Modern Guide to Witchcraft* I discussed in depth the process of setting up an altar. Here I'll offer a condensed version. Your altar is your basic "workbench" where you will do magick—just as a carpenter cuts, sands, glues, and nails at his workbench. It provides a focal point when you're casting spells, performing rites and rituals, meditating, communing with deities, or conducting any other magickal practices you may wish to engage in, either alone or with other people. You can set up a permanent altar or a temporary one within your sacred space, depending on your circumstances and preferences.

What Constitutes an Altar?

You can fashion an altar from just about anything—your intention is what's important and your understanding that the altar you've established is sacred. Perhaps you'd like to designate a handsome piece of furniture as your altar. Or, you can simply lay a pretty piece of cloth on a shelf, TV table, or cardboard box. If you choose to work outside, you could dedicate a large stone or a tree stump as your altar. If you decide to erect a temporary altar for spellworking, dismantle it when you're finished doing your spell.

Many people display their magick tools on their altars and store them there when not in use. Whether you opt to leave your tools in place more or less permanently or can only do this temporarily, display items that represent all four elements, for balance: earth, air, fire, and water. This could mean placing your pentagram, athame (ritual dagger), wand, and chalice on your altar. (We'll talk more about these tools in Chapter 6.) Or you could set a crystal there to signify earth, incense for air, a candle for fire, and a small bowl or vase of water for water. You can position anything on your altar that holds sacred or positive meaning for you: gemstones, statues of deities, images of totem animals, fresh flowers, etc., as well as the objects that you'll use in your spellwork. The most important thing is that you feel a sense of peace, joy, safety, and personal power when you do spells in your sacred space. Your altar serves as an anchor and a center of focus within that space.

Seasonal Altars

You may enjoy decorating your altar to celebrate the changing seasons or to mark special holidays, such as the eight sabbats (discussed in Chapter 8). Doing this will help you to attune yourself to the energies of the time and keep your altar looking fresh.

Positioning Your Altar

There's no right or wrong place within your sacred space to position your altar. Often the location of your altar depends on how much room you have, who will perform spells and rituals there (just you or other people as well), and what type of magick you'll do. Some people like to put the altar in the center of the space, which is convenient if a number of spellcasters will be doing magick together. Others prefer to set the altar in the north or the east. You can move your altar to different spots at different times of the year, or according to the moon's changing phases. Depending on your space, you may decide to erect more than one altar, perhaps a main one and smaller ones at each of the four directions. It's really up to you.

Directional Altars

If you opt to set up an altar at each of the four compass directions or "quarters," consider decorating each one to correspond to the nature of that direction. Witches associate the color yellow with the east, red with the south, blue with the west, and green with the north. You could put candles, flowers, fabric, gemstones, or other objects of the appropriate colors on your altars to signify their energies and enhance your awareness of your place within the whole.

Remember to cleanse everything before you bring it into your sacred space and place it on your altar(s). You can do this by washing items with mild soap and water, smudging them with the smoke of burning sage or incense, gently rubbing them with a piece of citrine (yellow quartz), or envisioning them surrounded and suffused with pure white light.

CASTING A CIRCLE

Nearly every book you read about magick and spellwork will discuss the importance of circle casting and offer suggestions for how to do it. Circles embody a wealth of symbolism, including wholeness, unity, completion, protection, eternity, and power. Some people say a circle protects those within it from evil forces, and although that may be true, it's not the main reason for casting a circle. Many traditions recommend doing magick within a psychic circle, for various reasons:

- A circle erects an energetic fence around the place where you do your magickal workings. This fence keeps unwanted energies out of your sacred space, so they can't disrupt or interfere with what you're doing.
- A circle contains the positive energy you raise during your spell or ritual. It holds and intensifies your power and intent until you're ready to release them into the larger world.
- If you are working with other people, a circle unites and enhances your energies, so that the group's power becomes greater than that of each individual within it.
- A circle brings you into closer contact with the sacred, moving you out of the mundane world temporarily and into the realm of magick and mystery. You realize that your actions are separated from your everyday existence and that increases the intensity of your focus. During the time you abide within the circle, you occupy a holy zone, nearer to the gods, goddesses, and spirits who can aid, guide, and protect you while you perform your spellwork.

As I've said before, casting a circle begins as an act of faith, to an extent—you *believe* the circle is there. Over time, or perhaps even on your very first attempt, you'll sense that the energy within the circle is very different from the energy outside it.

Preparing to Cast a Circle

Before you begin the physical part of casting a circle, it's important to ready the space where you'll erect your magick circle. This means cleansing it physically and psychically, just as you would any sacred space. Clear out anything that doesn't play a part in the spell or ritual you'll enact here. Sweep away old energies with a broom, as discussed earlier. Smudge the area with burning sage or incense.

Remove any distractions. Turn off all electronics: TV, phone, etc. Make sure people who won't be involved in your spell or ritual know not to disturb you. Put pets in a safe place where they won't interrupt. Cleanse all tools, spell ingredients, and other items that you'll use in your magick. Bring them into the area where you'll be working.

The Modern Witchcraft Spell Book

Ready yourself and all other participants. Go to the bathroom and tend to any personal needs, so you won't have to interrupt the spell/ritual once you get started. You may want to spend some time meditating or chanting to calm your mind and shift your focus. Smudge yourself and everyone else, to remove unwanted energies before entering the sacred space. You may wish to anoint participants with "holy" water, essential oils, or another substance that serves both to purify and to unite everyone involved.

Circle Casting 101

The ritual of casting a circle can be as simple or as complex as you want (or need) it to be. Some magick groups engage in elaborate and intricate ceremonies that contain many precise steps and ingredients. But you can also cast a perfectly effective circle by simply envisioning the area surrounded by a wall of pure white light. For many years, I worked within a large stone labyrinth that I'd built in the woods behind my house; it served as both my sacred space and a permanent magick circle. The directions offered here are suggestions only—feel free to design your own method according to your own preferences.

1. Gather all participants into the area where you'll be working, so that once you've cast the circle everyone will be inside it. After you've entered this sacred space, do not talk unless what you say is part of the ritual or spell.
2. Walk around the perimeter (often three times) of your intended workspace, beginning in the east and moving clockwise until you've made a complete circle and come back to your starting point. If you wish, draw the circle using a ceremonial sword, wand, or athame. Delineate the outer edge of the circle by holding the wand or blade parallel to the ground and pointing it outward. This physical act defines the circle in your mind.
3. To expand the circle so that it exists both in the physical realm and in the spiritual one, visualize energy being channeled into the space defined by the circle. Then expand it further, so that you envision a sphere of energy that encompasses you above, below, and around. With your imagination, you draw up energy from the earth and draw

down energy from the sky, blending them so that the combination fills the space.

4. If you choose to invite any spirits, guides, deities, ancestors, etc. to join in your spell/ritual, now is the time to call upon them. We'll address this practice in Chapter 7.

Once the circle is cast, no one should leave or enter it. If it becomes absolutely necessary to admit or dismiss someone, use your athame (or your hand) to "cut" an opening in the circle in the shape of a door, so that the person can enter or depart. Seal the opening afterward.

Opening the Circle

After you've finished your ritual or spellwork, you must open the circle so that the energy you've raised within it can flow out and materialize in the greater world. Basically, you'll reverse the steps you took to cast the circle.

1. If you've called upon any god/desses, angels, spirits, totems, or other nonphysical entities, thank them for their assistance and release them (we'll talk more about this in Chapter 7).

2. If you used a ritual athame, wand, or sword to draw the circle, take it up again and hold it with the point facing out, as you did to cast the circle. Retrace the path you used to create the circle, only in reverse— walk counterclockwise (three times if that's what you did to cast the circle) until you've removed all the psychic energy with which you built the circle.

3. Envision the magickal energy you raised during your spell/ritual flowing out into the universe, where it will manifest in accordance with your intentions. Sense that all is as it should be and trust that your objectives will come about in harmony with your will and that of Divine Will.

4. Extinguish candles and/or other flames. Gather up your tools (unless you prefer to leave them in your sacred space) and anything else you brought into the sacred space for the purposes of this spell/ritual. All participants can now leave the circle and return to their ordinary world.

In a nutshell, that's it. You can adapt this very basic pattern to make it more personal, embellish it to give it more drama, or interpret it as your own beliefs dictate. In later chapters, we'll talk more about other possibilities you may want to consider including. I also encourage you to read other books and to use your creativity to devise ways to enrich your circle casting to make it more meaningful for you. There are probably as many options as there are magickal workers—you're limited only by your imagination.

Chapter 4

NATURE'S MAGICK

Today, few people use eye of newt and toe of frog in spells. They're more likely to choose everyday ingredients they can find in any supermarket or New Age store—or better yet, in the natural environment. Using objects from nature is a wonderful way to enhance your connection with Mother Earth and to increase the power of your spells by adding the energies of plants, stones, etc. Since ancient times, witches, shamans, sorcerers, and other magick workers have looked to nature for spell materials. They used herbs and flowers to make healing potions, salves, poultices, and tonics. Gemstones and crystals provided protection, augmented personal powers, and attracted blessings. The natural world still provides a cornucopia of plants, minerals, and other treasures that you can use in your own magickal workings.

Many of the spells in Part II of this book include botanicals and/or gemstones. At the beginning of most chapters, you'll find lists that recommend the best plants, herbs, essential oils, and stones to use for specific types of spells.

SYMPATHETIC MAGICK

The basic philosophy of sympathetic magick is quite simple: like attracts like. This means that in spellwork, an item can serve as a representative or stand-in for another item that's similar to it in some way. It also means that the similarities are not coincidental and that they signify a connection—physical, spiritual, energetic, or otherwise—between the two items. Ginseng root, for example, resembles the human body, a similarity that some healers believe contributes to ginseng's medicinal properties. When you do spells, you can use associations between objects in order to make your spells more effective. In some instances, you may be aware of these connections; in other cases, the understanding happens at a subconscious level.

Because similarities exist between items, you can often substitute one ingredient for another in a spell. For example, a sunflower represents the energy of the sun, so if you're doing a spell that calls for solar power you can use sunflower seeds or petals to represent that power. If you're doing a love spell, you could use a pink rose or a piece of rose quartz—both resonate with the vibration of love. The energy of the flower is quicker, the stone's more enduring; however, either can play a role in a love spell.

Symbolism Exercise

Take a moment to consider how you form associations. Because your mind is the most important factor in magick, the mental images you hold are tremendously important when you perform spells. What do the words in the following list signify for you? What ideas and connections do they conjure up in your mind?

- Rose
- Snake
- Diamond
- Silk
- Horse
- Cactus
- Waterfall

- Apple
- Box
- Arrow

Most likely, your mind instantly produced a picture of the object. Beyond that, though, your imagination probably spun off in other directions and started making associations. For example, the word *diamond* may have triggered images of marriage or wealth. The word *horse* may have brought to mind thoughts of freedom, power, grace, speed, or beauty. Because your subconscious just naturally forms associations of this kind, you can make it work for you in spellcasting by choosing objects that symbolize your intentions.

Throughout this book, you'll see many examples of sympathetic magick at work. Some of the spells in Part II recommend choosing objects that hold significance for you or relate to your goals, and incorporating them into your spell. As you grow in knowledge and experience as a spellworker, you'll just naturally start making connections of this type.

Color Connections

Colors surround and influence us in countless ways, whether or not we realize it. That's why colors play such an important role in spellwork. Green is often used for money spells in the United States, because U.S. paper money is green on one side. In nature, green also makes us think of new growth and healthy plants. These are powerful associations. Yellow reminds us of sunshine, warmth, and happiness, so magick workers use this color for spells to attract good luck and joy. We associate the color red with passion; hence, love spells often include red flowers and red gemstones. In sympathetic magick, what "seems like" often "is." The underlying message is to trust your instincts—if something intuitively seems right to you, go with it.

MAGICKAL BOTANICALS

Many plants possess medicinal and healing properties, but for our purposes, we'll focus here on the metaphysical attributes of herbs and flowers. The category "botanicals" includes flowers, herbs, trees, shrubs, fruits and vegetables, and all sorts of other plants. In spellcraft, each has its purpose and value. In fact, plants are probably the most frequently used ingredients in spells of all kinds.

Choosing and Preparing Botanicals

Five thousand years ago, the Chinese emperor Shen Nung compiled the earliest known herbal reference book. Although the original text no longer exists, many later herbals evolved from this compilation. Some 2,000 years before the birth of Christ, the Egyptians and Sumerians kept records regarding the properties and applications of plants. The Egyptians used herbs extensively for cosmetic, medicinal, and embalming purposes.

As the Mediterranean trade routes grew and flourished, the use of herbs spread to Greece. The noted Greek physician Hippocrates (circa 460–375 B.C.E.) included in his writings roughly 400 herbal remedies. His remedies reflected his belief that all illnesses and diseases were caused by imbalances in the four bodily humors, which reflect nature's four elements: earth, water, fire, and air. When imbalances occurred, physicians recommended herbal remedies to restore harmony and facilitate healing. In ancient Britain, the Druidic priests, who were also healers, understood the planetary influences inherent in botanicals and used that knowledge when treating illness.

Plants grown naturally, without the assistance or interference of an outside source (such as a gardener or farmer), are referred to as "wildcrafted." Though cultivated herbs are grown in a controlled environment, they can be just as effective and potent as wild ones. You can purchase herbs fresh, dried, or in bulk from most greengrocers and farmers' markets. Note that a special relationship develops between the plants and the person who tends to them, so if you do not live in an area where you can find wild herbs, consider growing your own in a pot garden or window box.

When selecting botanicals, make sure they are full of vitality. Choose organic plants if possible. If you are purchasing your herbs and do not know under what conditions they were grown, make sure you wash them thoroughly to remove any residual chemicals that may have been used. You don't want the poisonous vibes of pesticides present in your spellwork! If you're harvesting a plant that you've grown or found in the wild, ask the plant's permission before harvesting it. Thank it for its help, whether you intend to eat it or use it in a spell. You might also choose to leave an offering in return for what you've received, such as a poured libation or a small crystal to honor the earth. You can also say "thanks" to the earth by cleaning up litter or other debris.

If you don't intend to use a plant immediately after harvesting it, dry it properly so that it will retain as much of its life force as possible. The best way to dry herbs is to hang them upside down in bunches in a cool, dry, relatively dark place. You can also dry them flat by spreading them out on a plate or cutting board wrapped in cloth. If you choose the flat drying method, you will need to turn the leaves, stems, or flowers frequently so that they dry evenly and do not rot.

You can either leave plants hanging in bunches or remove the leaves and flowers and store them in airtight jars or bottles made of dark glass (amber and cobalt). This slows the damaging effects of light and will preserve the herbs for a longer period of time.

Dandelion Blossom Oil

You can use this basic flower oil recipe for anointing candles and talismans. Dandelions grow wild and you may not prize them highly because they're "weeds," but their commonplace nature doesn't diminish their magickal power.

INGREDIENTS/TOOLS:

Dandelion blossoms

Jar with a tight lid

Cold-pressed olive oil or grape seed oil (amount determined by size of jar)

1 chopstick

Gather the dandelions at high noon on a sunny day—this imbues them with the radiant energy of the sun, and for practical purposes ensures that the blossoms will be dry. Fill your jar completely with the dandelion blossoms and pour in enough oil to completely fill the jar. Press out the air bubbles with the chopstick. Cap the jar and keep it in a cool, dry area. For the first two weeks, you'll need to open the jar every few days to press out the air bubbles and refill the jar with oil up to the top, making sure that the lid is tightly closed afterward. After that, you can use this lovely flower oil to anoint any objects you may use in your spellwork.

Using Botanicals in Magick

You can use botanicals, whether fresh or dried, in numerous ways. Put dried plant material in pouches to make amulets and talismans, or choose especially fragrant herbs and flowers for sachets and potpourri. Many of the spells in Part II use botanicals in this way.

Some plants may be burned in ritual fires, as offerings, or for purification. Sage is one of the most popular plants to use for this purpose. Many botanicals also come in the form of incense (sticks, cones, coils), which you can burn in spells and rituals—lots of the spells in Part II involve burning incense.

You can make an herbal infusion by boiling water, removing the water from the heat, and then adding herbs or flowers to the water. Let the plant material steep in the water for several minutes, and then strain and pour the water into a glass container. If you wish, set flowers in water and leave them in the sun to "steep." The essence of the flowers will be imparted to the water. Add a tiny amount of liquor such as brandy or vodka to the water to preserve it. Mist a room with flower water to purify it or sprinkle a little on an amulet or talisman to charge it.

You can prepare essential oils from plants if you like (although many people find it easier to purchase the oils). Oils are often used for anointing, consecrating, and blessing. You can add them to baths, too, and some may be ingested (but check first, as some are toxic). Each type of oil, like the plant from which it is derived, has its unique associations that enhance the power of your spell.

Burning a Ritual Fire

The Druids revered trees and understood the magickal nature of different types of trees. Oaks, for instance, symbolize strength and longevity; ashes and rowans provide protection; cedars attract prosperity; pines purify. You can burn a single type of wood or combine several in a ritual fire to produce a desired effect. If you decide to cut a twig or branch from a tree, remember to ask the tree's permission first and thank it afterward. Leaving an offering for the tree, such as some organic fertilizer, is also a nice idea.

THE POWER OF STONES

Long before people prized gems for monetary reasons, they valued stones for their magick properties. Spellworkers still do. You've probably already used gems for spells, although you may not have realized it at the time. Have you ever worn a piece of jewelry that contained your birthstone? Birthstones resonate with the energy of your zodiac sign and they've been worn since ancient times to enhance, modify, and balance a person's astrological makeup.

The dense nature of stones and their great endurance allows them to hold energy for a very long time. A gem that belonged to your great-grandmother probably still retains some of her energy resonance. This means that you can cast a spell using a stone and it will last for years. It also means that you need to cleanse stones before you work with them to remove any lingering vibes from people who handled them before you.

Just as each plant embodies certain characteristics and qualities that you can tap in spellwork, so does each stone. Often a stone's magickal properties relate to its color(s), perhaps even more than its mineral composition. Again, this is an example of sympathetic magick and the associations we place on colors. The following list shows the relationships between a stone's color and its magickal meaning:

- Red stones: Passion, courage, vitality
- Orange stones: Enthusiasm, good luck, self-confidence
- Yellow stones: Happiness, creativity (citrine or yellow quartz is used for cleansing)
- Green stones: Prosperity, growth, physical healing
- Blue stones: Peace, communication, psychic ability
- Purple stones: Wisdom, vision, connection with higher powers
- Pink stones: Love, friendship, social interactions, emotional balance
- White stones: Purity, cleansing, clarity, protection
- Black stones: Stability/permanence, banishing negativity, establishing boundaries

Gems are sacred in and of themselves, whether we choose to acknowledge them as such or not. They're not inert lumps; they possess life energy. That energy will manifest in your spells, so consider the gems you select and your connection with them carefully.

Preparing Stones for Spellwork

Amulets, talismans, and other types of spells frequently include stones. You may choose to use only one stone in a spell or combine several to fine-tune your objectives. Let's say, for example, that you're doing a love spell and you want to generate both passion and affection. In this case, you could incorporate both carnelian and rose quartz. If you seek stability too, add a piece of onyx.

If you only use one stone in your spellwork, let it be a clear quartz crystal. These readily available stones can do it all. They hold ideas and intentions; they attract and send information; they augment, focus, and direct energy; they store material for future use; they let you gaze into the future and the past. Crystals come in a variety of colors, due to minerals in their composition. Those colors provide clues to the crystals' use in spells.

Warning!

Don't drill holes in the stones you choose for your magick work. Gemstones and crystals are life forms, and if you bore into them or break them you may kill them. Instead, wrap them with wire or have a jeweler set them if you plan to wear them. Loose stones are great for amulets and talismans. Large stones aren't necessarily better than smaller ones—use your intuition and let yourself be drawn to the right stone for the job.

Before you begin working with gems and crystals, clear the stones of any residual energy left over from someone who may have previously handled the gems. Try one of the following methods:

- Wash the stone with mild soap and water, then leave it in the sunshine to dry. If you can hold it in the running water of a lovely, unpolluted stream, even better.
- Let the stone sit in the moonlight overnight to clear it.
- Smudge the gem by holding it in the smoke of burning sage or nestle it in a bed of dried sage leaves.
- Rub your stone gently with a piece of citrine (yellow quartz).
- Bury the gemstone in the earth for several days, or if possible, for the whole lunar month, beginning on the full moon.

Using Gemstones and Crystals in Spells

At the beginning of most chapters in Part II, you'll find a list of specific stones that witches and other magicians typically use for spells of certain types. Generally speaking, opaque stones work well in spells that involve material things; cloudy or translucent stones are best for emotional situations; clear stones relate to mental or spiritual conditions.

Crystals and gemstones are among a spellcaster's most basic and versatile tools. You can apply them in virtually any spell, in a variety of ways according to your preferences and the nature of the spell:

- Slip one or more stones and/or crystals into a mojo pouch or medicine bag to create a talisman or amulet.
- Carry a meaningful stone in your pocket to augment your personal energy.
- Wear gemstones/birthstones to heighten, calm, strengthen, balance, or otherwise influence your own energy patterns.
- Infuse water with a stone that relates to your intention, then remove the stone and drink the water.
- Add stones to bathwater to boost its healthful qualities.
- Place stones or crystals in your home to provide protection, harmonize energy patterns, or attract conditions you desire.
- Offer stones to deities and spirits in return for their assistance.
- Put a protection stone or quartz crystal in your car to keep you safe while traveling.
- Position stones on your body's chakras (energy centers) to promote health and well being (see Chapter 15).
- Gaze into a crystal to see beyond your normal range of vision; this is known as scrying.
- Use a gemstone or crystal as a pendulum to dowse (see Chapter 6).
- Meditate with stones and/or crystals to deepen your concentration and relaxation.
- Take a crystal with you when you travel and let it record the memory of the trip.
- Imprint a crystal with a message or intention, then direct it toward someone you wish to contact. You can do this by first holding the crystal to your forehead and sending your thoughts into the crystal, or by holding it to your lips and telling it what you want it to do. Then aim the crystal away from you and envision your message flowing out through the pointed end toward the other person.

This list barely scratches the surface of the magickal possibilities available to you. In Part II of this book, you'll find lots of spells that incorporate the power of gemstones and crystals. The more you work with stones, the more you'll discover. Treat your stones with love and respect. Cleanse them frequently to remove unwanted vibes (unless

The Modern Witchcraft Spell Book

they'll remain in place permanently as part of a spell). When you're not using them, store your stones in a safe place—wrapping them in silk will help to prevent ambient vibrations from affecting them. If you prefer, display them with pride on your altar or in another place of honor. Treat your crystals and gemstones as valued partners, and they will gladly work with you for a lifetime.

Chapter 5

THE POWER OF WORDS

Each of us is born with a wonderful instrument that we can use for healing, transformation, and magick: the voice. The earliest spells were probably spoken ones. Ancient shamans, witches, and sorcerers understood that sound and resonance had the power to shift reality. They may have uttered words that held meaning in an evident way, but that also contained sounds that impacted the ethers when said aloud. Today, spellworkers still use chants, prayers, affirmations, and other types of verbal magick, as you'll see when you get to Part II of this book.

In the mid-1990s, Japanese scientist Masaru Emoto began experimenting with how words affected water. He discovered that words could visibly alter the water's structure. Just as each snowflake is unique, Emoto found that each word produced a unique shape when the water was frozen. When the words *love, gratitude,* and *peace* were projected into the water, it froze into beautiful shapes. Expressions such as "I hate you" caused distorted, broken forms. The vibrational energy actually changed the physical appearance and the molecular shape of the water. Interestingly, it didn't matter what language was used. The words *love*, *amour*, *amore*, and the kanji symbol for love all generated similar snowflakes.

Because the universe—and everything in it—is composed of vibrations, all sounds produce effects. When you consider that all words create results, it makes sense to choose your words wisely and to think before you speak.

THE POWER OF PRAYER

For thousands of years, in cultures around the world, people have sought divine intervention to relieve suffering and attract blessings via the use of prayers. John Bunyan, a seventeenth-century English preacher and writer, said that prayer is the "sincere, sensible, affectionate pouring out of the soul to God." American poet Ralph Waldo Emerson described prayer as "a study of truth." The Unity Church calls prayer an "inward, silent knowing of the soul . . . of the presence of God." Witches view prayer as a means of communicating with the Divine.

Healing with Prayer

Like meditation, praying calms the mind and body, placing you in a gently altered state of consciousness where you can receive insights and guidance. On the physical level, blood pressure drops, heartbeat slows, breathing rate is lowered, and the adrenal glands secrete fewer of the stress-response hormones. Consequently, not only the recipient of the prayer benefits; so does the person who's praying. Prayer is also a demonstration of hope, and as you already know, hopefulness and a positive attitude can manifest beneficial results.

Whether you pray for yourself or someone else, your words have amazing power. According to Larry Dossey, MD, author of *Prayer Is Good Medicine*, in cases of intercessory prayer (praying for someone else at a distance) the consciousness of the person doing the praying actually influences the body of the person who is being prayed for. Dossey discovered that "more than 130 controlled laboratory studies show that prayer, or a prayerlike state of compassion, empathy and love, can bring

The Modern Witchcraft Spell Book

about healthful changes." Numerous studies have shown that prayer can have a beneficial effect on a range of illnesses.

Prayer and Magick

Much of magickal work involves healing—doing spells for yourself or for others. Therefore, it's encouraging to realize that the results of your words and intentions can actually be measured scientifically. However, you can tap the power of prayer for virtually any purpose: to gain protection, to attract love, and so on.

When you pray to a higher power, it implies that you honor that higher power—God, Goddess, Spirit, your guardian angel, or however you envision it—and that an established relationship exists between you, which enables you to call on that higher power for aid. It also implies that you believe the higher power can remedy the situation. Prayer isn't begging or pleading with a deity to give you what you want—it's humbly aligning your personal will with Divine Will. You commit yourself to co-creating the best possible outcome, under the guidance of a higher power.

How to Pray

Prayer can take many forms, from the formal repetition in a church or temple of memorized verses taken from a religious text, to feeling grateful for a beautiful sunny day. You can pray silently or aloud, alone or with others, for yourself or someone else. You can pray first thing in the morning, before meals, at bedtime—or when you're stuck in traffic, in the shower, at your computer, or taking a walk in the park. You can even join an online prayer group. The Internet offers hundreds of sites where you can post a prayer request, respond to others who currently need help, or read the personal testimonies of people who believe they've been helped by prayers.

WORDS OF POWER

Spiritual and occult literature abounds with references to the power of the human voice. For millennia people have recited magick words as a way of evoking supernatural forces and petitioning them for assistance.

This is usually done by calling out the deities' names. Speaking someone's name is said to be an act of power, giving the namer influence over the named (which is why in some belief systems, individuals have "public" names and "private" names that are kept secret). In the Genesis story, Adam was allowed to name the animals on earth and thus was given dominion over them.

Witches and spellworkers recognize the power inherent in some words and use them in spells and rituals. You've undoubtedly heard the word *abracadabra*, but the word isn't just something a stage illusionist says before he pulls a rabbit out of a hat. It derives from the Aramaic *Avarah K'Davarah*, which translates to "I will create as I speak"; it expresses your intention to manifest a result. Ancient magicians wrote the word as an inverted pyramid and used it in healing spells. In Chapter 13, you'll learn how to do this, too.

Many witches end spells with the words "So mote it be." This phrase (like "So be it") seals a spell and instructs the universe to carry out your will. If you want to banish an entity or energy, you can order it to leave by saying, "Be gone." The expression "Blessed be" is a favorite greeting among witches and a magickal exchange of positive energy.

In spells, you can choose to speak or write a single word, a phrase, or a longer statement. Words such as *love, abundance, peace, happiness,* and *safety* instantly bring to mind the results you seek. When you say the words aloud, you send a ripple through the cosmos stating your intention. When you write the words, the acupressure points in your fingers trigger responses in your brain. Many of the spells in Part II use words as components.

I Am

One of the most powerful and sacred statements is also one of the shortest: I am. It connects you with your divine essence for creative purposes. You can consciously choose to form a sentence that begins with "I am" in order to manifest a desired condition. Be very careful how you use the phrase "I am." Whatever follows these words will be charged with magickal energy and intention. *Never* say hurtful or derogatory things such as "I am stupid" or "I am ugly"—these statements can materialize as unpleasant conditions.

AFFIRMATIONS

A good way to state your intention in a spell is to create what's called an affirmation. An affirmation is a short phrase or sentence that clearly and optimistically expresses whatever condition you desire to bring about. Affirmations leave no room for doubt, fear, or ambiguity. Whether you write affirmations or say them aloud, putting your intentions into words helps to focus your mind and empower your spells.

Creating Effective Affirmations

As is true with most things in life, there are "right" ways and "wrong" ways to design affirmations. These tips will help you to word yours effectively:

- Keep it short.
- Use only positive imagery.
- State your intention in the present tense, as if the condition already exists.

Let's try a couple examples to help you get a feel for designing affirmations.

Right: I am completely healthy in body, mind, and spirit.

Wrong: I don't have any illnesses or injuries.

See the difference? The first sentence affirms what you seek: health. The second makes you think of conditions you don't want: illnesses and injuries.

Right: I now have a job that's perfect for me.

Wrong: I will get the perfect job.

In the first sentence you state that the job you seek is yours right now. The second indicates that you'll eventually get the job you want, but it could be some time way off in the future.

Being specific is usually a good thing when creating affirmations. If your goal is to lose twenty-five pounds or you've got your heart set on acquiring a 1965 red Mustang convertible with black leather seats, for instance, list the pertinent details in your affirmation. But sometimes you don't know all the ins and outs of a situation, or you don't want to limit your options—as in the job example we just considered. Sometimes it's best to let the universe work out the fine points.

Here's a case in point. A friend of mine wanted to attract more money into her life, so she wrote this affirmation: "I now earn more than enough money for everything I need and desire." When I read what she'd written, I immediately noticed she'd limited her potential by using the word *earn*. I suggested she revise her affirmation so it said: "I now receive more than enough money for everything I need and desire." Soon afterward, she got an unexpected tax refund that fulfilled her affirmation.

Using Affirmations in Spells

When you cast a spell, you can say affirmations aloud if you like. Or you can write them on slips of paper and put them in mojo or medicine pouches, to use as talismans or amulets. Some people like to carve words into candles and then burn the candles during a spell. Another popular way to use affirmations is to write them on a vision board and place the board where you'll see it often. Each time you read the words, you'll be reminded of your objective. Once you understand the basics of creating affirmations, you'll probably find lots of original ways to include them in your spells and rituals.

INCANTATIONS

Want to kick an affirmation up a notch? Design it as an incantation. Incantations are written as rhymes. The catchy phrasing and rhythm make the incantation easy to remember. The rhythm also adds power to your statement by drawing upon nature's rhythmic patterns, e.g., waves breaking on the shore or the beat of your heart. Don't worry about the literary quality of your incantations; just follow the same guidelines for creating affirmations, then make your statements rhyme.

Incantations can be as short as two lines or as long as your imagination and intention dictate. You can use an incantation in the same way you'd use any other affirmation. Although it's perfectly okay to merely write an incantation, more often they are spoken aloud. Because incantations feature both rhyme and meter, you may enjoy putting them to music and singing them.

Here's an example of an incantation to attract love, from my book *Nice Spells/Naughty Spells*:

As the day fades into night
I draw a love that's good and right.
As the night turns into day
We are blessed in every way.

Okay, it's not going to win any awards for literary value, but it gets the message across and that's what counts. You'll find more incantations in Part II of this book. Creating incantations is fun—use your imagination to design your own. The more energy you infuse into your creation, the more effective it will be. If you do spellwork with other people, singing an incantation together raises the energy exponentially. Wiccans and witches often sing incantations at celebrations. Chanting a love incantation while dancing around a Maypole on Beltane, for instance, is a joyful and powerful form of magick.

CHANTS

When you think of chanting, your mind may produce an image of Buddhists uttering the Sanskrit phrase *Om Mani Padme Hum* or medieval monks intoning Gregorian chants in European cathedrals. Chants are typically phrases, words, or syllables repeated aloud for a particular purpose. Saying a rosary is a form of chanting, for example. Witches sometimes chant rhymes in their rituals to raise energy and to unify all the participants. Some shamans even use chanting to reconnect a person's soul with the physical body after a trauma has caused a separation.

Dr. Alfred Tomatis, a French eye, ear, and nose specialist affectionately known as "Dr. Mozart," noticed that the ear was the first sense organ to develop. According to Tomatis, frequencies in the range of 2,000 to 4,000 cycles per second—those found in the upper range of the human speaking voice—are the most beneficial in healing. These resonances stimulate vibrations in the cranial bones and the ear muscles, which then revitalize or "charge" the brain.

The repetitive nature of a chant, as well as the actual words that compose it, act on your subconscious to generate results. You may wish to accompany your chanting with drumming, clapping, rattles, dancing, or playing musical instruments, in order to increase psychic energy. The vibration of the chanting (as well as that of any other accompanying sound) has a measurable effect on the nervous system. At its height, chanting can even stimulate altered states of awareness, including ecstatic trances.

Some people chant mantras while meditating. A mantra is a group of sacred sounds repeated for spiritual purposes. The mantra not only helps you to focus, it lets you become aware of the spirit housed within your body. By recognizing this spirit and your connection with it, you move from the material world into the magickal realm. That's why it's often beneficial to meditate prior to doing spellwork.

You can chant to create circumstances you desire. You can also chant to enhance your link with divine entities or to call upon them for assistance. Chanting is a particularly good way to dispel unwanted energies. The cumulative power of the repeated sounds breaks down obstacles that might otherwise impede a spell's success, just as sound waves can break down obstructions such as kidney stones in the body.

SIGILS

Have you ever wanted to write in your own secret language? Guess what, you can. One way to do this is to design sigils to use in your spellwork. A sigil is a uniquely personal symbol you draw in order to produce a specific result. In a sense, a sigil is a way of communicating with yourself via secret code, because no one else can interpret the symbol. Although there are various techniques for designing sigils, the easiest one involves fashioning an image from letters.

Start by writing a word or a short affirmation that states your intention. Delete any letters that are repeated. For example, the word *SUCCESS* contains three Ss and two Cs, but you only need to put one of each into your sigil. Entwine the remaining letters to form an image. You can use upper- and/or lower-case letters, block or script. Position them right-side up, upside down, forward, or backward. The end result depicts your objective in a graphic manner that your subconscious understands, although it won't make sense to anyone else. Each time you look at the sigil, you'll instantly recognize its meaning at a deep level and that reinforces your intention.

The following sigil takes the letters L O V E and combines them to create an image (the L is inherent to the E). Of course, you could configure the letters in a zillion different ways, according to your own preferences, and each design would be uniquely powerful. That's what makes sigils so special.

The process of creating the sigil as well as applying it are magick acts. Treat them that way. You may wish to design the sigil as a magickal working in itself and then use the sigil later as a component of another spell. In this way, you both craft and cast, and produce two effects by doing so: the crafting part—drawing the sigil—produces an effect on the person who draws it; it can then be used in casting another spell, for example the sigil for LOVE could be added to a love talisman. You can incorporate sigils into spells in myriad ways, for instance:

- Draw a sigil on a piece of paper and slip it into a mojo or medicine bag.
- Display a sigil on your altar to remind you of your intention.
- Hang one on the door to your home to provide protection.
- Carve one on a candle, and then burn the candle to activate your objective.
- Draw or embroider a sigil on a dream pillow.
- Add them to paintings, collages, or other artwork you create.

- Paint one on a glass so it can imprint water, wine, or another beverage with your intent.
- Have a jeweler fabricate your sigil as a pendant or pin and wear it as a talisman.
- Get a sigil tattooed on your body.

In Part II of this book, you'll find suggestions for using sigils in spells. There's no limit to how many sigils you can draw or how many ways you can use them. Give your imagination free rein.

Chapter 6

MAGICK TOOLS AND ACCOUTREMENTS

Carpenters use hammers, saws, screwdrivers, and lots of other tools in their work. Chefs use knives, spoons, bowls, pots, and pans. What do spellworkers use? Technically speaking, you don't need anything except your mind to cast a spell. However, people who do magick generally use certain tools and accoutrements, in part because these help you to focus and therefore achieve greater success with your spells.

The tools you use to do magick speak to your subconscious mind. A tool's shape, material, and other features provide clues to its symbolism and thus its role in spellwork, according to the concept of sympathetic magick. Although some items may look familiar, their magickal purposes may differ significantly from their roles in the mundane world. In this chapter, we'll look at some of the most popular tools witches, wizards, and other spellworkers use and the roles these implements play in spells. Remember, however, that even the most elegant tool requires your will to empower it. You may decide to work with a few of these, all, or none—it's up to you entirely.

Masculine and Feminine Energies

When we speak of masculine and feminine energies, we don't mean man and woman. Instead, we're referring to the complementary forces that exist everywhere in our universe: action (masculine) and receptivity (feminine). You'll notice that a spellcaster's tools correspond to the human body, symbolically depicting those energies. The wand and the athame, which represent masculine power, look distinctly phallic. The chalice and cauldron signify feminine energy and the womb. The five rays of the pentagram stand for the five "points" of the body: the head, arms, and legs.

THE WAND

You're familiar with magick wands, no doubt. The fairy tales we loved as children told us that you could tap a guy on the head with a magick wand and turn him into a frog or make him disappear. That's not the reason spellworkers use wands, though. A wand's real purpose is to direct energy. You can either attract or send energy with your wand. Aim it at the heavens to draw down cosmic power. Point it toward a person, place, or thing to project energy toward your goal. Some magicians cast circles with their wands.

Choosing Your Wand

What material makes the best wand? Traditionally, magicians used wood for their wands, particularly willow, yew, hazel, or rowan. But you don't have to hold with tradition. If you prefer, select a wand fabricated from metal, glass, quartz, ceramic—whatever "calls" to you. If you decide you want a wooden wand and plan to cut a small branch from a tree, always ask the tree's permission first and thank it when you've finished. (It's nice to give the tree an offering in return, too.) Cutting a wand is a ritual in itself, so approach the task with the proper mindset.

Your wand should be at least six inches long, but no longer or heavier than you find comfortable to handle. Are you a down-to-basics kind of

The Modern Witchcraft Spell Book

person? If so, you might want to leave your wand in its natural state. Would you enjoy something more ornate? Then decorate your wand to suit your fancy. Again, the choice is yours; however, because the wand is considered a "fire" tool, you might like to enhance its fiery nature with appropriate adornments, such as:

- Red, orange, or gold paint
- Gold, brass, or iron accents
- Red or orange gemstones: garnet, ruby, carnelian, red jasper
- Astrological glyphs for the fire signs: Aries, Leo, Sagittarius
- Red or orange ribbons, feathers, beadwork, etc.

Charging Your Wand

Now it's time to infuse your wand with magickal power. This transforms it from a stick of wood or a metal rod into an awesome tool for spellwork. Witches, wizards, and other magicians often enact a ritual or ceremony to charge their tools. It can be as simple or elaborate as you wish; your intention and attitude are the most important factors. Part of my wand-charging ritual involved hanging my wand from a tree in the sunshine for a solar month. Because charging your wand is a magickal act, approach the ritual with the proper mindset and perform it within a circle.

You might consider one or more of the following techniques:

- Hold your wand in the smoke of a ritual fire.
- Anoint it with essential oil(s): cinnamon, sandalwood, clove, musk.
- Carve it with words and/or symbols of power.
- Chant an incantation you've composed for this purpose.
- Play energizing music.

Clearly and authoritatively instruct your wand to do your bidding. Command it to work with you and only you. Point it toward the south and invite the energy of fire to enter it. Breathe your own energy into the wand to bring it to life. When you've finished, state aloud: So mote it be!

Magick Wands at Hogwarts

What woods make the best magick wands? According to author J.K. Rowling, Harry Potter's first wand is made from holly, while Hermione Granger's is made from vine wood. Ron Weasley's first wand is fashioned from ash, and Draco Malfoy's from hawthorn. The evil Lord Voldemort chose yew for his wand—a wood that magicians link with longevity, but that also has associations with death.

These suggestions are just that: suggestions. The best and most powerful charging rituals are those you design yourself. Put lots of energy and enthusiasm into your work. Pull out all the stops. Make it as personal as you can—the more meaningful it is to you, the better.

PENTAGRAM

The pentagram is a five-pointed star with a circle around it. Many witches wear this symbol for protection. You might choose to display one on the door to your home or place of business as a safeguard. Keep a pentagram in your car and on your altar. Draw them on paper and slip them into mojo or medicine pouches to make amulets. Carve pentagrams into candles and burn them during spellwork. In circle casting, you can trace pentagrams in the air or on the ground at the four directions to ensure safety. Many of the protection spells in Chapter 11 use pentagrams.

Choosing a Pentagram

The pentagram represents the earth element and is linked with the feminine force. Consequently, you might like to have a pentagram made of silver (a metal ruled by the moon) or copper (which is ruled by Venus). Perhaps you'd like to decorate your pentagram with crystals or gemstones, especially if you plan to wear it as a piece of jewelry. No material is inherently right or wrong, better or worse—it really depends on how you intend to use your pentagram.

Although you will probably only use one magick wand, you can have as many pentagrams as you want. You might like one made of ceramic, glass, or wood on which to serve food during rituals, perhaps decorated with the astrological glyphs for the earth signs: Taurus, Virgo, and Capricorn. If you're handy, you can embroider pentagrams on ritual

The Modern Witchcraft Spell Book

clothing. If you plan to hang a pentagram outside, make sure it can with-stand weather conditions. Display your pentagram with one point up, two down, and two out at the sides.

Charging Your Pentagram

As discussed earlier, the ritual of charging your tools empowers them and transforms them into magickal instruments. Consider the act of charging your pentagram a spell, and do it with the appropriate intent. You may choose to create an intricate ritual to charge it, or keep it sim-ple. Here are a few suggestions:

- Mist it with flower water made with carnation, snapdragon, gera-nium, and/or hyacinth petals. (If your pentagram is made of metal, pat it dry to prevent tarnishing.)
- Anoint it with essential oil(s): amber, basil, pine, fennel.
- Bury it in the earth for a period of time, perhaps a week. (You may need to encase it in a protective container.)
- Lay it on your altar and place crystals at each of the five points and in the center.
- Chant an incantation you've composed for this purpose.
- Let it sit in the moonlight overnight.

Clearly and authoritatively instruct your pentagram to do your bid-ding. Command it to work with you and only you. Point it toward the north and invite the energy of earth to enter it. Breathe your own ener-gy into the pentagram to bring it to life. When you've finished, state aloud: So mote it be!

ATHAME

The origins of the word *athame* have been lost to history. Some peo-ple speculate that it may have come from *The Key of Solomon* (*Clavicula Salomonis*) (published in 1572), which refers to the knife as the *Arthana* (*athame* may be a subverted form of this term). Another theory proposes that *athame* derives from the Arabic word *al-dhamme* (blood-letter), a sacred knife in the Moorish tradition. In either case, manuscripts dating back to the 1200s imply the use of ritual knives in magick work.

The athame's main purpose is to symbolically clear negative energies from a space you'll use in spellworking. You can also slice through obstacles or sever bonds with it, again symbolically. It needn't be sharp—you won't be chopping veggies with it. Some Wiccans and witches like to cast a circle with an athame instead of a wand.

Choosing Your Athame

This ritual dagger is usually a double-edged knife about four to six inches long. Some Wiccans, however, prefer crescent-shaped athames that represent the moon. Most athames are made of metal, but yours can be crystal, glass, or another material. An ordinary kitchen knife will work, too. If you like something more elegant, choose one that's adorned with crystals or gemstones. Because this tool symbolizes the air element, consider stones associated with air, such as aquamarine, fluorite, or clear quartz.

If you decide to purchase a vintage dagger for your magick work, make sure it hasn't drawn blood in the past. Some magicians believe that an athame used to physically harm another will never again be functional in magick, although in ancient times witches often "fed" special knives by rubbing them with blood.

Charging Your Athame

Before you use your athame in spellwork, charge it to make it truly "yours" and to imbue it with magickal power. Remember, this is a spell in itself, so approach the process accordingly. How you go about charging your athame is up to you—you can simply command it to do your will, or design a ritual with all sorts of bells and whistles. Here are some possibilities:

- Hold it in the smoke of burning incense.
- Anoint it with essential oil(s): carnation, lavender, ginger.
- Attach feathers to its hilt and/or decorate the hilt with the astrological glyphs for the air signs: Gemini, Libra, or Aquarius.

- Tie yellow or light blue ribbons on it, and recite a prayer or incantation with each knot.
- Play flute music, ring a bell, or place your athame near wind chimes to receive their sounds.

Clearly and authoritatively instruct your athame to do your bidding. Command it to work with you and only you. Point it toward the east and invite the energy of air to enter it. Breathe your own energy into the athame to bring it to life. When you've finished, state aloud: So mote it be!

CHALICE

The fourth major tool in the witch's tool kit is the chalice, which symbolizes the element of water. During rituals and rites, witches often drink ceremonial beverages from a chalice—many chalices feature long stems so they can be passed easily from hand to hand. Sharing the cup with coven members or spellworkers signifies connectedness and unity of purpose. You may choose to drink magick potions you've concocted from your chalice. Spellworkers also serve magickal elixirs, for healing or other purposes, in a special chalice.

The most famous chalice of all is the Holy Grail. The Grail myths embody far more information than we can go into here, but you may wish to examine them to gain a greater understanding of the magickal meaning of the chalice. Shaped like the womb, the chalice represents feminine fertility, power, and creativity in the larger sense. This potent vessel holds the waters of life and nurtures the imagination that births all things in the manifest world.

Choosing Your Chalice

Your chalice is a sacred vessel from which you will sip magick potions and ceremonial beverages. As such, it should be reserved for these special occasions—don't drink Coke from it at lunchtime. Depending on your preferences, your chalice may be simple or ornate. Some people choose chalices made of silver, because silver is a metal ruled by the moon and the chalice is a feminine tool. Others prefer crystal, colored glass, or ceramic chalices—the choice is entirely yours. You could even use an ordinary water glass or coffee cup, but that might not be quite as much fun. The beauty of the chalice, the way it feels in your hand, and the sound it makes when you clink it to another chalice in a toast all contribute to the experience.

In Chapter 5, we talked about Japanese scientist Masaru Emoto's work with imprinting water with words. Because the liquids that go into your chalice will absorb the energy of whatever images are on the vessel, it's best to choose a plain chalice without pictures, words, or patterns, as those may affect your spells. If you wish, you can decorate your chalice with temporary images that relate to your intentions for a spell and remove those images when you've finished.

Charging Your Chalice

Until you charge your chalice, it's just an ordinary vessel. Once you've imbued it with your magickal energy, it becomes your own "Grail." The ritual you enact to charge your chalice may be simple or complex, depending on your preferences. I charged my chalice by submerging it in a sacred pool for a lunar month. Because this tool symbolizes the element of water, many magicians choose to charge it with water or another liquid. Here are some suggestions:

- Spritz it with flower water made from jasmine, rose, lotus, or gardenia blossoms.
- Sprinkle it with "holy" water from a well, spring, or lake that holds special meaning for you. (Pat metal chalices dry afterward to prevent tarnishing.)
- Nestle the chalice in a bed of white rose petals, and leave it overnight.
- Anoint it on the outside with essential oil(s): rose, jasmine, ylang-ylang, gardenia.
- Paint your chalice with the astrological glyphs for Cancer, Scorpio, or Pisces.
- Place a piece of rose quartz, amethyst, moonstone, or a pearl in the chalice and fill it with spring water. Let it sit overnight, then remove the gem and either drink the water or pour it into a clear glass jar for use later.

- Play a singing bowl near your chalice to infuse it with positive vibrations. Singing bowls are usually made of metal or crystal and they have different musical tones. You strike them or run a mallet around the rim to create sound, which can be used for meditation, healing, or other purposes.

Clearly and authoritatively instruct your chalice to do your bidding. Command it to work with you and only you. Hold it so that the bowl of the chalice faces west and invite the energy of water to enter it. Breathe your own energy into the chalice to bring it to life. When you've finished, state aloud: So mote it be!

Magick Tools and the Tarot

You can see these four main tools illustrated in the beautiful oracle known as the tarot (which we'll talk about later). Each suit in the deck of cards is named for one of these tools: wands (sometimes called rods or staves), swords (or daggers, meaning athames), cups (or chalices), and pentacles (or pentagrams, sometimes called coins or disks). As such, they describe fundamental life energies and ways of interacting with the world.

CANDLES

The most common and versatile tool you're likely to use in your magickal practice, candles play a role in lots of rituals and spells. They also brighten many of our secular and religious celebrations. The concept of illumination carries both a practical meaning—visible light that enables you to see to conduct your daily tasks—and an esoteric one—an inspiration or awakening that enlivens mundane existence and expands understanding. The flame represents the element of fire, inspiration, clarity, passion, activity, energy, and purification. It can also signify Spirit.

You can use candles to set the stage for magick; their soft, flickering glow transports the spellworker into another level of awareness. You can gaze into a candle's flame to see beyond the ordinary limits of vision, even into the past or future. Many witches and other magicians use candles to tap color relationships in spellwork—burning a candle of a relevant color can augment a spell or ritual. "Dressing" or anointing your candles with essential oils adds another sensory dimension. As you evolve in your work as a spellcaster, you'll probably want to stock up on candles in various colors, sizes, and shapes—tapers for creating moods, pillars for long-term spells, votives for shorter spells/rituals and circle casting, and so on.

Some witches like to make their own candles, blending the wax with herbs/flowers, essential oils, and dyes that represent their intentions. You can even form candle wax into shapes that signify your objectives. In Part II, you'll find lots of spells that use candles in various ways to produce magickal results.

INCENSE

For thousands of years, aromatic gums and resins have been used in sacred rituals. Ancient Chinese and Indian texts describe the therapeutic, philosophical, and spiritual properties of aromatics. Churches and temples use incense to clear the air and to honor deities. In Buddhist belief, burning an offering of incense invites the Buddha into a statue of the holy being. Incense also serves as a vehicle for conveying prayers to the spirit world—as the smoke rises, it carries your requests along with it.

Aromas trigger instantaneous reactions in the brain. Inhaling certain smells can cause measurable responses involving memory, emotions, awareness, and more. That's one reason magickal workers include scents in their spells.

Burning incense combines the elements of fire and air. You can use it to cast a circle by walking the perimeter and trailing the fragrant smoke behind you. For balance, walk the circle a second time while sprinkling saltwater to represent the elements of earth and water. You can also charge talismans, amulets, and other magickal tools with incense by holding them in the smoke for a few moments.

Many witches purify a sacred space with incense. Sage is the most frequently used herb for this purpose, but you can burn pine, frankincense, sandalwood, eucalyptus, or another scent if you prefer. The best incense is blended from pure gums and resins, without synthetic binders.

You can even make your own by grinding up aromatic wood or resin (with a mortar and pestle or a coffee grinder) and adding finely powdered herbs or dried flowers.

Choose a scent that matches your intentions. You'll find lists at the beginnings of most chapters in Part II that show which scents correspond to love, money, protection, and so on.

Essential Oils

Like incense, aromatic oils enhance your sensory experience during a spell or ritual. These plant extracts contain the life energy of the plant, its unique signature and "soul essence." Unlike commercial fragrances, they do not include synthetic ingredients in their composition. You can use essential oils to dress candles, anoint talismans and amulets, charge magick tools, add to ritual baths, perfume your skin, and lots more. Use caution, however, because some oils can cause allergic reactions and some are toxic if ingested. Because essential oils are volatile, store them in a cool, dark place to prevent deterioration.

CAULDRON

According to Norse mythology, the god Odin received wisdom and the gift of intuition from a cauldron. Celtic legend mentions a cauldron as a tool of regeneration for the gods, and artists often depict the Irish creativity goddess Brigid stirring a cauldron. Stories such as these give us clues to the symbolic value of the cauldron today. Its shape represents the womb from which all life flows and its three legs represent the three-fold nature of human existence: body, mind, spirit.

The cauldron performs both symbolic and practical functions. You can use a cauldron to cook ritual foods and to concoct magick potions. It also serves as a handy vessel for holding water, flowers, or other items at a ceremony or ritual. If you like, you can build a fire inside your cauldron and drop wishes written on paper into the flames—the cauldron's creative qualities nurture your requests and bring them to fruition. Build your fire of sacred woods that pertain to your purpose: cedar for prosperity, ash for protection, apple for love. Although usually iron, a cauldron can be made of any fireproof material including copper, steel, or terra cotta—you can even draft an ordinary cooking pot into duty if need be.

SPELL BOTTLES

Spell or "witch" bottles contain items with similar energies, brought together for a specific intention. Depending on your purpose, the bottle can be a temporary or permanent fixture. Select a glass bottle that's large enough to hold all the ingredients you plan to put in it, then wash and dry it to remove any unwanted energies. Make sure all the ingredients correspond to your objective. Add botanicals, gemstones, coins, milagros, shells, or anything else that symbolizes your intention. You may wish to write an affirmation or sigil on a slip of paper, roll the paper into a scroll, and then put it into the bottle, too.

When you're certain you've included everything you need for your spell, close the lid and seal the bottle with wax dripped from a candle that you've designated as part of the spell. Once the spell is cast, the bottle should remain sealed. You may choose to place your mark on the wax seal and/or decorate the outside of the bottle with symbols, words, images, ribbons, etc. that relate to your spell. Place the bottle on your altar or in another spot in your home or business, depending on its purpose. If you prefer, bury the bottle in a special place. Spell bottles also make great gifts—personalize them with good wishes for friends who won't think you're too weird.

OTHER TOOLS AND ACCOUTREMENTS

What else might you want to put into your magick chest? Anything that you feel adds to your craft as a spellcaster. If wearing elegant ritual clothing enhances your sense of power or makes you feel part of another dimension, by all means dress up. If music elevates your mood or takes you into another place emotionally, play your favorite CDs or an instrument, if you have musical talent.

Oracles

Divination is the art of predicting the future. The word literally means to "let the divine realm manifest." An oracle may be a person with special abilities to see beyond the limits of the visible world—a psychic, astrologer, or shaman. Physical tools such as tarot cards and runes are also called oracles; magick workers consult them to gain guidance and advice. You can also use them in spells, as you'll see when you get to Part II of this book:

- Tarot—As mentioned earlier, these beautiful cards typically contain four suits that correspond to the four major tools we talked about at the beginning of this chapter. Each of the seventy-eight cards in a tarot deck has a special meaning based on its suit, number, colors, and many other things. You can lay out patterns of cards known as "spreads" for divination purposes, or you can use a single card in a spell. (My books *The Everything® Tarot Book* and *The Only Tarot Book You'll Ever Need* offer in-depth information about the meanings of the cards and instructions for using them.)

- Runes—The word *rune* means "secret" or "mystery." Most people think of the early Norse alphabet when they hear "runes." If you're a fan of J.R.R. Tolkien's books, you've already heard about runes. The most popular alphabet contains twenty-four letters, and each letter is named for an animal, object, condition, or deity. They also convey deeper meanings that you can tap in spellwork, as you'll soon see. You might also enjoy working with Ogham runes. These twenty letters from the old Celtic alphabet correspond to different trees, and like Norse runes they hold secret meanings. The letters are composed of lines, or notches, cut along a central line or stave. A phrase written in Ogham looks like a tree limb with branches sprouting from it. You can cast runes made of wood, stone, ceramic, etc. for divination purposes, or choose individual runes for spellwork.

- Pendulum—A pendulum usually consists of a small weight, such as a crystal, hung from a short chain or cord. You hold the chain, letting the pendulum dangle at the end of it, while you ask a simple question. The pendulum's movement—back and forth, side to side, around and around—has meaning and answers your question. The pendulum swings of its own accord—you don't influence its movement. When you use a pendulum, you're doing a form of dowsing. Most people think of dowsing as searching for water hidden underground, but that's only one method. When you consult a pendulum for the purpose of divination, you're searching for answers hidden deep within yourself.

Ribbons and Ropes

I'm a big fan of knot magick, and I've recommended using ribbons and ropes in many of the spells in Part II. When you tie a knot, you capture the mental and emotional energy present at the time in the knot and hold that energy there until you're ready to use it. Ancient mariners tied the wind into knots; if they were becalmed at sea, they opened the knots to release the wind and continued on their way.

You can also use ribbons to secure mojo pouches and medicine bags, so your magick stays inside. You'll find spells in Part II that use this method. Magick cords can also tie people together in a personal or professional relationship. If you believe an enemy is trying to harm you, you can bind that person or spirit by symbolically tying up him, her, or it with rope. A quick study of numerology will reveal the significance of numbers in spellworking and help you determine how many knots you'll need to tie in order to support your intentions: two for love, four for security, etc.

Make a Joyful Noise

Drums and rattles serve various purposes in magickal work. They raise energy. They break up blockages and stimulate sluggish conditions. They send messages far and wide. They can induce trances. They unify the minds and emotions of a group of people who choose to work together. They connect you with the spirit realm, and much more.

Bells can signal steps in a ritual. Bells and wind chimes also disperse unwanted energies and inspire harmony. Singing bowls help to balance the body's energy centers (chakras). They also calm and focus your mind, and connect you with higher levels of being.

The Modern Witchcraft Spell Book

Keep a Record

A grimoire or book of shadows is a witch's collection of magick recipes, spells, charms, invocations, and rituals. Here's where you keep a record of the magick you perform, the ingredients and tools you use, the potions, formulae, and incantations you create—and, of course, the results you generate. It's also a good idea to date each entry and note whatever else you consider significant, such as the moon's phase, your feelings, and anyone who participated in the spell/ritual with you. Many people prefer physical books for this purpose—the more ornate the better—but you can keep a computer version of a grimoire if you choose. You might want to take a look online at some of the beautiful old grimoires from medieval Europe, and even as far back as ancient Babylonia.

Pretty much anything can become a magickal instrument if you deem it so. Use what you consider necessary and what feels right to you. Over time, you may wish to add other tools to your collection or to devise your own. Remember to treat your tools with respect. When not in use, place them in a safe spot where they won't get damaged or handled by other people. You may wish to wrap them in silk or store them in a pretty box to protect them from ambient vibrations, as well as ordinary dust and dirt. With proper care, they should last a long time and serve you well.

Chapter 7

SPELLWORKING WITH SPIRITS

Do you believe in angels? Ghosts? Other spirit beings? If so, you're not alone. Throughout history, people have believed in nonphysical entities of many kinds. The ancient Greek, Roman, and Egyptian pantheons, for example, included lots of gods, goddesses, and lesser deities who performed a variety of tasks in this world and beyond. The Celts, Norse, Chinese, Hindi, and Native Americans all looked to divine beings for guidance and aid. Christianity honors an assortment of saints, and many traditions speak of angels. Our ancestors even credited spirits with bringing about natural occurrences, such as lightning and floods, and wove intricate myths around these supernatural beings.

We've already talked a little about spellworking with spirits and how they can help you in your magickal practice. In fact, spirits may be giving you a hand even if you don't realize it or haven't specifically asked for their assistance. What do we mean by spirits? In a very general sense, for the purposes of this book, we're referring to nonphysical beings who exist in another level of reality and with whom you can interact in some way. That's a broad and overly simplistic definition, and it includes many more entities than we'll discuss here. Gods and goddesses, angels, guides and guardians, ancestors, elementals, spirit animals, fairies, nature spirits, friends and loved ones who've left the material world, and many more may connect with you from time to time across "the Great Divide." In some cases, you can call upon them to assist you in spellworking.

Magick Cats

The ancient Egyptians revered cats as deities, but the Celts also attributed supernatural powers to felines. In Irish folklore, cat sidhe (otherworldly beings) guard access to the Underworld and its treasure. Magick white cats accompany the Welsh goddess Ceridwin. Images of cats appear on special stones in Scotland, put there by an ancient race known as the Picts. Female fairies and witches have long been known to keep cats as familiars (magickal companions) and to shapeshift into cats.

GODS AND GODDESSES

Do you feel an affinity with a particular culture, race, religion, or nation? If so, you may wish to study those people and their gods and goddesses. If you feel drawn to ancient Egypt, for instance, you might want to learn more about Isis, Bast, Hathor, Osiris, or Thoth. If you're Irish, you may sense a connection with Brigid, Ceridwin, or Lugh. But you needn't look only to deities with whom you share some lineage or common ground.

The Right God/dess for the Job

My previous books, *The Modern Guide to Witchcraft* and *The Everything® Wicca and Witchcraft Book*, contain lists of gods and goddesses from various cultures, along with their attributes. If you plan to call upon deities for assistance in spellwork, look to those whose characteristics and special powers relate to your intention(s). For example:

• In love spells, seek aid from Venus, Aphrodite, Freya, or Aengus.

The Modern Witchcraft Spell Book

- For prosperity spells, call upon Lakshmi, Zeus, or the Green Man (a pagan woodland deity, associated with fertility and popular in Celtic mythology).
- Ask Brigid, Ceres, or Lugh for assistance with healing spells.
- If you seek protection, call on Artemis, Tara, or Horus.
- To gain wisdom or inspiration, ask Brigid, Ceridwin, Sophia, Mercury, Odin, or Thoth for help.
- Spells for courage or strength could benefit from the help of Mars, Sekhmet, or Ganesh.

Sometimes all you have to do to enlist a deity's aid is ask. However, you can show your sincerity by placing an image of the god or goddess on your altar, or in another place of honor. If the deity has a holiday associated with him or her, celebrate it. You can also make an offering to a deity—incense, flowers, gemstones, etc. Do a little research to see if the god/dess you wish to contact has a favorite.

Calling a God or Goddess

After you've determined which deity you want to work with, cast a circle and invite that god/dess to join you in your sacred space. You can do this alone or with a group. You may wish to devote your altar to the deity for the term of the spell, or longer. Light a candle and incense, if you like, to help transport you mentally into another level of reality.

1. Clear your mind, center yourself, feel your connection to the earth and the heavens.
2. Allow your intuition and your personal energy to expand, becoming lighter and more sensitive.
3. Hold your arms out to your side, palms open, as if to embrace the deity whose presence you seek.
4. Call to the deity by name and request that he or she join you. This petition can be as simple or as eloquent as you choose. Some people invite the deity into their own bodies, but that's not necessary in most instances and involves a bit more skill.
5. When you sense the presence of the god/dess, continue with whatever magick you've chosen to perform.

If you're working outdoors, the deity may manifest through a sign or natural occurrence, such as a clap of thunder if the day is stormy, the parting of clouds, an increase in the wind, or other such phenomena. Sometimes the token spirit animal associated with the deity appears—e.g., a deer if you've called upon Diana. Sometimes the god/dess will speak directly in the form of an oracle. Often you simply feel a heightened sense of energy, awareness, or power, and you know the deity is there with you.

After you've finished your spellwork, release the deity. Many people like to compose a poetic parting statement, but you can say something as simple as: "Thank you [NAME] for your assistance here today. May you return home safely, and may there be peace between us." Remember to show respect and gratitude, just as you would if a human being had given you assistance in your pursuit. Then open the circle, trusting that with the deity's aid your spell will succeed.

SPIRIT ANIMALS

In ancient times, people in many parts of the world believed spirit animals lived in an invisible realm that intersects with our own physical one. These spirit beings helped our ancestors in countless ways, from providing food and protection to offering healing wisdom to predicting the future. Early humans considered these animal guides and guardians as deities—somewhat like angels—and paid homage to them.

What Are Spirit Animals?

Some traditions say that animal guides once lived on earth as physical creatures and passed over into the spirit world after death. Other views suggest that spirit beings never actually existed in the flesh—although their earthly counterparts may embody the spirits' energies. Still others tell us that spirit animals can assume the forms of physical creatures when they want to and can move between the worlds of ordinary and non-ordinary reality at will. People who study and work with spirit animals generally agree on one thing, however: These entities willingly offer us their help, and you can tap their special powers to enhance your well-being.

You've probably heard of "totems." The term refers to an animal, bird, reptile, fish, or insect with which you feel a strong and perhaps inexplicable affinity. A totem is your primary spirit animal guardian, or the guardian of your family or group. That being is always with you, protecting and guiding you. However, your personal totem may invite other animals to assist on occasions when you need a little extra help or when you're facing a challenge that requires the special characteristics of another creature.

Working with Spirit Animals

Ask your primary animal guide to make itself known to you. Try not to hold any expectations about what creature will appear. Perhaps you'll see a vision of it in your mind's eye or sense its presence near you. It might show up in a dream, or you may encounter its physical counterpart in nature. Trust that it will appear when the time is right and that the experience will be a positive one.

Showing respect and admiration for your totem animal is an essential part of working with it. This creature has a great deal to offer you, so you'll want to express gratitude. You can do this in a variety of ways:

- Find pictures of your totem in magazines or online and display them in your home or workplace.
- Learn as much as you can about your animal.
- Draw, paint, or sculpt images of your totem.
- Write a poem or story about your spirit animal.
- Watch animal shows on TV.
- Wear jewelry or clothing with the animal's picture on it.
- Go to a park, beach, farm, wildlife sanctuary, zoo, or other place to see your totem in the flesh.
- Join an animal welfare organization.
- Give money to a charity that protects animals and/or their habitat.

Once you've established a close relationship with your spirit animal guide or guides, you can ask them to assist you in all sorts of magickal work. Spirit animals can teach you their unique skills, provide protection, aid in healing, carry messages to and from other worlds, and do much more. My book *The Secret Power of Spirit Animals* contains lots of information about these amazing beings and how to work with them.

Familiars, Totems, and Pets

The term *familiar* refers to a special animal, bird, or other creature that works with a person to produce magickal results. Remember Harry Potter's owl? A familiar's physical and spiritual qualities can help you in spellworking. Sometimes a beloved pet might be a familiar, but that's not always the case. Your totem might share its powers through a familiar, but your totem doesn't necessarily serve as your familiar, nor is your familiar necessarily your totem.

ANGELS

In 2011, a poll conducted by the Associated Press found that 77 percent of Americans believe in angels. Many people report having received help from angels, especially during times of crisis or in periods of hopelessness and despair. According to some sources, everyone has a personal guardian angel who hears your prayers, watches over you, and helps you handle the challenges in your life.

Angelic Hierarchies

In some traditions, a hierarchy of angelic forces exists, with many ethereal beings at ascending levels of power. The Old Testament of the Bible lists them in the following order, from the lowest to the highest:

Level 1: Personal guardian angels

Level 2: Archangels

Level 3: Principalities (Princes)

Level 4: Powers

Level 5: Virtues

Level 6: Dominions

Level 7: Thrones (Orphanim)

Level 8: Cherubim

Level 9: Seraphim

Connecting with Your Guardian Angel

Do you sense the presence of your own guardian angel? If not, you may want to try one or more of the following:

- Before falling asleep, ask your angel to appear to you in a dream.
- Light incense and send your request to your angel in the rising smoke.
- On a slip of paper write a message to your angel, fold it three times, then burn it in your cauldron, fireplace, barbecue grill, or other safe spot.
- Place a figurine or picture of an angel on your altar.
- Meditate and listen for your angel's "voice."
- Observe nature. You might see your angel in the clouds, a body of water, a flower, or elsewhere.

Spellworking with Angels

Magick workers often invite angels to participate in rituals, both to provide protection and to augment the powers of the people involved in the ritual. Usually the angel Raphael is associated with the east, Michael with the south, Gabriel with the west, and Uriel with the north. You can use the following circle casting technique to invite these angelic beings to join you in your spellwork or ritual. Feel free to elaborate on this basic formula—make it as evocative as you like. Use your imagination.

1. Face east and hold your wand outstretched before you. Say aloud: "Angel Raphael, guardian of the east, be here now."
2. Turn clockwise and face south. Hold your wand outstretched before you. Say aloud: "Angel Michael, guardian of the south, be here now."
3. Turn clockwise and face west. Hold your wand outstretched before you. Say aloud: "Angel Gabriel, guardian of the west, be here now."
4. Turn clockwise and face north. Hold your wand outstretched before you. Say aloud: "Angel Uriel, guardian of the north, be here now."
5. Turn clockwise again until you reach the point at which you started to complete the circle, then proceed with your spell.

At the end of the spell or ritual, release the angels you've called in and thank them for assisting you. Again, you can use a simple, straightforward statement or a more colorful one that you create yourself. Open the circle in reverse order from how you cast it.

ELEMENTALS

Elementals are so named because they represent the four elements: earth, air, fire, and water. Most of the time you can't see them, though occasionally they cross over into our range of vision. They often figure prominently in folklore, fairy tales, and legends. If you befriend them, elementals can serve as devoted helpers who will eagerly assist you in performing magick spells.

However, these capricious beings aren't above playing tricks on you—especially if they feel you've dissed them or they just don't like you. Treat elementals with consideration, respect, and a bit of caution. Always remember to thank the elementals who assist you in your spellworking, too, and perhaps offer them a small gift to show your appreciation.

Gnomes

Gnomes are earth spirits. Sometimes called trolls, elves, or leprechauns, these elementals are practical, no-nonsense creatures that may appear a bit gruff. However, they possess a wonderful appreciation for material things and can be valuable aides when you're doing prosperity spells. They can also assist you with practical and mundane matters. Gnomes enjoy a bit of bling, so give them a piece of jewelry, a pretty crystal, or a few shiny coins to thank them for their help.

Sylphs

What people often think of as fairies are most likely air spirits, known as sylphs. They often look like tiny lights or flickering sparks. Because their specialty is communication, they can help you with negotiating contracts, writing term papers, pitching ideas, or other matters that involve communication. Sylphs naturally gravitate to intelligent, literary, and analytical people. They're especially fond of flowers, so place fresh blossoms on your altar or lay them in a sacred spot outdoors as an offering.

Salamanders

No, I don't mean lizards. These are the fire spirits, lively entities who are naturally drawn to people who exhibit creativity and initiative. When you do spells that involve action, inspiration, daring, or passion, salamanders can serve as liaisons, marshaling the forces of the fire realm to assist you. Call on them when you need an infusion of courage or vitality; they can also help you initiate a project or embark on a risky venture. They're also adept at handling contests that involve will and strength, whether on the gridiron or in the boardroom. Burn candles or incense to honor these elementals.

Ondines (Undines)

Ondines are water spirits. Mermaids and water nymphs fall into this category. These beautiful but sometimes temperamental beings relate best to sensitive, artistic, and psychic people. Invite them to assist you when you're doing love spells. They can also help you with emotional issues and situations that require keen intuition. Ondines are fond of perfume—pour a few drops in a stream, lake, or other body of water as a thank-you gift.

As representatives of the natural world, elementals frown on people who disrespect or harm the earth or its creatures. To win the elementals' favor, treat animals, plants, and all of our planet's inhabitants kindly.

> "[I]n the solid earth element live spiritual beings of an elemental kind who are very much more clever than human beings. Even a person of extreme astuteness intellectually is no match for these beings . . . One could say that just as man consists of flesh and blood so do these beings consist of cleverness, of super-cleverness . . . We may take pleasure in a red rose or feel enchanted when trees unfold their foliage. But these beings go with the fluid which as sap rises in the rose bush and participate in the redness of the blossoms."
> —RUDOLF STEINER, "THE ELEMENTAL WORLD AND THE FUTURE OF MANKIND," THE GENERAL ANTHROPOSOPHICAL SOCIETY, 1922

Spirits of all sorts populate our earth and the universe beyond. The ancient Greeks believed that spirits known as dryads lived in trees, and that if you cut down a tree the dryad would die. Early Romans believed that beings called nymphs occupied all the waters of the world. You could say that everything in our world embodies spirit—and just to be on the safe side, assume that spirits abide everywhere, even though you may not see them.

Ancestors, ghosts, fairies, mythic creatures, and other supernatural entities have intrigued us since the dawn of time. We've sought to appease them, woo them, avoid their displeasure, and solicit their aid. Spellworkers today still do so. If you choose to do spellwork with spirits, it's a good idea to familiarize yourself with the beings you wish to contact. Some are nice guys, some aren't—and many can be just a bit slippery. The realms in which they function aren't the same as ours, nor do they abide by the same rules we do.

Usually you're better off calling on angels and eschewing demons in any sort of spellwork. Both exist, and both are willing to work with you. But before you invite any spirit to assist you, remember an old saying among magicians: Don't raise any power you can't put down.

Chapter 8

TIMING SPELLS FOR BEST RESULTS

"To every thing there is a season, and a time to every purpose under the heaven."

—ECCLESIASTES 3.1, KING JAMES BIBLE

You've heard the saying "timing is everything," right? In spellwork, sometimes *when* you cast a spell can be just as important as *how*. Think of it this way. Casting a spell is like planting seeds. In order for seeds to grow into healthy plants, you must sow them during optimal conditions. The same holds true for spells. Of course, if you feel a pressing need to do a spell or sense that the energies around you are compatible with your intention, by all means go ahead.

ASTROLOGY AND MAGICK

When doing magick spells, it's a good idea to take celestial influences into account in order to choose the most auspicious times to perform spells and rituals. The sun and moon, and their ever-changing relationships to our planet, have fascinated human beings since the beginning of time. Our ancestors noticed that the sun's apparent movement brought about the seasons and that the moon's phases altered the tides and affected fertility in both humans and animals. Even today, we can easily see how solar and lunar forces operate in everyday life.

The ancients believed gods and goddesses inhabited the heavenly bodies. From their celestial abodes, they governed every facet of life on earth. Each deity—and each planet—possessed certain characteristics and powers. Modern astrologers don't usually think of the planets as the homes of god/desses; however, they still connect each of the celestial spheres with specific properties, influences, and powers that affect human and earthly existence.

Planetary Powers

Aligning yourself with planetary powers that support the nature of your spells can improve the effectiveness of your magickal workings. The following table shows each planet's areas of influence. (Note: For convenience, astrologers often lump the sun and moon under the broad heading of "planets" although, of course, we know they're not.)

Planet	Areas of Influence
Sun	Sense of self/identity, public image, career, creativity, leadership, well-being, masculine power
Moon	Emotions, intuition, dreams, home/domestic life, family/children, feminine power
Mercury	Communication, mental skill/activity, learning, travel, commerce
Venus	Love, relationships, social interactions, art, creativity, beauty, women

Mars	Action, vitality/strength, competition, courage, men
Jupiter	Growth/expansion, good luck, knowledge, travel
Saturn	Limitations, responsibility, work/business, stability/permanence
Uranus	Change, independence, sudden or unexpected situations, unconventional ideas or behavior
Neptune	Intuition, dreams, imagination/creativity, the spirit realm
Pluto	Hidden power/forces, transformation, death and rebirth

When you're doing spells, you may want to refer to this table. Venus's energy, for instance, can enhance love spells. Jupiter's expansive power can be an asset when you're doing spells for career success or financial growth. You can use the planets' symbols on candles, in talismans and amulets, and lots of other ways.

PLANETS AND SYMBOLS			
Planet/Node	**Symbol**	**Planet/Node**	**Symbol**
Sun	☉	Jupiter	♃
Moon	☽	Saturn	♄
Mercury	☿	Uranus	♅
Venus	♀	Neptune	♆
Mars	♂	Pluto	♇

You may also wish to consult an astrologer or check an ephemeris (tables of daily planetary movements) to determine when the celestial energies are favorable for your magickal workings.

Power Days

The heavenly bodies also rule the days of the week. By casting a spell on the day that corresponds to your intention—based on the deity who presides over the day—you can increase your potential for success. Most love spells, for instance, should be done on Friday because Venus, the planet of love and relationships, governs that day. Perform spells to bring success or money on Thursday, when Jupiter encourages growth.

Day of the Week	Ruling Planet/Deity
Monday	Moon
Tuesday	Mars
Wednesday	Mercury
Thursday	Jupiter
Friday	Venus
Saturday	Saturn
Sunday	Sun

Your Personal Best

When's the best time for you to cast a spell? On your birthday. On that special day each year, the sun shines brightly on you (even if it's raining outdoors) and spotlights your unique talents and abilities. Its energy illuminates and enhances whatever you undertake. As a result, whatever spells you do on your birthday have a better than usual chance of succeeding.

Planets and Signs

Each planet rules one or more signs of the zodiac. You probably know your birth sign—that's the astrological sign in which the sun was positioned on the day you were born. What you may not know, though, is that the moon and all the planets in our solar system also spend periods of time in each of the twelve signs of the zodiac and they continually move through these signs/sectors of the heavens. These signs "color" the energy of the planets. Therefore, it's good to check the positions of the planets when you're doing spells—especially the placements of the sun and moon. In Part II, I frequently advise doing spells when the sun or moon is in a particular astrological sign, in order to tip the scales in your favor. The following table shows the connections between the planets and the signs they govern.

Planet	Zodiac Sign(s)
Sun	Leo
Moon	Cancer
Mercury	Gemini, Virgo
Venus	Taurus, Libra
Mars	Aries
Jupiter	Sagittarius
Saturn	Capricorn
Uranus	Aquarius
Neptune	Pisces
Pluto	Scorpio

Now, refer back to the table presented earlier in this chapter that lists the planets and their areas of influence. When the sun or moon is positioned in a sign, it takes on some of the characteristics of that sign and the planet that rules the sign, which can be important in spellwork. For example, it's usually best to do love spells when the sun or moon is in Taurus or Libra—signs ruled by the planet Venus. If you're doing a travel spell, consider casting it when the sun or moon is in Gemini or Sagittarius.

The moon remains in a sign for about two and a half days and completes a circuit of all twelve zodiac signs each month. Check an ephemeris or an online astrology site to determine which days will support your objectives.

Every four months, the planet Mercury goes retrograde for approximately three weeks and appears to be moving backward through the sky. Mercury rules communication and thinking in general, so your mind might not be as clear as usual during retrograde periods. Your ability to communicate with others may be hampered as well. Usually, these aren't good times to do magick, as confusion and mistakes can occur.

MOON MAGICK

In early agrarian cultures, our ancestors planted crops and bred animals in accordance with the moon's cycles. Today, we can still see the moon's influence on fertility cycles, crop growth, the ocean's tides, and mundane affairs. In terms of casting spells, the moon is the most important of the heavenly bodies to consider. Magick practitioners often time their spells to correspond to the movements of this so-called "lesser light," perhaps because the moon rules intuition and the emotions, two parts of the psyche that strongly influence magick.

Farmers' Almanac

For almost 200 years, the *Farmers' Almanac* has published information about lunar cycles. It's not uncommon for farmers who employ advanced technical methods to also take the *Almanac*'s advice when planting and harvesting crops. Spellworkers, too, realize that you can reap greater benefits if you sow seeds (physically or symbolically) when the moon's position supports growth.

The New Moon

The new moon supports beginnings: the inception of new ideas, plans, projects, relationships, and activities. Now is the time to plant symbolic seeds that represent whatever you wish to create in your life. Cast spells to launch a new business, begin a relationship, or start a family. As the moon moves toward its full phase, you can watch your endeavor develop. The new moon is a good time to do divination, too.

The Waxing Phase

The moon's waxing phase—the two weeks between the new and full moons—represents a period of growth. This is the best time to do spells designed to expand a business, attract new people, and encourage prosperity. If, for instance, you wish to earn more money or get a promotion at work, do a spell during the waxing moon. As the moon's light grows, so will your fortune.

The Full Moon

The full moon represents the time of culmination and harvest. Under the moon's bright light, you can see (or at least start to see) the results of whatever you initiated two weeks ago, during the new moon, and begin reaping the benefits. You have more clarity now to understand how your goals are shaping up and what steps you need to take (if any) to bring them to fruition. Things that were hidden before may now come to light.

The Waning Phase

During the two weeks from the full moon to the next new moon, the moon "wanes" and appears to diminish in size from our vantage point here on Earth. This is a good time to do spells that involve decrease or letting go. This two-week period is perfect for spells to break old romantic ties, lose weight, eliminate bad habits, and reduce responsibilities at home or work. As the moon visibly shrinks, so will the conditions you've targeted with your magick.

Black and Blue Moons

When a month contains two full moons, the second is called a "blue moon." When two new moons occur in one month, the second is known as a "black moon." In these instances, the second one is considered more powerful than a regular new or full moon, so spells you do now may manifest more quickly.

Keeping a Lunar Journal

You may find it useful to keep track of the moon's phases for a few months, to get a sense of how the energy shifts and how it affects you. In a notebook or computer file, write a paragraph or so about how you feel during each lunar phase—describe your emotions, experiences, thoughts, and anything unusual or especially meaningful that happens. You might also wish to record your dreams and examine them in connection with the moon's position.

If you're recording your magickal work in a grimoire or book of shadows, be sure to note the moon's phase and its zodiac sign at the time you cast each spell. This practice will enable you to keep track of the moon's impact on your spells, so you can work more successfully with lunar power in the future.

ESBATS

Witches often come together for esbats, or meetings of covens, usually on full and/or new moons, to enjoy community and fellowship. Each full moon has its own unique characteristics, often based on seasonal energies. Esbat rituals draw upon nature's patterns, as well as mythology, cultural traditions, and astrology. Whether or not your magickal practice involves other people, you may wish to mark the full moons with rituals and/or spellwork. The following list briefly describes some of the attributes of each full moon. (Note that different cultures call the moons by different names.)

1. January—Known as the Cold, Frost, Ice, and Quiet Moon, it marks a time for renewal, discovery, resolve, and focusing on your purpose. Now is the time to set goals and to do spells for wealth and prosperity.
2. February—Called the Wild, Snow, Ice, and Starving Moon, it represents a period of healing and purification. Spells that prepare you for initiation, encourage healing or new growth, or foster physical or financial well-being are appropriate at this time.
3. March—The Storm, Wind, or Death Moon ushers in a time of change and awakening after a bleak, dormant period. Goals set under January's Cold Moon now begin to manifest. Do spells for personal growth and change now.
4. April—The Seed, Water, Growing, or Awakening Moon is a time of opening to new opportunities and experiences. Do spells for love, cleansing, growth, and strength at this time.

5. May—Known as the Hare, Bright, Grass, and Corn-planting Moon, it encourages joy, pleasure, sexuality, and fertility. This is a good time to do love spells, as well as spells for healing from emotional trauma and loss.

6. June—During the Honey, Mead, Planting, or Horse Moon, focus on strengthening relationships of all kinds: love, family, friendship, etc. This is also a good time to do spells to enhance communication and domestic harmony.

7. July—The Wort, Raspberry, or Rose Moon represents a time of maturation and fulfillment. Spells for protection and prosperity can benefit from the energy of this full moon.

8. August—This harvest moon, known as the Barley, Gathering, or Lightning Moon, is a time for gathering together all that holds meaning for you. Celebrate your blessings now and show gratitude, which will bring more blessings your way. Work with others of like mind during this time to share ideas, goals, and information.

9. September—The Harvest, Singing, or Spiderweb Moon is another period of reaping rewards for your efforts, and for seeing your dreams come to fruition. Give thanks for goals realized, projects completed, and wisdom gained. Focus on completion and bringing your life into balance.

10. October—During the Blood, Harvest, or Leaf-falling Moon, release old patterns and clear away emotional/psychic debris. Do spells to help you let go of whatever or whoever is standing in your way of fulfillment. This is also a time to remember and honor loved ones who have moved on to another realm of existence.

11. November—The Snow, Dark, or Tree Moon is a time to look beyond the mundane world, into the magickal one. Scry to gaze into the future; do divination to gain guidance and wisdom that will aid you in the coming months. Open your mind to receive prophecies of things to come.

12. December—Under the Dark, Cold, or Long Night Moon, release your fears and banish those things in your life that are harmful or no longer useful. This is a time for silence, meditation, and introspection. Do spells to break old bonds, overcome obstacles, and end self-limiting habits/behaviors.

Whether you belong to a group of magick workers or are a solitary practitioner, you will experience during full moon nights the sense of community and fellowship of like-minded people. You can be certain that on any full moon, people around the world are casting circles and performing spells, celebrating and chanting, scrying and meditating. You are an integral part of this global community. By realizing your part in the whole, you will bring yourself into closer connection with your fellow beings and the Divine.

SABBATS

Our ancestors divided the sun's annual cycle, known as the Wheel of the Year, into eight periods of approximately six weeks each. Each "spoke" in the Wheel corresponds to a particular degree in the zodiac. Witches and other pagans refer to these dates as *sabbats*, and celebrate them as holidays (or holy days). These high-energy days offer special opportunities for performing magick spells and rituals.

Samhain

Better known as Halloween or All Hallow's Eve, this holy day is usually observed on the night of October 31. For witches, Samhain is a time to remember and honor loved ones who have passed over to the other side (hence the connection with death). You may also wish to contact spirits in other realms of existence on this eve, or request guidance from ancestors or guardians. Because the "veil" that separates the seen and unseen worlds is thinnest at Samhain, many people like to do tarot or rune readings now to gain insight into the future. Perform spells to break old bonds and shed old habits on Samhain. For example, on a piece of paper write down something you want to release from your life, then burn the paper in your cauldron or a ritual fire.

Yule, the Winter Solstice

Yule is celebrated on the day of the winter solstice, which usually occurs between December 20 and December 22. This is the shortest day of the year in the Northern Hemisphere, the time when the earth is farthest away from the sun in her orbit through space. Because Yule marks the turning point at which the days begin to lengthen again, witches hail it as the "return of the light." To celebrate, light candles to represent the sun and burn a Yule log (usually oak, which symbolizes strength and longevity). Save a piece of the log to start your Yule fire next year. Do spells for rebirth and new beginnings on this sabbat.

Imbolc, Brigid's Day, or Candlemas

This sabbat honors Brigid, the beloved Celtic goddess of healing, smithcraft, and poetry. Her holiday begins on the evening of January 31 and concludes on February 2. At this time, daylight is increasing and the promise of spring is in the air. Thus, Imbolc is considered a time of hope and renewal. Brigid is one of the fertility goddesses, often depicted stirring a cauldron, and *imbolc* means "in the belly." Witches connect her with all forms of creativity, so this sabbat is a good time to engage your own creative urges. Do spells to launch new ventures, kindle inspiration for a project, or spark your imagination.

Ostara, the Spring Equinox

Usually celebrated around March 21, Ostara marks the first day of spring, ushering in warmer weather and longer days in the Northern Hemisphere. The earth awakens from her long winter's sleep and new life begins to emerge once more. This sabbat celebrates the triumph of life over death, as well as fertility and creativity. A time for planting seeds—literally or figuratively—Ostara's energy supports spells for beginnings. Consider planting herbs and flowers now to use in future spells. You may also want to craft talismans to attract good fortune.

Beltane

Witches usually celebrate Beltane on May 1, when flowers bloom profusely and crops begin sprouting in the fields. The sabbat marks a period of fruitfulness, and honors sexuality and fertility. An old tradition says that on Beltane women who wished to become pregnant should build a small fire in a cauldron, and then jump over it. Do love spells on this sabbat—fashion good luck charms to attract a new partner or improve an existing relationship. This is also a good time to tap the earth's fertility for prosperity magick—plant herbs such as mint and parsley to use in money spells.

Midsummer, the Summer Solstice

In the Northern Hemisphere, the summer solstice is the longest day of the year, usually around June 21. This is a time of abundance, when the earth puts forth her bounty in all its radiance. Tap this period of fullness to boost the power of spells for wealth, success, or recognition. Legend says you can communicate with the elementals and fairies now, and solicit their help in spellwork (see Chapter 7). Midsummer is also a good time to collect herbs, flowers, and other plants to use in magick spells throughout the year.

Lughnasadh or Lammas

Named for the Irish Celtic god Lugh (Lew in Wales), Lughnasadh (pronounced *LOO-nah-sah*) is usually celebrated on August 1. It is the first of the harvest festivals; our ancestors saw it as a time to reap the fruits of their labors and to begin preparing for the winter months ahead. As you enjoy the earth's bounty, remember to show gratitude for your blessings. This is a good time to do spells for health and protection, and to concoct herbal potions from fresh, healthy plants.

Mabon, the Autumn Equinox

Usually occurring around September 22, the autumn equinox is a time of balance and harmony, when day and night are of equal length. During this second harvest festival, witches take stock of the year's successes and failures, and give thanks for the good things in their lives. Honor your accomplishments now and reassess situations that didn't turn out as you'd hoped. As the year wanes, do spells for letting go, reduction, and endings. Legal spells can also benefit from Maban's energy. This is also a good time to resolve conflict and establish boundaries, in both personal and professional areas.

My book *The Modern Guide to Witchcraft* discusses the Wheel of the Year in greater depth, and includes some of the traditions surrounding these sabbats. It also offers suggestions for celebrating these special days.

The Modern Witchcraft Spell Book

When *Not* to Cast a Spell

Unless you have a clear goal in mind, don't bother doing a spell. Not only is it a waste of time and energy, it can actually create more problems because the energy generated by your spell lacks focus and bounces around through your life randomly like a pinball. If you're distracted or worried, your state of mind will interfere with your focus and the effects of your spell. Usually it's not a good idea to do a spell when you're ill, either, because your personal energies are unbalanced and that could weaken your spell. You might even send unhealthy vibes into the universe or drain your own vitality. Of course, you may want to do a spell to regain your health; try something gentle, such as a healing bath (see Chapter 13).

As we now move into Part II of this book, you'll notice that I recommend the best time to perform each spell, taking into account the moon's phase and other astrological influences. Usually I suggest more than one option. If a situation warrants immediate action and you can't do a spell on the optimal date, don't despair. Go ahead, and remember that your intention is the most important part of any spell.

PART II

Spells for ALL REASONS AND SEASONS

Chapter 9

SPELLS FOR LOVE AND FRIENDSHIP

As you may suspect, love spells are the ones magicians cast most frequently. We even use magickal terms to describe being in love—we feel enchanted, under a spell, bewitched, charmed, and so on. Often when we think of love spells, our minds conjure images of magickal incantations and mysterious potions meant to kindle passion in a person the spell-crafter desires, especially if that person doesn't return the feeling. Fairy tales, poetry, popular songs, and Hollywood perpetuate this idea.

Keep in mind, however, that love spells aren't meant to enchant or bewitch someone into falling in love with you—especially if that certain someone is already involved in a romantic relationship with another person. Although it may be tempting, and more than a few magicians have used magick to manipulate another person, doing so can backfire, sometimes with disastrous results. We all have free will and nothing can violate that will—not even magick or spells. The true purpose of a love spell is to increase your own power and attractiveness, so you draw the individual who's best for you.

If your spell involves someone else, ask his or her permission before casting it. This may not be possible if you're trying to make peace with another person from whom you're separated or if you need to break an unwanted bond between you and someone else. Even then, explain your intentions to that person's higher self and make it clear that you seek only the best for everyone concerned. If it's appropriate, you might invite the other person to participate in your spell. This can be beneficial if your spell is intended to enhance some aspect of an existing relationship, such as heightening the passion or joy between you.

Spells for love are numerous and varied, and before you do any, it's important to define what you want. Are you trying to attract someone? Looking for your soul mate? Hoping to improve your current relationship? The clearer you are in your own mind, and the more specific you can be, the greater your chances of success. The tables in this chapter show which ingredients can lend more power to your love spells.

Steps for Successful Spellcasting

Whenever you cast a spell, remember to use a few tried-and-true measures, as described in Chapter 1. These precautions can help you avoid complications, mix-ups, delays, or disappointments:

1. Remove all distractions.
2. Collect the ingredients and tools you'll use in your spell and cleanse them.
3. Purify and sanctify your space.
4. Quiet your mind.
5. Cast a circle around the area where you'll do your spellworking.
6. Perform the spell.
7. If you've called upon deities or spirits to assist you, thank and release them.
8. Open the circle.
9. Store your tools in a safe place until you need them again.

COLORS FOR LOVE SPELLS

Try to incorporate the colors red (for passion), pink (for affection), and/or purple (for romance) into your love spells. The most popular ways to do this are to burn candles or craft talisman pouches in these colors. You may also want to wear red and/or pink gemstones as talismans, or add red, pink, or purple flower petals to mojo bags, ritual baths, sachets, or potions. Many of the spells in this chapter draw upon these color associations.

INGREDIENTS FOR LOVE SPELLS

Gemstones

Carnelian: Stimulates sexual desire

Diamond: Deepens commitment and trust in a love relationship

Garnet: Increases love and passion

Opal: Aids love and seduction

Pearl: Encourages love, happiness, and emotional balance

Quartz (rose): Attracts romance, affection, and friendship

Flowers

Daisy: Inspires playfulness in love and friendship

Geranium (rose-colored): Boosts fertility and love

Jasmine: Encourages love, harmony, seduction, and sensuality

Myrtle: Brings luck in love

Rose: Attracts love and friendship; pink for affection, red for passion

Essential Oils/Incense

Jasmine: Encourages love, harmony, seduction, and sensuality

Musk: Heightens sensuality and sexuality

Patchouli: Boosts passion and sensuality

Rose: Attracts love and friendship

Ylang ylang: Increases sensuality and attractiveness

Herbs and Spices

Cayenne: Sparks sexuality and desire

Ginger: Stimulates romance, excitement, and sexuality

Marjoram: Blesses a new union and brings happiness

Vanilla: Encourages a more joyful and lighthearted approach to love

The Modern Witchcraft Spell Book

A SIMPLE SPELL TO ATTRACT LOVE

This quick-and-easy love spell requires only a handful of rose petals (preferably given to you by a friend or loved one, so they're already imbued with good energy). Take them outside your house or apartment and scatter them on the walkway leading to your home, while you say aloud:

"Love find your way.
Love come to stay!"

Continue repeating the incantation until you reach your door. Save one rose petal to carry with you as a talisman to encourage love to follow you into your home.

SPELL TO ATTRACT YOUR SOUL MATE

You're looking for that special person, the one and only, your ideal mate who is right for you in every way. But where do you begin? By casting a spell, of course. This one sends out the message that you are open to receiving love—and your perfect partner will pick up your vibes.

INGREDIENTS/TOOLS:
- 1 red rose
- 1 vase of cold water
- 1 ballpoint pen
- 1 pink votive candle
- 1 red votive candle
- A few drops of ylang-ylang essential oil
- 1 copper bowl
- Matches or a lighter

BEST TIME TO PERFORM THE SPELL:
- On the new moon, preferably on a Friday, or when the sun or moon is in Libra

Place the rose, which symbolizes the love you're looking for, in a vase of water and set it on your altar. Use the ballpoint pen to inscribe the letter X—the Norse rune for love—on the candles. Anoint the candles, which represent you and your soul mate, with the essential oil. (Pink is the color of love and affection, red the color of passion.) Put the candles together in the bowl and place it on your altar. Light the candles and say aloud:

> *"Winds of love, come to me,*
> *Bring my soul mate, I decree.*
> *As I wish, so mote it be."*

Imagine yourself with your soul mate. Make your visualization as detailed and vivid as possible. Feel this person's presence forming in the air around you. Let the candles burn all the way down, so the pink and red wax flow together in the bowl. While the wax is still warm, shape it with your fingers to form a heart, mingling the pink and red. Empty the vase of cold water into the bowl so the wax doesn't stick, and then remove the wax heart. If you know feng shui, put the wax heart in your relationship sector; otherwise place it in your bedroom. Allow the rose petals to dry. Save them for other spells.

SPELL TO ATTRACT FRIENDS

You've got to have friends in this world. For many people, friends are just as important as a primary partner. Friends bring out your best side, share your interests, pitch in when times are tough, and create a community in which you can thrive.

INGREDIENTS/TOOLS:
- Several ribbons

BEST TIME TO PERFORM THE SPELL:
- During the waxing moon, preferably when the sun or moon is in Gemini or Aquarius

This is a good spell to perform when you move into a new neighborhood or enter a new school and don't know anybody. Collect several ribbons in various colors that you like. Each ribbon represents a friend. Tie the ribbons to the branches of a tree. As you tie each ribbon, focus on attracting a new friend into your life and say aloud: "I now have a friend whom I love, respect, trust, and enjoy." Repeat until you've tied all the ribbons on the tree, then thank the tree for adding its positive energy to your spell.

SPELL TO ENHANCE A ROMANTIC RELATIONSHIP

Is something lacking in your relationship? Do you seek more romance, harmony, joy, passion? Choose the ingredients that will increase what you desire. Pink candles, for example, represent love and affection, whereas red ones represent passion. Select the aromatic oil you like best—see the table at the beginning of this chapter for suggestions.

INGREDIENTS/TOOLS:
- 2 pink or red candles in candleholders
- A few drops of rose, ylang-ylang, jasmine, gardenia, vanilla, or patchouli essential oil
- Deck of tarot cards
- Matches or a lighter

BEST TIME TO PERFORM THE SPELL:
- During the waxing moon, preferably on a Friday, or when the sun or moon is in Taurus or Libra

During the waxing moon, anoint the candles with the essential oil. Put a dot of oil on your heart to open it. From your deck of tarot cards, select the king and the queen of cups (which stand for you and your partner) and the nine of cups (the wish card). Place the candles on your altar, and lay the three cards face up between the candles.

Light the candles and state your wish. Be specific. Imagine it coming true. After a few minutes, extinguish the candles and place them in the area where you and your beloved will be spending time together.

Whenever you're together in that room, make sure these candles are burning.

Variations on Tarot Spells

You can also choose tarot cards according to your astrological sun sign to represent you and the person you love. Wands correlate with fire signs (Aries, Leo, Sagittarius). Pentacles are associated with earth signs (Taurus, Virgo, Capricorn). Swords relate to air signs (Gemini, Libra, Aquarius). Cups are linked with water signs (Cancer, Scorpio, Pisces). If you're at least twenty-one years old, select a king or queen from the suit that corresponds to your sign to symbolize you and the other person. If you're under twenty-one or doing a spell for younger people, use the pages of the appropriate suits.

RELATIONSHIP RESCUE PIE

Even a really great relationship hits some slumps once in a while. Whenever your relationship is in need of a pick-me-up, whip up an apple pie to bring more sweetness into your union. Apples represent health and love. Cinnamon is a sweet-and-spicy love herb, vanilla inspires love and peace, and ginger stimulates whatever it touches. Make sure to hold loving thoughts in your mind while you bake this delicious treat.

SERVES 6

INGREDIENTS/TOOLS:
- 6 medium tart apples, peeled and sliced thin
- ½ teaspoon ginger
- ½ teaspoon cinnamon
- ½ teaspoon nutmeg (or to taste)
- ½ teaspoon vanilla
- ¼ cup flour
- 2 prepared piecrusts for a 9" pie, or make crusts from scratch
- 2 tablespoons butter

The Modern Witchcraft Spell Book

• On a Friday night, during the waxing moon, or when the moon is in Libra or Taurus

1. Preheat the oven to 425°F.
2. Toss the apple slices with the spices, vanilla, and flour, then put them into the bottom of the piecrust. Dot the top of the apples evenly with bits of butter.
3. Put the other half of the piecrust over the top of the pie, securing it at the edges while saying:

"Secured within,
My magick begins.
Sweeten our love,
With blessings from above."

4. Gently draw a heart in the top of the pie using a fork so that energy bakes into the crust.
5. Bake the pie in the preheated oven for about 45 minutes, or until the crust is brown and apple juice is bubbling through the heart pattern. Enjoy eating the pie with your beloved.

THE DRINK OF LOVE

Japanese scientist Masaru Emoto discovered that water picks up the vibrations of pictures, words, thoughts, and emotions that come into contact with it. The water holds on to those impressions—and when you drink the imprinted water, your body absorbs the energies. This spell uses the lovely imagery from The Lovers card in your favorite tarot deck to fill you with loving feelings.

INGREDIENTS/TOOLS:

- The Lovers card from a tarot deck
- 1 glass of spring water
- 1 silver (or silver plate) spoon
- 1 drop of melted honey or a pinch of sugar

BEST TIME TO PERFORM THE SPELL:

- On a Friday night, during the waxing moon, or when the sun or moon is in Libra

Place the tarot card face up on a windowsill where the moon will shine on it. Set the glass of water on top of the card and leave it overnight. The image of the card will be imprinted into the water. In the morning, use a silver spoon to stir the honey or sugar into the glass to sweeten the water and, symbolically, your relationship. Drink the water with your partner to strengthen the love between you.

LOVE BATH

A luxurious bath can soothe mind, body, and spirit, and help you let go of the stress of the day. This spell cleanses you of tension or unpleasantness in a love relationship, so you can enjoy the positive things and open yourself to more happiness.

INGREDIENTS/TOOLS:

- A tub filled with comfortably hot water
- 1 cup of bath salts
- A few drops of jasmine, ylang-ylang, patchouli, or rose essential oil
- The rest of the rose petals left from the Spell to Attract Your Soul Mate
- 1 red or pink candle in a candleholder
- Matches or a lighter
- Romantic music

BEST TIME TO PERFORM THE SPELL:

- On a Friday night, during the waxing moon

The Modern Witchcraft Spell Book

As you fill your bathtub with water, sprinkle the bath salts into it. Bath salts act as a purifying agent, dispersing any unwanted vibrations. It's also a symbol of the earth element, which is associated with stability, security, and sensuality. Add the essential oil to the bath water, then scatter the rose petals on top. Light the candle and turn on the music.

Get into the tub and soak pleasantly, as you think loving thoughts about your partner. If you don't yet have a romantic partner, think positive thoughts about the person you intend to attract. If you have a lover, invite him or her to join you in the love bath.

SPELL TO MEND A ROMANTIC RIFT

A lovers' quarrel has left you and your partner at odds. Maybe you've said or done things you wish you could take back. Pride, hurt feelings, anger, and other destructive emotions may be preventing you from making up. How can you mend the rift between you? By casting a magick spell, of course. The key to this spell's success is focusing your mind on positive images only.

INGREDIENTS/TOOLS:
- 1 clear quartz crystal
- 1 ballpoint pen
- 1 piece of paper
- A few drops of jasmine essential oil
- 2 pink candles
- Candleholders
- Matches or a lighter

BEST TIME TO PERFORM THE SPELL:
- As soon as possible

Wash the quartz crystal with mild soap and water, then pat it dry. On the piece of paper write down everything you like, admire, and enjoy about your partner. Include his or her positive qualities, things about the relationship that you're grateful for, good times you've shared, and so on.

When you've finished, put a drop of oil on each corner of the paper and fold it three times.

Use the ballpoint pen to inscribe your name on one of the candles and your beloved's name on the other. Dress the candles by rubbing a little oil on them (not on the wicks). Put the candles in their holders and position them on your altar, a table, or other flat surface, so they are about a foot apart. Lay the folded piece of paper between the candles and set the crystal on top of the paper. Light the candles.

Close your eyes and bring to mind an image of your partner. Say to that image: "I honor the divine within you. I forgive you and I forgive myself. I am grateful for all the good times we've known together. I bless you and love you." Let go of all anger, resentment, recrimination, criticism, and so forth that you have held toward your partner. Don't mentally rehash the problems that led to the rift; entertain only positive thoughts and feelings. When you're ready, open your eyes and snuff out the candles. If necessary, repeat the spell the next day, only this time move the two candles a little closer together. Do this spell daily, moving the candles closer each time, until you've mended the rift between you.

A SPELL FOR FIDELITY

This spell encourages fidelity, but before casting it consider your reasons for doing so. Do you just want to strengthen the bond of trust between you and a partner? Or do you suspect that your significant other is being unfaithful? If so, do you really want to remain with this person?

INGREDIENTS/TOOLS:
- 4 votive candles (1 yellow, 1 red, 1 blue, and 1 green) in glass containers
- 1 object that represents your lover
- 1 object that represents you
- Matches or a lighter

BEST TIME TO PERFORM THE SPELL:
- On the full moon

The Modern Witchcraft Spell Book

Be sure to position your candles in a safe spot, where they can't ignite anything flammable. Place the yellow candle in the east within the space where you'll do your spell. Set the red one in the south, the blue one in the west, and the green one in the north. This defines the perimeter of your circle, and as you light each candle—moving clockwise from the east—you cast the circle. But before you do this, make sure that you and the objects you've chosen to represent you and your partner are within the circle.

Face east and light the yellow candle. Breathe deeply and imagine your intellect as lucid, crystalline, capable of making good decisions. Face south and light the red candle. Envision yourself and your lover passionately embracing. Face west and light the blue candle, as you sense loving feelings flowing between you and your partner. Face north, light the green candle, and imagine a strong bond of devotion, respect, and caring uniting you. When you have finished lighting the candles, stand facing the east and say:

"Winds of the east and the mind, keep [name of person]'s thoughts with me. So mote it be."

Turn to face south and say:

"Fires of the south and passion, keep [name] close to me. So mote it be."

Face west and say:

"Waters of our hearts, never do us part. So mote it be."

Face north and say:

"Forces of the earth, keep our bodies together now and evermore. So mote it be."

Move to the center of the circle and say:

"This spell is done in harmony with Divine Will, our own true wills, and with good to all."

To open the circle, snuff out the candles in the reverse order, moving counterclockwise, then bury the remains together in your backyard. If you live in an apartment, put the candles in a wooden box and place it under your bed.

MAGICK NECKLACE TO STIMULATE PASSION

Do you seem to be losing interest in your partner? Perhaps you long for the day when your love affair was passionate and fun. Still, you're not ready to give up on the relationship. This talisman draws upon the energies of gemstones to help rekindle your enthusiasm. It's also a pretty piece of jewelry.

INGREDIENTS/TOOLS:
- Carnelian or garnet beads (as many as you want to use)
- Opal beads (as many as you want to use)
- Pink pearls (as many as you want to use)
- Jeweler's wire, enough to make a necklace
- A few drops of ylang-ylang or jasmine essential oil

BEST TIME TO PERFORM THE SPELL:
- During the waxing moon, preferably on a Tuesday or Friday, or when the sun or moon is in Aries, Taurus, or Scorpio

Wash all the gemstones with mild soap and water, then pat them dry. Begin stringing the beads on the jeweler's wire. String the stones in any combination, as many of each as you feel you need. Carnelians and garnets spark passion. Opals encourage romance. Pearls promote emotional balance, harmony, and joy.

As you work, remember the good times you've enjoyed with your beloved. Concentrate especially on the passionate, romantic, and exciting moments between you. Think about all the things you admire and like about your partner. Don't let your mind stray to negative thoughts. Make the necklace as long as you like. When you've strung all the beads, dot each bead with a little essential oil. Allow the scent to imprint itself on your subconscious. Wear your magick necklace to reawaken passion in your partnership. Whenever you feel your enthusiasm waning, finger the beads to remind you of your intention.

COMMITMENT TALISMAN

Is the one you love commitment phobic? Are you having trouble moving your relationship to the next level? This talisman helps deepen and stabilize the feelings between you. However, in order to make this spell succeed you'll have to act in a way that seems contrary to your intentions: Stop pushing for a commitment and give your beloved the space he or she needs.

INGREDIENTS/TOOLS:
- 1 small piece of rose quartz
- 1 small piece of smoky quartz
- 1 small piece of carnelian
- 1 small piece of hematite
- 1 gold, silver, or copper ring
- Rose or jasmine incense
- Incense burner
- Matches or a lighter
- 1 pink or rose silk pouch
- 1 of your hairs
- 1 of your beloved's hairs
- Rose, jasmine, and gardenia petals
- 1 red ribbon
- Saltwater

BEST TIME TO PERFORM THE SPELL:
- On a Friday during the waxing moon, preferably when the sun or moon is in Taurus or Libra

Wash the stones and the ring with mild soap and water, then pat them dry. Fit the incense into its burner and light it. Put the 4 stones into the silk pouch. Tie the hairs around the ring if they're long enough; if not, simply put the hairs and the ring into the pouch. Add the flower petals.

Close the pouch with the red ribbon, tying 8 knots. As you tie each knot, repeat this incantation:

"I love you and you love me
Together we shall always be
And live in perfect harmony."

When you've finished, sprinkle the talisman with saltwater then hold it in the incense smoke for a few moments to charge your charm. Say aloud: "This is done in harmony with Divine Will, our own true wills, and for the good of all."

If you know feng shui, place the talisman in the relationship sector of your home; otherwise put it in your bedroom. Now that you've completed the spell, let go and let the universe take over.

SPELL FOR A PEACEFUL RELATIONSHIP

No matter how hard you try to get along, you and your partner always seem to end up fighting about something. It's uncanny how you manage to push each other's buttons. This spell helps to sweeten the energy between you to promote peace and harmony in your relationship.

INGREDIENTS/TOOLS:
- 1 shell
- 1 oblong stone
- 1 cauldron, large ashtray, incense burner, or other fireproof container
- 1 cone of gardenia incense
- Dried pink rose petals
- A dab of honey
- Matches or a lighter
- 1 pink cloth pouch, preferably silk or velvet

- On a Friday, preferably when the sun or moon is in Libra

Wash the shell and stone with mild soap and water, then pat them dry. Set the fireproof container on your altar or in another safe place. Put the incense in the center of the container, then sprinkle the rose petals around the incense. Rub a little honey on the shell and the stone, then lay both in the container—the shell represents the feminine force, the oblong stone symbolizes the male force.

Call to mind your lover's face. Light the incense. As it burns, chant this incantation aloud three times as if you were speaking to your partner:

"Between me and thee
May there always be
Love, peace, and harmony."

Allow the incense to burn down completely. When everything has cooled, put the shell, stone, rose petals, and ashes into the pink pouch. Place the pouch under your pillow or between the mattress and box spring of your bed to encourage positive feelings.

SPELL TO INCREASE YOUR ATTRACTIVENESS

You can use this spell to attract a romantic partner, or to get the attention of people you'd like to have as friends. It enhances your physical beauty, your communication skills, or other qualities that others find attractive.

INGREDIENTS/TOOLS:
- 1 ripe strawberry
- 1 small bowl or saucer
- 1 fork

BEST TIME TO PERFORM THE SPELL:
- During the waxing moon, preferably on a Thursday or Friday, or when the moon is in Libra

Hold the strawberry as you visualize people looking twice at you, complimenting you on your appearance, approaching you to chat, and so on. Put the strawberry in the bowl or saucer and mash it gently with the fork. Then anoint your lips with the strawberry juice. Eat the crushed strawberry sensually, enjoying the feeling of the pulp on your tongue, the seeds between your teeth, and the sweetness of the juice.

Say aloud:

"The words I speak,
The smiles I smile,
Be made sweet.
As bee to flower,
As honey to fly,
I draw you nigh."

SPELL TO SPARK ROMANCE

This spell increases your "sparkle" in an intimate situation. It can help you draw a new love to you or add zest to an existing relationship.

INGREDIENTS/TOOLS:
- Champagne (or sparkling apple cider)
- 1 chalice (or pretty wineglass)
- 3 drops rosewater

BEST TIME TO PERFORM THE SPELL:
- During the waxing moon, preferably on a Friday or when the moon is in Libra

Pour the champagne into your chalice or glass. Add the first drop of rosewater to the glass and say aloud: "I dazzle."

Add the second drop of rosewater to your chalice or glass as you say: "I sparkle."

Add the third and final drop of rosewater and say: "Romance me!"

The Modern Witchcraft Spell Book

Swirl the champagne in the glass gently to blend the rosewater. Drink the champagne, visualizing exactly how you wish to be attractive and what sort of experience you'd like to enjoy with a partner. See yourself and your partner as happy and fulfilled. Make the visualization as vivid as possible.

VARIATIONS TO TRY:
- Float a fresh red rose petal on the surface of the champagne.
- Double the ingredients to serve two people, and drink it with your partner.
- Serve chocolate-covered strawberries to further enhance the atmosphere for love.

A SPELL TO SAFEGUARD LOVE

This spell uses three spellcasting techniques—verbal, written, and physical—to renew, strengthen, preserve, and energize your love.

INGREDIENTS/TOOLS:
- Red or purple construction paper (red and purple are colors of passion and romance respectively)
- Rose oil
- Scissors
- Glue or tape
- 1 picture of you and your mate
- 1 pen that writes red ink

BEST TIME TO PERFORM THE SPELL:
- Anytime

Dab the paper with the rose oil, while saying:

"Rose of love, this spell is begun
I and [name of your partner] will always be one!"

Cut the paper in the shape of a heart. In the middle of the paper heart affix the picture(s) of yourself and your beloved. Write your names underneath. Put the heart in the relationship sector of your home (if you know feng shui) or in your bedroom to keep love alive.

Chapter 10

MONEY AND ABUNDANCE SPELLS

Who couldn't use a little more money—or maybe a whole lot more? We all know that money can't buy love, health, friendship, happiness, or respect—but prosperity sure beats poverty. In our material world money may not be everything, but it's essential to our day-to-day existence. Of course, abundance consists of much more than money. You may possess abundant vitality or intellect or creativity—riches that don't depend on and can't be bought with money. However, financial prosperity can provide the space, security, and opportunity for you to express your other gifts, without having to spend the bulk of your time and energy just earning a living.

Are you tired of worrying about bills? Would you like a better living and/or working environment? Do you need more time to devote to your creative pursuits, but don't feel you can afford it? Do you want more financial freedom to travel, further your education, break out of an unhappy domestic situation, or start your own business? The spells in this chapter are designed to help you overcome obstacles to prosperity and to attract abundance of all kinds into your life. The tables that follow show which ingredients can lend more power to your spells—feel free to customize if you choose to make a spell more personal.

Steps for Successful Spellcasting

Whenever you cast a spell, remember to use a few tried-and-true measures, as described in Chapter 1. These precautions can help you avoid complications, mix-ups, delays, or disappointments:

1. Remove all distractions.
2. Collect the ingredients and tools you'll use in your spell and cleanse them.
3. Purify and sanctify your space.
4. Quiet your mind.
5. Cast a circle around the area where you'll do your spellworking.
6. Perform the spell.
7. If you've called upon deities or spirits to assist you, thank and release them.
8. Open the circle.
9. Store your tools in a safe place until you need them again.

COLORS TO USE IN MONEY SPELLS

To enhance the spells you do for money and prosperity, incorporate the colors gold and silver (to symbolize precious metals and coins) and green (the color of paper money in some cultures and the indicator of healthy plant growth). The most popular ways to bring in these colors are to burn candles or craft talisman pouches in these colors. You may also want to wear golden, silvery, or green gemstones as talismans or add golden flower petals to mojo bags, ritual baths, sachets, or potions. Many of the spells in this chapter draw upon these color associations.

INGREDIENTS FOR PROSPERITY SPELLS

Gemstones

Agate (green): Helps stabilize your finances

Aventurine: Attracts wealth and abundance

Quartz abundance crystal: Aids financial growth and attracts abundance of all kinds

Tiger's eye: Increases good fortune and prosperity

Flowers

Daffodil: Attracts good luck

Marigold: Encourages financial gain

Sunflower: Its numerous seeds represent abundance and its sunny yellow petals suggest gold

Tulip: The cuplike shape represents a vessel to hold money and treasures

Essential Oils/Incense

Cedar: Protects and enhances your assets

Cinnamon: Encourages financial gain from a successful career or business endeavor

Clove: Stimulates financial growth

Vervain: Helps your financial goals materialize

Herbs and Spices

Cinnamon: Revs up the spell's power

Dill (seed or weed): Attracts good fortune

Parsley: Encourages prosperity and success

Spearmint: One of the most popular, all-purpose money herbs

SPELL TO CREATE A PROSPERITY CONSCIOUSNESS

Before you can attract wealth, you have to feel you are worthy of it. Many of us have been taught to believe we don't deserve prosperity, but those ideas can hinder your ability to achieve financial security. This spell helps you rewrite and revise old, outworn beliefs—see Chapter 5 for information about writing affirmations correctly.

INGREDIENTS/TOOLS:
- 14 green candles
- 1 empty glass container
- An affirmation

BEST TIME TO PERFORM THE SPELL:
- On the new moon

Purchase 14 green candles scented with pine or cedar essential oils. Votives and tea light candles are good to use for this spell. On the night of the new moon, light one of the candles at your altar or special place. While it's burning, say your affirmation aloud and feel its truth. After 5 minutes, extinguish the candle and rub your hands in the smoke. Waft the smoke toward your face, your body, your clothes. Hold your palms to your nose and inhale the scent. Remember the fragrance, and associate it with abundance, prosperity, and your new belief. Set the candle aside.

Repeat this ritual each day for the next 13 days, using a new candle each time. Set each spent candle next to its predecessor at the back of your altar. On the night of the full moon, after you have burned the fourteenth candle, light all fourteen again and let them finish burning down completely. Then pour the melted wax left over from all the candles into a glass container, forming a new candle. This new candle symbolizes your new belief about prosperity. Once the wax has solidified, bury it, symbolically planting it in the ground to make your wealth grow. If you prefer, mold the wax from these other candles around a new wick and burn it to attract abundance.

SPELL TO ATTRACT PROSPERITY

This spell can be used for any kind of prosperity, but it works best for the fullness of inner peace, the source of all true prosperity. When you truly believe you deserve prosperity, it comes to you effortlessly. Sage is a good herb for getting rid of negativity and cinnamon is excellent for boosting your creativity. Green, as you know, represents money and growth.

INGREDIENTS/TOOLS:
- 1 green candle
- 1 cauldron, or a fireproof ceramic or copper bowl
- 1 sprig of sage
- Matches or a lighter
- A pinch of cinnamon

BEST TIME TO PERFORM THIS SPELL:
- On the new moon

On the night of the new moon, put the green candle in your cauldron or bowl, along with the sage. Light them both. Sprinkle cinnamon into the flame, as you say: "I embrace prosperity and inner peace." Repeat these words and keep sprinkling cinnamon into the flame, until the cinnamon is gone. Let the candle and the sage burn down, then bury the remains in your yard or another place that holds meaning for you.

The Color of Money

In some countries, green is the color of paper money; therefore, your mind automatically makes a connection between green and wealth. If you live in a country where a different color appears on your currency, use that color to symbolize money instead. Gold and silver, the colors of precious metals, are good choices, too.

FENG SHUI WEALTH SPELL

In the ancient Chinese magickal system known as feng shui, red and purple are considered lucky colors. Plants symbolize growth. This spell combines the two symbols to attract wealth.

INGREDIENTS/TOOLS:
- 1 plant with red or purple flowers

BEST TIME TO PERFORM THE SPELL:
- During the waxing moon

Stand at the door you use most often when going in and out of your home, facing inside. Locate the farthest left-hand corner of your home, from your vantage point. That's what's known as your wealth sector. Put the plant in that area to make your wealth grow. Water, feed, and care for the plant with loving kindness. Talk to it. Send it good thoughts. Play classical music for it to enjoy (it may dance even if you can't see it). As you tend the plant and watch it grow, you'll notice your fortune improves, too.

CAULDRON MANIFESTATION SPELL

Wishes don't always materialize overnight—some take a while to develop. Try not to get discouraged and remember that everything happens in its own good time. While you're waiting, cast this spell to nurture your wish and bring it to fruition.

INGREDIENTS/TOOLS:
- 1 sheet of paper
- Scissors
- 1 pen or pencil
- 1 cauldron (or other bowl-shaped container)
- A pinch of powdered ginger
- 1 capsule or tablet blessed thistle
- 1 green cloth

- The day after the new moon

Cut the sheet of paper into 12 strips. On one strip write your wish in the form of an affirmation (see Chapter 5). Fold the paper strip three times and put it in the cauldron. Sprinkle a little powdered ginger in the cauldron (to speed up results) and a little blessed thistle (to help your goal manifest). You can purchase blessed thistle herbal supplements online, in health food stores, and in some supermarkets. Open a capsule or grind a tablet into powder, then add it to the cauldron. Cover the cauldron with the green cloth.

Allow the spell to "simmer" overnight, then in the morning remove the cloth and repeat the spell. Continue in this manner for a total of 12 days. If your wish hasn't materialized by the time of the full moon, take a break during the waning moon period and begin again on the first day of the waxing moon. Don't give up—trust that your wish will indeed manifest when the time is right.

SPELL TO REPLENISH YOUR WEALTH

Traditionally, mint is associated with prosperity and lemon with cleansing. Combine them with pepper to create a powerful spell to replenish your finances. If you've been in a creative slump, your finances are stagnant, or you've hit a dry period, this spell can stimulate prosperity.

INGREDIENTS/TOOLS:
- 1 paring knife
- 1 lemon
- 1 handful fresh mint leaves
- 1 glass bowl
- 3 bay leaves
- 3 peppercorns
- 1 small piece of aventurine
- 1 small piece of tiger's eye

- During the waxing moon, especially on a Thursday or Friday, or when the sun or moon is in Taurus

Slice the lemon and dry the slices in the oven at a low temperature. Sprinkle the mint leaves over the bottom of a glass bowl, then lay the dry lemon slices over the mint. Place the bay leaves on top of the lemons. In the center, position the 3 peppercorns and then set the aventurine and the tiger's eye atop the peppercorns. Hold your hands, palms down, over the bowl and close your eyes. The bowl represents nourishment and fullness. Envision the bowl filled with money—an endless supply that replenishes itself whenever you dip into it. Imagine yourself plucking whatever you need from the bowl—the money actually rises into your hands, as if your palms were magnets. No matter how much you remove, more money flows in to fill the bowl again.

MINT YOUR OWN

Wouldn't it be nice if you could mint your own money? Then you'd never have to worry about having enough. Well now you can. No, we're not talking about counterfeiting. Instead, use magick to make your wealth grow.

INGREDIENTS/TOOLS:
- 1 likeness of a million-dollar bill
- 1 green ceramic flowerpot
- Potting soil
- Spearmint or peppermint seeds, or a small mint plant
- Water

BEST TIME TO PERFORM THE SPELL:
- During the waxing moon, preferably when the sun or moon is in Taurus

Make a likeness of a million-dollar bill—you can draw one or download one from the Internet (even though there aren't any real million-dollar bills, that big number gets your attention). Fold the bill three times and place it in the bottom of the ceramic flowerpot. Fill the pot with soil. Plant the seeds or seedling in the soil and water it.

As you work, repeat this incantation:

"Every day
In every way
Prosperity
Now comes to me."

Set the flowerpot in a spot in what feng shui calls your wealth sector (unless the conditions there aren't favorable for the plant). Continue caring for your mint plant and remember to recite the incantation daily. When you trim the plant, save the leaves and dry them to use in talismans. As the plant grows, so will your finances.

PROSPERITY BREW

This spell uses herbal magick plus the symbolism of growing plants, along with a little help from feng shui to attract prosperity. You can also drink this brew hot or cold, to increase your prosperity consciousness.

INGREDIENTS/TOOLS:
- 1 cup of water
- 1 saucepan
- Fresh, chopped parsley
- Fresh, chopped mint leaves
- 1 wooden spoon
- 1 strainer

BEST TIME TO PERFORM THE SPELL:
- On the new moon

On the night of the new moon, pour a cup of water into a pot and begin heating it on the stove. Put the parsley and mint in the water and say, "I embrace prosperity and open myself to receive abundance of all kinds." Stir the brew with a wooden spoon, making three clockwise circles to charge the mixture. Bring the water to a boil, then turn off the stove and allow the brew to cool. Strain, then pour the water on the plant you placed in your wealth sector (see the Feng Shui Wealth Spell) or use it to water other plants in your home or yard.

No Limits on Wealth

Does performing a prosperity spell take away someone else's prosperity? Not at all! Prosperity and abundance don't have limits—the universe's riches are infinite and available to everyone. These spells might not work, however, if you're attempting to swindle someone out of money or to profit from someone else's loss.

QUICK CASH POTION

Do you need cash in a hurry? This magick potion starts working as soon as you ingest it. You can either brew this potion as a hot tea or enjoy it as a cool drink. If you like, share it with someone else whose intention is linked with your own.

INGREDIENTS/TOOLS:
- 1 paring knife
- Fresh ginger root
- Fresh mint leaves
- Spring water
- Cinnamon
- 1 clear glass or cup (no designs)
- The ace of pentacles from a tarot deck or the ace of diamonds from a regular deck of playing cards

BEST TIME TO PERFORM THE SPELL:
- During the waxing moon, preferably on a Thursday, but in an emergency do the spell as necessary

Chop the ginger and mint leaves very fine—the amount you use is up to you. Sprinkle them in the spring water, then add a dash of cinnamon.

If you wish, heat the water to make a tea (but don't let it boil). Pour the herb water in a clear glass or cup. Lay the card face up on your altar, table, or countertop and set the glass of water on top of it. Leave it for 5 minutes to allow the image on the card to imprint the water with its vibrations, then drink the tea.

SPELL TO CURB SPENDING

Is money going out faster than it's coming in? This spell taps the magick of feng shui to slow your cash outflow and help you get a handle on spending.

INGREDIENTS/TOOLS:
- All your credit cards
- 1 black envelope
- A few drops pine essential oil
- 1 piece of tumbled hematite
- 1 small piece of tumbled onyx
- Your wallet or purse
- 1 large stone (one that weighs at least a pound or two)

BEST TIME TO PERFORM THE SPELL:
- During the waning moon, preferably on a Saturday, or when the sun or moon is in Capricorn

Sort through your credit cards and place the ones you don't need or don't use regularly—as many as possible—in the black envelope. (You might consider canceling some of them while you're at it.) Next, dab a little essential oil on each of the stones. After the oil dries, slip the hematite in your wallet or purse—each time you reach for your cash, touch the stone to remind you of your intention.

Stash the envelope containing your credit cards in a safe spot and set the piece of onyx on it to symbolically hold down spending. Finally, place the large stone in the wealth sector of your home. To locate this, stand at the entrance to your home (the one you use most often, not necessarily the front door) with your back to the door, so you're looking inside. The farthest left-hand corner is the wealth sector.

Additional suggestion: If you want to cut back on business expenditures, you could put another piece of hematite or onyx in your cash register or safe, and another large stone in the wealth sector at your place of business.

AMULET TO WARD OFF CREDITORS

Are annoying phone calls and angry demand letters from creditors driving you nuts? Although you may be doing the best you can, collection agencies can be as persistent as pit bulls. This amulet helps to ward off creditors the way ancient amulets repelled evil spirits.

INGREDIENTS/TOOLS:
- 1 image of a bear
- The rune *Eihwaz*
- 1 small piece of turquoise
- Dried basil leaves
- Dried fennel
- Dried parsley
- 1 black drawstring pouch, made of cloth or leather

BEST TIME TO PERFORM THE SPELL:
- During the waning moon, preferably on a Saturday, or when the sun or moon is in Capricorn

Gather all the ingredients listed. The image of a bear could be a magazine picture, a small figurine, a jewelry charm, or a drawing you sketch yourself. The rune *Eihwaz*, which means "defense," could be a piece of stone, ceramic, wood, or metal with the symbol carved or painted on it. (It looks a bit like a reversed Z tilted slightly.) Wash the turquoise with mild soap and water, then pat it dry.

Place the herbs, rune, and piece of turquoise in the pouch. Then hold the image of the bear in your hand and gaze at it. The bear represents protection and fortitude. Ask the spirit bear, symbolized by this image, to defend you against harassment and to give you the strength to "bear up" under the challenge you are facing. Add the bear to your pouch and close the pouch. Wear the amulet or carry it with you while you continue resolving your financial issues.

A FETISH TO FIGHT BAD LUCK

We've all run into streaks of bad luck. Fashion a few of these fetishes, and use them to help disperse negative energy that can wreak havoc with your finances.

INGREDIENTS/TOOLS:
- 3 pennies (or other coins of small denomination)
- 3 pieces of green, gold, or silver cloth
- 3 pieces of white string or ribbon

BEST TIME TO PERFORM THE SPELL:
- Anytime

Place the pennies into the pieces of cloth, then tie them with the string or ribbon. As you tie the knots, recite this incantation:

"In luck I trust,
In luck I believe,
Within this bundle,
Abundance weave!"

To activate the fetish, take it to a remote location away from water or trees, and bury it in the ground. Say aloud:

"Bad fortune's come,
But not to stay.
I command it now
To turn away."

Turn away from the place where you've buried the bundle and don't look back. Visualize leaving behind all negative energy that hindered you in the past.

KEEP IT COMING PROSPERITY CIRCLE

Even if your present financial situation is sound, you can't predict what the future may bring. This spell ensures that prosperity will continue flowing toward you and that you'll always have more than enough money to cover your expenses.

INGREDIENTS/TOOLS:
- 9 small jars (baby food jars are perfect)
- 1 piece of paper
- 1 pen that writes green, gold, or silver ink
- Coins (any denomination)

BEST TIME TO PERFORM THE SPELL:
- Daily, beginning during the waxing moon

Choose a spot in your home or workplace where you can leave the jars in position permanently, where they won't be disturbed. Arrange the empty jars in a circle. On the piece of paper write the following affirmation: "I now have plenty of money for everything I need and desire and plenty to share with others." Lay the paper in the center of the circle of jars and put a coin on top to secure it. Then beginning at the east, work in a clockwise direction and drop one coin in each jar. Repeat the affirmation aloud each time you place a coin in a jar.

The next day add another coin to each jar, again starting at the east and working in a clockwise direction. Continue in this manner, adding one coin per day to each jar. When all the jars are full, remove the coins and donate the money to your favorite charity. As you give the money away, repeat the following affirmation three times: "I offer this money with love and gratitude. I now receive my tenfold return, with good to all concerned."

Start filling the jars again, in the same manner as before. Continue performing this spell and sharing your wealth indefinitely, in order to keep prosperity coming your way forever.

WHEEL OF FORTUNE

Does it seem that you never have enough money left over after paying the bills to buy anything extra? You're just scraping by. Will you ever manage to get ahead so you can treat yourself to a few luxuries? This spell helps you attract good fortune and acquire the objects you desire.

INGREDIENTS/TOOLS:
- Pictures of things you'd like to have
- Scissors
- 1 sheet of heavy paper or poster board
- Glue, paste, or tape
- The Wheel of Fortune card from a tarot deck you don't use for readings

BEST TIME TO PERFORM THE SPELL:
- During the waxing moon, preferably on a Thursday

Cut out pictures from magazines or catalogs, or download images from the Internet that depict the goodies you covet: a new car, a designer wardrobe, jewelry, the latest computer—whatever strikes your fancy. Cut the paper into the shape of a circle or wheel. Glue or tape the Wheel of Fortune card in the center of the paper circle. Arrange the pictures you've selected around the tarot card and fasten them to the paper. As you work, imagine all these wonderful things belonging to you. See yourself driving that new car or donning those diamonds. Make your visions as real as possible.

Display your "wheel of fortune" in a place where you will see it often. You might want to put it in what feng shui calls the wealth sector of your home or workplace. To locate this, stand at the entrance to your home or workplace—the one you use most often, not necessarily the front door—with your back to the door, so you're looking inside. The farthest left-hand corner is the wealth sector. Each time you look at your collage, you'll reinforce your intention to draw abundance into your life.

MONEY TREE SPELL

Money may not grow on trees, but you can tap the growth symbolism inherent in trees to increase your income. Whether you need cash to cover an unexpected expense, seek extra money for something special, or just want to improve your financial status, this spell helps you attract abundance of all kinds.

INGREDIENTS/TOOLS:
- Gold and/or silver ribbons
- Small charms, earrings, beads, crystals, and/or other ornaments
- Bells or wind chimes

BEST TIME TO PERFORM THE SPELL:
- During the waxing moon, preferably on a Thursday or Friday, or when the sun or moon is in Taurus

Tie the ribbons loosely on the branches of a favorite tree. The tree can be one on your own property or in a place that's special to you. Hang the other adornments on the branches as well. These objects represent gifts or offerings to the nature spirits, in return for their assistance in bringing you wealth. The earth elementals called gnomes really like bling and will appreciate these trinkets. As you attach each item, state your intention aloud and ask the nature spirits to help you acquire what you desire. When you've finished, thank the tree and the nature spirits.

PROSPERITY FRUIT SALAD

This seasonal breakfast or dessert combines fruits associated with prosperity and abundance. When you eat them, you take their energy into your body, which symbolizes your willingness to accept prosperity into your life. Blend the fruits according to your own taste preferences and your personal associations with them.

INGREDIENTS/TOOLS:
- Fresh pineapple chunks
- Blueberries

The Modern Witchcraft Spell Book

- Cherries, pitted and sliced in half
- Grapes, sliced in half, seeds removed
- Apples, diced
- Pears, diced
- 1 glass bowl
- 1 teaspoon lemon juice
- ¼ cup sugar

BEST TIME TO PERFORM THIS SPELL:
- During the waxing moon

Wash, dry, and cut the fruit into bite-sized pieces. Combine the fruit in a bowl. Sprinkle the lemon juice over the fruit. Sprinkle the sugar over the fruit and let sit for 1 hour. Enjoy, while you envision prosperity flowing toward you.

Chapter 11

SPELLS FOR SAFETY AND PROTECTION

Spells to provide protection were among the earliest and most sought-after forms of magick. Hunters, warriors, travelers—and just about everyone else—hoped spells would safeguard them against injuries, illness, robbers, bad luck, natural calamities, and evil in all its many forms. Even in modern times, if you travel to Greece or Turkey you'll likely see "evil eye" amulets everywhere—usually depicted as blue eye-like symbols made of glass or ceramic—hanging in homes, businesses, and cars to ward off dangerous forces. And who among us hasn't thrown salt over his shoulder to protect against bad luck, or crossed herself in the face of adversity, or carried a special object along when starting a journey?

Today, danger lurks all around us, just as it did millennia ago. Even though we may no longer believe that someone will curse us with the "evil eye," we still seek protection from automobile accidents, criminal elements, physical ailments, and other types of harm. The spells in this chapter are designed to protect you (or someone you care about) from adversity. What if you can't find an item that's called for in a spell? The tables included here show which ingredients to substitute if necessary, or if you just want to make a spell more personal.

Steps for Successful Spellcasting

Whenever you cast a spell, remember to use a few tried-and-true measures, as described in Chapter 1. These precautions can help you avoid complications, mix-ups, delays, or disappointments:

1. Remove all distractions.
2. Collect the ingredients and tools you'll use in your spell and cleanse them.
3. Purify and sanctify your space.
4. Quiet your mind.
5. Cast a circle around the area where you'll do your spellworking.
6. Perform the spell.
7. If you've called upon deities or spirits to assist you, thank and release them.
8. Open the circle.
9. Store your tools in a safe place until you need them again.

COLORS TO USE IN PROTECTION SPELLS

To enhance the spells you do for safety and protection, incorporate the colors white or black—although if your aim is to improve your psychic ability for protection, use indigo. The most popular ways to bring in these colors are to burn candles or craft amulet pouches in these colors. You may also want to carry black or white gemstones as amulets, wear black or white clothing while performing protection spells, or add white flower petals to mojo bags, ritual baths, sachets, or potions. Many of the spells in this chapter use these color associations.

INGREDIENTS FOR PROTECTION SPELLS

Gemstones

Amber: Though not really a stone—it's fossilized sap—amber offers protection from physical or nonphysical threats

Bloodstone: Provides physical protection and bolsters courage; the ancients believed it stanched the flow of blood

Onyx: Gives you strength to stand up to your adversaries

Peridot: Repels negative energies and neutralizes toxins

Snowflake obsidian: Provides overall protection

Tourmaline: Shields you from unwanted energies in the environment, such as EMFs

Flowers

Carnation (white): Brings protection and strength

Geranium (white): Helps protect you and your home

Lilac (white): Offers general protection and banishes negative energy

Lily (white): Repels and removes hexes; guards the soul as it journeys into the afterlife

Snapdragon (white): Protects you from illusion or deception; safeguards your home

Essential Oils/Incense

Anise (star): Protects against negative energy

Fennel: Provides physical and psychic protection

Pine: Guards against negativity and evil spirits

Herbs and Spices

Angelica: Use it magickally for protection and purification

Basil: One of the most popular, all-round protection herbs

Caraway (seeds): Protects you and your home from thieves

Comfrey: Provides protection while traveling

Rosemary: Provides safety and clears negative vibes

GEMSTONE NECKLACE FOR A SAFE TRIP

Although statistics show that most accidents happen near home, it's natural to feel a little anxious about your safety when you're going on a long trip. This gemstone amulet is more than a pretty necklace; it also provides protection while you're traveling.

INGREDIENTS/TOOLS:
- Amber beads
- Jade beads
- Turquoise beads
- Bloodstone beads
- Agate beads
- Silver or gold charms in the shape of angels, stars, pentagrams, and so on (optional)
- Jeweler's elastic

BEST TIME TO PERFORM THE SPELL:
- At least 3 days before your trip

Cut a length of jeweler's elastic long enough to wear as a necklace (if you prefer, you can make a bracelet instead). Begin stringing the beads on the jeweler's elastic. You can alternate the beads on a single string or, if you prefer, make three separate strands and twist them together. Add charms that symbolize protection, if you like.

As you work, visualize yourself safe and sound, traveling with ease wherever you go. Imagine a ball of pure white light surrounding you and shielding you from harm. When you've finished, tie a knot in the elastic. As you tie it, say this affirmation aloud: "This necklace keeps me safe and sound at all times and in all situations, now and always." Wear the amulet to protect you when you travel.

HERBAL PROTECTION PILLOW

Are closet monsters and bad dreams preventing you from getting a good night's sleep? Do you keep hearing things go bump in the night? This fragrant protection pillow calms your nerves and helps you relax, so you can stop worrying about unwanted nightly visitors.

INGREDIENTS/TOOLS:
- 2 squares of dark blue cloth, 3" × 3" or larger
- White thread
- 1 needle
- Dried basil leaves
- Fennel seeds
- Rosemary
- Dried parsley
- Lavender flowers
- Lemongrass
- Sage

BEST TIME TO PERFORM THE SPELL:
- On the new moon

Collect the ingredients listed. Sew the squares of blue cloth together on three sides—it's best if you do it by hand, rather than with a sewing machine. After you've finished, fill the casing with the herbs. Sew the fourth side closed to make a tiny pillow. Place the herbal protection pillow under your regular bed pillow. If you prefer, lay the protection pillow beside you so you can smell its soothing scent during the night.

TOTEM ANIMAL SPELL TO PROTECT YOUR HOME

Do you have a totem animal? Totems serve as spirit guardians and helpers—you can call upon them to aid you in times of need. Your totem is an animal, bird, reptile, or insect with which you feel a strong sense of kinship and which, to you, represents protective power. (For more information about totem animals, see Chapter 7 and my book *The Secret Power of Spirit Animals*).

INGREDIENTS/TOOLS:
- 1 image of an animal totem

- Basil leaves
- Bowl (optional)

- 3 days before the new moon, or whenever you feel the need

Select an image of your totem animal—a figurine, drawing, photograph, or image downloaded from the Internet—and place it near your front door. Say aloud, to your animal guardian:

"Protect this home,
High to low,
Fence to fence,
Door to door,
Light to dense,
Roof to floor."

Next, scatter the basil leaves all around the outside of your home. If you live in an apartment, either scatter them around the entire building or, instead, place the leaves in a bowl and set the bowl and your animal image just inside the door to your apartment.

PROTECTION AMULET FOR YOUR HOME

Here's another way to protect your home. You can also do this spell to safeguard your business, car, or other possessions—simply substitute a picture of whatever you intend to protect.

INGREDIENTS/TOOLS:
- 1 white candle
- 1 picture of your house
- 1 silver pentagram
- Dried petals from a white carnation
- 1 ash leaf
- 1 quartz crystal
- 1 piece of white coral

- 1 moonstone
- 1 piece of amber
- 1 white pouch, preferably made of silk
- 1 black ribbon
- Saltwater

<small>BEST TIME TO PERFORM THE SPELL:</small>
- On a Saturday or when the sun or moon is in Capricorn; however, if you feel at risk, do the spell as soon as possible

Set the candle on your altar and light it. Lay the picture of your house on the altar in front of the candle and put the pentagram on it (or draw a pentagram on the back of the picture). Gaze at the picture and, at the same time, envision a sphere of white light completely surrounding your home. Say aloud,

"My home is now protected
At all times,
In all situations,
Always and all ways."

Place the flower petals, ash leaf, crystal, coral, moonstone, and amber in the white silk pouch. Add the picture of your home and the pentagram. Tie the pouch closed with the ribbon, making 8 knots. With each knot, repeat your affirmation while you hold the vision of your home, surrounded by white light, in your mind's eye. After you've finished, sprinkle the amulet with saltwater to charge it. Extinguish the candle. Hang the amulet inside the front door to safeguard your home and your possessions.

SPELL TO BANISH SPIRITS FROM YOUR HOME

Are unidentified spirits or bad vibes invading your home? Do you sense tension or animosity from neighbors, previous residents, or maybe even ghosts? This spell banishes unwanted energies and prevents "psychic intruders" from coming back.

- 1 stick of sage incense or a sage wand
- Matches or a lighter
- 1 large pot
- 2 or more quarts of water
- 1 large bunch of fresh basil
- 1 pitcher

BEST TIME TO PERFORM THE SPELL:

- On a Saturday at dusk, preferably when the sun or moon is in Cancer or Capricorn

Light the sage incense or wand and allow the smoke to waft through your home. Walk through each room, letting the smoke clear the air. Call out to the unwanted energies and order them: "Be gone." After you've finished, pour the water in the pot and heat it. Add the basil and let it simmer for 10 minutes. Allow the brew to cool. Strain the basil out and pour the water into a pitcher. Set the basil aside to dry; save it to use in other spells. Take the pitcher of basil-infused water outside and pour it on the ground near your front door, drawing a pentagram with the liquid. As you mark the ground with the pentagram, say this incantation aloud:

"Harmful spirits stay away.
Ill intentions keep at bay.
My home is safe all night and day."

Repeat the process at your back door (and any other doors that lead into your home).

Spicy Sachet for Protection

A sachet of rosemary, angelica, sage, 3 cloves, and a pinch of salt tied shut with white ribbon is a good all-purpose amulet to hang above a door or to keep in your car for protection.

The Modern Witchcraft Spell Book

SEALING OIL

Use this oil to protect any items you choose: your purse, jewelry, car, home, etc. You can even put it on your pet's collar to keep Fluffy or Fido safe.

INGREDIENTS/TOOLS:
- 1 glass jar or bottle
- 3 tablespoons olive oil
- 3 pinches salt
- 1 whole clove
- 1 basil leaf

BEST TIME TO PERFORM THE SPELL:
- As needed

Wash the jar or bottle. Combine all the ingredients in it. Place it in a sunny spot and allow the ingredients to infuse for 3 days. When the magick oil is ready, dip your finger in it and draw a line across or along whatever you are sealing (around a door or window frame, inside the opening of your purse, etc.).

FINANCIAL PROTECTION AMULET

Are rising expenses, bad investments, loss of work, or debts threatening your financial security? This amulet helps to protect your assets and your serenity.

INGREDIENTS/TOOLS:
- 1 black marker
- 1 circle of soft, flexible leather (deerskin is perfect) 8" in diameter
- 1 single-hole paper punch
- 1 leather cord
- Alfalfa
- Small pieces or wood chips of cedar, ash, or pine
- 1 cauldron
- Matches or a lighter
- 1 small piece of aventurine
- 1 small piece of onyx

• On a Saturday, or when the sun or moon is in Capricorn

Choose a place where you can burn a small fire safely. With the marker, draw a pentagram on the inside center of the leather circle. With the paper punch, make small holes around the outside of the leather circle, large enough that you can slide the cord through them. Thread the cord through the holes. Pull up the outer edges of the circle, tightening the cord to form a pouch (with the pentagram inside on the bottom).

Put the alfalfa and wood chips in the cauldron. Light them and let them burn completely. Allow the ashes to cool. Pour the ashes into the pouch, then add the gemstones. Close the pouch and tie 3 knots in the cord.

Place the amulet in the wealth sector of your home or business. To locate this, stand at the entrance to your home (the one you use most often, not necessarily the front door) with your back to the door, so you're looking inside. The farthest left-hand corner is the wealth sector. If you prefer, put the amulet in your safe, cash register, or purse to safeguard your finances.

PROTECTION BATH

This relaxing spell is good to do at night, before you go to bed, to remove any bad vibes you may have picked up during the day. It cleanses your body, mind, and spirit of unwanted energies and safeguards you while your spirit travels during sleep.

INGREDIENTS/TOOLS:
• 4 white candles in unbreakable holders
• Matches or a lighter
• 4 clear quartz crystals
• A bathtub full of comfortably hot water
• ½ cup Epsom salts
• A few drops of lavender essential oil
• A few drops of fennel, basil, or cedar oil—or a combination

- Every night, or as often as possible

Set the candles in their holders at the corners of your bathtub and light them. Place one quartz crystal beside each candle. Fill the tub with water while you pour in the Epsom salts. Add the essential oils. Soak in the fragrant, soothing water for as long as you wish, while you envision yourself cleansed and cleared of all negative, harmful, and/or unbalanced energies. See yourself surrounded by a bubble of white light that will continue to protect you even after you leave the bath.

Extinguish the candles and get out of the water; empty the tub. You can carry the crystals with you throughout the day, or leave them on the corners of the tub—your choice.

BRAVE HEART LOTION

If you suffer from stage fright or feel uncomfortable speaking in front of a group of people, whip up a batch of this magick lotion and use it to boost your confidence. You can also use it if you feel nervous about a job interview, important meeting, or big game.

INGREDIENTS/TOOLS:
- 1 small carnelian, garnet, or ruby
- 1 glass jar or bottle, preferably amber-colored, with a lid or stopper
- 4 ounces of almond oil
- 3 drops of fennel essential oil
- 3 drops of cedar essential oil
- ¼ teaspoon dried basil leaves

BEST TIME TO PERFORM THE SPELL:
- Several days before your public appearance, preferably on a Tuesday or Sunday; if you don't have that much time, do the spell as needed

Wash the gemstone and the bottle/jar with mild soap and water. Pour the almond oil into the bottle/jar. Add the essential oils and inhale the fragrance, allowing it to invigorate your mind. Crumble the basil leaves very fine and add them to the oil. Add the gemstone. Cap the bottle/jar and shake it three times to blend and charge the ingredients.

Each morning, pour a little of the magick oil into your palm and dip your index finger in it. Then rub the oil on your skin at your heart center. Feel it strengthening your confidence. Take several slow, deep breaths, inhaling the warm, spicy scent, letting it strengthen and vitalize you. Repeat each morning until your fear diminishes. Rub a little extra on your chest immediately before you must face your audience. On with the show!

OIL TO GUARD AGAINST SECRET ENEMIES

You may not realize that someone is working against your best interests, so consider making and using this protection oil regularly. If you do suspect someone is out to get you, this magick oil heightens your strength and helps increase your insight so you can protect yourself before the enemy can strike.

INGREDIENTS/TOOLS:
- 1 glass jar or bottle with a tight-sealing lid
- 3 cloves
- 1 small piece of hematite
- A pinch of salt
- 3 ounces of olive oil

BEST TIME TO PERFORM THE SPELL:
- Whenever you need it, but preferably on a Tuesday or Saturday

Wash the bottle, then place the cloves in the bottle one by one as you visualize the bottle filling with white light. Add the hematite, visualizing the silvery color of the stone weaving and swirling through the white light. Add the salt, and visualize the silver and white light growing brighter. Carefully pour the olive oil into the jar or bottle over the contents, then cap the bottle tightly. Shake it three times to blend and charge the ingredients.

The Modern Witchcraft Spell Book

Open the jar or bottle and dip your finger in the oil. Draw a pentagram with the oil on your third eye (the brow chakra) and on the center of your chest (your heart chakra). If you wish, draw additional pentagrams on your other chakras for added protection.

SAFETY SHIELD FOR YOUR CAR

Approximately 2 million people are injured in vehicular accidents each year in the United States (and nearly a quarter of all accidents involve cell phone use). That's a good reason to create this magick safety shield to protect you and your car from harm.

INGREDIENTS/TOOLS:
- 1 nail, nail file, small knife, or other sharp tool
- 1 black candle
- 1 candleholder
- Matches or a lighter
- 1 piece of white paper
- 1 pen that writes black ink

BEST TIME TO PERFORM THE SPELL:
- As needed, but preferably on a Thursday or Saturday

Use the nail or other tool to engrave a pentagram into the candle's wax. Fit the candle in its holder, set it on your altar or another surface, and light the candle. On the piece of paper, draw a circle and write, "I am safe" inside the circle. If you like, add symbols, words, or other images that represent safety to you. You could even draw a picture of your car or write your license plate number on the paper. Drip a bit of melted candle wax on each corner of the paper. Use the nail or other tool to inscribe a pentagram in the warm wax. Extinguish the candle and place the safety shield in your car's glove compartment or affix it to your dashboard. (And don't use your cell phone to text or talk while driving!)

POTION TO PROTECT A LOVED ONE

Are you worried about a friend or loved one's safety? This magick potion protects someone else from harm. However, before you do this spell, ask the other person—either directly or psychically—if it's okay for you to use magick to help him or her, so you don't interfere with another's free will.

INGREDIENTS/TOOLS:
- 1 clear glass bottle with a lid or stopper
- 1 small clear quartz crystal
- Black paint or nail polish
- Water
- 1 kettle or pot
- Dried comfrey or comfrey tea bags

BEST TIME TO PERFORM THE SPELL:
- On a Monday, or when the sun or moon is in Cancer

Wash the bottle and the crystal with mild soap and water, then let them dry. Paint a pentagram on the side of the bottle. Heat the water in a kettle or pot and add the comfrey to it to make a tea (you can purchase comfrey tea bags in health food stores and many supermarkets). Allow it to steep for several minutes, then let it cool. Pour the tea into the bottle. Add the quartz crystal. Put the lid or stopper on the bottle and shake it three times to charge it. Let the potion sit overnight, preferably where the moon can shine on it.

Remove the crystal and give the protection potion to your friend or loved one. If you're afraid this person will think you're weird, you can transfer the tea into another container *sans* pentagram—the tea will retain the imprint of the symbol. Instruct the person to drink a little each day. Additional suggestion: While you're at it, brew some for yourself, too.

QUICK AND EASY FLYING SPELL

This spell requires no tools—just your imagination—and you can do it in a minute or so, right before your plane taxis into position for takeoff. Close your eyes and breathe slowly and deeply. Envision a cocoon of pure white light surrounding the entire plane from nose to tail and out to the tips of the wings. See the light swirling around the plane in a clockwise direction, forming a protective barrier against the elements. Mentally repeat the following affirmation three times: "I now enjoy a comfortable trip and arrive safely at [name of destination airport]." Visualize the plane traveling through the sky and landing safely on the runway at your final destination.

STRENGTH AND SAFETY SOUP

Make this delicious recipe during those times when you feel you need a little extra protection or think you may be coming down with a cold. Garlic and onions are the key ingredients. Romans used garlic for strength, and many people valued it for its protective properties (not just against vampires). Egyptians used onions to keep away harmful spirits and fed onions to their slaves to ensure vitality. This recipe also relies on the number four for its stabilizing, earthy influence.

INGREDIENTS/TOOLS:
- 1 large Spanish onion
- 1 large red onion
- 1 bundle green onions
- 1 white onion
- Frying pan
- 1 tablespoon butter
- 4 small cloves garlic, peeled and crushed
- 4 sticks celery, diced (optional)
- Large saucepan
- 2 cups beef stock
- 2 cups chicken stock
- 2 cups water
- 1 tablespoon Worcestershire sauce (or to taste)
- Croutons and grated cheese (for garnish, optional)

Slice the onions and sauté them in a frying pan with the butter and garlic, until golden brown. For a heartier broth, add the celery and fry it with the onions. Magickally, celery enhances your psychic sight and sense of inner peace. Stir the vegetables counterclockwise as they cook to banish negative energies. Say aloud:

> *"Onions for health,*
> *And to keep harm at bay,*
> *Garlic for safety*
> *All through the day!"*

Keep repeating the incantation until the onions are done. Transfer the onion mixture into a large saucepan, then add the stock, water, and Worcestershire sauce. Cook this mixture down over medium-low heat until it is reduced by 2 cups. Serve the soup with croutons and fresh grated cheese, if desired. Visualize your body being filled with white light as you eat it. You may want to share your magick soup with friends or loved ones.

GUARDIAN ANGEL RITUAL

Numerous polls conducted by Associated Press, AOL, Gallup, and others have found that nearly 80 percent of Americans believe in angels. Here's a way to request angelic assistance and protection. With this ritual you call upon Raphael, Michael, Gabriel, and Uriel. Perform this ritual by itself to petition their aid, or do it in conjunction with other spells. You can also do it with other people, if you choose—just make sure you and your companions are in agreement about your beliefs and intentions.

INGREDIENTS/TOOLS:
- 1 yellow votive candle
- 1 red votive candle
- 1 blue votive candle
- 1 green votive candle
- Matches or a lighter

• Anytime

Stand facing east and set the yellow candle on the ground (or floor) in front of you, where it can burn safely. Light the candle and say aloud:

"Archangel Raphael, Guardian of the East,
Come and be with me in this sacred space.
I request your protection and guidance
In all I do, now and always."

Move clockwise until you are facing south, and set the red candle on the ground (or floor) in front of you. Light the candle and say aloud:

"Archangel Michael, Guardian of the South,
Come and be with me in this sacred space.
I request your protection and guidance
In all I do, now and always."

Move clockwise until you are facing west, and set the blue candle on the ground (or floor) in front of you. Light the candle and say aloud:

"Archangel Gabriel, Guardian of the West,
Come and be with me in this sacred space.
I request your protection and guidance
In all I do, now and always."

Move clockwise until you are facing north, and set the green candle on the ground (or floor) in front of you. Light the candle and say aloud:

"Archangel Uriel, Guardian of the North,
Come and be with me in this sacred space.
I request your protection and guidance
In all I do, now and always."

Move to the center of the circle you've cast. Close your eyes and envision the four archangels standing around you, like sentries protecting you from harm. Feel their power flowing into you, filling you with strength and confidence. Remain in the center of the circle for as long as you wish. If you like, you can perform another spell or ritual now, under the watchful guard of the archangels. When you are ready, release the archangels and open the circle in the following manner.

Go to the east and stand facing outward. Say aloud:

"Archangel Raphael, Guardian of the East,
I thank you for your presence here this night (or day).
Please continue to guide and protect me always and all ways,
Even after you return to your home in the heavens.
Hail, farewell, and blessed be."

Extinguish the yellow candle. Move counterclockwise to the north and stand facing outward. Say aloud:

"Archangel Uriel, Guardian of the North,
I thank you for your presence here this night (or day).
Please continue to guide and protect me always and all ways,
Even after you return to your home in the heavens.
Hail, farewell, and blessed be."

Extinguish the green candle. Go to the west and stand facing outward. Say aloud:

"Archangel Gabriel, Guardian of the West,
I thank you for your presence here this night (or day).
Please continue to guide and protect me always and all ways,
Even after you return to your home in the heavens.
Hail, farewell, and blessed be."

Extinguish the blue candle. Go to the south and stand facing outward. Say aloud:

"Archangel Michael, Guardian of the South,
I thank you for your presence here this night (or day).
Please continue to guide and protect me always and all ways,
Even after you return to your home in the heavens.
Hail, farewell, and blessed be."

Extinguish the red candle. Additional suggestion: You can substitute this longer and more intricate circle-casting ritual for the basic one described in Chapter 3, if you choose.

Chapter 12

SPELLS FOR PERSONAL AND PROFESSIONAL SUCCESS

Because your mind is the architect of your reality, it's inevitable that your thoughts about yourself will generate material conditions that correspond to your ideas. Your life is your mirror. What you see is a reflection of what you believe about yourself. As you evaluate your personal and professional success, look at your entire life situation: your finances, your job, your relationships, your position in your community, and your health. If you aren't happy with your situation, you can change it by changing your perceptions of yourself.

Remember, nobody else gets to decide whether you're worthy of success. Only you do. Consider this quote from Eleanor Roosevelt: "No one can make you feel inferior without your consent." Nor can anyone else limit your personal power without your consent.

The spells in this chapter cover a number of different factors that pertain to success in all areas of life, because really, all areas are connected.

Instead of only aiming for fame and fortune, these spells help you connect with your own power and correct circumstances that may be sabotaging your success. The Spell to Release Negativity, for instance, clears obstacles to success—which may be necessary before you can start attracting the good things and conditions you seek.

Steps for Successful Spellcasting

Whenever you cast a spell, remember to use a few tried-and-true measures, as described in Chapter 1. These precautions can help you avoid complications, mix-ups, delays, or disappointments:

1. Remove all distractions.
2. Collect the ingredients and tools you'll use in your spell and cleanse them.
3. Purify and sanctify your space.
4. Quiet your mind.
5. Cast a circle around the area where you'll do your spellworking.
6. Perform the spell.
7. If you've called upon deities or spirits to assist you, thank and release them.
8. Open the circle.
9. Store your tools in a safe place until you need them again.

COLORS TO USE IN SPELLS FOR SUCCESS

To enhance the spells you do for success, incorporate the colors yellow, gold, and/or orange into your workings. If your aim is to also attract money, you can include green and/or silver. The most popular ways to bring in these colors are to burn candles or craft talisman pouches in these colors. You may also want to carry gemstones in these colors as talismans, or wear yellow, gold, or orange clothing while performing protection spells. Add flower petals that remind you of the sun to mojo bags, ritual baths, sachets, or potions. Many of the spells in this chapter use these color associations.

INGREDIENTS FOR SUCCESS SPELLS
Gemstones
Hematite: Deflects negativity, encourages determination, and promotes justice in legal matters
Onyx: Gives you strength to stand up to your adversaries
Star sapphire: Strengthens hope and clarity of purpose
Topaz: Increases confidence and courage; attracts fame and financial success
Flowers
Clover: Attracts good luck
Iris: The iris's three petals are said to symbolize faith, wisdom, and valor—qualities necessary to success
Lily of the valley: Enhances concentration and mental ability
Marigold: Encourages recognition; brings success in legal matters
Essential Oils/Incense
Cedar: Encourages prosperity and protects against adversaries
Cinnamon: Speeds career success and wealth
Patchouli: Stimulates enthusiasm and success in any endeavor
Sandalwood: Aids mental ability; facilitates guidance and assistance from higher sources
Herbs and Spices
Allspice: Encourages prosperity and good luck
Bay (bay laurel): Used to crown the victor of games in ancient Rome; it enhances success and wisdom
Nettle: Mitigates thorny situations and shows you how to handle problems
Nutmeg: Brings success in financial ventures

SPELL TO RELEASE NEGATIVITY

According to the Law of Attraction, you draw circumstances to you that align with your thoughts and feelings. That means if you've got a negative attitude, you're probably going to attract negative situations and people. Want to turn things around? Swap that bad attitude for a positive one.

INGREDIENTS/TOOLS:
- 1 piece of white paper
- 1 pen that writes blue ink
- White carnations in a clear glass container
- Matches or a lighter

BEST TIME TO PERFORM THIS SPELL:
- During the waning moon

If you encounter a bad situation, this spell breaks the destructive cycle of negativity and restores peace. You may not be able to change what has happened, but you can alter your perspective about it, which can soften the impact. Letting go of negative thoughts and feelings allows fortunate, happier ones to come into your life.

Write the following intention on the paper:

"I now release [name the situation]
And create new, positive energy to carry me forward.
I trust this is for my highest good
And affirm my commitment to this new path."

Place the paper beneath the vase of flowers. Leave it there until the flowers wilt. When you throw out the flowers, burn the paper to complete the releasing process.

The Modern Witchcraft Spell Book

POINT OF POWER SPELL

With this spell, you affirm that your point of power is in the present, the "now." At this very moment you can start creating the circumstances you desire—it's your launching pad for the rest of your life. So, get busy!

INGREDIENTS/TOOLS:
- 1 vase of yellow flowers
- 1 piece of turquoise
- 1 green candle
- 1 purple candle
- Matches or a lighter

BEST TIME TO PERFORM THE SPELL:
- On a Thursday or Sunday, during a waxing moon

The yellow flowers symbolize self-esteem and optimism. The green candle represents growth and prosperity, and the purple candle signifies wisdom and power. Turquoise attracts abundance, success, and good fortune.

Place the plant and gemstone on your altar, between the 2 candles. Light the candles and say aloud:

"My point of power,
Like these flowers,
Some way, somehow
Lies in the now."

Extinguish the candles. Carry the gemstone in your pocket or purse to reinforce your sense of personal power. Leave the flowers on your altar until they wither, then collect the petals and dry them for use in future spells.

SIMPLE SPELL TO ATTRACT GOOD THINGS

This simple spell helps you recognize the areas in your life that are rich and satisfying. According to the Law of Attraction, if you perceive yourself as needy, you'll lack things. By counting your blessings and being grateful, you attract more of the same. Like attracts like, as the saying goes.

INGREDIENTS/TOOLS:
- 1 index card
- 1 pen that writes gold or silver ink

BEST TIME TO PERFORM THE SPELL:
- During the waxing moon, preferably on a Sunday, Thursday, or Friday

Write "thank you" on the index card—write it again and again, until you've filled the card. As you write, think about the many things you have to be thankful for. Put the card in a place where you will see it often, such as on your refrigerator, your desk, or your bathroom mirror. Each time you see it, pause and say, "Thank you for [name a blessing]." Give thanks for the little things. Lots of people think only the big things count. We often forget that the big things are made up of the little things. Say thanks for the song that you heard on the radio that made you remember a special day from your childhood. Say thanks for the pouring rain that nourishes your garden. Say thanks for the crossing guard who works near your child's school. Your attitude of gratitude will bring more blessings into your life.

SPELL TO RELEASE PERFECTIONISM

Yes, you read that right. By clinging to the belief that you have to be perfect, you automatically set yourself up to fall short. Instead, do the best you can—and do this spell to release any lingering guilt.

INGREDIENTS/TOOLS:
- 1 piece of vellum or paper
- 1 pen

BEST TIME TO PERFORM THIS SPELL:
- During the waning moon, at sunset

The Modern Witchcraft Spell Book

Design an official-looking certificate. On it, write the following:

"I hereby authorize [your name] to be imperfect."

Sign your name. Keep the certificate somewhere safe. Take it out and look at it when you feel guilty for not being a superhero in your daily life.

RAISE YOUR FLAG

This spell lets you "announce" yourself and your goal to the world. Like Buddhist prayer flags, this practice taps the power of the wind to carry your message far and wide.

INGREDIENTS/TOOLS:
- 1 piece of yellow or orange cloth at least 8" × 8" square
- 1 waterproof marker

BEST TIME TO PERFORM THE SPELL:
- During the waxing moon, especially when the sun or moon is in Gemini or Sagittarius, on a Wednesday, at midday

Write your name on the cloth with the marker. Under your name, write an affirmation that states what you wish to achieve. Remember to state your intention in the present tense, and in a positive way (see Chapter 5 for more information). You can add images that symbolize your objective, if you like. (If you have more than one objective, create a different flag for each one.) When you're finished, hang the flag where the wind will make it flutter: a clothesline, flagpole, fence, etc. If your goals change, or the cloth starts looking bedraggled, make another flag to replace it.

SPELL TO BEAT OUT THE COMPETITION

When competition gets brisk or you fear an adversary wants to nudge you out of the picture, remember you have a secret weapon: magick. This spell helps you rise above the rest of the pack and keeps infringers from gaining a foothold.

- Polymer clay
- 1 large needle
- Jewelry elastic
- 1 nonstick baking tray

BEST TIME TO PERFORM THE SPELL:

- On a Tuesday, or when the sun or moon is in Aries

Have you ever seen animals defend their territory? They usually attack with teeth and claws. This spell takes its cue from them. What animal represents courage and ferocity to you? A lion? Bear? Doberman? Maybe a mythological creature such as a dragon? Shamans and sorcerers might use the actual teeth or claws from a totem animal in order to embody that animal's characteristics. You're going to fabricate "teeth" and "claws" from polymer clay to draw on the same symbolism. Select white or ivory clay to simulate the real thing, or another color if you prefer (who knows what color dragon's teeth are?).

Follow the directions on the package of clay to form lots of pointy teeth and claws, each about an inch or two in length. With the needle, pierce each one at the thicker end, making a hole large enough so the jewelry elastic will fit through it. Arrange the teeth and claws on the baking tray, making sure they don't touch each other. Bake according to instructions on the package.

Cut a piece of jewelry elastic long enough to go over your head. When the teeth and claws have cooked and cooled, string them on the elastic to make a necklace. Tie the elastic in a knot at the back. Wear this warrior's necklace to bolster your own courage, so you can scare off the competition and defend what's yours.

SPELL TO SAVE YOUR JOB

If you fear your job is on the line, try not to worry—that will only make matters worse. Instead, use your time and energy more productively by casting this spell.

INGREDIENTS/TOOLS:

- 4 white stones
- Black paint, nail polish, or a black felt-tip marker with permanent ink

BEST TIME TO PERFORM THE SPELL:

- Anytime

Collect 4 white stones. They can all be similar in size and shape or they can be different; the choice is yours. After washing the stones with mild soap and water, allow them to dry in the sun. With the black paint, nail polish, or marker, draw a pentagram on each stone to provide protection and security.

Put 1 stone on the floor in each corner of your cubicle, office, or work area to stabilize your position. As you set each stone in place, say or think this affirmation: "My job here is safe and secure, and all is well."

TALISMAN TO MAKE A GOOD IMPRESSION

Whether you're going for a job interview, giving a presentation, or meeting with an important client, this lucky charm helps you make a good impression. Remember, the key to success is believing in yourself. Enthusiasm is catching—if you're enthusiastic about your abilities and ideas, other people will get excited, too.

INGREDIENTS/TOOLS:

- Sandalwood incense
- Incense burner
- Matches or a lighter
- Red nail polish or red paint
- 1 small brush
- 1 small stone
- 1 piece of paper
- 1 pen
- 1 orange cloth pouch, preferably silk
- Cedar chips
- Cinnamon

- Dried parsley
- 1 yellow ribbon
- Saltwater

- On a Sunday, or when the sun or moon is in Leo

Fit the incense in its burner and light it. Use the nail polish or paint to draw the rune *Inguz*, which looks like two Xs stacked one on top of the other, on the stone. This rune represents new beginnings, fertility, and great power.

While the nail polish or paint is drying, write on the paper what you intend to accomplish. Whom do you wish to impress? What results do you desire from this meeting or appearance? As you write your list of objectives, envision yourself already achieving them. When you've finished, fold the paper so it's small enough to fit into the pouch and say aloud: "This is now accomplished in harmony with Divine Will, my own true will, and for the good of all."

Put the stone, paper, cedar, cinnamon, and parsley into the pouch. Tie the pouch closed with the ribbon, making 3 knots. Hold the image of your success in your mind as you tie the knots. Sprinkle the talisman with saltwater, then hold it in the incense smoke for a few moments to charge the talisman. Carry it in your pocket, purse, or briefcase when you go to your meeting to bring you good luck. Just knowing it's there will increase your self-confidence and help you make a good impression.

SPELL TO OPEN NEW DOORS

If downsizing, outsourcing, or another situation beyond your control has eliminated your job, remember the old saying: When one door closes another one opens. This spell uses the familiar symbolism to bring new opportunities your way.

INGREDIENTS/TOOLS:
- Small bells, one for each door in your home
- 9"-long red ribbons, one for each door in your home

The Modern Witchcraft Spell Book

BEST TIME TO PERFORM THE SPELL:
- On the new moon

Tie 1 bell at the end of each ribbon, then tie 1 ribbon to each door in your home. As you work, envision yourself attracting new opportunities. If you already know the job you'd like to have, see yourself performing it. Or, if you prefer, let the universe provide a position that's right for you. Each time you tie a ribbon on a doorknob, say the following affirmation aloud: "I now have a job that's perfect for me in every way."

As you go through the doors in your home daily, you'll constantly be reminded of your intention. The red ribbons represent good luck. The tinkling bells send your request out into the world. Repeat your affirmation every time you open a door, until you land the job you desire.

SPELL TO DRUM UP NEW BUSINESS

During slow periods, you may need to step outside the box to attract new clients/customers and opportunities. Since ancient times, drums have been used as a form of communication. Drumming also breaks up stagnant conditions. This spell helps you get the word out magickally—and it won't cost you a fortune in advertising.

INGREDIENTS/TOOLS:
- 1 drum
- 1 picture, token, or other symbol that represents success in your business
- Something to attach the symbol to the drum (e.g., ribbons or tape)

BEST TIME TO PERFORM THE SPELL:
- On the new moon

Fasten the symbol to the drum, by whatever means you prefer. You may be able to simply slide the image beneath the drum's strings. If you prefer, tie it to the drum with a ribbon of an appropriate color. Or you could even paint the symbol on the drum.

Stand facing east and begin drumming. Imagine you are sending a message to the world, inviting one and all to come patronize your business. If you like, extend the invitation to them verbally, explaining all the good things you have to offer them, as if you were doing a commercial. Visualize people flocking to you and enjoying your products or services. After a few minutes, turn to face south and do the same thing. Keep drumming as you turn to face west, and finally to the north. Continue drumming for as long as you like. Repeat this spell as often as you wish, until you have all the business you can handle.

SPELL TO WIN A DECISION

If an upcoming decision will affect your job, your public image, or a project you're working on, use magick to tip the scales in your favor. This spell puts you in a strong position and ensures that you'll be judged fairly.

INGREDIENTS/TOOLS:
- Cinnamon incense
- Incense burner
- Matches or a lighter
- 1 old-fashioned set of scales or 2 white saucers
- The Judgment card from a tarot deck
- 1 picture of yourself
- 1 image that symbolizes "the other" (e.g., a person, issue, or contest)
- 1 piece of watermelon tourmaline
- 1 gold-colored cloth

BEST TIME TO PERFORM THE SPELL:
- During the waxing moon, or when the sun and/or moon is in Libra

Fit the incense in its burner and light it. Set the scale or the saucers on your altar or another spot where they can remain safely in place until the decision is final. If you're using a scale, lay the Judgment card face up in front of it. If you're using 2 saucers, position them next to each other, about 6" apart, and lay the Judgment card face up between them.

The Modern Witchcraft Spell Book

Put the picture of yourself on the right side of the scale or in the right saucer. Put the image that symbolizes "the other" on the left side of the scale or in the left saucer.

Place the piece of tourmaline on the right side of the scale or in the right saucer, along with your picture. If you're using a set of scales, the stone will actually tip it in your favor. If you're using saucers, imagine the tourmaline supporting and strengthening you, giving "weight" to your position and bringing you luck. Allow the incense to finish burning down completely while you visualize the decision being made so that you benefit. See yourself happy and successful, winning the challenge. Cover the spell components with the golden cloth. Leave the spell in place until the decision is final.

FENG SHUI SPELL FOR SUCCESS

The ancient Chinese magickal system known as feng shui associates areas of your home with areas of your life. When you stand at the door you use most often to enter and exit your home, facing in, the section halfway between the farthest right-hand corner and the farthest left-hand corner of your home represents your future, fame, career, and public image.

INGREDIENTS/TOOLS:
- 3 objects that represent success to you
- 1 mirror
- 1 bell

BEST TIME TO PERFORM THE SPELL:
- During the waxing moon

In this sector arrange the three objects you've chosen to represent your success. Position the mirror so it reflects these objects, symbolically doubling their impact. Each day, take a few moments to gaze at these objects. Ring the bell as you do this to activate positive energy in this portion of your home. The sound of the bell also triggers your attention and helps you focus on achieving success.

GEMSTONE TALISMAN FOR SUCCESS

This spell can help you succeed—e.g., land a new job, receive a promotion, win a contest, or get a place on the team. Its power comes from combining the magickal meanings of rune symbols with the energies inherent in gemstones—fueled by your desire.

INGREDIENTS/TOOLS:
- Book or list of rune symbols
- Gold paint or metallic gold nail polish
- 3 gemstones that correspond to your objective (see the table at the beginning of this chapter and in Chapter 4 for suggestions)
- 1 gold pouch
- 1 red ribbon 12" long

BEST TIME TO PERFORM THE SPELL:
- During the waxing moon, preferably when the sun or moon is in Leo

Look through a book or list of rune symbols and select 3 that represent goals, conditions, or outcomes you desire. Paint 1 rune on each of the gemstones. When the paint dries, put all the stones into the pouch and tie it closed with the ribbon. Make 3 knots in the ribbon, one for each stone, and think about the intentions you've chosen. Carry the talisman in your pocket, purse, or backpack. If you prefer, place it in a desk drawer or on your altar.

DRESS FOR SUCCESS

Clothes may not make the man or woman, but how you dress does influence the way people think about you and react to you. The President wouldn't address the nation in a pair of ragged jeans and a T-shirt, would he? If you aspire to a position of authority or prominence, start dressing as if you already have that position—even if your dream hasn't manifested yet. In this way, you not only make a statement to others, you send a message to your subconscious that you expect it to help you achieve your goal.

The Modern Witchcraft Spell Book

Ingredients/Tools:

• Clothing, jewelry, accessories, etc. befitting the position you desire

Best time to perform the spell:

• Each morning, during the waxing moon, when the sun and/or moon is in Leo, on Samhain Eve (October 31), or on your birthday

Each day before you go out into the world, look in your mirror and affirm that you have already achieved the position you seek. Envision yourself performing the role you desire with great skill and satisfaction. Close your eyes and imagine your aura (the energy field around your body) expanding until it extends at least 1' out from your body in every direction, then envision that aura glowing with radiant golden light. Don't just see this light, feel it tingling all around you, warming you with its power, permeating your entire being. Imagine other people noticing and responding favorably to this golden glow. Now, open your eyes and see the very best in yourself—others will, too.

Chapter 13

HEALTH AND HEALING SPELLS

Our ancestors didn't have the advantage of modern medical procedures and pharmaceuticals, as we do today. Instead, when people became ill they relied on plant-based remedies, magick potions, and healing spells to treat ailments and injuries. In many parts of the world, that's still the case. But even in the United States, herbal medicine, essential oils, and various types of holistic healing are gaining popularity. Doctors also acknowledge that our thoughts and emotions have a lot to do with our physical well-being. Numerous studies show that meditation, visualization, and prayer can have a positive effect on health, too.

To some, that may sound like magick—and perhaps it is. As you already know, harnessing your mental power is the key to spellworking. You also understand that working with the forces of nature—plants, minerals, and so on—and tapping the energies inherent in them can help to bring about the conditions you desire. You're aware, too, that you can call upon spiritual beings to assist you in your spells. So it makes sense that magick spells can influence your health and other people's. In this chapter, you'll find spells to aid a variety of problems. But remember, before you cast a spell for someone else, ask that person (either directly or through psychic communication) if it's okay to use magick to help. That way you won't interfere with his or her free will. Just to be on the safe side, it's a good idea to end a spell with a statement such as: "This is done for the good of all concerned." Of course, spells are not intended to replace professional medical care.

Steps for Successful Spellcasting

Whenever you cast a spell, remember to use a few tried-and-true measures, as described in Chapter 1. These precautions can help you avoid complications, mix-ups, delays, or disappointments:

1. Remove all distractions.
2. Collect the ingredients and tools you'll use in your spell and cleanse them.
3. Purify and sanctify your space.
4. Quiet your mind.
5. Cast a circle around the area where you'll do your spellworking.
6. Perform the spell.
7. If you've called upon deities or spirits to assist you, thank and release them.
8. Open the circle.
9. Store your tools in a safe place until you need them again.

COLORS TO USE IN SPELLS FOR HEALTH AND HEALING

To enhance the spells you do for success, incorporate the colors green and blue into your magickal workings. White signifies purification and protection, so you can use it in healing spells, too. Consider burning candles or crafting talisman/amulet pouches in these colors. You may also want to carry gemstones in these colors as talismans or amulets, and wear green or blue clothing while performing health and healing spells. Add green or blue botanicals to mojo bags, ritual baths, sachets, or potions. Many of the spells in this chapter use these color associations.

INGREDIENTS FOR HEALTH AND HEALING SPELLS

Gemstones

Amethyst: Increases relaxation

Chrysocolla: Eases emotional pain

Citrine: Promotes cleansing and dissolves impurities

Fluorite: Eases stress and stress-related problems

Jade: Encourages good health and longevity

Jasper: Brown jasper supports physical healing; poppy jasper breaks up blockages that prevent energy from circulating through the body

Flowers/Plants

Aloe: Aids burns; soothes stomach and intestinal problems

Calendula: Soothes cuts and skin conditions

Gardenia: Brings tranquility and harmony

Lavender: Calms body, mind, and spirit, and encourages relaxation and sleep

Essential Oils/Incense

Eucalyptus: Relieves congestion and soothes colds

Lavender: Encourages relaxation and sleep

Sweet marjoram: Eases muscle and joint pain/stiffness

Herbs and Spices

Chamomile: Aids stomach problems; eases stress and supports relaxation

Comfrey: Encourages bone health and healing

Ginger: Improves digestion, calms nausea

Peppermint: Aids digestion and heartburn, eases headaches

Yarrow: In a poultice, it helps stanch bleeding

How Healing Spells Work

When you do a healing spell, you first clear away the obstruction, disruption, or negative energy that is causing the problem. Then you impart positive energy and harmony to the person seeking aid, to support his or her immune system so the problem doesn't return.

ABRACADABRA

Everybody knows the magick word *Abracadabra*—if you say it aloud, will it make your troubles disappear? Actually, it's better if you write it the way ancient healers did. This spell is thousands of years old, but it's still powerful medicine today.

INGREDIENTS/TOOLS:
- 1 blue candle
- 1 candleholder
- Matches or a lighter
- 1 piece of paper or parchment
- 1 pen or marker

BEST TIME TO PERFORM THE SPELL:
- During the waning moon, preferably when the sun or moon is in Virgo or Pisces

Fit the candle in its holder and light it. On the paper or parchment write the word *Abracadabra* as a descending triangle, like this:

The Modern Witchcraft Spell Book

```
ABRACADABRA
ABRACADABR
ABRACADAB
ABRACADA
ABRACAD
ABRACA
ABRAC
ABRA
ABR
AB
A
```

When you've finished, extinguish the candle and open the circle. Place the paper on the afflicted part of your body for a few minutes. Envision the illness or injury being transmitted into the symbol. Then remove the paper and take it outside. Tuck the paper in the cleft of a tree, where it will be exposed to the elements. As the word and the paper perish, your discomfort disappears.

WEIGHT LOSS POTION

If your jeans are getting tight and you're not sure you want to be seen in a swimsuit just now, what can you do to shed those unwanted pounds? This magick potion works at a subconscious level to calm hunger pangs and help you stick to your diet.

INGREDIENTS/TOOLS:
• Spring water
• Unsweetened green apple tea (not spiced apple)
• 1 bright pink ceramic cup
• 1 bright pink candle
• 1 candleholder
• Matches or a lighter

- During the waning moon, preferably on a Saturday or when the sun or moon is in Virgo or Capricorn

When you feel hungry, instead of eating something you shouldn't, brew a pot of green apple tea. Pour the tea into the bright pink cup. Fit the candle into its holder, set it on the dining or kitchen table, and light it. Sit and gaze at the candle while you inhale the refreshing scent of the tea. Drink the cup of tea slowly, keeping your attention focused on the candle. Feel your hunger pangs gradually subside. Repeat as necessary.

PAIN, PAIN GO AWAY

After a stressful day, does your head feel like someone is tightening a clamp around it? The key to this spell is detaching yourself from the pain, rather than resisting it.

Ingredients/Tools:
- None

Best time to perform the spell:
- Anytime

Sit in a comfortable place. Close your eyes. Acknowledge the presence of the pain, rather than fighting it. Don't identify with it, however. Try to envision it as something that's not a part of you. Mentally step back, so that your awareness is slightly above and outside your head, and simply observe the pain without emotion.

Press your thumbs on the back of your neck where it joins the base of the skull, with one thumb on each side. Apply firm but comfortable pressure for a minute or more, while you breathe slowly and deeply. Each time you inhale, imagine taking clear light blue air into your lungs. See the soothing blue air rise into your head and gently swirl around inside your skull.

After a minute or so, let go of your neck and press one index finger to your "third eye" (located between the eyebrows where the nose and forehead join). Continue breathing in blue air for a minute or two. Release the pressure on your third eye and hold your index fingers to your temples. Apply pressure for at least a minute, while you inhale healing blue light, then release. Open your eyes. Repeat as necessary.

SPELL TO EASE A HEADACHE

Here's another spell to soothe a headache—especially one caused by tension or sleeplessness. Performing this relaxing ritual every day may also have a beneficial effect on blood pressure, anxiety, insomnia, digestive complaints, and other stress-related conditions.

> **INGREDIENTS/TOOLS:**
> * 1 smoky quartz crystal
> * 1 piece of rose quartz
> * Lavender-scented incense
> * Incense burner
> * Matches or a lighter

> **BEST TIME TO PERFORM THE SPELL:**
> * As needed

Wash the stones in running water, then charge them by letting them sit in the sunlight for several minutes. Place the incense in the burner and light it. Sit quietly in a comfortable spot and begin breathing slowly and deeply. Hold the rose quartz in your left hand and feel it gently emitting loving, peaceful vibrations. Hold the smoky quartz crystal to your forehead and imagine the quartz dispersing the pain. Spend as much time as you need in this calm, relaxed state. When you're finished, cleanse the stones again and set them in a sunny spot.

SPELL TO RELIEVE MOTION SICKNESS

Whether you're sailing, flying, or winding around the mountains in an RV, motion sickness can turn your dream trip into a nightmare. Motion sickness usually occurs when you feel you are out of control—notice that the driver of a car rarely gets sick. This spell helps balance your equilibrium and calm nausea.

INGREDIENTS/TOOLS:
- Sea-Bands (available online, and at some health food stores or pharmacies in packages of two)
- 1 small vial of peppermint essential oil
- Gemstone Necklace for a Safe Trip (see Chapter 11)

BEST TIME TO PERFORM THE SPELL:
- As needed

If you start to feel queasy—or worry that you might—slip the Sea-Bands onto your wrists. They should fit snugly, with the nub pressing firmly against the middle of the underside of your arm about two or three finger widths up from the bend at your wrist. Inhale a few whiffs of the peppermint essential oil—you can pour a little oil on a handkerchief or sniff it directly from the bottle.

Don your Gemstone Necklace for a Safe Trip. Feel its magick protecting you, keeping you safe despite rough seas, air turbulence, or treacherous roads. Envision yourself surrounded by a ball of pure white light that shields you from harm. If you wish, visualize guardian angels or other deities on all sides, guiding you to safety. Repeat the affirmation "I am safe and sound at all times and in all situations" until you stop feeling upset.

HEALING MILK BATH

Nearly 3,000 years ago, Hippocrates, the "father of medicine," recommended baths for all sorts of ailments, and for centuries people have "taken the waters" to remedy health problems of all kinds. This simple milk bath soothes body and mind—adapt it to your special needs by adding appropriate herbs or flowers, essential oils, bath salts, and other ingredients.

INGREDIENTS/TOOLS:

- 1 cup cornstarch
- 2 cups milk powder
- 2 tablespoons dry herbs (see the table at the beginning of this chapter for suggestions)
- 1 glass jar with lid that will hold 3 cups (24 ounces)

BEST TIME TO PERFORM THE SPELL:

- As needed

Place all the ingredients in a blender or food processor. Blend until combined and reduced to a fine powder. Pour into the jar. To use, add ½ cup of this magick blend to bathwater while the tub is filling. (Store the rest in your fridge.) Soak in the tub as long as you like. Alternate suggestion: Substitute essential oils for dry herbs: eucalyptus for colds, sandalwood for aches/pains, etc.

MAGICK HEALING BREW

You're feeling under the weather and could use a little magick to soothe what ails you. When you drink this healing brew, you nourish your body, mind, and spirit with herbal medicine and loving energy.

INGREDIENTS/TOOLS:

- Mint herbal tea
- 1 chalice (or cup)
- 1 echinacea capsule (available in health food stores and some supermarkets)
- Lemon juice, to taste
- Honey, to taste
- 1 spoon

BEST TIME TO PERFORM THE SPELL:

- As needed

Brew the mint tea and pour some into your chalice or cup. Open the echinacea capsule and sprinkle the herb into the tea. Add a little lemon juice and honey. Stir the tea in the chalice three times, in a clockwise direction, to charge it.

Gaze at the chalice and imagine a ray of pink light flowing into the chalice, infusing the tea with healing energy. Then slowly sip the tea. Feel its loving vibrations being absorbed into your body. Let them spread out from your stomach into your arms, legs, and head. Feel a tingling warmth radiating in your heart chakra. Allow the healing herbal blend to ease your discomfort and restore your sense of well-being. Repeat as necessary.

SWEET DREAMS SPELL

When you lie down to sleep at night, does your mind keep racing like a hamster on a treadmill? If you can't stop thinking about all the things you have to do tomorrow, try this bedtime ritual—it helps you relax and get a good night's sleep, so your mind and body can rejuvenate themselves.

INGREDIENTS/TOOLS:
- 1 piece of amethyst
- 1 dark blue votive candle
- Matches or a lighter
- White Chestnut flower essence (available from health food stores or online)
- 1 glass of spring water
- 1 piece of paper
- 1 pen or pencil

BEST TIME TO PERFORM THE SPELL:
- Before going to bed

Wash the amethyst with mild soap and water, and pat it dry. Light the votive candle and spend a few moments gazing into the flame to relax your mind. Put 4 drops of White Chestnut flower essence in the glass of water and sip it slowly. On the paper, make a list of all the things you must remember to do tomorrow. Once you've written down these tasks your mind can stop reminding you of them.

When you've finished noting everything you can think of, turn the paper over and draw the *I Ching* hexagram "T'ai/Peace" on it. This symbol consists of six lines stacked one on top of the other. Each of the top three lines looks like two dashes side by side. The bottom three lines are solid. Lay the piece of paper on your nightstand with the *I Ching* hexagram facing up. Set the amethyst on top of the symbol.

Extinguish the candle. Get into bed and feel the soothing resonances of the flower essence and the amethyst quieting your thoughts. If your mind strays to worrisome matters, gently stop yourself and replace those thoughts with a mental image of the symbol "T'ai." Additional suggestion: Do this spell at least 15 minutes after brushing your teeth, as mint toothpaste or mouthwash will nullify the effects of the White Chestnut.

SWEET DREAMS POTION

According to WebMD, lack of sleep can lead to coronary problems, stroke, diabetes, and automobile accidents. We need our sleep in order to thrive, yet a huge number of people report not getting enough quality shuteye. Here's another way to quiet your thoughts and emotions so you can sleep better. This magick potion also inspires prophetic dreams that can offer guidance in your waking hours.

INGREDIENTS/TOOLS:
- 1 bowl (preferably silver or clear glass)
- 1 moonstone
- Spring water
- 1 glass bottle with a cap or stopper, any size

BEST TIME TO PERFORM THE SPELL:
- On the night of the full moon; however, if you can't wait that long, do the spell as needed

Wash the bowl and the moonstone with mild soap and water, then place the stone in the bowl. Fill the bowl with spring water. Set it on a windowsill, countertop, table, or other surface where the moon will be reflected in the water. Allow the water to sit overnight. In the morning, remove the moonstone and pour the moon-imprinted water into the bottle.

Each night before retiring, sip a little of the potion to help you sleep better. Pay attention to your dreams, too—they may hold answers to daily dilemmas or offer glimpses into the future. Make a new batch of Sweet Dreams Potion at each full moon.

SPELL TO HEAL A MINOR WOUND

This spell uses a poppet or doll to represent the injured individual—whatever you do to the doll manifests in the person you seek to heal. Remember to obtain the permission of another person before you do the spell for him or her. (This spell is intended to assist healing, not to replace professional medical care or to treat serious injuries.)

INGREDIENTS/TOOLS:
- 1 piece of cotton or silk cloth, 12" × 12", that matches the skin color of the person who seeks healing
- Straight pins
- Markers in a variety of colors
- Scissors
- Needle and thread to match the cloth
- Filling to stuff the poppet (cotton batting, wool, straw, or other material)
- Yarn that matches the hair color of the individual (or, if possible, actual hair from the person for whom you are doing the spell)
- Paper or parchment
- Herbs and/or flowers that correspond to the nature of the wound
- Green, blue, or white cloth

BEST TIME TO PERFORM THE SPELL:
- As needed

Fold the skin-colored cloth in half and pin it together. With a marker trace a basic human shape on the top layer of the cloth. Don't make it too small; use as much space as you can on the cloth. Cut out the

The Modern Witchcraft Spell Book

human shape, cutting through both layers of cloth at the same time. You will have two flat, human-like shapes. Match the edges and pin the two shapes together. Sew them together with a small running stitch (it's better to do this by hand rather than with a sewing machine, because it's more personal and gives you more time to focus on your intention). Leave one side of the "body" open between the hip and the arm.

Stuff the poppet with whatever material you've chosen. Pin the hole shut temporarily. With the markers, personalize the poppet to look like the individual who will be healed. Add yarn for hair, or attach clippings of the person's real hair. Draw eyes, nose, mouth, and other features. Add any physical markings such as birthmarks or tattoos. Enrich the poppet's appearance with colors that correspond to the individual's own characteristics. Write the person's full name and birthdate on the slip of paper, and fold it up. Unpin the hole and tuck the folded paper inside the doll. Pin it shut again. Hold the doll in your hands and look it into its eyes. State aloud the person's name with confidence and awareness. Visualize him or her whole and well—don't focus on the injury.

Unpin the hole, and gather up pinches of the herbs you have selected to correspond with healing the wound. Tuck them into the doll. Sew the hole up, as you say:

"Needle and thread,
Knit bone to bone,
Flesh to flesh,
Cell to cell.
[Name], you are well."

Hold the poppet in your hands and hum a single note. (You may choose to hum a note that corresponds to the chakra linked with the injury; see Chapter 2.) As you hum, visualize healing energy flowing down your arms and into the doll. When you feel as if the doll holds as much energy as it can handle for the moment, wrap it gently in the cloth whose color you've chosen to represent healing. Place the poppet in a safe place.

You may repeat the healing hum once a day if the individual requires it. When the person has recovered and is well again, thank the doll for its help. Then hold it in your hands and look it in the eyes. State aloud, with confidence and awareness: "This is no longer [name]." Burn or bury the doll to symbolize that the healing is complete and the poppet has served its purpose. Alternate suggestion: If the individual is chronically ill, do not destroy the doll, but keep it as a focus for ongoing healing work. You may ask the person if he or she would like you to keep the poppet in order to strengthen the healing process.

EASY DOES IT LOTION

You've overdone it and now your muscles are making their displeasure known. This herbal balm helps soothe sore muscles and relieve minor aches and pains.

INGREDIENTS/TOOLS:
- 1 glass jar, bottle, or other container with a lid
- 1 small clear quartz crystal
- 4 ounces of olive, grape seed, or almond oil
- A few drops of camphor essential oil
- A few drops of clove essential oil
- A few drops of lavender essential oil
- 1 small amount of fresh ginger root, grated very fine

BEST TIME TO PERFORM THE SPELL:
- As needed

Wash the jar or bottle and the crystal with mild soap and water. Pour the olive, grape seed, or almond oil into the bottle. Add a few drops of each essential oil. Add the fresh ginger to the oil mixture. Hold the quartz crystal to your "third eye" (between your eyebrows) and send a vision of soothing, healing energy into the crystal. You might see it as blue or green light. Then put the crystal into the oil mixture and cap the jar/bottle. Shake the jar/bottle three times to charge it. Rub the healing lotion on your sore muscles to alleviate pain. Repeat as necessary.

HEAVEN AND EARTH RITUAL TO INCREASE VITALITY

This ritual invites the nurturing, supportive energy of the earth and the enlivening energy of the sun to blend within your body and bring balance. If possible, perform this ritual outside, in a safe place where you can burn candles.

INGREDIENTS/TOOLS:
- 4 bayberry candles in holders (votive candles in glass containers are good choices)
- Matches or a lighter
- 4 clear quartz crystals

BEST TIME TO PERFORM THIS SPELL:
- As needed

Place the candles at the four compass directions. Set the crystals between the candles to form a circle. You'll notice this eight-point circle resembles the Wheel of the Year (discussed in Chapter 8). Step inside the circle and light the candles, beginning in the east and working in a clockwise direction. Stand facing east, with your arms outstretched at your sides, parallel to the ground, palms up.

The candles represent the fire element and the masculine force. The crystals symbolize the earth element and the feminine force. Feel the balanced energy around you flowing into your body from every direction. Receive it in your open hands and allow it to fill you up, energizing you. Draw Mother Earth's nurturing energy upward through your feet, into your legs, torso, arms, and head. Feel the sun's vitalizing energy flowing into the top of your head and down through your body, all the way to your feet. Envision the two forces—yin and yang, heaven and earth—blending and balancing one another in your heart center.

Stand in the center of the circle as long as you choose. When you feel invigorated, extinguish the candles in a counterclockwise direction to open the circle, and pick up the crystals. Carry the crystals with you to continually charge yourself with positive energy, or place them at the corners of your home to provide extra energy. Repeat this spell as often as needed. If you wish, you can invite other people to join you in the healing circle.

KEEP YOUR COOL POTION

This magick potion helps you beat the heat, whether it's physical or psychological. The secret ingredient is aquamarine, a pale blue gem whose name comes from the Latin word for seawater. Wise men and women used this stone to calm anger, ease stress, lower blood pressure, and bring down fevers.

INGREDIENTS/TOOLS:
- 1 aquamarine
- 1 chalice (or clear glass)
- Spring water

BEST TIME TO PERFORM THE SPELL:
- Anytime

Wash the aquamarine and chalice/glass with mild soap and water to remove any ambient vibrations and/or dirt. Place the gem in the bottom of your chalice, then fill the chalice with water. Swirl the water in the chalice in a counterclockwise direction to charge it, while you chant the following incantation:

"I am healed
In body and mind
Of imbalances
Of any kind."

Remove the aquamarine. As you drink the potion, imagine you are immersing yourself in a refreshing pool of water to help you keep your cool. Store unused water in the fridge, preferably in a clear glass bottle, and keep some on hand for emergencies. Additional suggestion: You can also soak a clean cotton cloth in this magick potion to make a cooling poultice. Lay the cloth on your forehead to ease a headache, over your eyes to soothe eyestrain, or on your abdomen to aid hot flashes or menstrual cramps.

RITUAL TO RECLAIM YOUR ENERGY

Do you feel worn out at the end of the day, especially if you have to deal with a lot of people? When you're around a difficult person, do you notice your energy diminishing? According to ancient Toltec teachings, you leave a bit of your own vitality behind with every individual you meet during the day. This ritual lets you reclaim the energy you've given away, so you don't get depleted.

INGREDIENTS/TOOLS:
• None

BEST TIME TO PERFORM THE SPELL:
• At the end of each day, before going to sleep

Sit in a comfortable chair and close your eyes. Start breathing slowly and deeply. Begin recalling all the people you encountered and all the incidents that occurred during the day, one at a time.

Turn your head to the left and remember something that happened in which you participated in some way. Inhale as you revisit the thoughts and feelings you had, as well as the actions that took place. Then turn your head to the right and exhale, releasing the experience with your breath. Continue doing this until you've recapped every event of the day, from beginning to end, the little things as well as the big ones. Feel yourself relaxing and gaining strength with each memory you cast out.

HEALING CHICKEN AND VEGGIE SOUP

Soup is a delicious way to warm up in the winter—especially if you're suffering with a cold or flu. In this recipe, the chicken and vegetables support the immune system to fight illness. The magickal secret to this soup's healing power comes not only from the vitamins and minerals in the ingredients, but also from the positive, loving vibrations you focus into the brew while you're cooking it.

INGREDIENTS/TOOLS:
• 4 tablespoons butter

- Large saucepan
- 1 large white onion, chopped
- 3 cloves garlic, diced
- 3 tablespoons brown sugar
- 2 tablespoons flour
- 4 cups chicken stock
- 1 (14½-ounce) can of diced tomatoes with juice
- 2 large carrots
- 2 large potatoes
- 1 small bunch of kale, chopped
- 2 tablespoons fresh parsley, chopped
- Water, as needed
- Salt and freshly ground pepper, to taste
- ¼ cup sherry or port (optional)
- Baguette (French bread), or croutons
- 1 cup grated mozzarella cheese

1. Melt the butter in the saucepan. Add the onion, garlic, and sugar and cook over medium-high heat; stir constantly using a clockwise motion (to boost the soup's healing energy) for 15 minutes or until sticky and caramel-brown. Remove from the heat.
2. Stir in the flour. Slowly add the stock, again stirring constantly using a clockwise motion. Return to the heat and bring to a boil, stirring regularly.
3. Add the veggies—feel free to include or substitute other vegetables if you wish (see tables in Chapter 16 for magickal correspondences). If soup seems too thick, add water (or more chicken stock or vegetable juice) until you get the consistency you like. Add salt and pepper to taste.
4. Cover and simmer gently for a half-hour (or longer if you wish), stirring occasionally. Add the sherry or port (if using). Taste and adjust the seasoning if required. Serve hot in bowls. Garnish with a slice of toasted baguette or croutons; sprinkle with grated cheese and chopped parsley.

Chapter 14

SPELLS FOR SELF-IMPROVEMENT

Self-doubt and lack of self-worth are common problems for many people. Self-esteem issues can keep you from achieving success in your career, from becoming financially secure, or from finding the love you desire and deserve. They can even cause illness. Increasing your sense of your own worthiness will help you to enhance every area of your life. You'll also improve your magickal power so you can produce better, faster results.

> *"Think of yourself like this: There's a universal intelligence subsisting throughout nature inherent in every one of its manifestations. You are one of those manifestations. You are a piece of this universal intelligence—a slice of God, if you will."*
> —Dr. Wayne W. Dyer, *The Power of Intention*

Regardless of what area in your life you wish to improve—your appearance, your health, your musical or athletic ability, your intelligence or intuition—magick can help. The most important part of working magick is your intent, fueled by your desire and willpower. Spells may not build up your physical muscles—although they can increase your energy and determination to stick with your training program—but they work wonders for strengthening your mental "muscles." The very nature of spellcasting requires you to focus your mind and use your imagination to visualize outcomes.

The spells in this chapter cover a wide range of conditions and objectives, from strengthening your sense of security to clearing your skin to eliminating an old habit. The tables included here offer information about the ingredients to use in spellwork, according to your purposes. Feel free to substitute ingredients from these charts to customize your spells and make them more personal.

Steps for Successful Spellcasting

Whenever you cast a spell, remember to use a few tried-and-true measures, as described in Chapter 1. These precautions can help you avoid complications, mix-ups, delays, or disappointments:

1. Remove all distractions.
2. Collect the ingredients and tools you'll use in your spell and cleanse them.
3. Purify and sanctify your space.
4. Quiet your mind.
5. Cast a circle around the area where you'll do your spellworking.
6. Perform the spell.
7. If you've called upon deities or spirits to assist you, thank and release them.
8. Open the circle.
9. Store your tools in a safe place until you need them again.

The Modern Witchcraft Spell Book

COLORS TO USE IN SPELLS FOR PERSONAL IMPROVEMENT

To enhance the spells you do for personal improvement, incorporate the colors yellow or orange into your workings. If your intention includes healing of some sort, you might also use green and/or blue. If you feel a need for more self-love and acceptance, choose pink. The most popular ways to bring in these colors are to burn candles or craft talisman pouches in these colors. You may also want to carry gemstones in these colors as talismans, or wear these colors while performing spells. Add flower petals that remind you of your objectives to mojo bags, ritual baths, sachets, or potions. Many of the spells in this chapter use these color associations.

INGREDIENTS FOR PERSONAL IMPROVEMENT SPELLS

Gemstones

Aquamarine: Stimulates intuition, imagination, and creativity

Fluorite: Improves concentration and mental clarity

Lapis lazuli: Deepens insight and inner wisdom

Moldavite: Enhances your ability to communicate with spirits, deities, and extraterrestrials

Obsidian: Provides strength to face obstacles; helps you break old habits

Sapphire: Increases spiritual knowledge and connection with the Divine

Flowers

Carnation: Promotes strength and perseverance

Rose: Pink increases self-love and yellow enhances creativity

Sunflower: Boosts confidence

Essential Oils/Incense

Anise: Improves psychic vision

Bergamot: Elevates your mood and increases confidence

Lemon: Clears the mind and makes you more alert

Orange: Increases happiness and optimism

Herbs and Spices

Marjoram: Encourages cooperation; supports life changes

Sage: Improves memory; clears old attitudes

Thyme: Strengthens focus and concentration

Verbena: Increases skill in artistic areas, especially performance

The Modern Witchcraft Spell Book

SPELL TO STRENGTHEN THE FIRST CHAKRA

This spell focuses on the body's first major energy center, known as the root chakra, at the base of your spine, to strengthen your sense of security, stability, and inner power.

INGREDIENTS/TOOLS:
- 1 object that represents your "tribe"
- 1 pen
- 1 piece of paper
- 1 red candle in a holder
- Vial of clove essential oil
- Matches or a lighter

BEST TIME TO PERFORM THE SPELL:
- During the waxing moon, preferably when the sun or moon is in Aries or Leo

The tribe symbol should be an object that represents your support system—a family photo, a figurine of a totem animal, or a treasured heirloom or item from your past. Set this "power object" on your altar. Next, write an affirmation that describes your intention. For example, you might write: "I can handle any challenge that comes my way" or "I am capable of caring for myself and my loved ones." Fold the paper three times and slip it under the object that signifies your tribe.

Dress the candle with clove oil (not on the wick). If you wish, dab some oil on your power object, too, and at the base of your spine. As you light the candle, inhale the scent of clove and say your affirmation aloud. Focus on the spot at the base of your spine and imagine you are directing energy into it. Imagine a glowing ball of red light there. Allow the candle to burn down on its own, and then burn the paper, releasing your affirmation into the universe.

COLOR SPELL FOR REVISING YOUR LIFE

This spell helps improve your life—even if you can't put your finger on precisely what or how it might make things better. The key is remembering that you are in charge of your own life—not somebody else—and every moment you have the power to change the things you don't like about it.

Ingredients/Tools:
- 1 piece of white paper
- 1 box of crayons (with at least 7 colors in the box)

Best time to perform the spell:
- During the new moon, preferably when the sun or moon is in Aries, or on a Tuesday, Thursday, or Sunday

Draw a big circle on the paper. This circle represents your life. Divide the circle into pie-slice wedges, as many wedges as you feel are necessary. Designate each slice to represent a segment of your life: friends, money, family, health, career, love—whatever you deem important. Usually we associate certain colors with certain areas of our lives: pink with love and affection, gold with money, etc. (At the beginning of the chapters in Part II of this book, you'll find information about colors to use in various types of spells and their meanings—but if your personal associations are different, by all means go with them.)

Look at the wedges that you've identified in your circle. Which areas of your life are you happy with and which ones do you want to change? Then look at the colors in your box of crayons and consider how those colors relate to your objectives. For example, if you want to relieve job-related stress and you connect serenity with blue, color the job sector blue. If you seek more affection in your love life, color that wedge pink. If you aren't clear about what you want to change, choose the crayon(s) you feel most drawn to at this moment and let your intuition guide you.

As you color the wedges in your circle, visualize your life realigning and rebalancing to reflect your choices. Don't be concerned about staying in the lines. Life isn't neatly compartmentalized. It's messy. Recognize that, accept it, and embrace it. You can also decorate your circular chart with stickers, glitter, cut-out photos, words, or whatever you like to personalize it. It's your life—have fun! Display your finished drawing on your altar, your desk, the fridge, the bathroom mirror, or another place where you'll see it often. Each time you look at it, reaffirm your commitment to creating the ideal balance of energies in your life.

CLEAR SKIN RITUAL

Do you see pimples, wrinkles, or other "imperfections" when you look into your mirror? When you do this simple ritual you focus positive energy onto your face to clear and rejuvenate your skin.

INGREDIENTS/TOOLS:
• None

BEST TIME TO PERFORM THE SPELL:
• Every day

Close your eyes and begin breathing slowly and deeply. Rub your palms together vigorously, until they feel quite warm. Beginning at your collarbones, hold your hands an inch or so away from your body with your palms turned toward you. Move your hands upward, over your face, to the top of your head—but don't actually touch your face. When you get to the top of your head, flick your hands sharply as if throwing off water—you are actually shaking off unwanted energy.

As you move your hands, imagine you are drawing off all the tension and impurities that lead to wrinkles, pimples, dryness, discoloration, and other imperfections. Envision healing, invigorating energy infusing your skin with good energy. Repeat these movements six more times (for a total of seven passes). Perform this quick-and-easy ritual each morning and each night to stimulate your own inherent vitality and regenerative abilities.

USE AN ANIMAL TOKEN TO ENHANCE A QUALITY

If you'd like to enhance a particular quality in yourself, look at the animal kingdom to see which creature embodies the quality you seek. The owl, for example, symbolizes wisdom; the lion represents courage; the turtle displays determination.

INGREDIENTS/TOOLS:
- 1 candle of a color that corresponds to your intention or that reminds you of the animal you've chosen
- 1 candleholder
- Matches or a lighter
- 1 small square of aluminum foil, 4" × 4"
- 1 nail, dry ballpoint pen, or other sharp object

BEST TIME TO PERFORM THIS SPELL:
- On the new moon

Fit the candle in the candleholder and light it. Allow it to burn while you meditate upon the animal you have chosen. Consider the qualities you admire in this creature and how you will use those characteristics in your own life. Carefully pick up the candle and hold it horizontally. Allow the wax to drip onto the piece of aluminum foil, forming a circular shape about the size of a quarter. Make sure the wax is at least ⅛" thick, and try to keep it as even as possible. Allow the wax to cool and dry. Leave the candle to burn while you work.

Peel the wax off the aluminum foil and turn it over so that the smooth side is facing up. With the nail, pen, or other tool, lightly scratch a simple symbol into the wax that represents the animal you have chosen. Do not carve too deeply, or you will snap the wax disk. Hold the wax amulet in your hands and envision the animal you have chosen, as you say:

"O [animal], lend me your [quality]
[Quality] flow through me night and day, day and night.
These are my words, this is my will.
So mote it be."

If you like, you can even act like the animal to show that you are receiving the animal energy you desire. Roar like the lion, hoot like the owl, etc. Hold the wax circle to your heart as you visualize the quality you seek flowing into you, down your arms, and into the wax circle. Extinguish the candle. Carry the wax disk with you to continue bringing you wisdom, courage, or whatever quality you seek.

BANISH THE BLUES

If you've been singing the blues lately, this ritual helps you change your tune. Drumming stimulates acupressure and reflexology points on your hands to produce beneficial effects. Because the beats harmonize with the beating of your own heart, drumming makes you feel joyful and alive.

INGREDIENTS/TOOLS:
- Sandalwood incense
- Incense burner
- Matches or a lighter
- Brightly colored ribbons (number and colors optional)
- 1 hand drum (for instance, a djembe, doumbek, or conga)
- The Sun card from a tarot deck you don't use for readings

BEST TIME TO PERFORM THE SPELL:
- Anytime

Fit the incense in its holder and light it. Tie the ribbons on the drum, as many as you like, in whatever colors please you. Then attach the Sun card to the drum, with the image facing out (you may be able to simply slip it under the drum strings).

Begin playing the drum with both hands. Don't worry about how you sound or whether you're doing it right, just play. Feel the drum's vibrations resonating through your hands, arms, and body. Feel it breaking up the dense, depressing energy around you. Close your eyes if you like. Try a variety of beats, keeping your mind focused on your drumming. You may hear singing or sense the presence of nonphysical beings near you, for drumming attracts fun-loving spirits. If you wish, put on a CD of lively African or Caribbean music and play along with it. Continue playing as long as you like. Repeat this spell whenever you start feeling blue to quickly shift your emotions to a higher vibration.

A LIGHT IN THE DARKNESS

If you don't feel you're getting the attention or respect you deserve, perhaps it's because other people can't see the real you. This spell makes them sit up and take notice, as you shine your light into the darkness like a beacon.

INGREDIENTS/TOOLS:
- 1 tarot card that represents you (from a deck you don't normally use for readings)
- 7 purple candles in candleholders
- Matches or a lighter

BEST TIME TO PERFORM THE SPELL:
- Begin 7 days before the full moon

Choose a tarot card that you resonate with or that you feel depicts you. Lay the card face up on your altar or another spot where you can leave the spell components safely in place for a week. Arrange the candles in a tight circle around the card. Light the candles, starting with the candle at the top of the card and working your way around the circle in a clockwise direction until you've lit them all. Gaze at the setup for a few moments while you imagine yourself illuminated brilliantly, as if standing in a spotlight. See other people watching and admiring you. When you feel ready, extinguish the candles in a counterclockwise direction.

The next day, repeat the ritual. This time, however, widen the circle of candles by moving each candle outward an inch or two. Repeat the ritual for a total of 7 days, moving the candles apart a little more each day. As the circle of candles increases in size, you expand your personal power. The light you shine into the world burns brighter and touches more people. On the night of the full moon allow the candles to finish burning down completely to send your "light" out into the universe. (Remember not to leave lit candles unattended.)

SPELL TO RELEASE OUTMODED PATTERNS

Identify one or more patterns that are holding you back or limiting your ability to express yourself. Choose candles of a color that relates to your objective. If you want to be better at handling your financial investments, for instance, use gold or silver candles. If you want to be more

The Modern Witchcraft Spell Book

creative in your professional life, use orange candles. If you want to be kinder and more loving toward yourself and others, burn pink candles.

INGREDIENTS/TOOLS:
- 2 candles in a color that corresponds to your intentions
- 1 piece of string
- Matches or a lighter
- Scissors
- Cauldron (optional)

BEST TIME TO PERFORM THE SPELL:
- During the waning moon, on a Saturday, or when the sun or moon is in Capricorn

Set the candles on your altar and tie them together with the string. Light the candles. Imagine the string is a limiting force that binds you and keeps you from functioning as fully as you could. Feel the energy of that self-limiting bond. Let your emotions come to the surface until they reach a peak and you experience a strong desire to remove the fetters. Then cut the string and burn it in your cauldron. (If you don't have a cauldron, you can burn it in the fireplace, a barbecue grill, or other safe place.) Say aloud:

"My self-limiting beliefs and bonds
Are burned up in this cleansing fire.
I'm now free to express myself
In any way I choose and desire."

Sense the relief that accompanies this symbolic release. Know that you can do whatever you wish to do, now that you've removed the old restrictions.

ANGELIC SPELL FOR CREATIVE ENERGY

If you feel a special affinity with a certain angel or deity, invite him or her to participate in this spell with you. Or ask one of the deities associated with creativity—Brigid, Isis, Apollo, Lugh, Odin, or Thoth, for example—to assist you.

INGREDIENTS/TOOLS:
- 1 small statue, icon, charm, picture, or other likeness of the angel or deity
- An offering for the angel or deity (your choice)

BEST TIME TO PERFORM THE SPELL
- During the waxing moon, especially when the sun or moon is in Leo or Libra; at dawn on a Sunday or Friday

Stand in the center of your circle and hold the likeness of the angel or deity in your hands. Invite him or her to fill you with creative power and join you in whatever task you've chosen. Then call upon the spirits of the four elements to lend their energies, too. Say aloud:

"Spirits of Air, fill me with inspiration.
Spirits of Fire, fill me with passion.
Spirits of Water, fill me with imagination.
Spirits of Earth, fill me with patience."

Feel the energies of these spirits—under the direction of your angel or deity—flowing into you. Stand in the circle as long as you like. When you feel you've absorbed as much creative energy as you need, place the image of the angel or deity on your altar. Lay the offering (a flower, a gemstone, or whatever you've selected) in front of the image and express your thanks. Release the entities you've called upon, with gratitude. Whenever you feel a need for a creative boost, touch the image and know that your guardian will assist you.

FENG SHUI SPELL TO ENHANCE CREATIVITY

Maybe you don't think of yourself as being creative, but everyone has some creative talent. Often we stifle ourselves because we think we have

The Modern Witchcraft Spell Book

to be a Mozart or van Gogh. This spell uses the Chinese magickal art of feng shui to spark your imagination and get your creative juices flowing.

INGREDIENTS/TOOLS:
- 1 slip of paper
- 1 pen
- 3 coins (any denomination)
- 1 bowl
- Yellow rose petals

BEST TIME TO PERFORM THE SPELL:
- When the moon is waxing, preferably when the sun or moon is in Leo

To locate the area of your home that corresponds to creativity, stand at the doorway that you use most often to enter or exit your home, facing in. Halfway between the farthest right-hand corner and the nearest right-hand corner is the creativity sector.

Write an affirmation on a slip of paper, describing your intention. Remember to state it in the present tense. For example, you might write "A major publishing company now buys my novel and I am content with all aspects of the contract." Or you could state "I now land a role in the upcoming community play" or "My tulips win an award in the spring gardening show."

Place your written affirmation in the creativity sector of your home, then position the three coins on top of it. The coins symbolize receiving money (or other rewards) for your creativity. Next, set the bowl on top of the coins and the affirmation. The bowl represents your willingness to attract and hold on to creative ideas. Fill the bowl with the rose petals. Yellow, the color associated with creativity and self-esteem, suggests that your creative ideas are blossoming and taking shape in the material world. Leave this spell in place until the full moon or until your wish materializes.

FENG SHUI SPELL TO IMPROVE YOUR IMAGE

Have you ever noticed that the entrances to the homes of rich and powerful people—as well as doors leading into government buildings, successful businesses, and cathedrals—tend to be grand, easily accessible, and well lit? In feng shui, the entrance to your home corresponds to your self-image and identity. Observe your entryway. Is it attractive and inviting? Or is it nondescript, cluttered, dark, maybe even difficult to find? To change your image—and the impression you make on others— all you have to do is improve your home's entrance.

INGREDIENTS/TOOLS:
- Whatever you choose

BEST TIME TO PERFORM THE SPELL:
- During the waxing moon, preferably when the sun or moon is in Leo, or on the summer solstice

Here are some ways you can improve your image: Install better lighting. Put a large, attractive plant near the door. Paint the door a bright, cheerful color. Affix handsome brass numerals on the door. Hang a decorative wreath on the door. Clear away all clutter or obstacles. Fix broken steps and railings. Remember, this is the first impression your visitors get of you, so make it as appealing as possible.

While you're working, periodically repeat this incantation (or another that you've designed yourself):

"The updates that I make today
Enhance my image in every way."

Keep your intention in mind—that's the most important part of the spell.

TALISMAN TO INCREASE SELF-CONFIDENCE

Most of us tend to be a little too self-critical. We pay more attention to our shortcomings than to our strengths and talents. This spell combines

The Modern Witchcraft Spell Book

a selection of ingredients that encourage personal power and fire up self-confidence.

INGREDIENTS/TOOLS:

- 1 piece of paper
- 1 pen, marker, or colored pencil
- 1 gold-colored pouch, preferably made of silk
- 1 almond
- 1 pinch of sage
- 1 acorn
- 1 small piece of tiger's eye, carnelian, or red jasper
- 1 red ribbon
- Sandalwood incense in a holder
- Matches or a lighter

BEST TIME TO PERFORM THE SPELL:

- On the full moon, preferably a Sunday or a Thursday, or when the sun or moon is in Leo

As described in Chapter 5, design a magick sigil by entwining the letters that spell the word *power* so they form an image. Fold the paper three times, then slip it into the gold-colored pouch. Add the almond, sage, acorn, and stone. Tie the pouch with the red ribbon, making 9 knots. Each time you tie a knot, repeat this incantation:

> *"By the magick of three times three*
> *Divine power flows through me.*
> *I am all I wish to be."*

Light the incense. Hold the talisman in the smoke for a few moments to charge it. Carry the talisman with you to increase your self-confidence. Hold it in your hand whenever you feel a need for a confidence boost. If you prefer, put it on your altar or in a spot where you'll see it often.

QUICK AND EASY SPELL FOR EMPOWERMENT

This spell requires no tools except the belief that magick works and that it can work for you. As you're waking up in the morning, before you open your eyes, when you're still in that drowsy state halfway between dreams and full consciousness, visualize whatever it is that you desire. The first thoughts you have in the morning are very powerful, and they color your experiences throughout the day. Then say your wish silently to yourself, in the form of an affirmation.

Let's say you want to ace an exam. Visualize the end result as vividly as possible: a big red A at the top of your exam sheet. Pour emotion into it. Imagine how excited you'll be when you see the A. Then say to yourself, "I ace my exam," feeling confident that you will do just that. When you get out of bed, forget about it. Release the desire and don't worry. Assuming that you've done your part to get an A on the exam (studied or otherwise prepared yourself), your intention should come true.

TAKE BACK WHAT'S YOURS

If you've let other people drain your energy during the day, this ritual will help you take back what's yours. Do this colorful practice every evening to improve your vitality, strengthen your ability to accomplish your objectives, and enhance every area of your life.

INGREDIENTS/TOOLS:
• None

BEST TIME TO PERFORM THE SPELL:
• At the end of each day, before going to sleep

Sit in a comfortable chair and close your eyes. Start breathing slowly and deeply. Bring to mind someone you encountered during the day. Imagine that person standing in front of you. Notice any splotches of color that appear to be stuck onto that person's body—they represent pieces of your own vital energy that you gave away to someone else.

Pick one splotch and as you inhale, imagine you are pulling that colored energy patch off the person's body and drawing it toward yourself.

As you exhale, feel the energy being reabsorbed into your body. Notice how this makes you feel—you should experience a slight sensation of contentment and strength.

Continue in this manner until you've taken back all the energy you lost during the day. You'll know you're done when you don't see any more colored blotches remaining on that individual's body. Then call to mind another person and repeat the ritual. Do this for everyone with whom you interacted, so they don't keep draining your power.

TRUE COLORS

Have daily stress and worries thrown you off-balance? This magick visualization technique tones your chakras to restore harmony to your entire system. When your chakras are balanced, you feel better in body, mind, and spirit.

INGREDIENTS/TOOLS:
• None

BEST TIME TO PERFORM THE SPELL:
• Anytime

Sit in a comfortable chair and close your eyes. Start breathing slowly and deeply. Focus your attention on the base of your spine, the energy center known as the "root chakra." Imagine a ball of clear red light glowing there, and feel warmth radiating in this part of your body for a few moments. Next, focus on the "sacral chakra" about a hand's width below your belly button. Envision a sphere of orange light shining there. After a few moments shift your attention to your solar plexus; see yellow light radiating there and warming this part of your body.

Continue breathing rhythmically as you visualize bright green light glowing around your heart. Feel it calming your emotions. Move your attention up to the base of your throat and imagine blue light shining there for a few moments. This helps you speak up for yourself with confidence. Shift your focus to your "third eye" on your forehead between your eyebrows, while you envision indigo light at this point. Finally, allow your attention to go to the "crown chakra" at the top of your head. As you see purple light glowing there, sense your connection with a higher force. Feel power flowing from the heavens into the top of your head and down your spine, energizing your entire body.

Enjoy this pleasant, soothing sensation for as long as you wish. Repeat this revitalizing ritual whenever you feel off-center, stressed out, or tired.

SPELL TO RELEASE SADNESS

This spell helps to lift your spirits by bringing back carefree feelings from childhood. On a practical level, it gets you outside in the sunshine and fresh air, and gives you a little exercise—all of which can improve your mood.

INGREDIENTS/TOOLS:
- 1 kite
- Kite string
- Strips of paper or lightweight ribbon
- Tape
- Scissors
- Matches or a lighter
- 1 cauldron (optional)

BEST TIME TO PERFORM THE SPELL:
- At sunset

Attach the string to the kite, then affix the strips of paper or ribbon to the kite's tail. Each strip or ribbon represents something that is causing you sadness. Take the kite to an open area. Feel the wind flow around you. Feel the sorrow in your heart, and imagine it flowing down your arms into the kite. Allow the wind to catch the kite and lift it up into the air. If you've never flown a kite before, abandon yourself to the experience. It takes focus, and intuition, and patience—just as magick does. As you fly the kite, visualize the wind lifting your sorrow gently away.

Fly the kite for as long as you choose. When you are done, reel it in and cut off the paper strips or ribbons. Burn them in your cauldron (or a safe spot such as a fireplace or barbecue grill) to symbolically eliminate your sadness. Repeat as often as necessary.

SPELL TO RELEASE ANGER

In order to release something, you must first acknowledge it. Holding on to anger not only drains your personal power, it also prevents good things from coming to you. This spell helps you release anger that may be eating away at you and draining energy that you could use more productively.

INGREDIENTS/TOOLS:
- 1 piece of paper
- 1 pen
- Matches or a lighter
- 1 cauldron (optional)

BEST TIME TO PERFORM THE SPELL:
- During the waning moon, at sunset on a Saturday

Write a letter to the person with whom you are angry. Use profanity, excessive exclamation points, capital letters, and bad grammar if you wish. Tell that person exactly what you think of him or her and how you feel. When you are done, reread your letter. Allow yourself to feel as emotional as you like.

Then, take three deep breaths and exhale all your tension and stress. At the bottom of your letter, write "I release my anger. [Name], you no longer hold any power over me." Burn the letter in your cauldron (or a safe spot such as a fireplace or barbecue grill) to symbolically eliminate your anger. Envision your anger drifting away with the smoke. Repeat as often as necessary, whenever a person or situation arouses your anger.

Chapter 15

SPELLS TO DO WITH OTHERS

At some point in your magickal journey you may decide to try spell-working with other people—especially if you're the sociable type and enjoy the camaraderie of like-minded folks. You've probably heard of witches' covens, but lots of magickal brotherhoods and sisterhoods have existed in the past and still do today. The Freemasons, the Hermetic Order of the Golden Dawn, and the Ordo Templi Orientis are just a few of the famous ones.

Joining forces with other magicians can strengthen your power by combining your energies and directing them toward a common purpose. Quite likely, some people in the group will have certain talents and skills, whereas others have different abilities—and that can benefit everyone. The key is to connect with people you respect and trust and whose objectives and beliefs are in harmony with your own. Problems can arise when members of the group disagree about how things should be done or power struggles get in the way of the common good. It's like what sometimes happens in businesses or social organizations—except when you're working magick, things can really get out of hand.

The spells in this chapter are designed for two or more people to perform together. Some spells also invite deities, elementals, spirit animals, and other entities to participate with you.

Steps for Successful Spellcasting

Whenever you cast a spell, remember to use a few tried-and-true measures, as described in Chapter 1. These precautions can help you avoid complications, mix-ups, delays, or disappointments:

1. Remove all distractions.
2. Collect the ingredients and tools you'll use in your spell and cleanse them.
3. Purify and sanctify your space.
4. Quiet your mind.
5. Cast a circle around the area where you'll do your spellworking.
6. Perform the spell.
7. If you've called upon deities or spirits to assist you, thank and release them.
8. Open the circle.
9. Store your tools in a safe place until you need them again.

SPELL TO CONNECT WITH OTHER MAGICIANS

If you think you'd like to do magick with other people, but don't know where to find those people, do a spell to attract them. Be as specific as you choose when you design this spell. If you wish to work only with men or women, be sure to say so. If you are open to working with an online spellcasting group, leave out the geographical conditions. If you wish to work with people of a specific religious path, then indicate that. Be aware, however, that the more conditions you stipulate, the fewer people will fill them. You have every right to be picky about the people you draw to yourself—and of course, you don't have to work with everyone you meet who happens to be a magician. This spell increases your chances of meeting people who are open to working with other spell-casters, not to lock you into a partnership of any kind.

INGREDIENTS/TOOLS:
- 1 peach-colored candle
- A few drops of vanilla essential oil (or pure vanilla extract)
- Matches or a lighter
- 1 slip of paper
- 1 pen
- 1 cauldron (or heatproof bowl)
- Several little feathers

BEST TIME TO PERFORM THE SPELL:
- At dawn during the moon's first quarter, preferably when the sun or moon is in Aquarius

Anoint the candle with vanilla. Light it, visualizing the light expanding and serving as a beacon to guide fellow magicians to you. On the paper, write an invitation to your ideal future spellcasting partners. For example, you might write: "I, [your name], issue an invitation to honest, sincere, and true spellcasters of [your geographical area]. If you seek to meet new people with whom to work, let us find one another." Sign it. Read the invitation aloud. Visualize your words flowing out into the world.

Touch the edge of the invitation to the candle's flame. When the paper has caught fire, let it burn in the heatproof bowl or cauldron. As it burns, visualize the energy of your invitation being released to flow out into the world. Allow the bowl or cauldron to cool. Place the feathers into the cauldron. Take the cauldron outside and hold it so that the wind lifts and swirls the feathers and the ashes, carrying them out into the world. If necessary, scoop the feathers and ashes out with your hand and toss them into the air. Watch the wind whisk away the ashes and feathers, and know your request has been sent.

Finding the Right Connection

If you're operating within an established group of people who've gathered to cast a spell (sometimes referred to as a circle), then you'll have at least some sort of energy connection between you. The closer you are to one another, the easier it is to merge and balance your energies. This comes with practice, of course; blending energy doesn't happen perfectly on the first try, no matter how experienced you are. With practice, though, you'll find the right balance of personal energies to create the right mix.

CREATE A GROUP POWER BUNDLE

Consider doing this spell when you first start working with a group of other magicians to connect your powers. It also strengthens your sense of unity and responsibility as a circle, and can give you insight into the individuals in your group.

INGREDIENTS/TOOLS:
• Small objects of your choice
• 1 multicolored pouch that includes all 7 colors of the rainbow

BEST TIME TO PERFORM THE SPELL:
• Anytime

Ask the members of the circle to bring small objects that they feel represent them. One person might bring a small figurine of an animal, another a favorite stone or crystal, a twig from a tree, a feather—it can be anything that holds special significance for the person. If you wish, have the members explain what the objects mean to them. Place the objects in the center of your circle. Raise energy by chanting together:

"We are one, our power flows.
We are one, our power grows."

After a minute or two of chanting, you'll start to feel the energy around you growing stronger. Focus the energy with your minds and direct it into the objects. Then put the objects into the pouch to keep them safe and to contain the energy. This is your group's power bundle. If the group meets in someone's home regularly, store it there. If the location changes, assign a different person each month (or after each meeting) to take the bundle home and watch over it. Bring it out at each meeting to symbolize unity.

CHALICE SPELL TO BOND A SPELLCASTING CIRCLE

This is a great spell for making your commitment to the spellcasting group official and launching your circle. You may also want to do it periodically to reinforce your bond, for example at the eight sabbats in the Wheel of the Year.

INGREDIENTS/TOOLS:
- 1 small bottle, can, or box of fruit juice of your choice
- 1 glass pitcher
- Glasses (one for each participant)
- 1 long-handled spoon

BEST TIME TO PERFORM THE SPELL:
- During the waxing moon, preferably on a Friday or when the sun or moon is in Aquarius

Have everyone bring one kind of juice to the meeting—don't confer beforehand, let it be random. Clean the pitcher, glasses, and spoon and consecrate them for your purpose. Place the pitcher, glasses, and spoon on your altar (or a table within your circle). Ask each member to empower his or her personal juice with positive energy, perhaps by stating a brief affirmation. Then, one by one, pour your juice into the pitcher and stir it three times using a clockwise motion.

When all the juices have been poured into the pitcher, state in unison:

"This special potion
Blessed by each one
Joins us together
The magick's begun."

Fill your glasses, then toast one another and the successful future of your circle and your spells. Drink the magick potion.

COLLECT INGREDIENTS FOR SPELLS

Collecting the components for spells and rituals can be a joint activity that includes all participants in the magickal working. Not only does this process get everyone involved from the very beginning, it stimulates your imagination and heightens your anticipation.

INGREDIENTS/TOOLS:
• Depends on the spell

BEST TIME TO PERFORM THE SPELL:
• Depends on the spell

After you've decided upon a spell and have determined which objects you'll need, each person agrees to acquire one or more of those objects. As you seek out the ingredients for your spell, focus your mind on the outcome and how it will benefit all concerned. In this way, you start the magick even before you combine the components you've collected. When you've gathered all the necessary items, go through the steps of cleansing your magickal space, consecrating it, casting a circle, etc. together.

BUILD A PERMANENT CIRCLE

If your group is likely to work together for a while, you may decide to create a permanent circle in which to perform your magick spells and rituals. Stonehenge is an example of an ancient stone circle that archaeologists believe may have been a ritual site. Labyrinths are excellent configurations for magickal work, too. You needn't build something so elaborate, however. Consider these possibilities:

• Collect stones and lay them out in a circle that's large enough for your group to work inside. You may want to place four larger stones at the four compass directions.

- Plant flowers, shrubs, etc. in a circle.
- Erect a low wooden fence to form a circle.
- Install metal or wooden posts and string lights between them to form a circle.
- Indoors, you can paint a circle on the floor (if household members and/or your landlord agree).

Position an altar in the center of the circle—or in another spot if the group prefers. Over time, you can add to your circle, if you wish, or decorate it seasonally. Use your imagination!

SPELL TO FIND A HOME

Perform this spell with everyone who will occupy the home you seek—this is a joint effort, and the place in which you live will be important to all of you. Not only will your collective energies increase multiplicatively, you'll also clarify your intentions by working together to strengthen the bond between you.

INGREDIENTS/TOOLS:
- Pencils, pens, or markers
- Magazine pictures
- Scissors
- Glue or tape
- Poster board

BEST TIME TO PERFORM THE SPELL:
- On the new moon

Either sketch the house you're looking for (if you have artistic ability) or find pictures that depict features you seek in your new home. Glue these illustrations to a poster board and hang it where you'll see it often. Add words, symbols, and other objects that you consider meaningful. The goal is to create a visual tool that focuses your minds on your desire. Make it vivid and detailed. Kids love doing this sort of thing and often come up with great ideas. The more energy you pour into your intention, the quicker it will materialize.

GEMSTONE CHAKRA SPELL

As you learned in Chapter 2, the chakras are energy centers that run from the base of your spine to the top of your head. When they're balanced, you feel better physically, mentally, and emotionally. This spell uses the power of gemstones to help your chakras function harmoniously. Notice that the colors of the stones correspond to the colors associated with the 7 major chakras. Perform this spell with a friend or loved one.

INGREDIENTS/TOOLS:
- 1 piece of red jasper
- 1 piece of carnelian
- 1 piece of topaz
- 1 piece of jade
- 1 piece of aquamarine
- 1 piece of lapis lazuli
- 1 piece of amethyst

BEST TIME TO PERFORM THE SPELL:
- Anytime

Wash the stones with mild soap and water, then pat them dry. Find a comfortable place where you can lie down on your back undisturbed for about half an hour. Your partner in this spell first puts the red jasper on your pubic bone. Next, he or she sets the carnelian on your lower abdomen, about a hand's width below your belly button. The topaz goes on your solar plexus; the jade on the center of your chest near your heart; the aquamarine at the base of your throat; the lapis lazuli on your forehead, between your eyebrows. Finally, your partner places the amethyst so it touches the crown of your head.

Relax and sense the stones sending their healing vibrations into your body's energy centers, restoring harmony and well-being to your entire

The Modern Witchcraft Spell Book

system. When you feel ready, ask your partner to remove the stones. Wash and dry the stones again. Swap places, so that now your partner is the recipient and you are the one positioning the stones on his or her body. After you've finished, cleanse the stones and store them in a safe place until you want to use them again.

THE MAGICK BOX

Everyone in the household—family members, roommates, romantic partners—can participate in this spell. You'll need a shoebox or a similar container that's small enough to fit on a shelf, but large enough to accommodate lots of wishes. This spell offers you a way to combine your energies to help all your wishes come true.

> **INGREDIENTS/TOOLS:**
> - 1 box with a lid
> - Colored pens, pencils, or markers
> - Magazine pictures, colored paper, stickers, other decorations
> - Glue
> - Slips of paper
>
> **BEST TIME TO PERFORM THE SPELL:**
> - During the waxing moon

Decorate the box however you like, using positive designs that appeal to you. Write words and/or symbols on it. Draw pictures. Affix images from magazines or downloaded from the Internet. The point is to personalize the box and to have fun engaging in the creative experience. On the top, write the words *The Magick Box.*

Put the box in place where everyone in your home has access to it and can see it when they enter the house or apartment. When the box is completely decorated, ask each member of the group to write 1 wish on a slip of paper and read it aloud to the others. Place the wishes in the box. Sharing your wishes with each other galvanizes your collective power. This builds momentum and attracts what you want more quickly. As each wish comes true, remove it from the box. Then make another wish and slip it into the box.

SPELL TO CALL IN DEITIES

This spell allows members of a group to call upon the guidance of the archangels: Raphael, Michael, Gabriel, and Uriel. You may petition their assistance in general, or ask for help with a particular issue.

INGREDIENTS/TOOLS:
- Sage incense
- Incense burner
- Matches or a lighter
- A few drops of the essential oil that corresponds to your issue; for general assistance, use sandalwood
- 1 ounce (or more if necessary) of a carrier oil, such as olive or grape seed, in a small dish
- 1 white pillar candle
- 1 nail, empty ballpoint pen, nail file, or other sharp object for carving the candle
- 1 cauldron (or fireproof bowl or saucer)
- 1 hand drum (optional)

BEST TIME TO PERFORM THE SPELL:
- As needed (see Chapter 8)

After forming your circle, set the sage incense in its holder on your altar and light it, thereby cleansing your working space. Add a few drops of the essential oil into the carrier oil and stir with your finger. Anoint each member of the circle by drawing a pentagram on his or her forehead with the oil (make sure no one in the group is allergic to the oil you've chosen). Ask each person in the circle to "sign" the candle by making a mark (word, sigil, astrological glyph, etc.) on the candle with the sharp implement. When everyone has finished inscribing the candle, rub the remaining oil on it (not on the wick), set it in the cauldron (or bowl or saucer) on your altar, and light the candle.

Have everyone focus on the candle's flame while you unify your energies toward your common objective. If someone opts to be the drummer, he or she should start beating a slow, steady rhythm now. Begin a low hum involving all participants in order to gently raise the energy.

A member of the group (chosen beforehand) takes the candle from the altar and holds it up, while facing east, and says:

> *"Raphael, bless this circle with your guidance. Help us to do right for those in need, and to work only for good."*

Pass the candle to another member of the circle (chosen beforehand). This person faces south, holds up the candle, and says:

> *"Michael, bless this circle with your passion and strength. Help us to defend those in need, and to protect ourselves and our loved ones at all times and in all situations."*

Pass the candle to another member of the circle (chosen beforehand). This person faces west, holds up the candle, and says:

> *"Gabriel, bless this circle with your love and serenity. Help us to bring light, love, and peace to those in need."*

Pass the candle to another member of the circle (chosen beforehand). This person faces north, holds up the candle, and says:

> *"Uriel, bless this circle with your stability. Help us to provide comfort and healing for those in need."*

Place the pillar candle on the altar again. While everyone in the circle focuses on the candle, say together:

> *"Behold, we summon the light of Spirit to guide this circle."*

Allow time for everyone to gaze at the candle as it burns and flickers, opening your minds to visions, sensations, and guidance. Spend as much time as you need, or decide beforehand to end the spell after a certain amount of time has passed. At that time, a person selected in advance snuffs out the candle and releases the angelic presences (as described in Chapter 7).

Afterward, all members of the group sit together and discuss what they witnessed, thought, sensed, or otherwise gleaned from the session. This joint experience lets you gain insights from the higher realms regarding how to handle a particular matter or how to proceed with your magickal work.

CHOOSE YOUR TOTEM ANIMAL

Although we often associate totem animals with Native American tribes, clans throughout history and around the world have honored totem creatures and relied upon their assistance for protection, sustenance, and healing. Your spellworking circle may also benefit from the guidance of one or more totems.

INGREDIENTS/TOOLS:
- Book or list that describes spirit animals (such as my book *The Secret Power of Spirit Animals*)
- Paper
- Scissors
- Colored markers

BEST TIME TO PERFORM THE SPELL
- Anytime

Discuss the animals, birds, etc. with which you feel a strong affinity. Describe the characteristics of these creatures with which you resonate. You'll likely find that some members of the group identify with the same creatures. Also talk about the objectives you've set for your group, the path you intend to take, and/or what energies unite you. A frank discussion of this type will help you determine which animal guides are working with you—and which ones you wish to ask to assist you.

Try to narrow down your list of affiliate spirit animals to one, or at least no more than three. When everyone agrees on the totem(s) you want to work with, cut squares of paper for each person in your circle to draw images of the creature(s) you've elected as your group's totem(s). These images can be simple or elaborate, stylized or realistic—it's up to you. Carry these images with you or post them in a place where you'll see them often, so you can call upon the animal's energy whenever you need it.

Alternate suggestions: If you feel *really* dedicated and convinced that the creature(s) chosen are your lifelong totem(s), you may wish to have an image tattooed on your body. If you prefer a less painful (and less permanent) expression, draw the animal's image on your body with a marker.

HONORING YOUR SPIRIT ANIMAL TOTEM

This spell expands upon the previous one. It deepens your connection to your group's totem and to one another.

INGREDIENTS/TOOLS:
- Offerings for your totem animal
- 1 white pillar candle in a fireproof holder
- Matches or a lighter
- Individual candles, one for each member of the group (choose your preferred colors)

BEST TIME TO PERFORM THE SPELL:
- Anytime

As a group, shop for a figurine, wall hanging, or other image of your animal(s). Everyone should agree on the image you choose. Display the image on your altar or in another place of power where you meet to do spellwork. Place the white pillar candle in its holder on the altar and have one person light it. Say aloud as a group:

"Spirit guardian and guide
Now we seek your presence here.
Bring us wisdom from above
Fill us with your boundless love
And remain forever near."

Each person now steps up to the altar, one at a time, and first lays his or her offering before the image of your group totem, then lights his or her personal candle from the white pillar candle. If you have a specific request for your spirit guardian at this time, state it. If you wish to perform an additional spell or ritual at this time, go ahead. Otherwise, simply remain in this circle of light for as long as you choose, embracing the energy of your totem and the group. Then thank your totem and extinguish your candles.

Greet your group's totem each time you meet and before you perform a spell or ritual together, and thank it after you've finished.

INTIMACY LOTION

Does your lover seem distant lately? Is your sex life less fulfilling than usual? Are you often too busy or too tired to engage in true intimacy? Use this magick lotion with your partner to stimulate the senses, deepen your connection, and generate loving feelings between you.

INGREDIENTS/TOOLS:
- 1 copper bowl
- 1 spoon (silver or silver plate, if possible)
- 1 glass or china container with a lid (ideally the container should be pink or red, and/or decorated with designs that represent love to you, such as roses or hearts)
- Unscented massage oil or lotion
- A few drops of essential oils of rose, jasmine, ylang-ylang, patchouli, and/or musk—choose the scents you like: one, two, or all of them

BEST TIME TO PERFORM THE SPELL:
- During the waxing moon, preferably on a Friday

Wash the bowl, spoon, and container with mild soap and water. Pour the massage oil or lotion into the copper bowl. Add a few drops of one of the essential oils you've chosen. Using the silver spoon, stir the mixture, making three clockwise circles. Add a few drops of the second essential oil (if you've opted to include more than one). Again, make three clockwise circles to stir the blend. Repeat this process each time you add an essential oil. As you work, envision a beautiful pink light running from your heart to your lover's heart, growing to envelop you both in its radiant glow. After you've finished, pour the lotion/oil into the glass/china container and put the lid on.

Choose a time and place where you and your partner can spend an extended period of time together, undisturbed. Take turns massaging each other with the magick lotion. Relax and engage your senses. Allow the soothing touch and fragrant oils to enhance the connection between you.

LOVE POTION

After a while, many couples find that their relationships feel a little flat—like champagne without the bubbles. This spell pumps romance back into your partnership. Perform it with your beloved.

INGREDIENTS/TOOLS:
- 2 rose-colored candles in candleholders
- Matches or a lighter
- Sparkling apple cider or champagne
- 1 chalice (or pretty wine glass)

BEST TIME TO PERFORM THE SPELL:
- During the waxing moon, preferably on a Friday or when the sun and/or moon is in Libra

Set the candles on your altar (or a table, mantel, or other flat surface). Light one candle yourself and let your lover light the other. Pour the cider or champagne into your chalice. Share the drink, passing the chalice back and forth, while you focus on your desire for one another. If you wish, express your loving feelings for each other. After you've finished the drink, extinguish the candles. Repeat whenever you like.

Chapter 16

SEASONAL SPELLS AND MAGICKAL RECIPES

For centuries, earth-honoring cultures have followed the sun's apparent passage through the sky. Our ancestors divided the Wheel of the Year, as the sun's annual cycle is known, into eight periods of approximately six weeks each. As discussed in Chapter 8, each "spoke" corresponds to a particular degree in the zodiac. Wiccans and other pagans call these eight holidays (or holy days) "sabbats." It's no coincidence that many of our modern-day holidays fall close to these ancient, solar dates. Each of these special days affords unique opportunities for performing spells and rituals—the cosmic forces operating on these dates can increase the power of your magick.

Any day that holds special meaning for you can also be a good time for spellwork. Your birthday, for instance, is one of the most auspicious dates in the year for doing spells.

FOOD AND THE SEASONAL CYCLE

In our global village society, we can eat strawberries in January and tomatoes in November. We've forgotten that once upon a time people had to seize the opportunity to enjoy seasonal foods because they were only available for a short period of time. As different fruits and vegetables ripened, our ancestors were reminded of the changing seasons and their own place in nature's cycle.

You can explore the seasonal and spiritual aspects of food today by shopping regularly at a farmers' market. Week by week, the produce available will vary in supply and quality. By familiarizing yourself with what is in season at different times of the year in your region, you can gain a better understanding of how earth and cosmic energies influence the food you eat. In this way, preparing and ingesting food becomes a magickal experience, a way to align yourself with the Wheel of the Year and interact with the energies around you. Honor the spiritual force in the food you eat by acknowledging the consciousness that exists within all living substances and your connection with other life forms.

Blessing Hearth and Home

Food preparation takes on special meaning when you see each step of the process as magickal. As you cook and clean, use affirmations to bless your home and loved ones.

1. When you open the kitchen door say: "May only health, love, and joy come through this door into this home."
2. While stirring a pot say: "Thanks be to all beings who contributed to this meal."
3. While serving food say: "May the food I prepare nourish my loved ones in both body and soul."
4. While sweeping say: "May all harmful, disruptive, or unbalanced energy be removed from this place."
5. When you turn off the kitchen light at night say: "Bless this kitchen, and keep those of us who use it safe and healthy through the night."

The Modern Witchcraft Spell Book

HOLIDAY FOODS AND BEVERAGES

Our holiday celebrations usually include food and libation of some sort. We even associate certain foods with certain holidays—it just wouldn't be Thanksgiving without a turkey, for example. Most people don't realize, however, that fruits, vegetables, and other edibles contain magickal properties. You can combine them for specific purposes—in the same way you combine various ingredients to make amulets and talismans. Modern-day witches generally prefer soups, stews, and other "brews" made with ordinary food items instead of eye of newt and toe of frog, and in this chapter, you'll find a number of delicious magickal recipes you can enjoy at your holiday gatherings, in addition to other spells.

MAGICKAL FRUITS

Apple: love, health, longevity

Banana: fertility, strength

Blackberry: prosperity, protection, abundance

Blueberry: tranquility, peace, protection, prosperity

Cranberry: protection, healing

Grape: prosperity, fertility

Kiwi: fertility, love

Lemon: purification, protection, health

Lime: happiness, purification, healing

Mango: spirituality, happiness

Melons: love, peace

Orange: joy, health, purification

Peach: spirituality, fertility, love, harmony

Pear: love, health, prosperity

Pineapple: prosperity, luck, friendship

Plum: love, tranquility

Raspberry: strength, courage, healing (especially for women)

Strawberry: love, peace, happiness, luck

MAGICKAL VEGETABLES

Beans: love, family harmony

Broccoli: protection, abundance

Cabbage: prosperity

Carrot: fertility, healing (especially for men)

Cauliflower: fertility, protection

Celery: peace, concentration, mental clarity, health
Cucumber: fertility, healing
Garlic: protection, banishing, purification
Green pepper: prosperity
Lettuce: peace, harmony
Mushroom: strength, courage, protection
Onion: protection, exorcism, healing
Peas: love, abundance
Potato: fertility, abundance
Squash: abundance, harmony (consider the color/shape to understand correspondences)
Tomato: love, passion
MAGICKAL GRAINS
Barley: love, fertility
Corn: spirituality, security, prosperity, protection
Rice: fertility, happiness, love, protection
Rye: love, joy, affection
Wheat: strength, growth, abundance, success

Steps for Successful Spellcasting

Whenever you cast a spell, remember to use a few tried-and-true measures, as described in Chapter 1. These precautions can help you avoid complications, mix-ups, delays, or disappointments:

1. Remove all distractions.
2. Collect the ingredients and tools you'll use in your spell and cleanse them.
3. Purify and sanctify your space.
4. Quiet your mind.
5. Cast a circle around the area where you'll do your spellworking.
6. Perform the spell.
7. If you've called upon deities or spirits to assist you, thank and release them.
8. Open the circle.
9. Store your tools in a safe place until you need them again.

SAMHAIN CHILI

In many places, this sabbat coincides with deer-hunting season, so you may choose to make this delicious chili with venison rather than beef. Cooking this chili outdoors in an iron cauldron over a fire gives an added sense of magick and connection to the earth. Serve with cornbread or your favorite hearty whole-grain bread.

SERVES 6

INGREDIENTS/TOOLS:

- 4–6 large portobello mushrooms
- Bowl
- Red wine (approximately 1 cup, or more to taste)
- Large pot or iron cauldron
- Olive oil
- 2 onions, sliced
- 2 pounds ground beef or venison
- 2 (14½-ounce) cans diced tomatoes

- 1 (6-ounce) can tomato paste
- 2 (15-ounce) cans red kidney beans (or two cans mixed beans)
- Chili powder or dried chilies, to taste
- 2 bay leaves
- Salt and pepper, to taste
- Cheddar cheese, grated (optional)

BEST TIME TO MAKE THIS MAGICKAL MEAL:
- The evening of October 31

1. Chop the portobello mushrooms into small pieces, approximately ½" square, and place them in a mixing bowl.
2. Pour the red wine over the mushrooms. Allow to marinate in the refrigerator for at least 2 hours. Stir occasionally to make sure all the mushrooms have been marinated in the wine.
3. In a large pot or cauldron, heat the olive oil. Add the sliced onions, and cook until fragrant and soft. Add ground beef or venison, and cook until browned. Spoon off the fat. Stir in the tomatoes and tomato paste, then add the beans. Pour in the mushrooms and red wine and combine. Add the chilies and bay leaves. Adjust seasoning to taste, and add more red wine (or water) if desired.
4. Simmer for at least 3 hours. If desired, sprinkle grated sharp Cheddar on top of each bowl of chili before serving.

SPELL TO SEE THE FUTURE

Because the veils between the seen and unseen worlds are thinnest on Samhain, many witches and wizards practice divination at this time. This spell lets you glimpse the future and perhaps receive guidance from the other side.

INGREDIENTS/TOOLS:
- 1 black candle in a candleholder
- Matches or a lighter
- 1 tarot deck

• The evening of October 31

Quiet your mind, then light the candle and put it on your altar or another place where it can burn safely. Shuffle the tarot deck as you set an intention to receive guidance about the future. Select a card. Place the card face up in front of the candle. Take a few moments—or as long as you wish—to look at the card, allowing any impressions or insights to arise into your awareness. Try not to think of any preconceptions you may hold about this card's meaning—allow your intuition to speak to you.

Gaze at the candle's flame and let the flickering light calm your mind even further. Stare at the flame for as long as you wish, as visions, signals, sensations, emotions, etc. rise to the surface of your consciousness. You may notice a guardian spirit communicating with you. Ideas might pop into your mind that aren't like anything you've considered before. Let yourself glimpse impressions of the future, without apprehension. Continue for as long as you wish. When you feel ready, extinguish the candle and write down your experiences in your Book of Shadows.

YULE GOOD LUCK CHARM

Would you like to give your friends and loved ones the gift of good luck in the coming year? This Yuletide custom lets you make a unique magickal gift for everyone on your list.

INGREDIENTS/TOOLS:
• 1 Yule log (traditionally oak)
• Matches or a lighter
• Cloth drawstring pouches (1 for each person on your gift list)
• Dried pink rose petals (for love)
• Dried lavender flowers (for peace of mind)
• Dried basil (for protection)
• Dried mint leaves (for prosperity)
• Dried echinacea (for health)
• 1 sheet of paper

- Scissors
- 1 pen

BEST TIME TO PERFORM THE SPELL:
- Yule (usually December 21)

On the night of the winter solstice, build a Yule fire in a safe place and burn an oak log in it. Allow the fire to burn down completely. The next morning after the ashes have cooled, scoop some into each pouch. Add the dried botanicals. Cut the sheet of paper into slips, so you have one for each person on your list. Write a personalized wish on each slip of paper. Fold the papers three times and add them to the pouches. Tie the pouches closed, bless them, and give them to your loved ones.

HOLIDAY PROTECTION WREATH

Holidays can be stressful times, even under the best of circumstances. This special table wreath does double duty—it serves as a pretty decoration while emitting good vibes to protect your sanity during the hectic holiday season.

INGREDIENTS/TOOLS:
- 1 piece of cardboard or poster board
- Scissors
- Lots of dried bay leaves
- Tacky glue, double-sided tape, or other fixative
- 1 white pillar candle in a glass holder
- Matches or a lighter

BEST TIME TO PERFORM THE SPELL:
- As needed

Cut a circle from the cardboard or poster board, then cut a hole in the center to make a "donut" large enough to slip over the candle in its holder. Like all circles, this one is a symbol of protection. Attach the bay leaves to the cardboard circle to make a wreath. Think peaceful thoughts as you work. Position the candle on your table, altar, or mantel. Slide the bay leaf wreath over it, so it circles the base of the candle. Light the candle and gaze into its flame to relax your mind and calm your nerves.

BRIGID'S CROSS

The Celtic goddess Brigid is associated with creativity, fertility, smithcraft, and the hearth. Often, she's depicted stirring a cauldron over dancing flames—both symbols of creativity. You can celebrate Brigid's Day (also known as Imbolc and Candlemas) by fashioning what's known as Crios Bridghe or Brigid's Cross, even though it's really a circle. Jumping through the magick circle brings good fortune.

INGREDIENTS/TOOLS:
- Scissors or pruning shears
- 3 vines or lengths of raffia (available in crafts stores), each 5 feet long
- 2 pieces of white cord or ribbon

BEST TIME TO PERFORM THE SPELL:
- Between January 31 and February 2

Cut the vines or raffia. Think of 3 wishes you want to come true, and assign 1 wish to each vine or length of raffia. Tie the vines or raffia together with 1 piece of cord or ribbon. Braid the vines/raffia, focusing on your wishes as you work. When you reach the end, tie the braid with the other piece of cord/ribbon. Then bend the braid around to form a circle and tie the 2 pieces of cord/ribbon together, making 3 knots. Lay the circle on the ground or floor, and step into it. Then lift the circle up along your body and over your head as you imagine yourself receiving the 3 wishes you desire. Hang the wreath in your home to bring blessings your way.

OSTARA SPELL TO BIRTH A NEW PROJECT

Are you having a hard time getting a project off the ground? Do delays, deterrents, and disappointments keep interfering with your progress?

This spell "fertilizes" your idea and helps you bring your venture to fruition. The custom of painting eggs at Easter originated with the early festival of Ostara, which is held on the spring equinox. Eggs are symbols of birth, life, and fertility, and Ostara celebrates the Earth's renewal after the long, cold winter.

INGREDIENTS/TOOLS:
- 1 raw egg
- 1 straight pin or needle
- 1 bowl
- Acrylic or watercolor paints
- 1 small paintbrush
- Water

BEST TIME TO PERFORM THE SPELL:
- On the Spring Equinox

Gently wash the egg first to remove bacteria as well as unwanted energies. Carefully poke a hole in each end of the egg with a pin. Holding the egg above the bowl, place your mouth over one hole, and gently blow the contents of the egg out through the other hole. When you've finished, rinse out the eggshell and let it dry.

Paint symbols and images on the eggshell that represent your project, as well as your objectives. Consider including colors, numbers, runes, astrological glyphs, and other symbols that relate to your intentions. Make sure everything you include has positive connotations for you. While you work, visualize your project moving forward and receiving the support and recognition you seek. See your goals coming to fruition, your success assured. You don't have to understand all the steps between the inception of your idea and its fulfillment; just imagine the end result you desire coming true.

After you've finished decorating your egg, display it on your altar or in a place where you'll see it often. Each time you look at it, you'll be reminded of your goal and your intention to succeed. Alternate suggestion: Hard-boil the egg. After the egg has cooled, decorate it. As you paint the egg and as you eat it, focus on your goal; see yourself achieving it happily. Save the eggshell pieces to use in another spell.

SEASONAL POTPOURRI

Dry potpourri blends the energies and fragrances of herbs, flowers, and spices for sensory and magickal purposes. You can place an open dish of potpourri in a room to scent the air and to draw, enhance, or disperse energies according to your will. Don't chop up your plant material—if you intend to dry fresh botanicals yourself for your potpourri, try to keep them as unbruised as possible, as the natural oils give flowers and spices their scent. When dry, crumble the plant matter into chunks.

INGREDIENTS/TOOLS:
- Glass bowl
- Dried herbs, flowers, and spices—your choice, depending on your intentions and the season
- Powdered orris root (2 tablespoons orris root powder per cup of dry potpourri mix)
- Essential oil(s)—your choice, depending on your intentions and the season (6 drops of essential oil per cup of dry mix)

BEST TIME TO PERFORM THE SPELL:
- Anytime

Place all the dried plant matter (including the powdered orris root) in a bowl and stir with your hands to combine. Sprinkle with the essential oil and stir again. Keep the blend in a closed container for at least 2 weeks so it can mellow; this allows the scents to blend. Open the container and stir it once a day to keep it from going moldy. Even if you think your plant material is perfectly dry, sometimes a drop or two of moisture may be left in it. When it's ready, put your potpourri in an open container and place it in the area you wish to be affected by the energy. It's also a nice idea to set a small amount of potpourri in a dish on your altar as an offering to deities.

Don't forget about your dry potpourri once you've set it out. Dust collects in it, and exposure to air and the energy of the room will eventually weaken the herbal components. Make a new batch when you feel that the vitality of the old one has expired. You can bury used potpourri, add it to ritual fires, or compost it. Dry potpourri also makes a good stuffing for herbal pillows, sachets, and poppets.

BELTANE TALISMAN TO ATTRACT LOVE

This ancient spring festival is held on May 1, and celebrates love, sexuality, pleasure, and fertility. At this time in the Wheel of the Year, the earth is ripe with nature's beauty—flowers blossom, leaves appear on the trees, baby animals and birds are born. Not surprisingly, this is the ideal time to perform love spells.

INGREDIENTS/TOOLS:
- 2 pieces of red felt, about 4 inches square
- Scissors
- 1 piece of paper
- 1 pen
- 1 penny
- 1 seashell
- 1 small elongated stone
- Needle and red thread

BEST TIME TO PERFORM THE SPELL:
- The morning of May 1

Imagine that one piece of felt represents you and the other represents your partner. Fold one piece of felt in half and, using the scissors, cut out one lobe of a heart shape starting from the folded edge. Then cut the other piece of felt in the same manner. On the piece of paper, write words and draw pictures or symbols that symbolize love—as many as you can, until you've filled the entire piece of paper. Wrap the paper tightly around the penny (copper is linked with Venus, the planet and goddess of love). Lay the penny, shell, and stone between the two felt hearts. Sew them together, envisioning the two hearts becoming one. Sleep with the charm under your pillow until your love manifests.

SPRINGTIME SMOOTHIE

You've heard the expression "You are what you eat," right? For this spell, you choose the fruits and/or veggies (from the table at the beginning of this chapter) that represent things you want to incorporate into yourself—all living things embody energy and they influence your own energy when you ingest them.

INGREDIENTS/TOOLS:
- Fruits/veggies that contain the magickal qualities you desire (organic if possible)
- 1 paring knife
- Blender
- Fruit/vegetable juice that contains the magickal qualities you desire
- Plain yogurt

BEST TIME TO PERFORM THIS SPELL:
- On the morning of May 1

Before you begin, wash all the fruits you've chosen and pat them dry. Then close your eyes and hold your hands palms-down above the fruit. Feel the energy radiating from the fruit; sense your connection with the fruits you've chosen. State aloud that both the nutrients and the magickal components contained in the fruit you've selected will benefit you in every way. Cut the fruit into small pieces and put them into the blender. Add the fruit juice, as much as you need to create the consistency you like. Then add as much yogurt as you like and blend everything until smooth. As you drink the magickal smoothie you've concocted, envision it bringing you good fortune and fulfilling your desires.

Alternate suggestion: If you prefer, combine the fruits/veggies you've chosen for a refreshing salad. Then add a dollop of yogurt and sprinkle with the petals from edible flowers, such as violets or nasturtiums, that represent your intentions.

MIDSUMMER CANDLE SPELL FOR GOOD FORTUNE

On Midsummer (the summer solstice), daylight in the Northern Hemisphere is longer than at any other time of the year. Therefore, candles—which symbolize the fire element and the sun—often play a role in spells and rituals performed on this sabbat. Fire also represents the masculine force in the universe, whereas water represents the feminine force. This easy spell combines both elements to bring good fortune and balance into your life.

INGREDIENTS/TOOLS:
- 1 floating candle in a color that represents a particular wish or desire (see the color correspondence charts at the beginnings of earlier chapters), or choose a golden-yellow candle to signify the sun
- Matches or a lighter

BEST TIME TO PERFORM THE SPELL:
- Midsummer's Eve

Take your candle and matches or lighter to a body of water—a gently flowing stream, a pond or lake, a quiet ocean cove. With your intention, empower the candle to bring you whatever you seek—love, money, success, etc. Say aloud:

"I shine this light
Into the night,
The power of fire
Attracts my desire."

Set the candle in the water, keeping your intention clearly in your mind, and watch the flame until it burns down or the water extinguishes it.

"There are two ways of spreading light: to be
The candle or the mirror that reflects it."
—EDITH WHARTON, "VESALIUS IN ZANTE. (1564)"

SUMMER SOLSTICE GAZPACHO

This chilled vegetable soup is a refreshing, healthy summer solstice treat. Green peppers signify prosperity; cucumber is associated with peace, harmony, and health; tomatoes and avocados attract love; celery encourages peace; onions and garlic provide protection and health.

SERVES 8–10

INGREDIENTS/TOOLS:

- Blender
- 2 large green bell peppers, cored, seeded, and diced
- 1 large cucumber, peeled and chopped
- 2 pounds tomatoes, cored and diced
- 1 celery stalk, chopped
- 1 onion, chopped
- 2 garlic cloves, peeled
- 1 avocado, chopped (optional)
- 1 large glass bowl
- 1 teaspoon salt
- ¼ teaspoon cayenne pepper
- Pinch of basil
- Pinch of parsley
- ⅓ cup olive oil
- 1 tablespoon lemon juice
- ¼ cup red wine vinegar
- 2 cans (12- or 15-ounce) tomato juice
- Sour cream, plain yogurt, fresh cilantro as a garnish, and/or corn or tortilla chips (optional)

1. In a blender, combine the first seven ingredients in small batches and blend until smooth. Pour into a large bowl. Add seasonings, oil, lemon juice, vinegar, and tomato juice and stir well to combine. Cover and chill for at least 5 hours or overnight.
2. Stir well and taste before serving. Adjust seasonings as necessary. Serve in bowls or large mugs. Garnish the soup as desired with sour cream or yogurt, fresh cilantro, and/or corn or tortilla chips.

The Modern Witchcraft Spell Book

SEASONAL COLLAGES

The whole family can engage in this magick spell. Young children love participating. You can make one collage for each season, or choose holidays throughout the year that you'd like to recognize. You can make your collage any size, but if you use a 22" × 28" poster board you'll have plenty of room for images and found objects.

INGREDIENTS/TOOLS:
- Scissors
- Pictures from magazines, flyers, catalogs, old greeting cards, photographs; images downloaded from the Internet
- Crayons, markers, colored pencils
- Blank drawing paper or construction paper
- Glue
- Poster board (whatever color you like, or connect it to the season: green for spring, orange for fall)
- Found objects related to the season (seashells, pinecones, leaves, flower petals, etc.)

BEST TIME TO PERFORM THE SPELL:
- At the change of the season

Cut out images associated with the season (summer-themed images might include beach umbrellas, ice cream, swimming pools, sandals, the sun, and so forth). Draw pictures or write words on the blank paper and cut them out as well. Glue the images and words to the poster board. You may lay the images out first to find a pattern that pleases you, or you can begin gluing the images wherever you feel inspired and allow the collage to form on its own. Then attach "found" objects to the collage. Take the collage down at the end of a holiday or season and begin the next collage. If you wish, date and store your collages, or burn them in a ritual fire to symbolize releasing the past from your life in preparation for what's upcoming.

Alternate suggestion: You can explore themes or ideas that are meaningful to you through this collaging project. For example, create an ancestor collage that looks at your family's heritage and its ways of celebrating holidays, bringing in traditions from the countries and cultures of your past.

LUGHNASADH PEASANT BREAD

Corn, wheat, and other grains are typically harvested around Lughnasadh, the holiday of the Celtic god Lugh. In agrarian cultures, this was the time to begin preparing for the barren winter months that lay ahead. Our ancestors cut, ground, and stored grain, canned fruit and vegetables, and brewed wine and beer in late summer. In addition to making this ritual bread, you might want to consider brewing your own beer, too.

MAKES 1 LOAF

INGREDIENTS/TOOLS:
- Small bowl
- 3 tablespoons sugar, divided
- 1 cup warm water (around 110°F), divided
- 2 heaping teaspoons yeast (or one package)
- Large bowl
- 2 cups flour (with more for kneading)
- 1 tablespoon finely chopped fresh rosemary
- 1 tablespoon finely chopped fresh thyme
- 1 tablespoon finely chopped fresh dill
- 1 tablespoon finely chopped fresh chives
- Olive oil
- 1 clean cloth
- Baking sheet

BEST TIME TO PERFORM THE SPELL:
- August 1

1. In a small bowl, stir 1 teaspoon of sugar into ¼ cup of warm water. Sprinkle the yeast over the top and allow it to proof until foamy (about 5 minutes).
2. In a large bowl, stir the remaining sugar into the flour. Make a well in the flour and pour the yeast in. Add the herbs and 1 tablespoon olive oil to the flour mixture. Stir to combine all the ingredients.

The Modern Witchcraft Spell Book

3. Slowly add the warm water as you stir to create a firm dough ball. If you add too much water, simply add a bit of flour to compensate. Scrape the sides of the bowl and add the scrapings to the dough ball.

4. Sprinkle the ball and bowl with a bit of flour. Cover with a clean cloth and set to rise in a warm place with no drafts until the dough has doubled in size (approximately an hour and a half).

5. Remove the dough from bowl and place on a floured surface. Knead for approximately 5 minutes until smooth and elastic. Sprinkle flour onto the kneading surface as necessary so that the dough does not stick.

6. Form the dough into a loaf-shaped log. Place on the baking sheet or in a bread pan. Brush the entire top with olive oil and leave to rise to the height you desire. (Placing the dough in a barely warm oven is a good place for it to rise.) Heat the oven to 400°F. (If your bread is rising in the oven, remove it carefully and then heat the oven.) Bake the bread for 30–40 minutes, or until golden brown.

Alternate suggestion: Choose herbs for specific purposes: onion for protection, poppy seeds for happiness and insight, etc. See the table at the beginning of this chapter for a list of vegetables and their associations.

SPELL TO BLESS THE EARTH

In keeping with the traditional harvest theme of Lughnasadh, this spell uses corn, wheat, or straw in a ritual blessing for Mother Earth and to give thanks for her bounty. It also marks the decline of the sun's power as the Wheel of the Year turns toward winter.

INGREDIENTS/TOOLS:
- Dried corn leaves, straw, wheat, or another grain
- Scissors
- Twine (made from a natural fabric, not plastic or nylon)
- 1 large iron cauldron (optional)
- Matches or a lighter

BEST TIME TO PERFORM THE SPELL:
- August 1

Fashion the dried corn leaves (or other grain) into a humanlike shape to represent the Sun King, whose powers are now waning. Cut pieces of twine and tie it around the "corn doll" to form its head, arms, and legs. Trim as needed. Build a fire in your cauldron, fireplace, or other safe spot. Burn the doll in the fire as an offering to Mother Earth.

MABON SOUP

Serve this lovely soup on the autumn equinox, also called Mabon. Apples are associated with love, health, protection, and immortality—cut one in half, and you'll see that the seeds are configured as a star/pentagram. Almonds carry the energy of prosperity; curry offers strength and protection.

SERVES 4–6
INGREDIENTS/TOOLS:
- 1½ pounds apples
- Paring knife
- ¼ cup butter
- Large saucepan
- 1 onion, finely chopped
- 6 tablespoons ground almonds
- 4 cups chicken or vegetable stock
- ½ teaspoon curry powder
- Salt and freshly ground pepper, to taste
- Blender or food processor
- Strainer
- ½ cup light cream, plain yogurt, or almond milk
- Toasted sliced almonds for garnish

1. Core, peel, and dice the apples. Melt the butter in a saucepan. Add the onion and cook gently until softened (about 5 minutes). Add the apples and stir gently for 2–3 minutes. Sprinkle the ground almonds over the apple and onion mixture, and stir for another 1–2 minutes.
2. Pour in the stock and bring to a boil. Add the curry powder, and salt and pepper to taste.

The Modern Witchcraft Spell Book

3. Reduce the heat to low. Cover and simmer for 20 minutes. The apples should be tender.
4. Remove from the heat and allow to cool to room temperature. Pour the soup into the blender or food processor and blend until smooth.
5. Pour the soup through a strainer into a clean pan. Add the cream, yogurt, or almond milk and stir until blended. Taste for seasoning and adjust if necessary. If the soup is too thick, add a bit more stock. Reheat gently (don't boil). Serve hot, garnished with a few toasted sliced almonds and an additional pinch of curry powder on top, if you desire.

Chapter 17

MISCELLANEOUS SPELLS

Whatever your problem, concern, or desire, a spell probably exists to address it. If you can't find one that's exactly what you're looking for—or can't get your hands on the recommended ingredients—then create your own spell. In previous chapters you'll find tables of information about colors, gemstones, botanicals, and other ingredients that can add to the power of your spells. Use these suggestions, if you wish, to customize your spell.

Whenever you cast a spell, remember to use a few tried-and-true measures, as described in Chapter 1. These precautions can help you avoid complications, mix-ups, delays, or disappointments:

1. Remove all distractions.
2. Collect the ingredients and tools you'll use in your spell and cleanse them.
3. Purify and sanctify your space.
4. Quiet your mind.
5. Cast a circle around the area where you'll do your spellworking.
6. Perform the spell.
7. If you've called upon deities or spirits to assist you, thank and release them.
8. Open the circle.
9. Store your tools in a safe place until you need them again.

GOOD VIBRATIONS POTION

Virtually any place can benefit from this uplifting spell. Do it when you move into a new home or after an argument or party, in your workplace, in your car—wherever you choose. It can even help boost your mood if you're feeling down in the dumps. Not only does it clear away unwanted vibrations, it fills your space with the fresh scent of oranges.

INGREDIENTS/TOOLS:
• 1 spray bottle (preferably made of clear glass)
• Saltwater
• A few drops of orange essential oil

BEST TIME TO PERFORM THE SPELL:
• Anytime

Fill the spray bottle with saltwater (if you don't live near the ocean, just add a pinch of sea salt to spring water). Add the essential oil and shake the bottle three times to charge the water. Start in the east and mist each room with this potion to clear away negative energy and fill the air with good vibrations.

ALADDIN'S LAMP

Remember the fable about the boy Aladdin who found a magick lamp with a genie inside? Like the genie in the story, this spell grants you 3 wishes.

INGREDIENTS/TOOLS:
- Metal oil lamp or a covered incense burner
- Incense
- Matches or a lighter

BEST TIME TO PERFORM THE SPELL:
- Depends on your wishes (see Chapter 8)

Use an old-fashioned oil lamp made of brass, tin, copper, or silver if you can find one; otherwise, substitute an incense burner with a lid that has perforations in it to allow the smoke to float out. Fit the incense into the lamp or incense burner and light it. Put the lid on so the smoke rises from the spout or perforations. Hold your hands on either side of the lamp or incense burner (don't actually touch it if the sides are hot) and pretend to rub it. Envision the smoke as a powerful genie who has come to do your bidding. You might even see a figure form in the smoke.

State your 3 wishes aloud as affirmations. In your mind's eye, see them already coming true. Spend a few minutes focusing on your requests as you inhale the scent of the incense. When you're ready, thank the "genie" for its assistance.

FEAR OF FLYING SPELL

Does the idea of soaring eight miles above the earth in a metal cylinder make you feel weak in your knees? And what about all those terrorist stories you keep hearing? What can you do to calm your fears of flying? One way is to enlist the aid of the air spirits, known as *sylphs*. Here's how.

INGREDIENTS/TOOLS:
- White carnation petals
- 1 container in which to carry the carnation petals
- Clove incense
- Incense burner
- Matches or a lighter
- 1 fan made of feathers (or a single large feather)

BEST TIME TO PERFORM THE SPELL:
- On a Wednesday or Thursday, at least a day before your trip

If possible, perform this spell outside. Pluck the petals from several white carnations and place them in a bowl or other container. Fit the incense into its burner and light it. Waft the smoke toward you with the fan (or use the feather and your hand to guide the smoke toward you). Turn around, allowing the smoke to touch all sides of your body. Tap both shoulders with the fan, then tap your body at the places where the seven main chakras or energy centers are located, starting at the crown chakra and ending at the root chakra.

Invite the sylphs to join you. Sylphs are nature elementals who serve as ambassadors of the element of air. You may see faint flickering lights or feel a shift in the air around you as they come to answer your call. They might even appear to you as tiny winged beings. Request their assistance on your trip. Express your concerns and explain what you would like them to do for you. Speak to them with courtesy and respect, as you would to a human being from whom you sought aid. Tell them you've brought a gift to thank them in advance for helping you. Open the container and scatter the carnation petals in the wind. You may notice that the wind picks up or changes direction as the sylphs accept your offering.

If you wish, take the fan or feather with you when you fly, to remind you that you are protected by the spirits of the air. Additional suggestion:

Wear the Gemstone Necklace for a Safe Trip (see Chapter 11) on your trip.

SPELL FOR A HAPPY HOME

If you live with other people, you may want to invite them to do this easy spell with you (if you think they'd be open to it). If you think they might object if they knew you were doing magick, you don't have to tell them—they'll just think you're decorating your home.

INGREDIENTS/TOOLS:
- Lavender-scented incense
- Incense burner
- Matches or a lighter
- Several houseplants with round leaves
- 1 wreath

BEST TIME TO PERFORM THE SPELL:
- Anytime

Fit the incense into the incense burner and place it near the front door of your home. Fragrant lavender dissolves stress and promotes serenity. Position the plants throughout your home. Put at least one in each room, and set one on your altar (if you have one). The round leaves represent harmony and unity. Jade plants are excellent choices because they also attract wealth, prosperity, and good health. Hang the wreath on your door to welcome positive forces into your home. Continue caring for your plants, watering and feeding them to keep them healthy. Periodically, light incense to keep positive energy wafting through your home.

Wreaths for All Seasons

Consider hanging a festive, seasonal wreath on your door and changing it at least four times a year. This practice keeps you in touch with the Earth's natural cycles. Changing the wreath periodically also prevents stagnation and draws new opportunities to you and the occupants of your home.

SPELL TO FIND A PARKING PLACE

It's the day after Thanksgiving, an icy rain is falling, and the mall parking lot is jammed with cars. You'd hoped to find a parking spot close to the entrance, but it looks like the nearest spaces are half a mile away. Don't worry; ask the parking goddess Barbara to come to your aid.

INGREDIENTS/TOOLS:
- None

BEST TIME TO PERFORM THE SPELL:
- Anytime

Stop driving around in circles, close your eyes, and take a few slow, deep breaths. In your mind's eye, see an empty space waiting for you exactly where you want to park. Recite this incantation aloud:

"Goddess Barbara, fair of face
Guide me to my parking place."

Open your eyes and drive to the spot the goddess has provided for you.

SPELL TO OVERCOME AN OBSTACLE

Anytime a daunting challenge faces you and you fear you don't have the strength to deal with it, call in some extra muscle to help you handle the task—magickally, that is. Since ancient times, the people of India have drawn upon the power of the elephant god Ganesh to help them overcome seemingly insurmountable obstacles. So can you.

INGREDIENTS/TOOLS:
- 1 image of an elephant or of Ganesh (for example, a small figurine or an image downloaded from the Internet)
- 1 athame (or table knife)

- On a Saturday, preferably during the waning moon, or when the sun or moon is in Capricorn

Close your eyes and imagine you're in a dark, dense jungle. The faintest light shines down through the branches high overhead and the vegetation is so thick you can see only a foot or two ahead of you. All sorts of dangers lurk unseen. Your situation seems impossible. You feel trapped and helpless.

Suddenly you hear the trumpeting call of an elephant—it's Ganesh coming to your rescue. Pick up your athame or table knife. Without hesitation he rushes toward you and easily lifts you with his trunk onto his back. Explain to him the nature of your problem. The tangled vines and thick overgrowth represent the obstacles facing you. Now visualize yourself riding on Ganesh's back as he marches into the jungle, trampling everything in his path.

Reach out with your athame and begin slashing away at the vines and branches in your way. Envision yourself hacking through the obstacles that blocked you before. See space opening up before you. Feel Ganesh's strength, lifting you high above your problems. Together you are unstoppable. Keep chopping away at the thick vegetation, eliminating obstacles one by one. You don't have to see all the way to the end, just tackle each conundrum as it presents itself. When you feel ready, climb down from Ganesh's back and thank him for his assistance. You now realize you have the ability to handle whatever challenges arise.

SPELL TO MANIFEST A TRIP YOU DESIRE

Is there someplace you've always wanted to go? Don't worry about how you'll get the money or time for the trip—just do your magick and let the universe handle the arrangements.

INGREDIENTS/TOOLS:
- Magazine photos or other images of places you want to go
- Maps, travel brochures, etc.
- Other symbols that represent travel to you

- Colored markers or pens
- 1 large sheet of heavy paper or cardboard
- Glue or tape
- Sandalwood incense
- Incense burner
- Matches or a lighter

BEST TIME TO PERFORM THE SPELL:
- During the waxing moon, preferably when the sun or moon is in Sagittarius, or on a Thursday

Collect pictures from magazines and travel catalogs of a place you'd like to visit. Gather maps, brochures, and other information about this place. Find symbols and images that represent travel to you—a toy airplane, a tiny boat, a hotel from a Monopoly game, seashells, and anything that relates to the trip you're planning.

After you've gathered as many things as you feel you need, use the markers to draw a circle on the piece of paper or cardboard—it should be large enough that you can stand within it. Glue or tape all the symbols you've collected inside the circle. Also inside the circle you can draw additional pictures and/or write words that describe your intentions, such as the names of the places you plan to visit or affirmations stating your desires.

When your "wish board" is finished, light the incense. Stand in the middle of the board and envision yourself journeying to the place(s) you've chosen. Make your visualization as clear and vivid as possible. Try to intuit the mood of the place, the sights, sounds, and smells. Enjoy yourself. Remain in the circle, imagining your journey, until the incense finishes burning.

TRAVEL POTION

To ensure that your trip goes smoothly, and that you enjoy yourself, make this magick travel potion before you leave home.

- 1 clear glass bottle
- Water
- The knight of wands from a tarot deck
- 1 red ribbon

BEST TIME TO PERFORM THE SPELL:

- On a Thursday, before your trip

Fill the bottle with water. Lay the knight of wands (the tarot card of travel and adventure) face up on your altar and set the bottle of water on the card. Leave it there overnight. In the morning, tie the red ribbon around the neck of the bottle, making 3 knots. As you tie each knot, repeat an affirmation such as "I enjoy a lovely, relaxing vacation" and visualize the end result in your mind's eye.

If you're driving, carry the bottle of magickally imprinted water with you on your trip. Sip the water periodically throughout the journey. If you're flying, drink the water before you go to the airport. As you drink, feel yourself having the perfect trip and a wonderful time away.

MILK OF HUMAN KINDNESS SPELL

This spell gives energy back to the earth—our home that gives so much to us. Do this balancing spell once a month, to keep positive energy flowing between you and the planet. It's also good to do whenever a wish has been granted or an important spell has succeeded, to show your gratitude.

INGREDIENTS/TOOLS:

- 1 small pot
- 1 cup milk
- 1 teaspoon honey
- A pinch of dried lavender flowers
- 1 clean glass jar
- 1 small moonstone

- At dawn or dusk, preferably when the sun or moon is in Taurus

In a small pot, warm the milk, the honey, and the lavender over low heat until the honey has dissolved—don't let it boil. Remove from the heat and it cool to room temperature. Pour the liquid into the jar. Touch the moonstone to your forehead, to your lips, then to your heart, and then add the stone gently to the liquid. Dip your finger into the milk, touch your heart with it, then dip your finger back into the liquid. Visualize the peace and gratitude in your heart being transferred to the milk.

Cap the jar and carry it outside to a tree near your home, or a tree that is special to you. Bow to the tree, uncap the jar, and pour the milk and the stone out at the base of the tree on the roots, as you say aloud:

"I give to the earth
As the earth gives to me.
Bless all who live here
For eternity."

Bow again to the tree, and feel loving energy flowing between you. If you wish, sit and meditate beneath the tree, or even climb up into its branches.

SO MUCH TO DO, SO LITTLE TIME

Does it seem that no matter how hard you work, you never seem to get caught up? If stress and frustration are getting you down, this spell offers a welcome respite from the demands the world makes on you.

Ingredients/Tools:
- Lavender incense
- Incense burner
- 1 light blue candle
- 1 candleholder
- Matches or a lighter
- A bathtub full of comfortably hot water

- A few drops of vanilla essential oil
- 4 good-sized chunks of citrine

- Anytime

Fit the incense and candle in their respective holders, set them on your bathroom vanity, then light both. Fill the bathtub with water. Add several drops of vanilla essential oil to the bathwater. After washing the citrines with mild soap and water, set one at each corner of the bathtub. Climb into the tub and make yourself comfy. Feel the citrines—known for their clarifying ability—drawing off your stress and neutralizing it.

Feel your frustrations and anxieties dissolving into the bathwater. The trick is not to think about anything outside the walls of the bathroom. When you worry about the past or future, you block receptivity to new ideas and guidance that could help you resolve problems. If a troublesome thought pops into your mind, send it into the water or let the citrines dissolve it. Soak for as long as you like until you feel calm, rested, and confident that all is well.

When your peace of mind is restored, get out of the tub. As the water drains away, visualize your cares flowing away with it. Pick up the citrines and thank them. Then wash them with clean water (not the bathwater) and mild soap, and pat them dry. Allow the candle and incense to burn down safely.

DEITY ASSISTANCE SPELL

Are you faced with a challenging situation, and can't figure out how to handle it? Whatever your problem is, there's a deity who can help. This spell requests divine assistance through burning incense, which in some spiritual traditions is considered an offering to the deities. As the smoke rises, it carries your request into the heavens.

INGREDIENTS/TOOLS:
- A picture, figurine, or other image of your chosen deity
- Incense

- Incense burner
- Matches or a lighter
- 1 slip of paper
- 1 pen or pencil

BEST TIME TO PERFORM THE SPELL:
- Depends on your intention (see Chapter 8)

Determine which deity is best suited to help you with your problem. (You'll find lots of information online and in books.) Then acquire an image/figurine of that god or goddess and display it on your altar. Select an incense that corresponds to your intentions—cinnamon or clove for career success, rose or jasmine for love, and so on. (See tables at the beginnings of Chapters 9–14.) Fit the incense into its burner and light it. Write your request on the slip of paper, fold it three times, and lay it at the feet of the deity.

Envision your request floating up to the heavens, carried on the incense smoke to your chosen god or goddess. Quiet your mind and listen for an answer or guidance. (Note: The answer may not come immediately—it could take a few days—so don't grow impatient.) Allow the incense to burn down completely. Thank the deity for helping you and trust that aid will come at the appropriate time.

CLEAR THE AIR

Have you ever wondered why witches use brooms? No, not for flying. Brooms sweep away disruptive energy from a space. Perform this cleansing ritual after an argument, a party, or anytime you feel a need to clear the air.

INGREDIENTS/TOOLS:
- 1 broom
- 1 bowl
- Saltwater
- Sage (bundled, loose, or incense)
- 1 fireproof holder that you can carry easily
- Matches or a lighter

- As needed

If possible, open the windows and doors. Start sweeping your home (or other space) with a broom—not just the floor, but the air as well. Wave the broom through the entire area, side to side, up and down, until you feel you've whisked away the psychic "dirt." Next, fill a small bowl with saltwater. Sprinkle a little in each corner of your home, then flick some water in the center of each room. Finally, put the sage into the holder and light it. Blow out the flames and let it smoke. Carry the burning sage from room to room, allowing its cleansing smoke to clear the air and restore peace to your home.

SPELL TO PERPETUATE POSITIVE ENERGY

We all hit rough spots in life, when it's hard to stay optimistic. If you're in one of those low periods, let this spell give you a boost. After you've done it once, you can cast the spell in an abbreviated form anytime, simply through the power of fragrance.

TOOLS/INGREDIENTS:
- Music that lifts your mood
- A few drops of bay essential oil
- A few drops of frankincense essential oil
- A few drops of jasmine essential oil
- A few drops of eucalyptus essential oil
- 1 yellow candle in a holder
- 1 red candle in a holder
- 1 blue candle in a holder
- 1 green candle in a holder
- Matches or a lighter

BEST TIME TO PERFORM THE SPELL:
- On the new moon

The new moon is best for this spell because as the moon's light increases, so will your energy and optimism. But you can do this spell on any night, whenever you need a boost of positive energy. With your intent firmly in mind, put on your favorite uplifting music. Rub the essential oils on the candles (not on the wicks) in the order shown in the Ingredients/Tools list (bay oil on the yellow candle, frankincense on the red one, and so on).

Position the candles in the four cardinal points: yellow in the east, red in the south, blue in the west, green in the north. Light the candles in this order, casting a circle of light around you. Say aloud:

"I enter the flow of All That Is.
I am filled with loving kindness.
I release all negative and unbalanced energies
And I draw the best to me.
So mote it be."

While you're doing this spell, "fold" your wish or desire into your thoughts and feelings. Enjoy the scents of the essential oils and notice them lifting your emotions. Gaze at the soft, glowing candlelight and imagine it brightening your life. Envision positive, joyful vibrations flowing toward you and into you. Remain in the circle for as long as you like. When you're ready, extinguish the candles in the reverse order of how you lit them, to open the circle. Dab a little of your preferred oil on a cloth hanky and carry it with you during the day to sniff whenever you need a lift.

SIGNS OF THE TIMES

Long ago, Celtic prognosticators known as frithirs read signs of the times according to the first thing that caught their attention when they stepped outside. Try this ancient divination technique when you need guidance.

INGREDIENTS/TOOLS:
• None

The Modern Witchcraft Spell Book

- The first Monday after a solstice or equinox

Immediately after arising in the morning—before you do anything else—sit quietly for a few minutes and contemplate whatever you want advice about. Then go to your door and close your eyes. Take three slow, deep breaths then open the door and step outside (if you can do this safely with your eyes closed). Otherwise just stand in the open doorway facing out. Open your eyes. What's the first thing you see? What significance does it hold for you? A squirrel could suggest that you get busy gathering money, information, or other resources so you'll be prepared in difficult times ahead. A butterfly might mean a change for the better is coming or that you must transform the way you've been doing things in order to succeed.

Notice any impressions or feelings that arise into your awareness— they may be significant. If you don't sense an immediate answer, simply tuck away the memory of what you've seen and allow it to percolate in your subconscious. You might want to do some research into classic symbolism associated with the object that caught your attention. (My book *The Secret Power of Spirit Animals* gives lots of information about the meanings of animals and other creatures.) Pretty soon, perhaps in a dream, you'll receive the guidance you've been seeking.

HANG IN THERE SPELL

We all get discouraged at times. Instead of giving up, do this spell—it helps you hang in there until the situation improves.

INGREDIENTS/TOOLS:
- Oak flower essence (available in health food stores or online)
- 1 piece of yellow paper
- 1 pen or marker that writes red ink
- 1 black candle
- 1 candleholder
- Matches or a lighter
- 1 tarot card that represents you

- The tarot card Strength (which signifies inner and outer strength)
- The seven of wands tarot card (which represents the ability to hold firm when you're challenged or attacked)
- The Star tarot card (which symbolizes hope)
- The World tarot card (which indicates everything working out successfully)

BEST TIME TO PERFORM THE SPELL:
- As needed

Put a few drops of oak flower essence under your tongue; if you prefer, you can put the flower essence in a glass of water and drink it. On the paper, draw a red pentagram at least 1' in diameter. Lay it face up on your altar, a table, or another flat surface where it can remain for a time. Fit the candle in its holder, set it in the center of the pentagram, and light the candle.

Place the tarot card that represents you on the top point of the pentagram. Position the cards Strength and the seven of wands on the two side points of the pentagram. Put the Star and the World cards on the pentagram's bottom two points. Gaze at the cards and allow their symbolism to imprint your subconscious with positive imagery. Feel them stimulating the courage and confidence you need to face the challenges before you. Don't focus on your problems, just let your mind relax for a time. When you feel ready or start to lose your focus, extinguish the candle. Repeat as necessary, to reinforce your determination.

The Modern Witchcraft Spell Book

Chapter 18

TAKING THE NEXT STEP

If you've made it this far, congratulations. You've learned how to craft and cast all sorts of spells for all sorts of reasons. You've concocted potions and lotions, fashioned talismans and amulets, and mastered a variety of magick tools. Best of all, you've trained your mind and discovered your innate power to create effects in the manifest world. So where do you go from here?

KNOWLEDGE IS POWER

The world of magick is vast, maybe infinite. No matter how much you learn, there's always something else to explore just around the corner. One of the most respected astrologers of the twentieth century, Marc Edmund Jones, once said that he'd studied astrology for fifty years and barely scratched the surface. The same holds true for magick. Perhaps you've found a path that resonates with you. Or maybe you're still searching. Either way, you might wish to familiarize yourself with different schools of magick, even if you don't end up embracing them. Each can offer you something special, something you may not have known about before.

You may also like to delve deeper into fields such as astrology, numerology, feng shui, or tarot. These ancient arts will not only enhance your spellwork, they can open doors into fascinating realms and expand your understanding of yourself as well as the world around you.

Read as much as you can. You'll find a zillion books and online sites devoted to magickal practice and spellwork. Some focus on a particular area of interest, such as candle spells or goddess worship. Others provide a more comprehensive body of information. Each author and each teacher will likely approach things a bit differently, depending on his or her personal preferences and experiences. That's a good thing, because you don't want to limit yourself to only one perspective. Some you'll agree with, some you won't. Some you might decide to put aside for the time being and revisit later. That's okay, too.

Knowledge is power, as the saying goes. The more knowledge you have, the more powerful you'll become as a spellworker.

PRACTICE, PRACTICE, PRACTICE

Athletes and musicians know that in order to develop their talents they must practice. Spellcasters, too, must practice if they want to hone their craft and fulfill their potential. As I've said before, magick isn't a spectator sport. It's not for couch potatoes or the faint of heart. The more spells you do, the more comfortable you'll feel with the process and the more confident you'll become in your own ability. Try the following suggestions to sharpen your skills:

- Meditate regularly. Even ten minutes a day will help to focus your mind and ease stress.
- Practice sensing energy in plants, stones, places, people, etc. Everything in the world is composed of energy, so the more you can attune yourself to the energy patterns around you, the better you'll get at manipulating them with spells.

- Do spells often. Not only will frequent spellcasting help you to improve your life, it will make you more aware of how your thoughts, words, and deeds produce results.
- Try different types of spells.
- Practice working with various spell components: herbs, candles, crystals, etc.
- Pay attention to your dreams. As you delve into other levels of reality and expand your intuition, you may start having more vivid dreams and receive information in dream states. These insights can offer guidance in your waking life and in your magick practice.
- Keep a journal. We've already talked about the value of recording your spells and rituals in a book of shadows, but you may also want to keep a separate journal of your personal growth—because as you develop as a magician, your thinking and lots of other things may start to change as well. If you choose to include all this information in your book of shadows, that's fine, too.

MAKE FRIENDS WITH NATURE

Many of us spend so much time in climate-controlled offices, apartments, and automobiles that we've lost touch with the natural world. Kids play online games instead of softball. We text while walking instead of noticing the scenery around us.

Developing a rapport with the natural world can strengthen your skills as a spellworker, in part because many of the spell components you'll be using come from nature: herbs and flowers, gemstones and crystals. Additionally, you'll become more aware of your connection to the greater whole. You'll attune yourself to the cycles of earth and the heavens, so that you can work with them to empower your spells. You may even attract attention from the other creatures who share this planet with you and gain their help. How can you begin to tap nature's wisdom?

- Go for a walk without your cell phone or your tunes.
- Visit different places in nature—the woods, the waterfront, a hilltop—and experience the different energies in each of these places.
- Go outside at night and look at the sky for a while. Pretty awesome, huh?
- Pay attention to the moon's changing phases and their effects.
- Sit under a tree and try to sense it communicating with you.
- Sit beside a lake, stream, or other body of water and let it calm your mind.
- Hold different types of stones and see if you notice different resonances emanating from them.
- Watch birds, insects, and wildlife.
- Collect fallen leaves in autumn or press wildflowers in your book of shadows in the spring.
- Plant some seeds and watch them grow.

You might also like to welcome the sun each morning with a yoga practice known as the Sun Salutation. Or take a few minutes at dawn, noon, dusk, and midnight to sense the energy patterns around you. Even if you live in a high-rise in Manhattan, you can still walk in a park, grow plants in a container on a fire escape, and observe the changing seasons.

CREATING SPELLS FROM SCRATCH

After a while, you'll probably want to design some original spells. That's great. Following these steps will help you to create spells that can be just as effective as the ones you learn from this book and from other sources:

1. Boil down the purpose of the spell to a word or short phrase.
2. Find the ingredients suited to your goal.
3. Determine the best time to cast the spell.
4. Decide if you want to include an affirmation or incantation. If so, write one according to the instructions in Chapter 5.
5. Cleanse and purify all the objects you'll use in your spell.
6. Consider the order in which you'll do what you do.

7. Write your spell in your book of shadows, along with your experiences and outcome.

What kind of results can you expect from your spellwork? Well, that depends on you. Like a computer, spells do exactly what you tell them to do. So if you perform a spell to find a perfect companion and end up with a wonderful dog, your magick certainly has worked!

CRAFT IT YOURSELF

Want to kick your spells up a notch? Try crafting your own ingredients. When you do it yourself, you imbue the components of your spells with your personal energy and intention. From the very beginning, you empower these components to work with you to accomplish your goals. They become embodiments of your will. You might want to:

- Grow your own botanicals from seed. Start with a few hardy herbs, such as mint for prosperity spells, basil for protection, sage for purification, and marjoram for love and happiness. Gradually increase your magickal garden according to your needs and physical environment.
- Make your own candles. One of the easiest ways to do this is to purchase beeswax sheets and roll them into candles. You can also melt wax and pour it into molds, adding specially chosen essential oils and flower petals or leaves from your homegrown plants. Opt for soy wax rather than paraffin (which contains petroleum products), and use cotton wicks that don't have lead in them.
- Make your own loose incense. You can use any combination of resins and plant matter, so long as you're certain they're safe to inhale when burned. You will need: 1 part resin (combined or single resins) and 1 part dried plant matter. Grind the resin in a mortar and pestle or a coffee grinder, and then grind the plant material. Put the mix in a small bottle or jar, shake to combine, then cap and label your fragrant blend.
- Make your own herbal oils for anointing candles, gemstones, and talismans. Place a handful of your chosen plant material in a small saucepan, and pour a cup of light olive or safflower oil over it. Heat

the oil and plant matter gently over a low temperature for fifteen minutes, then pour the mixture into a clean jar. Cover the jar with a double layer of cheesecloth and fasten with a rubber band. Allow the oil to sit for ten days to two weeks, then strain it into a clean bottle; cap and label.

- Fashion seasonal wreaths and decorative arrangements from plants you've grown yourself, cuttings from favorite trees and shrubs, cones from evergreens, feathers you've found, and/or other natural materials.

You might also enjoy sewing pouches for amulets and talismans, sachets, and dream pillows, then stuffing them with botanicals from your garden. Learn to make your own paper for writing spells and affirmations—you can even add magick herbs or flowers to the mix. Craft ritual jewelry with gemstones and crystals. Have fun, but remember that each step of the process is an important part of your spellworking.

DOING MAGICK WITH OTHER PEOPLE

If you've been practicing solo, at some time you may consider spellworking with other like-minded people. If you already know someone you'd like to work with, great. If not, you might start checking around to see if a group of metaphysically oriented people already exists in your area. Yoga centers, health food cooperatives, and New Age stores can be good places to start.

Performing spells and rituals with other people can have advantages and disadvantages. Consider the plusses and minuses before you make any major commitments. On the plus side, for example:

- It can be fun to share ideas and spend time with "kindred spirits."
- You can learn a lot from other people's experiences.
- Combining your energy with someone else's can ramp up the power of a spell.

On the other hand:

- If your energies or intentions aren't compatible with those of the others in a group, your spells could get confused, diffused, or go totally awry.
- If you're working with people who tend to be domineering, or you're insecure about your own abilities, you might allow someone else to influence you unduly.

Being part of a group requires cooperation, respect, and tolerance, so choose your magickal companions carefully. They needn't be your close friends, but you should have some common ground and similar ideas about magick. Honesty, trust, and supportiveness between you are important. Make sure their ethics are compatible with yours. Establish boundaries and set guidelines for the rituals and spells you'll perform. Decide how you'll delegate responsibilities and iron out problems. Don't let anyone coerce you into doing anything that goes against your personal code. If something doesn't feel right, trust your instincts and bow out if necessary.

Perhaps you'd like to study with a teacher. Again, check out potential teachers carefully before you sign on with one:

- Find out as much as you can about his or her background.
- Discuss his or her expectations of you.
- Are you on the same wavelength spiritually?
- Do you hold similar magickal goals?
- Do you feel the teacher respects you and your opinions, instead of judging or trying to dominate you?
- Are the pace, schedule, and workload comfortable for you?
- If the teacher charges fees, are you comfortable with the amount and the reasons for the fees?

You might want to interview other spellcasters for recommendations. You can do some online research to find someone in your area who might be right for you to study with. Or you can do a spell to attract the perfect teacher. Remember the old saying "When the student is ready, the teacher will appear."

Between the time you began this book and now, you've come a long way. I hope that you feel the journey has been worthwhile, and that you've learned things you can build upon as you continue your work as a magician. Once you've started on this path, your life will never be the same. Magick transforms you. Your worldview changes, and as a consequence your interactions with everyone and everything you encounter in your daily life change, too. As Dr. Wayne Dyer often says, "When you change the way you look at things, the things you look at change."

In the process, you change the world. Remember that old saying about how a butterfly flapping its wings on one side of the globe influences the winds at the opposite side? It's true. Your energy, your thoughts, your actions impact everything else in the universe. And now that you possess a greater understanding of how this happens, you realize that you have the power to consciously create circumstances. That's an awesome responsibility and one you shouldn't take lightly. Every moment of every day, you have the ability to manifest the reality you desire, in yourself and the world around you—and every moment you'll be challenged to make choices about how you use that ability. The future resides with you. Embrace it!

APPENDIX: U·S·/METRIC CONVERSION CHARTS

VOLUME CONVERSIONS

U.S. Volume Measure	Metric Equivalent
⅛ teaspoon	0.5 milliliter
¼ teaspoon	1 milliliter
½ teaspoon	2 milliliters
1 teaspoon	5 milliliters
½ tablespoon	7 milliliters
1 tablespoon (3 teaspoons)	15 milliliters
2 tablespoons (1 fluid ounce)	30 milliliters
¼ cup (4 tablespoons)	60 milliliters
⅓ cup	90 milliliters
½ cup (4 fluid ounces)	125 milliliters
⅔ cup	160 milliliters
¾ cup (6 fluid ounces)	180 milliliters
1 cup (16 tablespoons)	250 milliliters
1 pint (2 cups)	500 milliliters
1 quart (4 cups)	1 liter (about)

WEIGHT CONVERSIONS

U.S. Weight Measure	Metric Equivalent
½ ounce	15 grams
1 ounce	30 grams
2 ounces	60 grams
3 ounces	85 grams
¼ pound (4 ounces)	115 grams
½ pound (8 ounces)	225 grams
¾ pound (12 ounces)	340 grams
1 pound (16 ounces)	454 grams

The Modern Witchcraft Spell Book

INDEX

The Modern Witchcraft Spell Book

The Modern Witchcraft Spell Book

The Modern Witchcraft Spell Book

The Modern Witchcraft Spell Book

ABOUT THE AUTHOR

Skye Alexander is the award-winning author of more than thirty fiction and nonfiction books, including *The Modern Guide to Witchcraft, The Everything® Wicca & Witchcraft Book, The Everything® Spells & Charms Book, Nice Spells/Naughty Spells, Good Spells for Bad Days,* and *The Everything® Tarot Book.* Her stories have been published in anthologies internationally, and her work has been translated into more than a dozen languages. The Discovery Channel featured her in the TV special *Secret Stonehenge* doing a ritual at Stonehenge. She divides her time between Texas and Massachusetts.